Name Construction
in
Mediæval Japan

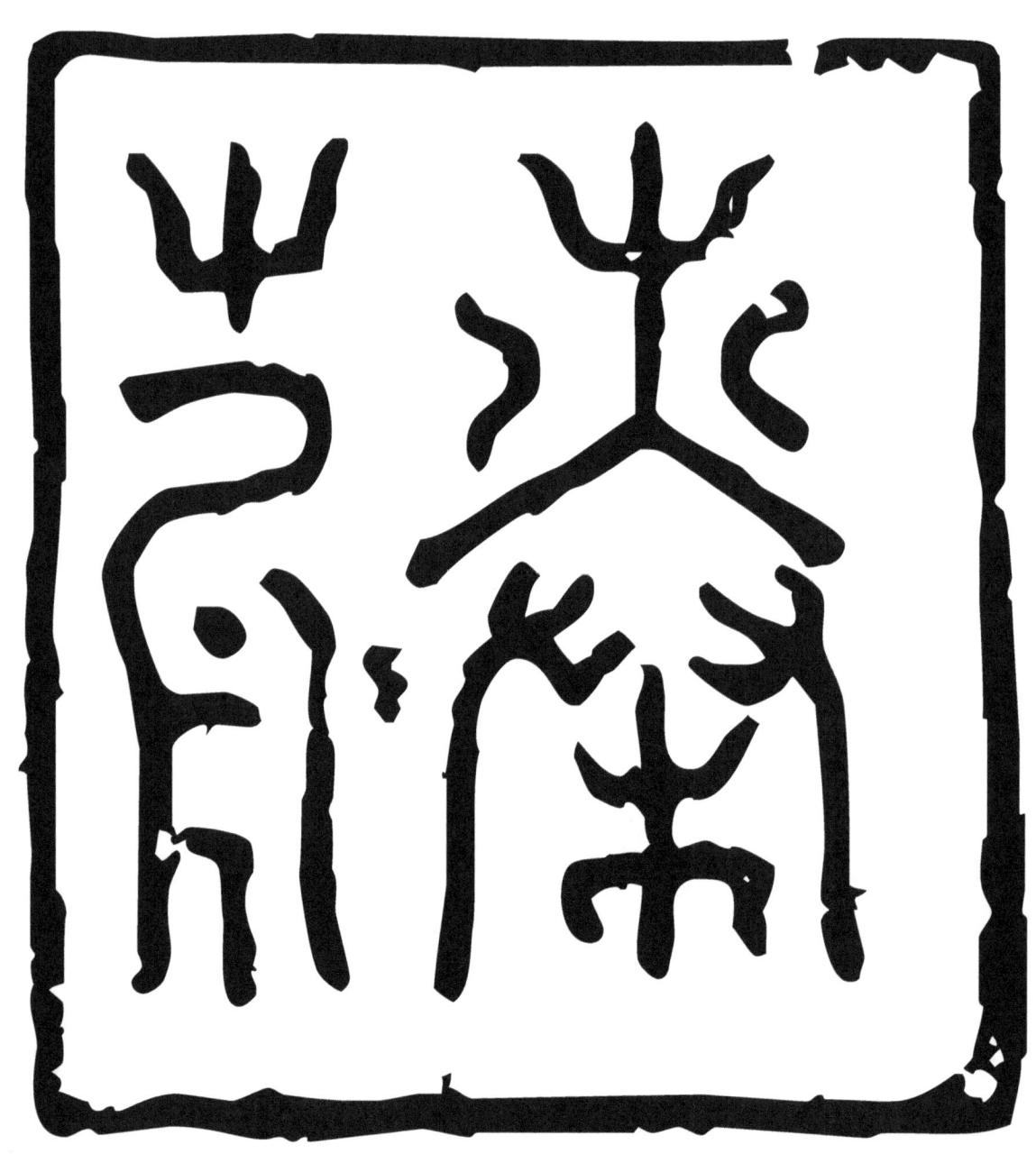

Inkan belonging to Fujiwara Tadahira (880-949)

Name Construction in Mediæval Japan

Revised Edition

Solveig Throndardottir

人名地名辞典 中世日本名制作・改訂版 北浜美雪

Gakumon
Syracuse, NY
2017

Author: Barbara Nostrand, Ph.D.
Publisher: Gakumon
Production: Lightning Source, La Vergne, TN 37089
Design: Bill Whitley and Barbara Nostrand
Technical Assistance: Dana Emery

Copyright © 2004 Barbara Nostrand
ALL RIGHTS RESERVED

The information in this publication is being made available for research purposes only. Other than short citations for onomastic research purposes, no part of this publication shall be reproduced in any way either printed or electronic without explicit written permission from the publisher acting as an agent for the author. Neither may it be stored in any information retrieval system or transmitted in any form or by any means electronic, mechanical, photographic, recording, or otherwise. All rights are retained by the author.

Library of Congress Cataloging-in-Publication Data

Throndardottir, Solveig
    Name Construction in Mediæval Japan / Solveig Throndardottir
    14, 464 p. 28 cm
    Includes bibliographical references and index

1. Names, Personal – Japan – Dictionaries	I Title
1. Names, Geographical – Japan – Dictionaries	
CS3000.T35 2004	2003-110774
929.4/0952/0902	CIP

Published by Gakumon, 2363 James Street, Syracuse, NY 13206-2840

22 21 20 19 18 17   10 9 8 7 6 5 4 3 2 1

ISBN 978-1-947401-00-6
Library of Congress Catalog Card No. 2003-110774

Review copies of portions of this work were privately circulated under the same title in 1991 and 1993. Copyright © 1991, 1993 Barbara Nostrand. Since the first printing of the original edition of Name Construction in Mediæval Japan on 1994 August 11, the text has been corrected, the section on titles expanded, and a glossary and name index added. Corrected Reprinting of Revised Edition Copyright © 2006 Barbara Nostrand ALL RIGHTS RESERVED. Reissued by Gakumon 2017.

TO OUR MOST NOBLE SOVEREIGN

東国五十一代 征夷大将軍 菊池 貫永 上

東洋帝国万歳

文成二十八年二月七日

ACKNOWLEDGMENT

The author wishes to thank the Carolingian Beneficium Pro Artibus and Baron Patri du Chat Gris without whose generous support compilation of this humble work would not have been possible.

Contents

	List of Tables	ix
	Preface	xi
	Preface to the Revised Edition	xiii
第一章	What is a Japanese Name?	1
第二章	Pronunciation Guide	9
第三章	Synopsis of Japanese History	13
第四章	Structure of Japanese Names	23
第五章	Surnames	31
第六章	Clan Names	35
第七章	Personal Names	41
第八章	Chinese Style Names	52
第九章	Christian Names	58
第十章	Titles and Offices	60
第十一章	Polite Speech	65
第十二章	Designing a Japanese Name	67
第十三章	How to Use the Name Tables	69

| 第十四章 | **Thematic Dictionary** | 73 |

    Table of Contents   73
    Semantic Index   84
    Phonetic Index   92

    Spacial Relationships   97
    Temporal Relationships   116
    Works Of Man   129
    Works Of Nature   145
    Celestial Phenomena   155
    Plants   159
    Beasts & Monsters   171
    Anatomy   176
    Light & Colour   179
    Groups & Relationships   185
    Rank & Status   192
    Peace & Security   208
    Number & Quantity   211
    Taste & Appearance   225
    Spiritual Traits   228
    Actions & Activities   237
    Perceiving & Communicating   250
    Feelings & Emotions   252
    Warfare   256
    Art & Letters   259
    Being & Existing   267
    Artifacts   271
    Textiles & Clothing   278
    Tools & Implements   280
    Purity   283
    Ethics   288
    Virtues   295
    Miscellaneous   305

| 第十五章 | **Japanese Names From Historical Sources** | 315 |

    Historical Surnames   315
    Historical Masculine Nanori   331
    Historical Masculine Yobina   370
    Historical Feminine Names   374
    Ancient & Mediæval Clans   390
    Historical Occupational Lineages   399
    Figures from History & Literature   403
    Japanese Emperors & Empresses   405
    Historical Nengou Since 990 CE   409

| 第十六章 | **Research Aids** | 413 |

    Glossary   413
    Bibliography   427
    Name Index   437
    General Index   459

List of Tables

Masculine Names Found in Heike Monogatari	6
Japanese Vowels & Diphthongs	9
Some Japanese Consonants	10
Japanese Phonetic Orthography	11
Verb Inflection in Thematic Elements	24
Categories of Given or Adopted Names	26
Hereditary Offices of the Fujiwara	32
Kanji Frequencies in Japanese Surnames Prior to 1600	33
Surnames of Daimyou During the Sengoku Period (ca. 1550)	34
Ancient Japanese Clans	36
Immigrant Clans	36
Common Tsuushou of Famous Clans	37
Historical Guilds	38
Names and Nicknames of Japanese Provinces	40
Simple Masculine Nanori	42
Kanji Frequencies in Masculine Nanori Prior to 1600 CE	43
Historical Tsuuji	44
Historical Osanana and Warawana	46
Yamato Period Feminine Suffixes	46
Feminine Names with Masculine Cognates	47
Feminine Root Names in Use Since Antiquity	48
Nara Period Suffixes	48
Kamakura Period Feminine Names	50
Habitats Found in Names of Monks and Artists	54
Origin of Imperial Posthumous Names	55
Kanji Commonly Found in Buddhist Names	56
Kanji Frequencies in Nengou after 990 CE	57
Names of Christian Daimyou	59
Common Names of Female Christians	59
Imperial Ranking System	60
Ministries of the Taihou and Yorou Codes	61
Ranks of the Palace Guards	62
Left Company of Gate Guards	62
Right Company of Gate Guards	62
Titular Offices of Provincial Governors	63

Ranks in Imperial Government Offices	64
Selected Ministries of the Imperial Government	64
Officers of Military Households	64
Officers in the Kamakura Bakufu	64
Recreating Military Titles & Offices	64
Pronouns	65
Honourific Suffixes	65
Honourific Prefixes	66
Addressing the Emperor	66
Polite Pronouns	66
Name Type Codes in the Thematic Dictionary	72

Preface

As with many things, this monograph had very humble beginnings. Like many other people who eventually joined the Society for Creative Anachronism, I grew up enjoying Robin Hood movies and read The Hobbit and The Lord of the Rings almost in a single sitting. In approximately AS V, I first heard of the SCA when the king and queen of the West Kingdom appeared as contestants on To Tell The Truth. Although I was not successful at guessing correctly during the show, I vividly recall the demonstration at the end of the game show. Although the society sounded very interesting to me, it was difficult at that time to actually meet people who belonged to it. Eventually, a coworker joined the company I was working at who was active in science fiction fandom who actually knew people in the society. However, she generally expressed low regard for people in the society and I was afraid to accept her offer to introduce me to members if I were interested. Thus, it was not for another year or two before I was actually invited to a society event. Regardless, I eventually joined the society in AS XI and later decided to try to learn Old Norse.

In AS XIII, many people in Carolingia were interested in learning mediæval languages which their "persona" would have known. As I was interested in Viking period Scandinavian culture, I decided to try to learn Old Norse. A friend of mine told me that there was a textbook for Old Norse and that it was available at the Harvard COOP. Hearing this, I went to the Harvard COOP and searched for this book for a long time, but failed to find it. What I did find was a small book which purported to teach Japanese in only thirty hours. As the book was relatively inexpensive and I enjoyed Japanese jidaigeki (period costume films), I decided to buy this book instead. Thus, began my exploits with attempting to learn Japanese. Later I was to join a culture exchange program and travel to Japan. And, when I returned, I enrolled in a Japanese class at Harvard University. Much to my surprise, I did well and decided to attend the Summer intensive Japanese language program at International Christian University the next Summer. Eventually, I was studying Japanese a second Summer in Japan when I was told that my father had died several weeks previously. I became rather depressed and simply stayed in Japan and eventually found work at an engineering company in Tokyo. While living in Japan, I was able to study a few art forms and collected books to bring back to use in the society. Unfortunately, my health deteriorated and I was forced to leave Tokyo. Thus, I decided to return to graduate school and complete my doctorate.

Before leaving Japan, I collected mediæval Japanese literature, books on architecture, heraldry and cooking and a fair amount of paraphernalia for calligraphy, the tea ceremony and the incense ceremony. As mediæval Japanese culture was very popular when I moved to Japan, I hoped to practice Japanese calligraphy and heraldry within the society. Although it is now many years since Shogun was a best seller and the Japanese middle ages are no longer as popular as they once was, I have been very fortunate to practice both calligraphy and heraldry within the East Kingdom. Soon after returning to Carolingia, I heard that there was to be a Known World Heraldic Symposium in the Kingdom of Atlantia. I thought that it would be a wonderful place to learn about heraldry and decided that I wanted to go. Unfortunately, I could find no way of traveling to the symposium, and so I resolved to contribute a short four to eight page paper on Japanese onomastics instead. When I was unable to finish my modest paper in time to submit it to the Atlantian KWHS, I continued working on the paper hoping to have it accepted as either a Pikestaff or Tournaments Illuminated article. But, as my little monster was quickly growing beyond the maximum word count for either of these publications my eyes began to focus up publication in Complete Anachronist.

Finally the "Japanese Names Project" became an end to itself. I began this project before I received my Ph.D. dissertation topic. Whenever my Ph.D. research was not going well (which was most of the time), I worked on the Japanese Names Project to reaffirm my validity as a scholar. I finally completed the Ph.D., but I am still working on this little project. There is a wealth to ancient and mediæval Japanese society which is partially revealed by this research. Several years ago, while working on this project at the East Asian Library at the University of Maryland, I was invited to join the Association for Asian Studies and have been a member ever since.

One problem with a project of this nature is that there are always more sources to go to, more names to collect and more analysis to do. Because of the relationship between Japanese names, the class structure of Japanese society, formal speech and governmental office, there are many things which I would like to learn. Thus, this work can never truly be complete. Last year, Meistari Fridrikr insisted that I publish a version of my work. One thing which I have learned from working on my Ph.D. thesis is that there is always more research to do and that it is necessary to occasionally report results. Last year, the Known World Heraldic Symposium was thrust upon me as an occasion for publishing what I have learned. This year I am letting Ice Dragon be such an occasion for me. For the last week when I should have been editing and polishing, I have still given in to the urge to research. However, an end must somehow be made of it. My consolation is that I can then begin afresh.

While this is the first edition of my work which shall be released to the general public, it is by no means either the first or the last. Review copies of an earlier edition were privately circulated among members of the College of Arms. Even after I wrote the words above and sent a copy of my manuscript to Ice Dragon, I continued to revise, correct and add to this present edition. Future editions will contain an expanded thematic dictionary, additional information concerning the history and construction of feminine names and a section on Japanese place names. All of this will take time both for research and for revising the present manuscript. Thus, in the interest of best serving both the College of Arms and our society as a whole, I am reluctantly releasing this more modest work to the winds of fortune.

As with any project which has lasted as long as this one has, there are many people to thank. Unfortunately, I have lost some of their names and can no longer do so properly. First I wish to thank my many patient Japanese instructors and especially Prof. Sakamoto Tadashi of Harvard University. I must also thank Lord Dana Stewart and another gentle who's name I unfortunately can no longer recall for helping me select the NISUS text editing system and for converting my manuscript from CPM to KANJITALK. NISUS was purchased under a grant generously provided by the Carolingian Beneficium Pro Artibus. I have been constantly encouraged by Meistari Fridrikr Tomasson av Knusslig Hamn who is currently Brigantia Principal Herald, by Master Arval Benicoeur and by Oohashi Katsutoshi Dono who has also given me much excellent advice about fonts, layout and printing. I am truly indebted to these few and to the many more who have helped and encouraged me over the years.

The primary objective of this monograph is to help people better understand and recreate Japanese names. To this end, it is necessary to begin to understand something of Japanese government, society, thought and belief as well. In short, you need to come to grips with the entire society and its values. This is more than can be faithfully reflected in a work on onomastics. Therefore, gentle reader I shall have to trust in your own scholarship to ferret out that which you need to know. I wish you only the very best in your journey. To those many people who have helped me with this project, I offer my most profound thanks. As always, I remain your most humble servant.

Solveig Throndardottir

Preface to the Revised Edition

Since its original publication, Name Construction in Mediæval Japan has undergone many corrections. Reprinting has often required font changes as electronic pre-press technology has evolved. Despite these changes in technology, I have in the past attempted to maintain a consistent table of contents and index with all previous editions. However, the time has come to shed the old indexing scheme. Many of the individual entries have moved about in the past so that exact page references have not always been consistent between print runs. Another mishap has intervened as well. The original for the 1999 reprinting by Potboiler Press was lost. This revised version is based on an earlier 1997 printing with some reorganization of tables, a new table of the names of Christian daimyou, textual corrections, and an additional name index. Many people have asked for an index of names appearing in this work. This revised version includes a first attempt at such an index. As always, I earnestly solicit corrections and comments from readers and users of this work.

Pursuing Japanese studies has lead me to meet many wonderful people. In particular, I wish to acknowledge Prof. Sakamoto of Harvard University Extension who first taught me Japanese, the anonymous curator of the East Asian Library at the University of Maryland who invited me to join the Association for Asian Studies, Prof. Kenneth L. Richard who tried to teach me Classical Japanese, and research and special collections librarians everywhere who let me use their books.

Solveig Throndardottir

文成三十八年夏至
Bunsei 38 Keshi

What is a Japanese Name?

The Society for Creative Anachronism sponsors events at which each participant assumes the role of a mediæval or renaissance person. At these events, people learn about mediæval and renaissance culture by experiencing it instead of merely reading about it in a book. They can also display the fruits of their own research and teach others what they have learned. Each person in the society adopts a "society name" for use at these events. Someone who is interested in Tudor England might choose a name such as "Henry Potter" which is appropriate for that time and place. His name may be quite different from that chosen by someone interested in twelfth century Italy. His name might also be very different from that born by somebody interested in a different period of English history. The society allows him a great range from which to choose a name. However, he is not allowed to choose a name belonging to a specific historical or literary figure. No one may call himself Catherine of Valois, Henry Tudor, Richard Plantagenet or Hildegard von Bingen. Instead, everyone must invent a novel name which is still somehow appropriate for a time and place that interests him.

Inventing a "society name" can be quite difficult. First of all, many of these names come from unfamiliar mediæval languages. Society names may also be put together quite differently from modern ones. Like the clothing worn at society events, the role of names and the way in which they are constructed differ from place to place and have changed over time. The way in which a name is constructed may also differ according to the gender or social status of the individual.

Anyone in the society may, if they desire, belong to the ruling elite of the culture which they are recreating. However, specific title and rank within the society are only awarded by regional officers who recreate titled nobility enjoying land tenure by virtue of legitimate succession. These kings, princes, and barons have the sole prerogative of granting rank to people, but may not do so to themselves. Nobody can award themselves title or status within the society, it must in all cases be conferred by superior authority or by one's own predecessor. While names peculiar to the nobility of any culture are appropriate, names which imply special rank or status should be avoided.

As with names from many other times and places, correctly constructing a Japanese name requires some understanding of the language used by the underlying culture and the significance of each component of a complete name. Names can convey either much or little information about the person bearing the name. A name can reveal the gender, approximate age, approximate social status, and much other information. As for many societies, Japanese names take on a spiritual dimension and can have almost magical significance. Just as the patriarchs of Israel had their names changed, a Japanese person might change his name several times during his life. Basil Hall Chamberlain tells in *Japanese Things* of an old friend suddenly presenting a business card with a new name on it. Similarly, a Japanese student might change his name during the middle of the school year. These name changes might result from rites of passage, adoption, a personal crises, changes of allegiance or simply a desire for improved fortune. Similarly, many places have enjoyed two or more names, complicating historical, geographic, and especially onomastic studies.

This book was written to help you create a plausible mediæval Japanese name. Specifically, it is limited to names born by members of the dominant culture of mediæval Japan. Names born by members of the indigenous Utari or Ainu population and inhabitants of Okinawa are excluded. This book is primarily concerned with Japanese names beginning with the Genpei War in 1185 and ending with the battle of Sekigahara in 1600. The Japanese middle ages, and indeed all of Japanese history, is customarily divided into distinct political and cultural periods. Often, onomastic sources only place names or even individuals roughly within these periods and do not give specific dates. While this book is not a comprehensive encyclopedia of Japanese cultural history, it does attempt a brief introduction to these periods. While it is not possible in these few pages to convey more than a superficial understanding of the Japanese language and the morphology of Japanese names, I hope that these few comments will help fellow members to construct authentic Japanese names.

Language and Orthography

While in Chinese a single character generally has a single pronunciation and meaning, Japanese is very different. Each Sino-Japanese ideographic character can be pronounced or "read" in one or more fundamentally different ways each of which may have more than one unrelated meaning. Specifically, a character may have one or more native Japanese readings or *kunyomi* 訓読み as well as one or more Sino-Japanese "Chinese readings" called *onyomi* 音読み. Typically, the Japanese readings are native Japanese words while the Chinese readings are used to form new words much as Latin and Greek roots are used in English. While Sino-Japanese ideograms are called *kanji* 漢字 (pronounced "kahn-gee") or Chinese letters, some of them such as *touge* 峠 (the word for mountain pass) were invented in Japan and are unknown in China. Chinese lacks the inflected endings and other grammatical features of Japanese. Thus, Japanese adapted *kanji* to write these. Simplified versions of these phonetic *kanji* evolved into *katakana* 片仮名 and *hiragana* 平仮名, the two syllabic alphabets of modern Japanese.

During the early classical period, Japanese documents were written exclusively in Chinese and later came to be written in Japanese. The Japanese simply applied Japanese words to the *kanji* with corresponding meaning. Language features not found in Chinese were written with *kanji* having the required sound with little regard for meaning. *Kanji* used in this way were simplified so that they could be written faster. Ultimately, two competing systems were developed with which to write Japanese phonetically. Both represent complete V (vowel), CV (consonant-vowel) or C (consonant) rhythmic units called mora with individual *kana* 仮名 characters derived from abbreviations for Chinese characters. After *kana* was developed, many documents had the correct pronunciation written next to the text in one of these two scripts. These annotations are called *furigana*. By reading *furigana* and by comparing Japanese with Chinese sources, we can reconstruct the way in which mediæval Japanese names were pronounced.

Since early Portuguese and Spanish contact with Japan in the sixteenth century, many different ways of writing Japanese with the "Roman" alphabet have been invented. Of these, the Hepburn system is probably the most popular and is largely responsible for the English versions of Japanese places names used outside of Japan. However, this system requires placing a macron above certain vowels which is difficult to type and is often left off. Thus, Tôkyô 東京 becomes Tokyo and Kyôto 京都 becomes Kyoto. Modern Japanese frequently use another system for writing personal names. Under this system, Itô 伊藤 becomes Itoh and Tôyama 陶山 becomes Tohyama.

This book uses its own system of romanization to better accommodate computer orthography and to facilitate retrieving the original Japanese phonetic orthography for the names listed. Our system departs from Hepburn in how it represents *long vowels*. Tôkyô 東京 is written as Toukyou, Kyôto 京都 as Kyouto, Itoh or Itô 伊藤 as Itou, and ôkii 大きい is written as *ookii*. Although the *long* **O** now sounds pretty much the same in all four, it is represented in Japanese syllabic orthography by an **OU** diphthong in the first three and by a repeated pure vowel in the last example. Until recently, the second half of long vowels was represented by a CV pair leading linguists to believe that old Japanese had a strict CV phonetic structure. This aspect of Japanese names is difficult to reconstruct. Except for a limited number of names where we have antique readings available, modern readings are used and CV phonetic structure is generally ignored. Japanese vowels are pure vowels much like those in Italian and **Y** is always a consonant and not a semi-vowel as in English. As most English speakers pronounce Japanese vowels and any word containing an **F**, **R**, or **Y** rather poorly, there is a separate chapter on Japanese pronunciation. While this chapter is not a definitive discussion of Japanese phonetics or dialects, you should read it carefully before trying to use this book. Regardless, since the introduction of Chinese ideographic writing to Japan, *kanji* 漢字 has been and continues to be the primary vehicle for understanding Japanese. Consequently, names are given both in *kanji* and in transliteration.

Each *kanji* is, by itself, a cluster of potential meanings and sound patterns. The same character may have several different meanings and several different ways of reading it. Similar meanings may be written with very different *kanji* which may or may not sound the same. As Japanese has a very limited phonetic system, words with very different meaning may have identical sound. This inherent ambiguity of the language is commonly resolved by references to the written form. This ambiguity is also a common theme in Japanese humor ranging from the *daimyou kyougen* play *Awataguchi*, through comic conversations in the Soseki novel *Wagahai Nekko de Aru* to contemporary *manzai* comic skits on Japanese television. Thus, a Japanese name is actually a collection of sound, meaning, and even the particular form of the *kanji* with which it is written. An example of calligraphically different names is 島田 Shimada and 嶋田 Shimada which have truly identical pronunciation and meaning. The only difference being the two forms for writing "island".

If you already own a *kanji* dictionary, you will quickly note that the *Thematic Dictionary* does not contain all of the *kanji* found in the name table in your dictionary. The *Thematic Dictionary* also includes many characters which were used in personal names prior to 1601, but which do not appear in the table in your dictionary. These *kanji* are no longer used in Japanese personal names. This is because the Japanese Ministry of Education has only approved 1000 general use *kanji* and an additional 166 *kanji* commonly found in names for use in modern Japanese names. The *kanji* in the *Thematic Dictionary* were selected using entirely different criteria. Every *kanji* which appears in a historical name in one of the alphabetical name lists at the end of this book also appears as an entry in the *Thematic Dictionary*.

In general, a Chinese character was included in the *Thematic Dictionary* if it was found in a Japanese name known to have been in use prior to 1600. A few additional *kanji* have been included to complete the Japanese zodiac and ordinal sequences. If you compare the *Thematic Dictionary* with the name table in a *kanji* dictionary, you will also discover that some of the "readings" given for *kanji* in the *Thematic Dictionary* can not be found in your table. This is because mediæval Japanese names frequently used archaic or specialized readings for these characters which are no longer in use. Further, the meanings associated with some of the *kanji* may not be the same as the ones with which you are familiar. Often this is the result of discovering either archaic meanings or meanings used in special combinations. Finally, the *Thematic Dictionary* is not a *kanji* dictionary. It does not explain the origin of the characters nor are there any instructions for writing them. There is no stroke index and no radical index with which to look up an unfamiliar character. Only those definitions which appear useful for composing names are given, and they are for the most part terse and evocative in nature rather than analytic. However, the *Thematic Dictionary* does contain, in addition to individual *kanji*, several standard *kanji* combinations commonly found in mediæval Japanese names.

The Individual in Japanese Society

In Japan, the family and not the individual forms the fundamental social unit. The family in its most atomic form is a group of people living together in a common dwelling. Unlike modern nuclear families, these families were based on residence and not parentage. Thus, there is an identification between "house" or *ie* 家 and "family" or *kazoku* 家族 which literally means "house-tribe". Japanese peasants lived together in large extended families often sharing a common building. Some of these buildings dating from the sixteenth century or earlier are very large. Peasant houses tended to be rather boxy and could be very tall with many floors. Urban commoners often lived in long houses called *nagaya* 長屋 which often had more than one door. While commoners were recorded by the census, they did not in general have true names. The occupants of each residential unit were recorded together on a common census form. The first entry was for the head of the residence who could be female. The remaining entries were generally in order of age. Men were often recorded by their birth order and women by a simple description. The census also recorded their titular membership in one of the ancient monopoly corporations or agricultural collectives.

The Japanese were and still are concerned with filial relationships and with comparative status. Both, of these were expressed in ancient and mediæval Japanese personal names. What constituted a personal name in classical and mediæval Japan remains rather elusive. Members of the warrior class typically changed their names several times during their life. Some people seem to have been known by different names at the same time. Finally, an accomplished Japanese warrior would have a collection of names and titular elements which would be used as circumstances dictated. The exact form of the name would depend upon social circumstances. Regardless, as the College of Arms registers names in a bureaucratic fashion and the crown issues edicts and official documents, it is important to construct a Japanese name corresponding to one of the historic official styles for naming people.

What is a Japanese Name?

A member of the mediæval Japanese aristocracy had a rich repertoire of names available to him. Having a family name and an official given name was a distinctive privilege of male members of the courtier and military classes. Of these, the official given name or *nanori* (pronounced "nah-noh-ree") was the more cherished privilege. A male Japanese aristocrat would also have an unofficial name called a *yobina* (pronounced "yoh-bee-nah") which he would use socially, but the *nanori* was the name which appeared on official documents and which he proclaimed before combat with a worthy adversary. A *yobina* is not a nickname. It is a less formal name which is used in conversation. A male aristocrat might also have a clan name, several artistic pseudonyms, nicknames, and other special names. Female Japanese aristocrats also had true names. Unfortunately, their names were not as extensively recorded as were the names of their brothers. In many cases they were simply recorded as the mothers, wives, or daughters of their men folk.

A masculine Japanese name can consist simply of a family name followed by a *yobina* and ending with a *nanori*. First, select a family name such as "Kajiwara" from the table of *Historical Surnames*. Second, the birth order should be decided upon. The birth order determines the substantive, or root, element of the *yobina*. A third born son could simply be called "Saburou" or might have an extra element placed before the birth order element. A birth order name can be selected from the numerical section of the *Thematic Dictionary* or any of the *tsuushou* in table of *Masculine yobina* can be selected. Birth order designations can be stacked. Thus, Tarousaburou is the third son of a first son. Finally, a *nanori* such as Mori'naka can be selected from the table of *Masculine nanori*. We have just constructed Kajiwara Saburou Mori'naka which is a plausible mediæval Japanese name.

While male Japanese aristocrats had distinctive *nanori* and *yobina*, their sisters were commonly referred to by their relationship to another person, a room, or their position. Although women occasionally adopted Chinese style composite *nanori* during the classical period, their *nanori* generally consisted of a single element either preceded by an honourific or followed by a quasi-titular element. A feminine Japanese name can consist simply of an *uji* or clan name followed by a *nanori*. First, select an *uji* such as Tachiba'na from the table of *Ancient & Mediæival Clans*. Then, select a *nanori* such as Hideko from the table of *Historical Feminine Names*. Tachiba'na no Hideko is also a plausible Japanese name. Unlike our masculine example, this name actually contains more information about the time period and social standing of the individual. This is because **-ko** is a quasi-titular element meaning "lady" which was common during the Kamakura Period. If she had lived earlier, she might have been known as Tachiba'na no Hideme instead. Later, she might have been known as Ohide. Names ending with **-ko** 子 once again became popular during the lifetime of Lafcadio Hearn at the end of the nineteenth century.

Many people like to invent their own names rather than merely selecting them from tables of historical names. In this way, people can express their own creativity and create names which are more expressive of their own personality. Like old Anglo-Saxon names, mediæval Japanese names are well suited for these urges. New Japanese names were often invented from a stockpile of root meanings. With a modest amount of effort, anyone can use the *Thematic Dictionary* to create a name which has both a pleasing meaning and a pleasing sound. To do this, you need only learn a bit about the structure of each of the components of a Japanese name. This will allow you to use the *Thematic Dictionary* to construct the names that you want.

Constructing a Japanese Surname

Chinese family names usually consist of a single thematic element and are thus written with a single *kanji* or Chinese character. Sheau-yueh J. Chao lists 534 single *kanji* names, 81 double *kanji* names, and only 2 three *kanji* names. While Japan adopted the Chinese system of writing, it has an almost limitless stockpile of potential family names. These names are constructed, much like the Chinese double word names, by agglutinating components each represented by a either a *kanji* or a *kanji* combination. Whether each of these thematic elements corresponds to a morpheme in the common linguistic sense will not be discussed here. Rather, we will rather freely call these atomic meaning units morphemes.

Many Japanese family names are simple locatives or descriptive places names. A small "river" or "brook" is Bach in German and Ogawa in Japanese. Consequently, it is easy to use the *Thematic Dictionary* to invent new Japanese surnames. Although the *Thematic Dictionary* contains many English synonyms, it is not a complete English Thesaurus. Consequently, if you do not find the first word that you look up, please try an equivalent. The *kanji* used in family names generally take their Japanese reading. These readings are written in lower case in the *Thematic Dictionary*. Regardless, you can refer to the examples in the *Thematic Dictionary* to see whether your reading was actually used in surnames. As the same *kanji* may have more than one Japanese reading, you should always do this before deciding upon a name.

Suppose you wish to call your family "rocky river" because you live near such a river or simply like that kind of place. Then, you look up "river" in the Semantic Index to the *Thematic Dictionary*. You quickly discover that there are two different ways of writing "river" one of which is used for larger rivers. You choose 川 **kawa** which can be used for smaller rivers. Then you look up "rock" and discover 石 **ishi** which means rock or stone. In Japanese, the substantive element always goes at the end so you put "rock" in front of "river" to create Ishikawa 石川 or Stonybrook. Once you have invented your name, you can then look it up and see whether it was used in the past. Our example is actually a very old name which was in use as early as the end of the Hei'an Period.

Constructing a Masculine Japanese Name

It is also very easy to invent masculine *nanori*. Such *nanori* are most often composed of two *kanji* the first descriptive and the second substantive. Together, they usually describe some moral attribute. In this way they strongly resemble Greek given names from the classical period. Of the two, the second one is generally the more important and should be selected first. As with surnames, the *kanji* used in these names generally take their Japanese reading. These readings are written in lower case in the *Thematic Dictionary*. Suppose you wish to express "strength" or "confidence" with your name. First you look up "confident" in the Semantic Index and select 康 from the *Thematic Dictionary*. The Japanese reading for this *kanji* is **yasu**. Now you can select one of the names listed in the *Thematic Dictionary*. You might choose Hideyasu 秀康 which means extraordinary strength or confidence.

You can also use the Semantic Index to choose your descriptive element just as you chose your substantive element. Suppose you want your *nanori* to mean "true strength". Maybe "true path" is close enough to the meaning that you want. If so, then you can simply choose Tsuneyasu 経康 from the list of document names including 康 in the *Thematic Dictionary*. However, you might want a *kanji* which simply means "true" or "correct". The *Thematic Dictionary* includes a section for 正 **masa** which means: "unerring", "genuine", "correct", or "true". The section for this *kanji* lists many examples where it is used as the descriptive element with a quality as the substantive element. Thus, we can confidently construct Masayasu 正康 as a novel *nanori*. There is even a different Masayasu with the same descriptive element listed in the *Thematic Dictionary*.

Sometimes people are more interested in how their name sound than what it means. While it is still important to consider the meaning of the name when putting it together, you can begin by looking up the desired sound pattern in the Phonetic Index to the *Thematic Dictionary*. Suppose that you like names ending in -**yoshi**. In this case there are actually over a dozen different *kanji* to choose from. Suppose you like -**yoshi** 吉 which means "lucky" or "fortunate". This is not the most common -**yoshi**, but it is easy to write and has an auspicious meaning. Again, you can simply choose a name such as Tadayoshi 忠吉 from the *Thematic Dictionary* or you can select the descriptive element either by its sound or by its meaning. However, remember that the meaning of a Japanese name is always important. Fortunately, many Japanese words sound the same, and you will usually be able to form a name with an auspicious meaning. **Tada-** 忠 means "faithful" or "loyal" so our name might mean "loyal fortune" or "good fortune through loyalty".

You may be familiar with the names of martial arts masters and other famous artists. These names are rather distinctive and are covered along with monastic names and posthumous names in the chapter on Chinese style names. While Buddhist monks used similar names, they did not customarily use family names. In fact, novitiates were sometimes known as *shukke* 出家 which signified their departure from their families. In contrast, masters of art forms often retained their family names. In general, Sino-Japanese artistic names were only adopted by masters of an art or by people who had retired from life to become lay Buddhist monks. All of these people originally had some other name and may have continued to use it throughout their life. Consequently, unless you have been awarded a peerage, these names are not appropriate for use within the Society for Creative Anachronism.

Thus far, we have constructed the name Ishikawa Hideyasu 石川秀康. Lord Hideyasu should also have a common use name or *yobina* 呼び名. These names are rather important as they were used in daily conversation. In a complete name, the family name comes first followed in order by: the *uji* or clan name, the *yobina*, and the *nanori*. Titles of office were usually attached to the *yobina* and not to any of the other names. Sometimes a possessive -**no**- appears in Japanese names. This -**no**- is never actually written, but is merely inserted by the speaker. This element has the same meaning as "of" in English names or "von" in German names. It most often occurs between a clan name and a *yobina* when both the *yobina* and the *nanori* are used together. It can also appear between the family name and a *yobina*, a *nanori*, or a Chinese style artistic name called a *houmyou*. Generally, it will appear at most once as part as a name an perhaps one more time embedded in a title of office.

During the Kamakura Period, masculine *yobina* or *tsuushou* 佐々木三郎秀義 usually indicated birth order. Generally, it is best to emulate this style and select a simple birth order name with perhaps a descriptive element attached to the front. The *Thematic Dictionary* is divided into major sections each of which is listed in the table of contents. Birth order names are classified in the section on Number & Quantity. The first three sons have special names which are listed separately. The remainder are named in a regular manner and their names are listed under their ordinal numbers. Most Japanese men bore *yobina* which were simply unmodified birth order names. Those bearing modified names usually prefixed the birth order name with a single *kanji*. These modifiers were often associated with the *uji* or clan to which the individual belonged. Regardless, these modifiers usually take their Chinese readings which are indicated by capital letters in the *Thematic Dictionary*. This may be the result of their association with Chinese literary *azana*.

Masculine Names Found in Heike Monogatari

- 梶原源太景景季   Kajihara no Genta Kagesuwe
- 佐々木三郎秀義   Sasaki no Saburou Hideyoshi
- 佐々木四郎高綱   Sasaki no Shirou Takatsuna
- 足利又太郎忠綱   Ashikaga no Matatarou Tadatsuna
- 武蔵三郎左衛門   Musashi no Saburousa'emon
- 薩摩守忠度   Satsuma nokami Tadanori
- 越中次郎   Etchuu no Jirou
- 今井四郎兼平   Imai no Shirou Kanehira

By the end of the sixteenth century, titular names such as Munesa'emon 宗左衛門 and Shirouhyou'ei'nojou 四郎兵衛尉 came into use. While Mu'nesa'emon does not contain a rank and should be acceptable to the College of Arms, Shirouhyou'ei'nojou does indicate specific rank and should be avoided. The "hyou'ei'nojou" at the end of the latter name is the culprit. Shirou 四郎 is a common *yobina* meaning number four son. Generally, names ending with -**nokami**, -**nosuke**, -**nojou**, -**nosakan**, and -**nodaibu** should be avoided.

Many people in the Society for Creative Anachronism form households in which they may have older and younger "brothers" and "sisters". For this reason, our young lord may consider himself to be a second son. In this case, he chooses Jirou 次郎 which literally means "next son". Simple *yobina* such as Jirou were born by most Japanese men. However, he is free to modify his *yobina* by attaching a descriptive element. He might wish to express "humility" or "smallness" and attach 小 **ko**- to his name. Thus, his *yobina* becomes Kojirou 小次郎.

We have now constructed a complete masculine Japanese name. We began by selecting a family name and proceeded to select both a *nanori* and a *yobina*. Our name is Ishikawa no Kojirou Hideyasu 石川小次郎秀康. He may be referred to simply as Kojirou in daily speech or as Ishikawa Hideyasu in official pronouncements. Later, when he is called into court and awarded arms, he will augment his *yobina* with his new title. If he excels as a warrior, he will be known as Kojirou U'emon no Daibu. If he excels as an artisan, he will be known as Kojirou Sa'emon no Daibu. While a complete discussion of office, rank, and status in mediæval Japan is properly speaking outside of the central topic of this book, a short discussion can be found in the chapter on Titles and Offices.

Constructing a Feminine Japanese Name

Begin by selecting an historical *uji* or clan from the table of *Ancient & Mediæval Clans*. While there were many *uji* before the Taika Reform in 645 CE, later most Japanese belonged to a relatively small number of *uji*. *Uji* which still claim members are indicated with a double circle in the table. Of theses, the Fujiwara are a fairly large and prominent *uji* and are an excellent choice. Now we require a personal name. Of course it is easiest to look up a name in the table of *Historical Feminine Names*. This table contains many names which are difficult to explain. First of all, it contains some names for which we lack *kanji*. Without *kanji* we can do little but guess at their meaning. It also contains a number of alliterative names and early period descriptive names. Some names which appear in this table occur both with and without a special honourific suffix. In general, you should select a name from no earlier than the Kamakura Period. You may be attracted to 梅 **ume** or "plum" which is one of the three lucky trees and represents "wifely devotion". This is the meaning for Umeme 梅女 which can be found in the table of *Historical Feminine Names*.

We have now selected 藤原梅女 Fujiwara no Umeme which is a complete feminine Japanese name. Unfortunately, women and their names are not as well documented as are men. Often, we know of a woman only by reference to her father, brother, husband, son, or family affiliation. While these women must have had other names by which they were called, census records and some histories often remain silent. In fact, very early census records are full of descriptive epithets such as "muddy legs" and "old hag".

An odd feature of Japanese phonology is that ancient name endings and a few personal pronouns suggest that **-ko** endings were masculine while **-me** endings were feminine. This is particularly interesting in that modern Japanese does not conjugate for gender. Examples include the words *musuko* 息子 (son) and *musume* 娘 (daughter), the names of the twin gods Iza'nami (female) and Iza'nagi (male) and the ancient name endings **-hime** (feminine) and **-hiko** (masculine). The importance lies in the column where the ending appears in the phonetic chart.

Many people are familiar with feminine Japanese names ending with 子 **-ko**. In classical Chinese, 子 means "son" and in names means "lord" or "master". 子 appears in the names of sages such as 告子 Gào Zi. In very early Japanese society, the suffix **-SHI** 子 was used to construct masculine names, but by the sixth or seventh century its use was rapidly spreading to feminine names as well. In these early names, most of which are associated with the imperial family and the court nobility, 子 continued to take its Chinese reading. This reading was in use as late as 1324 where it appears in the name Fujiwara Keishi 藤原経子. In later names, it takes **-ko** which is its Japanese reading. This reading appears as early as 1156 in the name Houjou Masako 北条政子.

What then can we say about women's names? That depends entirely upon the period of interest. While masculine *nanori* appear to have remained relatively unchanged from the time of the Genpei War till the battle of Sekigahara, the same can not be said for feminine names. However, probably the most enduring construction during the Japanese middle ages is very similar to the modern feminine names with which many are familiar. Instead of ending a name with 子 **-ko** one merely ends it with 女 **-me**. Although written with the *kanji* for woman, this ending is probably an abbreviation for daughter. Even today, woman are sometimes known generically as daughters or older sisters. Regardless, these names were in use as early as the Nara Period (ca. 800) and remained in use as late as the end of the Muromachi Period (ca. 1600). Later, attaching **o-** as an honourific prefix to the root name became popular. In 1884, almost no Japanese women attending the peers school had a name ending with the suffix 子 **-ko** as in Tsuko 津子. By 1941, the situation had reversed, and the percentage of these names relative to the general population had risen to 85 percent.

These names most frequently consist of a single *kanji* which usually has spiritual or moral significance within Japanese society. It can also express birth order or special blessings such as longevity. Consequently, feminine personal names can be constructed merely by selecting an appropriate thought from the *Thematic Dictionary*. One distinctive feature of women's names is the prevalence of the names of plants, beasts, and monsters. Although these elements are largely absent from masculine *nanori*, they appear quite frequently in names of women. You can also construct a feminine personal name using both a descriptive element and a substantive element much like a masculine *nanori*. In fact, some women bore names which are indistinguishable from masculine *nanori*. Regardless, whether your name uses one *kanji* or two to form its meaning, it should end with **-me** which can be written as either 賣 or 女. Of the two, 賣 is a rather older form than 女.

You can also use the Semantic Index to choose your descriptive element just as you chose your substantive element. Suppose you want to have your name mean "dragon" which is a very auspicious monster in East Asia. If so, then you can simply select **tatsu** 龍 from the *Thematic Dictionary*. Be careful to use the Japanese reading (written in lower case) and not the Chinese reading (written in upper case). Then simply attach **-me** 女 to the end to form Tatsume. We have just constructed 石川龍女 or Ishikawa no Tatsume. This may even be rather appropriate as Asian dragons are strongly associated with water.

Another construction became popular during the Nanboku Period (ca. 1350) and remained in use until the Meiji restoration in the nineteenth century. These names were very simple consisting of a single thematic idea to which an honourific **o-** 御 was prefixed by the speaker. This practice appears to have begun among the aristocracy and eventually spread to all of Japanese society. As there is great variety in the formation of feminine *nanori*, please consult the main text for more details. Even the main text is woefully inadequate. A particularly energetic reader may wish to consult the massive three volume work on the history of Japanese feminine names by Tsunoda Bunei. Unfortunately, this work is only available in Japanese.

There are many feminine names which do not require either a final honourific or an honourific prefix. Some of these names are quite ancient. In modern Japan, such names are typically longer than the root forms of other feminine names. Here we encounter names such as Midori or Miyuki.

Other Kinds of Names

Many other kinds of names were available to the Japanese aristocrat. Often they had childhood names which they exchanged for adult names upon reaching formal maturity. They also often had a collection of artistic names and upon retiring from the world would assume a monastic name in addition to their family name and *nanori*. These are generally dealt with in the chapter on Chinese style names. Similar names were also adopted by masters of various art forms. Within the context of the Society for Creative Anachronism, these names generally imply a degree of mastery appropriate for the peerage. Consequently, it is probably best to discourage people from adopting these names.

However, there is one kind of name which must be mentioned here. Buddhist monks had very distinctive names. First of all, regardless of birth, they generally did not use their family names. This sets them apart from lay monks and artisans who retained their family names. Most monks had a single name such as Shinran 親鸞 consisting of two *kanji* both of which took their Chinese reading. As with masculine *nanori*, the first *kanji* modifies the second one. These *houmyou* are often very similar to those adopted by lay monk and artisans. However, members of the various sects which practiced Zen meditation adopted a second Chinese style religious name. Thus, we encounter Tougen Zuisen 桃源瑞仙 (1433–1489) and Touzan Tanshou 東山湛照 (1231–1291). Zen monks often had a third informal name called a *dougou* or "path name", which expressed their own vision of enlightenment. These *dougou* typically end with one of a restricted collection of substantive elements.

Pronunciation Guide

Japanese has an undeserved reputation of being a "hard" language to learn. While there are thousands of Sino-Japanese *kanji* 漢字 and polite speech can be quite complex, Japanese has a relatively simple sound system. Further, you will not need to actually learn *kanji* or polite speech in order to construct Japanese names. In this book, we will be primarily concerned with grammatical and semantic issues. Japanese grammar, while fundamentally different from more familiar Western languages, is also relatively simple. However, before considering how to construct Japanese names, you must first gain a rudimentary understanding of Japanese phonetics. This will enable you to better pronounce the names which you construct and will also make it easier to read the Japanese technical terms used in this book.

While no book or audio recording can substitute for a live instructor, it is possible to explain the romanization of Japanese used in the text and the tables and to give some idea of how Japanese is pronounced. Japanese is an isochronos, non-stressed language which uses intonation accent. This means that when pronouncing Japanese, each syllable (which consists of a vowel, a consonant-vowel combination or syllabic **N**) should receive an equal amount of time. You should also be careful to pronounce the entire word with the same loudness of voice. This means that spoken Japanese is unstressed and may sound rather monotonous to someone who speaks a western language.

Japanese, has five vowels: **A, I, U, E, O** which are pronounced as in Italian or Spanish. Sometimes a vowel is pronounced twice as long. This is usually indicated by repeating the vowel. **O** is an exception to this rule. In the tables, an **O** of double duration is represented either by an "ou" or an "oo" depending upon how it is written in Japanese. This suggests that "ou" was originally a diphthong and should be pronounced slightly differently from "oo". However, the difference is only slight, and you will be understood if you pronounce them the same way. Unfortunately, neither Japanese phonetic writing nor any romanization completely reflects "long" vowels. This is because, when the same vowel brackets a semantic boundary, a short pause is introduced so as to pronounce them distinctly. This is one reason why you have to understand the meaning, or at least the structure, of Japanese names in order to pronounce them correctly. Finally, Japanese frequently subvocalize the **U** in "su", "tsu", or "zu". The effect is to lengthen the preceding consonant. While this may make the vowel hard to hear, these syllables still take a full time value.

Japanese Vowels

- A   as in "father," "saw", or "law not as in "at"
- I   as in "machine" or ", police" not as in "it"
- U   as in "flue," "rule", or "tune" not as in "fun"[1]
- E   as in "set" or "wet", or as in "whey not as in "set"[2]
- O   as in "joke" or "broke not as in "cot"

Japanese Diphthongs

- AI   as in the "y" in "my"
- EI   as in the "ay" of "may"
- AU   as in the "ow" of "cow"
- OU   as in the "o" of "sow"

---

[1] U is frequently subvocalized when it occurs in a CV (consonant-vowel) syllable. Thus, *sukiyaki* is pronounced more like "skiyaki".

[2] Which value E takes depends primary upon the dialect of the speaker. However, the first value is generally predominant over the second. The "e" in "whey", typically occurs at the beginning of words or as an isolated interjection. E is always pronounced and is never subvocalized. There are no "helping vowels" in Japanese.

Generally speaking, Japanese vowels are "pure" vowels. They are called "pure" because they take the same sound value throughout their duration. Many English vowels are actually diphthongs. A diphthong typically combines two vowels to make a composite sound. One example of this is the "a" in "say". This is actually a diphthong composed of an **E** followed by and **I**. This is precisely how this sound is written in Japanese phonetic orthography. Another common diphthong is the "y" in "fly". This diphthong is composed of an **A** followed by an **I**. Again, this is just how the sound is written in Japanese. Since these diphthongs are made up of two pure vowels, they automatically take two time values, one for each component sound. Thus, a diphthong is very much like a Japanese long vowel.

Most Japanese consonants sound very much like English consonants. Japanese has ten fundamental consonants: **K**, **S**, **T**, **N**, **H**, **M**, **Y**, **R**, and **W**. Of these, **K**, **S**, **T**, and **H** are unvoiced. A consonant can become voiced simply by voicing it with the vocal cords. This is how **G**, **Z**, **D**, and **B** are produced. You can tell the difference simply by feeling your neck while pronouncing either "good" or "could". While most Japanese consonants sound much like English consonants, some are a bit different. The most famous of these is the Japanese **R** which sounds much more like an **L** or even a **D** than the English **R** does. Technically, a Japanese **R** is produced by a single tongue tap on the hard palate.

Some Japanese consonants appear to change their sounds when they are followed by certain vowels. This is how Japanese gets its **SH**, **CH**, **TS**, and **F** sounds. While **SH** and **CH** may appear to be diphthongs, they are actually single sounds and do not contribute addition time values. Since Hei'an times, Japanese have tried to keep their mouths closed and especially hide their teeth even when talking. Consequently, while the English **F** is a labial-dental consonant, the Japanese **F** is a bilabial consonant. This means that it is produced by pursing the lips instead of biting the lower lip as in English. Another interesting variant is the super hard **G**. This **G** can be found in words like *naginata*. In this word, the **G** often sounds a bit more like an **NG** than it does in English.[3] Regardless, our romanization system does not require you to know when a consonant is transformed by the following consonant. Each English letter or letter combination is always pronounced in exactly the same way.

Some Japanese Consonants

G	as in "get" or the **NG**[4] in "sing"
J	as in "jet"
SH	as in "shall" or "shop"
CH	as in "church" or "cheap"
Y	as in "yacht", "youth" or "yo-yo"

Some controversy surrounds the reading of classical Japanese texts from the Hei'an Period. During this period, many verbs ending in **-u** were written with a **-fu** ふ instead of a final **-u** う as is the modern practice. Further, the conjugation of these endings in classical texts is consistent with the thesis that these words were actually pronounced with an aspirated **H** or bilabial **F** sound rather than with their modern pronunciation which uses a simple vowel. There is a related problem caused by the existence of obsolete *kana* characters which represent sounds patterns such as **we** ゑ and **wo** を which are used only rarely in the language. Since comparative linguistics indicates that the general trend in languages is toward simplification and there is evidence in Japanese itself for such simplification having taken place, we will assume that the historical documents correctly transcribe the pronunciation used at the time when they were produced. Thus, where *kana* transcriptions of names are available in the original documents, these older readings have been transliterated and used in preference to modern pronunciation.

---

[3] I had a lot of difficulty trying to master this particular sound and may never have learned it. Further, there is no distinct orthographic representation for this **NG** and it must be learned on a word by word basis. Fortunately, this sound appears to be more a feature of a regional dialect, and like the "nya" appearing in Sado speech or the "gya" appearing in Nagoya speech, can be avoided completely. (Nayaoya is a city between Tokyo and Kyoto with a well known dialect.)

[4] As already noted, the actual pronunciation depends on the dialect of the speaker. Generally, this consonant is a hard **G** in the Kansai area around Kyoto and more of an **NG** sound in the Kantou region around Tokyo. Please remember that any **I** sound between the **K** and the **Y** in Kyoto and Tokyo must be subvocalized.

Japanese Phonetic Orthography

N	W	R	Y	M	H	N	T	S	K	vowel
ん	わ	ら	や	ま	は	な	た	さ	か	あ A
	ゐ	り		み	ひ	に	ち	し	き	い I
		る	ゆ	む	ふ	ぬ	つ	す	く	う U
	ゑ	れ		め	へ	ね	て	せ	け	え E
	を	ろ	よ	も	ほ	の	と	そ	こ	お O

In the table above, ん is syllabic **N**. This is a voiced nasal consonant without a following vowel and receives a full time value. Most of the other syllables can be produced simply by following the consonant with the appropriate vowel. However, **si** is pronounced as **shi**, **ti** as **chi**, **tu** as **tsu**, and **hu** as **fu**. While some romanization systems write these sound patterns the first way, we will write them the second way which is more like how they are pronounced. Also, **shi** sounds like the English word "she" and **pi** like "pea".

The consonants of the **K**, **S**, **T**, and **H** columns are all unvoiced, but can become voiced. These consonants become: hard **G**, **Z**, **D**, and **B** respectively. Both **shi** and **chi** become **ji**, and both **su** and **tsu** become **zu**. All of these voiced consonants are written by adding a pair of short strokes to the character. Thus, **hi** ひ becomes **bi** び. The **H** sounds also have a half-voiced form in which case the **H** sound becomes a **P** sound. These are written by adding a small circle to the character. Thus, **hi** ひ becomes **pi** ぴ pronounced "pie". This **P** sound typically appears as a stop consonant while the fully voiced **B** does not.

We already saw that Japanese has diphthongs composed of two pure vowels which occupy two mora. Japanese also has single mora dipthongs made by combining an element from the **I** row with an element from the **Y** column. The element from the **I** row is pronounced first, and the element from the **Y** column second. For example, **gya** ぎゃ is a diphthong which combines **gi** and **ya**. The two parts should merge with the **I** of **gi** subvocalized. Although your are combining two distinct sounds, these dipthongs receive only one time value. Thus, *bugyou* ぶぎょう has three mora. In *kana*, a stop consonant is indicated by "small **tsu**" immediately before the stop consonant. We indicate a stop consonant by doubling the following consonant. A stop is produced by momentarily interrupting the air passage with either the lips or the glottis before the consonant. Thus, Nippon にっぽん contains four mora counting both the stop and syallabic n **N**.

Kanji and How to Read Them

In Japanese, each *kanji* frequently has more than one way to read it. An *onyomi* (pronounced "own-yoh-me") reading is the original Chinese way of reading the character while a *kunyomi* (pronounced "coon-yoh-me") reading is a Japanese word represented by the character. Further, in Japanese, the same character may have more than one meaning. And, the same meaning may be represented by more than one character even though they are pronounced identically. While Japanese family names and personal names are usually written with characters which take their *kunyomi* readings, Buddhist names and posthumous names are read using the *onyomi* readings for the characters used to write them. Artistic names adopted by adepts of art forms associated with Zen Buddhism are also frequently modeled after Chinese names and are read using *onyomi*. Although there is generally a preferred *onyomi* reading, some characters have multiple readings associated with different Chinese dynasties. Hence, the *onyomi* listed for a character in a Chinese Character Dictionary or *kanwajiten* reflects when the character was incorporated into the Japanese language.

Reading Chinese characters or *kanji* can be very difficult. For example, 成 actually has ten distinct *kunyomi* readings which can occur in *nanori*. This problem was solved during the Japanese middle ages by writing small *furigana* characters immediately to the right of the difficult *kanji* in the text. *Furigana* was written either using the *hiragana* 平仮名 (ordinary *kana*) syllabary shown above or the more formal looking *katakana* 片仮名 (half letter *kana*). This is very fortunate, as it allows us to better reconstruct what the names used during the Japanese middle ages actually sounded like.

Japanese names are not always constructed using the usual *kunyomi* readings of their constituent morphemes. For example, while *utsukushii* 美しい is the *kunyomi* for 美 which means "beautiful", it is not used in forming names. Rather, this character typically takes the *onyomi* **MI** or one of the special *kunyomi* **haru** or **yoshi** which are only used in names. Consequently, the preferred reading of a name may be rather different than if the component *kanji* characters were part of a sentence. One clue for determining the correct reading is that proper Japanese adjectives are conjugated, but Japanese names have no place for the *hiragana* used to conjugate them. Therefore, the conjugation is dropped which transforms the morpheme into a noun. If the corresponding noun exists, then we can construct a name from it. Thus, we can use *aoi* 青い which means "blue" to form Aomori 青森 which means "blue woods". However, the corresponding *kunyomi* noun for *utsukushii* 美しい or "beautiful" does not exist, and another reading must be substituted. Consequently, there are Japanese words such as *bijin* 美人 which means "beautiful person" and Japanese names such as Yoshiko 美子 which means "beautiful child".

Because of the complication in reading and writing Japanese names, *kanwajiten* often include an appendix on how to use Chinese characters in Japanese names. Further, Japanese commonly explain which letters are used in their names. This allows the listener to correctly understand the meaning of the speakers name and also allows them to write it down correctly in an adult manner. Because of the frequency of homophones and semi-homophones (words which although they are pronounced the same and have related meanings are none the less are written with different *kanji* characters depending on the context), Japanese are usually rather conscious of their written language. This, of course, carries over into names as well.

Repetition of Sound and Meaning

Many native Japanese words repeat either sound patterns or even morphemes. One example of this is animal sounds. In Japan, a dog barks "wan wan" and a cat cries "nya nya". This sort of repetition is so common that Japanese *kana* includes an abbreviation for repeating the preceding syllable. There is also a special *kana* for repeating a meaning unit which may consist of several syllables. Finally, when writing in *kanji*, the character 々 indicates a repetition of the previous *kanji* character. Both *kana* repetitions and 々 appear in onomastic sources. Of these, it is more important to understand the role of 々 in names such as Sasaki 佐々木. As with ordinary words, these words should be phrased so that each of the repeated patterns remains an atomic unit. Sometimes, the second phrase of such patterns is obscured by a phonetic transformation. For example, the **T** in the second half of "toki-doki" becomes voiced to produce a **D** due to coarticulation with the preceding vowel. Regardless, this word should be broken into "toki-doki" and in no other way. Although "toki-doki" is a native Japanese word, as with many other things in Japanese, this process is easier to understand if you know *kanji*. Consequently, the *kanji* version of a Japanese name or word is generally our best guide.

Rhythm, Syllables, and Mora

As mentioned previously, Japanese is *isochronous* which means that, unlike English, sound duration conveys meaning. Linguists believe that this is a comparatively recent development and that Old Japanese had a strict C-V structure. When isochronicity replaced consonant marking is unclear as *furigana* continued to mark internal rhythm units or mora with initial consonants long after the shift is believed to have occurred. Syllabic breaks coincide with meaning units represented by *kanji* which convey both sound and meaning. You can pause between *kanji*, but should not do so between mora belonging to the same *kanji*. For example, Kin'kaku'ji 金閣寺 (Temple of the Golden Pavilion) has five mora and three syllables which corresponds to the meaning units represented by the *kanji*. Although some languages use marks that look like apostrophes to mark accents, the romanization system in this monograph uses apostrophes to mark mora divisions to clarify rhythm. As marking all mora or syllable divisions would be distracting, only ones likely to be confused are marked. Under our system, 金閣寺 is written Kin'kaku'ji.

Intonation

Unlike Chinese, Japanese is not a tonal language. Rather, it is a pitch accented language where pitch patterns mark word boundaries and sentence phrasing. Japanese inflect questions much as in English by a rising pitch pattern at the end of a sentence. Thus, unless a question is intended, you should complete each word with either flat or falling pitch. Beyond this, you need not overly concern yourself with intonation as the intonation for specific words varies greatly. For example, the intonation of *ame* frequently depends upon whether the intended word is "rain" or "hard candy". However, this variation is reversed between the Kansai and Kantou regions of central Honshuu. Finally, Japanese dictionaries such as *Daijirin* include intonation tables which allow them to numerically indicate NHK broadcast standard intonation for each word entry.

Synopsis of Japanese History

From the dawn of Japanese history handed down to us by Chinese scholars to the present, Japanese history spans over fifteen centuries. Fortunately, many excellent texts are now available in English which cover either all or part of Japanese history. Thus, I will make no real attempt at a complete exposition of this vast subject. However, the text frequently refers to Japanese historical periods, and the early appearance of every onomastic entry is dated to one of these periods. Generally, once a name entered the pool of available names, it remained in use throughout the mediæval period. Thus, if a name was used in several different periods of Japanese history, the earliest period is given. Feminine given names are a notable exception to this maxim. Many women who lived during the early classical period and before bore descriptive names which seem to have disappeared by the Japanese middle ages. Regardless, this chapter is a brief account of Japanese history with a special emphasis on the evolution of names and titles. Its sole purpose is to provide a reference for the era notations in the onomastic tables.

Joumon Period — Joumon-jidai 縄文時代 **(7000 BCE–200 BCE)**

During this prehistoric age, Japan was populated by hunter-gatherer societies with some primitive agriculture using stone-age tools. Although some people believe that these people are the ancestors of the modern Japanese, it is a unlikely that the Joumon-jidai people were the cultural or even the direct linguistic ancestors of the Japanese. Regardless, this age saw the birth of the Japanese people.

Many people speculate about the ancestry of the Japanese. Apparently there were Caucasoid immigrants from Shakalin, Polynesian immigrants from the Pacific Islands, and immigrants from Southeast Asia who brought rice culture with them to Japan. The diverse background of the Japanese people is even today reflected by the genetic diversity stretched across the Japanese archipelago. Regardless, Japanese culture and history seems most tied to a group of people who migrated from central Asia through China and the Korean peninsula. The remains from this period primarily consist of stone artifacts including Venus figures. Around 300 BC, bronze and iron culture began to spread from Manchuria onto the Korean peninsula. Ultimately, iron culture was to swiftly overtake bronze culture as it moved across the Sea of Japan in about 200 BCE.

Yayoi Period — Yayoi-jidai 弥生時代 **(200 BCE–100 CE)**

This age saw the transformation of Japanese society from a neolithic culture to a metal culture. This period left may neolithic artifacts including stone agricultural tools such as the *magatama* or hand-scythe which is currently believed to have been used for harvesting grain. Material culture expanded, and this period left a variety of artifacts including wooden combs and bronze bells. In 108 BCE, the Han dynasty conquered North Korea and established a Chinese colony near modern Pyongyang. Shortly thereafter, the Japanese began to send missions to the Chinese colonial government. In 57 CE, the Japanese sent what was probably the first official envoy to China itself. This envoy was probably sent by one of the Kyuushuu "queendoms" as Northwest Kyuushuu remained for many years the principal route to the mainland. The Chinese court gave the envoy a gold seal which conferred title of kingship.

Thus began a long history of relations between Japan and Imperial China. Ultimately, Japan would look to China as a source for culture, scholarship, and institutions of government. Although Japan was destined to fight a long series of wars with China on the Korean peninsula, interest in China often waned whenever the Chinese government became weak. Specifically, Japanese interest in Chinese culture waned following the fall of the Wei dynasty in 265 CE. In general, Japanese cultural history expresses cycles of importation followed by assimilation and refinement. Later, we will see this pattern repeated when Japan imported Chinese imperial government.

Tumulus Period — Kofun-jidai 古墳時代 (100–562)

This age is named after the monumental tombs resembling small hills which were constructed for its aristocracy. During this time, the Japanese offered animal sacrifices to their gods. Chinese records attest to human sacrifices as late as 247 and oxen were still sacrificed much later. The Utari people (commonly called Ainu) continued to ritually kill bear cubs until the practice was abolished following the Meiji restoration in the nineteenth century. Under the influence of Buddhism, these sacrifices were replaced with food offerings of rice and fruit. But, occasionally fish would still be offered. In ancient times, the emperor was interred with living servants.

This period saw the arrival of the pony soldiers and possibly the beginnings of the aristocratic and warrior classes in Japan. Following the fall of the Wei dynasty in 265, China broke up into provinces. In Japan, the aristocracy and what became the imperial dynasty had emerged by 300. Thus, a vigorous Japan faced a weak China. The Japanese seized the advantage and invaded Korea in 369. With China in disorder, Korea broke up into three kingdoms. Thus the Japanese expeditionary force was able to establish a dependent kingdom in Korea and to rescue the king of Paikche in 391 from the king of Koguryö. As the Japanese began to keep their own annals at this time, this event marks the beginning of recorded Japanese history.

These events and other periods of civil disorder on the continent prompted many to emigrate to Japan. Often these immigrant groups included courtiers, scholars, and artisans who were integrated into Japanese aristocratic society. The *Nihongi* recounts the arrival of many such groups and gives details concerning their resettlement in Japan. The aristocracy of these immigrant groups appears to have been integrated into the native aristocracy while the peasants and artisans were settled on previously barren land. Thus, a new *uji* or clan arriving from the continent would be integrated into the federation of noble houses. When bureaucratic imperial government was instituted, the imperial government actively recruited Chinese scholars. Buddhist scholars and missionaries continued to arrive in Japan throughout the Japanese middle ages.

Prior to *Taika no kaishin* 大化の改新 or Taika Reform in 643, Japan was divided into independent clans called *uji* 氏 each holding its own territory and serving its own principal deity. As these were kinship groups, the *uji* were true "clans" unlike the military bands of the warring states period which are also sometimes called clans. Each *uji* had its own *uji no kami* 氏の上 or clan chief. At this time, the *uji no kami* was selected by the *uji* itself and not by any central government. Later, the imperial family gained control of the *uji* first by securing the right to approve appointment of the *uji no kami* and later by transforming them into appointed imperial offices. By the early eighth century, the clan chiefs were known as *uji no chouja* 氏の長者.

Like certain Germanic tribes, Japanese clans claimed a common relationship with a particular god. The gods were often personifications of natural forces. Unusual natural objects such as large trees or oddly shaped stones were considered divine as well. While the Japanese have a beastiary full of supernatural beasts and monsters, the Japanese did not invest the large trees and rocks which they worshiped with an anthropomorphic spirit. Rather, the Japanese gods are the divine antecedents of the Japanese race who preside over the well being of the nation. The Japanese gods live either in the mountains or in the sea. Consequently, the path to every shrine in Japan is said to lead either to the mountains or to the sea.

One of the chief functions of the clan head was conducting religious ceremonies. These ceremonies were primarily concerned with maintaining ritual purity and assuring agricultural production. Even a god could become ritually impure. The god Iza'nagi no Mikoto had to purify himself after viewing the decomposed corpse of the goddess Iza'nami no Mikoto in the land of the dead.[5] The god purified himself by washing himself in a river and putting on clean clothes. Thus, the native religion was essentially a purity cult. Physical uncleanliness of either body or clothing was counted as ritual defilement. Menstruation, sexual intercourse, child birth, wounds, and death all produced ritual impurity as well. Certain actions such as murder, inflicting wounds, incest, and bestiality resulted in impurity and where considered criminal acts.

---

[5] While Buddhism has elaborate notions concerning hell, paradise and reincarnation, Shintoh does not. While Japanese Buddhists follow the Indian tradition of cremating the dead, Shintoh practice was to bury the corpse. Thus, ghosts are much more commonly associated with Shintoh than with Buddhism. Eventually, Buddhist death and mourning practices superseded the native Shintoh customs.

Following the example of Iza'nagi no Mikoto, bathing became an important part of the native cult. Places and buildings could also be purified by waving wands or branches taken from sacred trees. Eventually, music, dance, and the Noh theatre evolved to entertain the gods and to aid in the purification rituals. So important was the ritual function of the aristocracy, that one of the primary attractions of Buddhism to the nobility was its more developed ritual.

The clan chiefs and their immediate families eventually coalesced into the emperor, his family, and the attendant nobles each claiming descent from a divine ancestor. Ama no Minakanushi no Mikoto 天御中主尊 was the founder of the divine race from which all of the gods and the clan chieftains were descended. The imperial family claimed descent from the sun goddess Amaterasu Oomikami[6] 天照大御神. Both the Nakatomi *uji* 中臣氏 and the Imibe 忌部 enjoyed important positions in the national cult as well. The Nakatomi were responsible for the "Great Purification" which was held twice each year while the Imibe performed rites of abstention and maintained taboos on behalf of the whole community. Clan rivalry eventually deposed the Nakatomi from power as other families seized upon the imperial family as a means for promoting the interests of their own families. By the fifth century, the emperor was creating, degrading, and even disbanding clans. As well as holding land, a clan could possess monopoly corporations of skilled artisans. The nobility were able to form new monopoly corporations rather freely. Others were created by the emperor and were often dedicated to the support of a an individual or a religious institution. There were also independent corporations which constituted a rival social structure. Corporations were of two types: guilds called *be* 部 and agricultural collectives called *tomo* 伴.

The *be* 部 were based upon skilled artisans such as weavers or scribes many of whom were immigrants from the continent. These were essentially closed occupational groups somewhat akin to European guilds. Unlike their European counterparts, these guilds might possess dependent agricultural estates. Further, these early monopoly corporations did not band together to form civic corporations. Frequently, immigrant groups included many skilled artisans and the resulting corporation would become a new *be*. This accounts for most of the clan names which end in -**be**. While it is tempting to read all such names as if they actually ended in -**be**, they were frequently read in entirely different ways. Consequently, we can not simply agglutinate the name for some object and the sound "be" and reliably form a name for one of these corporations or its noble house. Another way for an *uji* to acquire such a name was for a noble to obtain a preexisting corporation. In this case, he might choose to name his new *uji* after the corporation. While the *be* were frequently based upon skilled groups which owned villages of serfs, the *tomo* 伴 appear to have been strictly farming collectives.

From the beginning of the fifth century, clan chiefs began to give themselves special titles. Here there was a strong class distinction based upon presumed descent from one of the deities. That is, the hierarchy of the human nobility reflected the perceived hierarchy of their divine progenitors. Thus, the *omi* 臣 were thought to be descendents of the imperial family and through them the sun goddess. The *muraji* 連 claimed descent either from one of the other heavenly deities or from one of the earthly deities. The *kuni no miyatsuko* 国造 were provincial governors, the *tomo no miyatsuko* 伴造 administered monopoly corporations, and *inaki* 稲置 administered rural districts. Originally, these honours would be combined with the name of the district or occupation to form a complete title. Thus, we obtain titles such as Kashiwade no Omi 膳臣 who possessed the Kashiwadebe 膳部 guild charged with gathering and preparing oak leaves for food.

Among the noble class, marriage partners lived in separate residences and visited each other. This marriage pattern continued until the end of the Hei'an Period when both architectural styles and residential patterns of marriage partners began to change. In early Japan, women could ride astride horses, fight in battles, become clan chieftains, and generally enjoyed a great deal of autonomy. Women regularly fought in battle until the failure of the Joukyuu Disturbance during the Kamakura Period established the supremacy of the professional soldier. Female clan chiefs enjoyed the same titles as their masculine counterparts. Likewise, when a woman became emperor, she enjoyed the same title as her brothers.

---

[6] This is one of several titular forms which appear in the names of Japanese gods. It roughly translates as "supreme honourable god". While this is the name of a goddess, Japanese does not typically conjugate for either gender or number. **-nomikoto** 尊 is another titular form which is more commonly found in the names of gods. This "title" means "honourable" and is found in such names as Izanami no Mikoto and Iza'nagi no Mikoto.

Asuka Period — Asuka-jidai 飛鳥時代 (562–645)

This period begins with the collapse of Mima'na 任那 which was a Japanese colony in the southern part of the Korean peninsula. Inside Japan, the clan chiefs of the central clans instituted a census in order to govern their newly acquired possessions and the refugees arriving from the continent. Early census records were primarily interested in establishing the age and gender of the people occupying each building in a district. As peasants were not permitted to have official names, the houses themselves had names, but not the people. Houses were named either after a topographic feature, a monopoly corporation, or a local noble.

The imperial period did not really begin until the destruction of the Mo'no'nobe clan 物部氏 by Soga Umako 蘇我馬子 in 587. Prince Shoutoku Taishi 聖徳太子 (572–621) is probably the most famous figure from this period. He was a son of Emperor Youmei Tennou 用明天皇. He was originally known as Umaya no Ouji 厩戸皇子 which literally means "stable door". After his aunt, Empress Suiko Tennou 推古天皇 (554–628), ascended the throne in 593, he became crown prince and was called Shoutoko Taishi. Although he never became emperor, he administered the government as crown prince and *sesshou* 摂政 or regent until his death. Thus, even at this early time, we can see the Japanese principle of shadow government in action. Shoutoku Taishi introduced Chinese political ideology and institutions into the Japanese government. He was also an active supporter of Buddhism which was established in Japan during this period. The Buddhist temples were organized into a system of head temples such as Hou'ryuu'ji 法隆寺 with local temples scattered throughout the country. This was a period during which Japan imported much foreign culture including cultural elements from Western Asia, India, Greece, and Egypt.

The first written annals of Japanese history were compiled in 621. The *Kyuujiki* 旧事記 or "Annals of Ancient Things" compiled primarily from Chinese sources under the auspices of the court. It was entrusted to the Soga clan 蘇我氏, but was burned when the Soga 蘇我 themselves were destroyed in 645. Fortunately, a portion of the *Kyuujiki* called the *Kokuki* 国記 or "National Annals" was saved from destruction. Thus, from this era, it becomes possible to document Japanese names.

Hakuhou Period — Hakuhou-jidai 白鳳時代 (645–710)

The government was reorganized along Chinese lines in 645. The monopoly corporations and the territorial holdings of the nobility were abolished one year later in 646. The nobility became administrators in the central government and governors in the provinces. The government was divided into three departments under the emperor and the country was divided into administrative districts. While this system did not prove to be effective, it remained nominally in force until Kenmu Shinsei 建武新政 in 1334 when Emperor Go-Daigo Tennou 後醍醐天皇 briefly reestablished imperial control and reorganized the imperial government along Chinese lines. Even though the clan chiefs lost their holdings, they continued to use their old ranks and titles.

Naka no Ooe Ouji 中大兄皇子 was one of the most important figures in establishing supremacy of the imperial family. His name was Kuzuraki no Ouji 葛城皇子. He was known as "Naka no Oouji" to distinguish him from the other *ouji* or imperial princes. He was also known as Amemikoto Hirakasuwake 天命開別. Together with Nakatomi no Kamatari 中臣鎌足, Kuzuraki no Ouji destroyed the Soga uji 蘇我氏 in 645. He became the official heir and was known as Naka no Ooe Koutaishi 中大兄皇太子. Two years later, he succeeded his mother, Empress Saimei Tennou 斉明天皇, and moved the capital to Oumi 近江 where he reigned as emperor. He is known to history as Emperor Tenji Tennou 天智天皇. Thus, the imperial family[7] became preeminent in Japanese political life. Nakatomi no Kamatari was rewarded with high office in the new government and permission to form the Fujiwara *uji* 藤原氏. From this time, forming new clans required imperial dispensation. Years later, Toyotomi Hideyoshi 豊臣秀吉 sought imperial dispensation to form his new clan.

---

[7] While we can trace the history of the imperial family, it is difficult to find out anything about an "imperial clan". The imperial family may have possessed its own clan or it may simply have been a house within one of the major *uji* such as the Ootomo 大伴. Whatever the origin of the imperial family, it eventually acquired private estates during the Heian period.

In 682, Emperor Tenmu Tennou 天武天皇 commissioned a chronicle known as the *Kojiki* 古事記 or "Annals of Old Affairs" which was to contain a "history of the emperors and matters of high antiquity". This chronicle was finally completed in 712, thirty years after it was commissioned. In 684, Emperor Tenmu Tennou 天武天皇 finally abolished the old titular system used by the nobility replacing it with a system of twelve cap ranks and eight codified *kabane* 姓. These *kabane* were called *mahito* 真人, *asomi* 朝臣, *sukune* 宿禰, *imiki* 忌寸, and *michi no shi* 道師 which were new, and *omi* 臣, *muraji* 連, and *inaki* 稲置 which were from the old system. Thus, the old clan and corporate titles were transformed into offices in the new imperial government. Consequently, Azuma no Muraji 安曇連 and Kashiwade no Omi 膳臣 became ministerial titles for court officials charged with the emperor's table. These and other titles conveyed field allotments and other property to the holder of the title.

Throughout this time, the capital was moved upon the death of the old emperor and a new one constructed. With the coming of the Nara Period in a few years, Japan's replica of the Chinese imperial government would be complete. The *Taihouritsuryou* 大宝律令 Civic Code or Taihou Code was based on the Chinese Code of the Yung-Hwui. The Taihou Code was written by Fujiwara no Fuhito 藤原不比等 and promulgated by his grandson Emperor Monmu Tennou 文武天皇 in 702. Just before moving to its first permanent capital, the imperial government struck its first coinage in 708. Although the first issue included both copper and silver coins, subsequent issues were of copper only. Thus, the government was prepared to embark upon administering the nation through a system of civil servants, governmental allotments of fields, a regular census, and regulated taxation. However, Japanese society continued to be based upon family units and filial loyalty.

Nara Period — Nara-jidai 奈良時代 (710–794)

The first permanent capital was established under the reign of Empress Genmei Tennou 元明天皇. It was modeled after a Chinese imperial city and called Heijoukyou 平城京. The empress was called *Yamato neko amatsu mihiro toyokuni nari hime.* Like Tenmu Tennou, Genmei Tennou commissioned two annals. In 712, she commissioned the *Kojiki* 古事記 or "Annals of Old Things". In 713, Genmei Tennou commissioned the *Fudoki* 風土記. She also struck the first copper coinage. The *Kojiki* was published during the reign of her daughter, Empress Genshou Tennou 元正天皇. Like her mother, Genshou Tennou fostered the arts, the sciences, and agriculture. Buddhism flourished in Heijoukyou and large temples were built. Eventually, the monks became very powerful, and the capital was relocated in part to avoid their influence. Today, the old imperial city is known as Nara 奈良. Nara remains one of the cultural centers of Japan. Thus, the founding of Heijoukyou at Nara marks the true dawn of the classical period of Japanese culture. This was the period during which the Japanese attempted to emulate Chinese government which had a large civil service.

At first, the Japanese administered an examination system based upon the Chinese model. In principle, admission into the civil service was, as in China, dependent upon successfully sitting for a series of examinations. Prospective bureaucrats studied for these examinations at an academy, and the Japanese government imported instructors to open schools. While in theory open to all, admission to these academies was based in some degree upon parental rank and even upon the specific family that an aspiring young noble belonged to. Ultimately, appointment to one of these academies either to a teaching post or as a student became a hereditary prerogative. After the fall of the T'ang 唐 dynasty in China, the Japanese adopted an explicitly hereditary system. Finally, in 894 the government discontinued official missions to China.

Hei'an Period — Hei'an-jidai 平安時代 (794–1184)

To escape the depredations of the warrior monks, the capital was first relocated to Naga'oka'kyou 長岡京 in 784 and finally in 794 to Hei'ankyou 平安京. Many large temples were built on Mt. Hiei 比叡山 which overlooked the capital and classical Buddhism flourished during this period. Nara-jidai and Hei'an-jidai are the true classical periods of Japanese civilization. However, the monks living on Mt. Hiei 比叡山 constituted their own armies and frequently intervened in court politics. The imperial family managed to found their own "clan" with its own private holdings. Although the imperial family was able to make inroads into the Kamakura Bakufu, the emperor ultimately lost power to the *kuge* 公家 or court nobility and especially to the Fujiwara. In turn, the *kuge* lost power to their rusticated cousins and their retainers who constituted the emerging warrior houses or *buke* 武家.

The *kuge* maintained control of the emperor by forcing marriages, naming their own descendents heir, and by forcing the early retirement of each emperor so that the emperor was always an infant. Thus, the office of *kanpaku* 関白 or "imperial regent" for adult emperors and a similar guardianship for infant emperors were available to be filled by a member of the dominant noble family. The office of *kanpaku* was created in the ninth century by Emperor Koukou Tennou 光孝天皇 to reward Fujiwara Mototsune 藤原基経 for overthrowing Emperor Youzei Tennou 陽成天皇 in 884. During much of the Hei'an Period, this office was held by the Fujiwara family. Ironically, the Fujiwara attained prominence by helping the imperial family to destroy the Soga who had earlier attempted to attain power by the same means. The imperial family attempted to maintain influence by establishing a cloistered second court for the retired emperors in 1086. This shadow government by retired emperors or *insei* 院政 continued until the Mongol invasion caused the collapse of the Kamakura Bakufu making way for reinstituting direct imperial rule.

Although the equal-fields policy borrowed from the Chinese asserted that all lands ultimately belonged to the emperor. Lands were ceded by the emperor when establishing Buddhist temples. Further, lands came into the possession of various noble families[8] and through them to their rusticated retainers and cousins in the countryside. For the peasant, consigning their allotment to a temple or to one of the great families conferred the advantage of immunity to labor levies. Thus, the tax base of the imperial government gradually eroded. As the equal fields system collapsed, the imperial family built their own system of private temples and estates and even constructed detached palaces and administrative buildings outside of the imperial capital. Further, the rusticated nobility employed retainers called *samurai* 侍 who provided their territory with a military defense which the capital was increasingly incapable of. Samurai is derived from *saburau*, a verb meaning "to serve", and was originally applied to high ranking female retainers in the imperial palace.

- ❖ Creation of the *insei* 院政 Cloistered Court — 1069
- ❖ Taira no Kiyomori 平 清盛 becomes *daijoudaijin* 太政大臣 — 1167
- ❖ Genpei no Souran 源平の争乱 — 1180-5
- ❖ Mi'namoto no Yoritomo 源 頼朝 becomes 征夷大将軍 *sei'itaishougun* — 1192
- ❖ Mongol Invasion — 1279
- ❖ Ashikaga Bakufu 足利幕府 — 1336

The Japanese mediæval period begins with the Genpei War *Genpei no Souran* 源平争乱 between the Genji 源氏 or Mi'namoto clan and the Heike 平家 Taira family or Heishi 平氏 clan. The Heike secured control of the imperial government through palace intrigue and were eventually overthrown by the Genji. First, Taira Kiyomori 平 清盛 succeeded in having himself proclaimed *daijoudaijin* or "chancellor" and had one of his infant descendents proclaimed emperor. The Heike left the imperial government intact and ruled the country from their villas in Hei'ankyou 平安京 the imperial capital. Seeing their opportunity, the Genji rebelled and eventually destroyed the Heike and the infant emperor. The Genji established a military government at Kamakura 鎌倉 with Mi'namoto no Yoritomo 源頼朝 receiving a variety of imperial appointments including *sei'itaishougun* 征夷大将軍. We now call this military government the Kamakura Bakufu.

Kamakura Period — Kamakura-jidai 鎌倉時代 (1184–1333)

During this period the emperor in Hei'ankyou 平安京 usually abdicated when very young. Official functions were generally performed by the *kanpaku* who was the imperial regent. Although, the first three shoguns were from the Mi'namoto *uji*, later they were either taken from the Fujiwara *uji* which was one of the ancient noble clans or were princes of the imperial family itself. When Yoritomo died in 1199, the court asserted its authority by delaying appointing his son *shougun*. The *bakufu* responded by appointing a council of regents headed by Houjou Tokimasa 北条時政 who was a member of the Taira *uji*. Following the death of Mi'namoto Sa'netomo 源実朝 in 1219, the *bakufu* was controlled by a member of the Houjou clan 北条氏 who was appointed *shikken* 執権 or shougunal regent. Further, the retired emperors continued their attempts to influence Japanese politics as well.

---

[8] Japanese society was not strictly separated into castes until a formal caste system was instituted by the Tokugawa government in the seventeenth century. The caste system instituted in Japan was a greatly simplified version of the Indian caste system. The Indian caste system places the Brahmin caste at the top followed by the military caste.

The Kamakura Bakufu had its own structure and offices and acted in parallel to the imperial government. Although the court continued to appoint provincial governors,[9] the *bakufu* appointed a *soutsuibushi* 総追捕使 as "high constable" for each province. These men were responsible for keeping order in the provinces. Later, they were known as *shugo* 守護. Further, the *bakufu* obtained control over the *jitou* 地頭 who were originally appointed by the imperial government for each of the *shou'en* 荘園 private estates. These tax collectors were the local representative of governmental authority throughout most of the middle ages. In 1221, Retired Emperor Go-Toba Joukou 後鳥羽上皇 declared the *shikken* or shougunal regent an outlaw and sent his army of palace guards, warrior monks, and disaffected *samurai* to attack Kamakura. After suppressing the *Joukyuu Disturbance* 丞久の変, the *shikken* established a headquarters at Rokuhara 六波羅 to supervise the imperial court.[10] There, two *tandai* 探題 or "inspectors" governed the capital district. The *bakufu* rewarded its supporters with new *jitou* posts with greater revenue than before 1223. These offices gave the newly appointed *bakufu* official effective title to the land and these offices were accordingly passed on as heritable property. The emperor however continued to represent an important cultural property and was the imprimatur of legitimacy. Therefore the imperial capital and the imperial court remained important cultural objects in Japanese politics. The role of culture in Japanese politics must not be underestimated. Otherwise, the role of figures such as Sen no Rikyuu 千之利休 is incomprehensible. Beginning with this period, the emperor's family was gradually impoverished.

Despite the failure of Go-Toba Joukou to overthrow the *bakufu*, the *insei* cloistered government remained quite strong and the imperial family still controlled many great *shou'en* estates. In 1242, Emperor Go-Saga Tennou 御嵯峨天皇 ascended the throne. He abdicated in favor of his son, Emperor Go-Fukakusa Tennou 御深草天皇 in 1246, to ascend to the cloistered palace and control of the *insei*. He was an ally of the Houjou regents and succeeded in having one of his sons, Prince Mu'netaka Shinnou 宗尊親王 elected *shougun*. Unfortunately for the imperial family, he had Go-Fukakusa Tennou abdicate in favour of his younger brother, Emperor Kameyama Tennou 亀山天皇. The *bakufu* happily accepted the decision to perpetuate the imperial line through Kameyama in favour of Go-Fukakusa. When Go-Saga died, he left the very valuable *choukoudou* 長講堂 revenues and other substantial *shou'en* rights to Go-Fukakusa. Further, he instructed the *bakufu* to choose both the emperor and the senior retired emperor. The *bakufu* was unable to decisively select either, and two competing imperial lines emerged. Unable to suppress one line in favour of the other, the *bakufu* settled upon the two lines sharing the throne. Following the death of Go-Saga, each emperor reigned for only a short time before abdicating to yet another claimant. Thus, the imperial succession alternated between these two houses until they split completely following the Kenmu Restoration.

Upon the abdication of Emperor Ha'nazono Tennou 花園天皇 of the senior branch in 1318, Emperor Go-Daigo Tennou 後醍醐天皇 of the junior branch ascended the throne at the age of thirty. He was determined to abolish both the *bakufu* and the *insei*. His hope was to rule the country directly until his death. He abolished the *insei* in 1321 with the support of his father Go-Uda In 後宇多院 who resigned his position as senior retired emperor. At first, Prince Ku'ni'naga Shinnou 邦良親王 of the senior branch was elected crown prince. When Ku'ni'naga died, Go-Daigo nominated his own son, Prince Mori'naga Shinnou 護良親王, but the *bakufu* elected another member of the senior branch of the imperial family. Before Go-Daigo could assemble an army to attack Kamakura, the *bakufu* sent an expeditionary force against the capital in 1331. Go-Daigo escaped with the imperial sword and seal, but was later captured and taken to Rokuhara 六波羅. When, Kamakura sent orders to enthrone Prince Kazuhito Taishi 量仁太子 as Emperor Kougon Tennou 光厳天皇, Go-Daigo refused to abdicate and withheld the regalia. Thus, the Japanese consider the succession of Emperor Kougon Tennou and his court to be illegitimate. The *bakufu* held Emperor Go-Daigo at Rokuhara until the Houjou regent banished him to Oki island.

---

[9] These officials held titles consisting of the name of a province followed by *-nokami* 守. Thus, the governor of Musashi province would be called Musashi'nokami 武蔵守. Within the context of the Society for Creative Anachronism, this usage appears to be appropriate for landed barons who desire to recreate classical Japanese society. Those interested in later period should probably use *shugo* 守護 instead.

[10] Rokuhara was an old Taira estate located Southeast of the capital. The Houjou governors patterned their headquarters after the one which the Houjou family had already established in Kamakura to control the *bakufu*.

Prince Mori'naga Shinnou 護良新納 issued *ryouji* 令旨 enlisting disaffected warriors to the cause of the emperor. Many warriors responded and the *bakufu* was forced to raise its own army which depleted the defenses of Houjou territories. Hearing of the success of his supporters on the battlefield, Go-Daigo escaped and returned to the mainland. The *bakufu* sent an army under Ashikaga Taka'uji 足利尊氏 to attack the court established by Go-Daigo in Houki province. However, Taka'uji had accepted a commission from the imperial court in the South. He suddenly defected and attacked the Houjou garrison in the capital. Rokuhara was easily captured, but the members of the senior dynasty with their Houjou supporters escaped the city. The fleeing Houjou were trapped by imperial forces, and committed suicide. Upon hearing of the fall of the capital, the remainder of the *bakufu* army lifted their siege of the imperial forces and surrendered. Kamakura was finally captured by Nitta Yoshisada 新田義貞 acting under imperial decree.

Muromomachi Period — Muromachi-jidai 室町時代 (1333–1573)

In many ways, the Muromachi Period represents the "High Middle Ages" of Japan. It was during this period that many of the characteristic features of traditional Japanese society were developed. While this period actually began with an assertion of imperial authority, the military or *buke* class formed the dominant class during this period, and the old imperial government was totally eclipsed.

Kenmu Restoration — Kenmu Shinsei 建武新政 (1334–1336)

Emperor Go-Daigo was principally concerned with reinstituting imperial rule. After the fall of the *bakufu* and its Houjou regents, Go-Daigo abolished the office of *kanpaku*. He also refused to appoint a new *sei'itaishougun*. Unfortunately, the imperial government made prominent warriors governors of provinces, often at the expense of more capable men. Further, the imperial government was slow to distributed *onshou* 恩賞 awards for the services rendered by minor supporters. Many of these smaller families had never been fully compensated for repelling the Mongols and had hoped to profit from the fall of the *bakufu*. While the emperor had vast personal holdings, the government was impoverished and stuck new copper coins.

A surviving band of Houjou supporters seized Kamakura driving out Prince Nari'naga Shinnou 成良親王 along with his regent, Ashikaga Tadayoshi 足利置義 who was Taka'uji's brother. However, the court refused Taka'uji's request for an imperial warrant to march against Kamakura. This greatly angered Taka'uji, and he marched on Kamakura on his own initiative. After capturing Kamakura, Takuji established a court for himself and began to distribute territory to his supporters.

Go-Daigo declared Taka'uji and outlaw and issued a commission to suppress the eastern rebels. At first the imperial forces were successful, but Taka'uji understood the need to reward his commanders. At Ashigara pass, Taka'uji awarded estates to his men. These battlefield awards were an innovation which even Yoritomo had not arrogated to himself. This prospect of immediate reward not only encouraged the Ashikaga army, but persuaded unit commanders of the imperial army to defect as well. Further, the Ashikaga were a branch of the Mi'namoto *uji* or clan, and many warriors saw in Taka'uji a chance to reestablish the original Kamakura Bakufu.

The Ashikaga army marched on the capital, and the emperor was forced to flee once again. Although Taka'uji took up residence in the capital, loyalist forces soon retook the city. Taka'uji escaped to Kyuushuu, and the emperor reentered the imperial city. Taka'uji raised a new army and slowly advanced on the capital which he took after fighting a decisive battle at Mi'natogawa 湊川. The emperor once again took refuge in a monastery. After entrusting the imperial regalia to his son, Go-Daigo reentered with the capital with duplicate regalia to confer with Taka'uji. The regalia was given to Koumyou'in 光明院, a member of the senior branch of the imperial family, who was proclaimed emperor by Taka'uji. Although one of his sons was declared crown prince, Go-Daigo escaped to Yoshi'no 吉野 and established his own court.

Divided Court Period — Nanbokuchou-jidai 南北朝時代 (1336–1392)

The disputed imperial succession resulted in the establishment of rival courts. During this period there were two emperors and two courts called the *hokuchou* 北朝 Northern court and the *nanchou* 南朝 Southern Court. Each of the courts proclaimed *nengou* 年号 or era names. In this system, the ordinal number of the year is reckoned with respect to the most recently proclaimed era. These *nengou* are a special kind of *houmyou* or Buddhist name. These conflicting era names complicate chronology from this period.

Although the Northern Court of the senior branch of the imperial family was supported by the *bakufu*, the Southern Court held the legitimate line of succession. This perpetuated the rivalry between the two branches of the imperial house. Though with few resources, the Southern Court and its supporters proved to be quite tenacious. Several times, loyalist armies of the Southern Court seized the capital and the members of the senior branch of the imperial family. However, the loyalist armies were too small to withstand a siege by the *bakufu* army. The loyalist army was also unable to maintain a permanent capital for the Southern Court. Urban warfare spawned a new type of warrior. An *ashigaru* 足軽 was a light infantryman who carried only a single weapon. These troops, who came to specialize in surprise attacks, later played an important role in the Ou'nin War.

Eventually, the *bakufu* negotiated a union between the two imperial houses. Under the terms of union, the emperor was to abdicate in favour of the Northern pretender and succession would again alternate between the two houses. Emperor Go-Kameyama Tennou 後亀山天皇 went up to the capital from Yoshi'no bringing the imperial regalia. His intention was to solemnly abdicate according to prescribed ritual and surrender the regalia. However, the *bakufu* seized the emperor and the regalia which it transferred to the northern pretender without the *joukoku* 讓国 ceremony of "surrendering the state".

Muromachi Period — Muromachi-jidai 室町時代 (1336–1573)

Taka'uji was awarded the title *sei'itaishougun* when his military government was installed in the Muromachi district of the capital two years after his seizure of the government. During the interim, he assumed the imperial title of acting grand counsellor. Although Taka'uji hoped to restore the *bakufu* of Mi'namoto Yoritomo, the Ashikaga Bakufu was relatively weak with little influence much beyond the immediate precincts of the capital. Thus, the government was divided among the provincial military governors or *shugo* 守護. These governors, who were originally instituted during the Kamakura Bakufu, effectively supplanted the civilian governors of the old imperial government. Although theoretically appointed by the Muromachi Bakufu, the *shugo* became hereditary posts held by the *daimyou* 大名 families. This period also saw the development of a monetary economy which was to become prominent during the warring states period.

Warring States Period — Sengoku-jidai 戦国時代 (1467–1568)

The Ou'nin Ran 応仁乱 or "Ou'nin Conflict" derives its name from the era name of the year in which the war began. The Ou'nin Conflict itself lasted eleven years and destroyed half of the capital. In 1464, the *shougun*, Ashikaga Yoshimasa 足利義政, was without an heir and adopted his brother Ashikaga Yoshimi 足利義視. Soon thereafter, Yoshimasa had a son and sought to disinherit his brother. This might not have provoked a war had not several important warrior families had similar dynastic disputes at the same time. The dispossessed appealed to the *shugo daimyou*. Two factions emerged one headed by Hosokawa Katsumoto 細川勝元 and the other by Yama'na Mochitoyo 山名持豊.

The *shugo daimyou* left the capital to live in their provinces where they raised large private armies. Thus, the Ou'nin Insurrection brought about the effective collapse of the Muromachi Bakufu and inaugurated the Warring States Period. Constant warfare during this period not only disrupted the agrarian economy, but also enriched the trading and manufacturing houses which supplied weapons to the *daimyou*. Thus, the demands of the private armies brought about the emergence of a monetary economy with a revival of coinage. Economic disruption and constant warfare also destroyed or permanently altered the *buke* families which formally controlled the provinces. This is the Japan which was discovered by European explorers.

Momoyama Period — Azuchimomoyama-jidai 安土桃山時代 (1568–1603)

In 1568, Oda Nobunaga 小田 信長 entered the imperial capital Hei'ankyou 平安京 and installed Ashikaga Yoshi'aki 足利義昭 as a puppet *shougun* thus restoring effective national government. Yoshi'aki resented the effective power of Nobunaga and rebelled. Yoshi'aki was defeated, and the Muromachi Bakufu was finally abolished in 1573. Following the assassination of Oda Nobunaga in 1582, Toyotomi Hideyoshi attained military supremacy and became imperial regent or *kanpaku* in 1885. Hideyoshi completed the unification of Japan and launched an invasion of Korea, but died 1598 ending the Korean campaign. Following Hideyoshi's death, a war of succession broke out which culminated in the battle of Sekigahara and the two battles of Osaka castle. These battles established the Tokugawa family as the masters of post-mediæval Japan.

Edo Period — Edo-jidai 江戸時代 (1603–1868)

The closure of the Japanese middle ages can be variously dated to:

- ❖ National Unification under Oda Nobunaga   1568
- ❖ *Sekigahara Kasen* 関ヶ原合戦 (The Battle of Sekigahara)   1600
- ❖ Restoration of military government by Tokugawa Ieyasu 徳川 家康   1603
- ❖ Closure of Japan 鎖国の完成   1635

Of these, the investiture of Tokugawa Ieyasu 徳川 家康 as *sei'itaishougun* 征夷大将軍 is preferable, because it marks the institution of the post-mediæval government. Further, the institutionalization of Edo culture through the *iemoto* 家元 guild master system dates roughly from this time. Tokugawa Ieyasu was careful to redistribute fiefs so as to allow his supporters to subdue the minor *daimyou*. He also instituted the ruinous dual residency system wherein the *daimyou* had to regularly travel between their domains and the military capital. Ieyasu was also careful to remove the last vestige of political power from the emperor. All Europeans were expelled and Christianity was proscribed. Finally, the *bakufu* codified the classes and strictly regulated marriage and change in occupation.

During this period, the *daimyou* and their *samurai* retainers were systematically impoverished. Many *samurai* reverted to being farmers, others opened schools while others made fans or became actors. Those who remained in service to a lord become petty bureaucrats. The age of the *samurai* finally ended in the nineteenth century with their defeat by imperial conscripts during the Meiji Restoration and the following Satsuma Rebellion.

Meiji Restoration — Meiji'ishin 明治維新 (1868)

The *bakufu* imposed ruinous expenses upon its vassals. Inflation and devalued rice crops forced the *daimyou* to raise taxes and abrogate their debt. The Tenpou Famine of the early nineteenth century lead to peasant revolts and civic riots. As in the past, the *bakufu* instituted a series of reforms in 1841 designed to restore order and effective government. These reforms enacted strong sumptuary laws and dismissed corrupt officials and courtesans. The *bakufu* also attempted to regulate trade and repatriate runaway peasants.

The English victory in the Opium War of 1842 greatly alarmed the *bakufu* which hastened to strengthen coastal defenses. Although the Japanese were prepared for his arrival, the black ships of Commodore Perry in 1853 provoked a national crises. The treaties imposed on the *bakufu* seriously compromised Japanese sovereignty and were never approved by the imperial court. Vassals rose in open rebellion assassinating foreigners and firing on foreign vessels. The rebels turned to the emperor as the traditional source of legitimacy. The last *shougun* resigned leaving the *bakufu* in the hands of a short-lived council.

Imperially appointed *hanchou* 藩庁 took over administration of the *han* 藩 or feudal domains from the *daimyou* who received pensions and later titles of nobility. The old feudal *han* were formally abolished and replaced by prefectures in 1871. While the *samurai* received small pensions, many revolted against the new imperial government. In 1876, the samurai were forbidden to wear two swords, and in 1877 the *samurai* of the Satsuma Rebellion were defeated by imperial conscripts. Thus ended the age of the *samurai*.

Structure of Japanese Names

Before *myoujigomen* 名字御免 in the nineteenth century allowed all Japanese to bear official personal names, the structure of an official Japanese name depended upon the social status of the individual. This remains the case for the Japanese imperial family which does not have a surname. For this reason, we will discuss the overall structure of a complete name in terms of social considerations rather than in terms of syntax alone. To help us understand the different elementary names making up a complete name, we will look rather closely at the names born by Takeda Shingen 武田信玄 who lived during the sixteenth century. However, before proceeding with considering the individual elementary names in this name and their social significance, we will first consider the overall way in which the Japanese formed elementary names and strung them together.

Forming Elementary Names

The College of Arms requires individuals to devise complete names out of two or more elementary names. A complete Japanese name is constructed by stringing elementary names together so that preceding names or name groups modify succeeding names. Possessive **-no-** and enumerative **-ga-** sometimes appear between elementary names or even joining thematic elements within a single elementary name. Most of the time, this "possession" is only a grammatical construction wherein the first element modifies the second element. However, this "possession" can also reflect such things as group membership. Enumerative **-ga-** is used to fuse a description to a place name to form a new place name. Both, possessive **-no-** and enumerative **-ga-** are discussed elsewhere.

Some elementary names consist of a single thematic element. Others are formed from two or more elements. Japanese elementary names are formed by agglutinating thematic elements in much the same way as names are strung together to form a complete name. Essentially, the preceding elements possess, specify, or modify succeeding elements. Thus, the final element can be thought of as "substantive" and the preceding elements as "descriptive".

Thematic elements which are used to form combinations usually consist of one or two syllables. Although many of these elements take special readings when used in names, many of these apparently irregular forms appear to be descended from ordinary Japanese or Chinese words. Inventing thematic elements is very difficult. Fortunately, the *Thematic Dictionary* contains many elements taken from historical sources, and there should be little need to invent new ones. However, we can observe some patterns in how they appear to be formed. Almost all of the Chinese readings consist of either one or two syllables. Japanese nouns are used directly and Japanese adjectives are transformed into nouns either by dropping the final I or by taking a Chinese reading. Thus, *aoi* 青い becomes "ao" 青 and *utsukushii* 美しい becomes "mi" 美. Japanese verbs are more complicated.

How a Japanese verb is transformed into a thematic element depends on how it was conjugated in classical Japanese. The root is written ideographically and the inflection phonetically. A root or an inflection is "short" if it is just one syllable long, and "long" otherwise. Classical Japanese distinguished between many different classes of verbs, and most inflections began with a consonant. Later, the system of inflections was greatly simplified, and initial H and F disappeared from verb inflections. Classical Japanese dictionaries give the desired *renyou* inflection for each verb. For our purposes, which class a verb belongs to depends upon the initial consonant of the dictionary inflection for the modern counterpart of the verb.

Most modern Japanese verbs are regular verbs ending in **-ru**. Verbs ending in **-su** are also often quite regular. However, irregular verbs may have either of these endings. Regular verbs with long roots such as *sadameru* 定める are often simply pruned of their inflections. In this way we obtain names like Masasada 政定 and Naotomo 直朝. However, there are exceptional thematic elements which are formed by truncating a long root. The initial syllable of *tayoru* 頼る is dropped yielding **yoru**. The resulting form is then treated as a regular **R** form to produce the thematic element. This is how we obtain names such as Yori'aki 頼明. However, this apparently only happens when the final syllable would not otherwise correspond to one of our eight types. **Y** does not appear in our type list, but **R** does. Regular verbs with short roots such as *kaneru* 兼ねる are frequently inflected simply by preserving the initial syllable of the original inflection. This is commonly done when the initial consonant does not correspond to one of our verb types. This is how we obtain names like Kanemori 兼盛.

Verb Inflection in Thematic Elements

Consonant	Active	Inflected	Verb	Active	Inflected	Example	Reading
K	ku	ki	行く	yuku	yuki	行秀	Yukihide
S	su	shi	差す	sasu	sashi	江差	Esashi
T	tsu	tsu	勝つ	katsu	katsu	義勝	Yoshikatsu
H	fu	hi	咋ふ	ku(f)u	ku(h)i	咋女	Kuime
M	mu	mi	澄む	sumu	sumi	重澄	Shigezumi
R	ru	ri	成る	naru	nari	満成	Mitsunari
G	gu	gu	継ぐ	tsugu	tsugu	実継	Sanetsugu
B	bu	bu	宣べる	noberu	nobu	基宣	Motonobu

Gods and Goddesses

Although the names of Japanese deities are formed from the same morphemes as ordinary personal names, they are distinguished by the addition of distinctive prefixes and suffixes. Thus, the morphemes 天 (heavenly) which may be read either as **amano** or **amatsu** and 豊 (noble) which is read **toyo** are affixed to the beginning of a name. And, **mikoto** 命 (proclaim to assembled multitudes) and **himenomikoto** 媛命 (princess proclaimed to assembled multitudes) are appended to the end of a name. This meaning of the *kanji* 命 is used when forming the word *meirei* 命令 which means "command". Another important suffix is **oomikami** 大御神 which means "greatly honored god". This suffix appears in the name of the sun goddess, Amaterasu Oomikami 天照大御神 whose name means "heavenly shining greatly honoured god".

While *Kadokawa Saishin Kanwajiten* shows that in antiquity these morphemes used to form the names of deities also functioned as honourifics which were attached to the names of court nobles, the courtier families typically claimed divine descent. Further, in Shintoh, the morpheme 命 was also appended to the names of the dead to indicate their attainment of divine status. However, beginning as early as the Yamato Period, Buddhist burial practices largely replaced Shintoh 神道 burial practices. Thus, during the Japanese mediæval period, the dead typically received Buddhist posthumous names which imitated Chinese names.

Later, honourific prefixes which had been used to form the names of gods were sometimes incorporated into the personal and family names of commoners. Thus, surnames such as Amano 天野 and Toyoda 豊田 and given names such as Yutaka 豊 are not in any way presumptuous. However, the honourific suffixes retained their special status.

The Emperor and his Family

Jinmu Tennou 神武天皇 is the Chinese style posthumous name of the mythological first emperor of Japan. His name was Kamu Yamato Iwarebiko no Sumera Mikoto 神日本磐余彦天皇, and he was descended from the sun goddess. Structurally, "Yamato" appears to be part of a titular element in a Japanese style posthumous name. However, many early Japanese names were strongly titular, and we must conclude that the imperial family was thereby claiming a special titular relationship to the nation. In this name, "Yamato" is rendered as 日本 which is the Chinese name for the nation and not as 大和 which is how the name of the home province is rendered. Regardless, the imperial court originated in and around Yamato province, and both forms should be avoided. Jinmu Tennou was the divine founder of the imperial family. Thus, we find the imperial title *Tennou* being rendered as *sumera mikoto* 天皇 or "Lord of Heaven". The divine earthly sovereign perpetuated the divine title, but adopted a new *kanji* to differentiate it from his celestial counterparts.

Despite the appearance of Yamato in the imperial title, *Daijirin* fails to list Yamato uji 大和氏 and *Shinsen Kogojiten* asserts that Yamato 大和 is both the name of an ancient province and an alternate name for the nation as a whole. Neither makes any mention of a "Yamato clan". Regardless, by the Hei'an Period, the imperial family was not attached to a clan and did not use a family name. Henceforth, their names were composed solely of titular elements and either a *nanori* 名乗 or a Chinese style Buddhist name. A *nanori* is essentially an official given name. These are inherently very formal and were a privilege originally restricted to the nobility, certain members of the military class, and certain artisans. Since these names are structurally similar to Chinese given names and first appeared during a period of Chinese influence, we can guess that they were originally Chinese names read using native *kunyomi* readings for their *kanji*.

Historical emperors are typically known by a name which is constructed in Chinese style from two Chinese characters. This is an artifact of the institution of Buddhism in Japan. These names are not the *nanori* of the emperor. For example, Takaharu 尊治 was the *nanori* for Emperor Go-Daigo Tennou 後醍醐天皇. Thus, before his assumption of the throne, he was known as Prince Takaharu Koutaishi 尊治皇太子. Upon accession to the throne, he was known simply as the emperor. Following death or abdication, the emperor received a new name. These names like era names, the names of Buddhist monks, and posthumous names, are typically formed from the "Chinese" readings for their constituent *kanji*. In the *Thematic Dictionary*, these *onyomi* readings are distinguished by being written in capital letters while the native Japanese *kunyomi* readings are written in small letters. This convention conforms to common practice.

Notice that Go-Daigo sounds very "Chinese". Names constructed from Chinese readings sound more official than do names constructed from Japanese readings. One reason for this is that Chinese was the official court language for part of the classical period. Further, Chinese continued to be regularly taught as a classical language much as Latin was in Europe. Finally, the Chinese readings for *kanji* are generally shorter than the Japanese readings and are therefore more convenient for forming neologisms by agglutinating *kanji*. Forming neologisms is very common in Japan. However, many such words are never intended to be spoken, only read. They are called *yomikotoba* as distinct from the *ha'nashikotoba* used in spoken Japanese.

Like the emperor and the crown prince, the other members of the imperial family bore names which consisted of a *nanori* followed by a title. Princes belonging to the imperial family, bore names consisting of a *nanori* followed by either *shinnou* 親王 or simply *ou* 王. At first, all brothers and sons of the emperor were entitled to attach *shinnou* 親王 to their *nanori*. However, after the middle of the eighth century, a special proclamation called *shinnou senge* 親王宣下 was required before this title could be assumed. Those not receiving this accolade were only entitled to attach 王 -OU to their names. Thus, Tsugi'naga Shinnou 世良親王 was an imperial prince as was Isamitsu Ou 功満王, but of the two Tsugi'naga Shinnou enjoyed higher status. Similarly, an imperial princess who received *naishinnou senge* 内親王宣下 attached *naishinnou* 内新王 to her *nanori* while the rest simply attached *jo'ou* 女王 to their names. Thus, Kyuushi Naishinnou 久子内親王 was an imperial princess. Notice that while the *kanji* for this *nanori* can be read as "Hisako" which is a normative feminine *nanori*, this name actually takes its Chinese reading. This appears to have been a common practice for female relatives of the emperor. Regardless, their male counterparts commonly used native Japanese readings.

一品式部卿葛原親王

Ippon Shikibu Kyau Kazurahara no Shinnou

The court nobility enjoyed two systems of court rank. The first had four grades and was reserved to the imperial family. In our example above, *ippon* is the highest of these four imperial ranks. *Shikibu Kyau* (Shikibu Kyou) is the chief minister of the ritual department. Kazurahara is a special name given to the third son of the emperor. Finally, *shinnou* is a special honour given to favoured imperial princes.

As Japan was generally patrilineal, imperial princesses could not found families. Thus, female members of the imperial family were generally rusticated by being sent to live in Buddhist temples. Seikamon'in 西華門院 was an imperial princess who originally bore the feminine *nanori* Motoko 基子 or Kishi Naishinnou 基子内親王. As with male members of the imperial family, the written form of her *nanori* is indistinguishable from the *nanori* of other nobility. These names were only distinguished by the addition of titular elements. There are no other reserved name components for these names. Regardless, two *kanji* are strongly associated with members of the imperial court. Shared name elements called *tsuuji* 通字 recur in the imperial family and among the *kuge*. The *tsuuji* **-hito** 仁 commonly appears as the substantive element in the *nanori* of imperial princes and **kin-** 公 appears as the descriptive element in the *nanori* of high court nobles. Both of these *kanji* are rarely found in the *nanori* born by members of the *buke* class.

Categories of Given or Adopted Names

名乗	*nanori*	Official Name	Names used in proclamations and self introductions.
実名	*jitsumei*	True Name	One's real name. A legal name.
本名	*honmyou*	Genuine Name	Neither a artistic pseudonym nor an alias.
仮名	*kemyou*	Substitute Name	Names attached to the *eboshi* at the *genfuku* ceremony.
呼び名	*yobina*	Spoken Name	General use name other than the *nanori*.
童名	*warawana*	Childhood Name	Names used for children.
幼名	*osanana*	Infant Name	Names used for infants.
法名	*houmyou*	Buddhist name	Used by Buddhist adepts and others.
戒名	*kaimyou*	Posthumous Name	Chinese style name similar to a *houmyou*.
通称	*tsuushou*	Common Name	Names used in everyday conversation.
字	*azana*	Common Name	Informal names used by Monks and Chinese scholars.
雅号	*gagou*	Artistic Name	Born by poets, authors, artists, and artisans.
諡号	*shigou*	Posthumous Name	Posthumous names born by members of the imperial family.
院号	*ingou*	Palace Name	Augmentation to a posthumous name by the *shougun*.
尊号	*songou*	Honourific Name	Frequently granted by the Empress in early period.

Surnames and Nanori

The *shimei* 氏名 is the simplest form of a complete name. It consists simply of a clan or family name followed by a given name. According to Yoshida Taiyou, *shomin* 庶民 or commoners were first allowed to have *myouji* 苗字 or "true family names" by Prince Shoutoku Taishi. Following the Taika Reform in 645, the serfs and slaves formerly held by the *uji* were freed and were registered in the national census. Specifically, they and their lands became direct subjects of the emperor. In essence, they became public property. Thus, Yoshida argues, they all received family names. However, as we have seen, many scholars believe that these people did not receive true *myouji* (family names) at this time, but were merely registered by the house in which they dwelt. Japanese peasants lived either in large multi-floor dwellings or in long houses. They typically shared these dwellings with many other people. By the beginning of the Hei'an Period in 795, the courtier families were reasserting themselves by controlling the examination system and by obtaining special licenses for large private estates immune to land redistribution and taxation. As in Europe, loss of autonomy conferred some advantages for peasants as they were then immune to imperial labor levies. However, the peasants living on the private estates lost their family names. Ultimately, the only peasants retaining family names were the rustic *samurai* who lived in farming villages.

A monetary economy took hold in Japan during the Muromachi Period and became a significant feature of national life during the Edo Bakufu after 1600. A consequence of this was mercantile houses acquiring family names. Gradually more families acquired *myouji* until the Meiji Restoration when universal *myoujigomen* granted all Japanese the privilege of bearing a *myouji*. Regardless, as noted by Yoshida, until the Meiji Restoration in the 19th century, even if a commoner bore a family name, he did not bear a *nanori*. The *nanori* remained the unique province of the imperial family, the court nobility, the military class, and (only by special permission) of certain artists and artisans. While the Tokugawa Bakufu relegated craftsmen to a caste below the peasants, many crafts are considered high art forms in Japan. Adepts in certain crafts could therefore slightly sidestep the general relegation of craftsmen to lower social caste. Further, a very few crafts were considered to be appropriate occupations for members of the military caste.

Other Personal Names

A Japanese person has at his disposal a rich repertoire of names. Essentially, he has different names for different social situations. We shall chiefly concern ourselves with official names or *jitsumei* 実名; Buddhist names or *houmyou* 法名; common use names or *tsuushou* 通称; artistic names or *gagou* 雅号; palace names or *ingou* 院号; honourific names or *songou* 尊号; and posthumous names or *kaimyou* 戒名. There are generally two kinds of posthumous name. Those which refer to the individual during their life and those that refer to the individual after their death. The *jitsumei* is the most important name as it normally appears on all official documents and is used in proclamations and other official business. The sole exceptions are for those who have a name of superior status which might be more appropriate.

The importance of a *nanori* can not be emphasized too much. This is the name which a warrior announced to his adversary when giving battle. This name was the unique privilege of the Japanese upper class. All Japanese were registered by the census and in a sense had legal names, but family names and *nanori* were reserved to the *kuge* (court nobility), *buke* (warriors), and certain artistic adepts. Why did a military society which so valued the right to bear a name extend this privilege to artisans? Simply because artistic achievement often had as much political significance for Japanese as did prowess on the battlefield. Miyamoto Musashi was as much known for his artistic achievements as he was for his prowess with the sword.

Kabane

Titles called *kabane* 姓 originated among the ancient clans and persisted throughout the middle ages. Despite their longevity, or perhaps because of it, they are fairly mysterious. Although the Japanese adapted the Chinese character for family for writing *kabane*, they do not appear to be families. The *kabane* were originally titles assumed by clan nobility to distinguish their relative standing within society. As such, they were commonly attached as a suffix to territorial or clan names. Following the Taika Reform, these titles became ministerial titles within the new imperial government. Essentially, the newly expanded list of *kabane* were named ranks within imperial ministries. Thus, Kashiwade no Omi 膳臣 appears to have originally been a clan title which later became a ministerial title.

The *kabane* were very popular and the emperors at times created new *kabane* to reward their supporters. Consequently, it is very difficult to obtain a complete list of historical *kabane*. There are partial lists of important *kabane* in both the historical chapter and the chapter on titles. By the end of the Hei'an Period, private household officials had largely superseded public officials and we find the honourific *kabane* once again being attached to names. This accounts for much of the confusion surrounding the *kabane*. At the end of the Hei'an Period, *ason* 朝臣 (earlier called *asomi*) was an honourific title reserved for nobility belonging to the fifth rank or higher. As this was the rank to which the *shougun* and governors of great provinces, its use within the Society for Creative Anachronism should be reserved to reigning monarchs.

Ultimately, the military class emulated many of the practices of the court nobles. Although new titles and offices were added to the old ones, the old court titles remained important throughout Japanese history. The *shugo* 守護 or "High Constables" were provincial officers who reported to the Kamakura Bakufu. These officers essentially assumed many of the police powers of the *nokami* 守 or provincial governor. Later, during the Muromachi Period, the *shugo* were military governors appointed by the Ashikaga Bakufu. Eventually, the *shugo* obtained title to their provinces and became *daimyou*. Regardless, the *kabane* continued to appear in records of the Kamakura period and remained in use as late as the nineteenth century.

In general, the *kabane* appears to be quite formal and should only be used in conjunction with the *nanori*. This sets it apart from governmental offices which often appear with the *yobina*. Although *Heike Monogatari* sometimes places the *kabane* at the end of a name, it should appear immediately before the *nanori*. Regardless of placement, it should be preceded by possessive "no".

Titles and Offices

Beginning with the Hei'an Period, court nobles energetically sought employment both with the government and with other noble houses. These appointments often included opportunities for advancement in rank within the court hierarchy and other valuable political and economic connections. Further, although Japan instituted a system of examinations modeled after the one in China, success in examinations became dependent upon admission to special preparatory schools. Thus it is was very important for an aspiring young noble to apply for patronage to one of the great families. To apply for employment as a retainer, he would call upon his prospective patron at his residence. Once there, he would present his *myoubu* 名簿 which was a kind of placard with his name and other credentials written on it. He would then request an audience or *kenza* 件座 with his prospective lord. If his petition was granted, he then entered into a personal relationship with his lord. He henceforth addressed his master as *nushi* 主 or *shujin* 主人. Both of which mean "lord" or "master".

We will now consider a few specific examples to see how these various name elements fit together. In the early days of the Meiji Restoration, we find the following name on a roster of imperial appointments.

右納言 正二位行 源 朝臣 具視
Dai'nagon Shou'ni'igyou Mi'namoto no Asomi Tomomi

This document largely preserves the name and title structure found in the *Heike Monogatari* in which we can find the following name.

太政大臣平朝臣清盛公
Daijau Daijin Taira no Asson Kiyomori Kou

Both of these examples are court nobles enjoying the highest of court titles and rank. In both cases, the first thing that we encounter is the imperial office to which the noble was appointed. In the first example, the next element is the court rank of the noble. These ranks had numerical designations or grades. Each grade was in turn divided into a superior and an inferior division. Finally, after the first three ranks, each of the divisions was in turn divided into a superior and an inferior grade. These ranks are sometimes known as "cap ranks" because at one time each grade had a distinctive cap. *Ason*, *asomi*, and *asson* are *kabane* and when present immediately precede the *nanori*. Finally, we have an honourific title which is missing from the first example.

Now consider two names from the Warring States Period.[11]

武田 大膳 大夫 晴信 入道 信玄
Takeda Daizen no Daibu Haru'nobu Nyuudou Shingen

武田 四郎 勝頼
Takeda Shirou Katsuyori

The first name illustrates how to combine a *kamei* 家名 or "house name" with a title, a rank and a *nanori*. The title, *daizen no daibu* 大膳 大夫, is actually an office within the imperial government. The title consists of two elements. The first designates the division of the government and the second designates rank within that division. Together, they indicate a specific post within the imperial government which in turn has a corresponding "cap rank". Generally, it is these offices, and not the cap ranks, which are found in Japanese documents, literature, and graphic arts. As already mentioned, office could be conferred by any one of 1) the imperial government, 2) a princely household, 3) the military government, or 4) following conversion of their fiefs by the *shugo*, by territorial warlords as well. Although the military government eventually supplanted the imperial government, the imperial offices retained higher status.

These office titles invariably fell between the surname and the *nanori*. In this way, they emulate the *kabane* of the ancient aristocracy. The second example shows a *tsuushou* or "vulgar" name falling between the surname and the *nanori*. If there were also a title, it would immediately follow the vulgar name. In the example, the *tsuushou* means "number four son". This is the most common way for constructing vulgar names for Japanese males. Because of adoption and exchange of hostages, this name may not reflect the exact birth-order of the person bearing the name. Rather, it may reflect their relative standing within the district in which they live. This is particularly true for early in the Kamakura Period when surnames were not yet

---

[11] The first is taken from a painting of one of a series of battles at Kawa'nakajima which raged between Takeda Shingen and Uesugi Ka'ne'nobu over an eleven year period from 1553 to 1564. The second name can be found in a painting entitled, "Takedake Yuushou Iku Sahyoujou no Zu" which depicts the retainers of Takeda Shingen. Both paintings can be found at the Shingen Archives in Koufu Prefecture.

very stable and were often true locatives with parents and siblings each bearing different names. Thus it is easy to see how the title (which is really an office and therefore an occupational description) is primarily attached to the surname. This is because, with very early names in the military class, the surname is actually a locative component of the job title or office. Regardless, Japanese avoid referring to superiors by any of their names. Instead, they use honourifics and job titles. Naked honourifics were the most common form of address in mediæval Japan, and today the emperor is commonly referred to simply as Tennou Heika 天皇陛下 or "his majesty the emperor".

Warrior Families

At first, the only warriors who had hereditary surnames were rusticated court nobility. The various Mi'namoto families or Genji and the various Taira families or Heike are of imperial descent while the Fujiwara are descendents of one of the ancient clans. Thus, the imperial line's solution to it's population problem resulted in the creation of two powerful new clans. Of the Mi'namoto and the Taira, the Mi'namoto more energetically followed a policy of establishing themselves as a military clan. They acquired extensive provincial holdings and the head of the Mi'namoto family functioned as an *uji no kami* or "clan chief". Shortly before the Genpei War, the Mi'namoto established themselves as an autonomous country in the Kantou region. Ultimately, they offered clan membership in exchange for fealty. In contrast, the Heike were more interested in continuing life as an urban court family. They were primarily concerned with the intrigues of court politics and securing auspicious marriages.

Both the Genji and the Heike are actually descended from many different emperors. Often, an imperial prince receiving one of these names would found a new line. These lines were distinguished by placing a prefix before the common clan name. Thus, we meet the *Seiwa Genji* 清和源氏 who are descended from the rusticated sons of Emperor Seiwa Tennou 清和天皇. Eventually, a new lineage would either die out or would in turn spawn several new families with new inherited surnames. Thus, families with names such as: Ootake 大竹, Kirihara 桐原, and Wada 和田 can all be cadet branches of the Seiwa Genji. All of this suggests a solution for people who wish to construct names which incorporate both a clan name and a surname. If the clan name immediately follows the family name, then the family name will modify the clan name specifying which branch of the clan the individual belongs to. Thus a warrior could be called Ikeda no Mi'namoto Yoshi'nobu 池田 源 義信. Note first of all that Ikeda 池田 (pond-paddy) is a locative and localizes the Mi'namoto clan. Also, possessive **-no-** is never written. It is actually a somewhat optional conjunction placed between two nouns where the first noun modifies the second noun. Further, this particular warrior is asserting membership in a cadet house of the Genji 源氏 which might itself be known as the Ikeda Genji 池田源氏.

Within the Society for Creative Anachronism, a member of the *buke* class should bear a name consisting of a family name followed by a *yobina* and ending with a *nanori*. Only peers should bear *kabane*. These titles are attached either to the *uji* as in Taira no asson 平朝臣 or to the *nanori* as in Tadamori no ason 忠盛朝臣. The *uji* typically preceeds the surname when both are useed. Military and governmental honours awarded to armigeurs are attached to the *yobina*. This presents special problems for women as not all feminine *yobina* are appropriate vehicles for governmental titles. Generally, women should choose *yobina* related to masculine *yobina*. This is neither as difficult nor as unusual as it may sound. All a woman need do is attach an appropriate suffix to a name of correct form. Due to the social significance of distinctive suffixes in their names, women must be particularly careful to construct *nanori* appropriate to their rank.

Buddhist Names

Houmyou are Buddhist names and always take Chinese readings which, like Latin in Europe, was the language of scholarship. These names were born not only by Buddhist monks, but by artists and people who had retired from the world to become lay monks. Posthumous names are also Buddhist names. The emperor is much better known by his posthumous name and not by his other names. Emperor Tenmu Tennou 天武天皇 is a Chinese style Posthumous name. Before becoming emperor, he was known as Oo'ama Ouji 大海皇子. He also had a Japanese style posthumous name. It is Ama no Nunahara Oki no Mahito. Similarly, Emperor Tenji Tennou 天智天皇 was known as Kazuraki Ouji 葛城皇子 and posthumously as Amemikoto Hirakasuwake 天命開別.

Houmyou are a source for great confusion. This is because many martial arts masters and other famous people are more commonly known by their *houmyou* than they are by either their *nanori* or their *yobina*. However, these are really honourific artistic pseudonyms affected by masters of an art. As such, they are also sometimes called a *gagou* or "artistic" name. These names are in fact a token of mastery. In any of the artistic lineages, being awarded one of these names marks entry into the realm of the master. In the Urasenke tea society, a tea name or *chamei* is typically awarded after ten years of study.

Other individuals, such as Takeda Shingen, adopted a *houmyou* only late in life when they "retired from the world". Such individuals officially abdicated their offices in order to assure their succession and to better achieve the interests of their family. Thus, while it is easy to find documentary evidence for individuals with these names, they are generally presumptuous and should be discouraged. Many official portraits of Takeda Shingen give the following as the full form of his name.

武田 大膳 大夫 晴信 入道 信玄
Takeda Daizen no Daibu Harunobu Nyuudou Shingen

His name ends with a *houmyou* 法名 or Buddhist name which he assumed when he officially retired from life. Shingen 信玄 is the actual Buddhist name and *nyuudou* 入道 is an optional element which indicates that Takeda Shingen 武田信玄 is actually a lay monk who has retired from the world. Harunobu 晴信 is his *nanori*. Either the *nanori* or the *houmyou* may be used alone. However, if both are used, then the order given above should be observed.

While retired aristocrats simply attached a *houmyou* to their name, Buddhist monks were known only by one or more *houmyou*. Most monks bore names consisting of a single *houmyou*. Unfortunately, the College of Arms refuses to register names consisting of a single element. However, monks belonging to a Buddhist sect, such as Tendaishuu 天台宗 or any of the Zen sects, which practices *zazen* 座禅 or sitting mediation bore two or even three names. Of these two names, the first name is called an *azana* 字 and the second an *imi'na* 諱 or 諡号. Originally, *azana* were pseudonyms used by Chinese scholars. In Japan, these names retained their Chinese form and were primarily adopted by Buddhist monks and scholars. These names were typically bestowed upon students when they entered upon their studies. The *imi'na* is the true *houmyou* born by the adept. As such, it is a posthumous name. While secular Japanese generally received their posthumous names only after they died, Buddhist monks received theirs in life. Both of these names consist of two *kanji*, and take Chinese readings.

Names and Japanese Society

We have seen that a Japanese aristocrat held dearly both his right to a family name and to a *nanori*. We have also seen that the family and not the individual is the fundamental social unit in mediæval Japanese society. This in part accounts for the formal declarations of *nanori* upon the battlefield and the practice of ritual suicide in which the condemned demonstrates his own fundamental purity by exposing his soul through opening his abdomen.[12] The purpose of these acts was to affirm the worth of both family and the honour of the individual. While there were complex sociological and economic causes for these things, they are reflected in the importance of the death poem, formal names, and posthumous names. The remainder of this text examines each of the various elementary names born by an individual and attempts to relate it to the task of constructing a mediæval Japanese name and how such names can better reflect moral aspirations as well as kinship and alliance.

---

[12]Japanese believed that the soul resided in the abdomen. At the time, many Europeans believed that the brain was a useless organ and ascribed the residence of the soul to other organs of the body.

Surnames

Reflecting a fundamentally agrarian society, most Japanese surnames (family names) refer to either natural or agrarian geographical features. Even names which appear to represent the original occupation of a family are frequently rendered as place descriptions. This is because -**ya** 屋 (house) is the substantive element in many of these names. For example, Haginoya 萩乃屋 suggests that the family originally owned a candy store, but "candy house" is what it says. Similarly, Hariya 針屋 appears to have originated as the name of a needle maker. Generally, explicitly mercantile names should be avoided as they were most likely invented during the Meiji era following universal *myoujigomen* when all Japanese were permitted to have names.

Another, and much less important, source for family names is graphic design. Mitsubishi 三菱 literally means "three diamonds", and refers to the three diamond shapes in the Mitsubishi logo and not to crystalline carbon. While Mitsui 三井 means "three wells" and the logo consists of a representation of a well, it still is a valid locative. Thus, the name and the symbol of a family are often identified. However, it is important to understand that these symbols are always ones which can be painted or printed onto fabric. The *bushi* 武士 or warriors did carry standards consisting of a long baton to which were attached streamers. These are similar to those carried by companies of fire-fighters in modern Japan. They also carried windsocks similar to those seen on Boy's Day in Japan. However, the military class did not employ standards of the type used by the Roman legions and subsequently throughout European history. Rather, they employed a design known as a *kamon* 家紋 which was monochromatically[13] printed or painted on banners, clothes, lanterns, and other equipment. Consequently, while it is possible to construct a name such as Sanwa 三和, which can be graphically represented as three circles, it is not reasonable to construct a name like Kinshishi 金獅 meaning "golden lion" which cannot be monochromatically represented.

The ancient guilds, collectives, and monopoly corporations are yet another source for family names. Specifically, names such as Abe 阿部 which end with -**be** 部 appear to be rooted in these ancient associations discussed in the historical synopsis. Some of these corporations date from as early as the tumulus period ca. 350 when the Japanese nobility was active on the Korean peninsula. Many of these groups arrived in Japan as refugees from the political instability and warfare then prevalent in China and Korea.

Finally, a family name can indicate that the family has migrated or changed its status. Thus, Wata'nabe 渡辺 means "crossed over", but does not indicate where the family actually lives or where it came from. Similarly, Wata'nabe 渡部 literally means "cross over the ranks" which could indicate that a defection has occurred. It could also simply be the name of one of the ancient monopoly corporations responsible for transportation. Many Japanese names such as Naitou 内藤, which has the improbable literal meaning of "inside the wisteria", actually indicate a presumed relationship with the Fujiwara 藤原 clan.[14] Essentially these names are abbreviations of a specifier followed by the clan name. However, some families bearing these names appear to be descended from other clans. Further, Japanese kinship patterns were based more on formal arrangement, relative social status, and cohabitation than they were on physical descent. As many families came to hold hereditary office, a family name served to locate the family either within space or within human society.

---

[13] Although essentially monochromatic, these banners could be quite vivid. Red, white, blue and black were the colours most commonly used in these banners. Even yellow was used. While the *kamon* itself was monochromatic, the banner could be divided or have bars added to the field.

[14] The Fujiwara were instrumental in the Taika Reform and the attempt to abolish the *uji*, however they behaved very much like one of the surviving *uji* and actively acquired *shou'en* estates and exercised private government.

Houses Named After Provinces and Individuals

In *Heike Monogatari* 平家物語, the *kamei* 家名 or "house name" commonly appears as the initial element and the *nanori* commonly appears as the final element of a name. At this early date, some of these names may not be true *kamei* but rather the name of the province to which the warrior was posted. However, these names have the same form as Japanese family names. Genealogical trees reveal that these names often became stable family names, but that cadet branches of the family would later produce new family names by a similar mechanism.

Houses of the Fujiwara Clan

The names of the various branches of the Fujiwara clan illustrate how a clan name and either a locative or a fragmentary job title can combine to form family names. However, not all families with names ending with 藤 (TOU) and adopting the wisteria for their *kamon* currently claim membership in the Fujiwara clan. Some families named Andou 安藤, Naitou 内藤, or Kondou 近藤 claim Genji membership while some families with the name Endou 遠藤 claim Heishi membership. In the table below, the name of each family is followed the name of its hereditary office and the duties of that office.

Hereditary Offices of the Fujiwara

Family Name		Hereditary Office		
斎藤	Saitou	斎宮頭	Saiguu no kami	Warden of the Imperial Residence
内藤	Naitou	内蔵助	Naizou no suke	Deputy Treasurer
進藤	Shindou	修理之進	Shuuri no jou	Adjunct Administrator
工藤	Kudou	木工頭	Mokku no kami	Warden of Carpenters
首藤	Shudou	主馬首	Shume no suke	Warden of Horses
春藤	Toutou	春宮亮	Touguu no suke	Deputy Warden of Maidens
佐藤	Satou	左衛門尉	Sa'emon no jou	Adjunct Palace Guard
衛藤	Etou	兵衛佐	Hyou no suke	Deputy Palace Guard
安藤	Andou	案墓房	Anbo no fusa	Warden of Tombs and Cemeteries
近藤	Kondou	近江介	Oumi no suke	Lt. Governor of Oumi
遠藤	Endou	遠江介	Tootoumi no suke	Lt. Governor of Tootoumi
加藤	Katou	加賀介	Kaga no suke	Lt. Governor of Kaga
伊藤	Itou	伊豆介	Izu no suke	Lt. Governor of Izu
後藤	Gotou	備後介	Bingo no suke	Lt. Governor of Bingo
山藤	Santou	山城介	Yamashiro no suke	Lt. Governor of Yamashiro
須藤	Sutou	那須介	Nasu no suke	Lt. Governor of Nasu
武藤	Mutou	武蔵介	Musashi no suke	Lt. Governor of Musashi
尾藤	Bitou	尾張介	Owara no suke	Lt. Governor of Owara

Common Elements Used in Surnames

Japanese surnames typically consist of a locative substantive element preceded by one or more modifiers. There are 551 surnames dated from before 1601 listed in the appendix. The following *kanji* frequency table does not list all of the *kanji* appearing in the name list, but it does list every *kanji* which appears at least five times. These *kanji* are listed in descending order of overall frequency. The first of the three numerical entries for each *kanji* gives the total number of occurrences, the second the number of occurrences in initial position, and the third the number of occurrences in final position. Note that the frequencies in this study may not agree with the frequencies produced by Koop and Inada. Koop and Inada were only interested in the *kanji* used as the final and therefore substantive element of a surname. There are curious differences between the relative frequencies of individual *kanji* reported by the two lists. Although both agree on -ta 田 (rice paddy) as the most prevalent substantive element, differences appear with the second substantive *kanji*. While Koop and Inada report -yama 山 (mountain) as being the second most common substantive element, it only ranks fifth as a substantive element in this study. It achieves its higher overall ranking from occurring as a modifying element in names such as Yamada 山田 (mountain paddy).

Kanji Frequencies in Japanese Surnames Prior to 1600

Kanji	Frequencies			Usage			Meaning
田	71	07	64	-ta	-da		Paddy Field
山	34	15	19	-yama			Mountain
大	30	30	00	TAI-	oo-		Big
井	25	00	25	-i			Well
野	21	00	21	-no			Wide Plain
原	20	00	20	-hara	-bara	-wara	Meadow
川	18	00	18	kawa-	-kawa		River
木	18	07	11	ki-	-ki	-gi	Tree
河	15	09	06	kawa-	-KA	-kawa	Big River
小	15	15	00	ko-			Small
上	13	05	08	-ue	-noue	-kami	Above
長	13	13	00	CHOU-	naga-	osa-	Long
高	12	12	00	KOU-	taka-		Tall / High
松	12	07	05	-matsu			Pine Tree
島	12	00	12	-shima	-jima		Island
中	11	08	03	-naka			Middle
藤	11	00	11	-tou	-dou		Wisteria
部	10	00	10	-be			A Division
谷	10	00	10	-ya	-tani	-dani	Valley
岡	08	00	08	-oka			Hill
伊	08	08	00	I-			Rule / Conquer
崎	08	00	08	-saki			Slope
佐	08	08	00	SA-			Military Deputy
村	08	00	08	-mura			Village
内	08	00	08	NAI-	-uchi		Inside
賀	07	00	07	-KA	-GA		Celebrate A Gain
口	07	00	07	-guchi			Entrance / Exit
三	07	07	00	SAI-	mi-	-ZOU	Three
石	07	07	00	-SEKI	ishi-	iha- iwa-	Rock
沢	07	00	07	sawa-	-sawa		Glen / Run
平	07	07	00	hira-	-taira		Tranquil / Flat
堀	07	07	00	hori-	-hori		Dug Out / Excavation
安	06	06	00	A-	AN-	yasu-	Safe / Gentle / Secure
本	06	00	06	HON-	-moto		Main / Original / Base
吉	05	05	00	KICHI-	KITSU-		Lucky / Fortunate
加	05	05	00	KA-			Join Up / Enlist
金	05	05	00	kane-			Gold / Metal / Money
今	05	05	00	ima-			Now
東	05	00	05	-TOU			East
飯	05	05	00	ii-			Cooked Rice
尾	05	00	05	BI-	-o		Tail
間	04	00	04	-ma			Room / Space
戸	04	00	04	to-	-to		Door
見	04	00	04	-mi			Vantage / View / Vista
条	04	00	04	-JOU			Branch / Line
良	04	00	04	-RA			Good / Superior
利	04	00	04	-RI	-kaga		Produce Results
江	03	00	03	E-	-E		Large River
多	03	00	03	TA-	-TA		Many

Surnames of Daimyou During the Sengoku Period (ca. 1550)

青木	Aoki	赤松	Akamatsu	秋月	Akizuki
秋田	Akita	浅井	Asai	朝倉	Asakura
浅野	Asano	足利	Ashikaga	有馬	Arima
生駒	Ikoma	池田	Ikeda	石川	Ishikawa
石田	Ishida	石橋	Ishibashi	伊東	Itou
伊藤	Itou	稲葉	Inaba	今川	Imakawa
宇喜多	Ukita	上杉	Uesugi	氏家	Ujiie
浦上	Urakami	小川	Ogawa	小田	Oda
小野寺	Onodera	大内	Oouchi	大崎	Oosaki
大谷	Ootani	大友	Ootomo	大村	Oomura
岡本	Okamoto	奥山	Okuyama	織田	Oda
加藤	Katou	河野	Kawano	木下	Ki'noshita
木曾	Kiso	黒田	Kuroda	小笠原	Kokasahara
小西	Konishi	小早川	Kobayakawa	小山	Koyama
佐々木	Sasaki	佐竹	Satake	佐藤	Satou
佐野	Sano	斎藤	Saitou	島津	Shimazu
杉原	Sugihara	相馬	Souma	多賀	Taga
伊達	Date	田中	Ta'naka	田丸	Tamaru
高田	Takata	高橋	Takahashi	武田	Takeda
立花	Tachiba'na	龍川	Tatsukawa	丹羽	Tanba
千葉	Chiba	筒井	Tsutsui	寺沢	Terazawa
寺西	Teranishi	戸沢	Tozawa	徳川	Tokugawa
富山	Toyama	中川	Nakakawa	中村	Nakamura
長尾	Nagao	鍋島	Nabeshima	成田	Narita
南部	Nanbu	二階堂	Nikaidou	西尾	Nishio
原	Hara	早川	Hayakawa	福島	Fukushima
福原	Fukuhara	北条	Houjou	細川	Hosokawa
掘	Hori	堀尾	Horio	堀田	Horita
本多	Honda	本間	Honma	前田	Maeda
増田	Masuda	松浦	Matsuura	松平	Matsudaira
三浦	Miura	三木	Miki	三好	Miyoshi
水谷	Mizutani	皆川	Minakawa	宮部	Miyabe
武藤	Mutou	村上	Murakami	毛利	Mouri
最上	Mogami	森	Mori	山内	Yamauchi
山崎	Yamazaki	山名	Yama'na		

Names Formed using "ga" and "no"

Although many places names in Japan can be used for Japanese family names, some are not used in this way. These names are constructed by enumerating geographical objects such as barriers or fields with attributes. This construction is used in forming the places names: Kasumigaseki 霞ヶ関, Utsukushigahara 美ヶ原, Yumigahama 弓ヶ浜, and Sekigahara 関ヶ原. In these places names, both elements take the form of proper Japanese words or places names. The morpheme used to accomplish this is the counter -**ko** 箇 which is abbreviated as -**ka**- ヶ when used in places names. Although the root sound is -**ka** , coarticulation with the final phoneme in the preceding modifier vocalizes the **K** to produce -**ga**-. Similarly, Utsukushi'nomori 美の森 is formed from two native Japanese words conjoined by the formally "possessive" particle -**no**-. Also, while *no* 乃 is explicitly written in 萩乃屋, it is frequently implied by the surname and is not actually written. For example, Ki'noshita 木下 is correct while 木の下 are 木乃下 are not.

Clan Names

Like China, Japan developed clans called *uji* 氏 which were extended kinship groups encompassing many distinct families. Originally, each *uji* held territory and had its own titular deity. Each also had a name which the clan nobility or *gouka* 豪家 bore in common. These names were primarily derived from either the territory held by the clan or the occupation controlled by the clan. Other members of the clan and its holdings generally belonged to either a guild or monopoly corporation and used names formed from the clan name by adding **-be** 部. Thus, they were known by names such as Sogabe 蘇我部, Ootomobe 大伴部 and Heguribe 平群部. In 815, Emperor Kanmu Tennou 桓武天皇 ordered a genealogical tree for the nation constructed. This tree included some 1,182 *uji* most of which were extinct by the end of the Hei'an Period. While it may be difficult to properly construct occupational clan names, with the exception of Yamato which is believed to be the *uji* associated with the imperial family, many of the ancient "legal" provincial or district names are available for use. Thus, Izumo 出雲 may be used, but no Unshuu 雲州.

When a clan name is included in the name of a person, it is placed between the surname (family name) and the given name of the individual. The family name can be understood as qualifying the clan name, specifying a particular lineage within the clan or otherwise identifying the named individual within the context of clan membership. Thus,

西山 平 仁左衛門
Nishiyama no Taira Hitoshisa'emon

means Hitoshisa'emon of the Nishiyama branch of the Taira Clan. As seen in the example, the possessive particle -no- is inserted between the family name and the clan name when the name is spoken, but is not actually written. As this name does not include a formal *nanori*, this name is an example of an *tsuushou* or *yobina* with "hitoshi" 仁 as its descriptive element. While 仁 frequently appears in the *nanori* of members of the imperial family, this person was definitely a commoner.

Although the *uji* were officially abolished in 646 along with the *be* and *tomo*, several of them remained powerful and were able to acquire extensive private holdings which were immune to taxation by the national government. Thus, while most clan names died out, a very few of them survived. Further, two new clans were created to accommodate rusticated members of the imperial family. This was done to thin the ranks of the imperial family which could not accommodate all of its descendents. Thus, any Japanese person with a family name is not officially a member of the imperial family (regardless of actual descent). Further, unless a person assumes one of the princely titles such as *shinnou* 親王, *ou* 王, *naishinnou* 内親王, *jo'ou* 女王, or *taishi* 太子, no such claim is being made.

The bands of retainers which formed around warlords during the Japanese middle ages were not clans in the sense that they were not kinship groups. Thus, membership in one of these bands did not necessarily effect ones name. The Genji were an exception to this because they constituted themselves as a classical *uji* complete with a clan chief. When the Genji established the Kamakura Bakufu, Mi'namoto Yoritomo offered clan membership to a large number of individuals in exchange for fealty. This was done to help establish the new government. As clan members, these individuals were part of the extended kinship structure and were entitled to use the clan name.

Ancient Clans

The ancient clans predate the Taika Reform when the clans were abolished. Certain of these clans held hereditary titles as well as their clan name. The hereditary title was generally held by the clan chieftain. Thus, the *uji no kami* 氏上 of the Soga was known as the *oo'omi* 大臣 or "great" *omi*, and the clan chief of the Ootomo was known as the *oomuraji* 大連 or "great" *muraji*. Although each was the supreme ritualist within their own clan, the *oo'omi* took precedence over the *oomuraji* in national ritual affairs. While the *oomuraji* was preeminent in police matters. Thus, while they shared the government, the *oo'omi* held higher status than the *oomuraji*. These two offices or *kabane* corresponded to clan offices, each clan having is own *omi* and *muraji*.

Ancient Japanese Clans

大伴	Ootomo	Controlled the government until supplanted by the Mo'no'nobe
物部	Mo'no'nobe	Controlled the armorers and the government until destroyed by the Soga
蘇我	Soga	Controlled the government until destroyed by Fujiwara no Kamatari.
中臣	Nakatomi	Nakatomi no Kamatari founded a new clan called the Fujiwara.
平群	Heguri	Originated in the Nara area.
葛城	Kazuraki	Originated in the Nara area. Currently, this name is read as "Katsuragi"
忌部	Inbe	Court ritualists descended from the deity Futodama no Mikoto 太玉命.
斎部	Inbe	Alternate name for the Inbe 忌部 after the beginning of the Hei'an Period.

Foreign Clans

Some of the clans did not originate in Japan, but arrived as immigrants. These clans generally held somewhat inferior status to the ancient clans. These groups included many skilled artisans and were treated somewhat like monopoly corporations. Thus, each of these names can take **-be** 部 as a suffix.

Immigrant Clans

漢	Aya	Settled in Yamato	文	Fumi	Settled in Kawachi
史	Fubito	Settled in Yamato	秦	Hata	Settled in Yamashiro

New Clans

A few clans survived the Taika Reform of 645 and the abolition of clans in 646. These stalwart clans went on to acquire hereditary offices and territorial holdings immune from taxation by the national government. In addition, a few new clans were founded after the territorial governors replaced the clan chiefs and local nobility as the effective government of the nation. Some of these new clans were created by rusticating imperial princes. As the imperial government could not absorb all of the emperor's children, many of them were "rusticated" and either sent to live in a Buddhist temple or given family names and allowed to form their own noble houses. Many of these houses continued to live in the capital district and competed with the traditional court nobility.

Rusticated imperial princes were given any one of several family names reserved for them. Each rusticated prince founded his own lineage within one of these clans or great houses. Of these new clans, the Mi'namoto and the Taira are the most famous. While the Mi'namoto built a true clan collectively called the Genji complete with a clan chief, the Taira remained relatively autonomous and only founded a great house collectively called the Heike. Formation of a new clan was primarily of import to the old imperial government. Thus, Hideyoshi sought the imperial imprimatur of legitimacy for founding the Toyotomi. The warrior bands attached to the *daimyou* were part of a band and not a kinship based *uji*. Finally, clans took their names either from places as did the Fujiwara and the Kazuraki or they took names descriptive of the import of the clan itself as did the Nakatomi, the Ootomo and the Toyotomi.

Clan Names & Tsuushou

While a member of the *kuge* or *buke* classes would have a *nanori*, he would commonly be called by a *tsuushou* or *yobina*. Yoshida Taiyou notes in *Kamon Kakei Jiten* that Fujiwara Hidesato 藤原秀郷 was also known as Tahara no Fujitaka 田原藤太). The 太 in this name reflects Hidesato's standing as most senior member of the Fujiwara clan. While there are several different ways to form a *tsuushou*, they were frequently related to the name of the "clan" to which the individual belonged. An easy way to construct these names is to prefix a simple birth order name with a character borrowed from the clan name. Clan members shared a common repertoire of emblematic *kanji* called *tsuuji* 通字. This *tsuuji* was combined with unique attributes of the individual to form a personal name. Thus, the clan name provides the descriptive element and seniority the substantive element in these names. We will encounter *tsuuji* again when we consider *nanori*. However, the repertoire of *tsuuji* available to an individual for forming *tsuushou* was independent of the *tsuuji* inherited to form the *nanori*. The *tsuuji* in the *tsuushou* represents clan membership, while the *tsuuji* in the *nanori* represents personal lineage. Late in the Muromachi Period, names of old the *efu* guard units were often used as the substantive element of a *tsuushou*. These *tsuushou* include quasi-titular names such as Tairasa'emon 平左衛門 and Kiyo'u'emon 清右衛門.

Common Tsuushou of Famous Clans

Clan	Reading	Tsuushou	Reading	Tsuushou	Reading
源	Mi'namoto	源	GEN	源太	Genta
		源	GEN	源三	Gensan
		源	GEN	源内	Gen'uchi
平	Taira	平	HEI	平次	Heiji
藤原	Fujiwara	藤	TOU	藤一郎	Tou'ichirou
		藤	TOU	藤兵衛	Touheei
橘	Tachiba'na	橘	KITSU	橘次	Kitsuji
		吉	yoshi	吉政	Yoshimasa
菅原	Sugahara	官	KAN	官兵衛	Kanhei'ei
		菅	KAN	example not available	
		勘	KAN	example not available	
大江	Oo'e	江	KOU	江一	Kou'ichi
		郷	GOU	郷造	Gouzou
清原	Kiyohara	清	SEI	清二	Seiji
安部	Abe	安	A	安兵衛	Ahei'ei
		安	A	安太郎	Atarou
中原	Nakahara	忠	CHUU	忠造	Chuuzou
忠助	Tada'notsuke	中	CHUU	example not available	

Monopoly Corporations

A *be* 部 was a monopoly corporation of skilled artisans. At one time, there were more than 180 of these guilds each with attendant land holdings and agricultural workers. These groups can be divided into several types. One type worked on imperial estates some of which were established to support specific members of the imperial family. The *minashiro* groups were established as memorials. Their primarily purpose was to perpetuate the name of a prince or princess either directly or indirectly. Private labour groups belonged to *uji*. Often these groups were named simply by attaching -*be* to the name of the *uji*. Both imperial and private agricultural *be* might be named simply by attaching -*be* to the end of the name of their locale. Some of these occupational groups were established to support specialists in such things as pottery and brocade weaving and various service groups in the imperial court such as the court ladies.

Some of these guilds took on the proportions of clans. The seamen and the mountain wardens even owned private armies. Other monopoly corporations were simply memorial endowments. In 480, the emperor created a guild of Palace Attendants, a guild of Palace Stewards, and a guild of Palace Archers. These guilds were to have holdings in every province and the agricultural output of their lands was dedicated to the memory of his three childless consorts. Land tenure was no accident. The income derived from these land grants significantly subsidized the artisans. The government regularly apportioned agricultural taxes to support court officials and finance operations. Compensating retainers by awarding them production rights to agricultural holdings continued throughout Japanese history. Following the Taika Reform, nobles and government officials were compensated by being awarded specified acreage. Later, the warrior class was to be compensated in terms of agricultural production measured in rice bales.

As guild names were sometimes adopted as surnames by *kuge* and *buke* families, the status of these names is determined by the overall construction of the complete name. Such names followed by a *yobina*, as in Fuhitobe no Tarou 史部太郎, are simply the names of peasants and artisans. In the census, this name was prefixed by a locative *kamei* 家名 or house name. When combined with a *nanori*, these are names used by the *kuge* and *buke* classes. Combining one of these names with a classical or pre-classical title clearly identifies the individual as a member of the *kuge* class. Thus, a guild name can be combined with a *kabane* to form a clan our court title. Within the Society for Creative Anachronism, these court titles may be appropriate for guild officers, holders of order of high merit, or members of the peerage. Local guild officers may append *miyatsuko* 造 to the name of the guild to form titles such as Nishi'oribe no Miyatsuko 錦織部造. This title could be used by the guildmaster of the local brocade weavers guild. After guild stewards became imperial officers, the guild names could appear as titular elements in names. Furuta Oribe Shige'nari 古田 織部 重然 was a sixteenth century *daimyou*. In this example, Oribe 織部 is actually a contraction of Oribe-no-kami 織部正 which is an imperial title.

Historical Guilds

海部	Amabe	Fishermen	膳部	Kashiwadebe	Oak Leaf Gatherers
画部	Ekakibe	Illuminators	楯縫部	Tate'nuibe	Shield Stitchers
磯部	Isobe	Seaweed Gatherers	酒部	Sakabe	Wine Makers
衣縫部	Ki'nu'nuibe	Court Tailors	鍛冶部	Ka'nuchibe	Blacksmiths
弓削部	Yugebe	Boyers	田部	Tabe	Imperial Serfs
鞍作部	Kuratsukuribe	Saddle Makers	服部	Hatori	Weavers
錦織部	Nishigoribe	Brocade Weavers	陶作部	Suetsukuribe	Potters
織部	Oribe	Weavers	鳥取部	Totoribe	Bird Catchers
史部	Fuhitobe	Chroniclers	鳥飼部	Torika(h)ibe	Bird Feeders
山守部	Yamamoribe	Mountain Wardens	矢矧部	Yahagibe	Fletchers

Guild names follow either of two regular patterns. A guild name can consist of either a noun or a noun followed by a verb (conjugated in the infinitive) to indicate an occupation. Whether a verb is necessary is hard to predict, but they occur in most cases. A good Japanese dictionary can help you find a two *kanji* occupational name. The name of an occupation is then followed by -**be** 部 which just says that we are talking about the group of people who practice a particular occupation.

Some of the guilds may seem a bit odd. A mountain warden was called a Yamamori 山守. In this name, *yama* 山 is simply the word for "mountain" and *mamoru* 守る is simply the act of guarding or defending something. Sometimes, this group is simply called the Yamabe 山部. Why would there be *yamamori*? There are several possible answers. One is that they were simply gate keepers or perhaps bandits who regulated trade through the mountains. Another possibility is that they were bands of priests and attendants guarding mountain shrines. Generally, Shintoh gods are believed to dwell in the sea, the mountains, and in impressive objects such as waterfalls or particularly ancient trees. Today, members of various *yamabushi* cults and other religious groups enengage in mountain pilgrimages dressed in ancient pilgrim costumes.

Agricultural Collectives

The remaining communal organization was the agricultural collective. These were independent of any group of skilled artisans and were not part of the extended kinship relationship of a clan. They did not share the origin myth or religion of the noble which gained control of them. Rather, these collectives appear to have arisen as federations of autonomous farming villages which eventually came under control of the court nobility. Other communes were the property of local nobility. Regardless, it appears that these names can be formed simply by attaching "tomo" 伴 to the end of either the name of the patron or a descriptive name for the location of the commune.

Although these agricultural collectives were abolished by the Taika Reform, they may have formed the basis for some of the later *shou'en* estates held by the court nobility. The imperial family also held land through a special agricultural guild. These imperial estates were called *agata* 県,[15] and their local nobility were called *agata no miyatsuko* 県造. The imperial estates were also called *miyake* 屯倉 after the imperial granaries standing on them. Members of the Tabe 田部 guild worked the imperial lands. Later, these imperial estates were nationalized along with the holdings of the court nobles. Regardless, the origin of land tenure appears to be the primary distinguishing features between the *be* and the *tomo*.

Agricultural collectives appear to have taken their names either from simple locatives describing where the collective was located or the surnames of their owners. Unfortunately, I have not been able to find any examples of these names. However, these names can probably be constructed simply by appending "no tomo" 伴 to any locative. This pattern is suggested by the titles adopted by local nobility and overseers.

As with the monopoly corporations, combining one of these names with a classical or pre-classical title clearly identifies the individual as a member of the *kuge* class. Thus, a simple place name can be combined with one of the ancient *kabane* to form an ancient clan title. These were the territorial sovereigns in ancient Japan. Within the Society for Creative Anachronism, these titles are appropriate for landed nobility. Just as the local nobility of the monopoly corporations were called *be-no-miyatsuko* 部造, the local nobility of the agricultural collectives were called *tomo no miyatsuko* 伴造. As the *tomo* were directly related to land tenure, they were completely replaced by the system of provincial governors and estate stewards.

Late Mediæval Feudal Domains[16]

While the ancient *uji* were extended kinship groups, the Mi'namoto admitted unrelated people to the Genji during the Genpei War. This presaged the warrior bands found in the later middle ages. After the twelfth century, military men came to possess heritable territorial rights which they eventually converted into feudal domains. Following the O'nin War 応仁乱 (1467–1477), local *buke* families asserted ownership of local estates effectively confiscating them from their absentee owners. These holdings formed a new territory-based social structure. The newly endowed landowners called *kokujin* 国人 formed compacts or protests called *ikki* 一揆 which means "one effort" or "one goal".

The *ikki* resisted claims made by the *bakufu* and interference by neighboring *shugo*. Many of the *ikki* were peasant movements and were known by names such as 土一揆 Land Band, 一向一揆 One Goal Band", 百姓一揆 Farmer's Band, and 白旗一揆 White Flag Band. The *ikki* were united not by common blood or even by shared land tenure, but by a shared commitment to perform some act.[17] These new groups were not kinship groups and did not contribute new name elements. However, a close vassal might be adopted into the lord's family. The *ikki* were fundamentally territorial and their leaders evolved into the *daimyou* of the Sengoku Period. Their domains were called *kokka* 国家 (lit. national family), a term which views these territories as an organic extension of the *kokujin's* household. These holdings evolved into the *han* 藩 which were feudal domains or fiefs formally instituted after 1600 under the *bakuhan* 幕藩 system of the Edo Period. For example, Kagahan 加賀藩 would be an Edo Period feudal holding of Kaga province

---

[15]Today, -ken 県 is used to form the names for prefectures which correspond to states or provinces.

[16]See the article "Muromachi Bakufu" by John Whitney Hall in the *Cambridge History of Japan* for an extended discussion of this period.

[17] David L. Davis wrote an excellent article called *"Ikki* in Late Mediæval Japan" which appeared in *Medieval Japan*, edited by Hall and Mass.

Names of Japanese Provinces

As part of the Taika Reform, the nation was divided into sixty seven *kuni* 国 or "provinces", and these provinces were in turn divided into *gun* 郡 or "districts". Although the "legal" names of the provinces typically consisted of a substantive element preceded by a descriptive element, "contracted names" were in common use. These names are composed of the principal element of the legal name followed by "shuu" 州 meaning province. Thus, provinces (much like people) had both common names and formal names. Another construction (which is unfortunately of indeterminate antiquity) is to suffix the formal name of a province with *kuni* 国 with the counter ヶ (ga) interposed. This is found in names such as Sado-ga-kuni 佐渡ヶ国 which resembles such names as Seki-ga-hara 関ヶ原 and Oni-ga-shima 鬼ヶ島. When ヶ is omitted, 国 is read as "koku" which is its Chinese reading instead of as "kuni" which is its Japanese reading.

NAMES AND NICKNAMES OF JAPANESE PROVINCES

Province		Nickname		Province		Nickname	
安芸	Aki	芸州	Geishuu	安房	Awa	房州	Boushuu
阿波	Awa	阿州	Ashuu	淡路	Awaji	淡州	Tanshuu
備後	Bingo	備州	Bishuu	備中	Bitchuu	備州	Bishuu
備前	Bizen	備州	Bishuu	豊後	Bungo	豊州	Houshuu
豊前	Buzen	豊州	Houshuu	筑後	Chikugo	筑州	Chikushuu
筑前	Chikuzen	筑州	Chikushuu	出羽	Dewa	羽州	Ushuu
越後	Echigo	越州	Esshuu	越前	Echizen	越州	Esshuu
越中	Etchuu	越州	Eshhuu	播磨	Harima	播州	Banshuu
飛騨	Hida	飛州	Hishuu	肥後	Higo	肥州	Hishuu
常陸	Hitachi	常州	Joushuu	日向	Hiuga	日州	Nichishuu
肥前	Hizen	肥州	Hishuu	伯耆	Houki	伯州	Kakushuu
伊賀	Iga	伊州	Ishuu	壱岐	Iki	壱州	Ishuu
因幡	Inaba	因州	Inshuu	伊勢	Ise	勢州	Seishuu
石見	Iwami	石州	Sekishuu	伊予	Iyo	予州	Yoshuu
伊豆	Izu	豆州	Zushuu	和泉	Izumi	泉州	Senshuu
出雲	Izumo	雲州	Unshuu	加賀	Kaga	加州	Kashuu
甲斐	Kai	甲州	Koushuu	河内	Kawachi	河州	Kashuu
上総	Kazusa	総州	Soushuu	紀伊	Kii	紀州	Kishuu
上野	Kouzuke	上州	Joushuu	三河	Mikawa	三州	Sanshuu
美作	Mimasaka	作州	Sakushuu	美濃	Mino	濃州	Noushuu
武蔵	Musashi	武州	Bushuu	陸奥	Mutsu	奥州	Oushuu
長門	Nagato	長州	Choushuu	能登	Noto	能州	Noushuu
隠岐	Oki	隠州	Inshuu	大隅	Oosumi	隅州	Guushuu
近江	Oumi	江州	Goushuu	尾張	Owari	尾州	Bishuu
佐渡	Sado	佐州	Sashuu	相模	Sagami	相州	Soushuu
讃岐	Sanuki	讃州	Sanshuu	薩摩	Satsuma	薩州	Sasshuu
摂津	Settsu	摂州	Sesshuu	志摩	Shima	志州	Shishuu
下野	Shimotsuke	野州	Yashuu	下総	Shimousa	総州	Soushuu
信濃	Shinano	信州	Shinshuu	周防	Su'ou	防州	Boushuu
駿河	Suruga	駿州	Sunshuu	但馬	Tajima	丹州	Tanshuu
丹波	Tanba	丹州	Tanshuu	丹後	Tango	丹州	Tanshuu
遠江	Tootoumi	遠州	Enshuu	土佐	Tosa	土州	Toshuu
対馬	Tsushima	対州	Taishuu	若狭	Wakasa	若州	Jakushuu
山城	Yamashiro	城州	Joushuu	大和	Yamato	和州	Washuu

Personal Names

Ideally, the *shimei* or "full name" consisting of a *myouji* 苗字 or family name followed by a *nanori* 名乗 or formal personal name should be both meaningful as a unit and euphonious. Like ancient Greek names Japanese names attempt to attribute spiritual qualities to the person named. Consequently, while Japanese given names are descriptive, they do not usually attempt to describe the physique of the individual. Thus, while names such as Akahige 赤髭 (red beard), Ookami 狼 (wolf), or Tako 蛸 (octopus) which in modern Japanese means "baldy", might be used as nicknames, they are not normative Japanese names. Japanese were commonly known by more official common use *zokumyou* 俗名 or *tsuushou* 通称 which could indicate the birth order of the person. Thus, Kentarou 健太郎 is the oldest son in the family. **KEN-** 健 means "healthy", and therefore Kentarou might express a parental wish for the health of their first born son. As a name given by his parents, 健太郎 may be considered a childhood name which is how the ordinal names are viewed today. The choice of descriptive element in a *tsuushou* could also be dictated by clan membership. We have already seen some of these in the chapter on clan names.

As fully ten percent of the Japanese populace belonged to the *buke* class and were entitled to personal and family names, the presumption of gentle rank which is common in the Society for Creative Anachronism easily justifies the use of a *myouji* and a *nanori*. A Japanese warrior would typically have at least three names in the course of their life. First, they would receive a childhood name when born. A baby boy would often be given a name indicating a virtue and possibly a birth order followed either 王 -**OU** (king) or 麿 -**maro**. (lord). Thus, Zen'ichimaru 善市麿 is clearly the name of a young boy. Originally, adult men bore names ending with either 麿 or 麻呂 both read "maro", but later these names were restricted to infants and children. This titular element means "young lord". Later, 丸 was substituted, but retained the same reading. Finally, the common reading for 丸 prevailed. Thus, -**maru** had replaced -**maro** by the Kamakura Period. The suffix "maru" 丸 means "chubby" which is how Japanese thought of healthy boys. At puberty, children would choose or have given to them an adult *nanori*.

Finally, after establishing a career and securing an heir, the Japanese adult could become a lay Buddhist monk and assume a *houmyou* which is a Buddhist name. Thus, men would normally retain their family names throughout life, but would change their given names several time. However, a member of the *kuge* (courtier class) or *buke* (warrior class) would occasionally be given permission by the emperor to found a new *uji* which would have its own name. New family names did not require imperial consent and were formed rather frequently. Male members of the *buke* class were sometimes adopted at which time they took the name of their adoptive family. Feudal lords were also known to change the family names of their vassals. Since Japanese does not conjugate gender, it can be difficult to determine the gender of the individual from their name. In fact, Tsu'noda Bun'ei documents many cases where women bore masculine *nanori*. Therefore, we must depend upon gender annotations in primary sources to determine gender.

Although Anthony Bryant asserts that "women did not change their names as did the men ... they kept theirs for life", women actually changed their names about as often as men did. Tsu'noda Bun'ei provides a list of twenty one different categories of personal names for women. Further, his list includes Buddhistic names, posthumous names and even names given as augmentations. In fact, as women continued to govern provinces, fight in battle, and otherwise conduct their business up until at least midway through the Kamakura Period, that women had a repertoire of names commensurate with their male counterparts should not be surprising. Finally, women customarily changed their names upon maturity as late as the early Showa Period. This is illustrated in the famous Japanese film about the experiences of a female schoolteacher in rural Japan. Prior to the seventeenth century, many Japanese women had names derived from their relationships with men. As they bore such names as "wife of Yoshi'nobu" which they certainly did not receive at birth.

Japanese Men

Because of our dependence on Chinese chronicles, learning about very early names is rather difficult. Regardless, we will first examine what little we can deduce about masculine names prior to the Hei'an Period. Outside of the imperial family, very early masculine names were either titles, occupational names, or locatives. Following the clan name and possessive -**no**-, a simple epithet such as "ugly" or a locative might be followed by *maro* 麿 meaning "lord". Other nobles might be known simply by their clan name and their *kabane* or by their domain followed by the *kabane no miyatsuko* 造. Later we find -**maro** 麿 and -**ko** 子 being used as titular suffixes to mono-thematic masculine names such Nakachiko 仲子. Still later the -**ko** 子 names are applied to females.

坂上田村麻呂	Sakanno'ue no Tamura Maro	The Sakano'ue Lord of Tamura
安曇連浜子	Azumi no Muraji Hamako	Hamako Lord of Azumi

Names ending in -**maro** 麿, -**hiko** 孫, -**hiko** 彦, and -**ko** 子 appear to be a transitional stage on the road to developing true masculine *nanori* which begin to appear during the Nara Period.[18] While we encounter names ending in -**maro** 麿 as late as the early Hei'an Period in 823, widespread use of *nanori* roughly dates from the removal of the capital from Heijoukyou (Nara) to Hei'ankyou (Kyôto) in 794. The ascendancy of the *nanori* is partly due to the popularity of Chinese culture and especially Buddhism following the Taika no kaishin 大化の改新 Taika Reform of 643. Following the emergence of *nanori*, -**maro** 麿 continued to be used in names for infants and children, while -**ko** 子 became a titular element in feminine names. Gradually, -**maru** 丸 came to replace -**maro** 麿. Later, during the Muromachi Period, men stopped using these suffixes entirely. Since the beginning of the Kamakura Period, men had been using their birth order as the substantive element of their *yobina*. At the end of the sixteenth century, we begin to see men's names ending in -**o**. Many modern Japanese masculine names end in -**o** written either 男 (man), 夫 (husband), or 雄 (male).

Nanori

The *nanori* was the special provenance of men belonging to the *kuge* and the *buke* classes. *Nanori* first appear at about the time of the Taika Reform in 645 and were well established by the reign of Emperor Montoku in 850 who established the custom of emperors having *nanori*. During the Hei'an Period, these names were also acquired by prominent artists and artisans. As the word *nanori* implies, these were the names announced in battle and other formal occasions. Jeffrey Mass[19] shows that mediæval Japanese men treasured their personal names and in particular their *nanori*. These names were always used in documents. These names appear to be the result of applying Japanese readings to Chinese given names. While the majority of *nanori* consisted of a substantive element preceded by a descriptive element, there are a few rare *nanori* written with more than two *kanji* and several *nanori* written with a single *kanji*. Several of these single *kanji nanori* are shown below.

Simple Masculine Nanori

Nanori	Kanji	Notes	Nanori	Kanji	Notes
Hikaru	光	Bright / Shining	Shitagau	順	Order / Sequence
Hitoshi	等	Rank / Level	Susumu	進	Continue
Kisou	競	Strive	Tamotsu	保	Guarantee
Kotau	答	Answer / Reply	Terasu	照	Sparkling
Makoto	信	Belief / Faith	Tooru	融	Melt / Pass Through
Sadamu	定	Fix / Specify / Determine	Yoshi	義	Obligation / Fealty

---

[18] Fujiwara Fuyutsugu 藤原冬嗣 (775–826 CE) lived at the beginning of the Heian period. Fuyutsugu is identical in form to *nanori* encountered at the close of the sixteenth century.

[19] "Identity, Personal Names, and Kamakura Society" in Mass (1992) p. 101. This is different from the present condition where Japanese men commonly use their family names.

Common Elements Used in Masculine Nanori

Masculine *nanori* typically consist of a substantive element preceded by a single modifier. There are 2024 of these *nanori* in the table of *Historical nanori*. Every *kanji* which appears in at least forty names appears in the following table in descending order of overall frequency. The first number gives the total number of occurrences, the second the number of occurrences in initial (descriptive) position, and the third the number of occurrences in final (substantive) position.

Kanji Frequencies in Masculine Nanori Prior to 1600

Kanji	Frequencies			Usage		Meaning
義	123	100	23	yoshi-	-yoshi	Obligation / Fealty / Foster Child
宗	73	45	28	mune-	-mune	Master an Art
頼	83	56	27	yori-	-yori	Request / Ask
氏	81	36	45	uji-	-uji	Family / Clan
長	80	34	46	naga-	-naga	Long / Oldest
忠	74	42	32	tada-	-tada	Faithful / Loyal
宗	73	45	28	mu'ne-	-mu'ne	Master an Art
光	73	30	43	mitsu-	-mitsu	Bright / Shining
経	72	35	37	tsune-	-tsune	Sitar / True Path / Travel Straight
実	71	40	31	sa'ne-	-sa'ne	Seed or Center / Reality / Plentiful
盛	69	30	39	mori-	-mori	Plentiful / Piled Up
政	69	29	40	masa-	-masa	Govern / Rule / Instruct / Self-Control
親	69	35	34	chika-	-chika	Parent / Intimate
重	69	35	34	shige-	-shige	Heavy / Weighty / Serious
兼	69	45	24	ka'ne-	-ka'ne	Unite / Hold many Offices / Heavy Service
久	68	12	56	hisa-	-hisa	Longtime
通	67	42	27	michi-	-michi	Pass Through / Big Road
時	66	41	25	toki-	-toki	Hour / Time / Era
貞	63	46	17	sada-	-sada	Correct Spirit / Composure / Modesty
行	62	35	27	yuki-	-yuki	Go / Perform
清	61	28	33	kiyo-	-kiyo	Pure
家	60	34	26	ie-	-ie	Rural House / Family
朝	59	29	30	tomo-	-tomo	Morning / Dawn
定	59	26	23	sada-	-sada	Fix / Specify / Determine
基	57	35	22	moto-	-moto	Foundation / Earthen Dais
隆	53	28	25	taka-	-taka	Grow Tall / Pile Up
房	53	09	44	fusa-	-fusa	Monastic Cell
秀	53	22	31	hide-	-hide	Produce Good / Extraordinary / Bountiful
景	53	18	35	kage-	-kage	Bright / Magnificent
高	50	34	16	taka-	-taka	Tall / High
師	48	48	00	moro-	-moro	Teacher / Expert[20]
成	47	17	30	shige-	-shige	Become / Exist
直	34	15	19	nao-	-nao	Adjust / Correct (Action)[21]
直	11	08	03	tada-	-tada	Correct (Condition)
綱	45	01	44	tsu'na-	-tsu'na	Net[22]
教	44	25	19	nori-	-nori	Teaching / Dogma
正	40	28	12	masa-	-masa	Unerring / Genuine

---

[20] This character does not appear as the substantive element in documented *nanori*. One possible explanation for this is its role as the substantive element in many titles.

[21] Although the individual readings for 直 are given separately, the position of this character in the *kanji* frequency table was determined by its cumulative incidence.

[22] Nets are associated with physical strength. One of the rituals of modern *sumou* wrestlers involves hauling nets.

Dynastic Naming Practices

Members of the *kuge* and *buke* classes were concerned about their lineage and often reflected this concern in their *nanori*. Their *nanori* shared a common element called a *tsuuji* 通字. Many male members of the imperial family share **-hito** 仁 in their *nanori*. This practice also appears in artistic and religious names. Members of the Urasenke tea society, who have been granted permission to assume the family name and crest, place **SOU-** 宗 at the beginning of their "tea name". Similarly, the Chinese style religious names of Buddhist monks will share a common element. The *tsuuji* typically appears as the descriptive element in *nanori*, but it may appear as the substantive element such as the 仁 -hito in the names of imperial princes. While many members of a lineage may share a *tsuuji*, the *tsuuji* can skip generations and change over time. Often this happens when a father decides to pass on a different name element to his sons.

HISTORICAL TSUUJI

Kanji	Family	Tsuuji	Reading	Kanji	Example	Date
武田	Takeda	信	nobu	武田 信光	Takeda Nobumitsu	1162 - 1248
楠木	Kusunoki	正	masa	楠木 正季	Kusu'noki Masasue	? - 1336
島津	Shimatsu	久	hisa	島津 忠久	Shimatsu Tadahisa	1179 - 1227
小笠原	Ogasawara	長	naga	小笠原 長基	Ogasawara Nagamoto	1347 - 1407
織田	Oda	信	nobu	織田 信長	Oda Nobu'naga	1534 - 1582
毛利	Mouri	元	moto	毛利 元春	Mouri Motoharu	ca 1336
伊達	Date	宗	mu'ne	伊達 政宗	Date Masamu'ne	1353 - 1405
細川	Hosokawa	元	moto	細川 頼元	Hosokawa Yorimoto	1343 - 1397
千葉	Chiba	胤	ta'ne	千葉 宗胤	Chiba Mu'neta'ne	1265 - 1294

Men and Clan Names

Although Jeffrey Mass[23] shows that *uji* or clan membership passed from a father to his children during the Kamakura Period, adoption and matrilocal residence throughout the mediæval period often meant that clan membership was effectively passing from mothers or at least the maternal grandfather to their children. The prevalence of this practice is demonstrated by the popularity of *Funa Watashi Muko* 船渡聟 and other *muko kyougen* plays where a fathers seeks to marry their sons into a wealthy family. Regardless, men received *uji* or clan names at birth, and *kabane* titles were still being attached to these *uji* as late as the nineteenth century. Mass goes on to show that *uji* were extensively used in legal documents of the Kamakura Period. Simplified version of these clan names also appear as prefixes to birth order names throughout the middle ages. Mass goes on to note that the clan or *uji* names were more formal than the family name or *myouji*.

Tsuushou and Zokumyou

Yobina or *tsuushou* are common use given names which immediately precede military and governmental titles and offices in formal documents and can be thought of as carrying the title. These common names most often consist of simply a birth order such as Saburou 三郎 or a birth order preceded by a thematic element such as 与 (YO) which means "Team up". These thematic elements were often shared by members of a clan in much the same way as *tsuuji* are shared by the *nanori* within a lineage. As the *azana* is of Chinese origin, they were often constructed using the Chinese or *onyomi* readings of their constituent characters.

The *tsuushou* or *zokumyou* were the names used for social purposes. These names with their attached titles commonly appear between the *kamei* or *myouji* and the *nanori*. These names are typically constructed as a series of birth order names. There are many examples of such names in the section of the Thematic Dictionary devoted to numbers and quantities. These names can be combined with the parental birth order

---

[23]"Identity, Personal Names, and Kamakura Society" in Mass (1992).

preceding the child's birth order. Thus, Saburoutarou 三郎太郎 is the third son of a second son. The birth order elements can be preceded by the clan *tsuushou* so that Gentarousaburou 源太郎三郎 would be the third son of a first son and belong to the Genji 源氏 or Mi'namoto Clan. While the *kabane* titles are strongly associated with the *uji*, military titles are strongly associated with the *tsuushou*. In the late middle ages, titles for imperial guard appointments such as sa'emon 左衛門 became the basis for *tsuushou* such as Toraza'emon.

Since the Genpei War opened the Japanese middle ages, typical masculine *tsuushou* have ended with -ROU 郎. Like -maru, -ROU 郎 is a titular suffix whose reading changed over time. Earlier, this *kanji* was read as -RAU and only later took the reading -ROU. Unlike -maro 麿 which appears to be a Japanese invention, -ROU 郎 was a titular suffix imported from China. In China, -RAU 郎 was the title for the captain of a corps of imperial guards. From this, we may suppose that -ROU 郎 was originally used as a substantive element in titles. However, by the early Kamakura Period, it appears to have become a true name element and lost its titular import. The only remnant of its original titular use being the practice of attaching titles to the *tsuushou*. While it is difficult to date the emergence of -ROU in common names, we can posit that the popularity of these names grew as a result of Chinese influence in court life. Regardless, the popularity of these names appears to have supplanted the use of -maru in forming adult masculine names. Although these names contain what were originally titular elements in China, there is little evidence that 郎 was ever used in official titles in Japan. Further, as 郎 became nearly universal as the substantive element in masculine *tsuushou* of the *buke* class by the early Kamakura Period, these names should be permitted for use in the Society for Creative Anachronism.

Sometimes, the *zokumyou* is omitted and only the title or office appears. Thus, names such as Nagase no Hanguan Dairi Shigetsu'na 長瀬 判官代理 重綱[24] were extant during the Genpei War. The initial element is essentially a locative followed when spoken by the possessive particle -no-. The next element is a title which roughly translates to "deputy clan chief". The final element, Shigetsu'na 重綱, is the *nanori* or "official given name" of the individual. After retirement, a Japanese gentleman would adopt a Chinese style Buddhist name called a *houmyou*. These names are also typically constructed from two morphemes, but this time take their *onyomi* or Chinese reading. A familiar example of such a name is Takeda Shingen 武田 信玄 where Shingen 信玄 is a rather typical *houmyou* constructed from morphemes with theological and moral significance within Buddhism.

Infants, Children and Coming of Age

During the middle ages, a member of the warrior class would receive an infant name during the first year of their life. Baby boys usually received a birth name with a distinctive ending such as -maro 麿. Thus, Takamaru 孝丸 would normally be the name of a male child who has not yet under-gone his coming of age ceremony and received an adult name. This ceremony, called *genfuku* 元服, normally occurred when the young boy reached the age of twelve, but could occur somewhat later -maru. 丸 is shorthand for the native Japanese *kanji* -maro 麿 meaning "young lord" which we encountered in the Nara Period. *Maro* was originally written phonetically as 麻呂 and may have referred to a Polynesian symbol of kingship.[25]

As already noted, the *osanana* is a name given to infants and the *warawana* a name born by children. The *osanana* given to sons typically ended with either of three distinctive suffixes. The most typical of which is -maru 丸 which literally means "chubby" and connotes good health. And, -waka 若 is a common suffix which simply means "young". While -waka frequently appears before -maru, the converse is at best exceptionally rare. Like -waka, -chiyo 千代 is a suffix which can appear either as the final element in the name or before -maru. 千代 literally means "one thousand generations" and connotes preservation of the line. As these are suffixes, they are preceded by a substantive element. This substantive element can be either a single thematic element or it can be a complete *nanori*. While a normal *nanori* consists of only two *kanji*, a third *kanji* was sometimes added to these infantile *nanori*. An -OU 王 sometimes appears between the substantive name and the childhood suffixes. Generally, this is a title born by imperial princes before they received *shinnou senge*. This -OU 王 should be avoided in adult names used within the Society for Creative Anachronism.

---

[24] *Dairi* 代理 is a suffix attached to the titles of exofficio deputies, agents and "acting" appointees to office.

[25] Plutschow (1995).

Historical osanana and warawana

亀若丸	Kamewakamaru	Tortoise + Young + Chubby	Muromachi Period
竹若	Takewaka	Bamboo + Young	Nanboku Period
金王丸	Ka'nekimimaru	Gold + Lord + Chubby	Nanboku Period
永寿王丸	Nagahisa'oumaru	Long + Longevity + Lord + Chubby	Muromachi Period
勝永寿丸	Kachi'nagahisamaru	Victory + Long + Longevity + Chubby	Kamakura Period

While words for beasts and monsters are conspicuously absent from masculine *nanori*, they do appear as the substantive element in these names. Not only can animals appear as the substantive element in these names, but plants as well. The substantive element for an *osanana* or *warawana* can also be a virtue as in a *nanori* or a *tsuushou* and can even be composed of two elements the first of which is descriptive and the second substantive as in a *nanori*. In fact, the substantive element of an *osanana* can itself be a properly formed *nanori*. As noted in the section on clan names, this substantive element can be borrowed from the clan name. This practice is similar to the appearance of *tsuuji* in *nanori*. Finally, the imperial court title *ou* 王 can appear as a titular element between the substantive element its suffixes.

Japanese Women

While we encounter fully developed masculine *nanori* as early as 826, what about feminine names? Although masculine *nanori* appear to have remained largely unchanged throughout the Japanese middle ages, feminine names underwent significant chronological development. This parallels the evolution of masculine *azana* which came to incorporate previously titular elements. Consequently, there were several forms for constructing feminine names during each period. While Japanese women have formed their names in many different ways, these names spring from native Japanese sources. Except for baptismal names and *houmyou*, Japanese women did not import names from other cultures.

Yamato Period Feminine Suffixes

-hime	媛	秘	比賣			
-irashime	郎女	郎姫	女郎子	女郎	嬢	女郎
-tobe	戸邊					
-ko	子	児	古			
-kimi	君					

While we do encounter Japanese women with Chinese-inspired *nanori* similar to their brothers, this is unusual. Instead, their names appear to follow an earlier onomastic tradition. From ancient times, women bore names ending with distinctive suffixes. Thus, their names ended with -**hime** 姫,-**hime** 媛,-**me** 賣,-**me** 女 ,-**iratsume** 郎, and -**iratsume** 嬢. These are all native Japanese readings. Later, under the influence of Chinese scholarship, 女 was read as "nyo" which is its Chinese reading. Originally, men bore names ending with -**ko** 子,-**maro** 麿, and -**maro** 麻呂. Later, noble women began to end their names with -**ko** 子 as well. While men invariably wrote their names ideographically, women felt free to write their names purely phonetically. However, this does not mean that their names lacked meaning. Since the earliest chronicles were written, Japanese women have been writing their names ideographically. Not only were all Buddhist names written ideographically, but the *kuge* were particularly fond writing their names this way.

Like their brothers, Japanese women often bore several names at the same time. You should never confuse this with the multiple or compound names born by European women. There is no Japanese equivalent to Mary-Elizabeth. While some of their names may appear to be compound names of this sort, each of the components modifies or describes the substantive component. Thus, while it might be possible to separate out part of the name and have a valid name, it looses its identity in a longer name.

We will consider the construction Japanese feminine names chronologically beginning with the Yamato Period and ending with the Warring States Period. Many of these names follow regular constructions in which a substantive element or root name is combined with an honourific suffix. Often, the same root name was used in more than one period.

The names used by the *kuge* were often distinct from those used by the *buke* and lower classes. Japanese women were using distinctive suffixes as early as the Yamato Period. While later names were more concerned with destiny and morals, these early names were often physically descriptive or occupational. We encounter names such as Furume 古賣 meaning "old" and Shirakamime 白髮賣 meaning "white hair". But, we can already find names of a more auspicious sort. Hime 日賣 may simply mean "sunny" while I'nume 犬賣 means "dog". Why is "dog" auspicious? Like American Indians, the Japanese developed folk beliefs about animals. Further, the Japanese imported the Chinese zodiac which was populated by beasts and monsters. Thus, a dog is "faithful", oxen are "strong" and rats signify a bountiful harvest.

During the Nara Period, most feminine names were ended with 賣 **-me** which literally means to "sell" or to "make and send forth".[26] Occasionally, women's names ended with **-me** 女 which means "woman". Tamateme 玉手賣, Tsuburame 都夫良賣, and Shikitame 志祁多女 are typical of names found in *koseki* 戸籍 or census records from the Nara Period. As census documents were primarily concerned with agricultural production, labour levies, and tax assessments, we don't really know whether these names were in common use. At this time, **-ko** 子 was becoming a popular feminine suffix among the *kuge* class, but had yet to migrate to the lower classes. Certain prefixes and suffixes will transform a root name into either the name of a great noble or the name of a deity. Japanese goddesses typically had names beginning with either **ama-** 天, **amatsu-** 天, or **toyo-** 豊 and ending with **-mikoto** 命 or **-hime'no'mikoto** 媛命. The first two prefixes both represent "high heaven" while the third means "noble". The first suffix simply means "life", and the second means "princess of life". Women belonging to great noble families bore names ending with either **-hime** 比賣, **-hime** 媛, or **-hime** 郎女. All of which simply mean "princess".

Feminine Names with Masculine Cognates

Feminine Name		Masculine Name		Feminine Name		Masculine Name	
牛賣	Ushime	牛麻呂	Ushimaro	赤賣	Akame	赤人	Akahito
猿手賣	Saruteme	猿手	Sarute	諸賣	Morome	諸人	Morohito
吉賣	Yoshime	吉麻呂	Yoshimaro	申賣	Sarume	猿麻呂	Sarumaro
久須理賣	Kusurime	久須里	Kusuri	小玉賣	Kodamame	小玉	Kodama
黒賣	Kurome	黒麻呂	Kuromaro	酒手賣	Sakateme	酒手	Sakate
広国賣	Hirokunime	広国	Hiroku'ni	虫賣	Mushime	虫麻呂	Mushimaro
広賣	Hirome	広人	Hirohito	弟賣	Otome	弟麻呂	Otomaro
咋賣	Ku(h)ime	咋麻呂	Ku(h)imaro	百枝賣	Momo'eme	百枝	Momo'e
根手賣	Neteme	根手	Nete				

Many early feminine names can be transformed into masculine names simply by removing its feminine suffix. Most feminine names related to masculine names consisted of two or more *kanji* followed by a feminine suffix. The resulting masculine name should have two thematic elements. Whenever the resulting name would have been too short, the feminine suffix was simply replaced with either **-maro** 麻呂 or **-hito** 人. Thus, we encounter many masculine names consisting of the name of a plant or an animal followed by one of these two suffixes. We can even find Marome 麻呂賣 used as a woman's name. This name consists simply of a masculine suffix followed by a feminine suffix. Later, after the *nanori* became fully developed, these masculine cognates were comparatively rare.

---

[26] This ending is difficult to explain. Perhaps it reflects payment of a bride price. Regardless, women generally enjoyed higher status and greater personal freedom in Japanese antiquity than they did in the Japanese middle ages. Phonetically writing *hime* (princess) as 比賣 may also help account for this popularity.

Feminine Root Names in Use Since Antiquity[27]

あさ	Asa	あや	Aya	いさ	Isa	いし	Ishi
きし	Kishi	きぬ	Ki'nu	くに	Ku'ni	くめ	Kume
くら	Kura	くろ	Kuro	こま	Koma	さき	Saki
さや	Saya	さよ	Sayo	すゑ	Suwe	たつ	Tatsu
たへ	Tahe	たま	Tama	たを	Tawo	ちよ	Chiyo
とき	Toki	とし	Toshi	とめ	Tome	とよ	Toyo
とら	Tora	なみ	Nami	ひさ	Hisa	ひめ	Hime
ひら	Hira	まき	Maki	ます	Masu	まつ	Matsu
まな	Ma'na	みゆき	Miyuki	もも	Momo	ももえ	Momoe
ゆき	Yuki	よし	Yoshi	より	Yori		

After you remove honourific prefixes and suffixes from a Japanese name, you are left with the root name. Very few of the root names used by women in ancient Japan survived the Japanese middles ages to still be in use today. Depending on the period, these root names may require that a prefix or suffix be attached. While very long names appear to be quite common in ancient Japan, in later times prefixes and suffixes were often suppressed so that the total name would not exceed three or four mora. In general, whether a root name can accept a suffix or not can be determined by counting the number of mora. If a root name ends in a vowel and has one or two mora, then it can accept a suffix otherwise it can not. Thus, Miyuki みゆき, Yuki ゆき, and Yukiko ゆきこ can be constructed, but Miyukiko みゆきこ and Midoriko みどりこ should be avoided.

Nara Period Feminine Suffixes

Reading	Suffix	Meaning	Usage
-hime	賣	—	Used with a masculine root name
-toujime	刀自賣	Elderly	Used with a single descriptive element
-mushime	虫賣	Snake	Used with a single descriptive element
-tsume	津賣	Harbour	Used with topographic descriptors
-nushime	主賣	Master	Used with locatives and agricultural produce
-hime	比賣	Strive	Used with "spiritual" descriptors
-shimame	島賣	Island	Used with topographic descriptors
-wakame	若賣	Young	Used with other suffix elements
-rame	良賣	Good	Used with one and two element names

Women's names evolved rapidly during the comparatively short Nara Period. *Kuge* women took over the honourific suffix -**ko** 子 meaning "child". The *kuge* developed titles called *kabane* which became part of the name. The imperial family adopted or invented Chinese titles. Female members of the family were given the titles 内親王 *naishinnou* and 女王 *jo'ou*. During the middle of the Nara Period, imperial princesses commonly bore names consisting of a locative followed by their title. At this time, princesses and other great ladies commonly lived in their own detached palaces. Thus, these locatives might refer to the location of their palace. Thus, there was a princess named Sawa'uchi Jo'ou 沢内女王. Other imperial princesses and ladies of the court bore names claiming possession of a monopoly corporation or an office within the imperial government. During the Nara Period, 式部 -**shikibu** frequently appears as a titular element following the names of ladies belonging to the imperial court. The *shikibu* was a ritual department within the imperial government. Consequently, we meet ladies called Murasaki Shikibu 紫式部 and Izumi Shikibu 和泉式部. Ladies of the court were frequently called just *shikibu* 式部. This reflects a general trend in Japanese to

---

[27] Tsunoda Bunei remarks that very few of the phonetic forms found in ancient feminine names have survived the ages. Once meaning is considered, these 43 phonetic patterns correspond to many more root names. However, despite the prevalence of homonyms in Japanese, the resulting inventory of root names remains rather restricted.

append offices or job titles to names, or to even replace names with titles. Gradually, the complicated Yamato Period suffixes fell out of use and most women had names which simply ended with 賣 -**me**. However, the courtier society at Heijoukyou developed its own group of distinctive suffixes.

By the Hei'an Period, names ending with -**ko** 子 had become ubiquitous among women belonging to the *kuge* class. Outside of the court, women were still ending their names with -**me** 賣,-**tojime**, and -**mushime** 虫賣,-**kome** 子賣,-**machime**,-**akome** 阿古女, and -**teme** 手賣 were popular new suffixes. They were also using -**kime** 屎女 which actually means "fæces". However, their names were generally simpler than they were before. Only -**me** 女 and -**akome** 阿古女 formed names with two element root names. While -**akome** 阿古女 converted two *kanji* place names and family names into given names, -**me** written either 賣 or 女 could convert either a place name or a single *kanji* descriptive element into a given name. The remaining suffixes always acted as substantive elements, thus taking single element descriptive elements. Of these, -**teme** 手賣 is particularly interesting. This suffix roughly translates as "handler" and can be combined with the names of animals to form new names.

The end of the Hei'an Period (ca. 1175) saw the rise of the great warrior houses. This new warrior society instituted changes in government, architecture, land tenure, and marriage patterns. The new warrior houses were very conscious of rank, seniority, lineage and clan membership. Ranking warrior families began to give their women names ending in -**ko** 子 which had previously been reserved to the court nobility. Names such as Nakako 仲子, which indicated birth order or relative status, became quite popular. The courtiers were quite rank-conscious as well. The courtiers frequently called each other simply by their birth order or court rank. Often warrior women simply attached 女 (now read as -**NYO** instead of -**me**) after a masculine birth-order name such as Saburou 三郎 to produce names such as Saburome 三郎女. Why the change in reading? This change was to accommodate the customary Chinese reading of the characters making up many of the birth order names. Owing to the importance of the clan membership, warrior women commonly bore given names consisting simply of their clan name followed by either -**no'uji** 氏子 or -**uji'nome** 氏女. Finally, many women bore given names consisting of a single semantic element. These given names could be the names of plants, beasts, or monsters. Later, **o-** 御 or **o-** 於 came be attached as an affectionate prefix to these simple names.

The Kamakura Period begins with the Genpei War and Mi'namoto Yoritomo establishing a warrior government at Kamakura. By this time -**nyou**, 女 had completely supplanted -**me** 賣 for forming simple given names for women. However,-**NYOU** 女 itself began to give way before -**nomae** 前, -**gozen** 御前, and -**do'no** 殿. Sometimes, as in the following example, these forms could be combined.

丹波氏女伊夜前

Tanba Uji no Nyou Iya no Mae

Tanba is a provincial name and the name of the *uji*. You can think of Uji-no-nyou 氏女 as simply meaning "clan's woman". Iya 伊夜 is a two element name. However, it takes its Chinese reading instead of a more customary Japanese reading. Again, this is probably to maintain euphony with -**NYOU** 女 which immediately precedes it. By this time, the *buke* were commonly using -**ko** 子 interchangeably with -**NYOU** 女 in their names. However, as 子 takes a *Japanese reading* and 女 a Chinese reading, this choice may effect the reading of the entire name. Generally, if the parts of a single name take different kinds of readings, one Chinese and the other Japanese, than a possessive -**no**- will be found inserted between the two parts.

Beginning with the Divided Court Period, we have much more information about women belonging to the *buke* caste than for earlier periods. Names during this period generally had one of the following suffixes: -**OU** 王 meaning "king",-**yasame** 夜叉女 or -**yasa** 夜叉 which refer to the evening,-**hime** 姫 meaning "princess", -**ko** 子 which originally meant "son" or "lord", or -**ako** 阿古 which literally means "treasured antiquity". The root name could also be followed by -**kusu** 楠 which refers to an evergreen tree with heart shaped leaves and was typically combined (after the root name) with the suffix -**me** 女 as in Kusume 楠女 which lacks any root name and Kusakumame 楠熊女. Aguri 阿久 (treasured long interval of time) is commonly found without a root name and can be followed by -**me** 女 to produce Agurime 阿久女. Additionally, during this period there wre many names which consisted of the name of a plant or an animal followed by a suffix such as 御前

-gozen or by 女 -me. *Gozen* also functioned as a pronoun. It was generally applied to the wives, mistresses, and lovers of prominent men at the close of the Hei'an Period. *Gozen* originated as a pronoun referring to the previous posting of an official.

Kamakura Period Feminine Names

Type	Suffix	Reading	Example	Combined With
Birth Order	子	ko	四郎子	Ordinal or masculine birth order name
Clan	氏女	uji'nonyou	藤原氏女	Clan or family name
Clan	氏子	uji'noko	清原氏子	Clan or family name
Flora & Fauna	若女	wakame	菊若女	Names of plants, beast & monsters
Flora & Fauna	女	nyou	紀松女	Names of plants, beast & monsters
Flora & Fauna	前	nomae	松前	Names of plants, beast & monsters
Flora & Fauna	子	ko	犬子	Names of plants, beast & monsters
Princess	姫	hime	楽師姫	Locative or celestial ordinal
Princess	子	ko	知子	"Spiritual" quality
Pearl	阿古	ako	阿古殿	Honourific prefix or suffix

During the Muromachi Period, the **o-** prefix to women's names became universal for the *buke* class. Further, their names were frequently followed by the common name of a father, a husband, or another male relative. Thus, names such as O-Natsu-Seijuurou お夏清十郎 and O-Aya-Tenhei'ei お綾伝兵衛 can be found in mediæval documents. Another common construction can be ascribed to names such as Yaoya-O-Na'na 八百屋お七 where the woman's name follows the place descriptor or trade name used by her father or husband with an intervening honourific. Thus, Toujin-O-Kitsu 唐人お吉 is presumably the daughter or wife of a Chinese immigrant and the previous example would be the seventh daughter of a greengrocer. The honourific **o-** in all of these names is most often written with the letter 御, but 阿 and 於 also appear in mediæval documents. Because of the regularity of honourific **o-**, it is generally omitted from feminine names in the table of *Historical Feminine Names*. This affords greater visibility of the root names.

The influence of Buddhism is evident in many feminine names during the mediæval period. Some women had names consisting of one or two morphemes followed by 阿弥 **-ami** which are the first two characters in Amida Buddha 阿弥陀仏, the merciful Buddha of the Pure Land sects. There were also similar names with just 弥 **-MI** as the final element. This construction is particularly interesting because, it was also used for masculine names. 阿弥 **-ami** can be found as the final element in the artistic names of an important group of masculine artistic connoisseurs and adepts during the fifteenth and sixteenth centuries. Regardless, it strong Buddhistic flavour and was thereby quite attractive to Japanese intellectuals.

Early in the Muromachi Period, root names followed by **-ujime** 氏女 or **-me** 女 lost their popularity, and names such as Torachiyome 虎千代女 were supplanted by names such as Tora 虎 and Chiyo 千代. While mediæval Japanese masculine names usually had rather noble meanings, this is not universally true for feminine names. For example, the *kanji* which is read "Kaka" is a vulgar word for "wife" and "Uba" means a "worthless old woman".[28] However, Kaka 呵々 means to laugh in a loud voice. These repetitive names are rather common names for mediæval Japanese women. Alliteration of this sort is characteristic of Japanese onomatopoeia which makes these names rather evocative.

The naming practices established during the Muromachi Period remained normative until the Meiji restoration in the nineteenth century. Consequently, for most of the *samurai* epoch, Japanese feminine names consisted of a root name to which an honourific o 御 was prefixed by the speaker. The root name consisted of a single idea which was often just a single morpheme. Thus, names such as Kiku 菊 (chrysanthemum), Aoi 葵 (hollyhock), or Tora 虎 (tiger) were in common use. There were also many alliterative names, such as Kaka 呵々, Ne'ne 禰々 and Nyanya 若々 (young-young) which sounds like the "meowing" of a cat. These names repeated a single idea.

---

[28] Such women were frequently bound and disposed of on the snowy slopes of mountains during the Winter. Frequently, a mountain was specially designated for this purpose and was called *ubasuteyama* 姥捨て山.

From the late mediæval period to shortly after the Meiji Restoration in the nineteenth century, the names of adult Japanese women were prefixed with **o-** so that a woman might be called Oharu お春, but shortly after the Meiji Restoration it became popular to add suffixes to the end of the names of adult Japanese women. Thus, names like Haruko 春子 and Sachiko 幸子 became popular. These names appear to emulate the names of female members of the Japanese aristocracy during the classical and early mediæval periods. As Japanese women were relatively autonomous during these periods, they have always enjoyed great popularity with Japanese women. Along with the familiar **-ko** 子 which literally means child, **-yo** 代 in Kazuyo 和代 meaning generation and the ending **-e** 枝 in Chie 千枝 are also in modern use. While masculine names appear to have enjoyed greater stability and a relatively limited language for constructing them, feminine names have taken many different forms during the Japanese middle ages.

Women and Clan Names

Women received their clan names at birth and retained them throughout life. Women were more strongly attached to their clans than their brothers. Their *uji*, and not family names, are the names that are customarily combined with their personal name during the Kamakura Period. Unlike men, women sometimes follow and ancient Chinese custom and are sometimes known simply by their clan name followed by *uji*. *Thus*, a woman might be known simply as Fujiwara no uji (1206).[29]

Prior to the Taika Reform in 645, there were at least a thousand *uji* and over a hundred *be*. However, nationalization of their land holdings and governmental jurisdiction resulted in a limited number of *ujizoku* families retaining their importance. The Taika Reform and later the Genpei War resulted in the preeminence of three *uji* during the Kamakura Period. These were: the Mi'namoto, the Taira, and the Fujiwara. While these three *uji* account for most mediæval Japanese people, other *uji* did persist with living descendants even today. Some of the more successful of these *uji* are noted in the section on Ancient and Mediæval Clans.

Patronymics and Other Relational Names

We have already seen *tsuuji* used to express kinship through the *nanori*. A man's membership in an *uji* could be expressed by affixing the short form of his clan name to the beginning of a birth-orders style *tsuushou*. For example, a first born member of the Mi'namoto might receive the name Gentarou 源太郎. These short forms typically take Chinese *onyomi* readings as do the other parts of the birth order name. Birth order names could be further elaborated to express multi-generational descent. Thus, Gen'saburou'tarou would be the first son of a third son belonging to the Mi'namoto.

Women were often recorded as the mother, daughter, wife, or sister of a named man. This was accomplished by placing the word for the relationship after the name of the male relative. She might be recorded simply as a woman belonging to a particular clan such as the Fujiwara and called Fujiwara no me 藤原女. Finally, although women seldom had *nanori*, a woman's *tsuushou* could be formed by taking a *tsuuji* from her father and adding a feminine suffix such as **-ko**. Thus, Masako 政子 might be a daughter of Masemu'ne 政宗.

---

[29]"Identity, Personal Names, and Kamakura Society" in Mass (1992) p. 113.

Chinese Style Names

Buddhism and the Chinese language play a role in Japan similar to that played by Christianity and Latin in Western Europe. The Buddha taught that life is full of struggle which is inherently painful. Thus, the goal for the Buddhist is to overcome the struggle of life by, among other things, vanquishing desire. Early Buddhist sects stressed the importance of monastic living and life long asceticism. Buddhism stood upon the three pillars of the Buddha, Buddhist teaching, and the monastic community. This Hînayâna or *shoujou* 小乗 "small vehicle" Buddhism taught that enlightenment was for the very few or for none at all. Japan embraced a later more optimistic variant called Mahâyâna or *daijou* 大乗 "great vehicle" Buddhism.

The courtier class provided the chief ritualists for their clans and the nation as a whole and was initially attracted to the magical rituals of Tantric Buddhism. Zen Buddhism preached a doctrine of sudden enlightenment through rigorous meditation and training in practical arts. This approach to religion was very popular with the military class. Another approach to Buddhism which became very popular with the peasant class was chanting the name of one sutra or another. Practitioners of these sects were supposed to achieve material reward as well as spiritual enlightenment.

Buddhism teaches that death can lead to *satori* or an awakening of the spirit. In Japan, family ancestors are commonly enshrined upon domestic Buddhist alters. In fact, most Japanese receive a Buddhist name after their death. These posthumous Buddhist names strongly resemble monastic names. The Buddhist monk is special in that he uses this kind of name during life. The "pure land" approach to Buddhism was very popular in mediæval Japan. These movements teach that it is too difficult to achieve enlightenment in this world, and that this ultimate goal of Buddhism is to be achieved after death in a pure land to the West. Entry into this pure land can be achieved by calling upon the name of the Amida Buddha with perfect faith. In one popular variant on this belief, "wanting to believe" and calling upon the Amida Buddha even one time is enough to guarantee salvation.

Shinran 親鸞 (1173–1262) lived through the Genpei War to found the *Joudou Shinshuu* 浄道真宗 or "true teaching" school of Buddhism. This school teaches that Buddhist salvation is only possible through the mercy of the Amida Buddha 阿弥陀仏. Shinran was of noble birth, but was deeply moved by the plight of the peasants in war-torn Japan. He left the monastic community, renounced celibacy, took a wife, and lived humbly among the peasants, but he remained a Buddhist priest. His sect went on to become the most prosperous in Japan with ten branches and almost 20,000 temples. A -**RAN** 鸞 is a semi-divine heavenly phoenix. While this mythical bird forms the substantive element of Shinran, **SHIN**- 親 is the descriptive element. This element means "intimate" or "familiar".

As Shinran was of noble birth, he was entitled to a family name and a *nanori*. Upon entering a monastery, he was simply known as Han'en 範宴. **HAN**- 範 appears to have been taken from his father's *nanori* by adopting the *onyomi* of one its component *kanji*.. Later, he was known as Shinran. This assumption of a single Chinese style Buddhist name was normative practice for Buddhist monks from all walks of life. This monastic practice is quite different from warriors adding a *houmyou* to their names when they shaved their heads and "retired from life".

Buddhist Monks

Just as many western scholars assumed Latinate names, Buddhist monks had *imi'na* 諱 or 諡号 which were used posthumously to refer to the monk during life. These names are composed of two *kanji*, both of which take their Sino-Japanese *onyomi* readings. As with *nanori*, the first *kanji* acts as a descriptive element and the second *kanji* as a substantive element. Both of these elements frequently have meanings with special significance in Buddhism. Thus, "road", "gate", "meditation", "sun", &c. are frequently found in these names.

Chinese Style Names

As with other segments of Japanese society, lineage is important for Buddhist monks. Thus, the monks in a particular lineage will often share a common character in their names just as warriors do in their *nanori*. Many of the monks in the various Nichiren 日蓮 sects have, since the end of the Kamakura Period, born names beginning with *nichi* 日 or sun. We can observe this practice in artistic names as well.

Buddhism brought with it many ancient myths and legends from China. These stories often included magical animals and monsters, exotic places, and strange plants. Thus, we encounter the dragon and the phoenix. Buddhist sages traveling to India in the company of magic using stone monkeys, and dragon kings dwelling at the bottom of the sea. While these exotic beasts and monsters are largely absent from *nanori*, *yobina*, *nengou* or era names and the posthumous names of emperors, they are quite prevalent in *houmyou* adopted in life by monks, artists, and artisans. As this is a *houmyou*, both *kanji* take one of their Chinese readings. As many *kanji* do not have Japanese readings, many more *kanji* are available for forming *houmyou* than for forming *nanori*.

Most Buddhist monks, like Shinran, bore only an *imi'na*. Modern Buddhist monks may continue to use their family names. Some Buddhist monks, and especially members of either the Tendai sect or one of the Zen sects, bore a secondary name called an *azana* 字. These names were originally used by Confucian scholars in China. The Chinese scholars adopted an *azana* when they first matriculated in an academy or under a master, and continued to use it as their common name throughout their life. Like the *imi'na*, the *azana* is composed of two *kanji*, the first descriptive and the second substantive. The monk used his *azana* in daily life, and we can think of it as a *yobina*. When taken together, the *azana* precedes the *imi'na* in a complete name. In the following example, Banri is the *azana* of a fifteenth century Rinzai Zen Buddhist monk Banri Shuuku 万里集九 (b. 1428).

Many Zen monks also adopted a secondary *yobina* called a *dougou* 道号 or "path name". They would assume a *dougou* when they enter upon the path to enlightenment. A monk's *dougou* would express either his own understanding of enlightenment or his wish to achieve enlightenment. A Zen monk would often use his *dougou* in place of his more formal *azana* in daily life. Consequently, the *dougou* precedes the *imi'na* when it is substituting for the *azana* in a complete name. As the *dougou* expresses a desire to achieve enlightenment or an understanding of what enlightenment, it is typically composed of two elements the first of which is descriptive while the second is the word for some type of human habitation. These are the elements which Koop and Inada report as commonly being found in Buddhist names. Thus we have Bai'an Shuuku 梅案集九. In this example, Bai'an is one of the *dougou* born by the same fifteenth century Rinzai Zen Buddhist monk as in the previous example. While a monk would only have one *azana*, he could enjoy many *dougou*.

Artists & Artisans

In addition to a *nanori*, an artist may acquire a *gagou* 雅号 which is a distinctive artistic name. These names are related to the *dougou* adopted by Zen masters. Since its introduction to Japan, Zen Buddhism has promoted study of various art forms as a path to enlightenment. Essentially, the Zen master sees the practice of these arts as a form of religious practice. Certificates of mastery in Japanese art forms are often issued by Zen temples. For example, the tea ceremony is strongly associated with Dai'toku'ji 大徳寺. Receiving a *gagou* is often the mark of substantial accomplishment not only in an art form, but in mastery of Zen Buddhism as well. These *gagou* usually contain a morpheme denoting mastery or indicating the art form practiced by the person who bears the name. The other morpheme may be taken from the adept's *nanori*. Thus, somebody named Kitahama Miyuki 北浜 美雪 may, after entering the world of tea and studying under a master for many years, be granted a *gagou* by the *iemoto* of the tradition which she has been studying. If she had joined Urasenke 裏千家, she might receive Soumi 宗美 as a *chamei* 茶名 or "tea name". The initial character in this name is held in common by all *Urasenke* tea masters. The second character is, in this case, taken from the first charter of her *nanori*.

Artistic names are normally granted only when the individual has attained mastery of an art and should be considered presumptuous for those who are not actually masters of the associated art form. Thus, distinctive *gagou* should only be assumed upon award of an award of high merit or the Laurel.

The number of characters available for constructing *houmyou* is, if anything, greater than the number available for constructing *nanori*. However, due to the way in which Japanese compresses the original Chinese sound system, the number of distinct Chinese readings is rather less than the number of distinct sound patterns available for use in *nanori*. Further, the Chinese readings have a somewhat distinctive sound which sets them apart from the Japanese readings.

Habitats Found in Names of Monks and Artists

堂	DOU	Hall	齋	SAI	Bring Something
軒	KEN	House	舎	SHA	House
亭	TEI	Gazebo	庵	AN	Thatched Hut
楼	ROU	Tall Building	房	BOU	Room/Cell
園	EN	Garden	洞	DOU	Small Cave
窟	KUTSU	Cellar/Cavern	館	KAN	Mansion
閣	KAKU	Wooden Pavilion	坊	BOU	Monastery

Note that 齋 is the only character in the list which does not have an obvious way of thinking of it as a place of human habitation. The remainder of them, even the cavern, can be thought of as a place where reflection is possible. Gone from the list are palaces and castles, only austere places for meditation and quite reflection are included. Remember that these characters are used as the substantive element of a *dougou* and are not normally used in *houmyou*. In Japanese *kanji* dictionaries, a Chinese reading is printed in *katakana* and a Japanese reading in *hiragana*. In this manual, as in English dictionaries such as Nelson's, a Chinese reading is printed all in capitals and a Japanese reading all in lower case.

Retirement

Official retirement from the world offered many advantages to the Japanese. First of all, it freed them from a variety of official responsibilities. They could then devote more of their energies to administration and power politics, and otherwise work toward achieving the goals of their kinship group. It also helped warlords assure their succession and the continuation of their lineage and domains. Following official retirement from public life, Japanese often became lay monks or nuns and assumed a Chinese style Buddhist name. When doing so, they would retain their old family name and substitute their new Buddhist name for their *nanori*. However, if they chose to do so, they could use both names. While Japanese has no concept of a "middle name", collecting different kinds of names was very common. There were even individuals who collected multiple *nanori*. But, they did not use their different *nanori* at the same time. Thus, we will again consider our example taken from the Warring States Period. Following official retirement, Takeda Haru'nobu took the Buddhist name "Shingen" and was known as

武田 大膳 大夫 晴信 入道 信玄

Takeda Daizen no Daibu Haru'nobu Nyuudou Shingen

In his complete name given above, Takeda 武田 is his family name, *daizen no daibu* 大膳 大夫 his titular court office, Haru'nobu 晴信 his *nanori*, and Shingen 信玄 his *houmyou*. Nyuudou 入道 is an optional element which indicates that he has "entered the path" (to enlightenment). This element can only precede a *houmyou* and is not an independent onomastic component. While there is no apparent difference in the form of the Buddhist names taken by men and women, women were more likely to bear names including certain thematic components than were men. During the Muromachi Period, it was common for Buddhist nuns to bear names including 愛 (AI) meaning "love". This thematic element can be found in names such as Aisu 愛寿.

Posthumous Names

The *Taihouritsuryou* 大宝律令 Civic Code or Taihou Code was promulgated by Emperor Monmu Tennou 文武天皇 in 702. This code remained the basis for Japanese civil law until the Meiji Restoration in the nineteenth century. The Taihou Code decreed that posthumous names would be given to the dead according to their "conduct and deeds" in life. At first Japanese style names were devised for the dead. Later, Chinese style names were adopted. In 784, Oumi Mifune 淡海三船 devised posthumous names for all of the deceased emperors. Papinot lists six different sources for these imperial posthumous names. Of these, I have not been able to find a mediæval example of an emperor posthumously bearing the name of the longest era during his reign. Modern Japanese emperors proclaim a new era name upon their ascension, and it remains unchanged until their death; whereupon, it becomes their posthumous name.

Origin of Imperial Posthumous Names

Name of an Imperial Residence	清和院	Seiwa'in	清和天皇	Seiwa Tennou
Name of a Buddhist Temple	花山院	Kazan'in	花山天皇	Kazan Tennou
Name of the Place of Burial	村上	Murakami	村上天皇	Murakami Tennou
Name of Preceding Emperor	一条天皇	Ichijou Tennou	後一条天皇	Go-Ichijou Tennou
Name of the Place of Banishment	鳥羽離宮	Toba Rikyuu	後鳥羽天皇	Go-Toba Tennou

While the posthumous names of emperors are generally unique, an emperor can have a posthumous name strongly related to the name of a previous emperor. These names are constructed by adding the prefix **GO-** 後 to the original name. Thus, we encounter Emperors Go-Daigo Tennou 後醍醐天皇 and Emperor Go-Murakami Tennou 後村上天皇. These names can be thought of in the same vein as George II, but as **GO-** 後 actually means "the latter", posthumous imperial names can only be used twice. These derivative imperial names are unusual in that they freely combine an *onyomi* prefix with the original name.

Generally, posthumous names consist of an *imi'na* and a posthumous title or *shigou* 諡号. Members of the imperial family were given special posthumous names called *okurina* 諡 with distinctive *shigou*. We have already seen that the emperor received a Chinese style posthumous name ending with *Tennou* 天皇 which roughly means "Lord of High Heaven", but which we usually translate as emperor. Other members of the imperial family typically received posthumous names ending with **-in** 院 or "palace". Otherwise, deceased males received names ending with **-shinji** 信士, and deceased females received names ending with **-shinnyou** 信女. Regardless, the *imi'na* typically reflects the sect of the deceased. Thus, one of the two *kanji* in this name will come from a limited repertoire of peculiar to the particular sect that the deceased belonged to during life.

Honourific Jou'ingou

Highly placed women at the imperial court sometimes received a special name called a *jou'ingou* 女院号 from the emperor. This was known as *mon'in senge* 門院宣下. These names always consisted of a Chinese style name similar to a *houmyou* with *mon'in* 門院 attached as a suffix. Thus, a *mon'in* is actually a titular suffix which is attached to a Chinese style name.

殷富門院

Inpu Mon'in (1147–1216)

Although these are attached to names which look like *houmyou*, they are actually yet another name, and the individual can have a completely different *houmyou* as well. As only about 108 *jou'ingou* were ever given, they were a high honour. These names should never be assumed with the Society for Creative Anachronism. They should only be given as an augmentation by the crown.

Kanji Commonly Found in Buddhist Names

Descriptive Elements

A	阿	Cleft / Crevice / A Bend
AN	安	Gentle / Safe / Secure
BEN	弁	Blossom
DOU	道	Road / Path
E	栄	Bountiful
EN	円	Circle
EN	淵	Abyss
GEN	元	Base / Original
GEN	源	Origin
GEN	玄	Dark / Black / Austere
HOU	法	Law
ICHI	一	One
KEI	慶	Rejoice / Deer Skin
KEN	兼	Unite / Heavy Service
KEN	憲	Example / Pattern
KEN	袈	Monk's Robe
KEN	賢	Genius
KEN	顕	High Status / Show Clearly
KI	希	Wish / Desire
KYOU	経	Sutra / True Path
MAN	満	Become Full / Abundant
MU	無	Nothing / The Void
SHOU	昭	Bright
SO	祖	Founder of a Tradition
SOU	宗	Master an Art
SOU	総	Everything / Entire
TAKU	沢	Glen / Run
TAKU	詫	Denounce Illusion
TAN	湛	Fill Up / Become Abundant

Substantive Elements

AI	愛	Love
AN	安	Gentle / Safe / Secure
CHI	智	Intelligent
CHOU	長	Long / Oldest
CHUU	忠	Faithful / Loyal
EN	円	Circle
GA	賀	Celebrate A Gain
GEN	元	Base / Original
GOU	裟	*kesa* / Buddhist Robe
IN	隠	Disappear / Retire
KAI	快	Good Feelings / Sleepy
KAKU	覚	Learn / Memorize
KEI	慶	Rejoice / Deer Skin
KEI	計	Measure / Count
KOU	興	Happen / Begin
KOU	幸	Happy / Tattoo
KUU	空	Sky / Air / Open / Empty
MON	円	Circle
NI	爾	Bobbin / Distaff
NIN	忍	Endure
RAKU	楽	Happiness (Joy)
SAI	済	Same Likeness
SAI	盛	Plentiful / Piled Up
SAN	山	Mountain
SAN	算	Calculate
SEN	仙	Hermit / Adept
SHIN	信	Belief / Faith
SHIN	真	Genuine
YUU	祐	Divine Help

Nengou

The Japanese have enumerated the years in many different ways. In ancient times, they often simply enumerated the years since the elevation of the ruling clan chief. Most recently, they have been enumerating years according to the Gregorian calendar. This system is known as *seireki* 西暦 or the Western calendar. Since antiquity, the imperial family and its followers have enumerated the years since the coronation of Jinmu Tennou as the first emperor of Japan in 660 BC. Traditionally, Jinmu Tennou was crowned emperor on the eleventh day of February which is the first day of the first month in the old agricultural calendar. In this way, the Japanese were very much like the Romans who counted the years from the founding of Rome.

In her early classical period, Japan imported Chinese calendar makers and astronomers. They brought with them two different systems for reckoning the years. The first system, was a sixty year cycle based upon the twelve animals of the zodiac and the five elements of nature. The five elements were: *ki* 木 (wood), *hi* 火 (fire), *tsuchi* 土 (earth), *ka* 金 (metal) and *mizu* 水 (water). The twelve signs of the zodiac are listed in the *Thematic Dictionary*. Each of the five elements had an "older brother" and a "younger brother". A year was spent visiting each of the brothers before the calendar passed on to the next element. Thus, the elements combined to form ten signs. The names for these ten passages consisted of the name of the element followed either by *noe* for the older brother or *noto* for the younger. Each of these combinations had its own distinctive sign for ten in all. The years were calculated from *koushi* 甲子 which is the first cycle of the year of the rat. They then continued in order to complete the entire sixty year cycle. 1966 is called Hi'noe Uma 丙午 under this system. It was the forty third year in the sixty year cycle and the year of the horse.

Chinese Style Names

Nengou (lit. year names) are "era names". These "eras" were formally proclaimed by the imperial court for almost any reason, good or bad. Emperor Koutoku Tennou 教徳天皇 first imported this system from China and named the first historical era Taika 大化, which commenced in 645. The first year of any historical era is known as *gan nen* 元年, after which they are enumerated with Chinese numbers beginning with *ni nen* 二年 or second year. Although, the era sometimes changes at the beginning of a calendar year, it usually changes sometime during the middle of the year. Thus, the first year of the Heisei era was Heisei gan nen 平成元年, and the first complete year was Heisei ni nen 平成二年. All dates before the era change are reckoned according to the old era, and all dates after the new era has been proclaimed are reckoned according to the new era. The *nengou* are devised according to Chinese principles of *yin* and *yang*. Ideally, they should achieve internal balance and harmony and at the same time express hopes for peace, stability, cultural attainment, and good government. These are the predominant themes found in historical *nanori*. As with other Chinese style names, *nengou* are composed of two thematic elements, the first of which is descriptive and the second substantive. Thus, 平成 means "achieving peace" (lit. Becoming tranquil). Currently, the East Kingdom reckons the years according to the Bunsei 文成 era (lit. creating a culture). *Bunsei gan nen* was 1966, and the year changes on May first each year.

KANJI FREQUENCIES IN NENGOU AFTER 990

Kanji	Frequencies			Reading	Meaning	Kanji	Frequencies			Reading	Meaning
永	26	13	13	EI	Forever	禄	06	00	06	ROKU	Blessing
元	24	14	10	GEN	Base / Original	平	05	02	03	HEI	Peace
治	21	03	18	JI	Govern / Rule	万	04	03	01	MAN	Ten Thousand
文	19	15	04	BUN	Culture	大	02	02	00	TAI	Big
正	19	13	06	SHOU	Unerring / Correct	大	01	01	00	DAI	Big
応	18	06	12	OU	Worthy / Suitable	丞	03	03	00	JOU	Rescue
長	17	11	06	CHOU	Long / Senior	安	03	03	00	AN	Gentle / Safe
保	16	05	11	HOU	Guarantee	宝	03	02	01	HOU	Treasure
暦	13	02	10	RYAKU	Calendar	寿	03	01	02	JU	Longevity
歴	01	00	02	REKI	Progress / History	中	03	00	03	CHUU	Middle
徳	14	01	13	TOKU	Righteous / Just	養	02	01	01	YOU	Nourish
天	13	13	00	TEN	Sky / Heaven	武	02	00	02	MU	Strong / Brave
寛	13	12	01	KAN	Domestic Bliss	政	02	00	02	SEI	Govern / Rule
和	13	00	13	WA	Peace	化	02	00	02	KA	Change
嘉	11	10	01	KA	Well Done	喜	02	00	02	KI	Rejoice
延	11	08	03	EN	Prolong	昭	01	01	00	SHOU	Cheerful
建	10	10	00	KEN	Build / Construct	至	01	01	00	SHI	Achieve
康	10	09	01	KOU	Strong / Confident	興	01	01	00	KOU	Happen
仁	10	03	07	NIN	Precious	乾	01	01	00	KEN	High Heaven
承	09	04	05	JOU	Humbly Receive	観	01	01	00	KAN	Perceive
亨	09	04	05	KYOU	Receive Smoothly	福	01	00	01	FUKU	Happiness
久	09	02	07	KYUU	Longtime	禎	01	00	01	TEI	Divine Fortune
明	07	05	02	MEI	Bright	授	01	00	01	JU	Grant / Bestow
貞	06	05	01	JOU	Tranquil	成	01	00	01	SEI	Become / Exist
弘	06	05	00	KOU	Spread Out	国	01	00	01	KOKU	Nation
慶	06	03	03	KEI	Rejoice	吉	01	00	01	KITSU	Fortunate

The table above lists every *kanji* which has been used in an era name since 990. During that time, 199 *nengou* have been proclaimed. These include the overlapping *nengou* proclaimed during the Nanboku Period when there were two imperial courts. During especially turbulent times, the emperor would change the era name quite often. As with the similar tables for *nanori* and family names, each *kanji* has three frequency numbers, the first being the sum of the latter two. These numbers simply record the number of occurrences of that *kanji* in a *nengou*. The second number gives the number of times that the *kanji* was used as a descriptive element, and the last number gives the umber of times that it was used as a substantive element.

Christian Names

Although Nestorian Christianity had been known in East Asia for centuries, it does not appear to have spread to Japan. This is partly because the social role occupied by Christianity in the West was occupied by Buddhism in Japan. Western Christianity was introduced into Japan by Francisco De Xavier (1506–1552) in 1549. By 1581, there were an estimated 150,000 Christians and 200 churches in Japan. Before Tokugawa Iemitsu banned foreign travel by Japanese in 1635, several Japanese legations were sent to Europe. In 1613, Date Masamu'ne sent Hasekura Tsu'ne'naga 支倉常長 on a seven year mission to Pope Paul V. In 1635, overseas travel by Japanese was prohibited. Japanese trading missions were demolished, and repatriation of overseas Japanese banned. In Kyuushuu and other places where Christianity was particularly popular, the entire population was required to step on Christian icons to prove that they were not Christians. These icons, called *fumie* 踏絵, were manufactured by the government for this purpose. They bore either pictures of Jesus or the Virgin Mary. Special offices were established for this purpose and each person's name was entered in a book of record. Across the country, officials attached to Buddhist temples examined the religious affiliations of the populace. These officials entered peoples names in special temple census books called *Shuumon Ninbetsu Aratamechou* 宗門人別改帳 or "Census of Individual Reconfirmation of Belief". In 1639, Portuguese traders were expelled from Japan and by 1641 the remaining Dutch and English traders were confined to an artificial island in Nagasaki harbour.

At the time of baptism, Japanese Christians received Christian names called *reimei* 霊名 or "spirit names" similar to those born by their European counterparts. These names were frequently taken from the Christian scriptures and from the names of saints and apostles. These baptismal names were generally substituted for native Japanese *nanori* in the names of Japanese Christians. Consequently, names such as Akechi Garashia 明智ガラシア and Naitou Juria 内藤ジュリア were extant during this period. Baptismal names were written in *katakana*. Writing these names in *katakana* reflects more the feeling of the Japanese toward these names than it does their actual origin. Fully assimilated loan words from European languages are frequently written with *hiragana* or even *kanji*. Thus, we know that these Christian names were perceived as foreign and of uncertain meaning.

Since European names use sounds which did not exist in the native Japanese sound system, it was necessary to adapt the Japanese phonetic orthography to represent these names. In the table below, E is subvocalized in order to approximate the desired European consonant followed by a Japanese I. This is because, as explained in the section on Japanese phonology, these consonants are normally modified when pronounced with the I vowel. The first column gives the original European name followed by the Japanese phonetic transcription and a romanization of the Japanese pronunciation.

Male Christians

Male Christians commonly bore the names of saints. Ootomo Yoshishige 大友義鎮 (1530–1587) was thus known as ドン・フランシスコ or Don Furanshisuko. This is simply a rendering of Don Francisco into the Japanese phonetic system. "Don" is of course a rendering of an Iberian honourific component. He was a Christian *daimyou* who together with the Oomura 大村 sent emissaries to Europe in 1587. Although he was a Christian, he was also known as 大友宗麟 Ootomo Sourin. While this is possibly an example of Japanese religious syncretism, it is also possible that he became a Christian after he cut his hair and assumed a Buddhist name. Following becoming a Christian, he placed a cross beneath his *kamon* on his banners. Another Japanese Christian was Ko'nishi Joachin 小西ジョアチン (ca. 1570) whose name is probably a Japanese variant on Josquin. Another Japanese man was known as Leon.

Names of Christian Daimyou

Ki'noshita Katsutoshi	木下勝俊	Pedoro	ペドロ
Gamou Ujisato	蒲生氏郷	Rean	レアン
Ikeda Norimasa	池田教正	Shime'an	シメアン
Oda Nagamasu	織田長益	Jo'an	ジョアン
Ko'nishi Yuki'naga	小西行長	Agusuchi'no	アグスチノ
Ichijou Ka'nesada	一条兼定	Pauro	パウロ
Kuroda Takataka	黒田孝高	Shimeon	シメオン
Oomura Sumitada	大村純忠	Barutoromeo	バルトロメオ
Ootomo Yoshishige	大友義鎮	Furanshisuko	フランシスコ
Arima Haru'nobu	有馬晴信	Purotajio	プロタジオ
Goshima Sumiharu	五島純玄	Ruisu	ルイス

Female Christians

While a Christian woman might be known by her Christian name in combination with her *myouji*, she might also be known simply by her Christian name with a titular element attached as a suffix. In particular, she might be known as Agata Fujin アガタ婦人 wherein "Agata" is the root name and "fujin" simply indicates that she is a married woman.

Common Names of Female Christians

Julia	ジュリア	Juria	Gracia	ガラシア	Garashia
Joan	ジョアン	Jo'an	Maria	マリア	Maria
Madalena	マダレナ	Madare'na	Regina	レジナ	Reji'na
Mensia	メンシア	Menshia	Lucia	ルシア	Rushia
Martha	マルタ	Maruta	Tecla	テクラ	Tekura
Catarina	カタリナ	Katari'na	Monica	モニカ	Mo'nika
Anna	アンナ	Anna	Agatha	アガタ	Agata
Elizabetta	エリザベッタ	Erizabetta	Sabina	サビナ	Sabi'na
Candida	カンディダ	Kand(e)ida	Diego	ディエゴ	D(e)iego
Madolin	マドレイヌ	Madorei'nu			

Titles and Offices

Just as in Europe some titles such as "King", "Earl" and "Duke" eventually became names, some Japanese titles and offices became name components. Further, many people who lived during the classical and early feudal periods of Japanese history are known by "names" which are either descriptive or partially titular. Throughout history, there has been a close connection between titles and Japanese names. In particular, many common name elements appear to have originally been titles. Consequently, any complete study of Japanese names must include a survey of Japanese titles. We have already examined some of these name suffixes in the chapter on personal names. Here we will investigate titles and rank a bit further.

Imperial Ranking System

Imperial Princes			Common Nobility		
Rank[30]		Level	Rank		Offices and Privileges
一品	ippon	First	一位	ichi'i	Dai'jou Daijin
二品	nippon	Second	二位	ni'i	Sadai'jin, Udai'jin, Naidai'jin
三品	sanbon	Third	三位	san'i	Dai'nagon and Chuu'nagon
四品	shihon	Fourth	四位	shi'i	Other members of the Dajoukan[31]
		Fifth	五位	go'i	Can attend the emperor[32]
		Sixth	六位	roku'i	Imperial bureaucrats
		Seventh	七位	shichi'i	Imperial bureaucrats
		Eighth	八位	hachi'i	District Chieftains
		Initiate	初位	sho'i	Lowest rank of imperial appointment

Rank

We will begin with imperial rank as rank often determined the career paths available to an individual. Court rank was guaranteed to members of the *kuge* whose fathers held rank five or better. These fortunate few could expect quick promotion to higher rank and office and guaranteed land allotments. Other sons of the elite could through diligence achieve appointment at low court rank and possibly progress to higher rank. The provincial chieftains enjoyed initiate rank and rank eight. Mi'namoto no Yoritomo was made *chuu'nagon* 中納言 and *taishou* 大将 and achieved third rank. However, members of the country gentry seldom achieved and rarely surpassed the fifth rank.

---

[30]These ranks were bestowed on members of the imperial family who had been granted *shinnou senge* or *naishinnou senge*.

[31]The *dajoukan* was established in 671 and abolished in 1871. After 705, it consisted of the *daijou daijin* and the *sadaijin*, *udaijin*, and *naidaijin* ministers along with the *chidaijoukanji* imperial family liaison, two *dai'nagon*, two *chuu'nagon*, and four *shou'nagon* counselors, and the *sangi* 参議 and the *hisangi* 非参議 advisors. While the *sadaijin* and the *udaijin* oversaw extensive ministries, the other members oversaw a secretariat. Several other offices were available to nobles of high rank which did not carry membership in the *dajoukan*. The *ritsuryou* system is more fully discussed by Joan Piggott (1997).

[32]This is the highest court rank that someone who was not born into an elite family could normally aspire to. This is the rank attached to the office of *sei'i'taishougun*. and the 国守 *kuni'nokami* provincial governors.

Rank was and is a significant feature of Japanese society. Japanese tend to place themselves into "ranks and levels" and see themselves as a member of a structured social group. Consequently, imperial rank often appears with names in official records. Further, this rank was included in the information on the calling cards presented when seeking employment during the Hei'an period. This system of ranking persisted until the nobility was reorganized along British lines following the Meiji Restoration. The *kuge* were finally abolished by the American occupation under Gen. Douglas Mac Arthur.

Ministries of the Taihou and Yorou Codes

	Sadaijin			Udaijin	
中務省	Nakatsukasashou	Central Affairs	兵務省	Hyoubushou	Military Affairs
式部省	Shikibushou	Personnel	刑務省	Gyoubushou	Justice
治部省	Chibe	Civil Affairs	大蔵省	Oukurashou	Treasury
民部省	Minbushou	Popular Affairs	宮内性省	Kunaishou	Household

Princes and Kuge in Government

We already encountered quite a few titles. The gods themselves sported a variety of titles such as *mikoto*, and the heads of the ancient *uji* used a variety of *kabane*. All of the imperial titles including *tennou* 天皇, *mikado* 帝, and *koutei* 皇帝 for the emperor and *taishi* 太子 for the crown prince were appointive. Similarly, *touguu* 東宮, *ouji* 皇子, *ou* 王, *shinnou* 親王, *naishinnou* 内親王, *jo'ou* 女王, and *koutaishi* 王丈皇太子 are all appointive titles specific to imperial princes and princesses. Following regulation of court titles in 684, the princes and princesses were divided into two grades. The upper grade was called *shinnou* 親王 and *naishinnou* 内親王 for princes and princesses respectively. While admission to this grade was at first automatic for all direct descendents of the emperor, it later required special appointment which was called *shinnou senge* 親王宣下. Those not receiving this edict were only entitled to the title *ou* 王 or *jo'ou* 女王 respectively. Those who attained *shinnou senge* were considered to be especially close to the person of the emperor. And, they automatically belonged to one of the top four ranks at court,. The *ou* and the *jo'ou* automatically belonged to one of the top five ranks at court but were vulnerable to being expelled from the imperial family. Members of the imperial family served in a variety of capacities including holding posts under the *ritsuryou* system along with offices in the *insei* cloistered government and *sei'itaishougun* in the Kamakura Bakufu.

The *kuge* enjoyed a variety of ranks and titles. The *kabane* continued under the *ritsuryou* system and were attached to the ancient *uji*. Guaranteed court rank and resulting guaranteed governmental appointment ultimately divested the upper *ritsuryou* offices of real government function. However, the lower levels remained active until well into the Kamakura Period. Further, the private *shou'en* governments of the *uji* and *insei* were quite efficient.

Under the *ritsuryou* system, not only did each of the offices had a specific rank, authority, and income associated with it, but the court rank itself carried a land allocation. Thus, rank at court was very important throughout the Kamakura Period. Actual practice for the nobility was to refer either to the court rank or the office somewhat interchangeably. Thus, for purposes of recreation within the Society for Creative Anachronism, the court offices should be used as they were explicitly tied to rank at court and they are more descriptive.

Buke in Government

During the Kamakura Period, members of both the *kuge* and *buke* classes were frequently known partly by their imperial or private office and rank. These titles and offices were frequently attached either to the name of a territory or to their *tsuushou*. While the imperial government had eight ministries and a central secretariat, more about 65 percent of the 7,000 posts under the *ritsuryou* system directly served the emperor in some capacity. Of these, the ones of greatest interest here are the various guard detachments. Service in these detachments was open to the provincial elite and played a significant role in organizing and securing services in the provinces.[33] The *sekimori* 関守 border guards were conscript foot soldiers with three year

---

[33] The various mechanisms for rewarding military service in the provinces are discuseed at length by William Wayne Farris (1995).

enlistment periods. The code provided for military units modeled after the Chinese army and emphasized training with the crossbow and the catapult. Each of the foot soldiers was to be equipped with armour, a bow and arrows, a flag, and a drum. They were commanded by mounted local elite units drawn from the families of the district magistrates. Despite the Chinese model, the foot soldiers were quickly dominated by the mounted elite troops.

RANKS OF PALACE GUARDS

Rank		Title	Office Duties
3	大将	Taishou	General
4	中将	Chuushou	Lieutenant
5	少将	Shoushou	General Affairs
6	将監	Shougen	Adjutant
7	将曹	Shousou	Officer

The *eji* 衛士 were guard companies created by the Taihou Code in 701. Initially, their ranks were drawn from the militia with one year terms of service. Later, the term of service was extended to three years. Initially, there were two 400 man companies of *eji* 衛士 capital guards, two 400 man companies of *hyou'e* 近衛 Palace Guards, and a 200 man company of *emon* 衛門 gate guards. The palace guards were descended from the *to'neri* 舎人 who were a personal imperial guard dating from the fifth century. The code specified that they were to be appointed from the sons and relatives of the district magistrates. The gate guards were descended from pre-645 *yugei* 靫負 archery companies. These troops were originally drawn from the Western provinces and had close personal connections with the Ootomo no Muraji 大伴連. The gate guards also actively recruited the sons of the district magistrates. As the palace guard was better connected than the other units, they enjoyed higher court rank and a separate title system.

LEFT COMPANY OF GATE GUARDS

Rank		Title		Office	Duties
4	督	no Kami	左衛門督	Sa'emon-no-Kami	Chief
5	佐	no Suke	左衛門佐	Sa'emon-no-Suke	Deputy
6	尉	no Jou	左衛門尉	Sa'emon-no-Jou	General Affairs
7	志	no Sakan	左衛門志	Sa'emon-no-Sakan	Scribe
8	大夫	no Taifu	左衛門大夫	Sa'emon-no Daibu	Officer

RIGHT COMPANY OF GATE GUARDS

Rank		Title		Office	Duties
4	督	no Kami	右衛門督	U'emon-no-Kami	Chief
5	佐	no Suke	右衛門佐	U'emon-no-Suke	Deputy
6	尉	no Jou	右衛門尉	U'emon-no-Jou	General Affairs
7	志	no Sakan	右衛門志	U'emon-no-Sakan	Scribe
8	大夫	no Taifu	右衛門大夫	U'emon-no Daibu	Officer

Conscription was abolished in 792, and centralized recruitment of border guards stationed in Kyûshû ended in 795. The *efu* 衛府 imperial guard was reorganized in 811 creating left and right companies of gate guards. The guard units largely lost their police functions to the *kebi'ishi* 検非違使 in 810 which consolidated the police functions of the *efu* and the judicial functions of the *danjoudai* 弾正台. The conscript forces were replaced by provincial military elites and private *kuge* forces. However, the *emon* gate guards retained a military role and continued to attract provincial military men.

Each of the gate guard divisions was organized into a system of ranks which were appended as a suffix to either *sa'emon* 左衛門 left company or *u'emon* 右衛門 right company. The *emonfu* titles were quite popular and were eventually granted to many individuals. Eventually, they became the components of names in their own right, independent of the their original use. The last title in the list is more commonly read as *daifu* and literally means "big man". The second element 夫 later acquires the *kunyomi* reading -**o** and along with 雄, 男, and 生 appears as a masculine suffix in many somewhat old-fashioned modern masculine names such as Akio 明夫. During the Muromachi Period, we encounter -**sa'emon** 左衛門 in *tsuushou* such as Munesa'emon 宗左衛門 and Tarousa'emon 太郎左衛門, -**u'emon** in Moto'u'emon 源右衛門, and -**nosuke** 助 in names such as Shigenosuke 茂助.

Provincial Government

The eight ministries, the three *efu* divisions, the *kebi'ishi*, and ten more departments constituted the central government. The imperial government also included provincial administration and expeditionary forces. We will briefly look at three of these. Dazaifu 太宰府 was a detached capital responsible for administering Kyûshû and deploying coastal defenses. It was administered by the *sochi* 帥 who was an official of the third rank. The *chinjufu* 鎮守府 was responsible for expeditionary forces against the Ainu of northeastern Honshuu and was commanded by the *sei'itaishougun* who held fifth rank. The *kokushi* 国司 were the imperial provincial governments. Often the titular heads of the various provincial organizations remained in the capital and dispatched their deputies to the actual duty posts. These deputies were often transferred from one distant outpost to another and formed the top layer of the provincial elite.

The *kokushi* 国司 or "provincial governors" provide an imperial model for landed nobility. While these governors bear titles which sound the same as those born by members of the *efu*, they are written with different *kanji*. While members of the *efu* attached their ranks to the name of the name of their division, the *kokushi* attached their ranks to the name of the province which they governed. These titles appear to be particularly appropriate for landed nobility and their heirs.

Titular Offices of Provincial Governors

Rank	Title	Office	Reading	Duties
5	守	no Kami	武蔵守	Musashi-no-Kami	Chief
6	介	no Suke	武蔵介	Musashi-no-Suke	Deputy
7	掾	no Jou	武蔵掾	Musashi-no-Jou	Scribe
8	目	no Sakan	武蔵目	Musashi-no-Sakan	Officer

Military Government

Starting around 1179, we encounter *jitou* 地頭 military estate stewards being appointed by Taira no Kiyomori for various *shou'en* estates. The *jitou* were basically tax farmers receiving a share of the taxes owed to absentee landlords in the capital and elsewhere. Following the Genpei War, Mi'namoto no Yoritomo obtained imperial sanction in 1185 to appoint *jitou* for the estates and constables called *shugo* 守護 for the provinces. While the *shugo* were a new office, they followed a tradition of appointing constables to make arrests. The *jitou* were attached to individual *shou'en* and continued as tax farmers while the *shugo* were responsible for provincial and capital guard duty and performed police functions. During the Kamakura Period, both the *jitou* and the *shugo* were directly appointed by Kamakura. General military affairs were overseen by a board called the *samuraidokoro* 侍所. Later, the Muromachi Bakufu[34] placed the *jitou* under the *shugo*. During the Muromachi Period, the *shugo* usurped title to their domains and became the *shugo daimyou*.

---

[34]See the article "Muromachi Bakufu" by John Whitney Hall in the *Cambridge History of Japan* for an extended discussion of this period.

Ranks in Imperial Government Offices

		Ministries 省	Provinces 国司	Districts 郡司	efu 衛府	Dazaifu 太宰府	Chancellery 坊・職	Experts 寮
1	no Kami	卿	守	大領	督	帥	大夫	頭
2	no Suke	輔	介	少領	佐	弐	亮	助
3	no Jou	丞	掾	主政	尉	監	進	允
4	no Sakan	録	目	主帳	志	典	属	属

Selected Ministries of the Imperial Government

中務	Nakatsukasa	Secretariat
式部	Shikibu	Court Ritual, Promotions, and the University
治部	Jibu	Probate, Theatre, and Foreign Affairs
民部	Minbu	National Census and Survey
兵部	Hyoubu	Ministry of War
刑部	Gyoubu	Ministry of Justice
大蔵	Ookura	Chamberlain
宮内	Ku'nai	Household Ministry and Exchequer

Officers of Military Households

1	別當	Bettou	Superintendent	Responsible for overall clan administration.
2	令	Rei	Deputy	Responsible for formulating orders.
3	案主	Anju	Secretary	Responsible for writing orders & keeping records.
4	知家事	Chikeji	Inspector	Dispatched to execute orders & make inquiries.

Officers in the Kamakura Bakufu

征夷大将軍	Sei'itaishougun	Barbarian Suppressing Generalissimo
執権	Shikken	Head of the Mandokoro (Civil Government)
執事	Shitsuji	Deputy chief of the Mandokoro
別當	Bettou	Head of the Samuraidokoro (Military Arm)

Recreating Military Titles & Offices

将軍	Sei'itaishougun	Generalissimo	King
執権	Shikken	Shougunal Regent	Queen
探題	Tandai	Regional Military Governor	Territorial Prince
守護	Shugo	Provincial Military Governor	Landed Baron
武将	Bushou	Military Commander	Court Baron
大将	Taishou[35]	General	Knight
武将	Bushou	Commander	Squire
武師	Bushi	Military Expert	Master at Arms
学士	Gakushi	Professor (Imperial Title)	Master of the Laurel
太老	Tairou	Great Elder	Master of the Pelican
舎人	Toneri	Servant in a High Noble House	Squire, Apprentice or Protege
将軍	Shougun	General	King

---

[35] The *taishou* were commanders of the left and right divisions of the *ko'noei'fu* 近衛府 or *chikakimamori'notsukasa* palace guards. The Ko'noe 近衛 family descended from the Northern Fujiwara may have taken their name from service in these detachments. Ko'noe Sakihisa 近衛前久 (1538-1612) was a member of the *kuge*.

Polite Speech

We are all familiar with the use of pronouns when addressing feudal lords in England. It is common to address someone of high rank as "sire", "your excellency", "your majesty", or "your highness". Japanese has a counterpart to this which reflects the Japanese penchant for vertical organization. Japanese reflects this sensitivity to relative rank and social status by incorporating a hierarchy of pronouns. It is important to understand that for Japanese honourific speech is independent of formal speech. You can be formal without being polite or polite without being formal. We shall begin by examining a hierarchy of pronouns all of which mean "you". In the following table, status is as viewed by the speaker. Thus, you should never address your superior as "mashi".

Pronouns

Highest Level	上	Uhe	personal monarch or chief officer
	君	Kimi	nobles, princes and monarchs
	おとど	Otodo	nobles and officers
	おこと	Okoto	intimate friends and relatives
	そこ	Soko	inferiors
	北の方	Kita no Kata	wife of a noble
	いまし	Imashi	equals or inferiors
Lowest Level	まし	Mashi	equals or inferiors

These are distinct from honourifics such as "sir" or "lord" such as precede names in English usage. In Japanese this type of honourific follows the complete name of an individual. In Japanese, it is relatively rare to apply honourifics to your own name. There are however instances in which this is done. In these cases the speaker is clearly referring to themselves in the third person and is typically comparing themselves to some perceived norm. Regardless, the same predilection toward expressing ranks and levels is found in these honourifics. Again, status is as viewed by the speaker. Thus, you should avoid attaching **-GO** to the end of your superior's name.

Honourific Suffixes

Highest Level	上	Kami
	君	Kimi
	殿	Do'no
	様	Sama
	氏	Uji
Lowest Level	御	Go

Of these, the one most frequently appearing in mediæval Japanese manuscripts is 殿 *do'no*. It is still commonly used in official Japanese documents. This particular suffix most closely corresponds to "lord". It appears in a diverse collection of documents ranging from the letters of Nichiren in the thirteenth century to records of tea ceremonies at the end of the sixteenth century. The early edicts of the Mi'namoto *shougun* residing in Kamakura began with the formula, "Kamakura do'no no tsukase ... " in which he is called the "Lord of Kamakura".

The *kanji* used to write "uhe" can also be read as "kami". Herein lies a particular problem. While Nakada Norio does not list "uhe" in his dictionary of classical and mediæval Japanese, Matsumura Akira does list this reading with the desired meaning as a post-positional honourific. Thus, "ue" can be attached to a name or pronoun used to refer to a recognized superior. One example is "Chichi-ue" which might be translated as "Horrible Father". What then of "kami"? Here we find 守 *kami* or "lord protector" which is used to form the titles for certain high ranking officials. This *kanji* can also be used as a pronoun when referring to the *mikado* (emperor) or the *sei'itaishougun* (barbarian suppressing generalissimo). Beyond these, we have already seen that a noble during the early classical period customarily addressed his lord as either *nushi* or *shujin*. However, neither of these appear to have been attached to names. Finally, a student will address his master as *sensei* and will attach this title to his name. Similarly, students address senior students as *senpai*. Regardless, *do'no* remains the most generally applicable of the available honourific suffixes.

It is also possible to attach an honourific to the beginning of a persons name. These lack a counterpart in European usage. Specifically, they are purely marks of honour and do not correspond to any rank, title or office. Some of them are, however, strongly associated with specific honourifics or individuals.

Honourific Prefixes

On	[Arisama - "appearance"]	Ohon	[Toki - "time"]
O	[mae - "present before"]	Go	[Honshou "origin"]
Mi	[Uji - "clan" or "family"]	Oho	[Kimi - "lord"]
Ohomi	[Uta - "song" or "poem"]	Son	[Chichi - "father"]
Ki	[Sho - "writing"]	Taka	[Mi - "view"]
Hau	[Mei - "name"]	Rei	[Ani - "elder brother"]

What then of titles? Titles in mediæval Japan appear to have been attached to the *yobina* or *zokumyou* (common name) of individuals. This formation appears as early as *Heike Monogatari* which recounts the Genpei War at the end of the twelfth century. Thus, a complete Japanese name begins with the family name, followed by the *zokumyou* with attached title of office and ending with the *nanori* or formal given name. While an honourific prefix may be thought of as being optional, the terminal honourific suffix attached to the *nanori* is mandatory. Thus, we have constructed

白鶴城主 菊地 右衛門佐 菊池 貫永
Hiratsurajoushu Kikuchi no U'emonnotsuke Tsura'naga Do'no

wherein, Hiratsurajoushu (Lord of White Crane Castle) precedes the name. The remainder consists of names, offices, and honourifics. The office (or formal title) is constructed by combining the name for the "ministry of the right" with the rank within the ministry. Thus, U'emonnotsuke is an officer of the second rank within the martial arm of the military government. In the example, the *zokumyou* has been omitted. In very formal records and histories, the *zokumyou* would appear after the possessive "no" before the formal title. We conclude with a look at pronouns. The imperial forms are from the *iseiryou* 儀制令 or Law of Decorum.

Addressing the Emperor

天子	Tenshi	Child of Heaven	**Most Formal**
天皇	Tennou	Heavenly Sovereign	
皇帝	Oudai	King of Kings	
陛下	Heika	Your Majesty	**Most Intimant**

Polite Pronouns

旦那	Danna	Husband/Father	殿	Do'no	Superior/Boss
先生	Sensei	Teacher/Master	城主	Joushu	Castle Overlord

Designing a Japanese Name

This book is a practical guide for constructing Japanese names for use within the Society for Creative Anachronism. It consists primarily of tables of elementary names such as surnames, formal given names, and religious names. Once you have decided upon what sort of name you want, you should list the individual component name types in order and then proceed to either construct or select an appropriate name for each slot. Most people using this book will be interested in recreating either court or military nobility. In this case, men should devote special selection to selecting an appropriate *nanori* and *tsuushou* while women should devote equal attention to selecting their *uji* or *kamei*. The *Thematic Dictionary* which is a thesaurus of onomastic components. *Kanji* convey both sound and meaning. The *Thematic Dictionary* allows you to construct an individual name or analyze a name which you have looked up. You do not have to learn to read *kanji* to use the *Thematic Dictionary*. The *kanji* are there to help you understand how the names are put together. This helps you when you want to invent or analyze a name or when you want to know how to correctly pronounce or write a name.

The *Thematic Dictionary* is organized into broad categories like a thesaurus. This differs somewhat from a *kanwajiten* which organizes *kanji* by the number of strokes in their principal radical. The individual *kanji* assigned to the same broad category are loosely grouped into subcategories. The entry for each *kanji* in the *Thematic Dictionary* is organized by reading with the Sino-Japanese *onyomi* readings appearing first followed by the *kunyomi* readings. Each reading may have many dated examples of names drawn from historical sources. These examples also appear in alphabetical name lists following the *Thematic Dictionary*. Entries in the *Thematic Dictionary* are indexed both by meaning and by sound. This will allow you to design component names to match either a desired meaning or a desired sound. Generally, you will achieve superior results if you design names based upon meaning and Japanese filial considerations.

The simplest form of an official Japanese name for members of the *kuge* and *buke* classes is a family name followed by a *nanori*. Fujiwara Noriyori (1170–1243) is a good example from *Heike Monogatari* of such a name. The *nanori* can also be preceded by the name of district which the individual governs. Thus, we meet someone called Izu'nokami Nakatsu'na in *Heike Monogatari*. Some families belonging to the *buke* class may derive their names from these posting to districts which eventually became hereditary fiefs. Later, members of the *buke* class were to bear fixed *kamei* with assumption of territorial names depending upon appointment. Regardless, many members of the *buke* class bore *kamei* or "house names" which differed from those born by their father or siblings. While the *nanori* is a distinctive feature of the names for members of the *kuge* and *buke* classes, it is possible to include a *zokumyou* and even an office within a personal name. Thus, we can find names such as Kazu no Tarou Hougan Tadatsu'na in *Heike Monogatari* as well. In this name Kazu is a locative, Tarou a *zokumyou*, Hougan a title, and Tadatsu'na a *nanori*. Generally, the policy of the College of Arms precludes the inclusion of titles within names and thus names of this form should be avoided.

Names such as Yasuda no Saburou Yoshisada should be encouraged. Here, Yasuda is the *kamei*, Saburou the *zokumyou*, and Yoshisada the *nanori*. As already suggested, the crown should grant a name augmentation to male Japanese when awarding arms. This augmentation comes from the ancient *u'emon/sa'emon* system of government and augments the *zokumyou* as a suffix. Thus, Saburou becomes Saburoza'emon. Current practice in the East Kingdom is to award a court rank such as *sa'emondaibu* 左衛門大夫 or *u'emondaibu* 右衛門大夫 to all recipients and a *nanori* to those who have not yet selected an official style name. Recently, such a *nanori* was constructed by agglutinating the initial morpheme in the *zokumyou* of the recipient with the final morpheme of the *nanori* of the monarch. Thus, Sou'ichirou 宗一郎 was granted 宗永 Mu'ne'naga as a *nanori*. Thus, he becomes Wake no Sou'ichirou u'emon no daibu Mu'ne'naga 和気 宗一郎右衛門大夫 宗永. Please note that the -no- is not actually written, but is inserted by the speaker.

While many members of the *kuge* (aristocratic class) bore *kamei* (house names) similar to those born by members of the *buke* (warrior class), there are many examples from the Hei'an, Kamakura and Muromachi Periods of members of the *kuge* class being known by the names of temples, shrines, and palaces. This appears to be reserved to the *kuge* class, *buke* class being restricted to more topographic *kamei* such as "Nakamura" (middle village), "Oda" (big field), or "Hatakeyama" (terraced mountain). As noted by Anthony Bryant, these locative family names are most frequently composed of two characters of which the first character modifies the second. That is, the second character is the substantive element of the name. An easy example is "Iguchi" (literally "well mouth") which is an easy topographic example. Another is "Ogawa" (literally "small river"). This pattern also prevails for *nanori* in which the final element should be thought of as substantive. Further, single character names such as "Mi'namoto" or "Taira" are most frequently associated with aristocratic families. The reason for this is that many of these families have continental origins on the Korean peninsula and inherited their names from the time when the Japanese court was involved with the affairs of the ancient Sillah kingdoms. Thus, these family names follow a pattern which is more truly normative of continental names found in China and Korea than those found in Japan.

Koop and Inada have documented the combination of both a clan and a family name in Japanese personal names. A member of a Japanese clan may also have the clan name attached to his name. Koop and Inada assert that when this is done it should immediately follow the family name. When the name is read, a possessive -**no**- is inserted between the two names showing that the first name modifies the second. Finally, all masters and teachers in the Society for Creative Anachronism should have their names followed with an honourific "sensei" (master), all others of higher rank should be addressed with the honourific *do'no* 殿 (lord) following their name. This is the simplest approximation to actual mediæval usage.

While peasants and others were registered in census records under clan names with a simple *yobina*, the College of Arms generally presumes that a person registering a name and device is of what corresponds to the *buke* class in mediæval Japanese society. Thus, emulation of the names used by members of this class should be encourage by members of the College of Arms. For females, this entails selecting an *uji* and an appropriate *jitsumei*. The *jitsumei* is then shorted to produce *yobina*. For males, assumption of both a birth-order *yobina* and an official *nanori* should be encouraged. However, gentles in either case should be cautioned against unwarranted use of *nanori* prior to an actual award of arms. This situation is somewhat analogous to the display of devices and the use of honourifics in ordinary speech. Many subjects of the Laurel Kingdoms feel a particular attachment to distinguishing between those who have received awards of arms and those who do not. Thus, while enforcement is generally beyond the scope of the College of Arms, it is judicious for the local pursuivant to instruct his client in the significance of *nanori*. Further, as family names were reserved to those with special status, the client should be encouraged to select a clan name to be used with the *zokumyou* unto an actual award of arms is bestowed upon the client by the crown. At this time, the crown will grant permission to use a family name. This is known as Myouji'gomen 苗字御免. Following the award of arms, male Japanese will be known by their family name followed by their *yobina* with title and terminated by their *nanori*. In casual conversation, the *yobina* will remain in use, but in official documents and court proceedings, either the *nanori* or the more complete form will be used.

Prior to the Meiji Restoration, *nanori* (official names) and family names were both the province of the *kuge* and *buke* classes. That is, they were distinctive of the hereditary nobility and the military caste. Normative practice for all others, as demonstrated by census records, was clan name followed by *zokumyou* (vulgar name). Thus, most members of the Society for Creative Anachronism will probably wish to adopt a name which emulates the naming practices of the military caste. It is important to understand that while this naming style was rare among artisans and peasants, it was not impossible for such an individual to attain a name of this form. While rigid caste distinctions and restricted social mobility was enforced by the government during the Edo Period, this was not generally the case during the periods of Japanese history which correspond to the scope of the Society for Creative Anachronism. Consequently, for males the name should consist of a family name followed by a *zokumyou* and ending in a *nanori*. For women, the *zokumyou* can be deleted as they will usually be either descriptive or a variant on the *nanori*. These Chinese style Buddhist names usually substitutes for a native *nanori*.

How to Use the Name Tables

The are separate historical name tables for each of the different types of names used to construct a normative mediæval Japanese name. These tables are arranged alphabetically and grouped into sections according to the first character in a *kana* transcription of the names. The *hiragana* character for this syllable along with its roman transcription appear as a section header. The table is further divided into six columns. Each name in the historical tables will have entries for each of the first five columns. The sixth column contains additional research notes, some of which may be in Japanese.

The first column renders the name in English letters. Please carefully read the pronunciation guide or consult an elementary Japanese textbook before attempting to use the English version of the name. The spelling which appears in this column is intended to reflect how the name would be written in one of the Japanese phonetic alphabets. As there are many systems for "romanizing" Japanese, it is not possible to simply check for the same spelling, but rather, it is necessary to actually sound out the names when attempting to determine whether a names sounds the same as the name of a famous person. Other systems represent long vowels with a "macron" rather than by auxiliary vowels as in Japanese orthography. Also, some systems will write the consonants and glottal stops somewhat differently. For example, "chi" is sometimes written as "ti" because it appears in the T line rectangular arrangements of the Japanese syllabaries.

は ❖❖❖❖❖ Ha

Nanori	Kanji	Period	Date		Notes
Hama'nari	浜成	Uncertain	不詳	1600	
Harufusa	春房	Muromachi	室町	1572	High Courtier Official
Haruhisa	治久	Kamakura	鎌倉	1332	
Haruhisa	晴久	Sengoku	戦国	1568	
Haru'naga	治長	Sengoku	戦国	1568	
Haru'nobu	晴信	Uncertain	不詳	1600	
Harutada	治忠	Sengoku	戦国	1568	
Harutomo	晴具	Uncertain	不詳	1600	
Haruyuki	晴幸	Uncertain	不詳	1600	

As Japanese has a very restricted sound system, there are many homonyms and, consequently, the orthography of Japanese names and their pronunciation are equally important. This is very different from the traditional approach to onomastics taken by the College of Arms. In Japan, people commonly suspend conversations to determine what is actually being said by referring to the orthographic representation in Chinese letters. There is no counterpart for this in Western culture. However, in Asian countries, a name is a combination of both sound and orthography and a name which differs in either of these is a different name. Thus, while the "Rules for Submission" adopted by the College of Arms may never recognize this important distinction, scholarship demands that the actual Japanese orthography be represented as well as the pronunciation in the historical name tables. Thus, the second column gives the actual representation of the name as found in historical sources.

The third column gives the name of the earliest era in which use of the name by a member of the *buke* class has been documented, and the fourth column renders this era in Japanese. Certain names have not yet been documented for this class, but follow the general style for these names. (This is mainly the case for masculine *nanori* which have a distinctive form.) In this case, the entry is followed by an annotation in

Japanese indicating the class for which documented usage exists. While it may be advisable to avoid names with usage annotations, these names do have historical precedent, and further research will probably find instances of their use by members of the *buke* class. These eras are of cultural and historical significance and are in general use in scholarly publications both in Japanese and in English. Finally, some names have evocative English renderings of their meanings appearing in the fifth column.

Example

Supposes a warrior wishes to have an appropriate Japanese name. Then, he needs to select a family name which can be any name from the table of *Historical Surnames*. However, the College of Arms has in the past discouraged the use of historically significant surnames such as Fujiwara 藤原, Mi'namoto 源, Taira 平, Houjou 北条, Ashikaga 足利, and Tokugawa 徳川. These names were used by many people and probably should be admissible for use in the Society for Creative Anachronism. Otherwise, the various family names of each branch of the Genji clan should be restricted as members of any of these families could become *shougun*. Only Yamato written either as 大和 or 日本 and Toyotomi 豊臣 should be reserved surnames. The first two names were names born by legendary members of the imperial family and the last name was granted to Toyotomi Hideyoshi 豊臣秀吉 by the emperor at the close of the sixteenth century.

Our warrior begins by selecting the surname Ikeda 池田 which represents a rice farm near a pond. He continues by selecting a *zokumyou* such as Saburou 三郎. Finally, he selects a *nanori* such as Noriza'ne 範実. Thus, his complete name would be, Ikeda no Saburou Noriza'ne 池田 三郎 範実. If he excels on the battlefield, he may be awarded arms and given the titular office of *u'emondaibu* 右衛門大夫. After which, he would be known as Ikeda no Saburou U'emondaibu Noriza'ne Do'no 池田 三郎右衛門大夫 範実 殿.

A merchant has a somewhat simpler task. The merchant or craftsman selects the name of one of the monopoly corporations. Suppose that the merchant is in the textile business. Then, he may wish to use Oribe 織部 as that is the name for the weavers. However, this might only reflect remote ancestry. He also selects a *zokumyou* such as Gorou 五郎 which means "number five son". Yes, it may seem odd, but Japanese really did and still do name their male children after their birth order. Thus, he would be recorded on the census records as yet another Oribe no Gorou 織部 五郎.

Using the Thematic Dictionary

While there are many pictographic an Chinese characters and many that are ideographs for atomic concepts, most Chinese characters are composed of a semiotic component (usually written on the left) and a phonetic component (usually written on the right). The characters in a *kanji* dictionary are typically arranged with letters sharing the same principal semiotic component grouped together. Thus, a *kanji* dictionary is not just a dictionary, but a thesaurus as well. The entries in the *Thematic Dictionary* are grouped into twenty eight major categories. Some of these categories have very many entries and are quite long. Others only have a few entries. Although these major categories do not correspond to the ones found in a *kanji* dictionary, hopefully they will help you find the thematic elements you want. Further, Ideas are grouped together within the major categories as well. While "plants" form a major category, generally all of the trees are grouped together.

The *Thematic Dictionary* has its own table of contents. The mnemonic translations for every thematic elements are sequentially listed within the appropriate major category. These mnemonic translations are alphabetically arranged in the Semantic Index. Finally, the Phonetic Index lists each of the principle readings for the thematic elements appearing in the *Thematic Dictionary*. Those which are Chinese readings are in capitals and those which are native Japanese readings are in lower case. Readings which are peculiar to individual names appear in the *Thematic Dictionary*, but not in the Phonetic Index. A few of the entries have additional notes following the header as seen in the following examples. In our first example, 天 means "sky" or "heaven" which are mnemonic translations. Its Chinese reading is "TEN" and its Japanese reading is "ama". 天 can be found by any of these or under "Celestial Phenomena".

天　Sky / Heaven

Note that Tenjiku 天竺 is the ancient name for India used by people in China, Korea, and Japan. It is not the name of a place in Japan and was included for historical interest only.

Reading	Type	Example	Kanji	Period	Date	Added Meaning
TEN	P	Tenjiku	天竺	Nara	784	Fat Bamboo
TEN	Y	Tenbun	天文	Sengoku	1532	Literature / Culture
TEN	Y	Tenei	天永	Hei'an	1110	Forever

The entries in the Thematic Table of Contents and the two indices correspond to the mnemonic translations in the first line of the entry and the "readings" appearing in the first column of each entry in the *Thematic Dictionary*. These same mnemonic translations appear as entries in the "Added Meaning" column. Whether this added meaning is a substantive or descriptive element depends upon the position of the corresponding *kanji* in a particular name. Thus, the **TEN-** 天 (heavenly) in Tenbun is the descriptive element, and **-BUN** 文 (literature) is the substantive element.

文　Literature / Culture = BUN / Writing = fumi / Colour Harmony = aya

While this *kanji* specifically refers to writing, it can also refer more generally to literature or culture as a whole.

Reading	Type	Example	Kanji	Period	Date	Added Meaning
BUN	S	Bun'ya	文屋	Uncertain	1600	Urban House / Artisan
BUN	Y	Bun'an	文安	Muromachi	1444	Gentle / Safe / Secure
MON	S	Ichimonji	一文字	Hei'an	1183	One + Letter
aya	F	Aya	文	Uncertain	1600	
aya	F	Ayame	文女	Kamakura	1332	[Woman]
fumi	N	Fumitoki	文時	Hei'an	981	Time / Era
fumi	N	Ka'nefumi	兼文	Kamakura	1266	Unite

Tenbun is an era name. As Japan imported its system of era names from China, these names are actually a kind of *houmyou*. Consequently, their *kanji* always assume an *onyomi* or Chinese reading. Just as "Literature" and "Culture" appeared as added meanings for the listing of Bunya under 天 (heaven), "Sky" and "Heaven" appear as added meanings for Tenbun in its listing under 文 (culture). Regardless, Tenmon 天文 means "Heavenly Culture". As the *onyomi* generally represents all of the available meanings, the intended meaning is usually more specific when a *kanji* takes its *kunyomi* than when it takes its *onyomi*.

The following entry for incense from the *Thematic Dictionary* illustrates many different kinds of elementary name and *kanji* readings. It is found in the major category devoted to "artifacts. The first line gives the *kanji* and one or more mnemonic translations. In an actual *kanji* dictionary, many more meanings will be found for some letters than appear in the *Thematic Dictionary*. This is because those meanings normally be used to form names. Some *kanji* even have special meanings that are reserved for use in names and those are the ones which appear in the *Thematic Dictionary*. The first column gives the reading used in the example on the same line. [Special] means that the reading is non-agglutinating. Chinese readings are given in capital letters and Japanese readings in lower case letters. The next column has a code letter indicating which kind of name appears in the example. Following that, is a transliteration of the name and the name written in *kanji*. The next two columns give the era name, by which the name was in use. If the available documentation only gives the era name, then the date for the end of the era is given. If the name was derived from a specific individual, then the date approximates the year in which they were twenty years old. Finally, the last column gives semantic equivalents for the other characters in the name in the order in which they appear in the name. Words separated by a slash are for the same *kanji*. A plus sign separates the entries for one *kanji* from the ones for the next in names with three or more *kanji* in the written form of the name. Remember, for Japanese people, the written form of the name is even more important than the spoken form, and this is even more true for classical and mediæval Japan than it is today. During part of the classical period, Chinese became the official court language. Finally, research notes replace the *kanji* references for the entries in the alphabetical listings which follow the *Thematic Dictionary*.

香 Incense

Like many other items appearing in Japanese names, incense is strongly associated with Buddhism. Further, the incense ceremonially was a popular pastime dating from the Hei'an Period. As such, it is strongly associated with *Genji Monogatari*.

Reading	Type	Example	Kanji	Period	Date	Added Meaning
KOU	S	Kouzai	香西	Kamakura	1332	West
ka	N	Ku'nika	国香	Uncertain	1600	Country / Rural Area
kaori	F	Kaorime	香賣	Nara	784	
[Special]	F	Takako	香子	Hei'an	1183	[Lady]

Name Type Codes in the Thematic Dictionary

B	Infants & Children	F	Women	M	Masculine Yobina	S	Surname
E	Emperors	H	Chinese Style Name	N	Masculine Nanori	Y	Era Names

Deriving Meaning

The meaning for any individual entry in the *Thematic Dictionary* can be derived by combining the mnemonic translations given for the section or main entry with the "added meaning" given for the specific name found under the main entry. When doing this, you must be careful to combine the semantic elements in the correct order. If there are multiple entries in the "added meaning column", then they must be agglutinated in the order given. Further, you must take care to insert the principal meaning for the section in its proper place. While you do not have to actually read the *kanji* to do this, you need to take careful note of the order of the semantic elements appear in the name.

久 Longtime

Reading	Type	Example	Kanji	Period	Date	Added Meaning
KU	F	Ku'nime	久爾賣	Nara	784	Bobbin / Distaff
KU	S	Sakuma	佐久間	Sengoku	1568	Military Deputy + Space
KYUU	Y	Bunkyuu	文久	Edo	1861	Literature / Culture
hisa	N	Haruhisa	治久	Kamakura	1332	Govern / Rule
hisa	N	Hisayoshi	久義	Nanboku	1392	Fealty
hisa	N	Kagehisa	景久	Kamakura	1332	Bright / Magnificent
hisa	S	Hisada	久田	Sengoku	1568	Rice Paddy

In the example above, the main entry has only a single mnemonic definition. Frequently, there are several alternative definitions given. In these cases, the alternatives usually share a common theme. For a very few entries, such as 文 on the preceding page, these meanings are less strongly related and the intended meaning is determined by the reading of the *kanji* actually used in the name. In the above example, the main entry carries the meaning of "longtime". In particular, the adjective *hisashii* 久しい connotes nostalgia or preservation of a desired condition. In Japanese grammar, **hisa** is a stem form which can be used to build adjectives, adverbs, and even nouns. Under the main entry, we encounter names such as Hisayoshi 久義 wherein **hisa-** 久 is the descriptive element. In our example, **-yoshi** 義 is the substantive element. Thus, Hisayoshi could mean "Old Fashioned Fealty" or "Enduring Fealty". In other examples such as Haruhisa 治久, **-hisa** 久 forms the substantive element. In these names, **-hisa** 久 can be thought of as connoting preservation of some virtue or quality.

Many Japanese nouns can be converted into verbs simply by appending the auxiliary verb *suru* する meaning "to do". Similarly, many Japanese nouns can be converted into adjectives with the meaning of "being like". Thus, the thematic elements have greater flexibility than is immediately apparent from their mnemonic definitions.

Thematic Dictionary

Spacial Relationships	97
Temporal Relationships	116
Works of Man	129
Works of Nature	145
Celestial Phenomena	155
Plants	159
Beasts & Monsters	171
Anatomy	176
Light & Colour	179
Groups & Relationships	185
Rank & Status	192
Peace & Security	208
Number & Quantity	211
Taste & Appearance	225
Spiritual Traits	228
Actions & Activities	237
Perceiving & Communicating	250
Feelings & Emotions	252
Warfare	256
Art & Letters	259
Being & Existing	267
Artifacts	271
Textiles & Clothing	278
Tools & Implements	280
Purity	283
Ethics	288
Virtues	295
Miscellaneous	305

Thematic Dictionary

Table of Contents

❖ SPACIAL RELATIONSHIPS ❖

Place	97		Location	97		Place	97
Location	97		Duty Station	97		Main	97
Original	97		Root	97		Base	97
Origin	97		Origin	98		Purpose	98
Country	98		Rural Area	98		Nation	99
Land	99		Big Country	99		Territory	99
Province	99		Soil	99		Country	99
China	99		Han Dynasty	99		Strong Country	99
Shin Region of China	99		Barrier	100		Mouth	100
Entrance	100		Exit	100		Enter	100
Entrance	100		Blocked Off	100		Obstructed	100
Spacious	100		Spread Out	100		Expansive	100
Cramped	101		Small Area	101		Big	101
Small	102		Above	102		Upper	102
Superior	102		Top	102		Middle	103
Under	103		Lower	103		Bottom	103
Inferior	103		Inside	103		Innermost	104
Antecedent	104		East	104		West	104
South	105		North	105		Left	105
Right	105		Quadrant	105		Rectangle	105
Regulated	105		Prolong	105		Stretch Out	105
Draw	106		Stretch	106		Spread Out	106
Fat	106		Rotund	106		Round	106
Thick (Flat Objects)	106		Narrow	106		Thin (Round Objects)	106
Tall	107		High	107		Tree Top	108
Grow Tall	108		Pile Up	108		Deep	109
Shallow	109		Flat (Countryside)	109		Flat and Thin (Objects)	109
Peace	110		Flat	110		Ordinary	110
Tranquility	110		Long	111		Oldest	111
Senior	111		Inch	113		Measure (Length)	113
Near	113		Edge	113		Bank	113
Near	113		Far	113		Corner	114
Horn	114		Corner	114		Nook	114
Confluence	114		Agreement	114		Concord	114
Stand Up	114		Towards	114		Direction	114
Method	114		Near	114		Edge	114
Divide	115		Fork	115		Split	115
Branch	115		Cleft	115		Crevice	115
A Bend	115						

❖ TEMPORAL RELATIONSHIPS ❖

Beginning	116	First	116	Happen	116
Begin	116	Continue	116	Repeat	116
Do Again	116	Most	116	Last	116
Final	116	Behind	117	After	117
Formerly	117	Ever	117	Previous	117
Forever	117	Permanent	118	Changeless	118
Enduring	118	Longtime	119	Long Life	120
Longevity	120	Short Time	120	In a Twinkling	120
Neglect	120	Old	120	Young	120
Young	121	Healthy	121	Fresh	121
Vivid	121	Clear	121	Bright	121
Brilliant	121	Splendid	121	New	121
Fast	122	Early	122	Fast	122
Rapid	122	Good Horse	122	Now	122
Hour	122	Time	122	Era	122
Year	124	Year	124	Age of a Person	124
Era	124	Generation	124	Generation	124
Life	124	Morning	125	Dawn	125
Long Ago	126	Evening	126	Season	126
Season	127	Spring (Season)	127	Summer	127
Autumn	127	Winter	128		

❖ WORKS OF MAN ❖

Vantage	129	View	129	Vista	129
Steep Road	129	Pass Through	129	Big Road	129
Road	131	Way	131	Well	131
Rampart	132	Border	132	Stop Up	132
Fence	132	Hedge	132	Gate	132
Large Roof	132	Cosmos	132	Ridge Pole	132
Door	133	Wall	133	Platform Bed	133
Kitchen	133	Chef	133	Room	133
Space	133	Monastic Cell	133	Stairs	134
Level	134	Story (Building)	134	Rank	134
Audience Hall	135	Sanctuary	135	Residence	135
Dwelling	135	Rural House	135	Family	135
Urban House	137	Artisan	137	Inn	137
Stay Over	137	Camp	137	Mansion	137
Hall	137	Castle	137	Warehouse	137
Storehouse	138	Shintoh Shrine	138	Palace	138
Buddhist Temple	138	Mansion	139	Temple	139
Palace	139	School	139	Pagoda	139
Mound	139	Tomb	139	Foundation	139
Earthen Dais	139	Hamlet	140	Hometown	140
Rural	141	Hometown	141	Village	141
Town	141	Town	141	Monastic Residence	141
Market	142	Metropolis	142	Beautiful	142
Capital City	142	Magnificent	142	Palace Garden	142
Garden	142	Courtyard	142	Atrium	142
Garden	142	Dry Field	142	Rice Paddy	143

Thematic Dictionary —Table of Contents

Flooded Field	143	Dike	144	Levy	144
Flume	144	Ditch	144	Gutter	144
Bridge	144				

❖ WORKS OF NATURE ❖

Mountain	145	Peak	146	Slope	146
Island	146	Island	146	Ridge	147
Rise	147	Crest	147	Hillock	147
Hill	147	Hole	147	Cleft	147
Valley	147	Woods	148	Forest	148
Water	148	Hot Water	148	Sea	148
Harbour	148	Pond	149	Wave	149
Aquatic Cliff	149	Deep Water	149	Abyss	149
Beach	149	Shore	149	Bay	149
Delta	149	Swamp	150	Glen	150
Run	150	River	150	Large River	151
Inlet	151	Harbour	151	Cove	151
Rapids	151	Waterfall	151	Sand (In Water)	151
Quick Sand	151	Mud	152	Muddy	152
Spring (Water)	152	Wide Plain	152	Meadow	152
Pasture	153	Dirt	153	Earth	153
Rock	153	Boulder	154	Wild	154
Untamed	154				

❖ CELESTIAL PHENOMENA ❖

Sky	155	Heaven	155	Sun	155
Day	155	Moon	155	Month	155
Rat (Zodiac)	156	Ox (Zodiac)	156	Tiger (Zodiac)	156
Hare (Zodiac)	156	Dragon (Zodiac)	156	Snake (Zodiac)	156
Horse (Zodiac)	157	Goat (Zodiac)	157	Monkey (Zodiac)	157
Cock (Zodiac)	157	Dog (Zodiac)	157	Boar (Zodiac)	157
Clear (Sky)	157	Hot & Humid	157	Hot	158
Heat	158	Cold	158	Cloud	158
Fog	158	Snow	158	Wind	158

❖ PLANTS ❖

TTree	159	Wooden	159	Pine Tree	159
Cedar Tree	160	Evergreen Oak	160	Willow Tree	160
Cherry	160	Peach	160	Hollyhock	160
Plum (*ume*)	161	Aphananthe Aspera	161	Persimmon	161
Pear Tree	161	Tangerine	161	Chestnut	161
Cinnamon Tree	161	Paulownia	162	Camphor Tree	162
Zelkova Tree	162	Boxwood	162	Mulberry Bush	162
Yellow Rose Tree	162	Camellia	162	Cleyera Ochnacea	162
Bamboo	162	Fat Bamboo	163	Thin Bamboo	163
Wisteria	163	Lotus	163	Chrysanthemum	164
Grove	164	Thicket	164	Bushes	164
Common Reed	164	Reed	164	Rush	164
Club Rush	164	Bush Clover	164	Grass	165

Grass	165	Ground Cover	165	Young Rice Plants	165
Flax	165	Linen	165	Arrowroot	165
The Mace Plant	165	Millet	166	Tea	166
Melon	166	Cucumber	166	Bloom	166
Bouquet	166	Overgrow	166	Lush Growth	166
Grow	166	Blossom	166	Blossoming	166
Rooted	167	Planted	167	Root	167
Base	167	Trunk	167	Stalk	167
Branch	168	Twig	168	Leaf	168
Flower	168	Cherry Blossoms	168	Plum Blossoms	168
Flower	168	Flowering Shrubs	168	Flowering Grass	168
Seed	168	Center	168	Reality	168
Plentiful	168	Seed	170	Cause	170
Reason	170	Shoot	170	Sprout	170
Seedling	170				

❖ BEASTS & MONSTERS ❖

Person	171	Human	171	Ogre	171
Troll	171	Monkey	171	Tiger	171
Bear	172	Boar	172	Horse	172
Pony	172	Cow	172	Ox	172
Deer	173	Goat	173	Dog	173
Rabbit	173	Hare	173	Bird	173
Male Phoenix	173	Crane	174	Hawk	174
Sparrow	174	Sea Gull	174	Bug	174
Insect	174	Worm	174	Snake	174
Bee	174	Wasp	174	Hornet	174
Dragon	174	Dragon	175	Turtle	175
Tortoise	175	Longevity	175	Fish	175
Mackerel	175	Shark	175	Whale	175
Sea Monster	175				

❖ ANATOMY ❖

Body	176	Pregnant	176	Hand	176
Foot	176	Sufficient	176	Nose	176
Tail	176	Backbone	177	Be in a Row	177
Long	177	Eye	177	Hair (Generic)	177
Fur	177	Wool	177	Hair (Scalp)	177
Feather	177	Fluff	177	Down	177
Silk	177	Claw	178	Sides	178
Ribs	178	Supporter	178	Buttocks	178
Hips	178	Anus	178	Feces	178

❖ LIGHT & COLOUR ❖

Bright	179	Bright	179	Cheerful	179
Well Controlled	179	Brilliant	179	Clear	180
Bright	180	Bright	180	Shining	180
Bright	182	Magnificent	182	Bright	183
Visible	183	Explicit	183	Star Light	183

Thematic Dictionary—Table of Contents   77

Pure Light	183	Colour	183	Black	183
Dark	183	Black	183	Austere	183
Shade	183	Shadow	183	Purple	184
White	184	White	184	Unused	184
Virgin	184	Red (Fire)	184	Young	184
Red (Flowers)	184	Dark Crimson	184	Blue	184
Green	184				

❖ GROUPS & RELATIONSHIPS ❖

Public Service	185	Everybody	185	Monopoly Corporation	185
Military Column	185	Department	185	Collective	185
Band	185	Cross Over	185	Join Up	186
Enlist	186	Team up	186	Together	186
Collaborate	186	Gather Together	186	Together	186
Team-Work	186	Connect	187	Adopt	187
Our	187	Us	187	We	187
We	187	Our	187	One's Self	187
Me	187	Myself	187	Us	187
Family	187	Clan	187	Branch	189
Line	189	Prestigous Residence	189	Avenue	189
Inherit	189	Help	189	Lineage	189
Govern	189	Govern	189	Rule	189
Instruct	189	Self-Control	189	Govern	191
Rule	191	Law	191	Precept	191

❖ RANK & STATUS ❖

Public Official	192	Officer	192	Noble	192
King	193	Emperor	193	King	193
Imperial Prince	193	Deity	193	Minister	193
Principal Vassal	193	Regional Governor	193	Regional Deputy	194
Master	194	Lord	194	Commander	194
Ministerial Deputy	194	Military Deputy	195	Support	195
Aid	195	Deputy	195	Rescue	195
Assist	195	Palace Regiment	196	Right Gate Guards	196
Palace Regiment	196	Left Gate Guards	196	Palace Regiment	196
Teacher	196	Expert	196	Queen	197
Empress	197	Princess	197	Consort	197
Princess	197	Child	197	Older Sister	198
Wife	198	Woman	198	Woman	199
Old Person	199	Aged	199	Elderly	199
Elder	199	Old Woman	199	Hag	199
Husband	200	Man	200	Founder	200
Grandfather	200	Boy	200	Young Scholar	200
Youth	200	Son	200	Daughter	200
Child	200	Child	200	Servant	200
Grandchild	200	Prosper	201	Son	201
Younger Sister	201	Companion	201	Similar	201
Friend	201	Honourable	201	High Status	202
Show Clearly	202	Highest	202	Exemplar	202
Admirable	202	Name	203	Famous	203

Admirable	203	Buddhist Nun	203	Member	203
Parent	203	Intimate	203	Hermit	205
Adept	205	Sage	205	Unite	205
Hold several Offices	205	Heavy Service	205	Rank	206
Level	206	Blood Heir	206	Successor	207

❖ PEACE & SECURITY ❖

Gentle	208	Safe	208	Secure	208
Quiet	208	Peace	209	Plenitude	209
Expansive	209	Peace	209	Tranquility	209
Harmony	209	Japan	209		

❖ NUMBER & QUANTITY ❖

Son	211	Lord	211	First Son	211
Second Son	211	Second Son	212	Next Son	212
Third Son	212	All	212	One of Two	212
Piece	212	Bit	212	Part	212
Half	212	One	212	One	213
Two	213	Pair	213	Two	213
Three	213	Three	214	Visit	214
Four	214	Five	214	Six	214
Seven	214	Eight	215	Nine	215
Branch	215	Ten	215	One Hundred	215
One Thousand	215	Ten Thousand	216	Order	216
Sequence	216	Event Number	216	Consult	216
Confer	216	Base	216	Original	216
Second	217	Middle of a Group	217	Next	218
Next	218	Again	218	Last	218
First	219	Helmet	219	Second	219
Cute	219	Third	219	Alter	219
Fourth	219	Adult	219	Fifth	219
Speak	219	Sixth	219	Self	219
Seventh	220	Age	220	Eighth	220
Bitter	220	Ninth	220	Found	220
Tenth	220	Menstruation	220	Every	220
Ordinary	220	Wide Spread	220	Typical	220
Ordinary	220	The Same	220	Identical	220
Equitable	220	Separate	221	Different	221
Small Amount	221	Minor	221	Many	221
Numerous	221	Grow Numerous	221	Multiply	221
Overflow	221	Grow Numerous	222	Live Long	222
Prosper	222	Fill Up	222	Become Abundant	222
Bountiful	222	Fruitful	222	Plentiful	222
Piled Up	222	Become Full	223	Abundant	223

❖ TASTE & APPEARANCE ❖

Taste	225	Sweet Taste	225	Sweet Scent	225
Magnificent	225	Seem	225	Appear	225
Appear Cultured	225	Appear Tall	225	Grand	225

Thematic Dictionary — Table of Contents 79

Taste	226	Elegance	226	Grand Effect	226
Thick	226	Turbid	226	Thin	226
Light	226	Thin	226	Pale	226
Weak	226	Light	226	Minor	226
Trifling	226	Simple	226	Easy	226
Form	226	Shape	226	Beauty	226
Form	227	Shape	227	Figure	227
Beautiful	227	Exotic Beauty	227	Mysterious	227
Beauty	227	Colour Harmony	227	Strange	227
Unusual	227	Unexpected	227		

❖ SPIRITUAL TRAITS ❖

God	228	Buddha	228	Wheel of Life	228
Offering	228	Courtesy	228	Banquet	228
Food Offering	228	Ceremony	228	Rite	228
Method	228	System	228	Worship	229
Study	229	Sanctify	229	Bless	229
Spirit	229	Breath	229	Health	229
Divine Help	229	Zen	229	Oracle	230
Precious	230	High Quality	230	Excellence	231
Noble	231	Happy	231	Felicitous	231
Gift of the Gods	231	Happy	231	Blessed	231
Lucky	232	Fortunate	232	Precious	232
Benevolence	232	Misfortune	232	Belief	233
Faith	233	Teaching	234	Dogma	234
Law	235	Vigor	235	Spirit	235
Elan Vital	235	Obligatory Path	236		

❖ ACTIONS & ACTIVITIES ❖

Going	237	Bound For	237	Bring	237
Go	238	Depart	238	Follow After	238
Chosen	238	Stop	238	Desist	238
Catch	239	Gather	239	Carry	239
Deliver	239	Bring Along	239	Carry	239
Take Along	239	Cross Over	239	Walk	239
Follow	240	Tour	240	Travel	240
Bountiful Land	240	Wander	240	Meander	240
Play	240	Visit	240	Mount	240
Multiply	240	History Text	240	Climb	240
Ascend	240	Fly	240	Fly	240
Jump	240	Adjust	241	Correct	241
Attach	242	Arrive	242	To Become	242
Arrive	242	Be Posted	242	Become Attached	242
Use	242	Utilize	242	Employment	242
Service	242	Endure a Duty	242	Daily Labour	242
Very Rapid Hard Work	242	Sow Seed	243	Paint	243
Prepare	243	Gather	243	Build	243
Construct	243	Dig	243	Carve	243
Excavation	243	Quench	243	Immerse	243
Temper Steel	243	Paint Colours	243	Make	243

Create	243	Make	244	Manufacture	244
Spin (Thread)	244	Tie	244	Bind	244
Hold One's Breath	244	Knit	244	Entwine	244
Weave	244	Sew	244	Dry	244
Care For	244	Exchange Money	244	Become Wealthy	245
Bountiful	245	Industrious	245	Celebrate A Gain	245
Answer	245	Reply	245	Request	245
Ask	245	Perform Well	247	Divine	247
Foretell	247	Prophesy	247	Fix	247
Specify	247	Determine	247	Leisure	248
Quiet	248	Rest	248	Leisure	248
Sit Quietly	249	Eat	249	Bite	249

❖ PERCEIVING & COMMUNICATING ❖

Perceive	250	Understand	250	Oversee	250
Inspect	250	See from Above	250	Perceive	250
View	250	Spectacle	250	Appearance	250
Sound	250	Proclamation	250	Imperial Decree	251
Admonishment	251	Demand	251	Confer	251
Consult	251	Meet in Council	251		

❖ FEELINGS & EMOTIONS ❖

Emotional	252	Deep Feeling	252	Happiness	253
Felicitude	253	Happiness	253	Joy	253
Happy	253	Tattoo	253	Pleasure	253
Enjoyment	253	Agreement	253	Good Health	253
Rejoice	253	Deer Skin	253	Rejoice	254
Nostalgic	254	Nostalgic	254	Wish	254
Desire	254	Heartfelt Wish	254	Desire	254
Long Term Desire	254	Plan	254	Love	255
Affection	255	Desire	255	Cold to the Touch	255
Unfeeling	255				

❖ WARFARE ❖

Guarantee	256	Protect	256	Defend	256
Win	257	Conquer	257	Triumph	257
Victory	257	Strong	257	Brave	257
Military Force	257	Samurai	258	Warrior	258

❖ ARTS & LETTERS ❖

Poem	259	Song	259	Literature	259
Culture	259	Writing	259	Colour Harmony	259
Symbol	260	Writing	260	Elucidate	260
State	260	Speak	260	Declare	260
Proclaim	260	Word	260	Speak Truthfully	260
Letter	260	Character	260	Symbol	260
Text Book	260	Sutra	260	True Path	260
Travel Straight	260	Explicit	262	Clear	262

Thematic Dictionary — Table of Contents 81

Master an Art	262	Polish	264	Refine	264
Practice (An Art	264	Genius	264	Reason	264
Logic	264	Divide	264	Partition	264
Understand	264	Intelligent	264	Knowledge	265
Artisan	265	Artistry	265	Craft	265
Skill	265	Talent	265	Ability	265
Wise	266	Well Traveled	266	Learned	266
Idea	266	Opinion	266		

❖ BEING & EXISTING ❖

Become	267	Exist	267	Life	268
Live	268	Living	268	Lives	268
Exists (Animate)	268	Exists (Inanimate)	268	This	269
Decide	269	Choose	269	Definite	269
This	269	Him	269	Her	269
Rule	269	Conquer	269	There	269
Have	269	Possess	269	This	270
Here	270	Now	270	Ponder	270
This	270	This Way	270		

❖ ARTIFACTS ❖

Thing	271	Artifact	271	Koto	271
Harp	271	Gold	271	Metal	271
Money	271	Iron	271	Toy Ball	271
Jewel	272	Sphere	272	Gem	272
Treasure	272	Bell	272	Small Bell	272
Flag	273	Banner	273	Paper	273
Incense	273	Umbrella	273	Drugs	273
Salt	273	Uncooked Rice	273	Sake	274
Rice Wine	274	Alcohol	274	Cook Pot	274
Cooked Rice	274	Board	274	Plank	274
Box	274	Letter Box	274	Barrel	274
Tubular Box	275	Mirror	275	Boat	275
Ship	275	Rudder	275	Thread	275
Cable	275	Rope	275	Rope	275
Cord	275	Strap	275	Thong	275
Functional Beginning	275	Twist	276	Braid	276
Rope	276	Net	276	Goods	277
Showpiece	277	Masterpiece	277	Pedestal	277
Dais	277				

❖ TEXTILES & CLOTHING ❖

Silk	278	Linen	278	Flax	278
Cloth	278	Brocade	278	Pretty Cloth	278
Tuft	278	Fringe	278	Tassel	278
Robe	279	Rain or Snow Cape	279		

❖ TOOLS & IMPLEMENTS ❖

Tool	280	Artisan	280	Tool	280
Implement	280	Bobbin	280	Distaff	280
Spool	280	Needle	280	Grindstone	281
Mortar (Implement)	281	Pestle	281	Whetstone	281
Grindstone	281	Flat	281	Scythe	281
Sword	281	Arrow	281	Bow	282
Cart Wheel	282	A Yoke	282		

❖ PURITY ❖

Pure	283	Purity	284	Cleanse	284
Purify	284	Clean	284	Beautiful	284
Nature	285	Attributes	285	Purity	285
Simple	285	Pure (Strong Image)	285	Destination	285
Objective	285	Simple	285	Easy	285
Natural	285	Pure	285	Uncontaminated	285
Well Done	285	Required Form	286	Example	286
Model	286	Example	286	Guide	286
Example	286	Pattern	286	Make an Example	287

❖ ETHICS ❖

Produce Good	288	Extraordinary	288	Bountiful	288
Good	289	Superior	289	Reason	290
Justification	290	Purpose	290	Goal	290
Genuine	290	Unerring	291	Genuine	291
Correct	291	True	291	Correct Spirit	292
Composure	292	Modesty	292	Tranquility	292
Equanimity	292	Make Correct	293	Produce Results	293
Work Well	293	Measure Up	294	Strive	294
Emulate	294	Compete	294	Surpass	294

❖ VIRTUES ❖

Obligation	295	Fealty	295	Foster Child	295
Produce Good	297	Kind	297	Gentle	297
Male Flower	297	Respectful	297	Reverent	297
Reverent	297	Serene	297	Steadfast	298
Honest	298	Natural	298	Perseverance	298
Continue	298	Perpetuate	298	Persist	298
Endurance	298	Deep Resolve	298	Perseverance	298
Industry	298	Diligence	298	Gentle	299
Generosity	299	Intelligence	299	Spirit	299
Generous	299	Kind	299	Honest	299
Tough	299	Strong	299	Faithful	299
Loyal	299	Heavy	301	Weighty	301
Serious	301	Determined	302	Filial Loyalty	302
Bravery	302	Courage	302	Strength	303
Courage	303	Bravery	303	Spirit	303

Thematic Dictionary—Table of Contents 83

Courage	303	Bravery	303	Valour	303
Liver	303	Valour	303	Intrepid	303
Anger	303	Rage	303	Furor	303
Strong	303	Confident	303	Righteous	304
Just	304				

❖ MISCELLANEOUS ❖

Moreover	305	Log	305	Timber	305
Lumber	305	Wood	305	Raw Matterial	305
Talent	305	Raw Matterial	305	Talent	305
Why?	306	How?	306	Do this	306
Necessity (Small)	306	Satisfy	306	Fill	306
Melt	306	Mooing of a Cow	307	Grasp	307
Span	307	Hand's Breadth	307	Quality	307
Type	307	Specialty	307	Contrary	307
Disobedient	307	Obstinant	307	Backwards	307
Decay	307	Rot	307	Summit	307
Pinnacle	307	Plan	307	Scheme	307
Trick	307	Total	307	Gauge	307
Childbirth	307	Native	307	Produce	307
Yield Up	307	Be Careful	308	Look Out	308
Meat	308	Flesh	308	Fate	308
Determined Amount	308	Bird Nest	308	Play	308
Rest	308	Other	308	Foreign	308
What	308	Whither	308	How	308
That	308	Propagate	309	Multiply	309
Grow Fat	309	Grow Muscle	309	Fertile	309
Prepare	309	Wrap	309	Bundle	309
Come Here	309	Immediate Future	309	Revelation	309
Insight	309	Learn	309	Memorize	309
Independent	309	Self	309	By One's Self	309
Employment	310	Occupation	310	Terrible	310
Head	310	First	310	Zenith	310
Level	310	Status	310	Station	310
Exists (Archaic)	310	Progress	310	Pass Through	310
Domestic Tranquility	311	Humbly Receive	311	Worthy	311
Suitable	311	Receive	312	Receive Smoothly	312
High Heaven	312	Ancient Times	312	Found	312
Build	312	Construct	312	Hit the Mark	313
Reach	313	Arrive	313	Rescue from a Pit	313
Rear	313	Raise	313	Nourish	313
Change	313	Transformation	313	Grant	313
Bestow	313	Gratitude	313	Blessing	313
Beneficence	313	Divine Fortune	314	Happy	314

Semantic Index

A

Ability	265
Above	102
Abundant	223
Abyss	149
Adept	205
Adjust	241
Admirable	202-203
Admonishment	251
Adopt	187
Adult	219
Affection	255
After	117
Again	218
Age	220
Age of a Person	124
Aged	199
Agreement	114, 253
Aid	195
Alcohol	274
All	212
Alter	219
Ancient Times	312
Anger	303
Answer	245
Antecedent	104
Anus	178
Aphananthe Aspera	161
Appear	225
Appear Cultured	225
Appear Tall	225
Appearance	250
Aquatic Cliff	149
Arrive	242, 313
Arrow	281
Arrowroot	165
Artifact	271
Artisan	137, 265, 280
Artistry	265
Ascend	240
Ask	245
Assist	195
Atrium	142
Attach	242
Attributes	285
Audience Hall	135
Austere	183
Autumn	127
Avenue	189

B

Dackbone	177
Backwards	307
Bamboo	162
Band	185
Bank	113
Banner	273
Banquet	228
Barrel	274
Barrier	100
Base	97, 167, 216
Bay	149
Be Careful	308
Be in a Row	177
Be Posted	242
Beach	149
Bear	172
Beautiful	142, 227, 284
Beauty	226-227
Become	267
Become Abundant	222
Become Attached	242
Become Full	223
Become Wealthy	245
Bee	174
Begin	116
Beginning	116
Behind	117
Belief	233
Bell	272
Bend	115
Beneficence	313
Benevolence	232
Bestow	313
Big	101
Big Country	99
Big Road	129
Bind	244
Bird	173
Bird Nest	308
Bit	212
Bite	249
Bitter	220
Black	183
Bless	229
Blessed	231
Blessing	313
Blocked Off	100
Blood Heir	206
Bloom	166
Blossom	166
Blossoming	166
Blue	184
Boar	172
Boar (Zodiac)	157
Board	274
Boat	275
Bobbin	280
Body	176
Border	132
Bottom	103
Boulder	154
Bound For	237
Bountiful	222, 245, 288
Bountiful Land	240
Bouquet	166
Bow	282
Box	274
Boxwood	162
Boy	200
Braid	276
Branch	115, 168, 189, 215
Brave	257
Bravery	302-303
Breath	229
Bridge	144
Bright	121, 179-180, 182-183
Brilliant	121, 179

Bring	237	Cleyera Ochnacea	162	**D**	
Bring Along	239	Climb	240	Daily Labour	242
Brocade	278	Cloth	278	Dais	277
Buddha	228	Cloud	158	Dark	183
Buddhist Nun	203	Club Rush	164	Dark Crimson	184
Buddhist Temple	138	Cock (Zodiac)	157	Daughter	200
Bug	174	Cold	158	Dawn	125
Build	243, 312	Cold to the Touch	255	Day	155
Bundle	309	Collaborate	186	Decay	307
Bush Clover	164	Collective	185	Decide	269
Bushes	164	Colour	183	Declare	260
Buttocks	178	Colour Harmony	227, 259	Deep	109
By One's Self	309	Come Here	309	Deep Feeling	252
		Commander	194	Deep Resolve	298
C		Common Reed	164	Deep Water	149
Cable	275	Companion	201	Deer	173
Camellia	162	Compete	294	Deer Skin	253
Camp	137	Composure	292	Defend	256
Camphor Tree	162	Concord	114	Definite	269
Capital City	142	Confer	216, 251	Deity	193
Care For	244	Confident	303	Deliver	239
Carry	239	Confluence	114	Delta	149
Cart Wheel	282	Connect	187	Demand	251
Carve	243	Conquer	257, 269	Depart	238
Castle	137	Consort	197	Department	185
Catch	239	Construct	243, 312	Deputy	195
Cause	170	Consult	216, 251	Desire	254-255
Cedar Tree	160	Continue	116, 298	Desist	238
Celebrate A Gain	245	Contrary	307	Destination	285
Center	168	Cook Pot	274	Determine	247
Ceremony	228	Cooked Rice	274	Determined	302
Change	313	Cord	275	Determined Amount	308
Changeless	118	Corner	114	Different	221
Character	260	Correct	241, 291	Dig	243
Cheerful	179	Correct Spirit	292	Dike	144
Chef	133	Cosmos	132	Diligence	298
Cherry	160	Country	98-99	Direction	114
Cherry Blossoms	168	Courage	302-303	Dirt	153
Chestnut	161	Courtesy	228	Disobedient	307
Child	197, 200	Courtyard	142	Distaff	280
Childbirth	307	Cove	151	Ditch	144
China	99	Cow	172	Divide	115, 264
Choose	269	Craft	265	Divine	247
Chosen	238	Cramped	101	Divine Fortune	314
Chrysanthemum	164	Crane	174	Divine Help	229
Cinnamon Tree	161	Create	243	Do Again	116
Clan	187	Crest	147	Do this	306
Claw	178	Crevice	115	Dog	173
Clean	284	Cross Over	185, 239	Dog (Zodiac)	157
Cleanse	284	Cucumber	166	Dogma	234
Clear	121, 180, 262	Culture	259	Domestic Tranquility	311
Clear (Sky)	157	Cute	219	Door	133
Cleft	115, 147				

Down	177	Exists (Animate)	268	Follow	240
Dragon	174-175	Exists (Archaic)	310	Follow After	238
Dragon (Zodiac)	156	Exists (Inanimate)	268	Food Offering	228
Draw	106	Exit	100	Foot	176
Drugs	273	Exotic Beauty	227	Foreign	308
Dry	244	Expansive	100, 209	Forest	148
Dry Field	142	Expert	196	Foretell	247
Duty Station	97	Explicit	183, 262	Forever	117
Dwelling	135	Extraordinary	288	Fork	115
		Eye	177	Form	226-227
				Formerly	117

E

		F		Fortunate	232
Early	122			Foster Child	295
Earth	153	Faith	233	Found	220, 312
Earthen Dais	139	Faithful	299	Foundation	139
East	104	Family	135, 187	Founder	200
Easy	226, 285	Famous	203	Four	214
Eat	249	Far	113	Fourth	219
Edge	113-114	Fast	122	Fresh	121
Eight	215	Fat	106	Friend	201
Eighth	220	Fat Bamboo	163	Fringe	278
Elan Vital	235	Fate	308	Fruitful	222
Elder	199	Fealty	295	Functional Beginning	275
Elderly	199	Feather	177	Fur	177
Elegance	226	Feces	178	Furor	303
Elucidate	260	Felicitous	231		
Emotional	252	Felicitude	253	**G**	
Emperor	193	Fence	132		
Employment	242, 310	Fertile	309	Garden	142
Empress	197	Fifth	219	Gate	132
Emulate	294	Figure	227	Gather	239, 243
Endurance	298	Filial Loyalty	302	Gather Together	186
Endure a Duty	242	Fill	306	Gauge	307
Enduring	118	Fill Up	222	Gem	272
Enjoyment	253	Final	116	Generation	124
Enlist	186	First	116, 219, 310	Generosity	299
Enter	100	First Son	211	Generous	299
Entrance	100	Fish	175	Genius	264
Entwine	244	Five	214	Gentle	208, 297, 299
Equanimity	292	Fix	247	Genuine	290-291
Equitable	220	Flag	273	Gift of the Gods	231
Era	122, 124	Flat	110, 281	Glen	150
Evening	126	Flat (Countryside)	109	Go	238
Event Number	216	Flat and Thin (Objects)	109	Goat	173, 290
Ever	117	Flax	165, 278	Goat (Zodiac)	157
Evergreen Oak	160	Flesh	308	God	228
Every	220	Flooded Field	143	Going	237
Everybody	185	Flower	168	Gold	271
Example	286	Flowering Grass	168	Good	289
Excavation	243	Flowering Shrubs	168	Good Health	253
Excellence	231	Fluff	177	Good Horse	122
Exchange Money	244	Flume	144	Goods	277
Exemplar	202	Fly	240	Govern	189, 191
Exist	267	Fog	158	Grand	225

Grand Effect	226	Here	270	Inside	103
Grandchild	200	Hermit	205	Insight	309
Grandfather	200	High	107	Inspect	250
Grant	313	High Heaven	312	Instruct	189
Grasp	307	High Quality	230	Intelligence	299
Grass	165, 168	High Status	202	Intelligent	264
Gratitude	313	Highest	202	Intimate	203
Green	184	Hill	147	Intrepid	303
Grindstone	281	Hillock	147	Iron	271
Ground Cover	165	Him	269	Island	146
Grove	164	Hips	178		
Grow	166	History Text	240	**J**	
Grow Fat	309	Hit the Mark	313	Japan	209
Grow Muscle	309	Hold One's Breath	244	Jewel	272
Grow Numerous	221-222	Hold several Offices	205	Join Up	186
Grow Tall	108	Hole	147	Joy	253
Gate Guards	196	Hollyhock	160	Jump	240
Guarantee	256	Hometown	140-141	Just	304
Guide	286	Honest	298-299	Justification	290
Gutter	144	Honourable	201		
		Horn	114	**K**	
H		Hornet	174	Kind	297, 299
Hag	199	Horse	172	King	193
Hair (Generic)	177	Horse (Zodiac)	157	Kitchen	133
Hair (Scalp)	177	Hot	157-158	Knit	244
Half	212	Hot Water	148	Knowledge	265
Hall	137	Hour	122	Koto	271
Hamlet	140	How	306, 308		
Han Dynasty	99	Human	171	**L**	
Hand	176	Humbly Receive	311	Land	99
Hand's Breadth	307	Humid	157	Large River	151
Happen	116	Husband	200	Large Roof	132
Happiness	253			Last	116, 218
Happy	231, 253, 314	**I**		Law	191, 235
Harbour	148, 151	Idea	266	Leaf	168
Hare	173	Identical	220	Learn	309
Hare (Zodiac)	156	Immediate Future	309	Learned	266
Harmony	209	Immerse	243	Left	105
Harp	271	Imperial Decree	251	Left Gate Guards	196
Have	269	Imperial Prince	193	Leisure	248
Hawk	174	Implement	280	Letter	260
Head	310	In a Twinkling	120	Letter Box	274
Health	229	Incense	273	Level	134, 206, 310
Healthy	121	Inch	113	Levy	144
Heartfelt Wish	254	Independent	309	Life	124, 268
Heat	158	Industrious	245	Light	226
Heaven	155	Industry	298	Line	189
Heavy	301	Inferior	103	Lineage	189
Heavy Service	205	Inherit	189	Linen	165, 278
Hedge	132	Inlet	151	Literature	259
Helmet	219	Inn	137	Live	268
Help	189	Innermost	104	Live Long	222
Her	269	Insect	174		

Liver 303
Lives 268
Living 268
Location 97
Log 305
Logic 264
Long 111, 177
Long Ago 126
Long Life 120
Long Term Desire 254
Longevity 120, 175
Longtime 119
Look Out 308
Lord 194, 211
Lotus 163
Love 255
Lower 103
Loyal 299
Lucky 232
Lumber 305
Lush Growth 166

M

Mackerel 175
Magnificent 142, 182, 225
Main 97
Make 243-244
Make an Example 287
Make Correct 293
Male Flower 297
Male Phoenix 173
Man 200
Mansion 137, 139
Manufacture 244
Many 221
Market 142
Master 194
Master an Art 262
Masterpiece 277
Me 187
Meadow 152
Meander 240
Measure (Length) 113
Measure Up 294
Meat 308
Meet in Council 251
Melon 166
Melt 306
Member 203
Memorize 309
Menstruation 220
Metal 271
Method 114, 228

Metropolis 142
Middle 103
Middle of a Group 217
Military Column 185
Military Deputy 195
Military Force 257
Millet 166
Minister 193
Ministerial Deputy 194
Minor 221, 226, 275
Misfortune 232
Model 286
Modesty 292
Monastic Cell 133
Monastic Residence 141
Money 271
Monkey 171
Monkey (Zodiac) 157
Monopoly Corporation 185
Month 155
Mooing of a Cow 307
Moon 155
Moreover 305
Morning 125
Mortar (Implement) 281
Most 116
Mound 139
Mount 240
Mountain 145
Mouth 100
Mud 152
Muddy 152
Mulberry Bush 162
Multiply 221, 240, 309
Myself 187
Mysterious 227

N

Name 203
Narrow 106
Nation 99
Native 307
Natural 285, 298
Nature 285
Near 113-114
Necessity (Small) 306
Needle 280
Neglect 120
Net 276
New 121
Next 218
Next Son 212
Nine 215

Ninth 220
Noble 192, 231
Nook 114
North 105
Nose 176
Nostalgic 254
Nourish 313
Now 122, 270
Numerous 221

O

Objective 285
Obligation 295
Obligatory Path 236
Obstinant 307
Obstructed 100
Occupation 310
Offering 228
Officer 192
Ogre 171
Old 120
Old Person 199
Old Woman 199
Older Sister 198
Oldest 111
One 212-213
One Hundred 215
One of Two 212
One Thousand 215
One's Self 187
Opinion 266
Oracle 230
Order 216
Ordinary 110, 220
Origin 97-98
Original 97, 216
Other 308
Our 187
Overflow 221
Overgrow 166
Oversee 250
Ox 172
Ox (Zodiac) 156

P

Pagoda 139
Paint 243
Paint Colours 243
Pair 213
Palace 138-139
Palace Garden 142
Palace Regiment 196
Pale 226

Paper	273	Principal Vassal	193	Regional Deputy	194
Parent	203	Proclaim	260	Regional Governor	193
Part	212	Proclamation	250	Regulated	105
Partition	264	Produce	307	Rejoice	253-254
Pass Through	129, 310	Produce Good	288, 297	Repeat	116
Pasture	153	Produce Results	293	Reply	245
Pattern	286	Progress	310	Request	245
Paulownia	162	Prolong	105	Required Form	286
Peace	110, 209	Propagate	309	Rescue	195
Peach	160	Prophesy	247	Rescue from a Pit	313
Peak	146	Prosper	201, 222	Residence	135
Pear Tree	161	Protect	256	Respectful	297
Pedestal	277	Province	99	Rest	248, 308
Perceive	250	Public Official	192	Revelation	309
Perform Well	247	Public Service	185	Reverent	297
Permanent	118	Pure	283, 285	Ribs	178
Perpetuate	298	Pure (Strong Image)	285	Rice Paddy	143
Perseverance	298	Pure Light	183	Rice Wine	274
Persimmon	161	Purity	284, 285	Ridge	147
Persist	298	Purple	184	Ridge Pole	132
Person	171	Purpose	98, 290	Right	105
Pestle	281			Right Gate Guards	196
Piece	212	**Q**		Righteous	304
Pile Up	108	Quadrant	105	Rise	147
Piled Up	222	Quality	307	Rite	228
Pine Tree	159	Queen	197	River	150
Pinnacle	307	Quench	243	Road	131
Place	97	Quick Sand	151	Robe	279
Plan	254, 307	Quiet	208, 248	Rock	153
Plank	274			Room	133
Planted	167	**R**		Root	97, 167
Platform Bed	133			Rooted	167
Play	240, 308	Rabbit	173	Rope	275-276
Pleasure	253	Rage	303	Rot	307
Plenitude	209	Rain	279	Rotund	106
Plentiful	168, 222	Raise	313	Round	106
Plum (*ume*)	161	Rampart	132	Rudder	275
Plum Blossoms	168	Rank	134, 206	Rule	189, 191, 269
Poem	259	Rapid	122	Run	150
Polish	264	Rapids	151	Rural	141
Pond	149	Rat (Zodiac)	156	Rural Area	98
Ponder	270	Raw Matterial	305	Rural House	135
Pony	172	Reach	313	Rush	164
Possess	269	Reality	168		
Practice (An Art)	264	Rear	313	**S**	
Precept	191	Reason	170, 264, 290	Safe	208
Precious	230, 232	Receive	312	Sage	205
Pregnant	176	Receive Smoothly	312	Sake	274
Prepare	243, 309	Rectangle	105	Salt	273
Prestigous Residence	189	Red (Fire)	184	Samurai	258
Pretty Cloth	278	Red (Flowers)	184	Sanctify	229
Previous	117	Reed	164	Sanctuary	135
Princess	197	Refine	264	Sand (In Water)	151

Thematic Dictionary — Semantic Index 91

Satisfy	306
Scheme	307
School	139
Scythe	281
Sea	148
Sea Gull	174
Sea Monster	175
Season	126-127
Second	217, 219
Second Son	211-212
Secure	208
See from Above	250
Seed	168, 170
Seedling	170
Seem	225
Self	219, 309
Self-Control	189
Senior	111
Separate	221
Sequence	216
Serene	297
Serious	301
Servant	200
Service	242
Seven	214
Seventh	220
Sew	244
Shade	183
Shadow	183
Shallow	109
Shape	226-227
Shark	175
Shin Region of China	99
Shining	180
Shintoh Shrine	138
Ship	275
Shoot	170
Shore	149
Short Time	120
Show Clearly	202
Showpiece	277
Sides	178
Silk	177, 278
Similar	201
Simple	226, 285
Sit Quietly	249
Six	214
Sixth	219
Skill	265
Sky	155
Slope	146
Small	102
Small Amount	221

Small Area	101
Small Bell	272
Snake	174
Snake (Zodiac)	156
Snow	158
Snow Cape	279
Soil	99
Son	200-201, 211
Song	259
Sound	250
South	105
Sow Seed	243
Space	133
Spacious	100
Span	307
Sparrow	174
Speak	219, 260
Speak Truthfully	260
Specialty	307
Specify	247
Spectacle	250
Sphere	272
Spin (Thread)	244
Spirit	229, 235, 299, 303
Splendid	121
Split	115
Spool	280
Spread Out	100, 106
Spring (Season)	127
Spring (Water)	152
Sprout	170
Stairs	134
Stalk	167
Stand Up	114
Star Light	183
State	260
Station	310
Status	310
Stay Over	137
Steadfast	298
Steep Road	129
Stop	238
Stop Up	132
Storehouse	138
Story (Building)	134
Strange	227
Strap	275
Strength	303
Stretch	106
Stretch Out	105
Strive	294
Strong	257, 299, 303
Strong Country	99

Study	229
Successor	207
Sufficient	176
Suitable	311
Summer	127
Summit	307
Sun	155
Superior	102, 289
Support	195
Supporter	178
Surpass	294
Sutra	260
Swamp	150
Sweet Scent	225
Sweet Taste	225
Sword	281
Symbol	260
System	228

T

Tail	176
Take Along	239
Talent	265, 305
Tall	107
Tangerine	161
Tassel	278
Taste	225-226
Tattoo	253
Tea	166
Teacher	196
Teaching	234
Team up	186
Team-Work	186
Temper Steel	243
Temple	139
Ten	215
Ten Thousand	216
Tenth	220
Terrible	310
Territory	99
Text Book	260
That	308
The Mace Plant	165
The Same	220
There	269
Thick	226
Thick (Flat Objects)	106
Thicket	164
Thin	226
Thin (Round Objects)	106
Thin Bamboo	163
Thing	271
Third	219

Third Son	212	Unerring	291	Why?	306
This	269-270	Unexpected	227	Wide Plain	152
This Way	270	Unfeeling	255	Wide Spread	220
Thong	275	Unite	205	Wife	198
Thread	275	Untamed	154	Wild	154
Three	213-214	Unused	184	Willow Tree	160
Tie	244	Unusual	227	Win	257
Tiger	171	Upper	102	Wind	158
Tiger (Zodiac)	156	Urban House	137	Winter	128
Timber	305	Us	187	Wise	266
Time	122	Use	242	Wish	254
To Become	242	Utilize	242	Wisteria	163
Together	186			Woman	198-199
Tomb	139	**V**		Wood	305
Tool	280	Valley	147	Wooden	159
Top	102	Valour	303	Woods	148
Tortoise	175	Vantage	129	Wool	177
Total	307	Victory	257	Word	260
Tough	299	View	129, 250	Work Well	293
Tour	240	Vigor	235	Work Hard	242
Towards	114	Village	141	Worm	174
Town	141	Virgin	184	Worship	229
Toy Ball	271	Visible	183	Worthy	311
Tranquility	110, 209, 292	Visit	214, 240	Wrap	309
Transformation	313	Vista	129	Writing	259-260
Travel	240	Vivid	121		
Travel Straight	260			**Y**	
Treasure	272	**W**		Year	124
Tree	159	Walk	239	Yellow Rose Tree	162
Tree Top	108	Wall	133	Yield Up	307
Trick	307	Wander	240	Yoke	282
Trifling	226	Warehouse	137	Young	120-121, 184
Triumph	257	Warrior	258	Young Rice Plants	165
Troll	171	Wasp	174	Young Scholar	200
True	291	Water	148	Younger Sister	201
True Path	260	Waterfall	151	Youth	200
Trunk	167	Wave	149		
Tubular Box	275	Way	131	**Z**	
Tuft	278	We	187	Zelkova Tree	162
Turbid	226	Weak	226	Zen	229
Turtle	175	Weave	244	Zenith	310
Twig	168	Weighty	301	Zodiac	156
Twist	276	Well	131		
Two	213	Well Controlled	179		
Type	307	Well Done	285		
Typical	220	Well Traveled	266		
		West	104		
U		Whale	175		
Umbrella	273	What	308		
Uncontaminated	285	Wheel of Life	228		
Uncooked Rice	273	Whetstone	281		
Under	103	White	184		
Understand	250, 264	Whither	308		

Phonetic Index

A

A	115, 208
afu	160
agata	99
ai	186, 226
aka	184
ake	179
aki	125, 127-128, 179, 202, 260, 262
akira	179, 260, 262
ama	155, 203, 225
ama'nei	220
AN	208
ana	147
ane	198
ao	184
ara	154
ari	268-269
asa	109, 125, 278
ashi	164, 176
ATSU	176
atsu	298-299
awa	166
aya	225, 259
ayumi	239

B

BA	172, 199
ba	97
BE	113
be	185
BETSU	221
BI	176, 309
BOU	141
BU	212, 231
BUN	259
BUTSU	228

D

DCHA	166
CHI	149, 264-265
chi	216
chika	113, 203-205, 240
CHOU	111
CHUU	103

D

DACHI	239
DAI	101, 277
DO	153, 185
DOU	135

E

E	229, 256
e	151
EI	117, 222, 297
emon	196
EN	105, 113, 273
ETSU	294

F

FU	200, 245, 278
fuchi	149
fuji	163
fuka	109
FUKU	231, 253
fumi	259
funa	275
fune	275
furu	120
fusa	133-134, 278
futa	213
fuyu	128

G

GA	187, 245
GE	168
GEN	183, 200, 216-217
GO	117, 157, 214
GOKU	307
gozen	198
guchi	100

H

HA	149
ha	168, 177
HACHI	215
hachi	174
hagi	164
hajime	116
hako	274
hama	149
HAN	212, 286
hana	168
hane	177
hara	152-153
hari	280
haru	127, 157-158, 191
hase	244
hashi	144
hata	273
hatake	142
haya	122
hayashi	148
HEI	110, 219
HI	227, 294
hi	144, 155
hide	222, 288-289, 297
hiko	200
hime	197
hira	110, 256, 282
hiro	100-101, 106, 220, 266, 297

hisa	119-120, 231	
hito	171, 220, 232, 309	
hitsuji	157	
HO	194, 256	
HOKU	105	
HON	97	
hori	243	
hoso	106	
HOU	174, 191, 235, 256, 272	

I

HI	269, 310
i	131-132, 135
ICHI	212-213
ichi	142
ie	135-136
iha	153
iho	164
ii	274
ike	149
iki	201
iku	268
ima	122
IN	139
ina	165
ino	172, 176
inu	173
iri	100
iro	183
isao	185
ishi	153
iso	242
ita	274
ito	275
ITSU	213
itsu	214
iwa	153-154

J

JI	99, 138, 191, 213, 260, 280, 309
JIKU	163
JIN	220
JOU	137, 189, 292, 311, 313
JU	120, 313
JUU	215

K

KA	102, 151, 168, 173, 186, 245, 272, 285, 313
ka	219, 273
kabe	133
kachi	257
kado	132, 290
kaga	293
kage	182-183
KAI	134, 148
kaji	275
kaki	132, 161
KAKU	309
kama	165, 281
kame	175
kami	102-103, 177, 228
KAN	228, 250, 311
kana	271
kane	132, 205-206, 271-272, 309
karu	226
kasa	101, 273
kashi	160
kata	114, 212, 226, 264, 299
KATSU	165, 219
katsu	257, 305
katsura	161
kawa	150-151, 264
kaze	158
kazu	203, 210, 213, 299, 307-308, 310
KE	103, 194
ke	177
KEI	253
KEN	243, 250, 312
KI	115, 175, 219, 229-230, 232, 244, 254, 265
ki	137, 159, 219, 305
KIKU	164
kimi	192-193
kimo	303
kin	192
kine	281
kinu	279
kiri	158, 162
kishi	149
kita	105
KITSU	232
kiyo	283-284
KO	120, 219, 221
ko	102, 197, 200
koe	294
KOKU	98
koma	172
KON	113
kore	269-270, 275
koto	260, 271
KOU	106-107, 116, 151, 180, 219, 273, 303, 312
KU	119, 215, 280, 310
ku	272
kujira	175
kuma	172
kumo	158
kuni	98-99
kura	137, 161
kuri	161
kuriya	133
kuro	183
kuru	309
kusa	165
kuso	178
kusu	162, 273
KUTSU	120
kuwa	162
kuzu	165
KYOU	142, 253, 312
KYUU	119, 248

M

MA	165
ma	133, 172, 290
machi	141
mae	104
maki	153
maku	243
MAN	216, 223
maro	187
maru	106, 121
masa	114, 180, 189-190, 194, 212, 230, 264, 290-293
masu	221-222
mata	218
matsu	159-160
ME	273
me	177, 198-199
MEI	179
MI	225, 227
mi	129, 176, 201, 213, 219-220, 308
michi	129-131
mina	185
mino	279

Thematic Dictionary — Phonetic Index

mitsu	124, 180-181, 214, 223-224, 306
miya	138
mizo	144
mizu	148
MO	177
mo	116
mochi	166-167, 202, 254, 269-270
momo	160, 215
MON	132, 259
mono	271
mori	148, 193, 222-223
moro	196-197
moto	97, 139-140, 167-168, 217, 310
MOTSU	271
MOU	177
MU	257, 307
mu	214
mune	132, 189, 226, 262-263
mura	141
murasaki	184
mutsu	214
MYOU	227

N

NA	308
na	203, 306
nabe	274
nae	170
naga	111-113, 117-118
NAI	103
naka	103, 217-218, 264
NAN	105
nao	231, 241
nari	240, 242, 267-268, 298-299, 307
naru	243
nashi	161
natsu	127
nawa	282
ne	152, 167, 230
NI	203, 213, 232, 280, 308
NICHI	155
nii	121
NIN	232
nishi	104
nishiki	278
NO	226, 265
no	152, 269

nobu	105, 202, 233-234, 238, 250-251, 260
nori	105, 124, 126-127, 191, 216, 228, 234-235, 240, 253-254, 260, 262, 286-287, 304
NU	303
nu	244
nuki	298
numa	150
nushi	194

O

o	102, 176, 200-201, 244, 258, 275, 303
ogi	164
ohoshi	220
oka	147
oke	274
oki	116
oku	104
omi	193
ON	250
oni	171
oo	101-102, 106
ori	244
osa	113
oto	219
OTSU	219, 294
OU	193, 311-312
oya	200

R

RA	289
REKI	310
REN	163
RI	293
RO	177
ROKU	214, 313
ROU	211
RU	137
RYAKU	310-311
RYUU	174

R

SA	105, 151, 195
sa	186, 286
sachi	253
sada	247-248, 292-293

saemon	196
SAI	104, 213, 229
saka	129, 222, 274
sakaki	162
saki	104, 146
SAKU	243
sakura	160
same	175
samu	158
SAN	145
sana	290
sane	168-169, 181, 290
saru	171
sasa	163
sato	140, 239
sawa	150
SE	235
se	151
SEI	189, 267, 283, 285
SEKI	153
seki	100
SEN	104, 205, 215
SHI	197, 214, 227, 258, 270, 302, 313
shiba	164
shibu	100
SHICHI	214
shige	166-167, 243, 245, 267-268, 301-302
SHIKI	183
shiki	227
shima	146-147
shimo	103
SHIN	203, 220
shina	134, 277, 307
shio	273
shira	184
shiri	117, 178
shiro	124, 137
shishi	308
shita	103
shizu	208, 248
shizuka	208
SHO	97
SHOU	141, 179, 183, 189, 291, 311
SHUU	186
SO	117, 184
so	215
SON	200
sono	142
SOU	186, 262
SU	113, 120, 251, 306

su	116	tomoe	228	wake	264
sue	108, 126, 218	too	109, 113	waki	178
suga	164	tora	156, 171	waku	120
sugi	160	tori	173, 239	waraha	200
SUI	148	torn	173	we	229
suke	105, 186, 194-195, 229, 305-306	toshi	124, 126, 231, 242, 252, 293-294	wi	172
suki	307	TOU	104, 139, 163, 240, 242	wo	102, 221, 266, 285, 308
SUKU	137	toyo	231	WOU	199
sumi	114, 284-285	TSU	142		
suru	122	tsu	148		
suzu	272	tsubo	142		
suzushi	255	tsuchi	153		

Y

ya	126, 137, 147, 160, 215, 254, 281
yabu	164
yaka	135-136
yama	145-146
yanagi	160
yasu	208-209, 253, 256, 290, 303-304
YO	186
yo	124, 255
yoko	109
yon	214
yone	273
yori	114, 240, 245-247
yoshi	121, 158, 180, 216, 225, 232, 247, 253-255, 265-266, 284-285, 289, 295-297, 306
YOU	313
YU	98, 148, 240
yuki	158, 225, 237-238, 244, 253
YUU	303

U

TA	106, 221	tsuge	162
ta	143-144	tsugi	213, 218
tachi	114, 137	tsugu	187, 207, 218, 298
tada	241, 264, 270, 276, 293, 299-301	tsuka	139, 307
tahe	227	tsuki	155, 162, 242
TAI	101	tsukuri	244
taira	110	tsuma	198
taka	107-109, 173-174, 202, 219, 225, 230, 297, 302	tsume	178
take	162, 243, 257, 312	tsuna	276
taki	151	tsune	118, 260-262
tama	272	tsunu	114
tame	290	tsura	130, 237, 239, 298
TAN	184, 222, 226	tsuru	174
tane	167, 170, 206-207	tsutsu	275
tani	147	tsutsumi	144
tari	176		
taru	240		
tate	137		
tatsu	114, 156, 174-175		
TE	282		
te	176		
TEI	219, 292, 314		
TEN	155		
tera	138		
teru	179		
TO	153, 173, 206, 216, 239, 281		
to	133, 215, 245, 281		
toki	122-124, 156, 260		
toko	133		
TOKU	304		
tomare	254		
tomi	201, 245		
tomo	125-126, 185-186, 192, 201, 206, 236, 265, 269, 280		

U

U	105, 132
uchi	103
ue	103
ueki	167
uemon	196
ui	244
uji	187-189
uma	172
ume	161
umi	148
uo	175
ura	149, 232, 247
uri	166
ushi	172
usu	226, 281

W

WA	209-210
wa	187
waka	120

Z

ZE	269
ZEN	229, 247
ZOU	138, 213
ZU	310

❖ Spacial Relationships ❖

場 Place / Location

While *tokoro* 所 refers to a place where an activity is performed and commonly refers to a building or even an individual room, *ba* 場 commonly refers to a piece of land or someplace located within larger geography.

Reading	Type	Example	Kanji	Period	Date	Added Meaning
ba	S	Aeba	饗場	Nanboku	1392	Banquet
ba	S	Baba	馬場	Uncertain	1600	Horse

所 Place / Location / Duty Station

This is an abstract substantive element referring to a place or location. Specifically, it is used to describe a place dedicated to performing some task such as cooking or administration.

Reading	Type	Example	Kanji	Period	Date	Added Meaning
SHO	S	Bessho	別所	Sengoku	1568	Separate / Different

本 Main / Original / Root / Base

Note that this character is also used as a "counter" of long thin things. These counters are derived from Chinese and take their Chinese readings. In Japanese, each kind of object has its distinctive counter. This used to be a common practice in English and is being lost from Japanese as well. Thus, this counter appears in names such as Roppongi 六本木 which means "Six Trees".

Reading	Type	Example	Kanji	Period	Date	Added Meaning
HON	S	Honda	本多	Momoyama	1529	Many
HON	S	Honjou	本庄	Kamakura	1332	Rural / Hometown
HON	S	Honma	本間	Kamakura	1332	Room / Space
moto	S	Kakimoto	柿本	Uncertain	1600	Persimmon
moto	S	Kimoto	木本	Nanboku	1392	Tree
moto	S	Matsumoto	松本	Sengoku	1468	Pine Tree
moto	S	Miyamoto	宮本	Sengoku	1568	Palace
moto	S	Okamoto	岡本	Sengoku	1568	Hill
moto	S	Yamamoto	山本	Hei'an	1183	Mountain

源 Origin

Reading	Type	Example	Kanji	Period	Date	Added Meaning
GEN	M	Genjirou	源次郎	Uncertain	1600	Second Son
moto	N	Moto'uji	源氏	Kamakura	1332	Family / Clan
moto	S	Mi'namoto	源	Hei'an	1183	

由 Origin / Purpose

Reading	Type	Example	Kanji	Period	Date	Added Meaning
YU	F	Yukime	由伎賣	Nara	784	Artisan / Artistry / Craft / Skill
YU	S	Yu'i	由井	Kamakura	1332	Well
YU	S	Yura	由良	Kamakura	1332	Good / Superior
YU	S	Yuri	由利	Kamakura	1332	Produce Results / Work Well

国 Country / Rural Area

Note that both *kuni* 国 and *kuni* 邦 are used in the names of countries. *Kuni* 邦 tends to be used in the names of federated republics such as the Soviet Union and Burma. *Kuni* 国 is used in the names of more homogeneous countries such as Japan and China.

Reading	Type	Example	Kanji	Period	Date	Added Meaning
KOKU	Y	Koukoku	興国	Nanboku	1340	Happen / Begin
KOKU	S	Kokubu	国分	Kamakura	1332	Piece / Bit / Part
kuni	F	Ku'niko	国子	Hei'an	1183	[Lady]
kuni	N	Akiku'ni	顕国	Nanboku	1392	High Status
kuni	N	Chikaku'ni	親国	Hei'an	1183	Intimate
kuni	N	Hisaku'ni	久国	Muromachi	1572	Longtime
kuni	N	Ku'nihira	国衡	Kamakura	1189	A Yoke
kuni	N	Ku'nihira	国平	Kamakura	1332	Tranquility
kuni	N	Ku'nika	国香	Uncertain	1600	Incense
kuni	N	Ku'nikiyo	国清	Nanboku	1392	Pure
kuni	N	Ku'nimoto	国基	Kamakura	1332	Foundation
kuni	N	Ku'ni'naga	国長	Nanboku	1392	Long
kuni	N	Ku'ni'nobu	国信	Muromachi	1572	Belief / Faith
kuni	N	Ku'nishige	国重	Kamakura	1332	Heavy / Serious
kuni	N	Ku'nitsu'na	国綱	Hei'an	1183	Net
kuni	N	Ku'niyasu	国泰	Nanboku	1392	Peace / Plentitude
kuni	N	Masaku'ni	政国	Muromachi	1572	Govern / Rule
kuni	N	Mitsuku'ni	光国	Kamakura	1332	Bright / Shining
kuni	N	Mochiku'ni	持国	Muromachi	1572	Have / Possess
kuni	N	Moriku'ni	盛国	Hei'an	1183	Plentiful / Piled Up
kuni	N	Motoku'ni	基国	Nanboku	1392	Foundation
kuni	N	Motoku'ni	元国	Muromachi	1572	Base / Original
kuni	N	Nakaku'ni	仲国	Kamakura	1332	Middle of a Group
kuni	N	Noriku'ni	範国	Nanboku	1392	Required Form / Pattern
kuni	N	Sadaku'ni	貞国	Muromachi	1572	Correct Spirit
kuni	N	Sa'neku'ni	実国	Hei'an	1183	Reality
kuni	N	Shigeku'ni	重国	Kamakura	1332	Heavy / Serious
kuni	N	Sukeku'ni	資国	Kamakura	1332	Raw Materials
kuni	N	Sukeku'ni	助国	Kamakura	1332	Deputy (Rescue / Assist)
kuni	N	Tadaku'ni	忠国	Nanboku	1392	Faithful / Loyal
kuni	N	Takaku'ni	隆国	Uncertain	1600	Grow / Pile Up
kuni	N	Tokiku'ni	言国	Muromachi	1572	Speak Truthfully
kuni	N	Tsu'neku'ni	経国	Kamakura	1332	True Path
kuni	N	Ujiku'ni	氏国	Kamakura	1332	Family / Clan
kuni	N	Yoshiku'ni	義国	Hei'an	1183	Fealty
kuni	S	Oku'ni	小国	Uncertain	1600	Small

邦 Nation / Land / Big Country

Note that both *kuni* 国 and *kuni* 邦 are used in the names of countries. *Kuni* 邦 tends to be used in the names of federated republics such as the Soviet Union and Burma. *Kuni* 国 is used in the names of more homogeneous countries such as Japan and China.

Reading	Type	Example	Kanji	Period	Date	Added Meaning
kuni	N	Ka'neku'ni	兼邦	Nanboku	1392	Unite
kuni	N	Kiyoku'ni	清邦	Hei'an	1183	Pure
kuni	N	Ku'nimichi	邦通	Kamakura	1332	Pass Through
kuni	N	Ku'nimichi	邦道	Hei'an	1183	Road / Way
kuni	N	Ku'nimitsu	邦光	Nanboku	1392	Bright / Shining
kuni	N	Ku'ni'nari	邦業	Kamakura	1332	Industry / Diligence
kuni	N	Ku'nitoki	邦時	Uncertain	1600	Time / Era
kuni	N	Ku'nitsu'na	邦綱	Hei'an	1183	Net

県 Territory / Province

These are land allocations and therefore are dependent upon superior authority. This appears to be a relic of the land allocation system instituted by the Taika Reform. Under this system, various offices and titles were to carry land allocations. These were strictly speaking dependencies of the central imperial government. Later, they reverted to being heritable land rights. An *agata* was one of the largest land subdivisions under this system and would include towns and villages. In modern Japan, this notion has been revived and this letter is used to form the names of Japanese prefectures.

Reading	Type	Example	Kanji	Period	Date	Added Meaning
agata	S	Yamagata	山県	Uncertain	1600	Mountain

地 Soil / Country

Reading	Type	Example	Kanji	Period	Date	Added Meaning
JI	F	Jizoumae	地蔵前	Kamakura	1332	Storehouse + Antecedent
JI	F	Jizoume	地蔵女	Kamakura	1332	Storehouse + [Woman]
JI	S	Kaji	加地	Uncertain	1600	Join Up / Enlist

漢 China (Han Dynasty)

While 漢 was originally a name for the Yangtze River, its meaning was extended to include all of the main part of China. *Kan* 漢 is also attached to one of the Chinese dynasties and to the Milky Way. Thus, Ayame is probably the name of the daughter of a Chinese immigrant or a classics scholar.

Reading	Type	Example	Kanji	Period	Date	Added Meaning
aya	F	Ayame	漢賣	Nara	784	

秦 Strong Country (Shin Region of China)

Reading	Type	Example	Kanji	Period	Date	Added Meaning
hata	S	Hata	秦	Nanboku	1392	

関 Barrier

Reading	Type	Example	Kanji	Period	Date	Added Meaning
seki	P	Sekigahara	関ヶ原	Momoyama	1600	Meadow
seki	S	Oozeki	大関	Sengoku	1568	Big
seki	S	Seki	関	Sengoku	1568	

口 Mouth / Entrance / Exit

The **K** in *kuchi* 口 is voiced following vowels and syllabic **N** to become a **G**. *Kuchi* is always substantive and never descriptive. Thus, it is always read as "guchi" in names.

Reading	Type	Example	Kanji	Period	Date	Added Meaning
guchi	S	Awataguchi	粟田口	Kamakura	1332	Millet + Paddy
guchi	S	Higuchi	樋口	Hei'an	1183	Flume
guchi	S	Horiguchi	堀口	Nanboku	1392	Dig / Carve / Excavation
guchi	S	Mizoguchi	溝口	Sengoku	1568	Ditch / Gutter
guchi	S	Okeguchi	桶口	Uncertain	1600	Barrel
guchi	S	Taguchi	田口	Hei'an	1183	Rice Paddy
guchi	S	Yamaguchi	山口	Sengoku	1568	Mountain

入 Enter / Entrance

Reading	Type	Example	Kanji	Period	Date	Added Meaning
iri	F	Irimashime	入坐賣	Nara	784	Sit Quietly

渋 Blocked Off / Obstructed

Reading	Type	Example	Kanji	Period	Date	Added Meaning
shibu	S	Shibukawa	渋川	Nanboku	1392	River
shibu	S	Shibuya	渋谷	Kamakura	1332	Valley

広 Spacious / Spread Out / Expansive

Reading	Type	Example	Kanji	Period	Date	Added Meaning
hiro	N	Akihiro	顕広	Hei'an	1183	High Status
hiro	N	Chikahiro	親広	Kamakura	1332	Intimate
hiro	N	Fujihiro	藤広	Sengoku	1568	Wisteria
hiro	N	Hiro'aki	広明	Kamakura	1332	Bright
hiro	N	Hirochika	広周	Muromachi	1572	Tour / Travel / Bountiful Land
hiro	N	Hirofusa	広房	Kamakura	1332	Monastic Cell
hiro	N	Hirokado	広門	Sengoku	1568	Gate
hiro	N	Hirokoto	広言	Kamakura	1332	Speak Truthfully
hiro	N	Hiromoto	広元	Kamakura	1332	Base / Original
hiro	N	Hirosada	広定	Sengoku	1568	Determine
hiro	N	Hirotsugu	広嗣	Uncertain	1600	Successor
hiro	N	Hirotsu'na	広綱	Kamakura	1332	Net
hiro	N	Hirotsu'ne	広常	Hei'an	1183	Permanent
hiro	N	Hirozumi	広澄	Sengoku	1568	Cleanse / Purify
hiro	N	Mu'nehiro	宗広	Kamakura	1332	Master an Art

Thematic Dictionary — Spacial Relationships 101

Reading	Type	Example	Kanji	Period	Date	Added Meaning
hiro	N	Nobuhiro	信広	Muromachi	1572	Belief / Faith
hiro	N	Norihiro	範広	Nanboku	1392	Required Form / Pattern
hiro	N	Sadahiro	貞広	Nanboku	1392	Correct Spirit
hiro	N	Shigehiro	重広	Kamakura	1332	Heavy / Serious
hiro	N	Tamehiro	為広	Sengoku	1568	Purpose / Goal
hiro	N	Tokihiro	時広	Kamakura	1332	Time / Era
hiro	N	Tomohiro	朝広	Kamakura	1332	Morning
hiro	N	Yoshihiro	嘉広	Higashiyama	1575	Well Done
hiro	N	Yukihiro	行広	Muromachi	1572	Going To / Bound For

狭 Cramped / Small Area

Reading	Type	Example	Kanji	Period	Date	Added Meaning
kasa	S	Nagasa	長狭	Hei'an	1183	Long / Oldest / Senior
kasa	S	Wakasa	若狭	Kamakura	1332	Young

大 Big

Reading	Type	Example	Kanji	Period	Date	Added Meaning
DAI	Y	Daiji	大治	Hei'an	1126	Govern / Rule
TAI	F	Taifu	大輔	Kamakura	1332	Ministerial Deputy
TAI	Y	Tai'ei	大永	Sengoku	1521	Forever
TAI	Y	Taishou	大正	Modern	1912	Unerring / Genuine
oo	F	Ohoneme	大根賣	Nara	784	Root / Base
oo	F	Ohotsume	大津女	Nara	784	Harbour + [Woman]
oo	F	Ohoyame	大家女	Nara	784	Family + [Woman]
oo	F	Oohime	大姫	Kamakura	1197	Princess
oo	F	Ooshiamame	大海賣	Nara	784	Sea
oo	S	Ooba	大庭	Hei'an	1183	Garden / Courtyard / Atrium
oo	S	Oobatake	大畠	Uncertain	1600	Dry Field
oo	S	Oobayashi	大林	Uncertain	1600	Forest
oo	S	Ooda	大田	Kamakura	1332	Rice Paddy
oo	S	Oodachi	大館	Nanboku	1392	Mansion / Hall
oo	S	Oo'e	大江	Hei'an	1183	Inlet / Harbour / Cove
oo	S	Oogimachi	大親広	Kamakura	1332	Intimate + Town
oo	S	Oohara	大原	Kamakura	1332	Meadow
oo	S	Oo'i	大井	Uncertain	1600	Well
oo	S	Oo'i'da	大井田	Kamakura	1332	Rice Paddy Well
oo	S	Oomiya	大宮	Nanboku	1392	Palace
oo	S	Oomori	大森	Nanboku	1392	Woods
oo	S	Oomura	大村	Sengoku	1568	Village
oo	S	Oo'naka	大中	Hei'an	1183	Middle
oo	S	Oo'nakatomi	大中友	Hei'an	1183	Middle + Friend
oo	S	Oo'no	大乃	Hei'an	1183	There
oo	S	Oo'no	大野	Sengoku	1568	Wide Plain
oo	S	Oosaki	大崎	Uncertain	1600	Slope
oo	S	Ooshima	大島	Uncertain	1600	Island
oo	S	Oosuga	大須賀	Kamakura	1332	Necessity + Celebrate A Gain
oo	S	Ootaka	大高	Nanboku	1392	Tall
oo	S	Ootani	大谷	Sengoku	1568	Valley
oo	S	Ootomo	大友	Kamakura	1332	Friend
oo	S	Ootsubo	大坪	Kamakura	1332	Palace Garden
oo	S	Ootsuka	大塚	Nanboku	1392	Mound / Tomb
oo	S	Oo'uchi	大内	Kamakura	1332	Inside

Reading	Type	Example	Kanji	Period	Date	Added Meaning
oo	S	Ooyama	大山	Sengoku	1568	Mountain
oo	S	Ooya'no	大矢野	Kamakura	1332	Arrow + Wide Plain
oo	S	Oozeki	大関	Sengoku	1568	Barrier
[Special]	S	Yamato	大和	Hei'an	1183	Peace / Tranquility

小 Small

Reading	Type	Example	Kanji	Period	Date	Added Meaning
ko	F	Kodamame	小玉賣	Nara	784	Jewel / Sphere
ko	F	Ko'imome	小妹賣	Nara	784	Younger Sister
ko	F	Ko'i'name	小稲賣	Nara	784	Young Rice Plants
ko	F	Kojimame	小嶋賣	Nara	784	Island
ko	F	Kokurome	小黒女	Nara	784	Black + [Woman]
ko	F	Ko'ne'neme	小子々女	Muromachi	1572	[Lady] + [Woman]
ko	F	Kosasa	小笹	Kamakura	1332	Thin Bamboo
ko	F	Kotori	小鳥	Kamakura	1332	Bird
ko	F	Koyakatoyome	小宅豊賣	Nara	784	Noble Residence
ko	S	Kobayakawa	小早川	Kamakura	1332	River Fast / Early
ko	S	Kokasahara	小笠原	Uncertain	1600	Umbrella+ Meadow
ko	S	Ko'nishi	小西	Sengoku	1568	West
ko	S	Koyama	小山	Uncertain	1600	Mountain
o	F	Ohirame	小比良賣	Nara	784	Strive + Good / Superior
o	F	Omi'nome	小蓑賣	Nara	784	Rain or Snow Cape
o	F	Omiyame	小宮賣	Nara	784	Palace
o	F	Owime	小猪賣	Nara	784	Boar
o	S	Obata	小幡	Uncertain	1600	Flag / Banner
o	S	Oda	小田	Nanboku	1392	Rice Paddy
o	S	Ogasawara	小笠原	Nanboku	1392	Umbrella + Meadow
o	S	Ogashima	小鹿島	Kamakura	1332	Small + Island
o	S	Ogawa	小川	Uncertain	1600	River
o	S	Ogura	小倉	Kamakura	1332	Warehouse
o	S	Oguri	小栗	Muromachi	1572	Chestnut
o	S	Oku'ni	小国	Uncertain	1600	Country / Rural Area
o	S	O'no	小野	Hei'an	1183	Wide Plain
o	S	O'nodera	小野寺	Uncertain	1600	Wide Plain Temple
o	S	Oyama	小山	Kamakura	1332	Mountain
o	S	Oyamada	小山田	Nanboku	1392	Mountain Rice Paddy
o	S	Ozuki	小槻	Kamakura	1332	Zelkova Tree
wo	F	Wogusome	小屎賣	Nara	784	Feces
wo	F	Wohirame	小比良賣	Nara	784	Strive + Good / Superior
wo	F	Womi'nome	小蓑賣	Nara	784	Rain or Snow Cape
wo	F	Wotome	小女	Hei'an	1183	[Woman]
[Special]	F	Sayo	小夜	Uncertain	1600	Evening

上 Above = ue / Upper or Superior or Top = kami

Reading	Type	Example	Kanji	Period	Date	Added Meaning
KA	S	Kazusa	上総	Kamakura	1332	Tuft / Fringe / Tassel
kami	S	Kamiyama	上山	Nanboku	1392	Mountain
kami	S	Mogami	最上	Uncertain	1600	Most
kami	S	Murakami	村上	Kamakura	1332	Village
kami	S	Nogami	野上	Nanboku	1392	Wide Plain
kami	S	Sakagami	坂上	Nanboku	1392	Steep Road
kami	S	Uragami	浦上	Muromachi	1572	Bay / Delta

Reading	Type	Example	Kanji	Period	Date	Added Meaning
kami	S	Urakami	浦上	Uncertain	1600	Bay / Delta
ue	S	Saka'no'ue	坂上	Kamakura	1332	Steep Road
ue	S	Ue'no	上野	Nanboku	1392	Wide Plain
ue	S	Uesugi	上杉	Kamakura	1332	Cedar Tree
ue	S	Ueta	上田	Sengoku	1568	Rice Paddy
ue	S	Yama'no'ue	山上	Nanboku	1392	Mountain

中 Middle

Reading	Type	Example	Kanji	Period	Date	Added Meaning
CHUU	Y	Bunchuu	文中	Nanboku	1372	Literature / Culture
CHUU	Y	Genchuu	元中	Nanboku	1384	Base / Original
CHUU	Y	Shouchuu	正中	Kamakura	1324	Unerring / Genuine
naka	S	Nakazawa	中澤	Muromachi	1572	Glen / Run
naka	S	Naka'e	中江	Sengoku	1568	Inlet / Harbour / Cove
naka	S	Nakagawa	中川	Sengoku	1568	River
naka	S	Nakahara	中原	Hei'an	1183	Meadow
naka	S	Naka'i	中井	Sengoku	1568	Well
naka	S	Nakajou	中条	Kamakura	1332	Branch / Line / Road
naka	S	Nakamura	中村	Kamakura	1332	Village
naka	S	Naka'no	中野	Kamakura	1332	Wide Plain
naka	S	Oo'naka	大中	Hei'an	1183	Big
naka	S	Oo'nakatomi	大中友	Hei'an	1183	Big + Friend
naka	S	Take'naka	竹中	Sengoku	1568	Bamboo
naka	S	Ta'naka	田中	Hei'an	1183	Rice Paddy

下 Under = shita / Lower or Bottom or Inferior = shimo

Note that the **K** in **KE** is voiced following vowels and syllabic **N**.

Reading	Type	Example	Kanji	Period	Date	Added Meaning
KE	S	Kuge	久下	Hei'an	1183	Longtime
shimo	S	Shimotsuma	下妻	Kamakura	1332	[Wife]
shita	S	Ki'no'shita	木下	Sengoku	1568	Tree
shita	S	Matsushita	松下	Sengoku	1568	Pine Tree

内 Inside

Please note that the 'u' in *uchi* can be subarticulated following a vowel.

Reading	Type	Example	Kanji	Period	Date	Added Meaning
NAI	S	Naitou	内藤	Kamakura	1332	Wisteria
uchi	N	Uchitsu'ne	内経	Kamakura	1332	True Path
uchi	N	Uchiza'ne	内実	Kamakura	1332	Reality
uchi	S	Hori'uchi	堀内	Sengoku	1568	Dig / Carve / Excavation
uchi	S	Kawachi	河内	Uncertain	1600	Large River
uchi	S	Kawa'uchihara	河内原	Uncertain	1600	Large River + Meadow
uchi	S	Ko'uchi	河内	Uncertain	1600	Large River
uchi	S	Oo'uchi	大内	Kamakura	1332	Big
uchi	S	Saka'uchi	坂内	Uncertain	1600	Steep Road
uchi	S	Yabu'no'uchi	藪内	Sengoku	1568	Grove / Thicket
uchi	S	Yama'no'uchi	山内	Hei'an	1183	Mountain
uchi	S	Yama'uchi	山内	Muromachi	1572	Mountain

奥 Innermost

Reading	Type	Example	Kanji	Period	Date	Added Meaning
oku	S	Okuyama	奥山	Sengoku	1568	Mountain

前 Antecedent

Reading	Type	Example	Kanji	Period	Date	Added Meaning
SEN	S	Bizen	備前	Hei'an	1183	Prepare
mae	S	Maeba	前波	Sengoku	1568	Wave
mae	S	Maeda	前田	Sengoku	1568	Rice Paddy
saki	F	Sakiko	前子	Momoyama	1590	[Lady]
saki	N	Fusasaki	房前	Uncertain	1600	Monastic Cell
saki	N	Sakiyori	前頼	Nanboku	1392	Request / Ask

東 East

Please note that the T in TO can be voiced to form DO following a vowel or syllabic N.

Reading	Type	Example	Kanji	Period	Date	Added Meaning
TOU	S	Andou	安東	Kamakura	1332	Gentle / Safe / Secure
TOU	S	Itou	伊東	Hei'an	1183	This
TOU	S	Kaitou	海東	Kamakura	1332	Sea
TOU	S	Katou	加東	Uncertain	1600	Join Up / Enlist
TOU	S	Koutou	厚東	Nanboku	1392	Thick
[Special]	F	Azuma	東	Nara	784	
[Special]	F	Azumame	東方賣	Nara	784	Direction / Method

西 West

Please note that the S in SAI can be voiced to form ZAI following a vowel.

Reading	Type	Example	Kanji	Period	Date	Added Meaning
SAI	S	Kasai	葛西	Kamakura	1332	Arrowroot
SAI	S	Kouzai	香西	Kamakura	1332	Incense
SAI	P	Sai'dai'ji	西大寺	Nara	765	Big + Temple
nishi	F	Nishi	西	Momoyama	1590	
nishi	N	Nishikintoki	西公時	Nanboku	1392	Noble + Time / Era
nishi	N	Nishikin'yasu	西公保	Muromachi	1572	Noble + Guarantee
nishi	N	Nishisa'netaka	西実隆	Muromachi	1572	Reality Grow / Pile Up
nishi	S	Ima'nishi	今西	Uncertain	1600	Now
nishi	S	Ko'nishi	小西	Sengoku	1568	Small
nishi	S	Nishimura	西村	Sengoku	1568	Village
nishi	S	Nishi'o	西尾	Sengoku	1568	Tail
nishi	S	Nishiyama	西山	Sengoku	1568	Mountain
nishi	S	Tera'nishi	寺西	Sengoku	1568	Temple

南 South

Reading	Type	Example	Kanji	Period	Date	Added Meaning
NAN	S	Nanbu	南部	Kamakura	1332	Monopoly Corporation
minami	F	Mi'namime	南賣	Nara	784	

北 North

The reading, "HOU" in Houjou, is due to a phonetic transformation.

Reading	Type	Example	Kanji	Period	Date	Added Meaning
HOKU	S	Houjou	北条	Kamakura	1332	Branch / Line / Road
kita	F	Kita	北	Momoyama	1590	
kita	S	Kitabatake	北畠	Nanboku	1392	Dry Field

左 Left

Note special use in Saemon.

Reading	Type	Example	Kanji	Period	Date	Added Meaning
SA	M	Genza'emon	源左衛門	Kamakura	1332	Origin + Ministry

右 Right

Note special use in Uemon.

Reading	Type	Example	Kanji	Period	Date	Added Meaning
U	M	Moto'u'emon	源右衛門	Uncertain	1600	Origin + Ministry
U	F	Ukon	右近	Uncertain	1600	Near
suke	N	Takasuke	隆右	Nanboku	1392	Grow / Pile Up

矩 Quadrant / Rectangle / Regulated

Reading	Type	Example	Kanji	Period	Date	Added Meaning
nori	N	Mu'ne'nori	宗矩	Kamakura	1332	Master an Art

延 Prolong / Stretch Out

Reading	Type	Example	Kanji	Period	Date	Added Meaning
EN	Y	Enbun	延文	Nanboku	1356	Literature / Culture
EN	Y	Engen	延元	Nanboku	1336	Base / Original
EN	Y	Enkyou	延慶	Kamakura	1308	Rejoice / Deer Skin
EN	Y	Enkyou	延享	Edo	1744	Receive
EN	Y	Enkyuu	延久	Hei'an	1069	Longtime
EN	Y	En'ou	延応	Kamakura	1239	Worthy / Suitable
EN	Y	Enpou	延宝	Edo	1673	Treasure
EN	Y	Entoku	延徳	Sengoku	1489	Righteous / Just
EN	Y	Hou'en	保延	Hei'an	1135	Guarantee
EN	Y	Kan'en	寛延	Edo	1748	Domestic Tranquility
EN	Y	Man'en	万延	Edo	1860	Ten Thousand
nobu	N	Mori'nobu	守延	Kamakura	1332	Protect / Defend
nobu	N	Nobu'nori	延礼	Muromachi	1572	Offering / Courtesy

弘 Draw / Stretch / Spread Out

Reading	Type	Example	Kanji	Period	Date	Added Meaning
KOU	Y	Kankou	寬弘	Hei'an	1004	Domestic Tranquility
KOU	Y	Kou'an	弘安	Kamakura	1278	Gentle / Safe / Secure
KOU	Y	Kouchou	弘長	Kamakura	1261	Long / Oldest / Senior
KOU	Y	Kouji	弘治	Sengoku	1555	Govern / Rule
KOU	Y	Kouka	弘化	Edo	1844	Change / Transformation
KOU	Y	Kouwa	弘和	Nanboku	1381	Peace / Tranquility / Harmony
hiro	N	Arihiro	在弘	Nanboku	1392	Lives / Exist
hiro	N	Hiroshige	弘茂	Muromachi	1572	Blossoming
hiro	N	Hiroyo	弘世	Nanboku	1392	Generation / Life
hiro	N	Kagehiro	景弘	Hei'an	1183	Bright / Magnificent
hiro	N	Masahiro	政弘	Sengoku	1568	Govern / Rule
hiro	N	Morihiro	盛弘	Muromachi	1572	Plentiful / Piled Up
hiro	N	Mu'nehiro	宗弘	Kamakura	1332	Master an Art
hiro	N	Nagahiro	修弘	Sengoku	1568	Polish / Refine / Practice
hiro	N	Norihiro	教弘	Muromachi	1572	Teaching / Dogma
hiro	N	Sukehiro	佐弘	Kamakura	1332	Military Deputy
hiro	N	Ujihiro	氏弘	Muromachi	1572	Family / Clan
hiro	N	Yoshihiro	義弘	Kamakura	1332	Fealty

太 Fat / Rotund

This character is commonly found as part of a suffix used to form the names of men and boys. Please refer to the entry "TAROU" for this usage. This *kanji* is generally applied to round people, animals, or objects.

Reading	Type	Example	Kanji	Period	Date	Added Meaning
TA	F	Tarime	太利賣	Nara	784	Produce Results
TA	N	Mu'neta	宗太	Uncertain	1600	Master an Art
oo	S	Oota	太田	Muromachi	1572	Rice Paddy

丸 Round

This *kanji* replaces *maro* 麿 or 麻呂 in modern names and is found as an affectionate suffix attached to the names of ships or young boys. Please refer to the entry for 丸 Young/Healthy on page 121 for an extended discussion of this usage. Here, 丸 is a physical descriptive originating in a pictograph of a stooped human body.

Reading	Type	Example	Kanji	Period	Date	Added Meaning
maru	S	Tamaru	田丸	Sengoku	1568	Rice Paddy

厚 Thick (Flat Objects)

Reading	Type	Example	Kanji	Period	Date	Added Meaning
KOU	S	Koutou	厚東	Nanboku	1392	East

細 Narrow / Thin (Round Objects)

This *kanji* is generally applied to long and generally round objects such as people, brushes, and, roads.

Reading	Type	Example	Kanji	Period	Date	Added Meaning
hoso	F	Hosomeme	細目賣	Nara	784	Eye
hoso	S	Hosokawa	細川	Nanboku	1392	River

高　Tall / High

Reading	Type	Example	Kanji	Period	Date	Added Meaning
KOU	S	Kousaka	高坂	Nanboku	1392	Steep Road
taka	F	Takai	高子	Hei'an	1183	[Lady]
taka	F	Takako	高子	Hei'an	1183	[Lady]
taka	N	Atsutaka	淳高	Kamakura	1332	Steadfast / Honest / Natural
taka	N	Ietaka	家高	Kamakura	1332	Rural House / Family
taka	N	Kagetaka	景高	Hei'an	1183	Bright / Magnificent
taka	N	Kiyotaka	清高	Kamakura	1332	Pure
taka	N	Masataka	政高	Muromachi	1572	Govern / Rule
taka	N	Mitsutaka	満高	Nanboku	1392	Become Full / Abundant
taka	N	Moritaka	盛高	Muromachi	1572	Plentiful / Piled Up
taka	N	Noritaka	教高	Nanboku	1392	Teaching / Dogma
taka	N	Sadataka	貞高	Muromachi	1572	Correct Spirit
taka	N	Sadataka	定高	Kamakura	1332	Determine
taka	N	Shigetaka	重高	Hei'an	1183	Heavy / Serious
taka	N	Taka'aki	高顕	Nanboku	1392	High Status
taka	N	Taka'aki	高詮	Nanboku	1392	Explicit / Clear
taka	N	Taka'aki	高明	Uncertain	1600	Bright
taka	N	Takachika	高親	Muromachi	1572	Intimate
taka	N	Takahide	高秀	Nanboku	1392	Extraordinary / Bountiful
taka	N	Takahira	高衡	Kamakura	1332	A Yoke
taka	N	Takahisa	高久	Uncertain	1600	Longtime
taka	N	Taka'ie	高家	Kamakura	1332	Rural House / Family
taka	N	Takakage	高景	Kamakura	1332	Bright / Magnificent
taka	N	Takakazu	高数	Muromachi	1572	Fate / Determined Amount
taka	N	Takakiyo	高清	Hei'an	1183	Pure
taka	N	Takamasa	高政	Sengoku	1568	Govern / Rule
taka	N	Takamitsu	高光	Muromachi	1572	Bright / Shining
taka	N	Takamochi	高望	Uncertain	1600	Heartfelt Wish
taka	N	Takamoto	高幹	Nanboku	1392	Trunk / Stalk
taka	N	Takamoto	高元	Nanboku	1392	Base / Original
taka	N	Takamu'ne	高宗	Nanboku	1392	Master an Art
taka	N	Taka'naga	高長	Uncertain	1600	Long
taka	N	Taka'nao	高直	Hei'an	1183	Adjust / Correct
taka	N	Taka'nobu	高信	Kamakura	1332	Belief / Faith
taka	N	Taka'nori	高詮	Nanboku	1392	Explicit / Clear
taka	N	Taka'nori	高徳	Nanboku	1392	Righteous / Just
taka	N	Takasada	高貞	Nanboku	1392	Correct Spirit
taka	N	Takashige	高重	Kamakura	1332	Heavy / Serious
taka	N	Takasuke	高資	Kamakura	1332	Raw Materials
taka	N	Takasuke	高祐	Sengoku	1568	Divine Help
taka	N	Takatoki	高時	Kamakura	1332	Time / Era
taka	N	Takatomo	高知	Kamakura	1332	Knowledge
taka	N	Takatora	高虎	Sengoku	1568	Tiger
taka	N	Takatsu'na	高綱	Hei'an	1183	Net
taka	N	Takatsu'ne	高経	Kamakura	1332	True Path
taka	N	Takatsura	高連	Nanboku	1392	Bring Along
taka	N	Taka'uji	高氏	Kamakura	1332	Family / Clan
taka	N	Tokitaka	時高	Kamakura	1332	Time / Era
taka	N	Tsu'netaka	経高	Hei'an	1183	True Path
taka	N	Yasutaka	泰高	Muromachi	1572	Peace / Plentitude
taka	N	Yoshitaka	義高	Hei'an	1183	Fealty
taka	N	Yukitaka	行高	Kamakura	1332	Going To / Bound For
taka	S	Ootaka	大高	Nanboku	1392	Big

Reading	Type	Example	Kanji	Period	Date	Added Meaning
taka	S	Takahashi	高橋	Sengoku	1568	Bridge
taka	S	Taka'i	高井	Kamakura	1332	Well
taka	S	Taka'ishi	高石	Kamakura	1332	Rock
taka	S	Takaki	高木	Sengoku	1568	Tree
taka	S	Takama	高間	Nanboku	1392	Room / Space
taka	S	Takamatsu	高松	Nanboku	1392	Pine Tree
taka	S	Takanashi	高梨	Uncertain	1600	Pear Tree
taka	S	Takashi'na	高階	Kamakura	1332	Level / Rank
taka	S	Takata	高田	Sengoku	1568	Rice Paddy
taka	S	Takatsu	高津	Nanboku	1392	Harbour
taka	S	Takaya	高賀谷	Muromachi	1572	Celebrate A Gain + Valley

標 Tree Top

This meaning for this *kanji* has been extended to signs and symbols. The basic idea is intentional public display.

Reading	Type	Example	Kanji	Period	Date	Added Meaning
sue	N	Takasue	孝標	Hei'an	1008	Filial Loyalty

隆 Grow Tall / Pile Up

Reading	Type	Example	Kanji	Period	Date	Added Meaning
taka	N	Chikataka	親隆	Hei'an	1183	Intimate
taka	N	Ietaka	家隆	Kamakura	1332	Rural House / Family
taka	N	Kagetaka	景隆	Kamakura	1332	Bright / Magnificent
taka	N	Ka'netaka	兼隆	Hei'an	1183	Unite
taka	N	Koretaka	惟隆	Hei'an	1183	This / Here
taka	N	Masataka	雅隆	Kamakura	1332	High Quality
taka	N	Michitaka	道隆	Uncertain	1600	Road / Way
taka	N	Mitsutaka	満隆	Muromachi	1572	Become Full / Abundant
taka	N	Moritaka	盛隆	Kamakura	1332	Plentiful / Piled Up
taka	N	Mototaka	基隆	Kamakura	1332	Foundation
taka	N	Mu'netaka	宗隆	Hei'an	1183	Master an Art
taka	N	Nagataka	長隆	Kamakura	1332	Long
taka	N	Nobutaka	信隆	Hei'an	1183	Belief / Faith
taka	N	Noritaka	教隆	Kamakura	1332	Teaching / Dogma
taka	N	Sa'netaka	実隆	Muromachi	1572	Reality
taka	N	Shigetaka	重隆	Kamakura	1332	Heavy / Serious
taka	N	Suketaka	資隆	Hei'an	1183	Raw Materials
taka	N	Taka'aki	隆顕	Kamakura	1332	High Status
taka	N	Taka'aki	隆章	Kamakura	1332	Writing / Illucidate
taka	N	Taka'atsu	隆敦	Muromachi	1572	Generous / Kind / Honest
taka	N	Takachika	隆親	Hei'an	1183	Intimate
taka	N	Takafusa	隆房	Kamakura	1332	Monastic Cell
taka	N	Takahira	隆衡	Kamakura	1332	A Yoke
taka	N	Takahiro	隆博	Kamakura	1332	Well Traveled / Learned
taka	N	Taka'ie	隆家	Uncertain	1600	Rural House / Family
taka	N	Takakage	隆蔭	Nanboku	1392	Shade / Shadow
taka	N	Takaka'ne	隆兼	Kamakura	1332	Unite
taka	N	Takakiyo	隆清	Kamakura	1332	Pure
taka	N	Taka'kuni	隆国	Uncertain	1600	Country / Rural Area
taka	N	Takamasa	隆政	Nanboku	1392	Govern / Rule
taka	N	Takamichi	隆通	Uncertain	1600	Pass Through
taka	N	Takamori	隆盛	Uncertain	1600	Plentiful / Piled Up
taka	N	Takamoto	隆職	Hei'an	1183	Employment / Occupation

Reading	Type	Example	Kanji	Period	Date	Added Meaning
taka	N	Taka'naka	隆仲	Nanboku	1392	Middle of a Group
taka	N	Taka'nobu	隆信	Hei'an	1183	Belief / Faith
taka	N	Takashige	隆重	Sengoku	1568	Heavy / Serious
taka	N	Takasue	隆季	Hei'an	1183	Season
taka	N	Takasuke	隆右	Nanboku	1392	Right
taka	N	Takasuke	隆資	Nanboku	1392	Raw Materials
taka	N	Takasuke	隆祐	Kamakura	1332	Divine Help
taka	N	Takatada	隆忠	Kamakura	1332	Faithful / Loyal
taka	N	Takatoshi	隆俊	Kamakura	1332	Emotional
taka	N	Takatsu'ne	隆経	Uncertain	1600	True Path
taka	N	Takayoshi	隆義	Hei'an	1183	Fealty
taka	N	Takayoshi	隆能	Hei'an	1183	Talent / Ability
taka	N	Tokitaka	時隆	Uncertain	1600	Time / Era
taka	N	Tsu'netaka	経隆	Kamakura	1332	True Path
taka	N	Yoritaka	頼隆	Kamakura	1332	Request / Ask
taka	N	Yoshitaka	義隆	Kamakura	1332	Fealty
taka	N	Yoshitaka	吉隆	Kamakura	1332	Lucky / Fortunate
taka	N	Yoshitaka	能隆	Kamakura	1332	Talent / Ability
taka	N	Yukitaka	幸隆	Uncertain	1600	Happy / Tattoo
taka	N	Yukitaka	行隆	Hei'an	1183	Going To / Bound For

深 Deep

Reading	Type	Example	Kanji	Period	Date	Added Meaning
fuka	S	Fukahori	深堀	Kamakura	1332	Dig / Carve / Excavation
too	N	Yoshitoo	義深	Nanboku	1392	Fealty

浅 Shallow

Reading	Type	Example	Kanji	Period	Date	Added Meaning
asa	S	Asahara	浅原	Kamakura	1332	Meadow
asa	S	Asa'i	浅井	Uncertain	1600	Well
asa	S	Asa'no	浅野	Sengoku	1568	Wide Plain
asa	S	Yu'asa	湯浅	Kamakura	1332	Hot Water

横 Flat (Countryside)

Reading	Type	Example	Kanji	Period	Date	Added Meaning
yoko	S	Yokose	横瀬	Muromachi	1572	Rapids
yoko	S	Yokota	横田	Uncertain	1600	Rice Paddy
yoko	S	Yokoyama	横山	Kamakura	1332	Mountain

枚 Flat and Thin (Objects)

Reading	Type	Example	Kanji	Period	Date	Added Meaning
hira	F	Hirame	枚賣	Nara	784	

平 Peace = HEI / Flat = taira / Ordinary = hira / Tranquility

Peace is one of the perennial civic virtues in Japan. This *kanji* appears in Heijoukyou 平城京 and Hei'ankyou 平安京 the names of Nara and Kyoto when they were imperial capitals. More recently, it appears in Hesei 平成 the name of the current era and the posthumous name of the current emperor.

Reading	Type	Example	Kanji	Period	Date	Added Meaning
HEI	P	Hei'ankyou	平安京	Hei'an	794	Peace + Capital (Kyoto)
HEI	Y	Heiji	平治	Kamakura	1159	Govern / Rule
HEI	P	Heijoukyou	平城京	Nara	710	Castle + Capital (Nara)
HEI	Y	Heisei	平成	Modern	1989	Become / Exist
HEI	Y	Kouhei	康平	Hei'an	1058	Strong / Confident
HEI	Y	Ninpei	仁平	Hei'an	1151	Precious
HEI	Y	Shouhei	正平	Nanboku	1346	Unerring / Genuine
hira	F	Hirame	平女	Hei'an	1183	[Woman]
hira	N	Fusahira	房平	Muromachi	1572	Monastic Cell
hira	N	Fuyuhira	冬平	Kamakura	1332	Winter
hira	N	Iehira	家平	Kamakura	1332	Rural House / Family
hira	N	Kagehira	景平	Kamakura	1332	Bright / Magnificent
hira	N	Ka'nehira	兼平	Hei'an	1183	Unite
hira	N	Kiyohira	清平	Muromachi	1572	Pure
hira	N	Korehira	維平	Kamakura	1332	Cable / Rope
hira	N	Ku'nihira	国平	Kamakura	1332	Country / Rural Area
hira	N	Masahira	政平	Kamakura	1332	Govern / Rule
hira	N	Masahira	正平	Uncertain	1600	Unerring / Genuine
hira	N	Michihira	道平	Kamakura	1332	Road / Way
hira	N	Morohira	師平	Kamakura	1332	Teacher / Expert
hira	N	Motohira	基平	Kamakura	1332	Foundation
hira	N	Mu'nehira	宗平	Nanboku	1392	Master an Art
hira	N	Nagahira	永平	Hei'an	1183	Forever
hira	N	Nakahira	仲平	Uncertain	1600	Middle of a Group
hira	N	Sadahira	定平	Kamakura	1332	Determine
hira	N	Sa'nehira	実平	Kamakura	1332	Reality
hira	N	Shigehira	茂平	Kamakura	1332	Blossoming
hira	N	Sukehira	資平	Kamakura	1332	Raw Materials
hira	N	Tadahira	忠平	Uncertain	1600	Faithful / Loyal
hira	N	Tokihira	時平	Uncertain	1600	Time / Era
hira	N	Toohira	遠平	Kamakura	1332	Far
hira	N	Toshihira	俊平	Hei'an	1183	Emotional
hira	N	Tsu'nehira	経平	Kamakura	1332	True Path
hira	N	Yorihira	頼平	Kamakura	1332	Request / Ask
hira	N	Yoshihira	義平	Hei'an	1183	Fealty
hira	N	Yoshihira	良平	Kamakura	1332	Good / Superior
hira	N	Yukihira	行平	Kamakura	1332	Going To / Bound For
hira	S	Hiraga	平賀	Kamakura	1332	Celebrate A Gain
hira	S	Hira'iwa	平岩	Sengoku	1568	Boulder
hira	S	Hira'no	平野	Momoyama	1590	Wide Plain
hira	S	Hirata	平田	Hei'an	1183	Rice Paddy
hira	S	Hiratsuka	平塚	Sengoku	1568	Mound / Tomb
hira	S	Hirayama	平山	Kamakura	1332	Mountain
hira	S	Matsudaira	松平	Muromachi	1572	Pine Tree
taira	S	Taira	平	Hei'an	1183	

長 Long / Oldest / Senior

Note that 長 has a special meaning when speaking of children. The oldest son and daughter are referred to as *chounan* 長男 and *choujo* 長女 respectively.

Reading	Type	Example	Kanji	Period	Date	Added Meaning
CHOU	S	Chousokabe	長宗我部	Uncertain	1600	Our + Monopoly Corporation
CHOU	Y	Chougen	長元	Hei'an	1028	Base / Original
CHOU	Y	Chouhou	長保	Hei'an	999	Guarantee
CHOU	Y	Chouji	長治	Hei'an	1104	Govern / Rule
CHOU	Y	Choukan	長寛	Kamakura	1163	Domestic Tranquility
CHOU	Y	Choukyou	長享	Sengoku	1487	Receive
CHOU	Y	Choukyuu	長久	Hei'an	1040	Longtime
CHOU	Y	Chouroku	長禄	Muromachi	1457	Gratitude / Beneficence
CHOU	Y	Chouryaku	長歴	Hei'an	1037	Progress / Pass Through
CHOU	Y	Choushou	長承	Hei'an	1132	Humbly Receive
CHOU	Y	Choutoku	長徳	Hei'an	995	Righteous / Just
CHOU	Y	Chouwa	長和	Hei'an	1012	Peace / Tranquility / Harmony
CHOU	Y	Eichou	永長	Hei'an	1096	Forever
CHOU	Y	Keichou	慶長	Momoyama	1596	Rejoice / Deer Skin
CHOU	Y	Kenchou	建長	Kamakura	1249	Found / Build / Construct
CHOU	Y	Kouchou	弘長	Kamakura	1261	Draw / Stretch / Spread Out
CHOU	Y	Ouchou	応長	Kamakura	1311	Worthy / Suitable
CHOU	Y	Shouchou	正長	Muromachi	1428	Unerring / Genuine
naga	F	Nagako	長子	Hei'an	1183	[Lady]
naga	F	Nagatoshime	長寿女	Kamakura	1332	Longevity + [Woman]
naga	F	Wosame	長賣	Nara	784	
naga	N	Aki'naga	顕長	Hei'an	1183	High Status
naga	N	Ari'naga	有長	Kamakura	1332	Exists
naga	N	Chika'naga	親長	Kamakura	1332	Intimate
naga	N	Haru'naga	治長	Sengoku	1568	Govern / Rule
naga	N	Hisa'naga	久長	Muromachi	1572	Longtime
naga	N	Ie'naga	家長	Hei'an	1183	Rural House / Family
naga	N	Kage'naga	景長	Kamakura	1332	Bright / Magnificent
naga	N	Kinnaga	公長	Kamakura	1332	Noble / Official
naga	N	Kiyo'naga	清長	Kamakura	1332	Pure
naga	N	Ku'ni'naga	国長	Nanboku	1392	Country / Rural Area
naga	N	Masa'naga	雅長	Hei'an	1183	High Quality
naga	N	Masa'naga	政長	Nanboku	1392	Govern / Rule
naga	N	Michi'naga	道長	Uncertain	1600	Road / Way
naga	N	Mitsu'naga	光長	Hei'an	1183	Bright / Shining
naga	N	Mochi'naga	持長	Muromachi	1572	Have / Possess
naga	N	Mori'naga	盛長	Hei'an	1183	Plentiful / Piled Up
naga	N	Moro'naga	師長	Hei'an	1183	Teacher / Expert
naga	N	Moto'naga	基長	Nanboku	1392	Foundation
naga	N	Moto'naga	元長	Muromachi	1572	Base / Original
naga	N	Mu'ne'naga	宗長キ	Kamakura	1332	Master an Art
naga	N	Nagachika	長親	Hei'an	1183	Intimate
naga	N	Nagafusa	長房	Kamakura	1332	Monastic Cell
naga	N	Nagahide	長秀	Muromachi	1572	Extraordinary / Bountiful
naga	N	Nagahisa	長久	Uncertain	1600	Longtime
naga	N	Nagaka'ne	長兼	Kamakura	1332	Unite
naga	N	Nagakata	長方	Hei'an	1183	Direction / Method
naga	N	Nagakatsu	長勝	Sengoku	1568	Conquer / Triumph
naga	N	Nagakiyo	長清	Kamakura	1332	Pure
naga	N	Nagamasa	長政	Kamakura	1332	Govern / Rule
naga	N	Nagamichi	長通	Kamakura	1332	Pass Through

naga	N	Nagamitsu	長光	Kamakura	1332	Bright / Shining	
naga	N	Nagamitsu	長充	Muromachi	1572	Satisfy / Fill	
naga	N	Nagamochi	長茂	Kamakura	1332	Blossoming	
naga	N	Nagamori	長守	Kamakura	1332	Protect / Defend	
naga	N	Nagamori	長盛	Uncertain	1600	Plentiful / Piled Up	
naga	N	Nagamoto	長基	Nanboku	1392	Foundation	
naga	N	Nagamoto	長幹	Kamakura	1332	Trunk / Stalk	
naga	N	Naga'nari	長成	Uncertain	1600	Become / Exist	
naga	N	Naga'oki	長興	Muromachi	1572	Happen / Begin	
naga	N	Nagasada	長定	Kamakura	1332	Determine	
naga	N	Nagashige	長重	Nanboku	1392	Heavy / Serious	
naga	N	Nagataka	長親	Muromachi	1572	Intimate	
naga	N	Nagataka	長隆	Kamakura	1332	Grow / Pile Up	
naga	N	Nagateru	長輝	Sengoku	1568	Brilliant	
naga	N	Nagatoki	長時	Kamakura	1332	Time / Era	
naga	N	Nagatoshi	長年	Kamakura	1332	Year	
naga	N	Naga'uji	長氏	Kamakura	1332	Family / Clan	
naga	N	Nagayo	長世	Kamakura	1332	Generation / Life	
naga	N	Nagayori	長頼	Kamakura	1332	Request / Ask	
naga	N	Nagayoshi	長慶	Sengoku	1568	Rejoice / Deer Skin	
naga	N	Nagayoshi	長可	Sengoku	1568	Do This	
naga	N	Nagayoshi	長良	Uncertain	1600	Good / Superior	
naga	N	Nagayuki	長幸	Nanboku	1392	Happy / Tattoo	
naga	N	Nagayuki	長行	Sengoku	1568	Going To / Bound For	
naga	N	Nageta'ne	長胤	Nanboku	1392	Blood Heir	
naga	N	Nob'naga	信長	Kamakura	1332	Belief / Faith	
naga	N	Nori'naga	範長	Nanboku	1392	Required Form / Pattern	
naga	N	Sada'naga	貞長	Nanboku	1392	Correct Spirit	
naga	N	Sada'naga	定長	Kamakura	1332	Determine	
naga	N	Sa'ne'naga	実長	Kamakura	1332	Reality	
naga	N	Shige'naga	重長	Kamakura	1332	Heavy / Serious	
naga	N	Shige'naga	茂長	Kamakura	1332	Blossoming	
naga	N	Sue'naga	季長	Kamakura	1332	Season	
naga	N	Suke'naga	佐長	Kamakura	1332	Military Deputy	
naga	N	Suke'naga	資長	Nanboku	1392	Raw Materials	
naga	N	Taka'naga	高長	Uncertain	1600	Tall	
naga	N	Tame'naga	為長	Kamakura	1332	Purpose / Goal	
naga	N	Ta'ne'naga	胤長	Kamakura	1332	Blood Heir	
naga	N	Ta'ne'naga	種長	Sengoku	1568	Cause / Reason	
naga	N	Toki'naga	時長	Kamakura	1332	Time / Era	
naga	N	Tomo'naga	朝長	Hei'an	1183	Morning	
naga	N	Tomo'naga	倫長	Kamakura	1332	Obligatory Path	
naga	N	Toshi'naga	俊長	Kamakura	1332	Emotional	
naga	N	Toshi'naga	利長	Sengoku	1568	Produce Results	
naga	N	Tsu'ne'naga	常長	Uncertain	1600	Permanent	
naga	N	Yasu'naga	康長	Uncertain	1600	Strong / Confident	
naga	N	Yori'naga	頼長	Uncertain	1600	Request / Ask	
naga	N	Yoshi'naga	義長	Nanboku	1392	Fealty	
naga	N	Yoshi'naga	幸長	Sengoku	1568	Happy / Tattoo	
naga	N	Yoshi'naga	芳長	Uncertain	1600	Sweet Scent / Magnificent	
naga	N	Yuki'naga	行長	Kamakura	1332	Going To / Bound For	
naga	S	Naga'i	長井	Kamakura	1332	Well	
naga	S	Naga'numa	長沼	Kamakura	1332	Swamp	
naga	S	Naga'o	長尾	Kamakura	1332	Tail	
naga	S	Naga'oka	長岡	Kamakura	1332	Hill	
naga	S	Nagasa	長狭	Hei'an	1183	Cramped / Small Area	
naga	S	Nagasaki	長崎	Kamakura	1332	Slope	

Thematic Dictionary — Spacial Relationships 113

Reading	Type	Example	Kanji	Period	Date	Added Meaning
naga	S	Nagase	長瀬	Nanboku	1392	Rapids
naga	S	Nagatsuka	長束	Sengoku	1568	Grasp / Span / Hand's Breadth
osa	S	Osada	長田	Hei'an	1183	Rice Paddy
osa	S	Osafu'ne	長船	Kamakura	1332	Boat / Ship
[Special]	S	Hasebe	長谷部	Hei'an	1183	Monopoly Corporation
[Special]	S	Hasegawa	長谷川	Sengoku	1568	Valley + River

寸 Inch (Three Centimeters) / Measure (Length)

This *kanji* and the reading appearing in the example are definitely vulgar.

Reading	Type	Example	Kanji	Period	Date	Added Meaning
SU	F	Ihosume	五百寸賣	Nara	784	Five + Hundred

辺 Near / Edge / Bank

Reading	Type	Example	Kanji	Period	Date	Added Meaning
BE	S	Yama'nobe	山辺	Uncertain	1600	Mountain

近 Near

Reading	Type	Example	Kanji	Period	Date	Added Meaning
KON	S	Kondou	近藤	Kamakura	1332	Wisteria
chika	N	Chikakatsu	近葛	Kamakura	1332	Arrowroot
chika	N	Chika'nori	近則	Kamakura	1332	Make an Example
chika	N	Chikaza'ne	近実	Kamakura	1332	Reality
chika	S	Chikamatsu	近松	Uncertain	1600	Pine Tree

遠 Far

Reading	Type	Example	Kanji	Period	Date	Added Meaning
EN	S	Endou	遠藤	Sengoku	1568	Wisteria
too	N	Masatoo	正遠	Nanboku	1392	Unerring / Genuine
too	N	Moritoo	盛遠	Kamakura	1332	Plentiful / Piled Up
too	N	Mu'netoo	宗遠	Hei'an	1183	Master an Art
too	N	Nobutoo	信遠	Hei'an	1183	Belief / Faith
too	N	Noritoo	教遠	Nanboku	1392	Teaching / Dogma
too	N	Tadatoo	匡遠	Nanboku	1392	Make Correct
too	N	Toochika	遠親	Kamakura	1332	Intimate
too	N	Toohira	遠平	Kamakura	1332	Tranquility
too	N	Tookage	遠景	Kamakura	1332	Bright / Magnificent
too	N	Toomitsu	遠光	Hei'an	1183	Bright / Shining
too	N	Toomochi	遠茂	Hei'an	1183	Blossoming
too	N	Toomoto	遠元	Kamakura	1332	Base / Original
too	N	Yasutoo	保遠	Kamakura	1332	Guarantee
too	N	Yoritoo	頼遠	Nanboku	1392	Request / Ask

角 Corner / Horn

Reading	Type	Example	Kanji	Period	Date	Added Meaning
tsunu	F	Tsunume	角女	Nara	784	[Woman]

隅 Corner / Nook

Reading	Type	Example	Kanji	Period	Date	Added Meaning
sumi	S	Misumi	三隅	Nanboku	1392	Three

合 Confluence / Agreement / Concord

Reading	Type	Example	Kanji	Period	Date	Added Meaning
[Special]	N	Umakai	宇合	Uncertain	1600	Cosmos

立 Stand Up

Reading	Type	Example	Kanji	Period	Date	Added Meaning
tachi	S	Adachi	足立	Kamakura	1332	Foot / Sufficient
tachi	S	Tachiba'na	立花	Uncertain	1600	Flower
tatsu	F	Tatsume	立賣	Nara	784	
tatsu	N	Tatsuhisa	立久	Muromachi	1572	Longtime

方 Towards / Direction / Method / Near

Reading	Type	Example	Kanji	Period	Date	Added Meaning
kata	F	Makinokata	牧方	Kamakura	1332	Pasture
kata	N	Ka'nekata	兼方	Kamakura	1250	Unite
kata	N	Kiyokata	清方	Muromachi	1572	Pure
kata	N	Korekata	惟方	Hei'an	1183	This / Here
kata	N	Michikata	通方	Kamakura	1332	Pass Through
kata	N	Mu'nekata	宗方	Kamakura	1332	Master an Art
kata	N	Nagakata	長方	Hei'an	1183	Long
kata	N	Nobukata	信方	Uncertain	1600	Belief / Faith
kata	N	Norikata	憲方	Nanboku	1392	Example / Pattern
kata	N	Norikata	憲方	Nanboku	1392	Example / Pattern
kata	N	Sadakata	貞方	Nanboku	1392	Correct Spirit
kata	N	Tomokata	朝方	Hei'an	1183	Morning
kata	N	Tomokata	友方	Uncertain	1600	Friend
kata	N	Yorikata	頼方	Hei'an	1183	Request / Ask
kata	N	Yoshikata	好方	Hei'an	1183	Affection / Desire
kata	N	Yukikata	行方	Kamakura	1332	Going To / Bound For
kata	S	Ogata	緒方	Hei'an	1183	Rope / Functional Beginning

縁 Edge

Reading	Type	Example	Kanji	Period	Date	Added Meaning
masa	N	Sadamasa	貞縁	Kamakura	1332	Correct Spirit
yori	N	Tsu'neyori	常縁	Muromachi	1572	Permanent

岐 Divide / Fork / Split / Branch

The image evoked by this *kanji* is a mountain cleft in two. Here the emphasis is not upon the slope of the mountains curing down to where they meet, but upon the cleavage of a mountain in twain.

Reading	Type	Example	Kanji	Period	Date	Added Meaning
KI	S	Toki	土岐	Kamakura	1332	Dirt / Earth

阿 Cleft / Crevice / A Bend

The image evoked by this *kanji* is a place where mountains curve down into a cleft or divide with the sides rising together.

Reading	Type	Example	Kanji	Period	Date	Added Meaning
A	F	Acha	阿茶	Muromachi	1572	Tea
A	F	Achacha	阿茶茶	Uncertain	1600	Tea
A	F	Achame	阿茶女	Nanboku	1392	Tea + [Woman]
A	F	Aguri	阿久里	Nanboku	1392	Longtime Hamlet
A	F	Ako	阿子	Muromachi	1572	[Lady]
A	F	Akome	阿古女	Nanboku	1392	Old + [Woman]
A	F	Akome	阿子女	Nanboku	1392	[Lady] + [Woman]
A	F	Akome	阿小女	Nanboku	1392	Small + [Woman]
A	F	Akume	阿久女	Nanboku	1392	Longtime + [Woman]
A	F	A'ne	阿泥	Uncertain	1600	Mud / Muddy
A	F	Arime	阿里賣	Nara	784	Hamlet
A	F	Ayuteme	阿由提賣	Nara	784	Purpose
A	S	Abiru	阿比留	Kamakura	1332	Strive / Strive + Camp
A	S	Aso	阿蘇	Nanboku	1392	Dark Crimson
A	S	Aso'numa	阿曾沼	Nanboku	1392	Former + Swamp

❖ Temporal Relationships ❖

初 Beginning / First

Reading	Type	Example	Kanji	Period	Date	Added Meaning
hajime	F	Hajime	初	Muromachi	1572	
hajime	F	Hajimeme	初女	Muromachi	1572	[Woman]

興 Happen / Begin

Reading	Type	Example	Kanji	Period	Date	Added Meaning
KOU	Y	Koukoku	興国	Nanboku	1340	Country / Rural Area
oki	N	Aki'oki	顕興	Nanboku	1392	High Status
oki	N	Naga'oki	長興	Muromachi	1572	Long
oki	N	Nori'oki	教興	Nanboku	1392	Teaching / Dogma
oki	N	Okikaze	興風	Uncertain	1600	Wind
oki	N	Okita'ne	興胤	Nanboku	1392	Blood Heir
oki	N	Okitsu'ne	興常	Muromachi	1572	Permanent
oki	N	Tada'oki	忠興	Sengoku	1568	Faithful / Loyal
oki	N	Tomo'oki	朝興	Uncertain	1600	Morning
oki	N	Yoshi'oki	義興	Nanboku	1392	Fealty

進 Continue

Reading	Type	Example	Kanji	Period	Date	Added Meaning
susumu	N	Susumu	進	Kamakura	1234	

最 Repeat / Do Again / Most

Reading	Type	Example	Kanji	Period	Date	Added Meaning
mo	S	Mogami	最上	Uncertain	1600	Superior

末 Last / Final

Reading	Type	Example	Kanji	Period	Date	Added Meaning
su	F	Sueko	末子	Nanboku	1392	[Lady]
su	N	Suetada	末忠	Nanboku	1392	Faithful / Loyal

後　Behind / After

Reading	Type	Example	Kanji	Period	Date	Added Meaning
GO	S	Gotou	後藤	Kamakura	1332	Wisteria
shiri	F	Shirimachime	後町女	Hei'an	1183	Town + [Woman]

曾　Formerly / Ever

Reading	Type	Example	Kanji	Period	Date	Added Meaning
SO	F	Kosoko	巨曾子	Nara	784	Numerous
SO	S	Aso'numa	阿曾沼	Nanboku	1392	Crevice + Swamp
SO	S	Kiso	木曾	Uncertain	1600	Tree
SO	S	So'ne	曾禰	Uncertain	1600	Oracle

曽　Previous

Reading	Type	Example	Kanji	Period	Date	Added Meaning
SO	S	Soga	曽我	Uncertain	1600	Our / Us / We

永　Forever

Reading	Type	Example	Kanji	Period	Date	Added Meaning
EI	Y	An'ei	安永	Edo	1772	Gentle / Safe / Secure
EI	Y	Bun'ei	文永	Kamakura	1264	Literature / Culture
EI	Y	Eichou	永長	Hei'an	1096	Long / Oldest / Senior
EI	Y	Eihou	永保	Hei'an	1081	Guarantee
EI	Y	Eiji	永治	Hei'an	1141	Govern / Rule
EI	Y	Eikyou	永享	Muromachi	1429	Receive
EI	Y	Eikyuu	永久	Hei'an	1113	Longtime
EI	Y	Eiman	永万	Kamakura	1165	Ten Thousand
EI	Y	Ei'nin	永仁	Kamakura	1293	Precious
EI	Y	Eiroku	永禄	Sengoku	1558	Gratitude / Beneficence
EI	Y	Eiryaku	永暦	Kamakura	1160	Progress / Pass Through
EI	Y	Eishou	永承	Hei'an	1046	Humbly Receive
EI	Y	Eishou	永正	Sengoku	1504	Unerring / Genuine
EI	Y	Eitoku	永徳	Nanboku	1381	Righteous / Just
EI	Y	Eiwa	永和	Nanboku	1375	Peace / Tranquility / Harmony
EI	Y	Gen'ei	元永	Hei'an	1118	Base / Original
EI	Y	Hou'ei	保永	Edo	1704	Guarantee
EI	Y	Jou'ei	貞永	Kamakura	1232	Correct Spirit
EI	Y	Ju'ei	寿永	Kamakura	1182	Long Life / Longevity
EI	Y	Ka'ei	嘉永	Edo	1848	Well Done
EI	Y	Kan'ei	寛永	Edo	1624	Domestic Tranquility
EI	Y	Ken'ei	建永	Kamakura	1206	Found / Build / Construct
EI	Y	Kou'ei	康永	Nanboku	1342	Strong / Confident
EI	Y	Ou'ei	応永	Muromachi	1394	Worthy / Suitable
EI	Y	Tai'ei	大永	Sengoku	1521	Big
EI	Y	Ten'ei	天永	Hei'an	1110	Sky / Heaven
naga	F	Nagako	永子	Hei'an	1183	[Lady]
naga	N	Hide'naga	秀永	Uncertain	1600	Extraordinary / Bountiful
naga	N	Ie'naga	家永	Kamakura	1332	Rural House / Family

Reading	Type	Example	Kanji	Period	Date	Added Meaning
naga	N	Ka'ne'naga	兼永	Muromachi	1572	Unite
naga	N	Ka'ne'naga	包永	Kamakura	1332	Wrap / Bundle
naga	N	Katsu'naga	勝永	Sengoku	1568	Conquer / Triumph
naga	N	Nagafuji	永藤	Muromachi	1572	Wisteria
naga	N	Nagahira	永平	Hei'an	1183	Tranquility
naga	N	Nagakatsu	永勝	Sengoku	1568	Conquer / Triumph
naga	N	Nagamasa	永昌	Kamakura	1332	Clear / Bright
naga	N	Nagasue	永季	Nanboku	1392	Season
naga	N	Nagayuki	永幸	Nanboku	1392	Happy / Tattoo
naga	N	Nagayuki	永行	Muromachi	1572	Going To / Bound For
naga	N	Sa'ne'naga	実永	Muromachi	1572	Reality
naga	N	Suke'naga	資永	Kamakura	1332	Raw Materials
naga	N	Tsu'ne'naga	経永	Kamakura	1332	True Path
naga	S	Matsu'naga	松永	Uncertain	1600	Pine Tree
naga	S	Toku'naga	徳永	Sengoku	1568	Righteous / Just

常 Permanent

Reading	Type	Example	Kanji	Period	Date	Added Meaning
tsune	N	Hirotsu'ne	広常	Hei'an	1183	Spacious / Expansive
tsune	N	Ietsu'ne	家常	Kamakura	1332	Rural House / Family
tsune	N	Morotsu'ne	師常	Kamakura	1332	Teacher / Expert
tsune	N	Naotsu'ne	直常	Nanboku	1392	Adjust / Correct
tsune	N	Okitsu'ne	興常	Muromachi	1572	Happen / Begin
tsune	N	Tadatsu'ne	忠常	Kamakura	1332	Faithful / Loyal
tsune	N	Tadatsu'ne	直常	Uncertain	1600	Adjust / Correct
tsune	N	Tomotsu'ne	朝常	Nanboku	1392	Morning
tsune	N	Tsu'neharu	常治	Kamakura	1332	Govern / Rule
tsune	N	Tsu'nehide	常秀	Kamakura	1332	Extraordinary / Bountiful
tsune	N	Tsu'nemori	常盛	Kamakura	1332	Plentiful / Piled Up
tsune	N	Tsu'nemoto	常基	Hei'an	1183	Foundation
tsune	N	Tsu'ne'naga	常長	Uncertain	1600	Long
tsune	N	Tsu'neshige	常重	Hei'an	1183	Heavy / Serious
tsune	N	Tsu'neta'ne	常胤	Hei'an	1183	Blood Heir
tsune	N	Tsu'netomo	常伴	Hei'an	1183	Collective / Band
tsune	N	Tsu'neyasu	常安	Kamakura	1332	Gentle / Safe / Secure
tsune	N	Tsu'neyori	常縁	Muromachi	1572	Edge
tsune	N	Tsu'neyoshi	常昌	Nanboku	1392	Clear / Bright
tsune	N	Tsu'nezumi	常澄	Hei'an	1183	Cleanse / Purify
tsune	N	Yoshitsu'ne	義常	Hei'an	1183	Fealty
[Special]	F	Tokiwagozen	常盤御前	Hei'an	1138	Antecedent

恒 Changeless / Enduring

Reading	Type	Example	Kanji	Period	Date	Added Meaning
tsune	N	Kagetsu'ne	景恒	Nanboku	1392	Bright / Magnificent
tsune	N	Mototsu'ne	基恒	Muromachi	1572	Foundation

久 Longtime

Reading	Type	Example	Kanji	Period	Date	Added Meaning
KU	F	Ku'nime	久爾賣	Nara	784	Bobbin / Distaff
KU	F	Kusome	久曾賣	Nara	784	Formerly / Ever
KU	S	Kuga	久我	Uncertain	1600	Our / Us / We
KU	S	Kuge	久下	Hei'an	1183	Inferior
KU	S	Sakuma	佐久間	Sengoku	1568	Military Deputy + Space
KYUU	Y	Bunkyuu	文久	Edo	1861	Literature / Culture
KYUU	Y	Choukyuu	長久	Hei'an	1040	Long / Oldest / Senior
KYUU	Y	Eikyuu	永久	Hei'an	1113	Forever
KYUU	Y	Enkyuu	延久	Hei'an	1069	Prolong / Stretch Out
KYUU	Y	Genkyuu	元久	Kamakura	1204	Base / Original
KYUU	Y	Joukyuu	丞久	Kamakura	1219	Rescue from a Pit
KYUU	Y	Kenkyuu	建久	Kamakura	1190	Found / Build / Construct
KYUU	Y	Kyuu'an	久安	Hei'an	1145	Gentle / Safe / Secure
KYUU	Y	Kyuuju	久寿	Kamakura	1154	Long Life / Longevity
hisa	N	Haruhisa	治久	Kamakura	1332	Govern / Rule
hisa	N	Haruhisa	晴久	Sengoku	1568	Clear (Sky)
hisa	N	Hisahide	久英	Uncertain	1600	Kind / Gentle
hisa	N	Hisahide	久秀	Uncertain	1600	Extraordinary / Bountiful
hisa	N	Hisaka'ne	久兼	Kamakura	1332	Unite
hisa	N	Hisaku'ni	久国	Muromachi	1572	Country / Rural Area
hisa	N	Hisa'naga	久長	Muromachi	1572	Long
hisa	N	Hisa'nobu	久信	Sengoku	1568	Belief / Faith
hisa	N	Hisatoki	久時	Kamakura	1332	Time / Era
hisa	N	Hisatoyo	久豊	Muromachi	1572	Noble
hisa	N	Hisatsu'na	久綱	Kamakura	1332	Net
hisa	N	Hisatsu'ne	久経	Kamakura	1332	True Path
hisa	N	Hisayoshi	久義	Nanboku	1392	Fealty
hisa	N	Kagehisa	景久	Kamakura	1332	Bright / Magnificent
hisa	N	Katsuhisa	勝久	Muromachi	1572	Conquer / Triumph
hisa	N	Korehisa	惟久	Kamakura	1332	This / Here
hisa	N	Korehisa	伊久	Nanboku	1392	This
hisa	N	Kyuuzou	久蔵	Sengoku	1568	Storehouse
hisa	N	Michihisa	通久	Kamakura	1332	Pass Through
hisa	N	Morihisa	盛久	Muromachi	1572	Plentiful / Piled Up
hisa	N	Morohisa	師久	Nanboku	1392	Teacher / Expert
hisa	N	Motohisa	元久	Nanboku	1392	Base / Original
hisa	N	Mu'nehisa	宗久	Kamakura	1332	Master an Art
hisa	N	Nagahisa	長久	Uncertain	1600	Long
hisa	N	Nobuhisa	信久	Sengoku	1568	Belief / Faith
hisa	N	Sadahisa	貞久	Kamakura	1332	Correct Spirit
hisa	N	Tadahisa	忠久	Kamakura	1332	Faithful / Loyal
hisa	N	Takahisa	高久	Uncertain	1600	Tall
hisa	N	Tamehisa	為久	Kamakura	1332	Purpose / Goal
hisa	N	Tatsuhisa	立久	Muromachi	1572	Stand Up
hisa	N	Tomohisa	朝久	Muromachi	1572	Morning
hisa	N	Tomohisa	有久	Kamakura	1332	Exists
hisa	N	Tsu'nehisa	経久	Sengoku	1568	True Path
hisa	N	Ujihisa	氏久	Nanboku	1392	Family / Clan
hisa	N	Yorihisa	頼久	Muromachi	1572	Request / Ask
hisa	N	Yoshihisa	義久	Uncertain	1600	Fealty
hisa	N	Yoshihisa	能久	Kamakura	1332	Talent / Ability
hisa	N	Yukihisa	行久	Kamakura	1332	Going To / Bound For
hisa	S	Hisada	久田	Sengoku	1568	Rice Paddy

寿 Long Life / Longevity

Reading	Type	Example	Kanji	Period	Date	Added Meaning
JU	Y	Ju'ei	寿永	Kamakura	1182	Forever
JU	Y	Kuuju	久寿	Kamakura	1154	Longtime
JU	Y	Manju	万寿	Hei'an	1024	Ten Thousand
SU	F	Sue	寿恵	Uncertain	1600	Sanctify / Bless
hisa	B	Nagahisagimimaru	永寿王丸	Muromachi	1572	Forever + King + Young
hisa	B	Takehisamaru	竹寿丸	Muromachi	1572	Bamboo + Young / Healthy
hisa	F	Hisako	寿子	Kamakura	1332	[Lady]

稍 Short Time

Reading	Type	Example	Kanji	Period	Date	Added Meaning
yaya	F	Yaya	稍	Muromachi	1572	

忽 In a Twinkling / Neglect

Although "KOTSU" is the standard *onyomi* for this *kanji*, it appears to take a variant pronunciation when used in names.

Reading	Type	Example	Kanji	Period	Date	Added Meaning
KUTSU	S	Kutsu'na	忽那	Kamakura	1332	What? / Whither? / How?

古 Old

Reading	Type	Example	Kanji	Period	Date	Added Meaning
KO	F	Kohime	古比賣	Nara	784	Measure Up / Strive
KO	F	Komame	古麻賣	Nara	784	Flax / Linen
KO	F	Kotame	古多賣	Nara	784	Many
KO	F	Kotekome	古手子賣	Nara	784	Hand + [Lady]
KO	F	Kotsume	古都賣	Nara	784	Beautiful (Cultured)
furu	F	Furume	古賣	Nara	784	
furu	S	Furuda	古田	Sengoku	1568	Rice Paddy
furu	S	Furuta	古田	Sengoku	1568	Rice Paddy

若 Young

Like *maru* 丸, this character is commonly found as an affectionate suffix attached to the names of boys. Please note that *waka* precedes *maru* in names in which both characters appear.

Reading	Type	Example	Kanji	Period	Date	Added Meaning
waka	B	Kamewakamaru	亀若丸	Muromachi	1572	Tortoise + Young / Healthy
waka	B	Mitsuwaka	満若	Muromachi	1572	Become Full / Abundant
waka	B	Otowakamaru	乙若丸	Muromachi	1572	Second (Cute) + Young
waka	B	Takewaka	竹若	Nanboku	1392	Bamboo
waka	B	Yoshiwakamaru	幸若丸	Nanboku	1392	Happy / Tattoo
waka	S	Umewaka	梅若	Muromachi	1572	Plum
waka	S	Wakasa	若狭	Kamakura	1332	Cramped / Small Area
waku	F	Wakame	若賣	Nara	784	
waku	F	Wakugo	若子	Nara	784	[Lady]
waku	F	Wakugome	若子賣	Nara	784	[Lady]

Thematic Dictionary — Temporal Relationships

丸 Young / Healthy

This *kanji* is commonly found as an affectionate suffix attached to the names of boys. While this *kanji* commonly refers to a ball or other spherical object, it was originally a descriptive applied to people. It retains a special domestic meaning when used in personal names. Here it actually means "young and healthy". Originally, men had names ending in *maro* 麿 or 麻呂. Both of these are phonetic renderings of an ancient Japanese word exclusively used in forming names. This name element may be derived from a Polynesian word for a red rope worn by princes and kings. 麿 is actually a contraction of 麻呂 and is unknown in China. While originally used by adults, -*maro* names were later used as juvenile names and especially baby names. Later, the Japanese substituted 丸 for writing this suffix. Finally, the more common reading of *maru* for 丸 replaced the original ending. Why did the Japanese use 丸, the Japanese word for "circle", to write this ancient Japanese affectionate suffix? There are two possible simple explanations. First, the original pictograph depicts a person bent over and might evoke an image of a child playing. The other, more probable, possibility is the fact that in agrarian societies, fat children are thought to be healthy and reflect the prosperity of the family. In one of her books, Pearl S. Buck tells of a Chinese mother who saved a piece of fat to rub on her children's lips each day so that people would think that they had eaten. In ancient Japan, this suffix took the reading *maro*, but by the Japanese middle ages it had acquired the reading *maru*. This character rarely appears as a spacial descriptive in family names. Please refer to the corresponding entry in the section on "Spacial Relationships" for this usage.

Reading	Type	Example	Kanji	Period	Date	Added Meaning
maru	B	Chikumaru	千宝丸	Kamakura	1332	Thousand + Treasure
maru	B	Chitakamaru	千鶴丸	Kamakura	1332	Crane
maru	B	Chiyokumamaru	千代熊丸	Muromachi	1572	Era + Bear
maru	B	Haruwaramaru	春丸	Muromachi	1572	Spring (Season)
maru	B	Hirokatamaru	普賢丸	Nanboku	1392	Genius
maru	B	Hirosasamaru	孔雀丸	Muromachi	1572	Sparrow
maru	B	Jirouhoujimaru	次郎法師丸	Muromachi	1572	Second Son + Law + Expert
maru	B	Kamewakamaru	亀若丸	Muromachi	1572	Tortoise (Longevity) + Young
maru	B	Ka'negimimaru	金王丸	Nanboku	1392	Gold / Metal + King
maru	B	Kesatsurumaru	袈裟鶴丸	Kamakura	1332	Crane
maru	B	Mahisamaru	万寿丸	Kamakura	1332	Longevity
maru	B	Matsugimimaru	松王丸	Nanboku	1392	Pine Tree + King
maru	B	Matsumaru	松丸	Nanboku	1392	Pine Tree
maru	B	Nagahisagimimaru	永寿王丸	Muromachi	1572	Forever + Longevity + King
maru	B	Otowakamaru	乙若丸	Muromachi	1572	Second (Cute) + Young
maru	B	Takehisamaru	竹寿丸	Muromachi	1572	Bamboo + Longevity
maru	B	Toyochiyomaru	豊千代丸	Muromachi	1572	Noble Era
maru	B	Wakainumaru	若犬丸	Nanboku	1392	Young + Dog
maru	B	Yasugimimaru	安王丸	Muromachi	1572	Gentle + King / Imperial Prince
maru	B	Yoshigimimaru	王丸	Muromachi	1572	King / Imperial Prince / Deity
maru	B	Yoshiwakamaru	幸若丸	Nanboku	1392	Happy / Tattoo Young

鮮 Fresh / Vivid / Clear / Bright / Brilliant / Splendid

Reading	Type	Example	Kanji	Period	Date	Added Meaning
yoshi	F	Yoshiko	鮮子	Hei'an	1183	[Lady]

新 New

Note the phonetic transformation from the long vowel in "nii" to the glottal stop in Nitta.

Reading	Type	Example	Kanji	Period	Date	Added Meaning
nii	S	Nitta	新田	Kamakura	1332	Rice Paddy

早 Fast / Early

Reading	Type	Example	Kanji	Period	Date	Added Meaning
haya	S	Hayakawa	早川	Uncertain	1600	River

駿 Fast / Rapid / Good Horse

Although this *kanji* takes both "takashi" and "toshi" as *kunyomi*, no premodern instances of these readings has yet been found.

Reading	Type	Example	Kanji	Period	Date	Added Meaning
suru	S	Suruga	駿河	Kamakura	1332	Large River

今 Now

Reading	Type	Example	Kanji	Period	Date	Added Meaning
ima	F	Ima	今	Muromachi	1572	
ima	F	Imako	今子	Nanboku	1392	[Lady]
ima	S	Imagawa	今川	Nanboku	1392	River
ima	S	Ima'i	今井	Hei'an	1183	Well
ima	S	Imakawa	今川	Uncertain	1600	River
ima	S	Ima'nishi	今西	Uncertain	1600	West
ima	S	Ima'oka	今岡	Nanboku	1392	Hill

時 Hour / Time / Era

Reading	Type	Example	Kanji	Period	Date	Added Meaning
toki	F	Tokiko	時子	Hei'an	1183	[Lady]
toki	F	Tokime	時賣	Nara	784	
toki	F	Tokime	時賣	Nara	784	
toki	N	Akitoki	顕時	Kamakura	1332	High Status
toki	N	Aritoki	有時	Kamakura	1332	Exists
toki	N	Fumitoki	文時	Hei'an	981	Writing
toki	N	Hidetoki	英時	Kamakura	1332	Kind / Gentle
toki	N	Hisatoki	久時	Kamakura	1332	Longtime
toki	N	Ietoki	家時	Kamakura	1332	Rural House / Family
toki	N	Kagetoki	景時	Kamakura	1332	Bright / Magnificent
toki	N	Ka'netoki	兼時	Kamakura	1332	Unite
toki	N	Kintoki	公時	Nanboku	1392	Noble / Official
toki	N	Kiyotoki	清時	Kamakura	1332	Pure
toki	N	Koretoki	惟時	Nanboku	1392	This / Here
toki	N	Ku'nitoki	邦時	Uncertain	1600	Big Country
toki	N	Masatoki	正時	Nanboku	1392	Unerring / Genuine
toki	N	Michitoki	通時	Kamakura	1332	Pass Through
toki	N	Mitsutoki	光時	Kamakura	1332	Bright / Shining
toki	N	Moritoki	守時	Kamakura	1332	Protect / Defend
toki	N	Moritoki	盛時	Kamakura	1332	Plentiful / Piled Up
toki	N	Morotoki	師時	Kamakura	1332	Teacher / Expert
toki	N	Mototoki	基時	Kamakura	1332	Foundation
toki	N	Mu'netoki	宗時	Uncertain	1600	Master an Art
toki	N	Nagatoki	長時	Kamakura	1332	Long
toki	N	Nakatoki	仲時	Kamakura	1332	Middle of a Group

Thematic Dictionary — Temporal Relationships 123

toki	N	Naotoki	直時	Kamakura	1332	Adjust / Correct
toki	N	Naritoki	業時	Kamakura	1332	Industry / Diligence
toki	N	Nobutoki	信時	Kamakura	1332	Belief / Faith
toki	N	Nobutoki	宣時	Kamakura	1332	Proclamation
toki	N	Noritoki	季時	Kamakura	1332	Season
toki	N	Sadatoki	貞時	Kamakura	1332	Correct Spirit
toki	N	Sa'netoki	実時	Kamakura	1332	Reality
toki	N	Shigetoki	重時	Kamakura	1332	Heavy / Serious
toki	N	Shigetoki	茂時	Kamakura	1332	Blossoming
toki	N	Suetoki	季時	Kamakura	1332	Season
toki	N	Suketoki	資時	Kamakura	1332	Raw Materials
toki	N	Suketoki	祐時	Kamakura	1332	Divine Help
toki	N	Tadatoki	忠時	Kamakura	1332	Faithful / Loyal
toki	N	Takatoki	高時	Kamakura	1332	Tall
toki	N	Taketoki	武時	Kamakura	1332	Bravery / Military Force
toki	N	Tametoki	為時	Uncertain	1600	Purpose / Goal
toki	N	Toki'aki	時顕	Kamakura	1332	High Status
toki	N	Toki'akira	時章	Kamakura	1332	Writing / Elucidate
toki	N	Tokifusa	時房	Kamakura	1332	Monastic Cell
toki	N	Tokiharu	時治	Kamakura	1332	Govern / Rule
toki	N	Tokihide	時秀	Kamakura	1332	Extraordinary / Bountiful
toki	N	Tokihira	時平	Uncertain	1600	Tranquility
toki	N	Tokihiro	時広	Kamakura	1332	Spacious / Expansive
toki	N	Toki'ie	時家	Hei'an	1183	Rural House / Family
toki	N	Tokika'ne	時兼	Kamakura	1332	Unite
toki	N	Tokikiyo	時清	Kamakura	1332	Pure
toki	N	Tokimasa	時政	Hei'an	1183	Govern / Rule
toki	N	Tokimasu	時益	Kamakura	1332	Grow Numerous / Overflow
toki	N	Tokimichi	時通	Nanboku	1392	Pass Through
toki	N	Tokimochi	時茂	Kamakura	1332	Blossoming
toki	N	Tokimori	時盛	Kamakura	1332	Plentiful / Piled Up
toki	N	Tokimoto	時基	Kamakura	1332	Foundation
toki	N	Tokimu'ne	時宗	Kamakura	1332	Master an Art
toki	N	Tokimu'ne	時致	Kamakura	1332	Taste / Elegance / Grand Effect
toki	N	Tokimura	時村	Kamakura	1332	Village
toki	N	Toki'naga	時長	Kamakura	1332	Long
toki	N	Toki'nao	時直	Kamakura	1332	Adjust / Correct
toki	N	Toki'nari	時業	Kamakura	1332	Industry / Diligence
toki	N	Toki'nari	時成	Kamakura	1332	Become / Exist
toki	N	Toki'nobu	時信	Kamakura	1332	Belief / Faith
toki	N	Tokisada	時貞	Nanboku	1392	Correct Spirit
toki	N	Tokisada	時定	Hei'an	1183	Determine
toki	N	Tokishige	時重	Nanboku	1392	Heavy / Serious
toki	N	Tokishige	時茂	Kamakura	1332	Blossoming
toki	N	Tokisuke	時輔	Kamakura	1332	Ministerial Deputy
toki	N	Tokitada	時忠	Hei'an	1183	Faithful / Loyal
toki	N	Tokitaka	時高	Kamakura	1332	Tall
toki	N	Tokitaka	時隆	Uncertain	1600	Grow / Pile Up
toki	N	Tokitsugu	時継	Kamakura	1332	Connect / Adopt
toki	N	Tokitsu'na	時綱	Kamakura	1332	Net
toki	N	Tokitsura	時連	Kamakura	1332	Bring Along
toki	N	Toki'uji	時氏	Kamakura	1332	Family / Clan
toki	N	Tokiyori	時頼	Kamakura	1332	Request / Ask
toki	N	Tokiyoshi	時能	Nanboku	1392	Talent / Ability
toki	N	Tokiyuki	時幸	Kamakura	1332	Happy / Tattoo
toki	N	Tokiyuki	時行	Kamakura	1332	Going To / Bound For
toki	N	Tokiza'ne	時実	Kamakura	1332	Reality

Reading	Type	Example	Kanji	Period	Date	Added Meaning
toki	N	Tomotoki	朝時	Kamakura	1332	Morning
toki	N	Tsu'netoki	経時	Kamakura	1332	True Path
toki	N	Ujitoki	氏時	Nanboku	1392	Family / Clan
toki	N	Yasutoki	泰時	Kamakura	1332	Peace / Plenitude
toki	N	Yoritoki	頼時	Nanboku	1392	Request / Ask
toki	N	Yoshitoki	義時	Kamakura	1332	Fealty
toki	N	Yukitoki	行時	Nanboku	1392	Going To / Bound For

年 Year

Reading	Type	Example	Kanji	Period	Date	Added Meaning
toshi	N	Nagatoshi	長年	Kamakura	1332	Long

載 Year

This *kanji* also refers to loading cargo onto a cart or ship.

Reading	Type	Example	Kanji	Period	Date	Added Meaning
nori	N	Sada'nori	貞載	Nanboku	1392	Composure / Modesty

歳 Age of a Person

Reading	Type	Example	Kanji	Period	Date	Added Meaning
mitsu	F	Mitoshime	参歳賣	Nara	784	Three

代 Era / Generation

Reading	Type	Example	Kanji	Period	Date	Added Meaning
shiro	S	Tashiro	田代	Nanboku	1392	Rice Paddy
yo	B	Chiyokumamaru	千代熊丸	Muromachi	1572	Era + Bear
yo	B	Toyochiyomaru	豊千代丸	Muromachi	1572	Noble + 1000 generations
yo	F	Chiyo'inu	千代犬	Momoyama	1590	Era + Dog

世 Generation / Life

Reading	Type	Example	Kanji	Period	Date	Added Meaning
yo	N	Ariyo	有世	Nanboku	1392	Exists
yo	N	Chikayo	親世	Muromachi	1572	Intimate
yo	N	Hiroyo	弘世	Nanboku	1392	Draw / Stretch
yo	N	Ka'neyo	兼世	Nanboku	1392	Unite
yo	N	Masayo	雅世	Nanboku	1390	High Quality
yo	N	Mochiyo	持世	Muromachi	1572	Have / Possess
yo	N	Nagayo	長世	Kamakura	1332	Long
yo	N	Sadayo	貞世	Nanboku	1392	Correct Spirit
yo	N	Sa'neyo	実世	Kamakura	1332	Reality
yo	N	Tameyo	為世	Kamakura	1332	Purpose / Goal
yo	S	Serada	世良田	Kamakura	1332	Superior + Rice Paddy

朝 Morning / Dawn

Reading	Type	Example	Kanji	Period	Date	Added Meaning
aki	N	Aki'nobu	朝信	Sengoku	1568	Belief / Faith
aki	N	Akitada	朝忠	Uncertain	1600	Faithful / Loyal
aki	N	Aki'uji	朝氏	Uncertain	1600	Family / Clan
aki	N	Akiyasu	朝康	Uncertain	1600	Strong / Confident
aki	N	Uji'aki	氏朝	Nanboku	1392	Family / Clan
aki	N	Yori'aki	頼朝	Nanboku	1392	Request / Ask
aki	N	Yoshi'aki	義朝	Hei'an	1183	Fealty
asa	F	Asahi	朝日	Uncertain	1600	Sun / Day
asa	S	Asahi'na	朝比奈	Uncertain	1600	Measure Up / Strive
asa	S	Asakura	朝倉	Muromachi	1572	Warehouse
asa	S	Asayama	朝山	Nanboku	1392	Mountain
tomo	N	Chikatomo	親朝	Nanboku	1392	Intimate
tomo	N	Hidetomo	秀朝	Kamakura	1332	Extraordinary / Bountiful
tomo	N	Kagetomo	景朝	Kamakura	1332	Bright / Magnificent
tomo	N	Ka'netomo	兼朝	Muromachi	1572	Unite
tomo	N	Kimitomo	公朝	Kamakura	1332	Noble / Official
tomo	N	Michitomo	通朝	Nanboku	1392	Pass Through
tomo	N	Mitsutomo	満朝	Muromachi	1572	Become Full / Abundant
tomo	N	Mochitomo	持朝	Muromachi	1572	Have / Possess
tomo	N	Naotomo	直朝	Nanboku	1392	Adjust / Correct
tomo	N	Noritomo	教朝	Muromachi	1572	Teaching / Dogma
tomo	N	Noritomo	範朝	Kamakura	1332	Required Form / Pattern
tomo	N	Sadatomo	貞朝	Kamakura	1332	Correct Spirit
tomo	N	Sa'netomo	実朝	Kamakura	1332	Reality
tomo	N	Shigetomo	重朝	Muromachi	1572	Heavy / Serious
tomo	N	Shigetomo	成朝	Muromachi	1572	Become / Exist
tomo	N	Suketomo	資朝	Kamakura	1332	Raw Materials
tomo	N	Suketomo	助朝	Nanboku	1392	Deputy (Rescue / Assist)
tomo	N	Takatomo	孝朝	Nanboku	1392	Filial Loyalty
tomo	N	Taketomo	武朝	Nanboku	1392	Bravery / Military Force
tomo	N	Tametomo	為朝	Uncertain	1600	Purpose / Goal
tomo	N	Ta'netomo	胤朝	Muromachi	1572	Blood Heir
tomo	N	Tomofusa	朝房	Nanboku	1392	Monastic Cell
tomo	N	Tomohiro	朝広	Kamakura	1332	Spacious / Expansive
tomo	N	Tomohisa	朝久	Muromachi	1572	Longtime
tomo	N	Tomokage	朝景	Kamakura	1332	Bright / Magnificent
tomo	N	Tomokata	朝方	Hei'an	1183	Direction / Method
tomo	N	Tomokatsu	朝葛	Kamakura	1332	Arrowroot
tomo	N	Tomomasa	朝雅	Kamakura	1332	High Quality
tomo	N	Tomomasa	朝政	Kamakura	1332	Govern / Rule
tomo	N	Tomomitsu	朝光	Kamakura	1332	Bright / Shining
tomo	N	Tomomori	朝盛	Kamakura	1332	Plentiful / Piled Up
tomo	N	Tomomu'ne	朝宗	Nanboku	1392	Master an Art
tomo	N	Tomomu'ne	朝棟	Nanboku	1392	Ridge Pole
tomo	N	Tomomura	朝村	Kamakura	1332	Village
tomo	N	Tom'naga	朝長キ	Hei'an	1183	Long
tomo	N	Tomo'nao	朝直	Kamakura	1332	Adjust / Correct
tomo	N	Tomo'nari	朝業	Kamakura	1332	Industry / Diligence
tomo	N	Tomo'nori	朝範	Nanboku	1392	Required Form / Pattern
tomo	N	Tomo'oki	朝興	Uncertain	1600	Happen / Begin
tomo	N	Tomosada	朝定	Nanboku	1392	Determine
tomo	N	Tomotada	朝忠	Nanboku	1392	Faithful / Loyal
tomo	N	Tomotoki	朝時	Kamakura	1332	Time / Era

Reading	Type	Example	Kanji	Period	Date	Added Meaning
tomo	N	Tomotoshi	朝俊	Kamakura	1332	Emotional
tomo	N	Tomotsu'na	朝綱	Kamakura	1332	Net
tomo	N	Tomotsu'ne	朝経	Kamakura	1332	True Path
tomo	N	Tomotsu'ne	朝常	Nanboku	1392	Permanent
tomo	N	Ujitomo	氏朝	Muromachi	1572	Family / Clan
tomo	N	Yasutomo	泰朝	Kamakura	1332	Peace / Plenitude
tomo	N	Yoritomo	頼朝	Kamakura	1332	Request / Ask
tomo	N	Yoshitomo	義朝	Hei'an	1183	Fealty
tomo	N	Yukitomo	行朝	Nanboku	1392	Going To / Bound For
toshi	N	Taketoshi	武朝	Nanboku	1392	Bravery / Military Force

呉 Long Ago

Note that this also refers to a Chinese Dynasty and to China in general.

Reading	Type	Example	Kanji	Period	Date	Added Meaning
kure	F	Kure	呉	Uncertain	1600	

夜 Evening

Reading	Type	Example	Kanji	Period	Date	Added Meaning
ya	F	Yabushime	夜夫志賣	Nara	784	Husband + Determined
ya	F	Yaweme	夜恵賣	Nara	784	Sanctify / Bless
ya	S	Yasu	夜須	Hei'an	1183	Necessity

季 Season

Reading	Type	Example	Kanji	Period	Date	Added Meaning
nori	N	Noritoki	季時	Kamakura	1332	Time / Era
sue	N	Chikasue	親季	Kamakura	1332	Intimate
sue	N	Kagesue	景季	Kamakura	1332	Bright / Magnificent
sue	N	Ka'nesue	兼季	Kamakura	1332	Unite
sue	N	Kinsue	公季	Uncertain	1600	Noble / Official
sue	N	Masasue	正季	Nanboku	1392	Unerring / Genuine
sue	N	Mitsusue	光季	Kamakura	1332	Bright / Shining
sue	N	Mitsusue	満季	Muromachi	1572	Become Full / Abundant
sue	N	Nagasue	永季	Nanboku	1392	Forever
sue	N	Narisue	成季	Kamakura	1332	Become / Exist
sue	N	Norisue	範季	Kamakura	1332	Required Form / Pattern
sue	N	Sadasue	貞季	Kamakura	1332	Correct Spirit
sue	N	Suefusa	季房	Kamakura	1332	Monastic Cell
sue	N	Sueka'ne	季兼	Kamakura	1332	Unite
sue	N	Suemitsu	季光	Kamakura	1332	Bright / Shining
sue	N	Sue'naga	季長	Kamakura	1332	Long
sue	N	Suetoki	季時	Kamakura	1332	Time / Era
sue	N	Suetsugu	季継	Kamakura	1332	Connect / Adopt
sue	N	Suetsu'na	季綱	Muromachi	1572	Net
sue	N	Suetsu'ne	季経	Hei'an	1183	True Path
sue	N	Sueyasu	季保	Muromachi	1572	Guarantee
sue	N	Sueyoshi	季能	Kamakura	1332	Talent / Ability
sue	N	Sukesue	資季	Kamakura	1332	Raw Materials
sue	N	Tadasue	忠季	Kamakura	1332	Faithful / Loyal
sue	N	Takasue	隆季	Hei'an	1183	Grow / Pile Up
sue	N	Tsu'nesue	経季	Kamakura	1332	True Path
sue	N	Yoshisue	義季	Nanboku	1392	Fealty

紀 Season

Reading	Type	Example	Kanji	Period	Date	Added Meaning
nori	N	Nori'uji	紀氏	Muromachi	1572	Family / Clan

春 Spring (Season)

Reading	Type	Example	Kanji	Period	Date	Added Meaning
haru	F	Haru	春	Kamakura	1332	
haru	F	Haruhime	春日女	Nara	784	Sun / Day + [Woman]
haru	F	Harukiri	春霧	Muromachi	1572	Fog
haru	F	Harumatsu	春松	Kamakura	1332	Pine Tree
haru	F	Harutoshime	春寿女	Kamakura	1332	Longevity + [Woman]
haru	N	Harufusa	春房	Muromachi	1572	Monastic Cell
haru	N	Kageharu	景春	Muromachi	1572	Bright / Magnificent
haru	N	Michiharu	通春	Muromachi	1572	Pass Through
haru	N	Mochiharu	持春	Muromachi	1572	Have / Possess
haru	N	Motoharu	元春	Nanboku	1392	Base / Original
haru	N	Nobuharu	信春	Nanboku	1392	Belief / Faith
haru	N	Noriharu	憲春	Nanboku	1392	Example / Pattern
haru	N	Shigeharu	滋春	Hei'an	1183	Grow / Blossom
haru	N	Sukeharu	祐春	Kamakura	1332	Divine Help
haru	N	Ujiharu	氏春	Nanboku	1392	Family / Clan
haru	N	Yoriharu	頼春	Nanboku	1392	Request / Ask
haru	S	Harumichi	春道	Uncertain	1600	Road / Way
[Special]	F	Kasugame	春日女	Nanboku	1392	Sun / Day + [Woman]
[Special]	S	Kasuga	春日	Nanboku	1392	Sun / Day

夏 Summer

Reading	Type	Example	Kanji	Period	Date	Added Meaning
natsu	F	Natsu	夏	Momoyama	1438	
natsu	F	Natsu	夏女	Hei'an	1183	[Woman]
natsu	N	Moro'natsu	師夏	Nanboku	1392	Teacher / Expert
natsu	N	Sa'ne'natsu	実夏	Nanboku	1392	Reality
natsu	N	Yoshi'natsu	義夏	Muromachi	1572	Fealty

秋 Autumn

Reading	Type	Example	Kanji	Period	Date	Added Meaning
aki	F	Akime	秋女	Nara	784	[Woman]
aki	F	Akiyamame	秋山賣	Nara	784	Mountain
aki	N	Aki'ie	秋家	Kamakura	1332	Rural House / Family
aki	N	Akimoto	秋元	Kamakura	1332	Base / Original
aki	N	Akiyori	秋依	Kamakura	1332	Follow
aki	N	Hide'aki	英秋	Nanboku	1392	Kind / Gentle
aki	N	Ka'ne'aki	兼秋	Kamakura	1332	Unite
aki	N	Moro'aki	師秋	Nanboku	1392	Teacher / Expert
aki	N	Mu'ne'aki	統秋	Muromachi	1572	Lineage / Govern
aki	N	Naka'aki	仲秋	Nanboku	1392	Middle of a Group
aki	N	Nori'aki	憲秋	Nanboku	1392	Example / Pattern

Reading	Type	Example	Kanji	Period	Date	Added Meaning
aki	N	Tatsu'aki	竜秋	Kamakura	1332	Dragon
aki	S	Akimatsu	秋松	Uncertain	1600	Pine Tree
aki	S	Akita	秋田	Uncertain	1600	Rice Paddy
aki	S	Akiyama	秋山	Uncertain	1600	Mountain
aki	S	Akizuki	秋月	Nanboku	1392	Moon / Month

冬 Winter

Reading	Type	Example	Kanji	Period	Date	Added Meaning
fuyu	F	Fuyume	冬女	Hei'an	1183	[Woman]
fuyu	N	Fuyufusa	冬房	Muromachi	1572	Monastic Cell
fuyu	N	Fuyuhira	冬平	Kamakura	1332	Tranquility
fuyu	N	Fuyu'ie	冬家	Nanboku	1392	Rural House / Family
fuyu	N	Fuyumichi	冬通	Nanboku	1392	Pass Through
fuyu	N	Fuyu'nori	冬教	Kamakura	1332	Teaching / Dogma
fuyu	N	Fuyusuke	冬資	Nanboku	1392	Raw Materials
fuyu	N	Fuyutsugu	冬嗣	Uncertain	1600	Successor
fuyu	N	Fuyu'uji	冬氏	Kamakura	1332	Family / Clan
fuyu	N	Fuyuyasu	冬康	Kamakura	1332	Strong / Confident
fuyu	N	Kinfuyu	公冬	Muromachi	1572	Noble / Official
fuyu	N	Michifuyu	通冬	Nanboku	1392	Pass Through
fuyu	N	Morofuyu	師冬	Nanboku	1392	Teacher / Expert
fuyu	N	Norifuyu	教冬	Nanboku	1392	Teaching / Dogma
fuyu	N	Sa'nefuyu	実冬	Nanboku	1392	Reality
fuyu	N	Tadafuyu	直冬	Nanboku	1392	Adjust / Correct
fuyu	N	Tamefuyu	為冬	Kamakura	1332	Purpose / Goal
fuyu	N	Ujifuyu	氏冬	Nanboku	1392	Family / Clan
fuyu	N	Yoshifuyu	義冬	Nanboku	1392	Fealty

❖ WORKS OF MAN ❖

見 Vantage / View / Vista

Many places in Japan are named after particularly pleasant vistas. One example is Fujimi 富士見 which is renowned for its view of Mt. Fuji. 見 is included in this section because it can be used as the substantive element of a locative. Further, as such a place is not the scenery which is being a viewed and not the scenery itself, it is best thought of as a work of man and not a work of nature.

Reading	Type	Example	Kanji	Period	Date	Added Meaning
mi	N	Iwami	石見	Muromachi	1572	Rock
mi	N	Morimi	盛見	Muromachi	1572	Plentiful / Piled Up
mi	N	Satomi	里見	Kamakura	1332	Hamlet
mi	N	Tajimi	多治見	Kamakura	1332	Many + Govern / Rule
mi	N	Tsu'nemi	経見	Nanboku	1392	True Path
mi	N	Yoshimi	吉見	Kamakura	1332	Lucky / Fortunate
[Special]	F	Akiko	見子	Nanboku	1392	[Lady]

坂 Steep Road

Reading	Type	Example	Kanji	Period	Date	Added Meaning
saka	S	Kousaka	高坂	Nanboku	1392	High
saka	S	Sakagami	坂上	Nanboku	1392	Top
saka	S	Sakano'ue	坂上	Kamakura	1332	Top
saka	S	Saka'uchi	坂内	Uncertain	1600	Inside
saka	S	Wakisaka	脇坂	Sengoku	1568	Sides / Ribs / Supporter

通 Pass Through / Big Road

Reading	Type	Example	Kanji	Period	Date	Added Meaning
michi	N	Fuyumichi	冬通	Nanboku	1392	Winter
michi	N	Iemichi	家通	Hei'an	1183	Rural House / Family
michi	N	Ka'nemichi	兼通	Uncertain	1600	Unite
michi	N	Kimimichi	公通	Hei'an	1183	Noble / Official
michi	N	Kinmichi	公通	Hei'an	1183	Noble / Official
michi	N	Ku'nimichi	邦通	Kamakura	1332	Big Country
michi	N	Masamichi	雅通	Uncertain	1600	High Quality
michi	N	Michi'aki	通顕	Kamakura	1332	High Status
michi	N	Michi'aki	通昭	Kamakura	1332	Bright
michi	N	Michi'ari	通有	Kamakura	1332	Exists
michi	N	Michi'atsu	通淳	Muromachi	1572	Steadfast / Honest / Natural
michi	N	Michichika	通親	Hei'an	1183	Intimate
michi	N	Michifuyu	通冬	Nanboku	1392	Winter
michi	N	Michiharu	通春	Muromachi	1572	Spring (Season)

michi	N	Michiharu	通治	Kamakura	1332	Govern / Rule
michi	N	Michihide	通秀	Muromachi	1572	Extraordinary / Bountiful
michi	N	Michihiro	通博	Muromachi	1572	Well Traveled / Learned
michi	N	Michihisa	通久	Kamakura	1332	Longtime
michi	N	Michikata	通方	Kamakura	1332	Direction / Method
michi	N	Michikiyo	通清	Kamakura	1332	Pure
michi	N	Michimasu	通増	Nanboku	1392	Live Long / Prosper
michi	N	Michimitsu	通光	Kamakura	1332	Bright / Shining
michi	N	Michimori	通守	Muromachi	1572	Protect / Defend
michi	N	Michimori	通盛	Kamakura	1332	Plentiful / Piled Up
michi	N	Michi'nao	通直	Nanboku	1392	Adjust / Correct
michi	N	Michi'nari	通成	Kamakura	1332	Become / Exist
michi	N	Michi'nobu	通信	Kamakura	1332	Belief / Faith
michi	N	Michi'nori	通憲	Hei'an	1183	Example / Pattern
michi	N	Michi'o	通雄	Kamakura	1332	Strength / Courage / Bravery
michi	N	Michisada	通貞	Nanboku	1392	Correct Spirit
michi	N	Michishige	通重	Kamakura	1332	Heavy / Serious
michi	N	Michisuke	通相	Nanboku	1392	Together / Team Work
michi	N	Michisuke	通資	Kamakura	1332	Raw Materials
michi	N	Michitada	通忠	Kamakura	1332	Faithful / Loyal
michi	N	Michitaka	通尭	Nanboku	1392	Appear Tall or Grand
michi	N	Michita'ne	通種	Nanboku	1392	Cause / Reason
michi	N	Michitoki	通言	Nanboku	1392	Speak Truthfully
michi	N	Michitoki	通時	Kamakura	1332	Time / Era
michi	N	Michitomo	通具	Kamakura	1332	Tool / Implement
michi	N	Michitomo	通朝	Nanboku	1392	Morning
michi	N	Michitoshi	通俊	Uncertain	1600	Emotional
michi	N	Michitou	通任	Nanboku	1392	Endure a Duty
michi	N	Michitsugu	通継	Kamakura	1332	Connect / Adopt
michi	N	Michitsu'ne	通経	Kamakura	1332	True Path
michi	N	Michi'uji	通氏	Nanboku	1392	Family / Clan
michi	N	Michiyori	通頼	Kamakura	1332	Request / Ask
michi	N	Michiyoshi	通能	Nanboku	1392	Talent / Ability
michi	N	Michiyuki	通行	Muromachi	1572	Going To / Bound For
michi	N	Michiyuki	通之	Muromachi	1572	Go / Depart
michi	N	Mochimichi	持通	Muromachi	1572	Have / Possess
michi	N	Moromichi	師通	Uncertain	1600	Teacher / Expert
michi	N	Motomichi	基通	Hei'an	1183	Foundation
michi	N	Nagamichi	長通	Kamakura	1332	Long
michi	N	Norimichi	教通	Uncertain	1600	Teaching / Dogma
michi	N	Sadamichi	貞通	Sengoku	1568	Correct Spirit
michi	N	Sadamichi	定通	Kamakura	1332	Determine
michi	N	Tadamichi	忠通	Hei'an	1183	Faithful / Loyal
michi	N	Takamichi	隆通	Uncertain	1600	Grow / Pile Up
michi	N	Ta'nemichi	胤通	Kamakura	1332	Blood Heir
michi	N	Tokimichi	時通	Nanboku	1392	Time / Era
michi	N	Tomomichi	具通	Nanboku	1392	Tool / Implement
michi	N	Toshimichi	俊通	Hei'an	1183	Emotional
michi	N	Toyomichi	豊通	Muromachi	1572	Noble
michi	N	Tsu'nemichi	経通	Nanboku	1392	True Path
michi	N	Yasumichi	康通	Sengoku	1568	Strong / Confident
michi	N	Yasumichi	泰通	Hei'an	1183	Peace / Plenitude
michi	N	Yorimichi	頼通	Uncertain	1600	Request / Ask
michi	N	Yoshimichi	良通	Hei'an	1183	Good / Superior
michi	N	Yukimichi	行通	Nanboku	1392	Going To / Bound For
tsura	F	Tsurako	通子	Nanboku	1392	[Lady]

道 Road / Way

Note that this is the "DOU" which appears in the names of Japanese art forms.

Reading	Type	Example	Kanji	Period	Date	Added Meaning
michi	F	Michime	道女	Nara	784	[Woman]
michi	N	Koremichi	維道	Muromachi	1572	Cable / Rope
michi	N	Ku'nimichi	邦道	Hei'an	1183	Big Country
michi	N	Michiga'ne	道兼	Uncertain	1600	Unite
michi	N	Michihira	道平	Kamakura	1332	Tranquility
michi	N	Michi'ie	道家	Kamakura	1332	Rural House / Family
michi	N	Michimasa	道雅	Uncertain	1600	High Quality
michi	N	Michimasa	道政	Nanboku	1392	Govern / Rule
michi	N	Michi'naga	道長	Uncertain	1600	Long
michi	N	Michi'naga	道良	Kamakura	1332	Good / Superior
michi	N	Michi'nobu	道信	Uncertain	1600	Belief / Faith
michi	N	Michi'nori	道教	Nanboku	1392	Teaching / Dogma
michi	N	Michitaka	道隆	Uncertain	1600	Grow / Pile Up
michi	N	Michitoki	道辰	Nanboku	1392	Dragon (Zodiac)
michi	N	Michitsugu	道嗣	Kamakura	1332	Successor
michi	N	Michitsu'na	道綱	Nanboku	1392	Net
michi	N	Michitsu'ne	道経	Kamakura	1332	True Path
michi	N	Michiza'ne	道真	Hei'an	903	Genuine
michi	N	Tadamichi	忠道	Uncertain	1600	Faithful / Loyal
michi	N	Ta'nemichi	種道	Nanboku	1392	Cause / Reason
michi	S	Harumichi	春道	Uncertain	1600	Spring (Season)

井 Well

Reading	Type	Example	Kanji	Period	Date	Added Meaning
i	F	Iteme	井手賣	Nara	784	Hand
i	S	Asa'i	浅井	Uncertain	1600	Shallow
i	S	Asuka'i	飛鳥井	Kamakura	1332	Bird
i	S	Fuji'i	藤井	Hei'an	1183	Wisteria
i	S	Haki'i	波木井	Kamakura	1332	Wave + Tree
i	S	Ichi'no'i	一井	Kamakura	1332	One
i	S	Ida	井田	Kamakura	1332	Rice Paddy
i	S	I'i	井伊	Nanboku	1392	This
i	S	I'i	飯井	Uncertain	1600	Cooked Rice
i	S	Ima'i	今井	Hei'an	1183	Now
i	S	Ishi'i	石井	Nanboku	1392	Rock
i	S	Kaga'i	加賀井	Sengoku	1568	Enlist + Celebrate A Gain
i	S	Kame'i	亀井	Sengoku	1568	Tortoise (Longevity)
i	S	Matsu'i	松井	Sengoku	1568	Pine Tree
i	S	Momo'no'i	桃井	Nanboku	1392	Peach
i	S	Mura'i	村井	Uncertain	1600	Village
i	S	Naga'i	長井	Kamakura	1332	Long
i	S	Naka'i	中井	Sengoku	1568	Middle
i	S	Oo'i	大井	Uncertain	1600	Big
i	S	Saka'i	酒井	Sengoku	1568	Sake / Rice Wine
i	S	Sakura'i	桜井	Higashiyama	1482	Cherry Tree
i	S	Seto'i	瀬戸井	Kamakura	1332	Rapids + Door
i	S	Shima'i	島井	Uncertain	1600	Island
i	S	Taka'i	高井	Kamakura	1332	Tall
i	S	Tama'i	玉井	Nanboku	1392	Jewel / Sphere

Reading	Type	Example	Kanji	Period	Date	Added Meaning
i	S	Tsutsu'i	筒井	Muromachi	1572	Tubular Box
i	S	Usu'i	臼井	Nanboku	1392	Grind Stone
i	S	Yu'i	由井	Kamakura	1332	Purpose

封 Rampart / Border / Stop Up

Reading	Type	Example	Kanji	Period	Date	Added Meaning
kane	F	Ka'neko	封子	Hei'an	1183	[Lady]

垣 Fence / Hedge

Noble estates in Japan were typically surrounded by a solid fence approximately two meters high. The estate was entered through a gate which admitted one to the inferior precincts of the estate. The interior of an estate could be further divided by additional fences and gates. The innermost precincts of Japanese estates and houses are considered the most exalted.

Reading	Type	Example	Kanji	Period	Date	Added Meaning
kaki	S	Itagaki	板垣	Kamakura	1332	Board / Plank

門 Gate

Reading	Type	Example	Kanji	Period	Date	Added Meaning
MON	S	Boumon	坊門	Kamakura	1332	Monastic Residence
MON	S	Hamoda	羽門田	Higashiyama	1575	Feather + Rice Paddy
kado	N	Hirokado	広門	Sengoku	1568	Spacious / Expansive
kado	N	Masakado	将門	Uncertain	1600	Commander
kado	N	Yoshikado	良門	Uncertain	1600	Good / Superior

宇 Large Roof / Cosmos

Reading	Type	Example	Kanji	Period	Date	Added Meaning
U	F	Umagome	宇麻古賣	Nara	784	Flax / Linen + Old
U	F	Urime	宇利賣	Nara	784	Produce Results
U	F	Uteme	宇提賣	Nara	784	
U	N	Umakai	宇合	Uncertain	1600	Concord
U	S	Uda	宇多	Sengoku	1568	Many
U	S	Ukita	宇喜多	Uncertain	1600	Rejoice + Many
U	S	Usa	宇佐	Hei'an	1183	Military Deputy
U	S	Utsu'nomiya	宇都宮	Kamakura	1332	Metropolis + Palace

棟 Ridge Pole

This *kanji* especially refers to the ridge pole of a house.

Reading	Type	Example	Kanji	Period	Date	Added Meaning
mune	F	Mu'neko	棟子	Kamakura	1332	[Lady]
mune	N	Tomomu'ne	朝棟	Nanboku	1392	Morning / Dawn

戸 Door

Reading	Type	Example	Kanji	Period	Date	Added Meaning
to	F	Toto	戸々	Uncertain	1600	
to	S	Edo	江戸	Kamakura	1332	Inlet / Harbour / Cove
to	S	Kido	木戸	Muromachi	1572	Tree
to	S	Mito	三戸	Nanboku	1392	Three
to	S	Seto'i	瀬戸井	Kamakura	1332	Rapids + Well
to	S	Shishido	宍戸	Kamakura	1332	Meat / Flesh (Vulgar)
to	S	Toda	戸田	Sengoku	1568	Rice Paddy
to	S	Tokawa	戸川	Sengoku	1568	River
to	S	Tozawa	戸澤	Sengoku	1568	Glen / Run

壁 Wall

Reading	Type	Example	Kanji	Period	Date	Added Meaning
kabe	S	Makabe	真壁	Nanboku	1392	Genuine

床 Platform Bed

Reading	Type	Example	Kanji	Period	Date	Added Meaning
toko	F	Tokoyome	床世賣	Nara	784	Generation / Life

厨 Kitchen / Chef

Reading	Type	Example	Kanji	Period	Date	Added Meaning
kuriya	F	Kuriyako	厨子	Hei'an	1183	[Lady]
kuriya	F	Kuriyame	厨賣	Nara	784	

間 Room / Space

Reading	Type	Example	Kanji	Period	Date	Added Meaning
ma	S	Honma	本間	Kamakura	1332	Main / Base
ma	S	Noma	野間	Momoyama	1438	Wide Plain
ma	S	Sakuma	佐久間	Sengoku	1568	Military Deputy + Longtime
ma	S	Takama	高間	Nanboku	1392	Tall

房 Monastic Cell

Reading	Type	Example	Kanji	Period	Date	Added Meaning
fusa	F	Fusako	房子	Kamakura	1242	[Lady]
fusa	N	Akifusa	顕房	Muromachi	1572	High Status
fusa	N	Akifusa	章房	Kamakura	1332	Writing / Elucidate
fusa	N	Arifusa	有房	Kamakura	1332	Exists
fusa	N	Chikafusa	親房	Kamakura	1332	Intimate
fusa	N	Fujifusa	藤房	Kamakura	1332	Wisteria
fusa	N	Fusa'aki	房顕	Muromachi	1572	High Status
fusa	N	Fusahira	房平	Muromachi	1572	Tranquility

Reading	Type	Example	Kanji	Period	Date	Added Meaning
fusa	N	Fusakage	房景	Muromachi	1572	Bright / Magnificent
fusa	N	Fusamasa	房昌	Hei'an	1183	Clear / Bright
fusa	N	Fusa'nari	房成	Hei'an	1183	Become / Exist
fusa	N	Fusasaki	房前	Uncertain	1600	Antecedent
fusa	N	Fusashige	房繁	Muromachi	1572	Bloom / Bouquet
fusa	N	Fusatsugu	房嗣	Muromachi	1572	Successor
fusa	N	Fusaza'ne	房実	Kamakura	1332	Reality
fusa	N	Fuyufusa	冬房	Muromachi	1572	Winter
fusa	N	Harufusa	春房	Muromachi	1572	Spring (Season)
fusa	N	Hirofusa	広房	Kamakura	1332	Spacious / Expansive
fusa	N	Iefusa	家房	Kamakura	1332	Rural House / Family
fusa	N	Ka'nefusa	兼房	Kamakura	1332	Unite
fusa	N	Kinfusa	公房	Kamakura	1332	Noble / Official
fusa	N	Kiyofusa	清房	Hei'an	1183	Pure
fusa	N	Korefusa	伊房	Uncertain	1600	This
fusa	N	Masafusa	匡房	Uncertain	1600	Make Correct
fusa	N	Mochifusa	持房	Muromachi	1572	Have / Possess
fusa	N	Morofusa	師房	Uncertain	1600	Teacher / Expert
fusa	N	Motofusa	基房	Hei'an	1183	Foundation
fusa	N	Nagafusa	長房	Kamakura	1332	Long
fusa	N	Nakafusa	仲房	Nanboku	1392	Middle of a Group
fusa	N	Narifusa	業房	Hei'an	1183	Industry / Diligence
fusa	N	Nobufusa	信房	Kamakura	1332	Belief / Faith
fusa	N	Nobufusa	宣房	Kamakura	1332	Proclamation
fusa	N	Norifusa	教房	Muromachi	1572	Teaching / Dogma
fusa	N	Norifusa	憲房	Nanboku	1392	Example / Pattern
fusa	N	Sadafusa	貞房	Kamakura	1332	Correct Spirit
fusa	N	Sadafusa	定房	Kamakura	1332	Determine
fusa	N	Sa'nefusa	実房	Hei'an	1183	Reality
fusa	N	Shigefusa	重房	Kamakura	1332	Heavy / Serious
fusa	N	Suefusa	季房	Kamakura	1332	Season
fusa	N	Sukefusa	資房	Muromachi	1572	Raw Materials
fusa	N	Tadafusa	忠房	Hei'an	1183	Faithful / Loyal
fusa	N	Takafusa	隆房	Kamakura	1332	Grow / Pile Up
fusa	N	Takefusa	武房	Kamakura	1332	Bravery / Military Force
fusa	N	Ta'nefusa	胤房	Muromachi	1572	Blood Heir
fusa	N	Tokifusa	時房	Kamakura	1332	Time / Era
fusa	N	Tomofusa	朝房	Nanboku	1392	Morning
fusa	N	Toyofusa	豊房	Muromachi	1572	Noble
fusa	N	Tsugufusa	嗣房	Nanboku	1392	Successor
fusa	N	Tsu'nefusa	経房	Hei'an	1183	True Path
fusa	N	Yorifusa	頼房	Nanboku	1392	Request / Ask
fusa	N	Yoshifusa	義房	Nanboku	1392	Fealty
fusa	N	Yoshifusa	良房	Uncertain	1600	Good / Superior
fusa	N	Yukifusa	行房	Nanboku	1392	Going To / Bound For

階 Stairs / Level / Story (Building) / Rank

Reading	Type	Example	Kanji	Period	Date	Added Meaning
KAI	S	Nikaidou	二階堂	Kamakura	1332	Two + Sanctuary
shina	S	Takashi'na	高階	Kamakura	1332	Tall

堂 Audience Hall / Sanctuary

Reading	Type	Example	Kanji	Period	Date	Added Meaning
DOU	S	Nikaidou	二階堂	Kamakura	1332	Two + Story

宅 Residence

Reading	Type	Example	Kanji	Period	Date	Added Meaning
yaka	F	Yakame	宅賣	Nara	784	
[Special]	S	Atagi	安宅	Nanboku	1392	Gentle / Safe / Secure

居 Dwelling

This *kanji* literally means to "live" someplace.

Reading	Type	Example	Kanji	Period	Date	Added Meaning
i	S	Do'i	土居	Nanboku	1392	Dirt / Land

家 Rural House / Family

Reading	Type	Example	Kanji	Period	Date	Added Meaning
ie	N	Aki'ie	顕家	Kamakura	1332	High Status
ie	N	Aki'ie	秋家	Kamakura	1332	Autumn
ie	N	Ari'ie	有家	Kamakura	1332	Exists
ie	N	Chika'ie	親家	Hei'an	1183	Intimate
ie	N	Fuyu'ie	冬家	Nanboku	1392	Winter
ie	N	Hide'ie	秀家	Uncertain	1600	Extraordinary / Bountiful
ie	N	Hiro'ie	博家	Kamakura	1332	Well Traveled / Learned
ie	N	Iefusa	家房	Kamakura	1332	Monastic Cell
ie	N	Iehide	家栄	Muromachi	1572	Bountiful / Fruitful
ie	N	Iehira	家平	Kamakura	1332	Tranquility
ie	N	Iekage	家景	Kamakura	1187	Bright / Magnificent
ie	N	Ieka'ne	家兼	Nanboku	1392	Unite
ie	N	Iekata	家賢	Nanboku	1392	Genius
ie	N	Iemasa	家政	Kamakura	1332	Govern / Rule
ie	N	Iemichi	家通	Hei'an	1183	Pass Through
ie	N	Iemitsu	家光	Kamakura	1332	Bright / Shining
ie	N	Iemoto	家基	Kamakura	1332	Foundation
ie	N	Ie'naga	家永	Kamakura	1332	Forever
ie	N	Ie'naga	家長‡	Hei'an	1183	Long
ie	N	Ie'nari	家成	Uncertain	1600	Become / Exist
ie	N	Ie'nori	家教	Kamakura	1332	Teaching / Dogma
ie	N	Iesada	家貞	Hei'an	1183	Correct Spirit
ie	N	Iesada	家定	Kamakura	1332	Determine
ie	N	Ietada	家忠	Kamakura	1332	Faithful / Loyal
ie	N	Ietaka	家高	Kamakura	1332	Tall
ie	N	Ietaka	家隆	Kamakura	1332	Grow / Pile Up
ie	N	Ietoki	家時	Kamakura	1332	Time / Era
ie	N	Ietoyo	家豊	Muromachi	1572	Noble
ie	N	Ietsugu	家継	Hei'an	1183	Connect / Adopt
ie	N	Ietsugu	家嗣	Uncertain	1600	Successor
ie	N	Ietsu'ne	家経	Kamakura	1332	True Path

ie	N	Ietsu'ne	家常	Kamakura	1332	Permanent	
ie	N	Ietsura	家連	Kamakura	1332	Bring Along	
ie	N	Ie'uji	家氏	Kamakura	1332	Family / Clan	
ie	N	Ieyasu	家康	Hei'an	1183	Strong / Confident	
ie	N	Ieyasu	家泰	Nanboku	1392	Peace / Plenitude	
ie	N	Ieyoshi	家義	Kamakura	1332	Fealty	
ie	N	Ieyoshi	家良	Kamakura	1332	Good / Superior	
ie	N	Ieyuki	家行	Kamakura	1332	Going To / Bound For	
ie	N	Ieza'ne	家実	Kamakura	1332	Reality	
ie	N	Iezumi	家純	Muromachi	1572	Natural / Pure	
ie	N	Kage'ie	景家	Hei'an	1183	Bright / Magnificent	
ie	N	Ka'ne'ie	兼家	Muromachi	1572	Unite	
ie	N	Kata'ie	片家	Uncertain	1600	One of Two	
ie	N	Katsu'ie	勝家	Uncertain	1600	Conquer / Triumph	
ie	N	Masa'ie	雅家	Kamakura	1332	High Quality	
ie	N	Masa'ie	政家	Muromachi	1572	Govern / Rule	
ie	N	Masa'ie	正家	Nanboku	1392	Unerring / Genuine	
ie	N	Masa'ie	昌家	Nanboku	1392	Clear / Bright	
ie	N	Michi'ie	道家	Kamakura	1332	Road / Way	
ie	N	Mitsu'ie	光家	Kamakura	1332	Bright / Shining	
ie	N	Mitsu'ie	満家	Muromachi	1572	Become Full / Abundant	
ie	N	Mochi'ie	持家	Muromachi	1572	Have / Possess	
ie	N	Mori'ie	盛家	Kamakura	1332	Plentiful / Piled Up	
ie	N	Moro'ie	師家	Hei'an	1183	Teacher / Expert	
ie	N	Moto'ie	基家	Kamakura	1332	Foundation	
ie	N	Mu'ne'ie	宗家	Kamakura	1332	Master an Art	
ie	N	Naka'ie	仲家	Kamakura	1332	Middle of a Group	
ie	N	Nao'ie	直家	Kamakura	1332	Adjust / Correct	
ie	N	Nari'ie	成家	Kamakura	1332	Become / Exist	
ie	N	Nori'ie	範家	Hei'an	1183	Required Form / Pattern	
ie	N	Sada'ie	貞家	Nanboku	1392	Correct Spirit	
ie	N	Sada'ie	定家	Kamakura	1332	Determine	
ie	N	Suke'ie	資家	Muromachi	1572	Raw Materials	
ie	N	Suke'ie	助家	Nanboku	1392	Deputy (Rescue / Assist)	
ie	N	Tada'ie	忠家	Kamakura	1332	Faithful / Loyal	
ie	N	Taka'ie	高家	Kamakura	1332	Tall	
ie	N	Taka'ie	隆家	Uncertain	1600	Grow / Pile Up	
ie	N	Tame'ie	為家	Kamakura	1332	Purpose / Goal	
ie	N	Ta'ne'ie	胤家	Kamakura	1332	Blood Heir	
ie	N	Toki'ie	時家	Hei'an	1183	Time / Era	
ie	N	Tomo'ie	知家	Kamakura	1332	Knowledge	
ie	N	Toshi'ie	利家	Sengoku	1568	Produce Results	
ie	N	Tsu'ne'ie	経家	Kamakura	1332	True Path	
ie	N	Uji'ie	氏家	Muromachi	1572	Family / Clan	
ie	N	Yasu'ie	泰家	Kamakura	1332	Peace / Plenitude	
ie	N	Yasyu'ie	保家	Hei'an	1183	Guarantee	
ie	N	Yori'ie	頼家	Kamakura	1332	Request / Ask	
ie	N	Yoshi'ie	義家	Uncertain	1600	Fealty	
ie	N	Yuki'ie	行家	Kamakura	1332	Going To / Bound For	
ie	S	Uji'ie	氏家	Uncertain	1600	Family / Clan	
yaka	F	Yakako	家児	Nara	784	Youth / Son or Daughter	
yaka	F	Yakame	家女	Nara	784	[Woman]	
yaka	F	Yakanarime	家成賣	Nara	784	Become / Exist	

Thematic Dictionary — Works of Man 137

屋 Urban House / Artisan

Reading	Type	Example	Kanji	Period	Date	Added Meaning
ya	F	Yayorime	屋依賣	Nara	784	Follow
ya	S	Bun'ya	文屋	Uncertain	1600	Literature / Culture
ya	S	Hariya	針屋	Uncertain	1600	Needle
ya	S	Tsuchiya	土屋	Hei'an	1183	Dirt / Earth
ya	S	Wakiya	脇屋	Nanboku	1392	Sides / Ribs / Supporter

宿 Inn

Reading	Type	Example	Kanji	Period	Date	Added Meaning
SUKU	F	Suku'name	宿奈女	Nara	784	[Woman]

留 Stay Over / Camp

This *kanji* denotes temporary lodging. Specifically, it denotes stopping over someplace. Originally, this *kanji* evoked the image of the bit and bridle of a horse being cinched. This idea was extended to the notion of coming to rest with subsequent lack of motion.

Reading	Type	Example	Kanji	Period	Date	Added Meaning
RU	S	Abiru	阿比留	Kamakura	1332	Crevice + Stay Over / Camp

館 Mansion / Hall

Reading	Type	Example	Kanji	Period	Date	Added Meaning
tachi	S	Oodachi	大館	Nanboku	1392	Big
tate	P	Hakodate	函館	Modern	1983	Letter Box

城 Castle

Note that *shiro* 城 takes its Chinese reading "JOU" when used in the names of castles. As with other place names, *shiro* 城 forms a final substantive element following a locative or other nominative.

Reading	Type	Example	Kanji	Period	Date	Added Meaning
JOU	P	Heijoukyou	平城京	Nara	710	Castle + Capital (Nara)
JOU	H	Jou'ichi	城一	Nanboku	1392	One
ki	S	Yuuki	結城	Kamakura	1332	Tie / Bind / Hold One's Breath
shiro	S	Yamashiro	山城	Uncertain	1600	Mountain

倉 Warehouse

Reading	Type	Example	Kanji	Period	Date	Added Meaning
kura	S	Asakura	朝倉	Muromachi	1572	Morning
kura	S	Hasekura	支倉	Uncertain	1600	Exchange Money
kura	S	Ogura	小倉	Kamakura	1332	Small

蔵 Storehouse

Note that Musashi 武蔵 is the name of a Japanese province and is not a *nanori*. Thus, Musashi does appear as the initial element of many Japanese place names. While there are examples of provincial names used as locatives in personal names, I have not been able to find a case for Musashi being used in this way. While Miyamoto Musashi 宮本 武蔵 is an historical person, Musashi was neither his *yobina*, his *nanori*, nor his *gagou* (art name). Musashi appears to be uniquely applied to this individual. And, as the battle of Sekigahara occurred in 1600, it is likely that he acquired this appellation after 1601. Finally, as with most entries marked as [Special], *kura* 蔵 does not take any of its normative readings in Musashi. Thus, *kura* 蔵 should not be read as "sashi" in other combinations.

Reading	Type	Example	Kanji	Period	Date	Added Meaning
ZOU	N	Kyuuzou	久蔵	Sengoku	1568	Longtime
ZOU	N	Takezou	武蔵	Sengoku	1568	Bravery / Military Force
[Special]	P	Musashi	武蔵	Nara	710	Bravery / Military Force

宮 Shintoh Shrine / Palace

Reading	Type	Example	Kanji	Period	Date	Added Meaning
miya	F	Miyame	宮賣	Nara	784	
miya	S	Miyabe	宮部	Uncertain	1600	Monopoly Corporation
miya	S	Miyamoto	宮本	Sengoku	1568	Main / Base
miya	S	Miyazaki	宮崎	Kamakura	1332	Slope
miya	S	Oomiya	大宮	Nanboku	1392	Big
miya	S	Utsu'nomiya	宇都宮	Kamakura	1332	Large Roof +Metropolis

寺 Buddhist Temple

Note that Ryuu'zou'ji is actually the name of a Buddhist temple. There are many examples of higher nobility known by their association with a temple or shrine. Further, some members of the merchant class appear to have been known by their association with temples during the 16th century. However, *tera* 寺 does appear in the names of members of the military class. Generally, it does not appear to be part of the name of any particular temple. Rather, it appears to indicate a general association either with a particular (unidentified) temple or with Buddhism in general. As Buddhism strongly influences much of the Japanese language and is reflected in many Japanese names, the latter is probably most often the case. That said, a warrior in service to a temple might be known by the name of the temple in the same way as a warrior attached to a private estate. Because temple names are Sino-Japanese in nature, this usage would tend to remain informal and not change into heritable family names.

Buddhist temples generally have two names. Since Buddhism was imported from China, these names are typically constructed using *onyomi* 音読 or Sino-Japanese readings. The first name always ends with 山 (mountain) which is pronounced as "ZAN" in most names. The second name ends with 寺 (temple) which may take either its Sino-Japanese *onyomi* reading as in Saidaiji 西大寺 or its native Japanese *kunyomi* reading as in Kiyomizudera 清水寺. Typically each of the gates and the major buildings of a Buddhist temple has its own name as well.

Reading	Type	Example	Kanji	Period	Date	Added Meaning
JI	P	Dai'toku'ji	大徳寺	Uncertain	1600	Big + Righteou / Just
JI	P	Gou'toku'ji	豪徳寺	Sengoku	1480	Righteous / Just
JI	P	Myou'hou'ji	妙法寺	Uncertain	1600	Law
JI	P	Sai'dai'ji	西大寺	Nara	765	Big
JI	S	Ryuu'zou'ji	竜造寺	Nanboku	1392	Dragon
tera	F	Terame	寺賣	Nara	784	
tera	S	O'nodera	小野寺	Uncertain	1600	Small + Wide Plain
tera	S	Terada	寺田	Kamakura	1332	Rice Paddy
tera	S	Tera'nishi	寺西	Sengoku	1568	West
tera	S	Terazawa	寺澤	Sengoku	1568	Glen / Run

院 Mansion / Temple / Palace / School

After the *insei* 院政 or "cloistered government" of retired emperors was established, the retired emperor was referred to as the In 院 and his administrative headquarters was known as the In no Chou 院庁.

Reading	Type	Example	Kanji	Period	Date	Added Meaning
IN	S	Ijuu'in	伊集院	Nanboku	1392	Rule + Gather Together

塔 Pagoda

In Buddhist architecture, a pagoda is a tall building which houses a relic in its topmost spire. The remainder of the building is not actually used and was evolved from *stupah* tombs found in India. Most Buddhist temples were originally built with two pagodas, but many of these have since been destroyed by fires other disasters.

Reading	Type	Example	Kanji	Period	Date	Added Meaning
TOU	S	Ishidou	石塔	Nanboku	1392	Rock

塚 Mound / Tomb

Reading	Type	Example	Kanji	Period	Date	Added Meaning
tsuka	S	Hiratsuka	平塚	Sengoku	1568	Flat / Even
tsuka	S	Ootsuka	大塚	Nanboku	1392	Big

基 Foundation / Earthen Dais

Reading	Type	Example	Kanji	Period	Date	Added Meaning
moto	F	Motoko	基子	Hei'an	1183	[Lady]
moto	N	Akimoto	明基	Hei'an	1183	Bright
moto	N	Iemoto	家基	Kamakura	1332	Rural House / Family
moto	N	Ka'nemoto	兼基	Kamakura	1332	Unite
moto	N	Kinmoto	公基	Kamakura	1332	Noble / Official
moto	N	Ku'nimoto	国基	Kamakura	1332	Country / Rural Area
moto	N	Masamoto	政基	Muromachi	1572	Govern / Rule
moto	N	Mochimoto	持基	Muromachi	1572	Have / Possess
moto	N	Moromoto	師基	Nanboku	1392	Teacher / Expert
moto	N	Motochika	基親	Kamakura	1332	Intimate
moto	N	Motofusa	基房	Hei'an	1183	Monastic Cell
moto	N	Motohide	基秀	Muromachi	1572	Extraordinary / Bountiful
moto	N	Motohira	基衡	Uncertain	1600	A Yoke
moto	N	Motohira	基平	Kamakura	1332	Tranquility
moto	N	Moto'ie	基家	Kamakura	1332	Rural House / Family
moto	N	Motoka'ne	基兼	Hei'an	1183	Unite
moto	N	Motokiyo	基清	Kamakura	1332	Pure
moto	N	Motoku'ni	基国	Nanboku	1392	Country / Rural Area
moto	N	Motomasa	基政	Kamakura	1332	Govern / Rule
moto	N	Motomichi	基通	Hei'an	1183	Pass Through
moto	N	Motomori	基盛	Hei'an	1183	Plentiful / Piled Up
moto	N	Motomu'ne	基宗	Kamakura	1332	Master an Art
moto	N	Mot'naga	基長ｷ	Nanboku	1392	Long
moto	N	Moto'nari	基成	Kamakura	1332	Become / Exist
moto	N	Moto'nobu	基宣	Kamakura	1332	Proclamation
moto	N	Moto'nori	基教	Kamakura	1332	Teaching / Dogma
moto	N	Moto'nori	基範	Hei'an	1183	Required Form / Pattern

Reading	Type	Example	Kanji	Period	Date	Added Meaning
moto	N	Motoshige	基重	Hei'an	1183	Heavy / Serious
moto	N	Motosuke	基佐久間	Sengoku	1568	Military Deputy
moto	N	Motosuke	基輔	Kamakura	1332	Ministerial Deputy
moto	N	Mototada	基忠	Kamakura	1332	Faithful / Loyal
moto	N	Mototaka	基隆	Kamakura	1332	Grow / Pile Up
moto	N	Mototoki	基時	Kamakura	1332	Time / Era
moto	N	Mototsugu	基嗣	Kamakura	1332	Successor
moto	N	Mototsu'na	基綱	Kamakura	1332	Net
moto	N	Mototsu'ne	基経	Uncertain	1600	True Path
moto	N	Mototsu'ne	基恒	Muromachi	1572	Changeless / Enduring
moto	N	Moto'uji	基氏	Kamakura	1332	Family / Clan
moto	N	Motoyasu	基康	Uncertain	1600	Strong / Confident
moto	N	Motoyori	基頼	Kamakura	1332	Request / Ask
moto	N	Motoyoshi	基義	Uncertain	1600	Fealty
moto	N	Motoyoshi	基能	Nanboku	1392	Talent / Ability
moto	N	Motoyuki	基行	Kamakura	1332	Going To / Bound For
moto	N	Motoza'ne	基実	Hei'an	1183	Reality
moto	N	Nagamoto	長基	Nanboku	1392	Long
moto	N	Nakamoto	仲基	Hei'an	1183	Middle of a Group
moto	N	Norimoto	教基	Muromachi	1572	Teaching / Dogma
moto	N	Norimoto	憲基	Muromachi	1572	Example / Pattern
moto	N	Sa'nemoto	実基	Kamakura	1332	Reality
moto	N	Sukemoto	資基	Kamakura	1332	Raw Materials
moto	N	Tamemoto	為基	Hei'an	1183	Purpose / Goal
moto	N	Tokimoto	時基	Kamakura	1332	Time / Era
moto	N	Toshimoto	俊基	Kamakura	1332	Emotional
moto	N	Tsu'nemoto	常基	Hei'an	1183	Permanent
moto	N	Yasumoto	康基	Uncertain	1600	Strong / Confident
moto	N	Yorimoto	頼基	Kamakura	1332	Request / Ask
moto	N	Yoshimoto	義基	Uncertain	1600	Fealty
moto	N	Yoshimoto	良基	Nanboku	1392	Good / Superior

里 Hamlet

Reading	Type	Example	Kanji	Period	Date	Added Meaning
sato	N	Chisato	千里	Uncertain	1600	One Thousand
sato	S	Satomi	里見	Kamakura	1332	Vantage / View / Vista
sato	S	Satomura	里村	Sengoku	1568	Village

郷 Hometown

Reading	Type	Example	Kanji	Period	Date	Added Meaning
sato	F	Satoko	郷子	Nanboku	1392	[Lady]
sato	N	Hidesato	秀郷	Uncertain	1600	Extraordinary / Bountiful
sato	N	Koresato	惟郷	Muromachi	1572	This / Here
sato	N	Mitsusato	光郷	Nanboku	1392	Bright / Shining
sato	N	Ujisato	氏郷	Sengoku	1568	Family / Clan
sato	N	Yoshisato	義郷	Muromachi	1572	Fealty
sato	N	Yoshisato	能郷	Kamakura	1332	Talent / Ability

庄 Rural / Hometown

Reading	Type	Example	Kanji	Period	Date	Added Meaning
SHOU	S	Honjou	本庄	Kamakura	1332	Main / Base

村 Village

Traditionally, families or more properly households are the fundamental social unit in Japan. Households consisted of those people living together in a shared residence. The *mura* 村 is the smallest grouping of households. Following the Taika Reform, the *mura* were reorganized into *gou* and then into *ri* of five households. The *mura* was reinstated in the Hei'an period and persists as a social unit to the present.

Reading	Type	Example	Kanji	Period	Date	Added Meaning
mura	N	Koremura	惟村	Nanboku	1392	This / Here
mura	N	Masamura	政村	Kamakura	1332	Govern / Rule
mura	N	Mitsumura	光村	Kamakura	1332	Bright / Shining
mura	N	Murashige	村重	Uncertain	1600	Heavy / Serious
mura	N	Norimura	則村	Kamakura	1332	Make an Example
mura	N	Sadamura	貞村	Muromachi	1572	Correct Spirit
mura	N	Sukemura	資村	Kamakura	1332	Raw Materials
mura	N	Ta'nemura	種村	Kamakura	1332	Cause / Reason
mura	N	Tokimura	時村	Kamakura	1332	Time / Era
mura	N	Tomomura	朝村	Kamakura	1332	Morning
mura	N	Yasumura	泰村	Kamakura	1332	Peace / Plenitude
mura	N	Yoshimura	義村	Kamakura	1332	Fealty
mura	N	Yukimura	幸村	Sengoku	1568	Happy / Tattoo
mura	N	Yukimura	行村	Kamakura	1332	Going To / Bound For
mura	S	Kawamura	河村	Kamakura	1332	Large River
mura	S	Kimura	木村	Sengoku	1568	Tree
mura	S	Mura'i	村井	Uncertain	1600	Well
mura	S	Murakami	村上	Kamakura	1332	Superior
mura	S	Murata	村田	Uncertain	1600	Rice Paddy
mura	S	Murayama	村山	Nanboku	1392	Mountain
mura	S	Nakamura	中村	Kamakura	1332	Middle
mura	S	Nishimura	西村	Sengoku	1568	West
mura	S	Oomura	大村	Sengoku	1568	Big
mura	S	Satomura	里村	Sengoku	1568	Hamlet
mura	S	Sawamura	澤村	Kamakura	1332	Glen / Run
mura	S	Tamura	田村	Nanboku	1392	Rice Paddy

町 Town

Reading	Type	Example	Kanji	Period	Date	Added Meaning
machi	F	Machime	町女	Hei'an	1183	[Woman]
machi	S	Oogimachi	大親町	Nanboku	1392	Big + Intimate

坊 Town / Monastic Residence

Originally, this *kanji* denoted a rectangular district such as a Chinese city.

Reading	Type	Example	Kanji	Period	Date	Added Meaning
BOU	S	Boumon	坊門	Kamakura	1332	Gate

市 Market

Reading	Type	Example	Kanji	Period	Date	Added Meaning
ichi	F	Ichi	市	Momoyama	1590	
ichi	S	Ichikawa	市河	Nanboku	1392	Large River

都 Metropolis = TO / Beautiful = TSU

Reading	Type	Example	Kanji	Period	Date	Added Meaning
TSU	F	Tsume	都女	Nara	784	[Woman]
TSU	F	Tsutomeme	都刀米賣	Nara	784	Sword
TSU	S	Utsu'nomiya	宇都宮	Kamakura	1332	Large Roof + Palace
[Special]	F	Ku'niko	都子	Hei'an	1183	[Lady]

京 Capital City / Magnificent

Reading	Type	Example	Kanji	Period	Date	Added Meaning
KYOU	P	Hei'ankyou	平安京	Hei'an	794	Peace + Capital (Kyoto)
KYOU	S	Kyougoku	京極	Kamakura	1332	Summit / Pinnacle
[Special]	F	Atsuko	京子	Hei'an	1183	[Lady]

坪 Palace Garden

Reading	Type	Example	Kanji	Period	Date	Added Meaning
tsubo	S	Ootsubo	大坪	Kamakura	1332	Large

庭 Garden / Courtyard / Atrium

Reading	Type	Example	Kanji	Period	Date	Added Meaning
[Special]	S	Ooba	大庭	Hei'an	1183	Large

園 Garden

Reading	Type	Example	Kanji	Period	Date	Added Meaning
sono	S	Sonoda	園田	Kamakura	1332	Rice Paddy

畠 Dry Field

Reading	Type	Example	Kanji	Period	Date	Added Meaning
hatake	S	Hatakeyama	畠山	Kamakura	1332	Mountain
hatake	S	Kitabatake	北畠	Nanboku	1392	North
hatake	S	Oobatake	大畠	Uncertain	1600	Big

田 Rice Paddy / Flooded Field

Reading	Type	Example	Kanji	Period	Date	Added Meaning
ta	F	Tadako	田子	Hei'an	1183	[Lady]
ta	F	Ta'nushime	田主女	Nara	784	Master + [Woman]
ta	F	Tasukime	田次女	Nara	784	Next + [Woman]
ta	S	Akita	秋田	Uncertain	1600	Autumn
ta	S	Awata	粟田	Hei'an	1183	Millet
ta	S	Awataguchi	粟田口	Kamakura	1332	Millet + Mouth
ta	S	Eda	江田	Nanboku	1392	Inlet / Harbour / Cove
ta	S	Fu'nada	船田	Kamakura	1332	Boat / Ship
ta	S	Furuda	古田	Sengoku	1568	Old
ta	S	Furuta	古田	Sengoku	1568	Old
ta	S	Hamoda	羽門田	Sengoku	1568	Feather + Gate
ta	S	Ha'neda	羽田	Higashiyama	1575	Feather
ta	S	Harada	原田	Nanboku	1392	Meadow
ta	S	Hatta	八田	Hei'an	1183	Eight
ta	S	Hirata	平田	Hei'an	1183	Flat / Even
ta	S	Hisada	久田	Sengoku	1568	Longtime
ta	S	Horita	堀田	Sengoku	1568	Dig / Carve / Excavation
ta	S	Hotta	堀田	Kamakura	1332	Dig / Carve / Excavation
ta	S	Ida	井田	Kamakura	1332	Well
ta	S	Iida	飯田	Kamakura	1332	Cooked Rice
ta	S	Ikeda	池田	Hei'an	1183	Pond
ta	S	Ishida	石田	Sengoku	1568	Rock
ta	S	Itoda	糸田	Kamakura	1332	Thread
ta	S	Kamata	鎌田	Hei'an	1183	Scythe
ta	S	Katata	堅田	Sengoku	1568	Tough / Strong
ta	S	Kishita	岸田	Sengoku	1568	Shore
ta	S	Kita	木田	Uncertain	1600	Tree
ta	S	Kuroda	黒田	Sengoku	1568	Black
ta	S	Maeda	前田	Sengoku	1568	Antecedent
ta	S	Makuta	蒔田	Sengoku	1568	Sow Seed / Paint
ta	S	Masuda	益田	Nanboku	1392	Grow Numerous / Overflow
ta	S	Masuda	増田	Uncertain	1600	Live Long / Prosper
ta	S	Matsuda	松田	Nanboku	1392	Pine Tree
ta	S	Morita	森田	Momoyama	1438	Woods
ta	S	Murata	村田	Uncertain	1600	Village
ta	S	Narita	成田	Kamakura	1332	Become / Exist
ta	S	Nigita	和田	Nanboku	1392	Peace / Tranquility
ta	S	Nitta	新田	Kamakura	1332	New
ta	S	Numada	沼田	Muromachi	1572	Swamp
ta	S	Oda	御田	Uncertain	1600	Honourable
ta	S	Oda	小田	Nanboku	1392	Small
ta	S	Oda	織田	Sengoku	1568	Weave
ta	S	Ooda	大田	Kamakura	1332	Big
ta	S	Oo'i'da	大井田	Kamakura	1332	Big + Well
ta	S	Oota	太田	Muromachi	1572	Fat
ta	S	Osada	長田	Hei'an	1183	Long
ta	S	Oyamada	小山田	Nanboku	1392	Mountain Small
ta	S	Sakurada	桜田	Uncertain	1600	Cherry Tree
ta	S	Sa'nada	佐奈田	Hei'an	1183	How? + Military Deputy
ta	S	Sa'nada	真田	Uncertain	1600	Genuine
ta	S	Sata	佐田	Muromachi	1572	Military Deputy
ta	S	Serada	世良田	Kamakura	1332	Generation + Good
ta	S	Shibata	柴田	Uncertain	1600	Bushes

Reading	Type	Example	Kanji	Period	Date	Added Meaning
ta	S	Shimada	島田	Muromachi	1572	Island
ta	S	Sonoda	園田	Kamakura	1332	Garden
ta	S	Tabara	田原	Nanboku	1392	Meadow
ta	S	Tada	多田	Hei'an	1183	Many
ta	S	Taguchi	田口	Hei'an	1183	Mouth / Entrance
ta	S	Tajiri	田尻	Kamakura	1332	Buttocks / Hips / Anus
ta	S	Takata	高田	Sengoku	1568	Tall
ta	S	Takeda	武田	Kamakura	1332	Bravery / Military Force
ta	S	Tamaru	田丸	Sengoku	1568	Round / Circle
ta	S	Tamura	田村	Nanboku	1392	Village
ta	S	Ta'naka	田中	Hei'an	1183	Middle
ta	S	Tashiro	田代	Nanboku	1392	Era
ta	S	Terada	寺田	Kamakura	1332	Temple
ta	S	Toda	戸田	Sengoku	1568	Door
ta	S	Tokuda	徳田	Nanboku	1392	Righteous / Just
ta	S	Toyoda	豊田	Sengoku	1568	Noble
ta	S	Tsuda	津田	Sengoku	1568	Harbour
ta	S	Ueta	上田	Sengoku	1568	Upper
ta	S	Wada	和田	Kamakura	1332	Peace / Tranquility
ta	S	Wosada	他田	Hei'an	1183	Other / Foreign
ta	S	Yamada	山田	Hei'an	1183	Mountain
ta	S	Yasuda	安田	Hei'an	1183	Gentle / Safe / Secure
ta	S	Yokota	横田	Uncertain	1600	Flat

堤 Dike / Levy

Reading	Type	Example	Kanji	Period	Date	Added Meaning
tsutsumi	S	Tsutsumi	堤	Hei'an	1183	Middle of a Group

樋 Flume

Reading	Type	Example	Kanji	Period	Date	Added Meaning
hi	S	Higuchi	樋口	Hei'an	1183	Mouth / Entrance
hi	S	Hizume	樋爪	Hei'an	1183	Claw

溝 Ditch / Gutter

Reading	Type	Example	Kanji	Period	Date	Added Meaning
mizo	S	Mizoguchi	溝口	Sengoku	1568	Mouth / Entrance

橋 Bridge

Note that *hashi* 橋 takes its Japanese reading when used in the names of bridges such as Nihonbashi 日本橋. As with other place names, *hashi* forms a final substantive element following a locative or other nominative.

Reading	Type	Example	Kanji	Period	Date	Added Meaning
hashi	S	Akahashi	赤橋	Uncertain	1600	Red (Fire) / Young
hashi	S	Ishibashi	石橋	Nanboku	1392	Rock
hashi	S	Takahashi	高橋	Sengoku	1568	Tall

❖ WORKS OF NATURE ❖

山 Mountain

When used in names for mountains, 山 forms the substantive element and may take either its Sino-Japanese reading as in Fujisan 富士山 or its Japanese reading as in Nishiyama 西山. Generally, the reading for the substantive element 山 agrees with the reading for the descriptive element. While some towns have names in which 山 takes its Sino-Japanese *onyomi* reading, the Japanese reading is normative for surnames.

山 also forms the substantive element in one of the names for Buddhist temples. Buddhist temples generally have two names. Since Buddhism was imported from China, these names are typically constructed using Sino-Japanese *onyomi* readings. The first name always ends with *yama* 山 (mountain) which generally takes the reading "ZAN" in these names. The second name ends with *tera* 寺 (temple) which may take either its Chinese reading as in Saidaiji 西大寺 or its Japanese reading as in Kiyomizudera 清水寺. Typically each of the gates and the major buildings of a Buddhist temple has its own name as well.

Reading	Type	Example	Kanji	Period	Date	Added Meaning
SAN	P	Enzan	塩山	Modern	1983	Salt
SAN	P	Fujisan	富士山	Modern	1674	Industry
yama	S	Akiyama	秋山	Uncertain	1600	Autumn
yama	S	Anayama	穴山	Uncertain	1600	Hole / Cleft
yama	S	Asayama	朝山	Nanboku	1392	Morning
yama	S	Hatakeyama	畠山	Kamakura	1332	Dry Field
yama	S	Hirayama	平山	Kamakura	1332	Flat / Even
yama	S	Kameyama	亀山	Kamakura	1332	Tortoise (Longevity)
yama	S	Kamiyama	上山	Nanboku	1392	Superior
yama	S	Koyama	小山	Uncertain	1600	Small
yama	S	Kuwayama	桑山	Sengoku	1568	Mulberry Bush
yama	S	Moriyama	守山	Nanboku	1392	Protect / Defend
yama	S	Murayama	村山	Nanboku	1392	Village
yama	S	Nishiyama	西山	Sengoku	1568	West
yama	S	Okuyama	奥山	Sengoku	1568	Innermost
yama	S	Ooyama	大山	Sengoku	1568	Big
yama	S	Oyama	小山	Kamakura	1332	Small
yama	S	Oyamada	小山田	Nanboku	1392	Rice Paddy Small
yama	S	Sakurayama	桜山	Uncertain	1600	Cherry Tree
yama	S	Toriyama	鳥山	Uncertain	1600	Bird
yama	S	Toyama	富山	Uncertain	1600	Industry
yama	S	Yamada	山田	Hei'an	1183	Rice Paddy
yama	S	Yamagata	山形	Uncertain	1600	Form / Shape / Beauty
yama	S	Yamagata	山県	Uncertain	1600	Territory / Province
yama	S	Yamagi	山木	Hei'an	1183	Tree
yama	S	Yamaguchi	山口	Sengoku	1568	Mouth / Entrance
yama	S	Yamakawa	山川	Sengoku	1568	River
yama	S	Yamamoto	山本	Hei'an	1183	Main / Base
yama	S	Yama'na	山名	Kamakura	1332	Famous / Admirable

Reading	Type	Example	Kanji	Period	Date	Added Meaning
yama	S	Yama'nobe	山辺	Uncertain	1600	Near
yama	S	Yama'no'uchi	山内	Hei'an	1183	Inside
yama	S	Yama'no'ue	山上	Nanboku	1392	Upper
yama	S	Yama'oka	山岡	Uncertain	1600	Hill
yama	S	Yamashiro	山城	Uncertain	1600	Castle
yama	S	Yama'uchi	山内	Muromachi	1572	Inside
yama	S	Yamazaki	山崎	Momoyama	1590	Slope
yama	S	Yokoyama	横山	Kamakura	1332	Flat

岳 Peak

Reading	Type	Example	Kanji	Period	Date	Added Meaning
[Special]	S	Mu'nawoka	宗岳	Hei'an	1183	Master an Art

崎 Slope

Reading	Type	Example	Kanji	Period	Date	Added Meaning
saki	S	Ishizaki	石崎	Muromachi	1572	Rock
saki	S	Miyazaki	宮崎	Kamakura	1332	Palace
saki	S	Nagasaki	長崎	Kamakura	1332	Long
saki	S	Okazaki	岡崎	Hei'an	1183	Hill
saki	S	Oosaki	大崎	Uncertain	1600	Big
saki	S	Shiozaki	塩崎	Uncertain	1600	Salt
saki	S	Takezaki	竹崎	Kamakura	1332	Bamboo
saki	S	Yamazaki	山崎	Momoyama	1590	Mountain

嶋 Island

The difference between 島 and 嶋 appears to be purely stylistic.

Reading	Type	Example	Kanji	Period	Date	Added Meaning
shima	F	Shimame	嶋賣	Nara	784	
shima	F	Shima'nushime	嶋主女	Nara	784	Master + [Woman]
shima	S	Kawashima	河嶋	Uncertain	1600	Large River

島 Island

The difference between 島 and 嶋 appears to be purely stylistic.

Reading	Type	Example	Kanji	Period	Date	Added Meaning
shima	F	Shimatarume	島乗賣	Nara	784	Mount / Multiply
shima	P	Kagoshima	鹿児島	Hei'an	1183	Child + Deer
shima	P	Tokushima	徳島	Hei'an	1183	Righteous / Just
shima	S	Fukushima	福島	Sengoku	1568	Happy / Blessed
shima	S	Goshima	五島	Sengoku	1568	Fifth
shima	S	Kashima	鹿島	Muromachi	1572	Deer
shima	S	Kojima	児島	Nanboku	1392	Youth / Son or Daughter
shima	S	Kurushima	来島	Sengoku	1568	Come Here / Immediate Future
shima	S	Nabeshima	鍋島	Uncertain	1600	Cook Pot
shima	S	Ogashima	小鹿島	Kamakura	1332	Small + Deer
shima	S	Ooshima	大島	Uncertain	1600	Big
shima	S	Samejima	鮫島	Kamakura	1332	Shark
shima	S	Shima	島	Sengoku	1568	
shima	S	Shimada	島田	Muromachi	1572	Rice Paddy

Thematic Dictionary — Works of Nature

Reading	Type	Example	Kanji	Period	Date	Added Meaning
shima	S	Shima'i	島井	Uncertain	1600	Well
shima	S	Shimazu	島津	Kamakura	1332	Harbour
shima	S	Toshima	豊島	Hei'an	1183	Noble
shima	S	Yoshima	好島	Kamakura	1332	Affection / Desire

塙 Ridge / Rise / Crest

This *kanji* can represent any sudden change in elevation.

Reading	Type	Example	Kanji	Period	Date	Added Meaning
hanawa	S	Ha'nawa	塙	Sengoku	1568	

丘 Hillock

Reading	Type	Example	Kanji	Period	Date	Added Meaning
oka	P	Koto'oka	琴丘	Modern	1983	Koto (Harp)
oka	P	Narabigaoka	双ヶ丘	Modern	1983	Pair / Two

岡 Hill

Reading	Type	Example	Kanji	Period	Date	Added Meaning
oka	S	Ima'oka	今岡	Nanboku	1392	Now
oka	S	Kata'oka	片岡	Kamakura	1332	One of Two
oka	S	Naga'oka	長岡	Kamakura	1332	Long
oka	S	Okabe	岡部	Kamakura	1332	Monopoly Corporation
oka	S	Okamoto	岡本	Sengoku	1568	Main / Base
oka	S	Okazaki	岡崎	Hei'an	1183	Slope
oka	S	Yama'oka	山岡	Uncertain	1600	Mountain

穴 Hole / Cleft

Reading	Type	Example	Kanji	Period	Date	Added Meaning
ana	S	Anayama	穴山	Uncertain	1600	Mountain

谷 Valley

Reading	Type	Example	Kanji	Period	Date	Added Meaning
tani	S	Mizutani	水谷	Sengoku	1568	Water
tani	S	Ootani	大谷	Sengoku	1568	Big
tani	S	Sugitani	杉谷	Sengoku	1568	Cedar Tree
tani	S	Ta'ni	谷	Sengoku	1568	
ya	S	Kamiya	神谷	Uncertain	1600	God
ya	S	Ka'naya	金谷	Nanboku	1392	Gold / Metal
ya	S	Kumagaya	熊谷	Sengoku	1568	Bear
ya	S	Shibuya	渋谷	Kamakura	1332	Blocked Off / Obstructed
ya	S	Takaya	高賀谷	Muromachi	1572	Tall + Celebrate A Gain
[Special]	S	Kumagai	熊谷	Hei'an	1183	Bear
[Special]	S	Hasebe	長谷部	Hei'an	1183	Monopoly Corporation
[Special]	S	Hasegawa	長谷川	Sengoku	1568	Long + River

森 Woods

Reading	Type	Example	Kanji	Period	Date	Added Meaning
mori	F	Moriko	森子	Nanboku	1392	[Lady]
mori	S	Ka'namori	金森	Sengoku	1568	Gold / Metal
mori	S	Mori	森	Uncertain	1600	
mori	S	Morita	森田	Momoyama	1590	Rice Paddy
mori	S	Oomori	大森	Nanboku	1392	Big

林 Forest

Reading	Type	Example	Kanji	Period	Date	Added Meaning
hayashi	S	Hayashi	林	Uncertain	1600	
hayashi	S	Oobayashi	大林	Uncertain	1600	Big

水 Water

Reading	Type	Example	Kanji	Period	Date	Added Meaning
SUI	S	Kikusui	菊水	Uncertain	1600	Chrysanthemum
mizu	S	Mizu'no	水野	Sengoku	1568	Wide Plain
mizu	S	Mizutani	水谷	Sengoku	1568	Valley
mizu	S	Yoshimizu	吉水	Nanboku	1392	Lucky / Fortunate

湯 Hot Water

Reading	Type	Example	Kanji	Period	Date	Added Meaning
YU	S	Yu'asa	湯浅	Kamakura	1332	Shallow

海 Sea

Reading	Type	Example	Kanji	Period	Date	Added Meaning
KAI	S	Kaitou	海東	Kamakura	1332	East
umi	S	Unno	海野	Kamakura	1332	Wide Plain

津 Harbour

Reading	Type	Example	Kanji	Period	Date	Added Meaning
tsu	S	Shimazu	島津	Kamakura	1332	Island
tsu	S	Takatsu	高津	Nanboku	1392	Tall
tsu	S	Tsuda	津田	Sengoku	1568	Rice Paddy
tsu	S	Tsugaru	津軽	Sengoku	1568	Light / Minor / Trifling / Easy

Thematic Dictionary — Works of Nature   149

池 Pond

Reading	Type	Example	Kanji	Period	Date	Added Meaning
CHI	S	Kikuchi	菊池	Kamakura	1332	Chrysanthemum
ike	F	Ikeko	池子	Nanboku	1392	[Lady]
ike	S	Ike	池	Uncertain	1600	
ike	S	Ikeda	池田	Hei'an	1183	Rice Paddy

波 Wave

Reading	Type	Example	Kanji	Period	Date	Added Meaning
HA	F	Hakome	波古賣	Nara	784	Old
HA	F	Hatame	波太賣	Nara	784	Eldest
HA	S	Haki'i	波木井	Kamakura	1332	Tree + Well
HA	S	Hata'no	波多野	Kamakura	1332	Many + Wide Plain
HA	S	Maeba	前波	Sengoku	1568	Antecedent
HA	S	Shiba	斯波	Kamakura	1332	This Way

淵 Aquatic Cliff / Deep Water / Abyss

Reading	Type	Example	Kanji	Period	Date	Added Meaning
fuchi	S	Ha'nebuchi	羽淵	Higashiyama	1575	Feather

浜 Beach

Reading	Type	Example	Kanji	Period	Date	Added Meaning
hama	F	Hamame	浜女	Nara	784	[Woman]
hama	N	Hama'nari	浜成	Uncertain	1600	Become / Exist

岸 Shore

Reading	Type	Example	Kanji	Period	Date	Added Meaning
kishi	S	Kishita	岸田	Sengoku	1568	Rice Paddy

浦 Bay / Delta

Reading	Type	Example	Kanji	Period	Date	Added Meaning
ura	S	Matsu'ura	松浦	Muromachi	1572	Pine Tree
ura	S	Mi'ura	三浦	Kamakura	1332	Three
ura	S	Uragami	浦上	Muromachi	1572	Superior
ura	S	Urakami	浦上	Uncertain	1600	Upper

沼 Swamp

Reading	Type	Example	Kanji	Period	Date	Added Meaning
numa	S	Aso'numa	阿曾沼	Nanboku	1392	Aso (A region in Kyushu)
numa	S	Naga'numa	長沼	Kamakura	1332	Long
numa	S	Numada	沼田	Muromachi	1572	Rice Paddy

澤 Glen / Run

A *sawa* 澤 is actually a kind of swamp in that the water table is at or above ground level. However, a typical example can be found in the mountains where water seeps out of the ground along a rock trail going up the side of a mountain. In general, a *sawa* does not have the brackish or stagnant connotations which "swamp" does in the English language.

Reading	Type	Example	Kanji	Period	Date	Added Meaning
sawa	S	Isawa	伊澤	Kamakura	1332	This
sawa	S	Ka'nazawa	金澤	Uncertain	1600	Gold / Metal
sawa	S	Ka'nezawa	金澤	Uncertain	1600	Gold / Metal
sawa	S	Nagazawa	中澤	Muromachi	1572	Middle
sawa	S	Sawa	澤	Nanboku	1392	
sawa	S	Sawamura	澤村	Kamakura	1332	Village
sawa	S	Terazawa	寺澤	Sengoku	1568	Temple
sawa	S	Tozawa	戸澤	Sengoku	1568	Door
sawa	S	Aizawa	相澤	Modern	1782	Together / Team Work

川 River

Reading	Type	Example	Kanji	Period	Date	Added Meaning
kawa	S	Kobayakawa	小早川	Kamakura	1332	Small + Fast / Early
kawa	N	Momokawa	百川	Uncertain	1600	One Hundred
kawa	S	Arakawa	荒川	Nanboku	1392	Wild / Untamed
kawa	S	Hasegawa	長谷川	Sengoku	1568	Long + Valley
kawa	S	Hayakawa	早川	Uncertain	1600	Fast / Early
kawa	S	Horikawa	堀川	Nanboku	1392	Dig / Carve / Excavation
kawa	S	Hosokawa	細川	Nanboku	1392	Thin
kawa	S	Imagawa	今川	Nanboku	1392	Now
kawa	S	Imakawa	今川	Uncertain	1600	Now
kawa	S	Ishikawa	石川	Hei'an	1183	Rock
kawa	S	Kawakatsu	川勝	Sengoku	1568	Conquer / Triumph
kawa	S	Kawashiri	川尻	Sengoku	1568	Buttocks / Hips / Anus
kawa	S	Kikkawa	吉川	Nanboku	1392	Lucky / Fortunate
kawa	S	Mi'nakawa	皆川	Uncertain	1600	Everybody
kawa	S	Nakagawa	中川	Sengoku	1568	Middle
kawa	S	Ogawa	小川	Uncertain	1600	Small
kawa	S	Shibukawa	渋川	Nanboku	1392	Blocked Off / Obstructed
kawa	S	Takikawa	瀧川	Uncertain	1600	Waterfall
kawa	S	Tatsukawa	龍川	Uncertain	1600	Dragon
kawa	S	Tokawa	戸川	Sengoku	1568	Door
kawa	S	Tokugawa	徳川	Uncertain	1600	Righteous / Just
kawa	S	Yamakawa	山川	Sengoku	1568	Mountain
kawa	S	Yoshikawa	吉川	Sengoku	1568	Lucky / Fortunate

河 Large River

This kanji is associated with the Yellow River which is the second largest river in China.

Reading	Type	Example	Kanji	Period	Date	Added Meaning
KA	S	Ohoshika	凡河	Uncertain	1600	Every / Ordinary
KA	S	Suruga	駿河	Kamakura	1332	Fast / Rapid
KOU	S	Ko'uchi	河内	Uncertain	1600	Inside
KOU	S	Kou'no	河野	Kamakura	1332	Wide Plain
kawa	S	Aikawa	淡河	Kamakura	1332	This / Pale / Weak
kawa	S	Ichikawa	市河	Nanboku	1392	Market
kawa	S	Kawachi	河内	Uncertain	1600	Inside
kawa	S	Kawagoe	河越	Kamakura	1332	Surpass
kawa	S	Kawamura	河村	Kamakura	1332	Village
kawa	S	Kawa'no	河野	Uncertain	1600	Wide Plain
kawa	S	Kawara	河原	Hei'an	1183	Meadow
kawa	S	Kawashima	河嶋	Uncertain	1600	Island
kawa	S	Kawa'uchihara	河内原	Uncertain	1600	Inside + Meadow
kawa	S	Samukawa	寒河	Muromachi	1572	Cold
kawa	S	Shi'nagawa	品河	Kamakura	1332	Goods
kawa	S	Teshigawara	勅使河原	Nanboku	1392	Decree + Meadow

江 Inlet / Harbour / Cove

An *e* 江 is a place where the sea or a lake cuts into the land and provides safe anchorage for ships and boats.

Reading	Type	Example	Kanji	Period	Date	Added Meaning
e	S	Eda	江田	Nanboku	1392	Rice Paddy
e	S	Edo	江戸	Kamakura	1332	Door
e	S	Naka'e	中江	Sengoku	1568	Middle
e	S	Nao'e	直江	Sengoku	1568	Adjust / Correct
e	S	Oo'e	大江	Hei'an	1183	Big

瀬 Rapids

Reading	Type	Example	Kanji	Period	Date	Added Meaning
se	S	Iwase	岩瀬	Hei'an	1183	Boulder
se	S	Nagase	長瀬	Nanboku	1392	Long
se	S	Seto'i	瀬戸井	Kamakura	1332	Door + Well
se	S	Yokose	横瀬	Muromachi	1572	Flat

瀧 Waterfall

Reading	Type	Example	Kanji	Period	Date	Added Meaning
taki	S	Takikawa	瀧川	Uncertain	1600	River

沙 Sand (In Water) / Quick Sand

Reading	Type	Example	Kanji	Period	Date	Added Meaning
SA	F	Sabame	沙婆賣	Nara	784	Old Woman / Hag
SA	F	Sashime	沙姿賣	Nara	784	Form / Shape / Figure

泥 Mud / Muddy

Reading	Type	Example	Kanji	Period	Date	Added Meaning
ne	F	Nebame	泥婆賣	Nara	784	Old Woman / Hag
ne	F	Neshime	泥姿賣	Nara	784	Form / Shape / Figure
[Special]	F	Nume	泥賣	Nara	784	

泉 Spring (Water)

Reading	Type	Example	Kanji	Period	Date	Added Meaning
izumi	S	Izumi	泉	Kamakura	1213	

野 Wide Plain

Note that a Japanese Plain can be either grasslands or forested.

Reading	Type	Example	Kanji	Period	Date	Added Meaning
no	S	Ama'no	天野	Kamakura	1332	Sky / Heaven
no	S	Asa'no	浅野	Sengoku	1568	Shallow
no	S	Hata'no	波多野	Kamakura	1332	Waves + Many
no	S	Hine'no	日根野	Nanboku	1392	Sun / Day + Root / Base
no	S	Hira'no	平野	Momoyama	1590	Flat / Even
no	S	Ii'no	飯野	Nanboku	1392	Cooked Rice
no	S	Kawa'no	河野	Uncertain	1600	Large River
no	S	Kou'no	河野	Kamakura	1332	Large River
no	S	Kusa'no	草野	Kamakura	1332	Grass
no	S	Mizu'no	水野	Sengoku	1568	Water
no	S	Naka'no	中野	Kamakura	1332	Middle
no	S	Nogami	野上	Nanboku	1392	Superior
no	S	Noma	野間	Momoyama	1590	Room / Space
no	S	Ogi'no	荻野	Nanboku	1392	Common Reed
no	S	O'no	小野	Hei'an	1183	Small
no	S	O'nodera	小野寺	Uncertain	1600	Small + Temple
no	S	Oo'no	大野	Sengoku	1568	Big
no	S	Ooya'no	大矢野	Kamakura	1332	Big + Arrow
no	S	Sa'no	佐野	Kamakura	1332	Military Deputy
no	S	Shige'no	滋野	Hei'an	1183	Grow / Blossom
no	S	Take'no	武野	Sengoku	1568	Bravery / Military Force
no	S	Tomi'no	富野	Hei'an	1183	Industry
no	S	Ue'no	上野	Nanboku	1392	Upper
no	S	Unno	海野	Kamakura	1332	Sea

原 Meadow

A Japanese Meadow is large, relatively flat and covered with flowers. A *kougen* 高原 is an alpine meadow.

Reading	Type	Example	Kanji	Period	Date	Added Meaning
hara	S	A'ihara	栗飯原	Nanboku	1392	Chestnut + Cooked Rice
hara	S	Asahara	浅原	Kamakura	1332	Shallow
hara	S	Fuji'wara	藤原	Nara	784	Wisteria
hara	S	Fukuhara	福原	Sengoku	1568	Happy / Blessed
hara	S	Hara	原	Hei'an	1183	
hara	S	Harada	原田	Nanboku	1392	Rice Paddy

Thematic Dictionary — Works of Nature 153

Reading	Type	Example	Kanji	Period	Date	Added Meaning
hara	S	Ihohara	蘆原	Hei'an	1183	Reed / Rush
hara	S	Inuhara	犬原	Hei'an	1183	Dog
hara	S	Kajiwara	梶原	Kamakura	1332	Rudder
hara	S	Kasawara	笠原	Uncertain	1600	Umbrella
hara	S	Kawara	河原	Hei'an	1183	Large River
hara	S	Kawa'uchihara	河内原	Uncertain	1600	Large River Inside
hara	S	Kiyohara	清原	Kamakura	1332	Pure
hara	S	Kokasahara	小笠原	Uncertain	1600	Small + Umbrella
hara	S	Kuzurahara	葛原	Uncertain	1600	Arrowroot
hara	S	Nakahara	中原	Hei'an	1183	Middle
hara	S	Ogasawara	小笠原	Nanboku	1392	Small
hara	S	Oohara	大原	Kamakura	1332	Big
hara	S	Sahara	佐原	Hei'an	1183	Military Deputy
hara	S	Sakakibara	榊原	Sengoku	1568	Camellia / Cleyera Ochnacea
hara	S	Sugihara	杉原	Sengoku	1568	Cedar Tree
hara	S	Tabara	田原	Nanboku	1392	Rice Paddy
hara	S	Teshigawara	勅使河原	Nanboku	1392	Decree + Large River

牧 Pasture

Reading	Type	Example	Kanji	Period	Date	Added Meaning
maki	F	Makime	牧賣	Nara	784	
maki	F	Makinokata	牧方	Kamakura	1332	Direction / Method
maki	S	Maki	牧	Kamakura	1332	

土 Dirt / Earth

Reading	Type	Example	Kanji	Period	Date	Added Meaning
DO	S	Dohi	土肥	Kamakura	1332	Fertility / Grow Fat
DO	S	Do'i	土居	Nanboku	1392	Dwelling
TO	S	Toki	土岐	Kamakura	1332	Bend in the Road / Divide
tsuchi	F	Tsuchi	土	Momoyama	1590	
tsuchi	F	Tsuchime	土賣	Nara	784	
tsuchi	S	Tsuchiya	土屋	Hei'an	1183	Urban House / Artisan

石 Rock

Reading	Type	Example	Kanji	Period	Date	Added Meaning
SEKI	S	Senseki	仙石	Sengoku	1568	Hermit / Adept
iha	F	Ihamime	石身賣	Nara	784	Body / Pregnant
ishi	F	Ishi	石	Muromachi	1572	
ishi	F	Ishime	石女	Kamakura	1332	[Woman]
ishi	S	Akashi	赤石	Nanboku	1371	Red (Fire) / Young
ishi	S	Ishibashi	石橋	Nanboku	1392	Bridge
ishi	S	Ishida	石田	Sengoku	1568	Rice Paddy
ishi	S	Ishidou	石塔	Nanboku	1392	Pagoda
ishi	S	Ishi'i	石井	Nanboku	1392	Well
ishi	S	Ishikawa	石川	Hei'an	1183	River
ishi	S	Ishizaki	石崎	Muromachi	1572	Slope
ishi	S	Taka'ishi	高石	Kamakura	1332	Tall
iwa	S	Iwami	石見	Muromachi	1572	Vantage / View / Vista

岩 Boulder

Reading	Type	Example	Kanji	Period	Date	Added Meaning
iha	F	Iha	岩	Muromachi	1572	
iwa	F	Iwa	岩	Uncertain	1600	
iwa	F	Iwatsurume	岩鶴女	Nanboku	1392	Crane + [Woman]
iwa	S	Hira'iwa	平岩	Sengoku	1568	Flat / Even
iwa	S	Iwamatsu	岩松	Muromachi	1572	Pine Tree
iwa	S	Iwase	岩瀬	Hei'an	1183	Rapids

荒 Wild / Untamed

Reading	Type	Example	Kanji	Period	Date	Added Meaning
ara	S	Arakawa	荒川	Nanboku	1392	River
ara	S	Araki	荒木	Muromachi	1572	Tree

❖ Celestial Phenomena ❖

天 Sky / Heaven

Note that Tenjiku 天竺 is the ancient name for India used by people in China, Korea and Japan. It is not the name of a place in Japan and was included for historical interest only.

Reading	Type	Example	Kanji	Period	Date	Added Meaning
TEN	P	Tenjiku	天竺	Nara	784	Fat Bamboo
TEN	Y	Tenbun	天文	Sengoku	1532	Literature / Culture
TEN	Y	Ten'ei	天永	Hei'an	1110	Forever
TEN	Y	Tengi	天喜	Hei'an	1053	Rejoice
TEN	Y	Tenji	天治	Hei'an	1124	Govern / Rule
TEN	Y	Tenju	天授	Nanboku	1375	Grant / Bestow
TEN	Y	Tenmei	天明	Edo	1781	Bright
TEN	Y	Tenna	天和	Edo	1681	Peace / Tranquility / Harmony
TEN	Y	Tennin	天仁	Hei'an	1108	Precious
TEN	Y	Tenpou	天保	Edo	1830	Guarantee
TEN	Y	Tenpuku	天福	Kamakura	1233	Happiness (Felicitity)
TEN	Y	Tenshou	天承	Hei'an	1131	Humbly Receive
TEN	Y	Tenshou	天正	Momoyama	1573	Unerring / Genuine
TEN	Y	Ten'you	天養	Hei'an	1144	Rear / Raise / Nourish
ama	S	Ama'no	天野	Kamakura	1332	Wide Plain

日 Sun / Day

Reading	Type	Example	Kanji	Period	Date	Added Meaning
NICHI	F	Nikkouhime	日光姫	Kamakura	1332	Bright / Shining + Princess
NICHI	H	Nichiren	日蓮	Kamakura	1332	Lotus
NICHI	P	Nikkou	日光	Modern	1983	Bright / Shining
hi	F	Hime	日賣	Nara	784	
hi	F	Hisame	日佐賣	Nara	784	Military Deputy
hi	F	Hishimame	日嶋女	Nara	784	Island + [Woman]
hi	S	Hine'no	日根野	Nanboku	1392	Root / Base + Wide Plain
[Special]	S	Kasuga	春日	Nanboku	1392	Spring (Season)

月 Moon / Month

Reading	Type	Example	Kanji	Period	Date	Added Meaning
suki	F	Tsukime	月賣	Hei'an	1183	
tsuki	S	Akizuki	秋月	Nanboku	1392	Autumn

子 Rat (Zodiac)

The sign of the rat is the first of the twelve houses in Chinese astrology. This is a very propitious sign as it connotes wealth and good fortune. Rats are a sign that the store houses are full of grain and there is plenty of food to eat. Lin Shan says that people born in this year or under this sign are optimistic, generous and congenial. Names associated with human beings, dwellings, store houses and food are especially appropriate for these people.

Reading	Type	Example	Kanji	Period	Date	Added Meaning
ne	F	Ne'neme	子々女	Muromachi	1572	[Woman]

丑 Ox (Zodiac)

The sign of the ox is the second of the twelve houses in Chinese astrology. Oxen are very strong and are still used as draft animals in much of Asia. Court nobles commonly employed ox carts fitted out as small rooms. Inside cities, these carts were sometimes pulled by retainers and in all cases the oxen are lead by retainers. The wheel of an ox cart is strongly associated with *Genji Monogatari* in which case it is depicted half submerged in water. Lin Shan says that people born in this year or under this sign are destined to work hard throughout their lives. Supposably, such people are also destined to live in comfort if they are born at night. Oxen are also stable, determined and not at all impetuous.

Reading	Type	Example	Kanji	Period	Date	Added Meaning
ushi	No examples of names using this *kanji* have yet been found. *Kanji* included for completeness.					

寅 Tiger (Zodiac)

The sign of the tiger is the third of the twelve houses in Chinese astrology. Tigers are very ferocious and so are tiger people. They are believed to be strong, independent and self assured. These people are destined to live eventful lives. Lin Shan says that these traits are more pronounced for people born during the night. In China, names containing an element associated with mountains such as are especially propitious for these people. In Japan, these elements primarily appear in surnames.

Reading	Type	Example	Kanji	Period	Date	Added Meaning
tora	F	Tora	寅	Muromachi	1572	
tora	F	Tora'inu'me	寅犬	Nanboku	1392	Dog
tora	F	Torame	寅女	Hei'an	1183	[Woman]

卯 Hare (Zodiac)

Reading	Type	Example	Kanji	Period	Date	Added Meaning
u	No examples of names using this *kanji* have yet been found. *Kanji* included for completeness.					

辰 Dragon (Zodiac)

Reading	Type	Example	Kanji	Period	Date	Added Meaning
tatsu	F	Tatsuko	辰子	Muromachi	1572	[Lady]
toki	N	Michitoki	道辰	Nanboku	1392	Road / Way

巳 Snake (Zodiac)

Reading	Type	Example	Kanji	Period	Date	Added Meaning
mi	No examples of names using this *kanji* have yet been found. *Kanji* included for completeness.					

Thematic Dictionary — Celestial Phenomena 157

午 Horse (Zodiac)

Reading	Type	Example	Kanji	Period	Date	Added Meaning
GO	M	Heigo	丙午	Modern	1983	Third (Alter)
uma	No examples of names using this reading have yet been found. Reading included for completeness.					

未 Goat (Zodiac)

Reading	Type	Example	Kanji	Period	Date	Added Meaning
hitsuji	F	Hitsujime	未女	Constructed	800	[Woman]

申 Monkey (Zodiac)

Reading	Type	Example	Kanji	Period	Date	Added Meaning
saru	F	Sarume	申賣	Nara	784	

酉 Cock (Zodiac)

Reading	Type	Example	Kanji	Period	Date	Added Meaning
tori	F	Torime	酉女	Constructed	800	[Woman]

戌 Dog (Zodiac)

Reading	Type	Example	Kanji	Period	Date	Added Meaning
inu	No examples of names using this *kanji* have yet been found. *Kanji* included for completeness.					

亥 Boar (Zodiac)

Reading	Type	Example	Kanji	Period	Date	Added Meaning
i	No examples of names using this *kanji* have yet been found. *Kanji* included for completeness.					

晴 Clear (Sky)

Reading	Type	Example	Kanji	Period	Date	Added Meaning
haru	N	Haruhisa	晴久	Sengoku	1568	Longtime
haru	N	Haru'nobu	晴信	Uncertain	1600	Belief / Faith
haru	N	Harutomo	晴具	Uncertain	1600	Tool / Implement
haru	N	Haruyuki	晴幸	Uncertain	1600	Happy / Tattoo
haru	N	Nariharu	斉晴	Nanboku	1392	Prepare / Gather
haru	N	Yoshiharu	可晴	Sengoku	1568	Do This

蒸 Hot & Humid

Reading	Type	Example	Kanji	Period	Date	Added Meaning
musu	F	Musu	蒸	Uncertain	1600	

温 Hot / Heat

Reading	Type	Example	Kanji	Period	Date	Added Meaning
yoshi	F	Yoshiko	温子	Hei'an	1183	[Lady]

寒 Cold

Reading	Type	Example	Kanji	Period	Date	Added Meaning
samu	S	Samukawa	寒河	Muromachi	1572	Large River

雲 Cloud

Reading	Type	Example	Kanji	Period	Date	Added Meaning
kumo	F	Kumoko	雲子	Hei'an	1183	[Lady]
kumo	F	Kumome	雲女	Nara	784	[Woman]

霧 Fog

Reading	Type	Example	Kanji	Period	Date	Added Meaning
haru	F	Harukiri	春霧	Muromachi	1572	Spring (Season)
kiri	P	Kirishima	霧島	Modern	1983	Island

雪 Snow

Reading	Type	Example	Kanji	Period	Date	Added Meaning
yuki	F	Miyukime	三雪女	Nara	784	Three + [Woman]
yuki	F	Yukiko	雪子	Nanboku	1392	[Lady]

風 Wind

Reading	Type	Example	Kanji	Period	Date	Added Meaning
kaze	N	Okikaze	興風	Uncertain	1600	Happen / Begin

❖ Plants ❖

木   Tree / Wooden

Reading	Type	Example	Kanji	Period	Date	Added Meaning
ki	S	Aoki	青木	Sengoku	1568	Blue / Green
ki	S	Araki	荒木	Muromachi	1572	Wild / Untamed
ki	S	Haki'i	波木井	Kamakura	1332	Wave + Well
ki	S	Kido	木戸	Muromachi	1572	Door
ki	S	Kimoto	木本	Nanboku	1392	Main / Base
ki	S	Kimura	木村	Sengoku	1568	Village
ki	S	Ki'no'shita	木下	Sengoku	1568	Below
ki	S	Kiso	木曾	Uncertain	1600	Formerly / Ever
ki	S	Kita	木田	Uncertain	1600	Rice Paddy
ki	S	Kozukuri	木造	Nanboku	1392	Make / Manufacture
ki	S	Kusu'noki	楠木	Nanboku	1392	Camphor Tree
ki	S	Kutsuki	朽木	Kamakura	1332	Decay / Rot
ki	S	Miki	三木	Kamakura	1332	Three
ki	S	Motegi	茂木	Nanboku	1392	Blossoming
ki	S	Niki	仁木	Kamakura	1332	Precious
ki	S	Sasaki	佐々木	Kamakura	1332	Military Deputy
ki	S	Suzuki	鈴木	Uncertain	1600	Small Bell
ki	S	Takaki	高木	Sengoku	1568	Tall
ki	S	Yagi	矢木	Kamakura	1332	Arrow
ki	S	Yamagi	山木	Hei'an	1183	Mountain

松   Pine Tree

The pine tree is one of the felicitous trees in Japan. As pine trees are green all year, they are associated with Winter and old age. The pine tree is especially associated with the month of December and the Noh play Okina. A famous Japanese saying holds that "bamboo is straight and pine trees are gnarled", and other has that "pine trees break in the wind while bamboo bends in the wind.".

Reading	Type	Example	Kanji	Period	Date	Added Meaning
matsu	F	Matsu	松	Kamakura	1332	
matsu	F	Matsume	松女	Muromachi	1572	[Woman]
matsu	F	Matsume	松賣	Hei'an	1183	
matsu	N	Takatoshi	高松	Uncertain	1600	Tall
matsu	S	Akamatsu	赤松	Nanboku	1392	Red (Fire) / Young
matsu	S	Akimatsu	秋松	Uncertain	1600	Autumn
matsu	S	Chikamatsu	近松	Uncertain	1600	Near
matsu	S	Iwamatsu	岩松	Muromachi	1572	Boulder
matsu	S	Matsuda	松田	Nanboku	1392	Rice Paddy
matsu	S	Matsudaira	松平	Muromachi	1572	Flat
matsu	S	Matsu'i	松井	Sengoku	1568	Well

Reading	Type	Example	Kanji	Period	Date	Added Meaning
matsu	S	Matsumoto	松本	Sengoku	1468	Main / Base
matsu	S	Matsu'naga	松永	Uncertain	1600	Forever
matsu	S	Matsushita	松下	Sengoku	1568	Below
matsu	S	Matsu'ura	松浦	Muromachi	1572	Bay / Delta
matsu	S	Takamatsu	高松	Nanboku	1392	Tall

杉 Cedar Tree

Reading	Type	Example	Kanji	Period	Date	Added Meaning
sugi	P	Suginome	杉目	Suginome	1593	Eye
sugi	S	Sugihara	杉原	Sengoku	1568	Meadow
sugi	S	Sugitani	杉谷	Sengoku	1568	Valley
sugi	S	Uesugi	上杉	Kamakura	1332	Upper

樫 Evergreen Oak

Reading	Type	Example	Kanji	Period	Date	Added Meaning
kashi	S	Togashi	富樫	Muromachi	1572	Become Wealthy

柳 Willow Tree

Reading	Type	Example	Kanji	Period	Date	Added Meaning
ya	S	Yagyuu	柳生	Sengoku	1568	Life / Live / Living
yanagi	P	Oniyanagi	鬼柳	Modern	1983	Ogre

桜 Cherry

Cherry trees are primarily appreciated for their blossoms. Since ancient times, Japanese have congregated under cherry trees to drink, play games, sing and write poems. Many organizations sponsor drinking parties known as *hanami* 花見 for this purpose. Typically an honourific is attached and modern Japanese speak of *ohanami*.

Reading	Type	Example	Kanji	Period	Date	Added Meaning
sakura	S	Sakurada	桜田	Uncertain	1600	Rice Paddy
sakura	S	Sakura'i	桜井	Higashiyama	1482	Well
sakura	S	Sakurayama	桜山	Uncertain	1600	Mountain

桃 Peach

Momotarou 桃太郎 is the national folk hero of Japan. He is miraculously born from a large peach and goes on to conquer the oni 鬼 or ogres which plagued Japan. Peaches remain a popular offering at Buddhist and Shintoh alters.

Reading	Type	Example	Kanji	Period	Date	Added Meaning
momo	F	Momoko	桃子	Uncertain	1600	[Lady]
momo	S	Momono'i	桃井	Nanboku	1392	Well

葵 Hollyhock

Reading	Type	Example	Kanji	Period	Date	Added Meaning
aoi	F	Aoi	葵	Hei'an	1001	(Modern reading)
afu	F	Afui	葵	Hei'an	1001	(Older reading)

梅 Plum (Japanese Apricot)

Even before the cherry blossoms, the plum blossoms herald the coming of Spring.

Reading	Type	Example	Kanji	Period	Date	Added Meaning
ume	F	Mume	梅	Nanboku	1392	
ume	F	Umeme	梅女	Kamakura	1332	[Woman]
ume	S	Umewaka	梅若	Muromachi	1572	Young

椋 Aphananthe Aspera (Flowering Tree)

Reading	Type	Example	Kanji	Period	Date	Added Meaning
kura	F	Kurame	椋賣	Nara	784	
kura	F	Kurateme	椋手賣	Nara	784	Hand

柿 Persimmon

Reading	Type	Example	Kanji	Period	Date	Added Meaning
kaki	S	Kakimoto	柿本	Uncertain	1600	Main / Base

梨 Pear Tree

Reading	Type	Example	Kanji	Period	Date	Added Meaning
nashi	S	Takanashi	高梨	Uncertain	1600	Tall

橘 Tangerine

In modern Japan, tangerines and *omochi* (pounded sweet rice cakes) are festive foods eaten at New Year.

Reading	Type	Example	Kanji	Period	Date	Added Meaning
KITSU	F	Kitsume	橘賣	Nara	784	
tachibana	S	Tachiba'na	橘	Hei'an	1183	

栗 Chestnut

Reading	Type	Example	Kanji	Period	Date	Added Meaning
kuri	F	Kuri	栗	Uncertain	1600	
kuri	S	Oguri	小栗	Muromachi	1572	Small
[Special]	S	A'ihara	栗飯原	Nanboku	1392	Cooked Rice + Meadow

桂 Cinnamon Tree

Reading	Type	Example	Kanji	Period	Date	Added Meaning
katsura	P	Katsuragawa	桂川	Modern	1983	River

桐 Paulownia

Reading	Type	Example	Kanji	Period	Date	Added Meaning
kiri	S	Katagiri	片桐	Sengoku	1568	One of Two

楠 Camphor Tree

Reading	Type	Example	Kanji	Period	Date	Added Meaning
kusu	S	Kusu'noki	楠木	Nanboku	1392	Tree

槻 Zelkova Tree

Reading	Type	Example	Kanji	Period	Date	Added Meaning
tsuki	S	Ozuki	小槻	Kamakura	1332	Small

柘植 Boxwood

Reading	Type	Example	Kanji	Period	Date	Added Meaning
tsuge	P	Tsuge	柘植	Modern	1983	Rooted / Planted

桑 Mulberry Bush

Reading	Type	Example	Kanji	Period	Date	Added Meaning
kuwa	S	Kuwayama	桑山	Sengoku	1568	Mountain

山吹 Yellow Rose Tree

Reading	Type	Example	Kanji	Period	Date	Added Meaning
yamabuki	F	Yamabukime	山吹女	Muromachi	1572	[Woman]

榊 Camellia / Cleyera Ochnacea

This is a sacred tree in Shintoh.

Reading	Type	Example	Kanji	Period	Date	Added Meaning
sakaki	S	Sakakibara	榊原	Sengoku	1568	Meadow

竹 Bamboo

Reading	Type	Example	Kanji	Period	Date	Added Meaning
take	F	Take	竹	Momoyama	1438	
take	F	Takeme	竹女	Kamakura	1332	[Woman]
take	S	Satake	佐竹	Kamakura	1332	Military Deputy
take	S	Take'naka	竹中	Sengoku	1568	Middle
take	S	Takezaki	竹崎	Kamakura	1332	Slope

Thematic Dictionary — Plants 163

竺 Fat Bamboo

Note that Tenjiku 天竺 is the ancient name for India used by people in China, Korea and Japan. It is not the name of a place in Japan and was included for historical interest only.

Reading	Type	Example	Kanji	Period	Date	Added Meaning
JIKU	P	Tenjiku	天竺	Nara	784	Sky / Heaven

笹 Thin Bamboo

This *kanji* is also a euphemism for sake.

Reading	Type	Example	Kanji	Period	Date	Added Meaning
sasa	F	Kosasa	小笹	Kamakura	1332	Small

藤 Wisteria

This wisteria largely owes its popularity as a name element to the Fujiwara family. The Fujiwara were a *kuge* family founded by Nakatomi Kamatari 中臣 鎌足 (614-669). They claimed descent from Ame no Koya'ne no Mikoto one of the faithful followers of Amaterasu no Mikoto.

Reading	Type	Example	Kanji	Period	Date	Added Meaning
TOU	S	Bitou	尾藤	Kamakura	1332	Tail
TOU	S	Endou	遠藤	Sengoku	1568	Far
TOU	S	Gotou	後藤	Kamakura	1332	After
TOU	S	Itou	伊藤	Sengoku	1568	This
TOU	S	Katou	加藤	Kamakura	1332	Join Up / Enlist
TOU	S	Kondou	近藤	Kamakura	1332	Near
TOU	S	Kudou	工藤	Kamakura	1332	Tool / Artisan
TOU	S	Mutou	武藤	Kamakura	1332	Bravery / Military Force
TOU	S	Naitou	内藤	Kamakura	1332	Inside
TOU	S	Saitou	斎藤	Kamakura	1332	Worship / Study
TOU	S	Satou	佐藤	Kamakura	1332	Military Deputy
fuji	F	Fujiko	藤子	Hei'an	1183	[Lady]
fuji	F	Fujime	藤賣	Hei'an	1183	
fuji	N	Fujifusa	藤房	Kamakura	1332	Monastic Cell
fuji	N	Fujihiro	藤広	Sengoku	1568	Spacious / Expansive
fuji	N	Fujiyori	藤頼	Muromachi	1572	Request / Ask
fuji	N	Mitsufuji	満藤	Muromachi	1572	Become Full / Abundant
fuji	N	Mu'nefuji	宗藤	Kamakura	1332	Master an Art
fuji	N	Nagafuji	永藤	Muromachi	1572	Forever
fuji	N	Norifuji	憲藤	Nanboku	1392	Example / Pattern
fuji	N	Norifuji	教藤	Nanboku	1392	Teaching / Dogma
fuji	N	Sadafuji	貞藤	Kamakura	1332	Correct Spirit
fuji	N	Sukefuji	資藤	Nanboku	1392	Raw Materials
fuji	N	Yorifuji	頼藤	Nanboku	1392	Request / Ask
fuji	N	Yukifuji	行藤	Kamakura	1332	Going To / Bound For
fuji	S	Fuji'i	藤井	Hei'an	1183	Well
fuji	S	Fujiwara	藤原	Nara	784	Meadow

蓮 Lotus (Associated with the Lotus Sutra)

Reading	Type	Example	Kanji	Period	Date	Added Meaning
REN	H	Nichiren	日蓮	Kamakura	1332	Sun / Day

菊 Chrysanthemum

Reading	Type	Example	Kanji	Period	Date	Added Meaning
KIKU	F	Kiku	菊	Muromachi	1572	
KIKU	F	Kikumatsu	菊松	Kamakura	1332	Pine Tree
KIKU	F	Kikume	菊女	Kamakura	1332	[Woman]
KIKU	S	Kikuchi	菊池	Kamakura	1332	Pond
KIKU	S	Kikusui	菊水	Uncertain	1600	Water

薮 Grove / Thicket

Reading	Type	Example	Kanji	Period	Date	Added Meaning
yabu	S	Yabuno'uchi	薮内	Sengoku	1568	Inside

柴 Bushes

Reading	Type	Example	Kanji	Period	Date	Added Meaning
shiba	S	Shibata	柴田	Uncertain	1600	Rice Paddy

荻 Common Reed

Reading	Type	Example	Kanji	Period	Date	Added Meaning
ogi	S	Ogi'no	荻野	Nanboku	1392	Wide Plain

蘆 Reed / Rush

Reading	Type	Example	Kanji	Period	Date	Added Meaning
ashi	S	Ashi'na	蘆名	Kamakura	1332	Famous / Admirable
iho	S	Ihohara	蘆原	Hei'an	1183	Meadow

菅 Club Rush

Reading	Type	Example	Kanji	Period	Date	Added Meaning
suga	P	Suga	菅	Modern	1983	
suga	P	Suga'ura	菅浦	Modern	1983	Bay / Delta
suga	P	Sugashima	菅島	Modern	1983	Island
suga	P	Sugadaira	菅平	Modern	1983	Tranquility
suga	P	Sugaya	菅谷	Modern	1983	Valley

萩 Bush Clover

Reading	Type	Example	Kanji	Period	Date	Added Meaning
hagi	P	Hagi	萩	Modern	1983	
hagi	P	Hagi'no	萩野	Modern	1983	Wide Plain
hagi	P	Hagihara	萩原	Modern	1983	Meadow
hagi	P	Hagiyama	萩山	Modern	1983	Mountain

Thematic Dictionary — Plants

草 Grass

Reading	Type	Example	Kanji	Period	Date	Added Meaning
kusa	S	Kusa'no	草野	Kamakura	1332	Wide Plain

芝 Grass / Ground Cover

Shiba 芝 refers to the grass and small plants found in Japanese gardens and similar places. Normally, such plants grow in clumps to simulate nature. Japanese translate "lawn" as *shibafu* 芝生 in which an entire area is uniformly covered with vegetation.

Reading	Type	Example	Kanji	Period	Date	Added Meaning
shiba	S	Shiba	芝	Kamakura	1332	

稲 Young Rice Plants

Reading	Type	Example	Kanji	Period	Date	Added Meaning
ina	F	I'nako	稲子	Hei'an	1183	[Lady]
ina	F	I'name	稲賣	Nara	784	
ina	S	I'naba	稲葉	Sengoku	1568	Leaf
ina	S	I'nage	稲毛	Kamakura	1332	Wool

麻 Flax / Linen

Reading	Type	Example	Kanji	Period	Date	Added Meaning
MA	F	Ma	麻	Uncertain	1600	
MA	F	Maeme	麻得女	Nara	784	[Woman]
MA	F	Makayame	麻何夜賣	Nara	784	Evening
MA	F	Marime	麻里賣	Nara	784	Hamlet
MA	F	Mashime	麻志女	Nara	784	Determined + [Woman]
MA	F	Mawayame	麻我夜賣	Nara	784	Our / Us / We + Evening
MA	N	Nakamaro	仲麻呂	Uncertain	1600	Middle of a Group Backbone

葛 Arrowroot

Reading	Type	Example	Kanji	Period	Date	Added Meaning
KATSU	N	Chikakatsu	近葛	Kamakura	1332	Near
KATSU	N	Tomokatsu	朝葛	Kamakura	1332	Morning
KATSU	S	Kasai	葛西	Kamakura	1332	West
kuzu	S	Kuzurahara	葛原	Uncertain	1600	Meadow

蒲 The Mace Plant

Reading	Type	Example	Kanji	Period	Date	Added Meaning
kama	P	Kamata	蒲田	Modern	1983	Rice Paddy
[Special]	S	Gamou	蒲生	Sengoku	1568	Life / Live / Living

粟 Millet

Reading	Type	Example	Kanji	Period	Date	Added Meaning
awa	S	Awata	粟田	Hei'an	1183	Rice Paddy
awa	S	Awataguchi	粟田口	Kamakura	1332	Rice Paddy + Entrance

茶 Tea

Reading	Type	Example	Kanji	Period	Date	Added Meaning
CHA	F	Acha	阿茶	Uncertain	1600	Crevice
CHA	F	Achacha	阿茶茶	Uncertain	1600	Crevice
CHA	F	Chako	茶子	Muromachi	1572	[Lady]
SA	F	Sasa	茶々	Uncertain	1600	
[Special]	F	Sakuma	茶阿	Uncertain	1600	Crevice

瓜 Melon / Cucumber

Kyuuri 胡瓜 is the actual word for cucumber in modern Japanese. The progenitor of the Uryuu family may have been a melon farmer.

Reading	Type	Example	Kanji	Period	Date	Added Meaning
uri	S	Uryuu	瓜生	Kamakura	1332	Life / Live / Living

繁 Bloom / Bouquet / Overgrow / Lush Growth

Shigeru 繁る is a verb which describes the blossoming and growth of trees, bushes and grass.

Reading	Type	Example	Kanji	Period	Date	Added Meaning
shige	N	Fusashige	房繁	Muromachi	1572	Monastic Cell
shige	N	Kageshige	景繁	Kamakura	1332	Bright / Magnificent
shige	N	Nobushige	信繁	Uncertain	1600	Belief / Faith
shige	N	Norishige	則繁	Muromachi	1572	Make an Example
shige	N	Shigemasa	繁昌	Kamakura	1332	Clear / Bright
shige	N	Shige'uji	繁氏	Nanboku	1392	Family / Clan
shige	N	Yoshishige	義繁	Nanboku	1392	Fealty

滋 Grow / Blossom

Reading	Type	Example	Kanji	Period	Date	Added Meaning
shige	N	Shigeharu	滋春	Hei'an	1183	Spring (Season)
shige	N	Tomoshige	具滋	Kamakura	1332	Tool / Implement
shige	S	Shige'no	滋野	Hei'an	1183	Wide Plain

茂 Blossoming

Shigeru 茂る is a verb which describes the growth spreading to blanket the fields.

Reading	Type	Example	Kanji	Period	Date	Added Meaning
mochi	N	Kagemochi	景茂	Kamakura	1332	Bright / Magnificent
mochi	N	Koremochi	維茂	Uncertain	1600	Cable / Rope
mochi	N	Mochiza'ne	茂実	Uncertain	1600	Reality

Thematic Dictionary — Plants   167

Reading	Type	Example	Kanji	Period	Date	Added Meaning
mochi	N	Moromochi	師茂	Nanboku	1392	Teacher / Expert
mochi	N	Nagamochi	長茂	Kamakura	1332	Long
mochi	N	Shigemochi	重茂	Nanboku	1392	Heavy / Serious
mochi	N	Sukemochi	祐茂	Kamakura	1332	Divine Help
mochi	N	Tokimochi	時茂	Kamakura	1332	Time / Era
mochi	N	Toomochi	遠茂	Hei'an	1183	Far
mochi	N	Yoshimochi	義茂	Kamakura	1332	Fealty
shige	N	Hiroshige	弘茂	Muromachi	1572	Draw / Stretch
shige	N	Kinshige	公茂	Kamakura	1332	Noble / Official
shige	N	Masashige	政茂	Kamakura	1332	Govern / Rule
shige	N	Mitsushige	光茂	Muromachi	1572	Bright / Shining
shige	N	Moroshige	師茂	Nanboku	1392	Teacher / Expert
shige	N	Mu'neshige	宗茂	Sengoku	1568	Master an Art
shige	N	Nobushige	信茂	Uncertain	1600	Belief / Faith
shige	N	Norishige	範茂	Kamakura	1332	Required Form / Pattern
shige	N	Sadashige	貞茂	Muromachi	1572	Correct Spirit
shige	N	Sa'neshige	実茂	Muromachi	1572	Reality
shige	N	Shigehira	茂平	Kamakura	1332	Tranquility
shige	N	Shigekatsu	茂勝	Sengoku	1568	Conquer / Triumph
shige	N	Shigemitsu	茂光	Hei'an	1183	Bright / Shining
shige	N	Shige'naga	茂長	Kamakura	1332	Long
shige	N	Shigetoki	茂時	Kamakura	1332	Time / Era
shige	N	Shigeza'ne	茂実	Nanboku	1392	Reality
shige	N	Sukeshige	祐茂	Kamakura	1332	Divine Help
shige	N	Tadashige	直茂	Sengoku	1568	Adjust / Correct
shige	N	Tokishige	時茂	Kamakura	1332	Time / Era
shige	N	Tsu'neshige	経茂	Nanboku	1392	True Path
shige	N	Yasushige	保茂	Kamakura	1332	Guarantee
shige	N	Yorishige	頼茂	Kamakura	1332	Request / Ask
[Special]	S	Motegi	茂木	Nanboku	1392	Tree

植 Rooted / Planted

Reading	Type	Example	Kanji	Period	Date	Added Meaning
tane	N	Yoshita'ne	義植	Uncertain	1600	Fealty
ueki	P	Ueki	植木	Modern	1983	Tree

根 Root / Base

Reading	Type	Example	Kanji	Period	Date	Added Meaning
ne	F	Neme	根賣	Nara	784	
ne	F	Nemushime	根虫賣	Nara	784	Bug / Insect / Snake

幹 Trunk / Stalk

Reading	Type	Example	Kanji	Period	Date	Added Meaning
moto	N	Akimoto	顕幹	Nanboku	1392	High Status
moto	N	Hidemoto	秀幹	Muromachi	1572	Extraordinary / Bountiful
moto	N	Masamoto	政幹	Nanboku	1392	Govern / Rule
moto	N	Motoshige	幹重	Nanboku	1392	Heavy / Serious
moto	N	Nagamoto	長幹	Kamakura	1332	Long
moto	N	Norimoto	憲幹	Kamakura	1332	Example / Pattern

Reading	Type	Example	Kanji	Period	Date	Added Meaning
moto	N	Tadamoto	忠幹	Kamakura	1332	Faithful / Loyal
moto	N	Takamoto	高幹	Nanboku	1392	Tall
moto	N	Yoshimoto	義幹	Kamakura	1332	Fealty

枝 Branch / Twig

Reading	Type	Example	Kanji	Period	Date	Added Meaning
[Special]	S	Saigusa	三枝	Uncertain	1600	Three

葉 Leaf

Reading	Type	Example	Kanji	Period	Date	Added Meaning
ha	S	Chiba	千葉	Kamakura	1332	One Thousand
ha	S	I'naba	稲葉	Sengoku	1568	Young Rice Plants

花 Flower (Cherry or Plum Blossoms)

Reading	Type	Example	Kanji	Period	Date	Added Meaning
hana	F	Ha'nako	花子	Nanboku	1392	[Lady]
hana	F	Ha'name	花賣	Hei'an	1183	
hana	S	Tachiba'na	立花	Uncertain	1600	Stand Up

華 Flower (Flowering Shrubs & Grass)

Reading	Type	Example	Kanji	Period	Date	Added Meaning
KA	P	Chuuka	中華	Modern	1983	Middle
GE	P	Gesan	華山	Modern	1983	Mountain
hana	F	Ha'nako	華子	Modern	1983	[Lady]

実 Seed or Center / Reality / Plentiful

Reading	Type	Example	Kanji	Period	Date	Added Meaning
SANE	N	Chikaza'ne	近実	Kamakura	1332	Near
sane	N	Chikaza'ne	親実	Kamakura	1332	Intimate
sane	N	Fusaza'ne	房実	Kamakura	1332	Monastic Cell
sane	N	Ieza'ne	家実	Kamakura	1332	Rural House / Family
sane	N	Ka'neza'ne	兼実	Hei'an	1183	Unite
sane	N	Masaza'ne	雅実	Uncertain	1600	High Quality
sane	N	Mochiza'ne	茂実	Uncertain	1600	Blossoming
sane	N	Moroza'ne	師実	Uncertain	1600	Teacher / Expert
sane	N	Motoza'ne	基実	Hei'an	1183	Foundation
sane	N	Motsuza'ne	以実	Sengoku	1480	Highest
sane	N	Mu'neza'ne	宗実	Hei'an	1183	Master an Art
sane	N	Nahoza'ne	直実	Uncertain	1600	Adjust / Correct
sane	N	Naoza'ne	直実	Hei'an	1183	Adjust / Correct
sane	N	Nobuza'ne	信実	Kamakura	1332	Belief / Faith
sane	N	Noriza'ne	教実	Kamakura	1332	Teaching / Dogma
sane	N	Noriza'ne	憲実	Muromachi	1572	Example / Pattern
sane	N	Noriza'ne	範実	Nanboku	1392	Required Form / Pattern

Thematic Dictionary — Plants

sane	N	Sadaza'ne	定実	Kamakura	1332	Determine
sane	N	Sa'neatsu	実淳	Muromachi	1572	Steadfast / Honest / Natural
sane	N	Sa'nechika	実親	Kamakura	1332	Intimate
sane	N	Sa'nefusa	実房	Hei'an	1183	Monastic Cell
sane	N	Sa'nefuyu	実冬	Nanboku	1392	Winter
sane	N	Sa'nehide	実秀	Muromachi	1572	Extraordinary / Bountiful
sane	N	Sa'nehira	実平	Kamakura	1332	Tranquility
sane	N	Sa'nehiro	実博	Muromachi	1572	Well Traveled / Learned
sane	N	Sa'neka'ne	実兼	Kamakura	1332	Unite
sane	N	Sa'nekazu	実員	Kamakura	1332	Member
sane	N	Sa'nekazu	実量	Muromachi	1572	Generosity / Spirit
sane	N	Sa'neku'ni	実国	Hei'an	1183	Country / Rural Area
sane	N	Sa'nemasa	実雅	Kamakura	1332	High Quality
sane	N	Sa'nemasa	実政	Kamakura	1332	Govern / Rule
sane	N	Sa'nemitsu	実光	Kamakura	1332	Bright / Shining
sane	N	Sa'nemori	実盛	Hei'an	1183	Plentiful / Piled Up
sane	N	Sa'nemoto	実基	Kamakura	1332	Foundation
sane	N	Sa'nemu'ne	実宗	Kamakura	1332	Master an Art
sane	N	Sa'ne'naga	実永	Muromachi	1572	Forever
sane	N	Sa'ne'naga	実長	Kamakura	1332	Long
sane	N	Sa'ne'naka	実仲	Kamakura	1332	Middle of a Group
sane	N	Sa'ne'nao	実直	Nanboku	1392	Adjust / Correct
sane	N	Sa'ne'natsu	実夏	Nanboku	1392	Summer
sane	N	Sa'ne'nori	実教	Kamakura	1332	Teaching / Dogma
sane	N	Sa'ne'o	実雄	Kamakura	1332	Strength / Courage / Bravery
sane	N	Sa'nesada	実定	Hei'an	1183	Determine
sane	N	Sa'neshige	実重	Kamakura	1332	Heavy / Serious
sane	N	Sa'neshige	実茂	Muromachi	1572	Blossoming
sane	N	Sa'netada	実忠	Kamakura	1332	Faithful / Loyal
sane	N	Sa'netaka	実隆	Muromachi	1572	Grow / Pile Up
sane	N	Sa'netoki	実時	Kamakura	1332	Time / Era
sane	N	Sa'netomo	実朝	Kamakura	1332	Morning
sane	N	Sa'netoshi	実俊	Nanboku	1392	Emotional
sane	N	Sa'netsugu	実継	Kamakura	1332	Connect / Adopt
sane	N	Sa'netsu'na	実綱	Hei'an	1183	Net
sane	N	Sa'netsu'ne	実経	Kamakura	1332	True Path
sane	N	Sa'ne'uji	実氏	Kamakura	1332	Family / Clan
sane	N	Sa'neyasu	実康	Uncertain	1600	Strong / Confident
sane	N	Sa'neyasu	実泰	Kamakura	1332	Peace / Plenitude
sane	N	Sa'neyo	実世	Kamakura	1332	Generation / Life
sane	N	Sa'neyori	実頼	Uncertain	1600	Request / Ask
sane	N	Shigeza'ne	茂実	Nanboku	1392	Blossoming
sane	N	Sukeza'ne	資実	Kamakura	1332	Raw Materials
sane	N	Tadaza'ne	忠実	Hei'an	1183	Faithful / Loyal
sane	N	Takeza'ne	武実	Nanboku	1392	Bravery / Military Force
sane	N	Tameza'ne	為実	Kamakura	1332	Purpose / Goal
sane	N	Tokiza'ne	時実	Kamakura	1332	Time / Era
sane	N	Toshiza'ne	俊実	Kamakura	1332	Emotional
sane	N	Uchiza'ne	内実	Kamakura	1332	Inside
sane	N	Yoriza'ne	頼実	Kamakura	1332	Request / Ask
sane	N	Yoshiza'ne	義実	Hei'an	1183	Fealty
sane	N	Yoshiza'ne	良実	Kamakura	1332	Good / Superior
sane	N	Yukiza'ne	行実	Kamakura	1332	Going To / Bound For
sane	N	Nishisa'netaka	西実隆	Muromachi	1572	Grow / Pile Up West

種 Seed / Cause / Reason

Reading	Type	Example	Kanji	Period	Date	Added Meaning
tane	N	Kiyota'ne	清種	Kamakura	1332	Pure
tane	N	Masata'ne	真種	Nanboku	1392	Genuine
tane	N	Michita'ne	通種	Nanboku	1392	Pass Through
tane	N	Tameta'ne	為種	Muromachi	1572	Purpose / Goal
tane	N	Ta'nemichi	種道	Nanboku	1392	Road / Way
tane	N	Ta'nemura	種村	Kamakura	1332	Village
tane	N	Ta'nenaga	種長	Sengoku	1568	Long
tane	N	Ta'neshige	種重	Kamakura	1332	Heavy / Serious
tane	N	Ta'nesuke	種佐	Nanboku	1392	Military Deputy
tane	N	Ta'netsugu	種継	Uncertain	1600	Connect / Adopt
tane	N	Ta'neyasu	種保	Kamakura	1332	Guarantee
tane	N	Yoshita'ne	義種	Nanboku	1392	Fealty

苗 Shoot / Sprout / Seedling

Reading	Type	Example	Kanji	Period	Date	Added Meaning
nae	F	Naeme	苗女	Hei'an	1183	[Woman]

❖ Beasts & Monsters ❖

人 Person / Human

Note that although this character can be read as "hito", it is not the character which commonly appears in the *nanori* of the imperial family.

Reading	Type	Example	Kanji	Period	Date	Added Meaning
hito	B	Hitomaru	人丸	Uncertain	1600	Young / Healthy
hito	N	Akahito	赤人	Uncertain	1600	Red (Fire) / Young
hito	N	Yoshihito	義人	Muromachi	1572	Fealty

鬼 Ogre / Troll

According to legend, trolls or ogres used to live in many places in Japan. Japanese trolls are large horned and hairy man like creatures who wear loin cloths and practice cannibalism. Further, they are often depicted as being intensely coloured. Their colourations is monochromatic so that an oni might be red all over or blue all over. Many places in Japan have folk stories about the ferocity of the local oni and there are many places named after them. The Japanese national folk hero, Momotarou 桃太郎 or "Peach Boy", conquered the oni with the aid of enchanted animals.

Reading	Type	Example	Kanji	Period	Date	Added Meaning
oni	P	Oniike	鬼池	Modern	1983	Pond
oni	P	Onigatsurayama	鬼面山	Modern	1983	Mountain
oni	P	Oniyanagi	鬼柳	Modern	1983	Willow Tree

猿 Monkey

Reading	Type	Example	Kanji	Period	Date	Added Meaning
saru	F	Saru	猿	Uncertain	1600	
saru	M	Sarumaru	猿丸	Uncertain	1600	Young / Healthy
saru	P	Saruhashi	猿橋	Modern	1983	Bridge

虎 Tiger

Reading	Type	Example	Kanji	Period	Date	Added Meaning
tora	F	Tora	虎	Uncertain	1600	
tora	F	Toramatsume	虎松女	Nanboku	1392	Pine Tree + [Woman]
tora	N	Kagetora	景虎	Uncertain	1600	Bright / Magnificent
tora	N	Masatora	正虎	Uncertain	1600	Unerring / Genuine
tora	N	Nobutora	信虎	Sengoku	1519	Belief / Faith
tora	N	Takatora	高虎	Sengoku	1568	Tall
tora	N	Toramasa	虎昌	Uncertain	1600	Clear / Bright
tora	N	Toramori	虎盛	Uncertain	1600	Plentiful / Piled Up
tora	N	Torata'ne	虎胤	Uncertain	1600	Blood Heir
tora	N	Torayasu	虎泰	Uncertain	1600	Peace / Plenitude

熊 Bear

Note that there are two different readings for identically written names. The second reading simply includes the unwritten formal geographic designator 箇 which is commonly abbreviated as ケ. This is an unusual construction in personal names and is rather more common for place names.

Reading	Type	Example	Kanji	Period	Date	Added Meaning
kuma	S	Kumagai	熊谷	Hei'an	1183	Valley
kuma	S	Kumagaya	熊谷	Sengoku	1568	Valley

猪 Boar

Note that "wi" is probably an antique Japanese reading for this character. In classical Japanese, both the "h" sounds and the "w" sounds had a more complete complement of vowels than they do in modern Japanese. Similarly, "ino" appears to be an antique form as well.

Reading	Type	Example	Kanji	Period	Date	Added Meaning
ino	P	Inohana	猪鼻	Modern	1983	Nose
wi	F	Owime	小猪賣	Nara	784	Small

馬 Horse

Reading	Type	Example	Kanji	Period	Date	Added Meaning
BA	S	Baba	馬場	Uncertain	1600	Place / Location
ma	F	Mamime	馬身賣	Nara	784	Body / Pregnant
ma	F	Mateme	馬手賣	Nara	784	Hand
ma	S	Arima	有馬	Sengoku	1568	Exists
ma	S	Souma	相馬	Kamakura	1332	Together / Team Work
uma	F	Mumatsume	馬都賣	Nara	784	Beautiful (Cultured)
uma	F	Uma	馬	Muromachi	1572	
uma	F	Umame	馬女	Nara	784	[Woman]
uma	F	Umatsume	馬都賣	Nara	784	Beautiful (Cultured)
uma	F	Umatsume	馬津賣	Nara	784	Harbour

駒 Pony

Reading	Type	Example	Kanji	Period	Date	Added Meaning
koma	F	Koma	駒	Muromachi	1572	
koma	F	Komame	駒賣	Nara	784	
koma	S	Ikoma	生駒	Sengoku	1568	Life / Live / Living

牛 Cow / Ox

Reading	Type	Example	Kanji	Period	Date	Added Meaning
ushi	F	Ushi	牛	Nara	784	
ushi	F	Ushime	牛賣	Nara	784	

Thematic Dictionary — Beats & Monsters

鹿 Deer

Reading	Type	Example	Kanji	Period	Date	Added Meaning
KA	P	Kagoshima	鹿児島	Hei'an	1183	Child + Island
KA	S	Kashima	鹿島	Muromachi	1572	Island
KA	S	Ogashima	小鹿島	Kamakura	1332	Small + Island

羊 Goat

Reading	Type	Example	Kanji	Period	Date	Added Meaning
hitsuji	F	Hitsujime	羊賣	Nara	784	

犬 Dog

Reading	Type	Example	Kanji	Period	Date	Added Meaning
inu	F	Inu	犬	Kamakura	1332	
inu	F	Inume	犬賣	Nara	784	
inu	F	Inume	犬女	Hei'an	1183	[Woman]
inu	F	Inuwaka	犬若	Uncertain	1600	Young
inu	F	Tora'inu'me	寅犬女	Nanboku	1392	Tiger (Zodiac) + [Woman]
inu	P	Inuyama	犬山	Uncertain	1600	Mountain
inu	S	Inuhara	犬原	Hei'an	1183	Meadow

兎 Rabbit / Hare

Supposably, a rabbit lives on the moon where he makes Omochi which is a confection made out of sweet rice.

Reading	Type	Example	Kanji	Period	Date	Added Meaning
TO	F	Toyome	兎世女	Muromachi	1572	Generation / Life + [Woman]

鳥 Bird

Asuka is the name of a district in the Kansai region where many of the early imperial cities were located. There are other place names in Japan which incorporate a bird as the substantive element. However, these names do not appear to have been directly used as family names. Rather, they appear as descriptive elements before a more specific substantive element. Asuka evokes a felicitous image of birds flying in the bright morning sky of a sweet smelling day.

Reading	Type	Example	Kanji	Period	Date	Added Meaning
torn	F	Torime	鳥女	Nara	784	[Woman]
tori	F	Torime	鳥賣	Nara	784	
tori	S	Toriyama	鳥山	Uncertain	1600	Mountain
[Special]	P	Asuka	飛鳥	Asuka	562	Flying
[Special]	S	Asuka'i[36]	飛鳥井	Kamakura	1332	Well

鳳 Male Phoenix

Reading	Type	Example	Kanji	Period	Date	Added Meaning
taka	F	Takako	鳳子	Hei'an	1183	[Lady]

---

[36] Asuka is a region in Nara Prefecture which was the nexus of early imperial government.

鶴 Crane

The crane like the tortoise is a symbol of longevity.

Reading	Type	Example	Kanji	Period	Date	Added Meaning
tsuru	F	Tsuru	鶴	Kamakura	1332	
tsuru	F	Tsurukome	鶴子	Kamakura	1332	[Lady]
tsuru	F	Tsurume	鶴女	Nanboku	1392	[Woman]

鷹 Hawk

Reading	Type	Example	Kanji	Period	Date	Added Meaning
taka	S	Takatori	鷹取	Nanboku	1392	Catch(er) / Gather(er)
taka	P	Mitaka	三鷹	Modern	1893	Three
taka	P	Taka'no	鷹野	Modern	1983	Wide Plain

雀 Sparrow

Reading	Type	Example	Kanji	Period	Date	Added Meaning
[Special]	S	Sasabe	雀部	Hei'an	1183	Monopoly Corporation

鴎 Sea Gull

Reading	Type	Example	Kanji	Period	Date	Added Meaning
HOU	H	Shou'ou	紹鴎	Uncertain	1600	Inherit / Help

虫 Bug, Insect, Worm, Snake

Reading	Type	Example	Kanji	Period	Date	Added Meaning
mushi	F	Mushime	虫賣	Nara	784	

蜂 Bee / Wasp / Hornet

Reading	Type	Example	Kanji	Period	Date	Added Meaning
hachi	S	Hachisuka	蜂須賀	Sengoku	1568	Necessity + Celebrate a Gain

竜 Dragon (New Kanji)

Asian dragons are strongly associated with water and are supposed to dwell in rivers and the ocean. The dragon king is a sea god and lives in a palace at the bottom of the ocean. There does not appear to be a semantic difference between the modern and the ancient forms of the *kanji* used to write dragon. Thus, the older form should be preferred. However, as some sources have recorded names using the modern version, they are listed here.

Reading	Type	Example	Kanji	Period	Date	Added Meaning
RYUU	S	Ryuu'zou'ji	竜造寺	Nanboku	1392	Temple
tatsu	N	Tatsu'aki	竜秋	Kamakura	1332	Autumn

Thematic Dictionary — Beats & Monsters   175

龍 Dragon (Old Kanji)

Asian dragons are strongly associated with water and are supposed to dwell in rivers and the ocean. The dragon king is a sea god and lives in a palace at the bottom of the ocean. Note that Ryuu'zou'ji is actually the name of a Buddhist temple. Temple names are usually constructed using the Sino-Japanese *onyomi* readings for their constituent characters. There does not appear to be a semantic difference between the modern and the ancient forms of the *kanji* used to write dragon. Thus, the older form should be preferred. However, as some sources have recorded names using the modern version, they are listed under the modern form.

Reading	Type	Example	Kanji	Period	Date	Added Meaning
tatsu	F	Tatsume	龍賣	Nara	784	
tatsu	F	Tatsutoshime	龍寿女	Kamakura	1332	Longevity + [Woman]
tatsu	N	Nobutatsu	信龍	Uncertain	1600	Belief / Faith
tatsu	N	Yoshitatsu	義龍	Uncertain	1600	Fealty
tatsu	S	Tatsukawa	龍川	Uncertain	1600	River

亀 Turtle / Tortoise (Longevity)

Reading	Type	Example	Kanji	Period	Date	Added Meaning
KI	Y	Bunki	文亀	Sengoku	1501	Literature / Culture
KI	Y	Genki	元亀	Momoyama	1570	Base / Original
kame	F	Kame	亀	Kamakura	1332	
kame	F	Kamematsu	亀松	Kamakura	1332	Pine Tree
kame	F	Kametsuru	亀鶴	Nanboku	1392	Crane
kame	F	Kameyo	亀夜	Momoyama	1590	Evening
kame	S	Kame'i	亀井	Sengoku	1568	Well
kame	S	Kameyama	亀山	Kamakura	1332	Mountain

魚 Fish

Reading	Type	Example	Kanji	Period	Date	Added Meaning
uo	F	Iwokome	魚子賣	Hei'an	1183	[Lady]
uo	F	Iwome	魚賣	Nara	784	

鯖 Mackerel

Reading	Type	Example	Kanji	Period	Date	Added Meaning
saba	F	Sabame	鯖賣	Nara	784	

鮫 Shark

Reading	Type	Example	Kanji	Period	Date	Added Meaning
same	S	Samejima	鮫島	Kamakura	1332	Island

鯨 Whale / Sea Monster

Reading	Type	Example	Kanji	Period	Date	Added Meaning
kujira	F	Kujirako	鯨子	Hei'an	1183	[Lady]

❖ ANATOMY ❖

身 Body / Pregnant

Reading	Type	Example	Kanji	Period	Date	Added Meaning
mi	F	Ihamime	石身賣	Nara	784	Rock
mi	F	Mamime	馬身賣	Nara	784	Horse
mi	F	Mime	身賣	Nara	784	

手 Hand

Reading	Type	Example	Kanji	Period	Date	Added Meaning
te	F	Kurateme	椋手賣	Nara	784	Flowering Tree
te	F	Tamochime	手持賣	Nara	784	Have / Possess
te	F	Teyorime	手依賣	Nara	784	Follow
te	P	Iwate	岩手	Modern	1983	Boulder

足 Foot = Ashi / Sufficient = Tari

Reading	Type	Example	Kanji	Period	Date	Added Meaning
ATSU	S	Asuke	足助	Kamakura	1332	Deputy (Rescue / Assist)
ashi	S	Adachi	足立	Kamakura	1332	Stand Up
ashi	S	Ashikaga	足利	Kamakura	1332	Produce Results / Work Well
tari	F	Tarime	足賣	Nara	784	
tari	N	Kamatari	鎌足	Uncertain	1600	Scythe

鼻 Nose

Reading	Type	Example	Kanji	Period	Date	Added Meaning
ino	P	Inohana	猪鼻	Modern	1983	Boar

尾 Tail

Reading	Type	Example	Kanji	Period	Date	Added Meaning
BI	S	Bitou	尾藤	Kamakura	1332	Wisteria
o	S	Hori'o	堀尾	Sengoku	1568	Dig / Carve / Excavation
o	S	I'no'o	飯尾	Muromachi	1572	Cooked Rice
o	S	Naga'o	長尾	Kamakura	1332	Long
o	S	Nishi'o	西尾	Sengoku	1568	West
o	S	Seno'o	妹尾	Hei'an	1183	Younger Sister

Thematic Dictionary — Anatomy 177

呂 Backbone / Be in a Row / Long

Reading	Type	Example	Kanji	Period	Date	Added Meaning
RO	S	Moro	毛呂	Kamakura	1332	Wool

目 Eye

Reading	Type	Example	Kanji	Period	Date	Added Meaning
me	F	Mememe	目々女	Hei'an	1183	[Woman]
me	F	Mezurame	目都良賣	Nara	784	Beautiful + Good
me	P	Suginome	杉目	Suginome	1593	Cedar Tree
me	S	Mega	目賀	Nanboku	1392	Celebrate A Gain

毛 Hair (Generic) / Fur / Wool

Note that many women bore names referring to their hair or other physical features. This is particularly true of peasants and artisans in classical Japan. Also note that 和岐毛賣 appears to be a complete name.

Reading	Type	Example	Kanji	Period	Date	Added Meaning
MO	F	Mochime	毛知賣	Nara	784	Knowledge
MO	F	Morime	毛里賣	Nara	784	Hamlet
MO	S	Moro	毛呂	Kamakura	1332	Backbone
MO	F	Na'nimome	奈爾毛賣	Nara	784	How? + Bobbin / Distaff
MOU	S	Mouri	毛利	Kamakura	1332	Produce Results / Work Well
ke	S	I'nage	稲毛	Kamakura	1332	Young Rice Plants
ke	F	Wakigeme	和岐毛賣	Nara	784	Peace
[Special]	F	Umishime	毛女	Nara	784	[Woman]

髪 Hair (Scalp)

Reading	Type	Example	Kanji	Period	Date	Added Meaning
kami	F	Shirakami	白髪	Uncertain	1600	White

羽 Feather

Reading	Type	Example	Kanji	Period	Date	Added Meaning
ha	S	Hamoda	羽門田	Higashiyama	1575	Rice Paddy Gate
ha	S	Tanba	丹羽	Uncertain	1600	Red (Flowers)
hane	F	Ha'netsume	羽津賣	Nara	784	Harbour
hane	S	Ha'nebuchi	羽淵	Higashiyama	1575	Abyss
hane	S	Ha'neda	羽田	Higashiyama	1575	Rice Paddy

羅 Fluff / Down / Silk

Reading	Type	Example	Kanji	Period	Date	Added Meaning
[Special]	F	Yosamime	依羅賣	Nara	784	Follow

爪 Claw

Reading	Type	Example	Kanji	Period	Date	Added Meaning
tsume	S	Hizume	樋爪	Hei'an	1183	Flume

脇 Sides / Ribs / Supporter

During the Hei'an Period, this *kanji* was used to denote the second highest Sumo rank and corresponds to the modern Sekiwaki 関脇 Sumo rank.

Reading	Type	Example	Kanji	Period	Date	Added Meaning
waki	S	Wakisaka	脇坂	Sengoku	1568	Steep Road
waki	S	Wakiya	脇屋	Nanboku	1392	Urban House / Artisan

尻 Buttocks / Hips / Anus

Reading	Type	Example	Kanji	Period	Date	Added Meaning
shiri	S	Kawashiri	川尻	Sengoku	1568	River
	S	Tajiri	田尻	Kamakura	1332	Rice Paddy / Flooded Field

屎 Feces

This *kanji* and the reading appearing in the example are definitely vulgar.

Reading	Type	Example	Kanji	Period	Date	Added Meaning
kuso	F	Wogusome	小屎賣	Nara	784	Small

❖ Light & Colour ❖

明 Bright

Reading	Type	Example	Kanji	Period	Date	Added Meaning
MEI	Y	Bunmei	文明	Sengoku	1469	Literature / Culture
MEI	Y	Meiji	明治	Modern	1868	Govern / Rule
MEI	Y	Mei'ou	明応	Sengoku	1492	Worthy / Suitable
MEI	Y	Meireki	明歴	Edo	1655	Progress / Pass Through
MEI	Y	Meitoku	明徳	Nanboku	1390	Righteous / Just
MEI	Y	Meiwa	明和	Edo	1764	Peace / Tranquility / Harmony
MEI	Y	Tenmei	天明	Edo	1781	Sky / Heaven
ake	S	Akechi	明智	Uncertain	1600	Intelligent
aki	M	Taka'akira	高明	Uncertain	1600	Tall
aki	N	Akihira	明衡	Uncertain	1600	A Yoke
aki	N	Akimoto	明基	Hei'an	1183	Foundation
aki	N	Akimu'ne	明宗	Nanboku	1392	Master an Art
aki	N	Akita'ne	明胤	Kamakura	1332	Blood Heir
aki	N	Akizumi	明純	Muromachi	1572	Natural / Pure
aki	N	Hiro'aki	広明	Kamakura	1332	Spacious / Expansive
aki	N	Kin'aki	公明	Kamakura	1332	Noble / Official
aki	N	Nobu'aki	宣明	Kamakura	1332	Proclamation
aki	N	Suke'aki	資明	Nanboku	1392	Raw Materials
aki	N	Suke'aki	祐明	Kamakura	1332	Divine Help
aki	N	Taka'aki	高明	Uncertain	1600	Tall
aki	N	Tame'aki	為明	Nanboku	1392	Purpose / Goal
aki	N	Uji'aki	氏明	Nanboku	1392	Family / Clan
aki	N	Yori'aki	頼明	Sengoku	1568	Request / Ask
akira	F	Akirakeiko	明子	Hei'an	1183	[Lady]
akira	N	Mori'akira	盛明	Kamakura	1332	Plentiful / Piled Up

昭 Bright / Cheerful / Well Controlled

Reading	Type	Example	Kanji	Period	Date	Added Meaning
SHOU	Y	Shouwa	昭和	Modern	1926	Peace / Tranquility / Harmony
aki	N	Michi'aki	通昭	Kamakura	1332	Pass Through
aki	N	Yoshi'aki	義昭	Uncertain	1600	Fealty

輝 Brilliant

Reading	Type	Example	Kanji	Period	Date	Added Meaning
teru	N	Nagateru	長輝	Sengoku	1568	Long
teru	N	Teru'aki	輝顕	Nanboku	1392	High Status
teru	N	Terumoto	輝元	Sengoku	1568	Base / Original

昌 Clear / Bright

Reading	Type	Example	Kanji	Period	Date	Added Meaning
masa	N	Chikamasa	親昌	Nanboku	1392	Intimate
masa	N	Fusamasa	房昌	Hei'an	1183	Monastic Cell
masa	N	Ka'nemasa	兼昌	Uncertain	1600	Unite
masa	N	Kazumasa	員昌	Uncertain	1600	Member
masa	N	Masa'ie	昌家	Nanboku	1392	Rural House / Family
masa	N	Masakage	昌景	Uncertain	1600	Bright / Magnificent
masa	N	Masamori	昌盛	Uncertain	1600	Plentiful / Piled Up
masa	N	Masa'nari	昌成	Hei'an	1183	Become / Exist
masa	N	Masa'nobu	昌信	Uncertain	1600	Belief / Faith
masa	N	Masata'ne	昌胤	Uncertain	1600	Blood Heir
masa	N	Masatoyo	昌豊	Uncertain	1600	Noble
masa	N	Masatsugu	昌次	Uncertain	1600	Next
masa	N	Masayoshi	昌能	Nanboku	1392	Talent / Ability
masa	N	Masayuki	昌幸	Sengoku	1568	Happy / Tattoo
masa	N	Nagamasa	永昌	Kamakura	1332	Forever
masa	N	Nobumasa	信昌	Sengoku	1465	Belief / Faith
masa	N	Shigemasa	繁昌	Kamakura	1332	Bloom / Bouquet
masa	N	Toramasa	虎昌	Uncertain	1600	Tiger
masa	N	Yasumasa	保昌	Uncertain	1600	Guarantee
masa	N	Yoshimasa	義昌	Kamakura	1332	Fealty
yoshi	N	Tsu'neyoshi	常昌	Nanboku	1392	Permanent

光 Bright / Shining

Reading	Type	Example	Kanji	Period	Date	Added Meaning
KOU	H	Kousa	光佐	Uncertain	1600	Military Deputy
KOU	P	Nikkou	日光	Modern	1983	Sun / Day
hikaru	N	Hikaru	光	Uncertain	1600	
mitsu	F	Mitsuko	光子	Hei'an	1183	[Lady]
mitsu	N	Arimitsu	有光	Muromachi	1572	Exists
mitsu	N	Chikamitsu	親光	Kamakura	1332	Intimate
mitsu	N	Iemitsu	家光	Kamakura	1332	Rural House / Family
mitsu	N	Kagemitsu	景光	Kamakura	1332	Bright / Magnificent
mitsu	N	Ka'nemitsu	兼光	Kamakura	1332	Unite
mitsu	N	Katsumitsu	勝光	Muromachi	1572	Conquer / Triumph
mitsu	N	Kinmitsu	公光	Hei'an	1183	Noble / Official
mitsu	N	Kiyomitsu	清光	Hei'an	1183	Pure
mitsu	N	Ku'nimitsu	邦光	Nanboku	1392	Big Country
mitsu	N	Masamitsu	政光	Hei'an	1183	Govern / Rule
mitsu	N	Michimitsu	通光	Kamakura	1332	Pass Through
mitsu	N	Mitsuchika	光親	Kamakura	1332	Intimate
mitsu	N	Mitsuhide	光秀	Sengoku	1568	Extraordinary / Bountiful
mitsu	N	Mitsuhiko	光比己	Uncertain	1600	Measure Up / Strive
mitsu	N	Mitsu'ie	光家	Kamakura	1332	Rural House / Family
mitsu	N	Mitsukazu	光員	Kamakura	1332	Member
mitsu	N	Mitsuku'ni	光国	Kamakura	1332	Country / Rural Area
mitsu	N	Mitsumasa	光政	Hei'an	1183	Govern / Rule
mitsu	N	Mitsumasa	光正	Nanboku	1392	Unerring / Genuine
mitsu	N	Mitsumori	光盛	Kamakura	1332	Plentiful / Piled Up
mitsu	N	Mitsumu'ne	光宗	Kamakura	1332	Master an Art
mitsu	N	Mitsumura	光村	Kamakura	1332	Village

mitsu	N	Mitsu'naga	光長	Hei'an	1183	Long
mitsu	N	Mitsu'nari	光成	Sengoku	1568	Become / Exist
mitsu	N	Mitsu'nobu	光信	Muromachi	1572	Belief / Faith
mitsu	N	Mitsu'nori	光範	Nanboku	1392	Required Form / Pattern
mitsu	N	Mitsusada	光定	Kamakura	1332	Determine
mitsu	N	Mitsusato	光郷	Nanboku	1392	Hometown
mitsu	N	Mitsushige	光重	Kamakura	1332	Heavy / Serious
mitsu	N	Mitsushige	光茂	Muromachi	1572	Blossoming
mitsu	N	Mitsusue	光季	Kamakura	1332	Season
mitsu	N	Mitsuta'ne	光胤	Nanboku	1392	Blood Heir
mitsu	N	Mitsutoki	光時	Kamakura	1332	Time / Era
mitsu	N	Mitsutsugu	光継	Nanboku	1392	Connect / Adopt
mitsu	N	Mitsutsu'ne	光経	Kamakura	1332	True Path
mitsu	N	Mitsuyasu	光泰	Nanboku	1392	Peace / Plenitude
mitsu	N	Mitsuyoshi	光吉	Kamakura	1332	Lucky / Fortunate
mitsu	N	Mitsuyoshi	光嘉	Sengoku	1568	Well Done
mitsu	N	Mitsuyoshi	光能	Hei'an	1183	Talent / Ability
mitsu	N	Mitsuyuki	光行	Kamakura	1332	Going To / Bound For
mitsu	N	Mochimitsu	以光	Muromachi	1572	Highest
mitsu	N	Mochimitsu	持光	Muromachi	1572	Have / Possess
mitsu	N	Morimitsu	盛光	Nanboku	1392	Plentiful / Piled Up
mitsu	N	Moromitsu	師光	Hei'an	1177	Teacher / Expert
mitsu	N	Motomitsu	元光	Muromachi	1572	Base / Original
mitsu	N	Mu'nemitsu	宗光	Kamakura	1332	Master an Art
mitsu	N	Nagamitsu	長光	Kamakura	1332	Long
mitsu	N	Nakamitsu	仲光	Muromachi	1572	Middle of a Group
mitsu	N	Naomitsu	直光	Hei'an	1183	Adjust / Correct
mitsu	N	Nobumitsu	信光	Kamakura	1248	Belief / Faith
mitsu	N	Norimitsu	範光	Nanboku	1392	Required Form / Pattern
mitsu	N	Sadamitsu	貞光	Uncertain	1600	Correct Spirit
sane	N	Sa'nemitsu	実光	Kamakura	1332	Center / Reality / Plentiful
mitsu	N	Shigemitsu	重光	Muromachi	1572	Heavy / Serious
mitsu	N	Shigemitsu	茂光	Hei'an	1183	Blossoming
mitsu	N	Suemitsu	季光	Kamakura	1332	Season
mitsu	N	Sukemitsu	佐光	Kamakura	1332	Military Deputy
mitsu	N	Tadamitsu	忠光	Hei'an	1183	Faithful / Loyal
mitsu	N	Takamitsu	高光	Muromachi	1572	Tall
mitsu	N	Takemitsu	武光	Nanboku	1392	Bravery / Military Force
mitsu	N	Tamemitsu	為光	Uncertain	1600	Purpose / Goal
mitsu	N	Tomomitsu	朝光	Kamakura	1332	Morning
mitsu	N	Toomitsu	遠光	Hei'an	1183	Far
mitsu	N	Toshimitsu	俊光	Kamakura	1332	Emotional
mitsu	N	Toyomitsu	豊光	Muromachi	1572	Noble
mitsu	N	Tsunamitsu	綱光	Muromachi	1572	Net
mitsu	N	Tsu'nemitsu	経光	Kamakura	1332	True Path
mitsu	N	Ujimitsu	氏光	Nanboku	1392	Family / Clan
mitsu	N	Yorimitsu	頼光	Uncertain	1600	Request / Ask
mitsu	N	Yoshimitsu	吉光	Kamakura	1332	Lucky / Fortunate
mitsu	N	Yoshiteru	義光	Kamakura	1332	Fealty
mitsu	N	Yukimitsu	行光	Kamakura	1332	Going To / Bound For
mitsu	S	Fukumitsu	福光	Kamakura	1332	Happy / Blessed

景 Bright / Magnificent

The image is of the sun rising over the lanterns of the capital city. The sun is bright and the view is magnificent. The native *kunyomi* reading for this character is "kage" which is the same as the Japanese word for shadow. This character is particularly interesting in that it actually takes both meanings depending on which Chinese reading is used. However, when used in personal names, this character appears mean "bright" and "magnificent" and not "shadow" as the permissible Chinese reading for this character in personal names represents "bright" and not "shadow".

Reading	Type	Example	Kanji	Period	Date	Added Meaning
kage	N	Chikakage	親景	Muromachi	1572	Intimate
kage	N	Fusakage	房景	Muromachi	1572	Monastic Cell
kage	N	Iekage	家景	Kamakura	1187	Rural House / Family
kage	N	Kagechika	景親	Hei'an	1183	Intimate
kage	N	Kageharu	景春	Muromachi	1572	Spring (Season)
kage	N	Kagehira	景平	Kamakura	1332	Tranquility
kage	N	Kagehiro	景弘	Hei'an	1183	Draw / Stretch
kage	N	Kagehisa	景久	Kamakura	1332	Longtime
kage	N	Kage'ie	景家	Hei'an	1183	Rural House / Family
kage	N	Kagekado	景廉	Kamakura	1332	Reason / Justification
kage	N	Kagekatsu	景勝	Uncertain	1600	Conquer / Triumph
kage	N	Kagekazu	景員	Hei'an	1183	Member
kage	N	Kagekiyo	景清	Hei'an	1183	Pure
kage	N	Kagemasa	景正	Kamakura	1332	Unerring / Genuine
kage	N	Kagemasu	景益	Kamakura	1332	Grow Numerous / Overflow
kage	N	Kagemitsu	景光	Kamakura	1332	Bright / Shining
kage	N	Kagemochi	景茂	Kamakura	1332	Blossoming
kage	N	Kagemori	景盛	Kamakura	1332	Plentiful / Piled Up
kage	N	Kagemu'ne	景宗	Nanboku	1392	Master an Art
kage	N	Kage'naga	景長	Kamakura	1332	Long
kage	N	Kage'naka	景仲	Muromachi	1572	Middle of a Group
kage	N	Kage'nobu	景信	Muromachi	1572	Belief / Faith
kage	N	Kageshige	景繁	Kamakura	1332	Bloom / Bouquet
kage	N	Kagesue	景季	Kamakura	1332	Season
kage	N	Kagesuke	景資	Kamakura	1332	Raw Materials
kage	N	Kagetada	景忠	Kamakura	1332	Faithful / Loyal
kage	N	Kagetaka	景高	Hei'an	1183	Tall
kage	N	Kagetaka	景隆	Kamakura	1332	Grow / Pile Up
kage	N	Kagetoki	景時	Kamakura	1332	Time / Era
kage	N	Kagetomo	景朝	Kamakura	1332	Morning
kage	N	Kagetora	景虎	Uncertain	1600	Tiger
kage	N	Kagetsugu	景継	Kamakura	1332	Connect / Adopt
kage	N	Kagetsu'na	景綱	Kamakura	1332	Net
kage	N	Kagetsu'ne	景経	Hei'an	1183	True Path
kage	N	Kagetsu'ne	景恒	Nanboku	1392	Changeless / Enduring
kage	N	Kageyasu	景泰	Kamakura	1332	Peace / Plenitude
kage	N	Kageyori	景頼	Kamakura	1332	Request / Ask
kage	N	Kageyoshi	景義	Kamakura	1332	Fealty
kage	N	Masakage	昌景	Uncertain	1600	Clear / Bright
kage	N	Morikage	盛景	Kamakura	1332	Plentiful / Piled Up
kage	N	Morokage	師景	Nanboku	1392	Teacher / Expert
kage	N	Mu'nekage	宗景	Muromachi	1572	Master an Art
kage	N	Norikage	教景	Muromachi	1572	Teaching / Dogma
kage	N	Sadakage	定景	Kamakura	1332	Determine
kage	N	Sukekage	輔景	Kamakura	1332	Ministerial Deputy
kage	N	Takakage	孝景	Nanboku	1392	Filial Loyalty
kage	N	Takakage	高景	Kamakura	1332	Tall
kage	N	Tomokage	朝景	Kamakura	1332	Morning

Thematic Dictionary — **Light & Colour**   183

Reading	Type	Example	Kanji	Period	Date	Added Meaning
kage	N	Tomokage	友景	Kamakura	1332	Friend
kage	N	Tookage	遠景	Kamakura	1332	Far
kage	N	Toshikage	敏景	Muromachi	1572	Very Rapid Hard Work
kage	N	Tsu'nekage	経景	Uncertain	1600	True Path
kage	N	Yoshikage	義景	Kamakura	1332	Fealty

照 Bright / Visible / Explicit

Reading	Type	Example	Kanji	Period	Date	Added Meaning
terasu	N	Terasu	照	Nanboku	1392	

晶 Star Light / Pure Light

This *kanji* evokes the image of three stars shining together.

Reading	Type	Example	Kanji	Period	Date	Added Meaning
SHOU	H	Shouji	晶爾	Uncertain	1600	Bobbin / Distaff

色 Colour

Reading	Type	Example	Kanji	Period	Date	Added Meaning
SHIKI	S	Isshiki	一色	Nanboku	1392	One
iro	S	Irobe	色部	Uncertain	1600	Monopoly Corporation

黒 Black

Reading	Type	Example	Kanji	Period	Date	Added Meaning
kuro	F	Hokurome	黒子賣	Hei'an	1183	[Lady]
kuro	F	Kurome	黒賣	Nara	784	
kuro	S	Kuroda	黒田	Sengoku	1568	Rice Paddy

玄 Dark / Black / Austere

Reading	Type	Example	Kanji	Period	Date	Added Meaning
GEN	H	Shingen	信玄	Sengoku	1568	Belief / Faith
kuro	F	Kuroko	玄子	Hei'an	1183	[Lady]

蔭 Shade / Shadow

Unlike *kage* 影 which refers to a shadow image, *kage* 蔭 is primarily concerned with an area without light. Literally, this kanji means a place where light does not strike. Ironically, this forms the basis for the common phrase *okage* 御蔭 which refers to help received from the Buddha. Thus, the notion of shadow extends to protection received from a senior member of society. This idea of "protection" extends to the notion of social advancement due to the stature of grandparents.

Reading	Type	Example	Kanji	Period	Date	Added Meaning
kage	N	Takakage	隆蔭	Nanboku	1392	Grow Tall / Pile Up

紫 Purple

Reading	Type	Example	Kanji	Period	Date	Added Meaning
murasaki	F	Murasaki'emon	紫衛門	Hei'an	1183	Palace Regiment

白 White

Reading	Type	Example	Kanji	Period	Date	Added Meaning
shira	F	Shirakamime	白髪賣	Nara	784	Scalp Hair
shiro	F	Shiro	白	Muromachi	1572	

素 White / Unused / Virgin

Reading	Type	Example	Kanji	Period	Date	Added Meaning
SO	H	Sosei	素性	Uncertain	1600	Nature / Attributes / Purity

赤 Red (Fire) / Young

Reading	Type	Example	Kanji	Period	Date	Added Meaning
aka	F	Akame	赤賣	Nara	784	
aka	N	Akahito	赤人	Uncertain	1600	Person / Human
aka	S	Akahashi	赤橋	Uncertain	1600	Bridge
aka	S	Akamatsu	赤松	Nanboku	1392	Pine Tree
aka	S	Akashi	赤石	Nanboku	1371	Rock

丹 Red (Flowers)

Reading	Type	Example	Kanji	Period	Date	Added Meaning
TAN	S	Tanba	丹羽	Uncertain	1600	Feather

蘇 Dark Crimson

Reading	Type	Example	Kanji	Period	Date	Added Meaning
SO	F	Soteme	蘇弓賣	Nara	784	Bow
SO	S	Aso	阿蘇	Nanboku	1392	Crevice

青 Blue / Green

Although the *kunyomi* for this *kanji* is "ao" 青 in modern Japanese, it was read as "awo" in classical Japanese, and the classical adjective was awoshi. While some argue that classical pronunciation persisted throughout period, others contend that it disappeared by the Hei'an period. See Hollyhock for Aoi 葵.

Reading	Type	Example	Kanji	Period	Date	Added Meaning
ao	P	Aoyama	青山	Modern	1983	Mountain
ao	S	Aoki	青木	Sengoku	1568	Tree
ao	S	Aoto	青砥	Kamakura	1332	Whetstone / Grindstone / Flat

❖ Groups & Relationships ❖

功 Public Service

Reading	Type	Example	Kanji	Period	Date	Added Meaning
isao	F	Isakome	功子賣	Nara	784	[Lady]

皆 Everybody

Reading	Type	Example	Kanji	Period	Date	Added Meaning
mina	S	Mi'nakawa	皆川	Uncertain	1600	River

部 Monopoly Corporation / Military Column / Department

This character was used to form the names of monopoly corporations associated with the noble clans. These corporate names were commonly used by peasants and artisans.

Reading	Type	Example	Kanji	Period	Date	Added Meaning
be	S	Chousokabe	長宗我部	Uncertain	1600	Long + Master an Art + Our
be	S	Hasebe	長谷部	Hei'an	1183	Long + Valley
be	S	Irobe	色部	Uncertain	1600	Colour
be	S	Miyabe	宮部	Uncertain	1600	Palace
be	S	Nanbu	南部	Kamakura	1332	South
be	S	Okabe	岡部	Kamakura	1332	Hill
be	S	Sakabe	酒部	Hei'an	1183	Sake / Rice Wine
be	S	Sasabe	雀部	Hei'an	1183	Sparrow
be	S	Takebe	建部	Kamakura	1332	Build / Construct
be	S	Urabe	卜部	Muromachi	1572	Divine / Foretell / Prophesy

伴 Collective / Band

Reading	Type	Example	Kanji	Period	Date	Added Meaning
tomo	N	Tsu'netomo	常伴	Hei'an	1183	Permanent

渡 Cross Over

Possibly the name for Sado Island derives from the fact that it was the place where imperial Japan exiled its nobles and scholars.

Reading	Type	Example	Kanji	Period	Date	Added Meaning
DO	P	Sado	佐渡	Kamakura	1332	Military Deputy

加 Join Up / Enlist

Reading	Type	Example	Kanji	Period	Date	Added Meaning
KA	F	Kahime	加比賣	Nara	784	Measure Up / Strive
KA	F	Kajime	加自賣	Nara	784	Independent
KA	F	Kakame	加々女	Hei'an	1183	[Woman]
KA	F	Karime	加利賣	Nara	784	Produce Results
KA	S	Kaga'i	加賀井	Sengoku	1568	Celebrate A Gain + Well
KA	S	Kagami	加賀美	Hei'an	1183	Celebrate A Gain + Beauty
KA	S	Kaji	加地	Uncertain	1600	Soil / Country
KA	S	Katou	加東	Uncertain	1600	East
KA	S	Katou	加藤	Kamakura	1332	Wisteria

与 Team up

Reading	Type	Example	Kanji	Period	Date	Added Meaning
YO	M	Yogotarou	与五太郎	Uncertain	1600	Fifth Son
YO	M	Yo'ichirou	与一郎	Modern	1983	First Son
YO	M	Yokurou	与九郎	Uncertain	1600	Ninth Son
YO	M	Yotarou	与太郎	Uncertain	1600	First Son

俱 Together / Collaborate

Reading	Type	Example	Kanji	Period	Date	Added Meaning
tomo	N	Ka'netomo	兼俱	Muromachi	1572	Unite / Heavy Service

集 Gather Together

Reading	Type	Example	Kanji	Period	Date	Added Meaning
SHUU	S	Ijuu'in	伊集院	Nanboku	1392	Rule + Mansion

相 Together / Team-Work

Reading	Type	Example	Kanji	Period	Date	Added Meaning
SOU	S	Souma	相馬	Kamakura	1332	Horse
ai	N	Yosh'aii	良相	Uncertain	1600	Good / Superior
ai	S	Aizawa	相澤	Modern	1782	Glen / Run
sa	F	Sakami	相模	Uncertain	1600	Model / Example / Guide
sa	S	Sagara	相良	Kamakura	1332	Good / Superior
suke	N	Kinsuke	公相	Kamakura	1332	Noble / Official
suke	N	Michisuke	通相	Nanboku	1392	Pass Through
suke	N	Tamesuke	為相	Kamakura	1332	Purpose / Goal
suke	N	Yoshisuke	良相	Uncertain	1600	Good / Superior

Thematic Dictionary — Groups & Relationships

継 Connect / Adopt

Reading	Type	Example	Kanji	Period	Date	Added Meaning
tsugu	N	Chikatsugu	親継	Kamakura	1332	Intimate
tsugu	N	Ietsugu	家継	Hei'an	1183	Rural House / Family
tsugu	N	Kagetsugu	景継	Kamakura	1332	Bright / Magnificent
tsugu	N	Kintsugu	公継	Kamakura	1332	Noble / Official
tsugu	N	Koretsugu	惟継	Kamakura	1332	This / Here
tsugu	N	Michitsugu	通継	Kamakura	1332	Pass Through
tsugu	N	Mitsutsugu	光継	Nanboku	1392	Bright / Shining
tsugu	N	Moritsugu	盛継	Uncertain	1600	Plentiful / Piled Up
tsugu	N	Sadatsugu	貞継	Nanboku	1392	Correct Spirit
tsugu	N	Sadatsugu	定継	Kamakura	1332	Determine
tsugu	N	Sa'netsugu	実継	Kamakura	1332	Reality
tsugu	N	Shigetsugu	重継	Kamakura	1332	Heavy / Serious
tsugu	N	Suetsugu	季継	Kamakura	1332	Season
tsugu	N	Ta'netsugu	種継	Uncertain	1600	Cause / Reason
tsugu	N	Tokitsugu	時継	Kamakura	1332	Time / Era
tsugu	N	Tsugu'nobu	継信	Kamakura	1184	Belief / Faith
tsugu	N	Ujitzugu	氏継	Uncertain	1600	Family / Clan
tsugu	N	Yoshitsugu	義継	Kamakura	1332	Fealty

我 Our / Us / We

Reading	Type	Example	Kanji	Period	Date	Added Meaning
GA	S	Kuga	久我	Uncertain	1600	Longtime
GA	S	Soga	曽我	Uncertain	1600	Formerly / Ever
wa	F	Wagimome	我妹賣	Nara	784	Younger Sister

吾 We / Our / One's Self

Reading	Type	Example	Kanji	Period	Date	Added Meaning
[Special]	F	Areme	吾女	Nara	784	[Woman]

麿 Me / Myself / Us

Originally used in names of adult men and written as 麻呂, *maro* 麿 is now commonly replaced by 丸 and read as *maru*. Please refer to the entry for 丸 Young/Healthy on page 121 for an extended discussion of this usage.

Reading	Type	Example	Kanji	Period	Date	Added Meaning
maro	N	Nakamaro	仲麿	Uncertain	1600	Middle of a Group

氏 Family / Clan

Reading	Type	Example	Kanji	Period	Date	Added Meaning
uji	F	Ujiko	氏子	Nanboku	1392	[Lady]
uji	N	Aki'uji	顕氏	Nanboku	1392	High Status
uji	N	Aki'uji	朝氏	Uncertain	1600	Morning
uji	N	Fuyu'uji	冬氏	Kamakura	1332	Winter
uji	N	Hide'uji	秀氏	Sengoku	1568	Extraordinary / Bountiful
uji	N	Hisa'uji	尚氏	Muromachi	1572	Excellence
uji	N	Ie'uji	家氏	Kamakura	1332	Rural House / Family

uji	N	Ka'ne'uji	兼氏	Kamakura	1332	Unite
uji	N	Kazu'uji	和氏	Nanboku	1392	Peace / Tranquility
uji	N	Kiyo'uji	清氏	Nanboku	1392	Pure
uji	N	Masa'uji	雅氏	Nanboku	1390	High Quality
uji	N	Masa'uji	政氏	Sengoku	1568	Govern / Rule
uji	N	Masa'uji	正氏	Uncertain	1600	Unerring / Genuine
uji	N	Michi'uji	通氏	Nanboku	1392	Pass Through
uji	N	Mitsu'uji	満氏	Muromachi	1572	Become Full / Abundant
uji	N	Mochi'uji	持氏	Muromachi	1572	Have / Possess
uji	N	Mori'uji	盛氏	Kamakura	1332	Plentiful / Piled Up
uji	N	Moro'uji	師氏	Nanboku	1392	Teacher / Expert
uji	N	Moto'uji	基氏	Kamakura	1332	Foundation
uji	N	Moto'uji	元氏	Nanboku	1392	Base / Original
uji	N	Moto'uji	源氏	Kamakura	1332	Origin
uji	N	Mu'ne'uji	宗氏	Kamakura	1332	Master an Art
uji	N	Naga'uji	長氏	Kamakura	1332	Long
uji	N	Nao'uji	直氏	Nanboku	1392	Adjust / Correct
uji	N	Nari'uji	成氏	Uncertain	1600	Become / Exist
uji	N	Nori'uji	紀氏	Muromachi	1572	Season
uji	N	Nori'uji	範氏	Nanboku	1392	Required Form / Pattern
uji	N	Sada'uji	貞氏	Kamakura	1332	Correct Spirit
uji	N	Sa'ne'uji	実氏	Kamakura	1332	Reality
uji	N	Shige'uji	重氏	Kamakura	1332	Heavy / Serious
uji	N	Shige'uji	成氏	Muromachi	1572	Become / Exist
uji	N	Shige'uji	繁氏	Nanboku	1392	Bloom / Bouquet
uji	N	Suke'uji	助氏	Nanboku	1392	Deputy (Rescue / Assist)
uji	N	Tada'uji	忠氏	Sengoku	1568	Faithful / Loyal
uji	N	Taka'uji	高氏	Kamakura	1332	Tall
uji	N	Taka'uji	尊氏	Kamakura	1305	Exemplar / Admirable
uji	N	Tame'uji	為氏	Kamakura	1332	Purpose / Goal
uji	N	Toki'uji	時氏	Kamakura	1332	Time / Era
uji	N	Tomo'uji	知氏	Nanboku	1392	Knowledge
uji	N	Tsu'ne'uji	経氏	Kamakura	1332	True Path
uji	N	Tsura'uji	貫氏	Muromachi	1572	Perseverance
uji	N	Uji'aki	氏詮	Nanboku	1392	Explicit / Clear
uji	N	Uji'aki	氏朝	Nanboku	1392	Morning
uji	N	Uji'aki	氏明	Nanboku	1392	Bright
uji	N	Ujifuyu	氏冬	Nanboku	1392	Winter
uji	N	Ujiharu	氏治	Nanboku	1392	Govern / Rule
uji	N	Ujiharu	氏春	Nanboku	1392	Spring (Season)
uji	N	Ujihide	氏秀	Nanboku	1392	Extraordinary / Bountiful
uji	N	Ujihiro	氏弘	Muromachi	1572	Draw / Stretch
uji	N	Ujihisa	氏久	Nanboku	1392	Longtime
uji	N	Uji'ie	氏家	Muromachi	1572	Rural House / Family
uji	N	Ujikiyo	氏清	Nanboku	1392	Pure
uji	N	Ujiku'ni	氏国	Kamakura	1332	Country / Rural Area
uji	N	Ujimitsu	氏光	Nanboku	1392	Bright / Shining
uji	N	Ujimitsu	氏満	Nanboku	1392	Become Full / Abundant
uji	N	Ujimori	氏盛	Sengoku	1568	Plentiful / Piled Up
uji	N	Ujimu'ne	氏宗	Sengoku	1568	Master an Art
uji	N	Uji'nao	氏直	Nanboku	1392	Adjust / Correct
uji	N	Uji'nari	氏成	Uncertain	1600	Become / Exist
uji	N	Uji'nobu	氏信	Kamakura	1332	Belief / Faith
uji	N	Uji'nori	氏憲	Muromachi	1572	Example / Pattern
uji	N	Uji'nori	氏範	Nanboku	1392	Required Form / Pattern
uji	N	Ujisato	氏郷	Sengoku	1568	Hometown
uji	N	Ujishige	氏鎮	Nanboku	1392	Quench / Immerse / Temper

Thematic Dictionary — Groups & Relationships

Reading	Type	Example	Kanji	Period	Date	Added Meaning
uji	N	Ujita'ne	氏胤	Nanboku	1392	Blood Heir
uji	N	Ujitoki	氏時	Nanboku	1392	Time / Era
uji	N	Ujitomo	氏朝	Muromachi	1572	Morning
uji	N	Ujitoshi	氏俊	Nanboku	1392	Emotional
uji	N	Ujitoshi	氏利	Muromachi	1572	Produce Results
uji	N	Ujitsu'na	氏綱	Nanboku	1392	Net
uji	N	Ujitsu'ne	氏経	Kamakura	1332	True Path
uji	N	Ujitzugu	氏継	Uncertain	1600	Connect / Adopt
uji	N	Ujiyasu	氏泰	Nanboku	1392	Peace / Plenitude
uji	N	Ujiyori	氏頼	Nanboku	1392	Request / Ask
uji	N	Ujiyoshi	氏能	Nanboku	1392	Talent / Ability
uji	N	Ujiyuki	氏幸	Nanboku	1392	Happy / Tattoo
uji	N	Ujiyuki	氏之	Muromachi	1572	Go / Depart
uji	N	Yasu'uji	泰氏	Uncertain	1600	Peace / Plenitude
uji	N	Yori'uji	頼氏	Kamakura	1332	Request / Ask
uji	N	Yoshi'uji	義氏	Kamakura	1332	Fealty
uji	N	Yoshi'uji	能氏	Kamakura	1332	Talent / Ability
uji	N	Yuki'uji	幸氏	Kamakura	1332	Happy / Tattoo
uji	N	Yuki'uji	行氏	Kamakura	1332	Going To / Bound For

条 Branch / Line / Prestigous Residence / Avenue

This *kanji* was used to count major roads in Hei'ankyou much like major avenues are counted in cities like New York. The avenues were numbered from North to South. Ichijou 一条 and defined districts in the capital. As the imperial palace was at the northern end of the city, a low avenue number signified a considerable connection to the imperial government and other sources of revenue and power.

Reading	Type	Example	Kanji	Period	Date	Added Meaning
JOU	S	Houjou	北条	Kamakura	1332	North
JOU	S	Ichijou	一条	Kamakura	1332	One
JOU	S	Nakajou	中条	Kamakura	1332	Middle
JOU	S	Shijou	四条	Kamakura	1332	Four
JOU	S	Kujou	九条	Kamakura	1219	Nnee

紹 Inherit / Help

Reading	Type	Example	Kanji	Period	Date	Added Meaning
SHOU	H	Shou'ou	紹鴎	Uncertain	1600	Sea Gull

統 Lineage / Govern

Reading	Type	Example	Kanji	Period	Date	Added Meaning
mune	N	Mu'ne'aki	統秋	Muromachi	1572	Autumn
mune	N	Yoshimu'ne	義統	Muromachi	1572	Fealty

政 Govern / Rule / Instruct / Self-Control

Reading	Type	Example	Kanji	Period	Date	Added Meaning
SEI	Y	Bunsei	文政	Edo	1818	Literature / Culture
SEI	Y	Kansei	寛政	Edo	1789	Domestic Tranquility
masa	F	Masako	政子	Kamakura	1332	[Lady]
masa	N	Chikamasa	親政	Uncertain	1600	Intimate
masa	N	Hidemasa	秀政	Sengoku	1568	Extraordinary / Bountiful

masa	N	Iemasa	家政	Kamakura	1332	Rural House / Family
masa	N	Koremasa	惟政	Nanboku	1392	This / Here
masa	N	Masachika	政親	Kamakura	1332	Intimate
masa	N	Masahira	政平	Kamakura	1332	Tranquility
masa	N	Masahiro	政弘	Sengoku	1568	Draw / Stretch
masa	N	Masa'ie	政家	Muromachi	1572	Rural House / Family
masa	N	Masakiyo	政清	Muromachi	1572	Pure
masa	N	Masaku'ni	政国	Muromachi	1572	Country / Rural Area
masa	N	Masamitsu	政光	Hei'an	1183	Bright / Shining
masa	N	Masamoto	政幹	Nanboku	1392	Trunk / Stalk
masa	N	Masamoto	政基	Muromachi	1572	Foundation
masa	N	Masamoto	政元	Nanboku	1392	Base / Original
masa	N	Masamu'ne	政宗	Nanboku	1392	Master an Art
masa	N	Masamura	政村	Kamakura	1332	Village
masa	N	Masa'naga	政長	Nanboku	1392	Long
masa	N	Masa'nori	政則	Muromachi	1572	Make an Example
masa	N	Masashige	政茂	Kamakura	1332	Blossoming
masa	N	Masasuke	政助	Uncertain	1600	Deputy (Rescue / Assist)
masa	N	Masasuke	政祐	Nanboku	1392	Divine Help
masa	N	Masataka	政高	Muromachi	1572	Tall
masa	N	Masatomo	政具	Uncertain	1600	Tool / Implement
masa	N	Masatomo	政知	Muromachi	1572	Knowledge
masa	N	Masatoyo	政豊	Muromachi	1572	Noble
masa	N	Masatsugu	政嗣	Kamakura	1332	Successor
masa	N	Masatsu'na	政綱	Kamakura	1328	Net
masa	N	Masatsu'ne	政経	Muromachi	1572	True Path
masa	N	Masa'uji	政氏	Sengoku	1568	Family / Clan
masa	N	Masayasu	政康	Muromachi	1572	Strong / Confident
masa	N	Masayasu	政泰	Kamakura	1332	Peace / Plenitude
masa	N	Masayoshi	政義	Kamakura	1332	Fealty
masa	N	Masayuki	政行	Nanboku	1392	Going To / Bound For
masa	N	Michimasa	道政	Nanboku	1392	Road / Way
masa	N	Mitsumasa	光政	Hei'an	1183	Bright / Shining
masa	N	Mitsumasa	満政	Muromachi	1572	Become Full / Abundant
masa	N	Mochimasa	以政	Hei'an	1183	Highest
masa	N	Morimasa	盛政	Kamakura	1332	Plentiful / Piled Up
masa	N	Motomasa	基政	Kamakura	1332	Foundation
masa	N	Mu'nemasa	宗政	Kamakura	1332	Master an Art
masa	N	Nagamasa	長政	Kamakura	1332	Long
masa	N	Nobumasa	信政	Kamakura	1332	Belief / Faith
masa	N	Norimasa	教政	Muromachi	1572	Teaching / Dogma
masa	N	Norimasa	範政	Muromachi	1572	Required Form / Pattern
masa	N	Sadamasa	貞政	Kamakura	1332	Correct Spirit
masa	N	Sa'nemasa	実政	Kamakura	1332	Reality
masa	N	Shigemasa	重政	Sengoku	1568	Heavy / Serious
masa	N	Tadamasa	忠政	Sengoku	1568	Faithful / Loyal
masa	N	Takamasa	高政	Sengoku	1568	Tall
masa	N	Takamasa	隆政	Nanboku	1392	Grow / Pile Up
masa	N	Takemasa	武政	Nanboku	1392	Bravery / Military Force
masa	N	Tokimasa	時政	Hei'an	1183	Time / Era
masa	N	Tomomasa	朝政	Kamakura	1332	Morning
masa	N	Toshimasa	俊政	Kamakura	1332	Emotional
masa	N	Tsu'nemasa	経政	Kamakura	1332	True Path
masa	N	Yasumasa	康政	Sengoku	1568	Strong / Confident
masa	N	Yorimasa	頼政	Hei'an	1183	Request / Ask
masa	N	Yoshimasa	義政	Kamakura	1332	Fealty
masa	N	Yukimasa	行政	Kamakura	1332	Going To / Bound For

治 Govern / Rule

Reading	Type	Example	Kanji	Period	Date	Added Meaning
JI	Y	Bunji	文治	Kamakura	1185	Literature / Culture
JI	Y	Chouji	長治	Hei'an	1104	Long / Oldest / Senior
JI	Y	Daiji	大治	Hei'an	1126	Big
JI	Y	Eiji	永治	Hei'an	1141	Forever
JI	Y	Genji	元治	Edo	1864	Base / Original
JI	Y	Heiji	平治	Kamakura	1159	Tranquility
JI	Y	Houji	保治	Kamakura	1247	Guarantee
JI	Y	Ji'an	治安	Hei'an	1021	Gentle / Safe / Secure
JI	Y	Jiryaku	治歷	Hei'an	1065	Progress / Pass Through
JI	Y	Jishou	治承	Kamakura	1177	Humbly Receive
JI	Y	Jouji	貞治	Nanboku	1362	Correct Spirit
JI	Y	Kanji	寬治	Hei'an	1087	Domestic Tranquility
JI	Y	Kenji	建治	Kamakura	1275	Found / Build / Construct
JI	Y	Kouji	康治	Hei'an	1142	Strong / Confident
JI	Y	Kouji	弘治	Sengoku	1555	Draw / Stretch / Spread Out
JI	Y	Manji	万治	Edo	1658	Ten Thousand
JI	Y	Meiji	明治	Modern	1868	Bright
JI	Y	Ninji	仁治	Kamakura	1240	Precious
JI	Y	Shouji	正治	Kamakura	1199	Unerring / Genuine
JI	Y	Tenji	天治	Hei'an	1124	Sky / Heaven
JI	Y	Tokuji	德治	Kamakura	1306	Righteous / Just
haru	F	Haruko	治子	Nanboku	1392	[Lady]
haru	N	Chikaharu	親治	Hei'an	1183	Intimate
haru	N	Haruhisa	治久	Kamakura	1332	Longtime
haru	N	Haru'naga	治長	Sengoku	1568	Long
haru	N	Harutada	治忠	Sengoku	1568	Faithful / Loyal
haru	N	Masuharu	泰治	Nanboku	1392	Peace / Plenitude
haru	N	Michiharu	通治	Kamakura	1332	Pass Through
haru	N	Motoharu	元治	Hei'an	1183	Base / Original
haru	N	Tokiharu	時治	Kamakura	1332	Time / Era
haru	N	Tsu'neharu	常治	Kamakura	1332	Permanent
haru	N	Ujiharu	氏治	Nanboku	1392	Family / Clan
haru	N	Yoriharu	賴治	Nanboku	1392	Request / Ask
haru	N	Yoshiharu	義治	Nanboku	1392	Fealty

法 Law

Note that "law" includes Buddhist teachings and that this is probably the sense in which this element most often occurs. Dharma (Law) along with Buddha, and Samgah (Community) are the three pillars of Buddhism.

Reading	Type	Example	Kanji	Period	Date	Added Meaning
HOU	P	Myou'hou'ji	妙法寺	Uncertain	1600	Temple
nori	F	Norime	法賣	Nara	784	Law

儀 Precept

Reading	Type	Example	Kanji	Period	Date	Added Meaning
nori	N	Masa'nori	正儀	Nanboku	1392	Unerring / Genuine

❖ Rank & Status ❖

公 Public Official / Officer / Noble / Duke (Classical Chinese)

This character is strongly associated with the higher court nobility. When read as "kimi", it is also an honourific used for persons of very high social status. Collectively, the court nobility were known as the *kuge* 公家 as opposed to the *buke* 武家 which formed the military class.

Reading	Type	Example	Kanji	Period	Date	Added Meaning
kimi	N	Kimi'nari	公業	Kamakura	1332	Industry / Diligence
kimi	N	Kimitomo	公朝	Kamakura	1332	Morning
kin	N	Kimimichi	公通	Hei'an	1183	Pass Through
kin	N	Kin'aki	公明	Kamakura	1332	Bright
kin	N	Kin'ari	公有	Muromachi	1572	Exists
kin	N	Kinnori	公教	Hei'an	1183	Teaching / Dogma
kin	N	Kin'o	公雄	Kamakura	1332	Strength / Courage / Bravery
kin	N	Kin'yasu	公保	Hei'an	1183	Guarantee
kin	N	Kin'yuki	公行	Muromachi	1572	Going To / Bound For
kin	N	Kinchika	公親	Kamakura	1332	Intimate
kin	N	Kinfusa	公房	Kamakura	1332	Monastic Cell
kin	N	Kinfuyu	公冬	Muromachi	1572	Winter
kin	N	Kinhide	公秀	Kamakura	1332	Extraordinary / Bountiful
kin	N	Kinhira	公衡	Kamakura	1332	A Yoke
kin	N	Kinkata	公賢	Kamakura	1332	Genius
kin	N	Kinkiyo	公清	Nanboku	1392	Pure
kin	N	Kinmasa	公雅	Kamakura	1332	High Quality
kin	N	Kinmichi	公通	Hei'an	1183	Pass Through
kin	N	Kinmitsu	公光	Hei'an	1183	Bright / Shining
kin	N	Kinmori	公守	Kamakura	1332	Protect / Defend
kin	N	Kinmoto	公基	Kamakura	1332	Foundation
kin	N	Kinmu'ne	公宗	Kamakura	1332	Master an Art
kin	N	Kinnaga	公長	Kamakura	1332	Long
kin	N	Kinnao	公直	Kamakura	1332	Adjust / Correct
kin	N	Kinsada	公定	Kamakura	1332	Determine
kin	N	Kinshige	公茂	Kamakura	1332	Blossoming
kin	N	Kinsue	公季	Uncertain	1600	Season
kin	N	Kinsuke	公相	Kamakura	1332	Together / Team Work
kin	N	Kintada	公忠	Nanboku	1392	Faithful / Loyal
kin	N	Kintoki	公時	Nanboku	1392	Time / Era
kin	N	Kintoshi	公俊	Muromachi	1572	Emotional
kin	N	Kintsu'na	公綱	Kamakura	1332	Net
kin	N	Kintsu'ne	公経	Hei'an	1183	True Path
kin	N	Kintsugu	公継	Kamakura	1332	Connect / Adopt
kin	N	Kintsura	公連	Muromachi	1572	Bring Along
kin	N	Nishikin'yasu	西公保	Muromachi	1572	Guarantee West
kin	N	Nishikintoki	西公時	Nanboku	1392	Time / Era West
tomo	N	Kiyotomo	清公	Hei'an	842	Pure

君 King / Emperor / Lord (Classical Chineses)

Reading	Type	Example	Kanji	Period	Date	Added Meaning
kimi	N	Nobukimi	信君	Uncertain	600	Belief / Faith

王 King / Imperial Prince / Deity

This element can be found a postpositional honourific in the names of gods and the names of members of the imperial family. Either Shinnou 親王 or Ou 王 is attached to the *nanori* of imperial princes. As 親 (SHIN) means "intimate", Shinnou is superior to Ou. In either case, there is no family name and the *nanori* with the attached titular form constitutes a complete name. Similarly, imperial princesses bore names consisting of a complete *nanori* followed by Naishinnou 内親王. Kyuushinaishinnou 久子内親王 was also known as Eiyoumonin 永陽門院 which consists of a typical Buddhistic name or *houmyou* 法名 followed by the titular form. As this is the name of a Buddhist nun, the characters take their Chinese readings. Similarly, Hanshinaishinnou 範子内親王 was known as Boumon'in 坊門院.

Reading	Type	Example	Kanji	Period	Date	Added Meaning
OU	F	Enshi Naishinnou	延子内親王	Kamakura	1291	[延明門院]
OU	F	Etsushi Naishinnou	悦子内親王	Kamakura	1259	[延政門院]
OU	F	Hanshi Naishinnou	範子内親王	Hei'an	1177	[坊門院]
OU	F	Kyuushi Naishinnou	久子内親王	Kamakura	1271	[永陽門院]
OU	N	Tsugi'naga Shinnou	世良親王	Kamakura	1330	Generation + Good
OU	N	Tsugiyoshi Shinnou	世良親王	Kamakura	1330	Generation + Good
OU	N	Tsuguhito Shinnou	継仁親王	Kamakura	1279	Connect / Adopt + Precious

臣 Minister / Principal Vassal / Servant (Classical Chinese)

Note that Omi 臣 was also the name of one of the powerful ruling clans of ancient Japan.

Reading	Type	Example	Kanji	Period	Date	Added Meaning
omi	N	Suke'omi	祐臣	Kamakura	1332	Divine Help

守 Regional Governor

As a title, this character appears after the locative. Thus, we have names like Tosa no Kami 土佐守 which means "Baron of Tosa" or "Sheriff of Tosa". Tosa is the name of a remote province featured in the story *Tosa Monogatari*.

Reading	Type	Example	Kanji	Period	Date	Added Meaning
mori	N	Kinmori	公守	Kamakura	1332	Noble / Official
mori	N	Michimori	通守	Muromachi	1572	Pass Through
mori	N	Morichika	守親	Uncertain	1600	Intimate
mori	N	Morimasa	守正	Kamakura	1332	Unerring / Genuine
mori	N	Morimori	盛守	Uncertain	1600	Plentiful / Piled Up
mori	N	Mori'nobu	守延	Kamakura	1332	Prolong / Stretch Out
mori	N	Moritoki	守時	Kamakura	1332	Time / Era
mori	N	Moritomo	守知	Sengoku	1568	Knowledge
mori	N	Moritomo	守友	Uncertain	1600	Friend
mori	N	Moromori	師守	Nanboku	1392	Teacher / Expert
mori	N	Nagamori	長守	Kamakura	1332	Long
mori	N	Tamemori	為守	Kamakura	1332	Purpose / Goal
mori	N	Tomomori	具守	Kamakura	1332	Tool / Implement
mori	S	Moriyama	守山	Nanboku	1392	Mountain

介 Regional Deputy

This *kanji* is also used to form the titles of lieutenant governors. Specifically, these deputies were part of the kokushi 国司 system of government. These officials governed the provinces. Often, the actual governors remained in the capital while the deputies, estate stewards and other representatives managed affairs in the provinces.

Reading	Type	Example	Kanji	Period	Date	Added Meaning
KE	F	Kesame	介佐賣	Hei'an	1183	Military Deputy
suke	N	Mu'nesuke	宗介	Kamakura	1332	Master an Art

主 Master / Lord

Reading	Type	Example	Kanji	Period	Date	Added Meaning
nushi	F	Shima'nushime	嶋主女	Nara	784	Island + [Woman]
nushi	F	Ta'nushime	田主女	Nara	784	Rice Paddy + [Woman]

将 Commander

As the single instance of reading this character as "suke" is poorly documented, this reading should be avoided. Also note that this character appears in bushou 武将 or "knight". In terms of the Society for Creative Anachronism, it may be argued that this rank most closely approximates knighthood.

Reading	Type	Example	Kanji	Period	Date	Added Meaning
masa	N	Masakado	将門	Uncertain	1600	Gate
masa	N	Norimasa	憲将	Uncertain	1600	Example / Pattern
masa	N	Sadamasa	貞将	Kamakura	1332	Correct Spirit
masa	N	Yoshimasa	義将	Muromachi	1572	Fealty
masa	N	Yoshimasa	良将	Uncertain	1600	Good / Superior
suke	N	Yoshisuke	良将	Uncertain	1600	Good / Superior

輔 Ministerial Deputy

The reading "tsuke" is used to form the titles for ministerial deputies. When this character takes the Chinese reading "HO", it means to assist or rescue.

Reading	Type	Example	Kanji	Period	Date	Added Meaning
HO	F	Hoshi	輔子	Hei'an	1182	[Lady]
suke	N	Akisuke	顕輔	Uncertain	1600	High Status
suke	N	Chikasuke	親輔	Kamakura	1332	Intimate
suke	N	Ka'nesuke	兼輔	Sengoku	1568	Unite
suke	N	Kiyosuke	清輔	Uncertain	1600	Pure
suke	N	Morosuke	師輔	Uncertain	1600	Teacher / Expert
suke	N	Motosuke	基輔	Kamakura	1332	Foundation
suke	N	Motosuke	元輔	Uncertain	1600	Base / Original
suke	N	Mu'nesuke	宗輔	Hei'an	1183	Master an Art
suke	N	Narisuke	成輔	Kamakura	1332	Become / Exist
suke	N	Norisuke	範輔	Kamakura	1332	Required Form / Pattern
suke	N	Sadasuke	定輔	Hei'an	1183	Determine
suke	N	Sukekage	輔景	Kamakura	1332	Bright / Magnificent
suke	N	Suketa'ne	輔胤	Muromachi	1572	Blood Heir
suke	N	Tokisuke	時輔	Kamakura	1332	Time / Era
suke	N	Toshisuke	俊輔	Muromachi	1572	Emotional
suke	N	Yorisuke	頼輔	Hei'an	1183	Request / Ask

佐 Military Deputy / Support / Aid

This character is also used to form the titles of military deputies. Specifically, these deputies were part of the emonfu 衛門府 system of government. This governmental office was responsible for the military class.

Reading	Type	Example	Kanji	Period	Date	Added Meaning
SA	F	Samiko	佐美子	Hei'an	1183	Beauty + [Lady]
SA	F	Samime	佐美賣	Nara	784	Beauty
SA	F	Sanko	佐子	Muromachi	1455	[Lady]
SA	F	Sasame	佐々賣	Nara	784	
SA	F	Sayome	佐夜賣	Nara	784	Evening
SA	H	Kousa	光佐	Uncertain	1600	Bright / Shining
SA	S	Sahara	佐原	Hei'an	1183	Meadow
SA	S	Sakuma	佐久間	Sengoku	1568	Longtime + Room
SA	S	Sa'nada	佐奈田	Hei'an	1183	Why? / How? + Rice Paddy
SA	S	Sa'no	佐野	Kamakura	1332	Wide Plain
SA	S	Sa'nuki	佐貫	Kamakura	1332	Perseverance
SA	S	Sasaki	佐々木	Kamakura	1332	Tree
SA	S	Sata	佐田	Muromachi	1572	Rice Paddy
SA	S	Satake	佐竹	Kamakura	1332	Bamboo
SA	S	Satou	佐藤	Kamakura	1332	Wisteria
SA	S	Usa	宇佐	Hei'an	1183	Large Roof
SA	S	Yusa	遊佐	Nanboku	1392	Wander / Meander / Play
suke	N	Motosuke	基佐	Higashiyama	1482	Foundation
suke	N	Sukehide	佐秀	Nanboku	1392	Extraordinary / Bountiful
suke	N	Sukehiro	佐弘	Kamakura	1332	Draw / Stretch
suke	N	Sukemasa	佐理	Uncertain	1600	Reason / Logic
suke	N	Sukemitsu	佐光	Kamakura	1332	Bright / Shining
suke	N	Suke'naga	佐長	Kamakura	1332	Long
suke	N	Sukeyoshi	佐吉	Kamakura	1332	Lucky / Fortunate
suke	N	Ta'nesuke	種佐	Nanboku	1392	Cause / Reason
suke	N	Yukisuke	行佐	Kamakura	1332	Going To / Bound For

助 Deputy (Rescue / Assist)

Reading	Type	Example	Kanji	Period	Date	Added Meaning
suke	N	Masasuke	雅助	Muromachi	1572	High Quality
suke	N	Masasuke	政助	Uncertain	1600	Govern / Rule
suke	N	Morosuke	師助	Nanboku	1392	Teacher / Expert
suke	N	Suke'ie	助家	Nanboku	1392	Rural House / Family
suke	N	Sukekazu	助員	Kamakura	1332	Member
suke	N	Sukeku'ni	助国	Kamakura	1332	Country / Rural Area
suke	N	Sukemoto	助職	Kamakura	1332	Employment / Occupation
suke	N	Suke'nobu	助信	Kamakura	1332	Belief / Faith
suke	N	Sukeshige	助重	Nanboku	1392	Heavy / Serious
suke	N	Suketomo	助朝	Nanboku	1392	Morning
suke	N	Suketsu'na	助綱	Kamakura	1332	Net
suke	N	Suke'uji	助氏	Nanboku	1392	Family / Clan
suke	N	Sukeyoshi	助能	Kamakura	1332	Talent / Ability
suke	N	Yorisuke	頼助	Uncertain	1600	Request / Ask
suke	N	Yoshisuke	義助	Nanboku	1392	Fealty
suke	S	Asuke	足助	Kamakura	1332	Foot / Sufficient

右衛問 Palace Regiment — Right Company of Gate Guards

Reading	Type	Example	Kanji	Period	Date	Added Meaning
uemon	M	Moto'u'emon	源右衛門	Uncertain	1600	Origin

左衛問 Palace Regiment — Left Company of Gate Guards

Reading	Type	Example	Kanji	Period	Date	Added Meaning
saemon	M	Mu'nesa'emon	宗左衛門	Uncertain	1600	Master an Art
saemon	M	Gorousa'emon	五郎左衛門	Uncertain	1600	Fifth Son
saemon	M	Tarousa'emon	太郎左衛門	Uncertain	1600	First Son
saemon	M	Sukesa'emon	助左衛門	Uncertain	1600	Rescue

衛問 Palace Regiment

The weimonfu 紫衛門 was one of three regiments of palace guards and was divided into a left company and a right company of gate guards. During the Hei'an period, women with guards were sometimes called Uwemon or Sawemon.

Reading	Type	Example	Kanji	Period	Date	Added Meaning
emon	F	Murasaki'emon	紫衛門	Hei'an	1183	Purple

師 Teacher / Expert

Reading	Type	Example	Kanji	Period	Date	Added Meaning
moro	F	Morome	師女	Hei'an	1183	[Woman]
moro	N	Moro'aki	師顕	Kamakura	1332	High Status
moro	N	Moro'aki	師秋	Nanboku	1392	Autumn
moro	N	Moro'akira	師詮	Nanboku	1392	Explicit / Clear
moro	N	Morochika	師親	Kamakura	1332	Intimate
moro	N	Morofusa	師房	Uncertain	1600	Monastic Cell
moro	N	Morofuyu	師冬	Nanboku	1392	Winter
moro	N	Morohide	師英	Muromachi	1572	Kind / Gentle
moro	N	Morohide	師秀	Nanboku	1392	Extraordinary / Bountiful
moro	N	Morohira	師平	Kamakura	1332	Tranquility
moro	N	Morohisa	師久	Nanboku	1392	Longtime
moro	N	Morohisa	師尚	Hei'an	1183	Excellence
moro	N	Moro'ie	師家	Hei'an	1183	Rural House / Family
moro	N	Morokage	師景	Nanboku	1392	Bright / Magnificent
moro	N	Moroka'ne	師兼	Kamakura	1332	Unite
moro	N	Morokata	師賢	Kamakura	1332	Genius
moro	N	Morokawa	師賢	Uncertain	1600	Genius
moro	N	Morokazu	師員	Kamakura	1332	Member
moro	N	Moromichi	師通	Uncertain	1600	Pass Through
moro	N	Moromitsu	師光	Hei'an	1177	Bright / Shining
moro	N	Moromochi	師茂	Nanboku	1392	Blossoming
moro	N	Moromori	師守	Nanboku	1392	Protect / Defend
moro	N	Moromori	師盛	Hei'an	1183	Plentiful / Piled Up
moro	N	Moromoto	師基	Nanboku	1392	Foundation
moro	N	Moro'naga	師長	Hei'an	1183	Long
moro	N	Moro'naka	師仲	Hei'an	1183	Middle of a Group
moro	N	Moro'nao	師直	Hei'an	1183	Adjust / Correct
moro	N	Moro'natsu	師夏	Nanboku	1392	Summer
moro	N	Moro'nobu	師信	Kamakura	1332	Belief / Faith

Thematic Dictionary — Rank & Status   197

Reading	Type	Example	Kanji	Period	Date	Added Meaning
moro	N	Moro'nori	師教	Kamakura	1332	Teaching / Dogma
moro	N	Moro'o	師緒	Kamakura	1332	Rope / Functional Beginning
moro	N	Moroshige	師重	Kamakura	1332	Heavy / Serious
moro	N	Moroshige	師茂	Nanboku	1392	Blossoming
moro	N	Morosuke	師助	Nanboku	1392	Deputy (Rescue / Assist)
moro	N	Morosuke	師輔	Uncertain	1600	Ministerial Deputy
moro	N	Morotada	師忠	Kamakura	1332	Faithful / Loyal
moro	N	Morotoki	師時	Kamakura	1332	Time / Era
moro	N	Morotsugu	師嗣	Muromachi	1572	Successor
moro	N	Morotsu'na	師綱	Nanboku	1392	Net
moro	N	Morotsu'ne	師経	Kamakura	1332	True Path
moro	N	Morotsu'ne	師常	Kamakura	1332	Permanent
moro	N	Morotsura	師連	Kamakura	1332	Bring Along
moro	N	Moro'uji	師氏	Nanboku	1392	Family / Clan
moro	N	Moroyasu	師泰	Nanboku	1392	Peace / Plenitude
moro	N	Moroyori	師頼	Uncertain	1600	Request / Ask
moro	N	Moroyoshi	師義	Nanboku	1392	Fealty
moro	N	Moroyoshi	師良	Nanboku	1392	Good / Superior
moro	N	Moroyuki	師行	Nanboku	1392	Going To / Bound For
moro	N	Moroza'ne	師実	Uncertain	1600	Reality

妃 Queen / Empress / Princess / Consort

The more common 姫 implies a rather young woman. Otherwise, the two *kanji* have similar meaning.

Reading	Type	Example	Kanji	Period	Date	Added Meaning
hime	F	Masahime	正妃	Hei'an	1183	Unerring / Genuine

姫 Princess

This is one of the characters commonly found at the end of the names of high ranking women. Like 子 (ko), it appears to be an honourific suffix. For this reason, only a partial list of documentable names is given below.

Reading	Type	Example	Kanji	Period	Date	Added Meaning
hime	F	Hime	姫	Uncertain	1600	
hime	F	Himekurome	姫黒女	Nanboku	1392	Black + [Woman]
hime	F	Himeme	姫賣	Nara	784	
hime	F	Himeshirome	姫代女	Nanboku	1392	Era + [Woman]
hime	F	Himewakame	姫若女	Nanboku	1392	Young + [Woman]

子 Child / Son or Master (Classical Chineses)

This is one of the characters commonly found at the end of the names of high ranking women. It was originally attached to the names of men and was later attached to the names of women. It appears to be an honourific suffix similar to hime 姫 or princess. For this reason, only a partial list of documentable names is given below.

Reading	Type	Example	Kanji	Period	Date	Added Meaning
SHI	F	Hoshi	輔子	Hei'an	1182	Ministerial Deputy [Lady]
SHI	N	Teishi	定子	Uncertain	1600	Determine
ko	F	Akiko	見子	Nanboku	1392	Vantage / View / Vista
ko	F	Akiko	詮子	Hei'an	1183	Explicit / Clear
ko	F	Akirakeiko	慧子	Hei'an	1183	Wise
ko	F	Akirakeiko	明子	Hei'an	1183	Bright
ko	F	Ako	阿子	Muromachi	1572	Crevice
ko	S	Amako	尼子	Sengoku	1568	Buddhist Nun
ko	S	Ka'neko	金子	Kamakura	1332	Gold / Metal

姉 Older Sister

Reading	Type	Example	Kanji	Period	Date	Added Meaning
ane	F	A'ne'noko	姉子	Hei'an	1183	[Lady]
ane	F	A'netsume	姉都賣	Nara	784	Beautiful (Cultured)

妻 Wife / Principal Wife (Classical Chinese)

This is one of the characters commonly found at the end of women's names. Unlikely, 子 and 賣, it appears to be purely descriptive and not honourific. This element can be attached to the names of men. Since it appears in regular constructions, only a partial list of documentable names is given below.

Reading	Type	Example	Kanji	Period	Date	Added Meaning
tsuma	F	Tsuma	妻	Uncertain	1600	
tsuma	S	Shimotsuma	下妻	Kamakura	1332	Inferior

婦 Wife

Marriage patterns underwent many changes throughout Japanese history. During the Hei'an period, noble Japanese women often lived in separate palaces and were visited by their husbands. Following the Hei'an period, both Japanese architecture and marriage customs underwent significant changes. This particular *kanji* depicts a wife in the role of a domestic servant who holds a broom cleaning the house.

Reading	Type	Example	Kanji	Period	Date	Added Meaning
[Special]	F	Omi'nako	婦子	Kamakura	1332	[Lady]

御前 Wife

Marriage patterns underwent many changes throughout Japanese history. During the Hei'an period, noble Japanese women often lived in separate palaces and were visited by their husbands. Following the Hei'an period, both Japanese architecture and marriage customs underwent significant changes. "Gozen" is a polite titular form applied to women's names during the close of the Hei'an period. These women were either the wives, mistresses, or lovers of prominent men, and Gozen was often used as a pronoun to referring to them. *Gozen* originated as a pronoun referring to the previous location of an official, and its use in names may reflect a change in marriage patterns.

Reading	Type	Example	Kanji	Period	Date	Added Meaning
gozen	F	Tokiwagozen	常盤御前	Hei'an	1138	Permanent + Antecedent
gozen	F	Tomoegozen	巴午前	Hei'an	1184	Wheel of Life
gozen	F	Shizukagozen	静御前	Hei'an	1185	Quiet

賣 Woman

Note that this character is actually the old form for 売 which means to sell goods. Despite this inauspicious meaning, it appears to be an honourific suffix.

Reading	Type	Example	Kanji	Period	Date	Added Meaning
me	F	Ha'name	花賣	Hei'an	1183	Flower
me	F	Ha'netsume	羽津賣	Nara	784	Feather + Harbour
me	F	Harime	針賣	Nara	784	Needle
me	F	Hatame	波太賣	Nara	784	Wave + Eldest
me	F	Hikome	比古賣	Nara	784	Measure Up / Strive + Old
me	F	Hime	肥賣	Nara	784	Fertility / Grow Fat
me	F	Hime	比賣	Nara	784	Measure Up / Strive
me	F	Hime	日賣	Nara	784	Sun / Day

Thematic Dictionary — Rank & Status   199

me	F	Himeme	姫賣	Nara	784	Princess
me	F	Hirame	枚賣	Nara	784	Flat and Thin
me	F	Hisame	日佐賣	Nara	784	Sun + Military Deputy
me	F	Hisatsume	比佐豆賣	Nara	784	Strive + Military Deputy
me	F	Hitsujime	羊賣	Nara	784	Goat
me	F	Hokurome	黒子賣	Hei'an	1183	Black + [Lady]
me	F	Hosomeme	細目賣	Nara	784	Thin + Eye
me	F	Ihamime	石身賣	Nara	784	Rock + Body / Pregnant
me	F	Ihosume	五百寸賣	Nara	784	Five Hundred + Inch
me	F	Ikuheme	伊久倍賣	Nara	784	This + Longtime + Propagate

女 Woman

This is one of the characters commonly found at the end of women's names. Unlike 子 and 賣, 女 appears to be purely descriptive and not honourific. This element can be attached to the names of men. Since it appears in regular constructions, only a partial list of documentable names is given below.

Reading	Type	Example	Kanji	Period	Date	Added Meaning
NYO	F	Zennyo	善女	Kamakura	1332	Perform Well
NYO	F	Mitsu'nyo	満女	Kamakura	1332	Become Full / Abundant
NYOU	F	Saka'nyou	尺女	Kamakura	1332	A cubit
me	F	Achame	阿茶女	Nanboku	1392	Crevice + Tea
me	F	Akime	秋女	Nara	784	Autumn
me	F	Akome	阿古女	Nanboku	1392	Old Crevice
me	F	Akome	阿子女	Nanboku	1392	Crevice + [Lady]
me	F	Akome	阿小女	Nanboku	1392	Crevice Small
me	F	Akume	阿久女	Nanboku	1392	Longtime Crevice
me	F	Arame	安良女	Hei'an	1183	Safe / Secure + Good
me	F	Areme	吾女	Nara	784	
me	F	Ayame	文女	Kamakura	1332	Writing
me	F	Ayumime	歩女	Hei'an	1183	
me	F	Chiyotsurume	千世鶴女	Nanboku	1392	Generation / Life
me	F	Fuyume	冬女	Hei'an	1183	Winter
me	F	Hajimeme	初女	Muromachi	1572	First
me	F	Hime	比女	Nara	784	Measure Up / Strive
me	F	Meme	女々	Uncertain	1600	
me	F	Nebame	泥婆賣	Nara	784	Mud / Muddy + Hag
me	F	Sabame	沙婆賣	Nara	784	Sand (In Water) + Hag
me	F	Wobame	乎婆賣	Nara	784	Destination / Objective + Hag

老 Old Person / Aged / Elderly / Elder

This *kanji* currently takes "ROU" as its *onyomi*. The "na" in the name appears to transform "wo" into a "na-form" adjective. Thus, Wouname appears to be a descriptive name.

Reading	Type	Example	Kanji	Period	Date	Added Meaning
WOU	F	Wouname	老女	Nara	784	[Woman]

婆 Old Woman / Hag

Census records show that people with these rather unattractive names were not necessarily old.

Reading	Type	Example	Kanji	Period	Date	Added Meaning
BA	F	Nebame	泥婆賣	Nara	784	Mud / Muddy
BA	F	Sabame	沙婆賣	Nara	784	Sand (In Water)
BA	F	Wobame	乎婆賣	Nara	784	Destination / Objective

夫 Husband / Man

The image evoked by this *kanji* is hearing and faithfully performing orders.

Reading	Type	Example	Kanji	Period	Date	Added Meaning
FU	F	Yabushime	夜夫志賣	Nara	784	Evening + Determined
o	M	Toshi'o	十四夫	Modern	1983	Ten + Four (Fourteen)

祖 Founder / Grandfather

This *kanji* also denotes a guardian spirit of roadways. The single occurrence of this *kanji* in a name may be a case where it is substituted for 親 which usually means "intimate" in names. Here, the variant reading "oya" for 親 appears. This reading usually refers to parents. It may have been that the *kanji* was substituted to make the meaning more clear.

Reading	Type	Example	Kanji	Period	Date	Added Meaning
oya	F	Oyako	祖子	Nara	784	[Lady]

彦 Boy / Young Scholar

This is a particularly ancient *kanji* for boy. It is customarily used as an honourific pronoun. Further, it refers to a boy who has excelled in such things as scholarship and the arts.

Reading	Type	Example	Kanji	Period	Date	Added Meaning
GEN	M	Genkutarou	彦九太郎	Uncertain	1600	Ninth Son
hiko	M	Hikosaburou	彦三郎	Muromachi	1572	Third Son
hiko	M	Katsuhiko	甲彦	Modern	1983	First (Helmet)
hiko	M	Otohiko	乙彦	Modern	1983	Second (Cute)
hiko	N	Hikoyoshi	彦良	Nanboku	1392	Good / Superior

児 Youth / Son or Daughter / Child

This *kanji* specifically refers to young or "small" children.

Reading	Type	Example	Kanji	Period	Date	Added Meaning
ko	P	Kagoshima	鹿児島	Hei'an	1183	Deer + Island
ko	S	Kojima	児島	Nanboku	1392	Island

童 Child / Servant

This *kanji* refers to older children who have not yet officially become adults by undergoing *genfuku no shiki*. Please note that "waraha" represents an older pronunciation and that "warawa" is the modern reading.

Reading	Type	Example	Kanji	Period	Date	Added Meaning
waraha	F	Warahako	童子	Hei'an	1183	[Lady]

孫 Grandchild

This *kanji* can also be read as "hiko" in the names of gods. Presumably, this element was used as a suffix for forming the names of high ranking males in antiquity.

Reading	Type	Example	Kanji	Period	Date	Added Meaning
SON	M	Songorou	孫五郎	Uncertain	1600	Fifth Son
SON	M	Sonjirou	孫次郎	Uncertain	1600	Second / Next + Son

息 Prosper / Son

The reading for the single example of this *kanji* appears to be "iki" as that is one its standard readings. If this is true, then the initial "o" is merely the honourific initial "o" discussed in the text. As already noted, 子 is a quasi-titular final name element.

Reading	Type	Example	Kanji	Period	Date	Added Meaning
iki	F	Okiko	息子	Hei'an	1183	[Lady]

妹 Younger Sister

Reading	Type	Example	Kanji	Period	Date	Added Meaning
[Special]	F	Wagimome	我妹賣	Nara	784	Our / Us / We
[Special]	S	Seno'o	妹尾	Hei'an	1183	Tail

類 Companion / Similar

While 類 emphasizes the similarity of two people or things, 友 emphasizes togetherness.

Reading	Type	Example	Kanji	Period	Date	Added Meaning
tomo	F	Tomoko	類子	Hei'an	1183	[Lady]

友 Friend

While 類 emphasizes the similarity of two people or things, 友 emphasizes togetherness.

Reading	Type	Example	Kanji	Period	Date	Added Meaning
tomi	S	Oo'nakatomi	大中友	Hei'an	1183	Big / Middle
tomo	N	Akitomo	顕友	Nanboku	1392	High Status
tomo	N	Moritomo	守友	Uncertain	1600	Protect / Defend
tomo	N	Nobutomo	信友	Uncertain	1600	Belief / Faith
tomo	N	Sumitomo	純友	Uncertain	1600	Natural / Pure
tomo	N	Tomokage	友景	Kamakura	1332	Bright / Magnificent
tomo	N	Tomokata	友方	Uncertain	1600	Direction / Method
tomo	N	Tomo'nori	友則	Uncertain	1600	Make an Example
tomo	S	Ootomo	大友	Kamakura	1332	Big

御 Honourable

Before Nanbokuchou Jidai 南北朝時代 or Divided Court Period when the imperial line split into a southern and a northern court, this character formed an honourific prefix for women of very high rank. In this case it was read as "mi". Following the spit of the court, this character became a universal prefix for women belonging to the military class. However, it came to take "o" as its reading. This element also helps form other honourifics such as gozen 御前.

Reading	Type	Example	Kanji	Period	Date	Added Meaning
mi	F	Mihime	御比賣	Nara	784	Measure Up / Strive
mi	F	Mikeshi	御衣	Nara	784	Robe
mi	F	Mimime	御々女	Nanboku	1392	[Woman]
mi	F	Mitomime	御富賣	Nara	784	Industry
mi	F	Miyukime	御由支賣	Nara	784	Purpose + Exchange Money
o	F	Oda	御田	Uncertain	1600	Rice Paddy

顕 High Status / Show Clearly

Reading	Type	Example	Kanji	Period	Date	Added Meaning
aki	N	Akifusa	顕房	Muromachi	1572	Monastic Cell
aki	N	Akihide	顕秀	Kamakura	1332	Extraordinary / Bountiful
aki	N	Akihiro	顕広	Hei'an	1183	Spacious / Expansive
aki	N	Aki'ie	顕家	Kamakura	1332	Rural House / Family
aki	N	Akika'ne	顕兼	Kamakura	1332	Unite
aki	N	Akiku'ni	顕国	Nanboku	1392	Country / Rural Area
aki	N	Akimasa	顕雅	Kamakura	1332	High Quality
aki	N	Akimori	顕盛	Kamakura	1332	Plentiful / Piled Up
aki	N	Akimoto	顕幹	Nanboku	1392	Trunk / Stalk
aki	N	Aki'naga	顕長	Hei'an	1183	Long
aki	N	Aki'nobu	顕信	Nanboku	1392	Belief / Faith Belief / Faith
aki	N	Aki'oki	顕興	Nanboku	1392	Happen / Begin
aki	N	Akisada	顕定	Muromachi	1572	Determine
aki	N	Akisuke	顕輔	Uncertain	1600	Ministerial Deputy
aki	N	Akitoki	顕時	Kamakura	1332	Time / Era
aki	N	Akitomo	顕友	Nanboku	1392	Friend
aki	N	Akitoshi	顕俊	Uncertain	1600	Emotional
aki	N	Akitsu'na	顕綱	Nanboku	1392	Net
aki	N	Aki'uji	顕氏	Nanboku	1392	Family / Clan
aki	N	Akiyasu	顕泰	Nanboku	1392	Peace / Plenitude
aki	N	Akiyoshi	顕能	Nanboku	1392	Talent / Ability
aki	N	Chika'aki	親顕	Nanboku	1392	Intimate
aki	N	Fusa'aki	房顕	Muromachi	1572	Monastic Cell
aki	N	Michi'aki	通顕	Kamakura	1332	Pass Through
aki	N	Moro'aki	師顕	Kamakura	1332	Teacher / Expert
aki	N	Nao'aki	直顕	Kamakura	1332	Adjust / Correct
aki	N	Nori'aki	憲顕	Nanboku	1392	Example / Pattern
aki	N	Sada'aki	貞顕	Kamakura	1332	Correct Spirit
aki	N	Tada'aki	忠顕	Nanboku	1392	Faithful / Loyal
aki	N	Taka'aki	高顕	Nanboku	1392	Tall
aki	N	Taka'aki	隆顕	Kamakura	1332	Grow / Pile Up
aki	N	Teru'aki	輝顕	Nanboku	1392	Brilliant
aki	N	Toki'aki	時顕	Kamakura	1332	Time / Era
aki	N	Tsu'ne'aki	経顕	Nanboku	1392	True Path
aki	N	Yoshi'aki	義顕	Hei'an	1183	Fealty

以 Highest

Reading	Type	Example	Kanji	Period	Date	Added Meaning
mochi	N	Mochimasa	以政	Hei'an	1183	Govern / Rule
mochi	N	Mochimitsu	以光	Muromachi	1572	Bright / Shining
mochi	N	Mochimori	以盛	Muromachi	1572	Plentiful / Piled Up
mochi	N	Motsuza'ne	以実	Sengoku	1480	Reality

尊 Exemplar / Admirable

Reading	Type	Example	Kanji	Period	Date	Added Meaning
nobu	F	Nobuko	尊子	Hei'an	1183	[Lady]
taka	N	Taka'uji	尊氏	Kamakura	1305	Family / Clan

名 Name / Famous / Admirable

Reading	Type	Example	Kanji	Period	Date	Added Meaning
na	F	Nakako	名子	Nanboku	1392	[Lady]
na	F	Na'na	名々	Nanboku	1392	
na	F	Natoko	名門子	Hei'an	1183	Gate + [Lady]
na	N	Suke'na	資名	Kamakura	1332	Raw Materials
na	S	Ashi'na	蘆名	Kamakura	1332	Reed / Rush
na	S	Fuji'na	富士名	Kamakura	1332	Industry
na	S	Nawa	名和	Kamakura	1332	Peace / Tranquility
na	S	Yama'na	山名	Kamakura	1332	Mountain

尼 Buddhist Nun

Reading	Type	Example	Kanji	Period	Date	Added Meaning
NI	F	I'nishi	伊尼斯	Uncertain	1600	This + This Way
ama	S	Amako	尼子	Sengoku	1568	[Lady]

員 Member

Reading	Type	Example	Kanji	Period	Date	Added Meaning
kazu	F	Kazuko	員子	Nanboku	1392	[Lady]
kazu	N	Kagekazu	景員	Hei'an	1183	Bright / Magnificent
kazu	N	Kazumasa	員昌	Uncertain	1600	Clear / Bright
kazu	N	Mitsukazu	光員	Kamakura	1332	Bright / Shining
kazu	N	Morikazu	盛員	Kamakura	1332	Plentiful / Piled Up
kazu	N	Morokazu	師員	Kamakura	1332	Teacher / Expert
kazu	N	Sa'nekazu	実員	Kamakura	1332	Reality
kazu	N	Sukekazu	助員	Kamakura	1332	Deputy (Rescue / Assist)
kazu	N	Yorikazu	頼員	Kamakura	1332	Request / Ask
kazu	N	Yoshikazu	能員	Kamakura	1332	Talent / Ability

親 Parent / Intimate

This element can be found a postpositional honourific in the names of gods and the names of rusticated members of the imperial family. In the names of rusticated members of the imperial family, Shinnou 親王 is attached to a normally constructed *nanori*. As this is a regular construction, only a partial list of documentable names is given below. Please also note the variant readings of 世良親王.

Reading	Type	Example	Kanji	Period	Date	Added Meaning
SHIN	F	Shinshi	親子	Kamakura	1332	[Lady]
SHIN	H	Gishin	義親	Hei'an	1099	Fealty
SHIN	N	Tsugi'nagashinnou	世良親王	Kamakura	1330	Generation + Superior
SHIN	N	Tsugiyoshishinnou	世良親王	Kamakura	1330	Generation + Superior
SHIN	N	Tsuguhitoshinnou	継仁親王	Kamakura	1279	Connect / Adopt + Precious
chika	F	Chikako	親子	Nanboku	1392	[Lady]
chika	N	Arichika	有親	Kamakura	1332	Exists
chika	N	Chika'aki	親顕	Nanboku	1392	High Status
chika	N	Chikafusa	親房	Kamakura	1332	Monastic Cell
chika	N	Chikaharu	親治	Hei'an	1183	Govern / Rule
chika	N	Chikahide	親秀	Kamakura	1332	Extraordinary / Bountiful
chika	N	Chikahira	親衡	Kamakura	1213	A Yoke

chika	N	Chikahiro	親広	Kamakura	1332	Spacious / Expansive
chika	N	Chika'ie	親家	Hei'an	1183	Rural House / Family
chika	N	Chikakage	親景	Muromachi	1572	Bright / Magnificent
chika	N	Chikakiyo	親清	Kamakura	1332	Pure
chika	N	Chikaku'ni	親国	Hei'an	1183	Country / Rural Area
chika	N	Chikamasa	親雅	Kamakura	1332	High Quality
chika	N	Chikamasa	親政	Uncertain	1600	Govern / Rule
chika	N	Chikamasa	親昌	Nanboku	1392	Clear / Bright
chika	N	Chikamitsu	親光	Kamakura	1332	Bright / Shining
chika	N	Chikamoto	親元	Muromachi	1572	Base / Original
chika	N	Chikamoto	親職	Kamakura	1332	Employment / Occupation
chika	N	Chikamu'ne	親宗	Hei'an	1183	Master an Art
chika	N	Chikamu'ne	親致	Kamakura	1332	Taste / Elegance / Grand Effect
chika	N	Chika'naga	親長	Kamakura	1332	Long
chika	N	Chika'nobu	親信	Hei'an	1183	Belief / Faith Belief / Faith
chika	N	Chika'nori	親教	Muromachi	1572	Teaching / Dogma
chika	N	Chika'nori	親範	Hei'an	1183	Required Form / Pattern
chika	N	Chikasue	親季	Kamakura	1332	Season
chika	N	Chikasuke	親輔	Kamakura	1332	Ministerial Deputy
chika	N	Chikataka	親隆	Hei'an	1183	Grow / Pile Up
chika	N	Chikata'ne	親胤	Nanboku	1392	Blood Heir
chika	N	Chikatomo	親朝	Nanboku	1392	Morning
chika	N	Chikatoshi	親俊	Muromachi	1572	Emotional
chika	N	Chikatsugu	親継	Kamakura	1332	Connect / Adopt
chika	N	Chikatsu'ne	親経	Kamakura	1332	True Path
chika	N	Chikayasu	親康	Kamakura	1332	Strong / Confident
chika	N	Chikayo	親世	Muromachi	1572	Generation / Life
chika	N	Chikayoshi	親能	Kamakura	1332	Talent / Ability
chika	N	Chikayuki	親行	Kamakura	1332	Going To / Bound For
chika	N	Chikaza'ne	親実	Kamakura	1332	Reality
chika	N	Kagechika	景親	Hei'an	1183	Bright / Magnificent
chika	N	Ka'nechika	兼親	Kamakura	1332	Unite
chika	N	Kinchika	公親	Kamakura	1332	Noble / Official
chika	N	Korechika	惟親	Kamakura	1332	This / Here
chika	N	Masachika	雅親	Sengoku	1490	High Quality
chika	N	Masachika	政親	Kamakura	1332	Govern / Rule
chika	N	Michichika	通親	Hei'an	1183	Pass Through
chika	N	Mitsuchika	光親	Kamakura	1332	Bright / Shining
chika	N	Mitsuchika	満親	Nanboku	1392	Become Full / Abundant
chika	N	Morichika	守親	Uncertain	1600	Protect / Defend
chika	N	Morochika	師親	Kamakura	1332	Teacher / Expert
chika	N	Motochika	基親	Kamakura	1332	Foundation
chika	N	Motochika	元親	Uncertain	1600	Base / Original
chika	N	Mu'nechika	宗親	Kamakura	1332	Master an Art
chika	N	Nagachika	長親	Hei'an	1183	Long
chika	N	Nakachika	仲親	Kamakura	1332	Middle of a Group
chika	N	Narichika	成親	Hei'an	1183	Become / Exist
chika	N	Nobuchika	信親	Muromachi	1572	Belief / Faith Belief / Faith
chika	N	Sadachika	貞親	Kamakura	1332	Correct Spirit
chika	N	Sadachika	定親	Kamakura	1332	Determine
chika	N	Sa'nechika	実親	Kamakura	1332	Reality
chika	N	Shigechika	重親	Uncertain	1600	Heavy / Serious
chika	N	Sukechika	資親	Nanboku	1392	Raw Materials
chika	N	Sukechika	祐親	Hei'an	1183	Divine Help
chika	N	Tadachika	忠親	Hei'an	1183	Faithful / Loyal
chika	N	Takachika	高親	Muromachi	1572	Tall
chika	N	Takachika	隆親	Hei'an	1183	Grow / Pile Up

Reading	Type	Example	Kanji	Period	Date	Added Meaning
chika	N	Toochika	遠親	Kamakura	1332	Far
chika	N	Tsu'nechika	経親	Kamakura	1332	True Path
chika	N	Yasuchika	康親	Sengoku	1568	Strong / Confident
chika	N	Yasuchika	泰親	Hei'an	1183	Peace / Plenitude
chika	N	Yorichika	頼親	Kamakura	1332	Request / Ask
chika	N	Yoshichika	義親	Uncertain	1600	Fealty

仙 Hermit / Adept / Sage

A *sennin* 仙人 is an ageless and immortal Taoist sage. These sages are frequently associated with mountains. According to legend, many of these sages, as well as many Buddhist monks, grow wings and long noses to become *tengu*.

Reading	Type	Example	Kanji	Period	Date	Added Meaning
SEN	F	Sen	仙	Uncertain	1600	
SEN	S	Senseki	仙石	Sengoku	1568	Rock
SEN	P	Sendai	仙台	Modern	1983	Pedestal / Dais

兼 Unite / Hold several Offices / Heavy Service

Reading	Type	Example	Kanji	Period	Date	Added Meaning
KANE	F	Ka'neko	兼子	Hei'an	1155	[Lady]
kane	N	Akika'ne	顕兼	Kamakura	1332	High Status
kane	N	Akika'ne	章兼	Nanboku	1392	Writing / Elucidate
kane	N	Hisaka'ne	久兼	Kamakura	1332	Longtime
kane	N	Ieka'ne	家兼	Nanboku	1392	Rural House / Family
kane	N	Ka'ne'aki	兼秋	Kamakura	1332	Autumn
kane	N	Ka'ne'atsu	兼敦	Nanboku	1392	Generous / Kind / Honest
kane	N	Ka'nechika	兼親	Kamakura	1332	Intimate
kane	N	Ka'nefumi	兼文	Kamakura	1266	Writing
kane	N	Ka'nefusa	兼房	Kamakura	1332	Monastic Cell
kane	N	Ka'nehira	兼衡	Hei'an	1183	A Yoke
kane	N	Ka'nehira	兼平	Hei'an	1183	Tranquility
kane	N	Ka'ne'ie	兼家	Muromachi	1572	Rural House / Family
kane	N	Ka'nekata	兼方	Kamakura	1250	Direction / Method
kane	N	Ka'neku'ni	兼邦	Nanboku	1392	Big Country
kane	N	Ka'nemasa	兼雅	Hei'an	1183	High Quality
kane	N	Ka'nemasa	兼昌	Uncertain	1600	Clear / Bright
kane	N	Ka'nemichi	兼通	Uncertain	1600	Pass Through
kane	N	Ka'nemitsu	兼光	Kamakura	1332	Bright / Shining
kane	N	Ka'nemori	兼盛	Uncertain	1600	Plentiful / Piled Up
kane	N	Ka'nemoto	兼基	Kamakura	1332	Foundation
kane	N	Ka'nemoto	兼元	Muromachi	1572	Base / Original
kane	N	Ka'nemu'ne	兼宗	Kamakura	1332	Master an Art
kane	N	Ka'ne'naga	兼永	Muromachi	1572	Forever
kane	N	Ka'ne'naka	兼仲	Kamakura	1332	Middle of a Group
kane	N	Ka'ne'nobu	兼信	Kamakura	1332	Belief / Faith Belief / Faith
kane	N	Ka'ne'nobu	兼宣	Muromachi	1572	Proclamation
kane	N	Ka'ne'nori	兼教	Kamakura	1332	Teaching / Dogma
kane	N	Ka'nera	兼良	Muromachi	1572	Good / Superior
kane	N	Ka'neshige	兼重	Nanboku	1392	Heavy / Serious
kane	N	Ka'nesue	兼季	Kamakura	1332	Season
kane	N	Ka'nesuke	兼輔	Sengoku	1568	Ministerial Deputy
kane	N	Ka'netada	兼忠	Kamakura	1332	Faithful / Loyal
kane	N	Ka'netaka	兼隆	Hei'an	1183	Grow / Pile Up
kane	N	Ka'neta'ne	兼胤	Muromachi	1572	Blood Heir

Reading	Type	Example	Kanji	Period	Date	Added Meaning
kane	N	Ka'netoki	兼時	Kamakura	1332	Time / Era
kane	N	Ka'netomo	兼倶	Muromachi	1572	Together / Collaborate
kane	N	Ka'netomo	兼朝	Muromachi	1572	Morning
kane	N	Ka'netou	兼任	Hei'an	1183	Endure a Duty
kane	N	Ka'netsugu	兼嗣	Nanboku	1392	Successor
kane	N	Ka'netsugu	兼続	Sengoku	1568	Continue / Perpetuate / Persist
kane	N	Ka'netsu'na	兼綱	Hei'an	1183	Net
kane	N	Ka'netsu'ne	兼経	Kamakura	1332	True Path
kane	N	Ka'netsura	兼連	Nanboku	1392	Bring Along
kane	N	Ka'ne'uji	兼氏	Kamakura	1332	Family / Clan
kane	N	Ka'neyasu	兼康	Hei'an	1183	Strong / Confident
kane	N	Ka'neyo	兼世	Nanboku	1392	Generation / Life
kane	N	Ka'neyori	兼頼	Kamakura	1332	Request / Ask
kane	N	Ka'neyoshi	兼好	Uncertain	1600	Affection / Desire
kane	N	Ka'neza'ne	兼実	Hei'an	1183	Reality
kane	N	Michiga'ne	道兼	Uncertain	1600	Road / Way
kane	N	Mitsuka'ne	満兼	Muromachi	1572	Become Full / Abundant
kane	N	Moriga'ne	盛兼	Sengoku	1568	Plentiful / Piled Up
kane	N	Morika'ne	盛兼	Kamakura	1332	Plentiful / Piled Up
kane	N	Moroka'ne	師兼	Kamakura	1332	Teacher / Expert
kane	N	Motoka'ne	基兼	Hei'an	1183	Foundation
kane	N	Nagaka'ne	長兼	Kamakura	1332	Long
kane	N	Narika'ne	業兼	Kamakura	1332	Industry / Diligence
kane	N	Nobuka'ne	信兼	Hei'an	1183	Belief / Faith Belief / Faith
kane	N	Norika'ne	範兼	Uncertain	1600	Required Form / Pattern
kane	N	Sa'neka'ne	実兼	Kamakura	1332	Reality
kane	N	Sueka'ne	季兼	Kamakura	1332	Season
kane	N	Tadaka'ne	忠兼	Nanboku	1392	Faithful / Loyal
kane	N	Takaka'ne	隆兼	Kamakura	1332	Grow / Pile Up
kane	N	Tameka'ne	為兼	Kamakura	1332	Purpose / Goal
kane	N	Tokika'ne	時兼	Kamakura	1332	Time / Era
kane	N	Toshika'ne	俊兼	Kamakura	1332	Emotional
kane	N	Tsu'neka'ne	経兼	Nanboku	1392	True Path
kane	N	Yorika'ne	頼兼	Hei'an	1183	Request / Ask
kane	N	Yoshika'ne	義兼	Kamakura	1332	Fealty

等 Rank / Level

Reading	Type	Example	Kanji	Period	Date	Added Meaning
TO	F	To'ime	等伊賣	Nara	784	This
TO	F	To'noko	等能子	Nara	784	Talent + [Lady]
hitoshi	N	Hitoshi	等	Uncertain	1600	
tomo	N	Tomotsu'na	等綱	Muromachi	1572	Net

胤 Blood Heir

Reading	Type	Example	Kanji	Period	Date	Added Meaning
tane	N	Akita'ne	明胤	Kamakura	1332	Bright
tane	N	Chikata'ne	親胤	Nanboku	1392	Intimate
tane	N	Hideta'ne	秀胤	Kamakura	1332	Extraordinary / Bountiful
tane	N	Ka'neta'ne	兼胤	Kamakura	1332	Unite
tane	N	Kiyota'ne	清胤	Nanboku	1392	Pure
tane	N	Masata'ne	昌胤	Uncertain	1600	Clear / Bright
tane	N	Mitsuta'ne	光胤	Nanboku	1392	Bright / Shining

Thematic Dictionary — Rank & Status   207

Reading	Type	Example	Kanji	Period	Date	Added Meaning
tane	N	Mitsuta'ne	満胤	Muromachi	1572	Become Full / Abundant
tane	N	Motota'ne	元胤	Muromachi	1572	Base / Original
tane	N	Mu'neta'ne	宗胤	Kamakura	1332	Master an Art
tane	N	Nageta'ne	長胤	Nanboku	1392	Eldest
tane	N	Narita'ne	成胤	Kamakura	1332	Become / Exist
tane	N	Nobuta'ne	信胤	Nanboku	1392	Belief / Faith
tane	N	Norita'ne	憲胤	Nanboku	1392	Example / Pattern
tane	N	Okita'ne	興胤	Nanboku	1392	Happen / Begin
tane	N	Sadata'ne	貞胤	Kamakura	1332	Correct Spirit
tane	N	Shigeta'ne	重胤	Kamakura	1332	Heavy / Serious
tane	N	Suketa'ne	輔胤	Muromachi	1572	Ministerial Deputy
tane	N	Ta'nefusa	胤房	Muromachi	1572	Monastic Cell
tane	N	Ta'ne'ie	胤家	Kamakura	1332	Rural House / Family
tane	N	Ta'nemasa	胤正	Kamakura	1332	Unerring / Genuine
tane	N	Ta'nemichi	胤通	Kamakura	1332	Pass Through
tane	N	Ta'nemori	胤盛	Kamakura	1332	Plentiful / Piled Up
tane	N	Ta'nemu'ne	胤宗	Kamakura	1332	Master an Art
tane	N	Ta'ne'naga	胤長	Kamakura	1332	Long
tane	N	Ta'ne'nao	胤直	Hei'an	1183	Adjust / Correct
tane	N	Ta'ne'nobu	胤信	Kamakura	1332	Belief / Faith
tane	N	Ta'netomo	胤朝	Muromachi	1572	Morning
tane	N	Ta'netsu'na	胤綱	Kamakura	1332	Net
tane	N	Ta'neyori	胤頼	Kamakura	1332	Request / Ask
tane	N	Ta'neyoshi	胤義	Kamakura	1332	Fealty
tane	N	Ta'neyuki	胤行	Kamakura	1332	Going To / Bound For
tane	N	Torata'ne	虎胤	Uncertain	1600	Tiger
tane	N	Tsu'neta'ne	常胤	Hei'an	1183	Permanent
tane	N	Ujita'ne	氏胤	Nanboku	1392	Family / Clan
tane	N	Yasuta'ne	泰胤	Kamakura	1332	Peace / Plenitude
tane	N	Yorita'ne	頼胤	Kamakura	1332	Request / Ask
tane	N	Yoshita'ne	義胤	Kamakura	1332	Fealty

嗣 Successor

Reading	Type	Example	Kanji	Period	Date	Added Meaning
tsugu	N	Fusatsugu	房嗣	Muromachi	1572	Monastic Cell
tsugu	N	Fuyutsugu	冬嗣	Uncertain	1600	Winter
tsugu	N	Hirotsugu	広嗣	Uncertain	1600	Spacious / Expansive
tsugu	N	Ietsugu	家嗣	Uncertain	1600	Rural House / Family
tsugu	N	Ka'netsugu	兼嗣	Nanboku	1392	Unite
tsugu	N	Masatsugu	政嗣	Kamakura	1332	Govern / Rule
tsugu	N	Michitsugu	道嗣	Kamakura	1332	Road / Way
tsugu	N	Moritsugu	盛嗣	Hei'an	1183	Plentiful / Piled Up
tsugu	N	Morotsugu	師嗣	Muromachi	1572	Teacher / Expert
tsugu	N	Mototsugu	基嗣	Kamakura	1332	Foundation
tsugu	N	Nobutsugu	信嗣	Kamakura	1332	Belief / Faith
tsugu	N	Noritsugu	教嗣	Muromachi	1572	Teaching / Dogma
tsugu	N	Sadatsugu	定嗣	Kamakura	1332	Determine
tsugu	N	Tadatsugu	忠嗣	Muromachi	1572	Faithful / Loyal
tsugu	N	Tsugufusa	嗣房	Nanboku	1392	Monastic Cell
tsugu	N	Tsugu'nori	嗣教	Muromachi	1572	Teaching / Dogma
tsugu	N	Tsu'netsugu	経嗣	Nanboku	1392	True Path
tsugu	N	Yoritsugu	頼嗣	Kamakura	1332	Request / Ask
tsugu	N	Yoshitsugu	義嗣	Muromachi	1572	Fealty
tsugu	N	Yoshitsugu	良嗣	Muromachi	1572	Good / Superior

❖ Peace & Security ❖

安 Gentle / Safe / Secure

Note that this character represents yet another variation on "Peace". However, it also has the conotations of "Safe" and even "Inexpensive". When read as "yasu", this character also means "Gentle". This is a meaning which it aquired in Japan.

Reading	Type	Example	Kanji	Period	Date	Added Meaning
A	F	Amako	安万子	Hei'an	1183	[Lady]
A	F	Arame	安良女	Hei'an	1183	Good / Superior
A	S	Abe	安倍	Hei'an	1183	Propagate / Multiply
A	S	Adachi	安達	Kamakura	1332	Carry / Deliver
A	S	Andou	安東	Kamakura	1332	East
A	S	Atagi	安宅	Nanboku	1392	Residence
AN	H	Dou'an	道安	Uncertain	1600	Road / Way
AN	S	Andou	安藤	Modern	1762	Wisteria
AN	Y	An'ei	安永	Edo	1772	Forever
AN	Y	Angen	安元	Kamakura	1175	Base / Original
AN	Y	Antei	安貞	Kamakura	1227	Correct Spirit
AN	Y	Bun'an	文安	Muromachi	1444	Literature / Culture
AN	Y	Hou'an	保安	Hei'an	1120	Guarantee
AN	Y	Ji'an	治安	Hei'an	1021	Govern / Rule
AN	Y	Jou'an	承安	Kamakura	1171	Humbly Receive
AN	Y	Kei'an	慶安	Edo	1648	Rejoice / Deer Skin
AN	Y	Kou'an	康安	Nanboku	1361	Strong / Confident
AN	Y	Kou'an	弘安	Kamakura	1278	Draw / Stretch / Spread Out
AN	Y	Kyuu'an	久安	Hei'an	1145	Longtime
AN	Y	Nin'an	仁安	Kamakura	1166	Precious
AN	Y	Ou'an	応安	Nanboku	1368	Worthy / Suitable
AN	Y	Shou'an	正安	Kamakura	1299	Unerring / Genuine
yasu	F	Yasuko	安子	Hei'an	1183	[Lady]
yasu	F	Yasukome	安子賣	Hei'an	1183	[Lady]
yasu	N	Ariyasu	有安	Hei'an	1183	Exists
yasu	N	Shigeyasu	重安	Sengoku	1568	Heavy / Serious
yasu	N	Tsu'neyasu	常安	Kamakura	1332	Permanent
yasu	N	Yasusada	安定	Uncertain	1600	Determine
yasu	N	Yasutoshi	安俊	Kamakura	1332	Emotional
yasu	N	Yasutsugi	安次	Sengoku	1568	Next
yasu	S	Yasuda	安田	Hei'an	1183	Rice Paddy
yasu	S	Yasutomi	安富	Nanboku	1392	Industry

静 Quiet

Reading	Type	Example	Kanji	Period	Date	Added Meaning
shizu	F	Shizuko	静子	Hei'an	1183	[Lady]
shizuka	F	Shizukagozen	静御前	Hei'an	1185	[Madam]

泰 Peace / Plenitude / Expansive

Reading	Type	Example	Kanji	Period	Date	Added Meaning
yasu	N	Akiyasu	顕泰	Nanboku	1392	High Status
yasu	N	Ieyasu	家泰	Nanboku	1392	Rural House / Family
yasu	N	Kageyasu	景泰	Kamakura	1332	Bright / Magnificent
yasu	N	Ku'niyasu	国泰	Nanboku	1392	Country / Rural Area
yasu	N	Masayasu	政泰	Kamakura	1332	Govern / Rule
yasu	N	Masayasu	正泰	Kamakura	1332	Unerring / Genuine
yasu	N	Mitsuyasu	光泰	Nanboku	1392	Bright / Shining
yasu	N	Moroyasu	師泰	Nanboku	1392	Teacher / Expert
yasu	N	Mu'neyasu	宗泰	Kamakura	1332	Master an Art
yasu	N	Sadayasu	貞泰	Kamakura	1332	Correct Spirit
yasu	N	Sa'neyasu	実泰	Kamakura	1332	Reality
yasu	N	Sukeyasu	資泰	Hei'an	1183	Raw Materials
yasu	N	Sukeyasu	祐泰	Hei'an	1183	Divine Help
yasu	N	Torayasu	虎泰	Uncertain	1600	Tiger
yasu	N	Toshiyasu	俊泰	Muromachi	1572	Emotional
yasu	N	Tsu'neyasu	経泰	Nanboku	1392	True Path
yasu	N	Ujiyasu	氏泰	Nanboku	1392	Family / Clan
yasu	N	Yasuchika	泰親	Hei'an	1183	Intimate
yasu	N	Yasuharu	泰治	Nanboku	1392	Govern / Rule
yasu	N	Yasuhide	泰秀	Kamakura	1332	Extraordinary / Bountiful
yasu	N	Yasuhira	泰衡	Hei'an	1155	A Yoke
yasu	N	Yasu'ie	泰家	Kamakura	1332	Rural House / Family
yasu	N	Yasukiyo	泰清	Kamakura	1332	Pure
yasu	N	Yasumichi	泰通	Hei'an	1183	Pass Through
yasu	N	Yasumori	泰盛	Kamakura	1332	Plentiful / Piled Up
yasu	N	Yasumura	泰村	Kamakura	1332	Village
yasu	N	Yasu'nori	泰範	Nanboku	1392	Required Form / Pattern
yasu	N	Yasusada	泰貞	Nanboku	1392	Correct Spirit
yasu	N	Yasushige	泰重	Nanboku	1392	Heavy / Serious
yasu	N	Yasutaka	泰高	Muromachi	1572	Tall
yasu	N	Yasuta'ne	泰胤	Kamakura	1332	Blood Heir
yasu	N	Yasutoki	泰時	Kamakura	1332	Time / Era
yasu	N	Yasutomo	泰朝	Kamakura	1332	Morning
yasu	N	Yasutsu'na	泰綱	Kamakura	1332	Net
yasu	N	Yasutsu'ne	泰経	Hei'an	1183	True Path
yasu	N	Yasu'uji	泰氏	Uncertain	1600	Family / Clan
yasu	N	Yoriyasu	頼泰	Kamakura	1332	Request / Ask
yasu	N	Yukiyasu	行泰	Kamakura	1332	Going To / Bound For

和 Peace / Tranquility / Harmony / Japan

Reading	Type	Example	Kanji	Period	Date	Added Meaning
WA	F	Wakako	和香子	Hei'an	1183	Incense + [Lady]
WA	F	Wakigeme	和岐毛賣	Nara	784	Wool
WA	F	Wakume	和賣	Nara	784	
WA	S	Nawa	名和	Kamakura	1332	Famous / Admirable
WA	S	Wada	和田	Kamakura	1332	Rice Paddy
WA	S	Waki	和気	Nanboku	1392	Spirit / Breath
WA	Y	Bunna	文和	Nanboku	1352	Literature / Culture
WA	Y	Chouwa	長和	Hei'an	1012	Long / Oldest / Senior
WA	Y	Eiwa	永和	Nanboku	1375	Forever

WA	Y	Genna	元和	Edo	1615	Base / Original
WA	Y	Jouwa	貞和	Nanboku	1345	Correct Spirit
WA	Y	Kouwa	康和	Hei'an	1099	Strong / Confident
WA	Y	Kouwa	弘和	Nanboku	1381	Draw / Stretch / Spread Out
WA	Y	Kyouwa	享和	Edo	1801	Receive
WA	Y	Meiwa	明和	Edo	1764	Bright
WA	Y	Shouwa	正和	Kamakura	1312	Unerring / Genuine
WA	Y	Shouwa	昭和	Modern	1926	Bright / Cheerful
WA	Y	Tenna	天和	Edo	1681	Sky / Heaven
WA	Y	Youwa	養和	Kamakura	1181	Rear / Raise / Nourish
kazu	F	Kazuko	和子	Hei'an	1183	[Lady]
kazu	F	Nagokome	和子賣	Nara	784	[Lady]
kazu	N	Kazu'uji	和氏	Nanboku	1392	Family / Clan
kazu	N	Kazuyoshi	和義	Nanboku	1392	Fealty
kazu	S	Nigita	和田	Nanboku	1392	Rice Paddy
[Special]	S	Yamato	大和	Hei'an	1183	Big

❖ Number & Quantity ❖

Before Myoujigomen 名字御免 in the nineteenth century, the majority of Japanese did not have names in the same sense that members of the *kuge* or *buke* classes did. As mentioned elsewhere, members of lower classes were recorded in census record by their affiliation to one of the ancient monopoly corporations. Not only could they not have family names, but they were denied *nanori* as well. Since the nineteenth century, the former distinction has been lost and there are books published in Japanese which lump all of these names together and call them *nanori*. Many modern masculine names employ substantive elements which distinguish them from normative practice for forming *nanori* before the nineteenth century. Others which became common during the twentieth century were rarely used earlier.

郎 Son / Lord / Commander (Classical Chinese)

Originally, this *kanji* was attached to place names. Later, place names combined with birth order came to be used as informal personal names. Effectively, this *kanji* is a "counter" for sons when used in forming names. It is usually preceded by a number, but may be preceded by a purely descriptive or "spiritual" element. Because of the relative importance of the first three sons, there are special names for these three. Three of the ordinal names have special typical forms. These are: Tarou, Jirou, and Saburou. These forms are more common than those constructed using the standard *onyomi* ordinals: ICHI, NI and SAN.

During the Han dynasty in China, this word was applied to military district commanders by their troops. Later, it came to be used to refer to any master.. In modern Japan, the word has been used as a pet name for young boys and for husbands by their wives. The classical Chinese meaning explains the popularity of this name element in *Heike Monogatari* in which it is frequently connected with districts. The prominence of this element is *tsuushou* reflects the Japanese preference to use titles.

Reading	Type	Example	Kanji	Period	Date	Added Meaning
ROU	M	Ichirou	壱郎	Modern	1983	Son

太郎 First Son

Reading	Type	Example	Kanji	Period	Date	Added Meaning
TA	M	Tarou	太郎	Uncertain	1600	
TA	M	Genkutarou	彦九太郎	Uncertain	1600	Boy / Young Scholar
TA	M	Kentarou	健太郎	Uncertain	1600	Build / Construct
TA	M	Kutarou	久太郎	Sengoku	1568	Longtime
TA	M	Matatarou	又太郎	Uncertain	1600	Next
TA	M	Tarousa'emon	太郎左衛門	Uncertain	1600	Ministry of the Left
TA	M	Yatarou	弥太郎	Momoyama	1438	Nostalgic
TA	M	Yo'ichitarou	与一太郎	Hei'an	1183	Team Up + One
TA	M	Yogotarou	与五太郎	Uncertain	1600	Team Up
TA	M	Yotarou	与太郎	Uncertain	1600	Team Up

二郎 Second Son

Reading	Type	Example	Kanji	Period	Date	Added Meaning
JI	M	Jirou	二郎	Modern	1983	
JI	M	Kyoujirou	教二郎	Modern	1983	

次郎 Second Son / Next Son

Reading	Type	Example	Kanji	Period	Date	Added Meaning
JI	M	Jirou	次郎	Uncertain	1600	
JI	M	Genjirou	源次郎	Uncertain	1600	Origin
JI	M	Kojirou	小次郎	Sengoku	1568	Small
JI	M	Matajirou	又次郎	Uncertain	1600	Next
JI	M	Sonjirou	孫次郎	Uncertain	1600	Grandchild
JI	M	Soujirou	宗次郎	Uncertain	1600	Master an Art
JI	M	Zenjirou	善次郎	Uncertain	1600	Perform Well

三郎 Third Son

Reading	Type	Example	Kanji	Period	Date	Added Meaning
SABU	M	Saburou	三郎	Muromachi	1572	
SABU	M	Gensaburou	源三郎	Momoyama	1438	Origin
SABU	M	Hikosaburou	彦三郎	Muromachi	1572	Boy / Young Scholar

全 All

Reading	Type	Example	Kanji	Period	Date	Added Meaning
masa	F	Masatsuguko	全継子	Hei'an	1183	Connect / Adopt [Lady]

片 One of Two

Reading	Type	Example	Kanji	Period	Date	Added Meaning
kata	N	Kata'ie	片家	Uncertain	1600	Rural House / Family
kata	S	Katagiri	片桐	Sengoku	1568	Paulownia Tree
kata	S	Kata'oka	片岡	Kamakura	1332	Hill

分 Piece / Bit / Part

Reading	Type	Example	Kanji	Period	Date	Added Meaning
BU	S	Kokubu	国分	Kamakura	1332	Country / Rural Area

半 Half

Reading	Type	Example	Kanji	Period	Date	Added Meaning
HAN	S	Handa	半田	Modern	1983	Rice Paddy

一 One

Reading	Type	Example	Kanji	Period	Date	Added Meaning
ICHI	M	Ichirou	一郎	Modern	1983	Son
ICHI	M	Yo'ichitarou	与一太郎	Hei'an	1183	Team Up + First Son
ICHI	S	Ichijou	一条	Kamakura	1332	Branch / Line / Road

Thematic Dictionary — **Number & Quantity** 213

Reading	Type	Example	Kanji	Period	Date	Added Meaning
ICHI	S	Ichimonji	一文字	Hei'an	1183	Writing + Letter
ICHI	S	Ichino'i	一井	Kamakura	1332	Well
ITSU	S	Isshiki	一色	Nanboku	1392	Colour
hajime	F	Hajime	一	Modern	1983	
hitoshi	M	Hitoshi	一	Modern	1983	
kazu	M	Kazu'nari	一也	Modern	1983	Exists
kazu	N	Hidekazu	秀一	Sengoku	1568	Extraordinary / Bountiful
kazu	N	Kazushige	一重	Sengoku	1568	Heavy / Serious
kazu	N	Kazutada	一直	Sengoku	1568	Adjust / Correct
kazu	N	Kazutoyo	一豊	Sengoku	1568	Noble

壱 One

This *kanji* is commonly used in contracts as it is harder to change to a different number than is the simpler *kanji* with the same meaning.

Reading	Type	Example	Kanji	Period	Date	Added Meaning
ICHI	M	Ichirou	壱郎	Modern	1983	Son

二 Two

Reading	Type	Example	Kanji	Period	Date	Added Meaning
JI	M	Jihei	二平	Modern	1983	Peace
JI	M	Tomiji	富二	Modern	1983	Industry
NI	S	Nikaidou	二階堂	Kamakura	1332	Story + Sanctuary
futa	P	Futagawa	二川	Modern	1983	River
tsugi	M	Tsugi'o	二雄	Modern	1983	Strength / Courage / Bravery

双 Pair / Two

Reading	Type	Example	Kanji	Period	Date	Added Meaning
futa	P	Futaba	双葉	Modern	1983	Leaf
futa	P	Futama	双三	Modern	1983	Three
futa	S	Futami	双海	Modern	1983	Sea
narabi	P	Narabigaoka	双ヶ丘	Modern	1983	Hillock

三 Three

Reading	Type	Example	Kanji	Period	Date	Added Meaning
SAI	S	Saigusa	三枝	Uncertain	1600	Branch / Twig
ZOU	S	Bunzou	豊三	Hei'an	1183	Noble
mi	F	Miyukime	三雪女	Nara	784	Snow
mi	N	Mitsu'nari	三成	Uncertain	1600	Become / Exist
mi	P	Mitaka	三鷹	Modern	1893	Hawk
mi	S	Miki	三木	Kamakura	1332	Tree
mi	S	Misumi	三隅	Nanboku	1392	Corner / Nook
mi	S	Mito	三戸	Nanboku	1392	Door
mi	S	Mi'ura	三浦	Kamakura	1332	Bay / Delta
mi	S	Miyoshi	三好	Sengoku	1568	Affection / Desire
mi	S	Miyoshi	三善	Kamakura	1332	Perform Well

参 Three / Visit

This *kanji* is commonly used in contracts as it is harder to change to a different number than is the simpler *kanji* with the same meaning. Although "mitsu" is listed as the *kunyomi* for this *kanji*, this is actually a special reading which is used when 参 is substituting for 三 and is not a normative reading. This substitution arises, because they both have three strokes and share "SAN" as a common *onyomi*. Thus, "mitsu" is a *kunyomi* transferred from 三 to this *kanji*.

Reading	Type	Example	Kanji	Period	Date	Added Meaning
mitsu	F	Mitoshime	参歳賣	Nara	784	Age of a Person

四 Four

Reading	Type	Example	Kanji	Period	Date	Added Meaning
SHI	S	Shijou	四条	Kamakura	1332	Branch / Line / Road
yon	F	Yochiko	四千子	Hei'an	1183	[Lady]

五 Five

Reading	Type	Example	Kanji	Period	Date	Added Meaning
GO	M	Fujigorou	藤五郎	Uncertain	1600	Wisteria
GO	M	Gengorou	源五郎	Uncertain	1600	Origin
GO	M	Gorou	五郎	Higashiyama	1575	Son
GO	M	Gorousa'emon	五郎左衛門	Uncertain	1600	Ministry of the Left
GO	M	Jogorou	助五郎	Uncertain	1600	Rescue
GO	M	Songorou	孫五郎	Uncertain	1600	Grandchild
GO	M	Yogotarou	与五太郎	Uncertain	1600	Team Up + Fifth Son
GO	M	Zengorou	善五郎	Sengoku	1568	Perform Well
GO	S	Goshima	五島	Sengoku	1568	Island
itsu	F	Itsu'i	五位	Muromachi	1572	Level / Status / Station
itsu	F	Itsu'itsu	五々	Muromachi	1572	
[Special]	F	Ihosume	五百寸賣	Nara	784	Hundered + Inch
[Special]	F	Isogamime	十五上女	Nara	784	Superior
[Special]	F	Satsukime	五月賣	Hei'an	1183	Moon / Month

六 Six

Reading	Type	Example	Kanji	Period	Date	Added Meaning
ROKU	M	Rokurou	六郎	Kamakura	1332	
ROKU	P	Roppongi	六本木	Modern	1983	Trees
mu	S	Muta	六田	Modern	1983	Rice Paddy
mutsu	F	Mutsuko	六子	Uncertain	1600	[Lady]
mutsu	F	Mutsumi	六美	Modern	1983	Beauty
[Special]	F	Mi'nazuki	六月賣	Hei'an	1183	Moon / Month

七 Seven

Reading	Type	Example	Kanji	Period	Date	Added Meaning
SHICHI	M	Shichirou	七朗	Modern	1983	
SHICHI	M	Shichirou	七郎	Modern	1983	

八 Eight

Reading	Type	Example	Kanji	Period	Date	Added Meaning
HACHI	M	Hachirou	八郎	Modern	1983	
HACHI	S	Hatta	八田	Hei'an	1183	Rice Paddy
ya	P	Yagi	八木	Modern	1983	Tree

九 Nine

Reading	Type	Example	Kanji	Period	Date	Added Meaning
KU	M	Genkutarou	彦九太郎	Uncertain	1600	Young Scholar + Son
KU	M	Jinkurou	甚九郎	Sengoku	1568	Terrible + Son
KU	M	Kurou	九郎	Kamakura	1332	Son
KU	M	Yokurou	与九郎	Modern	1983	Team Up
KU	N	Kubutsu	九仏	Muromachi	1572	Buddha
KU	S	Kujou	九条	Kamakura	1219	Branch / Road / Avenue

十 Ten

Reading	Type	Example	Kanji	Period	Date	Added Meaning
JUU	H	Juubutsu	十仏	Muromachi	1572	Buddha
JUU	M	Juurou	十郎	Kamakura	1332	Son
so	M	Soroku	十六	Modern	1983	Six
to	M	Toshi'o	十四夫	Modern	1983	Four + Husband / Man
[Special]	F	Isogamime	十五上女	Nara	784	Superior

百 One Hundred

Reading	Type	Example	Kanji	Period	Date	Added Meaning
momo	F	Momoe	百恵	Uncertain	1600	Sanctify / Bless
momo	F	Momoko	百子	Hei'an	1183	[Lady]
momo	F	Momome	百賣	Nara	784	
momo	F	Momote	百手	Uncertain	1600	Hand
momo	F	Momoteme	百手賣	Nara	784	Hand
momo	N	Momokawa	百川	Uncertain	1600	River

千 One Thousand

Recently, an article appeared in *Tankou* 淡交 which discussed whether Sen 千 is a Japanese name. The problem being that SEN is the Chinese reading for the character. This, combined with the fact that 千 is a single character surname makes this a very unusual name in Japan. There is some evidence that the family was originally called Tanaka 田中 Aand that the name was changed by Sen no Rikyuu 千利休. The article concluded by asserting that the 千 (Sen) family is Japanese. However, the name remains problematic. Members of the Sen family are married to daughters of the imperial family. Regardless, Sen no Rikyuu 千利休 did live in Japan during the sixteenth century and was an advisor to Toyotomi Hideyoshi 豊臣 秀吉.

Reading	Type	Example	Kanji	Period	Date	Added Meaning
SEN	F	Senchiyo	千千代	Momoyama	1590	Era
SEN	P	Senzu	千頭	Modern	1983	Head / First / Zenith
SEN	S	Sen	千	Uncertain	1600	

Reading	Type	Example	Kanji	Period	Date	Added Meaning
chi	B	Chikumaru	千宝丸	Kamakura	1332	Treasure + Young / Healthy
chi	F	Chime	千賣	Nara	784	
chi	F	Chiyo	千代	Momoyama	1590	Era
chi	F	Chiyo'inu	千代犬	Momoyama	1590	Era + Dog
chi	F	Chiyorime	千依賣	Nara	784	Follow
chi	F	Chiyotsurume	千世鶴女	Nanboku	1392	Generation + Crane + [Woman]
chi	N	Chisato	千里	Uncertain	1600	Hamlet
chi	P	Chiga'no'ura	千賀浦	Modern	1983	Celebrate a Gain + Bay / Delta
chi	S	Chiba	千葉	Kamakura	1332	Leaf

万 Ten Thousand

Reading	Type	Example	Kanji	Period	Date	Added Meaning
MAN	F	Manme	万女	Hei'an	1183	[Woman]
MAN	Y	Eiman	永万	Kamakura	1165	Forever
MAN	Y	Man'en	万延	Edo	1860	Prolong / Stretch Out
MAN	Y	Manji	万治	Edo	1658	Govern / Rule
MAN	Y	Manju	万寿	Hei'an	1024	Long Life / Longevity

順 Order / Sequence

Reading	Type	Example	Kanji	Period	Date	Added Meaning
yoshi	N	Hisayoshi	尚順	Sengoku	1568	Excellence
shitagau	N	Shitagau	順	Uncertain	1600	

度 Event Number = TO / Consult / Confer = nori

Reading	Type	Example	Kanji	Period	Date	Added Meaning
TO	F	Tomoko	度茂子	Hei'an	1183	Blossoming + [Lady]
nori	N	Masa'nori	正度	Uncertain	1600	Unerring / Genuine
nori	N	Tada'nori	忠度	Hei'an	1183	Faithful / Loyal
nori	N	Tomo'nori	知度	Hei'an	1183	Knowledge

元 Base / Original

Reading	Type	Example	Kanji	Period	Date	Added Meaning
GEN	Y	Angen	安元	Kamakura	1175	Gentle / Safe / Secure
GEN	Y	Chougen	長元	Hei'an	1028	Long / Oldest / Senior
GEN	Y	Engen	延元	Nanboku	1336	Prolong / Stretch Out
GEN	Y	Genbun	元文	Edo	1736	Literature / Culture
GEN	Y	Genchuu	元中	Nanboku	1384	Middle
GEN	Y	Gen'ei	元永	Hei'an	1118	Forever
GEN	Y	Genji	元治	Edo	1864	Govern / Rule
GEN	Y	Genki	元亀	Momoyama	1570	Tortoise (Longevity)
GEN	Y	Genkou	元亨	Kamakura	1321	Receive Smoothly
GEN	Y	Genkou	元康	Kamakura	1331	Strong / Confident
GEN	Y	Genkyuu	元久	Kamakura	1204	Longtime
GEN	Y	Genna	元和	Edo	1615	Peace / Tranquility / Harmony
GEN	Y	Gennin	元仁	Kamakura	1224	Precious
GEN	Y	Gen'ou	元応	Kamakura	1319	Worthy / Suitable
GEN	Y	Genroku	元禄	Edo	1688	Gratitude / Beneficence

Thematic Dictionary— Number & Quantity 217

Reading	Type	Example	Kanji	Period	Date	Added Meaning
GEN	Y	Genryaku	元歴	Kamakura	1184	Progress / Pass Through
GEN	Y	Gentoku	元徳	Kamakura	1329	Righteous / Just
GEN	Y	Hougen	保元	Kamakura	1156	Guarantee
GEN	Y	Jougen	丞元	Kamakura	1207	Rescue from a Pit
GEN	Y	Kagen	嘉元	Kamakura	1303	Well Done
GEN	Y	Kangen	寛元	Kamakura	1243	Domestic Tranquility
GEN	Y	Kengen	乾元	Kamakura	1302	High Heaven / Ancient Times
GEN	Y	Kougen	康元	Kamakura	1256	Strong / Confident
GEN	Y	Shougen	正元	Kamakura	1259	Unerring / Genuine
moto	F	Motoko	元子	Nanboku	1392	[Lady]
moto	N	Akimoto	秋元	Kamakura	1332	Autumn
moto	N	Chikamoto	親元	Muromachi	1572	Intimate
moto	N	Hidemoto	秀元	Sengoku	1568	Extraordinary / Bountiful
moto	N	Hiromoto	広元	Kamakura	1332	Spacious / Expansive
moto	N	Ka'nemoto	兼元	Muromachi	1572	Unite
moto	N	Katsumoto	且元	Sengoku	1568	Moreover
moto	N	Katsumoto	勝元	Muromachi	1572	Conquer / Triumph
moto	N	Masamoto	政元	Nanboku	1392	Govern / Rule
moto	N	Mitsumoto	満元	Muromachi	1572	Become Full / Abundant
moto	N	Motochika	元親	Uncertain	1600	Intimate
moto	N	Motoharu	元治	Hei'an	1183	Govern / Rule
moto	N	Motoharu	元春	Nanboku	1392	Spring (Season)
moto	N	Motohisa	元久	Nanboku	1392	Longtime
moto	N	Motokiyo	元清	Nanboku	1392	Pure
moto	N	Motoku'ni	元国	Muromachi	1572	Country / Rural Area
moto	N	Motomasa	元雅	Muromachi	1572	High Quality
moto	N	Motomitsu	元光	Muromachi	1572	Bright / Shining
moto	N	Moto'naga	元長	Muromachi	1572	Long
moto	N	Moto'nari	元就	Uncertain	1600	To Become / Be Posted
moto	N	Moto'nobu	元信	Uncertain	1600	Belief / Faith
moto	N	Motoshige	元重	Muromachi	1572	Heavy / Serious
moto	N	Motosuke	元資	Muromachi	1572	Raw Materials
moto	N	Motosuke	元輔	Uncertain	1600	Ministerial Deputy
moto	N	Motota'ne	元胤	Muromachi	1572	Blood Heir
moto	N	Mototsu'na	元綱	Sengoku	1568	Net
moto	N	Mototsura	元連	Muromachi	1572	Bring Along
moto	N	Moto'uji	元氏	Nanboku	1392	Family / Clan
moto	N	Motoyoshi	元喜	Uncertain	1600	Rejoice
moto	N	Motoyoshi	元良	Uncertain	1600	Good / Superior
moto	N	Mu'nemoto	宗元	Nanboku	1392	Master an Art
moto	N	Nobumoto	信元	Muromachi	1572	Belief / Faith
moto	N	Shigemoto	重元	Sengoku	1568	Heavy / Serious
moto	N	Takamoto	高元	Nanboku	1392	Tall
moto	N	Terumoto	輝元	Sengoku	1568	Brilliant
moto	N	Toomoto	遠元	Kamakura	1332	Far
moto	N	Yorimoto	頼元	Nanboku	1392	Request / Ask
moto	N	Yoshimoto	義元	Uncertain	1600	Fealty
moto	S	Arimoto	有元	Kamakura	1332	Exists

仲 Second / Middle of a Group

Reading	Type	Example	Kanji	Period	Date	Added Meaning
naka	F	Naka'noko	仲子	Hei'an	1183	[Lady]
naka	N	Kage'naka	景仲	Muromachi	1572	Bright / Magnificent
naka	N	Ka'ne'naka	兼仲	Kamakura	1332	Unite
naka	N	Mitsu'naka	満仲	Uncertain	1600	Become Full / Abundant

Reading	Type	Example	Kanji	Period	Date	Added Meaning
naka	N	Mochi'naka	持仲	Muromachi	1572	Have / Possess
naka	N	Mori'naka	盛仲	Uncertain	1600	Plentiful / Piled Up
naka	N	Moro'naka	師仲	Hei'an	1183	Teacher / Expert
naka	N	Naka'aki	仲秋	Nanboku	1392	Autumn
naka	N	Nakabumi	仲文	Uncertain	1600	Writing
naka	N	Nakachika	仲親	Kamakura	1332	Intimate
naka	N	Nakafusa	仲房	Nanboku	1392	Monastic Cell
naka	N	Nakahira	仲平	Uncertain	1600	Tranquility
naka	N	Naka'ie	仲家	Kamakura	1332	Rural House / Family
naka	N	Nakaki	仲材	Sengoku	1568	Raw Matterial / Talent
naka	N	Nakaku'ni	仲国	Kamakura	1332	Country / Rural Area
naka	N	Nakamaro	仲麻呂	Uncertain	1600	Flax / Linen + Backbone
naka	N	Nakamaro	仲麿	Uncertain	1600	Together / Team Work
naka	N	Nakamitsu	仲光	Muromachi	1572	Bright / Shining
naka	N	Nakamoto	仲基	Hei'an	1183	Foundation
naka	N	Nakamu'ne	仲宗	Hei'an	1183	Master an Art
naka	N	Naka'nari	仲業	Kamakura	1332	Industry / Diligence
naka	N	Naka'nari	仲成	Uncertain	1600	Become / Exist
naka	N	Nakasada	仲貞	Nanboku	1392	Correct Spirit
naka	N	Nakatoki	仲時	Kamakura	1332	Time / Era
naka	N	Nakatsu'na	仲綱	Hei'an	1183	Net
naka	N	Nakayori	仲頼	Hei'an	1183	Request / Ask
naka	N	Sa'ne'naka	実仲	Kamakura	1332	Reality
naka	N	Taka'naka	隆仲	Nanboku	1392	Grow / Pile Up
naka	N	Tsu'ne'naka	経仲	Kamakura	1332	True Path
naka	N	Yoshi'naka	義仲	Muromachi	1572	Fealty
naka	N	Yoshi'naka	能仲	Kamakura	1332	Talent / Ability

次 Next

Reading	Type	Example	Kanji	Period	Date	Added Meaning
tsugu	F	Tsugume	次女	Nara	784	[Woman]
tsugu	N	Hidetsugu	秀次	Uncertain	1600	Extraordinary / Bountiful
tsugu	N	Masatsugu	昌次	Uncertain	1600	Clear / Bright
tsugu	N	Masatsugu	正次	Muromachi	1572	Unerring / Genuine
tsugu	N	Shigetsugu	重次	Momoyama	1549	Heavy / Serious
tsugi	N	Nobutsugi	信次	Uncertain	1600	Belief / Faith
tsugi	N	Tadatsugi	直次	Sengoku	1568	Adjust / Correct
tsugi	N	Yasutsugi	安次	Sengoku	1568	Gentle / Safe / Secure
tsugu	N	Yoritsugu	頼次	Nanboku	1392	Request / Ask

又 Next / Again

Reading	Type	Example	Kanji	Period	Date	Added Meaning
mata	M	Matajirou	又次郎	Uncertain	1600	Second / Next + Son

末 Last

Reading	Type	Example	Kanji	Period	Date	Added Meaning
sue	F	Sueko	末子	Modern	1983	[Lady]

甲 First (Helmet) / 木兄 (Kinoe)
Used in the ancient Japanese calendric system. Elder of the 木兄 / 木弟 pair.

Reading	Type	Example	Kanji	Period	Date	Added Meaning
KATSU	M	Katsuhiko	甲彦	Modern	1983	Boy / Young Scholar
KOU	M	Koujirou	甲子郎	Modern	1983	Child + Son
ka	S	Kai	甲斐	Muromachi	1572	Beauty / Colour Harmony
ki	M	Ki'ne'o	甲子男	Modern	1983	Child

乙 Second (Cute) / 木弟 (Kinoto)
Used in the ancient Japanese calendric system. Junior of the 木兄 / 木弟 pair.

Reading	Type	Example	Kanji	Period	Date	Added Meaning
OTSU	M	Otsuto	乙人	Modern	1983	Person / Human
oto	M	Otohiko	乙彦	Modern	1983	Boy / Young Scholar
oto	N	Otomuro	乙牟漏	Uncertain	1600	Mooing of a Cow
taka	F	Takaharu	乙春	Hei'an	1183	Spring (Season)

丙 Third (Alter) / 火兄 (Hinoe)
Used in the ancient Japanese clendric system. Elder of the 火兄 / 火弟 pair.

Reading	Type	Example	Kanji	Period	Date	Added Meaning
HEI	M	Heigo	丙午	Modern	1983	Horse (Zodiac)
hinoe	M	Hinoe	丙	Modern	1983	

丁 Fourth (Adult) / 火弟 (Hinoto)
Used in the ancient Japanese calendric system. Junior of the 火兄 / 火弟 pair.

Reading	Type	Example	Kanji	Period	Date	Added Meaning
TEI	M	Teizou	丁三	Modern	1983	
TEI	F	Tei	丁	Uncertain	1600	

戊 Fifth (Speak) / 土兄 (Tsuchinoe)
Used in the ancient Japanese calendric system. Elder of the 土兄 / 土弟 pair.

Reading	Type	Example	Kanji	Period	Date	Added Meaning
BO	No examples of names using this *kanji* have yet been found. *Kanji* included for completeness.					

己 Sixth (Self) / 土弟 (Tsuchinoto)
Used in the ancient Japanese calendric system. Junior of the 土兄 / 土弟 pair.

Reading	Type	Example	Kanji	Period	Date	Added Meaning
KI	F	Kimorime	己母里賣	Nara	784	Hamlet
KI	M	Yukio	由己男	Modern	1983	Purpose
KO	N	Mitsuhiko	光比己	Modern	1983	Bright / Shining + Strive
mi	N	Masami	正己	Modern	1983	Unerring / Genuine

庚 Seventh (Age) / 金兄 (Kanenoe)
Used in the ancient Japanese calendric system. Elder of the 金兄 / 金弟 pair.

Reading	Type	Example	Kanji	Period	Date	Added Meaning
KOU	No examples of names using this *kanji* have yet been found. *Kanji* included for completeness.					

辛 Eighth (Bitter) / 金弟 (Kanenoto)
Used in the ancient Japanese calendric system. Junior of the 金兄 / 金弟 pair.

Reading	Type	Example	Kanji	Period	Date	Added Meaning
SHIN	M	Shin'ichi	辛一	Modern	1983	

壬 Ninth (Found) / 水兄 (Mizunoe)
Used in the ancient Japanese calendric system. Elder of the 水兄 / 水弟 pair.

Reading	Type	Example	Kanji	Period	Date	Added Meaning
JIN	M	Jin'ichi	壬一	Modern	1983	One
mi	S	Mifu	壬生	Uncertain	1600	Life / Live / Living

癸 Tenth (Menstruation) / 水弟 (Mizunoto)
Used in the ancient Japanese calendric system. Junior of the 水兄 / 水弟 pair.

Reading	Type	Example	Kanji	Period	Date	Added Meaning
KI	No examples of names using this *kanji* have yet been found. *Kanji* included for completeness.					

凡 Every / Ordinary

Reading	Type	Example	Kanji	Period	Date	Added Meaning
ohoshi	S	Ohoshika	凡河	Uncertain	1600	Large River
[Special]	F	Nifuko	凡生子	Hei'an	1183	Life / Live / Living + [Lady]

普 Wide Spread / Typical / Ordinary
The meaning of this *kanji* is influenced by which "reading" is used. "Hiro" relates strongly to the original meaning which was sun shining spreading out evenly over flat countryside. "Amanei" relates more to being ordinary. Regardless, Japanese are conscious of both meanings when they see this *kanji*.

Reading	Type	Example	Kanji	Period	Date	Added Meaning
ama'nei	F	Ama'neiko	普子	Hei'an	1183	[Lady]
hiro	F	Hiroko	普子	Hei'an	1183	[Lady]
	N	Hirotoshi	普利	Sengoku	1568	Produce Results / Work Well

同 The Same / Identical / Equitable
Note that 子 takes its *onyomi* in Hitoshi.

Reading	Type	Example	Kanji	Period	Date	Added Meaning
hito	F	Hitoshi	同子	Hei'an	1183	[Lady]

別 Separate / Different

This *kanji* evokes the image of meat being carved from a bones.

Reading	Type	Example	Kanji	Period	Date	Added Meaning
BETSU	S	Bessho	別所	Sengoku	1568	Locaton / Duty Station

少 Small Amount / Minor

This *kanji* appears to be substituted for 小 in the one name where it appears. Further, note the antique pronunciation of the initial syllable. This syllable becomes "o" in Modern Japanese. Essentially, classical Japanese appears to have avoided syllable consisting of naked vowels preceding them with either a "w" or an "f" sound. The "w" sound appears to be characteristic of initial syllables while the "f" sound appears in case endings for verbs.

Reading	Type	Example	Kanji	Period	Date	Added Meaning
wo	F	Wotome	少女	Nara	784	[Woman]

多 Many

Reading	Type	Example	Kanji	Period	Date	Added Meaning
TA	F	Masaru	多子	Hei'an	1183	[Lady]
TA	F	Taki	多喜	Hei'an	1183	Rejoice
TA	F	Tamiko	多美子	Hei'an	1183	Beauty + [Lady]
TA	F	Tarumime	多流美賣	Nara	784	Beauty
TA	F	Tata	多々	Nanboku	1392	
TA	F	Tawome	多乎賣	Nara	784	Destination
TA	S	Hata'no	波多野	Kamakura	1332	Wave + Wide Plain
TA	S	Honda	本多	Momoyama	1529	Main / Base
TA	S	Tada	多田	Hei'an	1183	Rice Paddy
TA	S	Taga	多賀	Sengoku	1568	Celebrate A Gain
TA	S	Tajimi	多治見	Kamakura	1332	Govern / Rule + Vista
TA	S	Tatara	多々良	Kamakura	1332	Good / Superior
TA	S	Uda	宇多	Sengoku	1568	Large Roof
TA	S	Ukita	宇喜多	Uncertain	1600	Large Roof + Rejoice

巨 Numerous

Reading	Type	Example	Kanji	Period	Date	Added Meaning
KO	F	Kosoko	巨曾子	Nara	784	Formerly / Ever + [Lady]

益 Grow Numerous / Multiply / Overflow

Reading	Type	Example	Kanji	Period	Date	Added Meaning
masu	N	Kagemasu	景益	Kamakura	1332	Bright / Magnificent
masu	N	Masuyuki	益之	Muromachi	1572	Go / Depart
masu	N	Mochimasu	持益	Muromachi	1572	Have / Possess
masu	N	Tokimasu	時益	Kamakura	1332	Time / Era
masu	N	Yorimasu	頼益	Muromachi	1572	Request / Ask
masu	S	Masuda	益田	Nanboku	1392	Rice Paddy

増 Grow Numerous / Live Long / Prosper

Reading	Type	Example	Kanji	Period	Date	Added Meaning
masu	N	Michimasu	通増	Nanboku	1392	Pass Through
masu	N	Nobumasu	信増	Nanboku	1392	Belief / Faith
masu	S	Masuda	増田	Uncertain	1600	Rice Paddy

湛 Fill Up / Become Abundant

Reading	Type	Example	Kanji	Period	Date	Added Meaning
TAN	H	Soutan	宗湛	Uncertain	1600	Master an Art

栄 Bountiful / Fruitful

Reading	Type	Example	Kanji	Period	Date	Added Meaning
EI	F	Eishi	栄子	Kamakura	1332	[Lady]
hide	N	Iehide	家栄	Muromachi	1572	Rural House / Family
hide	N	Nobuhide	宣栄	Nanboku	1392	Proclamation
saka	N	Nobusaka	信栄	Sengoku	1568	Belief / Faith
saka	N	Norisaka	憲栄	Uncertain	1600	Example / Pattern

盛 Plentiful / Piled Up

Reading	Type	Example	Kanji	Period	Date	Added Meaning
mori	N	Akimori	顕盛	Kamakura	1332	High Status
mori	N	Arimori	有盛	Hei'an	1183	Exists
mori	N	Atsumori	敦盛	Hei'an	1183	Generous / Kind / Honest
mori	N	Kagemori	景盛	Kamakura	1332	Bright / Magnificent
mori	N	Ka'nemori	兼盛	Uncertain	1600	Unite
mori	N	Kiyomori	清盛	Hei'an	1183	Pure
mori	N	Koremori	維盛	Hei'an	1183	Cable / Rope
mori	N	Masamori	昌盛	Uncertain	1600	Clear / Bright
mori	N	Masamori	正盛	Uncertain	1600	Unerring / Genuine
mori	N	Michimori	通盛	Kamakura	1332	Pass Through
mori	N	Mitsumori	光盛	Kamakura	1332	Bright / Shining
mori	N	Mochimori	以盛	Muromachi	1572	Highest
mori	N	Mori'akira	盛詮	Muromachi	1572	Explicit / Clear
mori	N	Mori'akira	盛明	Kamakura	1332	Bright
mori	N	Moriga'ne	盛兼	Sengoku	1568	Unite
mori	N	Morihide	盛秀	Uncertain	1600	Extraordinary / Bountiful
mori	N	Morihiro	盛弘	Muromachi	1572	Draw / Stretch
mori	N	Morihisa	盛久	Muromachi	1572	Longtime
mori	N	Mori'ie	盛家	Kamakura	1332	Rural House / Family
mori	N	Morikage	盛景	Kamakura	1332	Bright / Magnificent
mori	N	Morika'ne	盛兼	Kamakura	1332	Unite
mori	N	Morikazu	盛員	Kamakura	1332	Member
mori	N	Moriku'ni	盛国	Hei'an	1183	Country / Rural Area
mori	N	Morimasa	盛政	Kamakura	1332	Govern / Rule
mori	N	Morimi	盛見	Muromachi	1572	Vantage / View / Vista
mori	N	Morimitsu	盛光	Nanboku	1392	Bright / Shining
mori	N	Morimori	盛守	Uncertain	1600	Protect / Defend

Thematic Dictionary — Number & Quantity 223

Reading	Type	Example	Kanji	Period	Date	Added Meaning
mori	N	Mori'naga	盛長	Hei'an	1183	Long
mori	N	Mori'naka	盛仲	Uncertain	1600	Middle of a Group
mori	N	Mori'nao	盛直	Hei'an	1183	Adjust / Correct
mori	N	Mori'nobu	盛信	Uncertain	1600	Belief / Faith
mori	N	Moritaka	盛高	Muromachi	1572	Tall
mori	N	Moritaka	盛隆	Kamakura	1332	Grow / Pile Up
mori	N	Moritoki	盛時	Kamakura	1332	Time / Era
mori	N	Moritoo	盛遠	Kamakura	1332	Far
mori	N	Moritoshi	盛俊	Hei'an	1183	Emotional
mori	N	Moritsugi	盛継	Uncertain	1600	Connect / Adopt
mori	N	Moritsugu	盛嗣	Hei'an	1183	Successor
mori	N	Moritsu'na	盛綱	Hei'an	1183	Net
mori	N	Moritsura	盛連	Kamakura	1332	Bring Along
mori	N	Mori'uji	盛氏	Kamakura	1332	Family / Clan
mori	N	Moriyoshi	盛義	Uncertain	1600	Fealty
mori	N	Moromori	師盛	Hei'an	1183	Teacher / Expert
mori	N	Motomori	基盛	Hei'an	1183	Foundation
mori	N	Mu'nemori	宗盛	Hei'an	1183	Master an Art
mori	N	Nagamori	長盛	Uncertain	1600	Long
mori	N	Narimori	業盛	Hei'an	1183	Industry / Diligence
mori	N	Norimori	教盛	Hei'an	1183	Teaching / Dogma
mori	N	Sadamori	貞盛	Muromachi	1572	Correct Spirit
mori	N	Sa'nemori	実盛	Hei'an	1183	Reality
mori	N	Shigemori	重盛	Hei'an	1183	Heavy / Serious
mori	N	Sukemori	資盛	Hei'an	1183	Raw Materials
mori	N	Tadamori	忠盛	Hei'an	1183	Faithful / Loyal
mori	N	Takamori	隆盛	Uncertain	1600	Grow / Pile Up
mori	N	Ta'nemori	胤盛	Kamakura	1332	Blood Heir
mori	N	Tokimori	時盛	Kamakura	1332	Time / Era
mori	N	Tomomori	知盛	Hei'an	1183	Knowledge
mori	N	Tomomori	朝盛	Kamakura	1332	Morning
mori	N	Toramori	虎盛	Uncertain	1600	Tiger
mori	N	Tsu'nemori	経盛	Hei'an	1183	True Path
mori	N	Tsu'nemori	常盛	Kamakura	1332	Permanent
mori	N	Ujimori	氏盛	Sengoku	1568	Family / Clan
mori	N	Yasumori	康盛	Hei'an	1183	Strong / Confident
mori	N	Yasumori	泰盛	Kamakura	1332	Peace / Plenitude
mori	N	Yasumori	保盛	Kamakura	1332	Guarantee
mori	N	Yorimori	頼盛	Hei'an	1183	Request / Ask
mori	N	Yoshimori	義盛	Hei'an	1183	Fealty
mori	N	Yoshimori	能盛	Hei'an	1183	Talent / Ability
mori	N	Yukimori	行盛	Kamakura	1332	Going To / Bound For

満 Become Full / Abundant

Reading	Type	Example	Kanji	Period	Date	Added Meaning
MAN	H	Giman	義満	Uncertain	1600	Fealty
mitsu	N	Mitsu'aki	満詮	Muromachi	1572	Explicit / Clear
mitsu	N	Mitsuchika	満親	Nanboku	1392	Intimate
mitsu	N	Mitsufuji	満藤	Muromachi	1572	Wisteria
mitsu	N	Mitsuhide	満秀	Muromachi	1572	Extraordinary / Bountiful
mitsu	N	Mitsu'ie	満家	Muromachi	1572	Rural House / Family
mitsu	N	Mitsuka'ne	満兼	Muromachi	1572	Unite
mitsu	N	Mitsumasa	満雅	Muromachi	1572	High Quality
mitsu	N	Mitsumasa	満政	Muromachi	1572	Govern / Rule
mitsu	N	Mitsumoto	満元	Muromachi	1572	Base / Original

mitsu	N	Mitsu'naka	満仲	Uncertain	1600	Middle of a Group
mitsu	N	Mitsu'nao	満直	Muromachi	1572	Adjust / Correct
mitsu	N	Mitsu'nari	満成	Muromachi	1572	Become / Exist
mitsu	N	Mitsu'nori	満教	Muromachi	1572	Teaching / Dogma
mitsu	N	Mitsu'nori	満慶	Muromachi	1572	Rejoice / Deer Skin
mitsu	N	Mitsu'nori	満則	Muromachi	1572	Make an Example
mitsu	N	Mitsu'nori	満範	Muromachi	1572	Required Form / Pattern
mitsu	N	Mitsusada	満貞	Nanboku	1392	Correct Spirit
mitsu	N	Mitsushige	満重	Muromachi	1572	Heavy / Serious
mitsu	N	Mitsusue	満季	Muromachi	1572	Season
mitsu	N	Mitsusuke	満祐	Muromachi	1572	Divine Help
mitsu	N	Mitsutada	満直	Muromachi	1572	Adjust / Correct
mitsu	N	Mitsutaka	満高	Nanboku	1392	Tall
mitsu	N	Mitsutaka	満隆	Muromachi	1572	Grow / Pile Up
mitsu	N	Mitsuta'ne	満胤	Muromachi	1572	Blood Heir
mitsu	N	Mitsutomo	満朝	Muromachi	1572	Morning
mitsu	N	Mitsutsu'na	満綱	Muromachi	1572	Net
mitsu	N	Mitsutsu'ne	満経	Muromachi	1572	True Path
mitsu	N	Mitsu'uji	満氏	Muromachi	1572	Family / Clan
mitsu	N	Mitsuyori	満頼	Hei'an	1183	Request / Ask
mitsu	N	Mitsuyuki	満幸	Nanboku	1392	Happy / Tattoo
mitsu	N	Mitsuzumi	満純	Muromachi	1572	Natural / Pure
mitsu	N	Nobumitsu	信満	Muromachi	1417	Belief / Faith
mitsu	N	Sadamitsu	貞満	Nanboku	1392	Correct Spirit
mitsu	N	Ujimitsu	氏満	Nanboku	1392	Family / Clan
mitsu	N	Yoshimitsu	義満	Muromachi	1572	Fealty

❖ Taste & Appearance ❖

味 Taste

"Taste" is meant in both the literal and the metaphorical sense. Metaphorically, it refers to both aesthetic appreciation and to experiencing something which is in some way sensual.

Reading	Type	Example	Kanji	Period	Date	Added Meaning
MI	F	Mitsu	味津	Uncertain	1600	Harbour

甘 Sweet Taste

Reading	Type	Example	Kanji	Period	Date	Added Meaning
ama	S	Amari	甘利	Uncertain	1600	Produce Results
[Special]	O	Ukaibe	鵜甘部	Ancient	645	

芳 Sweet Scent / Magnificent

Reading	Type	Example	Kanji	Period	Date	Added Meaning
yoshi	F	Yoshime	芳賣	Nara	784	
yoshi	N	Yoshi'naga	芳長	Uncertain	1600	Long

如 Seem / Appear

Reading	Type	Example	Kanji	Period	Date	Added Meaning
yuki	F	Yukime	如女	Hei'an	1183	[Woman]

郁 Appear Cultured

Reading	Type	Example	Kanji	Period	Date	Added Meaning
aya	F	Ayako	郁子	Hei'an	1183	[Lady]

尭 Appear Tall or Grand

Reading	Type	Example	Kanji	Period	Date	Added Meaning
taka	N	Michitaka	通尭	Nanboku	1392	Pass Through

致 Taste / Elegance / Grand Effect

This *kanji* also denotes humble service, exerting one's self and rendering assistance.

Reading	Type	Example	Kanji	Period	Date	Added Meaning
mune	N	Chikamu'ne	親致	Kamakura	1332	Parent / Intimate
mune	N	Tadamu'ne	忠致	Hei'an	1183	Faithful / Loyal
mune	N	Tokimu'ne	時致	Kamakura	1332	Hour / Time / Era

濃 Thick / Turbid

Reading	Type	Example	Kanji	Period	Date	Added Meaning
NO	P	Shi'na'no	信濃	Uncertain	1600	Belief / Faith

薄 Thin / Light

Reading	Type	Example	Kanji	Period	Date	Added Meaning
usu	S	Usu'i	薄井	Modern	1983	Well

淡 Thin / Pale / Weak

Among other things, this *kanji* relates to the aesthetics of the tea ceremony. Again this has significance within Buddhist thought. The Buddha preached against a false attachment to the world. Zen Buddhists attempt to achieve sudden enlightenment through immediate experience. Thus, adepts of Zen art forms develop a kind of detachment from the minutiae of the art form itself which is profoundly liberating.

Reading	Type	Example	Kanji	Period	Date	Added Meaning
TAN	H	Soutan	宗淡	Modern	1983	Master an Art
TAN	S	Tannawa	淡輪	Nanboku	1392	Cart Wheel (Karma)
ai	S	Aikawa	淡河	Kamakura	1332	Large River
[Special]	P	Augo	淡河	Modern	1983	Large River

軽 Light / Minor / Trifling / Simple / Easy

Karuizawa is the name of a famous Japanese resort area. This name dates from 1923 and is quite modern. It was included merely to indicate the *kunyomi* for 軽 without the initial syllable being voiced due to coarticulation with the preceding syllable.

Reading	Type	Example	Kanji	Period	Date	Added Meaning
karu	P	Karuizawa	軽井澤	Modern	1923	Well + Glenn / Run
karu	S	Tsugaru	津軽	Sengoku	1568	Harbour

形 Form / Shape / Beauty

This *kanji* relates to painting pictures and especially to representing the form of inanimate objects.

Reading	Type	Example	Kanji	Period	Date	Added Meaning
kata	S	Yamagata	山形	Uncertain	1600	Mountain

姿 Form / Shape / Figure

This *kanji* specifically relates to the form or shape of the human body.

Reading	Type	Example	Kanji	Period	Date	Added Meaning
SHI	F	Neshime	泥姿賣	Nara	784	Muddy
SHI	F	Sashime	沙姿賣	Nara	784	Sand (in Water)
SHI	F	Woshime	乎姿賣	Nara	784	Destination + Simple / Pure

美 Beautiful

Originally, this *kanji* evoked the image of a large unblemished ram. This idea was extended to all things that are beautiful. However, the nuance of strength remains to this day.

Reading	Type	Example	Kanji	Period	Date	Added Meaning
MI	F	Akemi	明美	Uncertain	1600	Bright
MI	F	Miyuki	美由喜	Uncertain	1600	Purpose + Rejoice
MI	S	Kagami	加賀美	Hei'an	1183	Enlist + Celebrate A Gain

妙 Exotic Beauty / Mysterious

Reading	Type	Example	Kanji	Period	Date	Added Meaning
MYOU	F	Myouhoume	妙法女	Kamakura	1332	[Woman]
tahe	F	Tahe	妙	Muromachi	1572	
tahe	F	Taheme	妙賣	Nara	784	

斐 Beauty / Colour Harmony

Reading	Type	Example	Kanji	Period	Date	Added Meaning
HI	S	Kai	甲斐	Muromachi	1572	First (Helmet)

奇 Strange / Unusual / Unexpected

Reading	Type	Example	Kanji	Period	Date	Added Meaning
shiki	N	Toshiki	俊奇	Kamakura	1244	Emotional

❖ Spiritual Traits ❖

神 God

Reading	Type	Example	Kanji	Period	Date	Added Meaning
KAN	P	Kanda	神田	Modern	1983	Rice Paddy
kami	S	Kamiya	神谷	Uncertain	1600	Valley
miwa	F	Miwame	神賣	Nara	784	

仏 Buddha

Reading	Type	Example	Kanji	Period	Date	Added Meaning
BUTSU	H	Juubutsu	十仏	Muromachi	1572	Ten
BUTSU	H	Kubutsu	九仏	Muromachi	1572	Nine
BUTSU	H	Shibutsu	士仏	Muromachi	1572	Samurai / Warrior

巴 Wheel of Life

Reading	Type	Example	Kanji	Period	Date	Added Meaning
tomoe	F	Tomoegozen	巴午前	Hei'an	1184	[Madam]

礼 Offering / Courtesy

Reading	Type	Example	Kanji	Period	Date	Added Meaning
nori	N	Nobu'nori	延礼	Muromachi	1572	Prolong / Stretch Out

饗 Banquet / Food Offering

Reading	Type	Example	Kanji	Period	Date	Added Meaning
[Special]	S	Aeba	饗場	Nanboku	1392	Place / Location

式 Ceremony / Rite / Method / System

Reading	Type	Example	Kanji	Period	Date	Added Meaning
nori	F	Noriko	式子	Hei'an	1183	[Lady]

斎 Worship / Study

Reading	Type	Example	Kanji	Period	Date	Added Meaning
SAI	S	Saitou	斎藤	Kamakura	1332	Wisteria

恵 Sanctify / Bless

Note that "we" is an obsolete syllable in the Japanese phonetic system. Thus, the name Yawe is likely to be from the Hei'an period or the Nara period.

Reading	Type	Example	Kanji	Period	Date	Added Meaning
E	F	E'nume	恵怒賣	Nara	784	Valor / Anger / Rage
E	S	Era	恵良	Nanboku	1392	Good / Superior
we	F	Yawe	夜恵	Uncertain	1600	Evening

気 Spirit / Breath / Health

Reading	Type	Example	Kanji	Period	Date	Added Meaning
KI	S	Kehi	気比	Nanboku	1392	Measure Up / Strive
KI	S	Waki	和気	Nanboku	1392	Peace / Tranquility

祐 Divine Help

Reading	Type	Example	Kanji	Period	Date	Added Meaning
suke	N	Masasuke	政祐	Nanboku	1392	Govern / Rule
suke	N	Mitsusuke	満祐	Muromachi	1572	Become Full / Abundant
suke	N	Mu'nesuke	宗祐	Nanboku	1392	Master an Art
suke	N	Norisuke	則祐	Nanboku	1392	Make an Example
suke	N	Suke'aki	祐明	Kamakura	1332	Bright
suke	N	Sukechika	祐親	Hei'an	1183	Intimate
suke	N	Sukeharu	祐春	Kamakura	1332	Spring (Season)
suke	N	Sukekiyo	祐清	Kamakura	1332	Pure
suke	N	Sukemochi	祐茂	Kamakura	1332	Blossoming
suke	N	Suke'nari	祐成	Kamakura	1332	Become / Exist
suke	N	Suke'nobu	祐信	Kamakura	1332	Belief / Faith
suke	N	Suke'nori	祐則	Muromachi	1572	Make an Example
suke	N	Suke'omi	祐臣	Kamakura	1332	
suke	N	Sukeshige	祐茂	Kamakura	1332	Blossoming
suke	N	Suketoki	祐時	Kamakura	1332	Time / Era
suke	N	Suketsu'ne	祐経	Kamakura	1332	True Path
suke	N	Sukeyasu	祐泰	Hei'an	1183	Peace / Plenitude
suke	N	Takasuke	高祐	Sengoku	1568	Tall
suke	N	Takasuke	隆祐	Kamakura	1332	Grow / Pile Up

禅 Zen

Reading	Type	Example	Kanji	Period	Date	Added Meaning
ZEN	F	Zenni	禅尼	Kamakura	1332	Buddhist Nun

禰 Oracle

Reading	Type	Example	Kanji	Period	Date	Added Meaning
ne	F	Neko	禰子	Nanboku	1392	[Lady]
ne	F	Ne'ne	禰々	Momoyama	1438	
ne	F	Ne'neme	禰々女	Nanboku	1392	[Woman]
ne	S	So'ne	曾禰	Uncertain	1600	Formerly / Ever

貴 Precious

Reading	Type	Example	Kanji	Period	Date	Added Meaning
KI	F	Miyuki	美由貴	Uncertain	1600	Beauty + Purpose
taka	F	Takako	貴子	Hei'an	1183	[Lady]

雅 High Quality

Reading	Type	Example	Kanji	Period	Date	Added Meaning
masa	F	Masako	雅子	Hei'an	1183	[Lady]
masa	N	Akimasa	顕雅	Kamakura	1332	High Status
masa	N	Arimasa	有雅	Kamakura	1332	Exists
masa	N	Chikamasa	親雅	Kamakura	1332	Intimate
masa	N	Hiromasa	博雅	Uncertain	1600	Well Traveled / Learned
masa	N	Ka'nemasa	兼雅	Hei'an	1183	Unite
masa	N	Kinmasa	公雅	Kamakura	1332	Noble / Official
masa	N	Masa'ari	雅有	Kamakura	1241	Exists
masa	N	Masachika	雅親	Sengoku	1490	Intimate
masa	N	Masa'ie	雅家	Kamakura	1332	Rural House / Family
masa	N	Masakata	雅賢	Hei'an	1183	Genius
masa	N	Masakiyo	雅清	Muromachi	1390	Pure
masa	N	Masamichi	雅通	Uncertain	1600	Pass Through
masa	N	Masa'naga	雅長	Hei'an	1183	Long
masa	N	Masasada	雅定	Hei'an	1183	Determine
masa	N	Masasuke	雅助	Muromachi	1572	Deputy (Rescue / Assist)
masa	N	Masatada	雅忠	Kamakura	1332	Faithful / Loyal
masa	N	Masataka	雅隆	Kamakura	1332	Grow / Pile Up
masa	N	Masatsu'na	雅綱	Uncertain	1600	Net
masa	N	Masatsu'ne	雅経	Kamakura	1332	True Path
masa	N	Masa'uji	雅氏	Muromachi	1390	Family / Clan
masa	N	Masayo	雅世	Muromachi	1390	Generation / Life
masa	N	Masayuki	雅幸	Muromachi	1390	Happy / Tattoo
masa	N	Masayuki	雅行	Kamakura	1332	Going To / Bound For
masa	N	Masaza'ne	雅実	Uncertain	1600	Reality
masa	N	Michimasa	道雅	Uncertain	1600	Road / Way
masa	N	Mitsumasa	満雅	Muromachi	1572	Become Full / Abundant
masa	N	Motomasa	元雅	Muromachi	1572	Base / Original
masa	N	Narimasa	成雅	Uncertain	1600	Become / Exist
masa	N	Sadamasa	定雅	Kamakura	1332	Determine
masa	N	Sa'nemasa	実雅	Kamakura	1332	Reality
masa	N	Tadamasa	忠雅	Hei'an	1183	Faithful / Loyal
masa	N	Tomomasa	朝雅	Kamakura	1332	Morning

尚 Excellence

Reading	Type	Example	Kanji	Period	Date	Added Meaning
hisa	F	Hisako	尚子	Hei'an	1183	[Lady]
hisa	F	Hisa'uji	尚氏	Muromachi	1572	Family / Clan
hisa	N	Hisa'nori	尚慶	Sengoku	1568	Rejoice / Deer Skin
hisa	N	Hisa'uji	尚氏	Muromachi	1572	Family / Clan
hisa	N	Hisayoshi	尚順	Sengoku	1568	Order / Sequence
hisa	N	Morohisa	師尚	Hei'an	1183	Teacher / Expert
hisa	N	Naozumi	尚純	Muromachi	1572	Natural / Pure
hisa	N	Shigehisa	重尚	Kamakura	1246	Heavy / Serious
hisa	N	Tomohisa	知尚	Kamakura	1332	Knowledge
hisa	N	Yorihisa	頼尚	Nanboku	1392	Request / Ask
hisa	N	Yoshihisa	義尚	Kamakura	1465	Fealty
nao	N	Nori'nao	宣尚	Muromachi	1572	Proclamation
nao	N	Nori'nao	則尚	Muromachi	1572	Make an Example

豊 Noble

Reading	Type	Example	Kanji	Period	Date	Added Meaning
BU	S	Bunzou	豊三	Hei'an	1183	Three
toshi	F	Toshimame	豊島賣	Nara	784	Island
toshi	N	Yoshitoyo	義豊	Muromachi	1572	Fealty
toshi	S	Toshima	豊島	Hei'an	1183	Island
toyo	F	Toyome	豊女	Hei'an	1183	[Woman]
toyo	N	Hisatoyo	久豊	Muromachi	1572	Longtime
toyo	N	Ietoyo	家豊	Muromachi	1572	Rural House / Family
toyo	N	Katsutoyo	勝豊	Muromachi	1572	Conquer / Triumph
toyo	N	Kazutoyo	一豊	Sengoku	1568	One
toyo	N	Masatoyo	政豊	Muromachi	1572	Govern / Rule
toyo	N	Masatoyo	昌豊	Uncertain	1600	Clear / Bright
toyo	N	Mochitoyo	持豊	Muromachi	1572	Have / Possess
toyo	N	Noritoyo	教豊	Muromachi	1572	Teaching / Dogma
toyo	N	Toyofusa	豊房	Muromachi	1572	Monastic Cell
toyo	N	Toyomichi	豊通	Muromachi	1572	Pass Through
toyo	N	Toyomitsu	豊光	Muromachi	1572	Bright / Shining
toyo	S	Toyoda	豊田	Sengoku	1568	Rice Paddy
toyo	S	Toyotomi	豊富	Uncertain	1600	Industry
yutaka	M	Yutaka	豊	Modern	1983	

祥 Happy / Felicitous / Gift of the Gods

Reading	Type	Example	Kanji	Period	Date	Added Meaning
sachi	F	Sachiko	祥子	Nanboku	1392	[Lady]

福 Happy / Blessed

Reading	Type	Example	Kanji	Period	Date	Added Meaning
FUKU	S	Fukuhara	福原	Sengoku	1568	Meadow
FUKU	S	Fukumitsu	福光	Kamakura	1332	Bright / Shining
FUKU	S	Fukushima	福島	Sengoku	1568	Island

吉 Lucky / Fortunate

Please note that Kikkawa has a glottal stop while Kira does not.

Reading	Type	Example	Kanji	Period	Date	Added Meaning
KI	S	Kikkawa	吉川	Nanboku	1392	River
KI	S	Kira	吉良	Kamakura	1332	Good / Superior
KITSU	Y	Kakitsu	嘉吉	Muromachi	1441	Well Done
yoshi	F	Yoshikome	吉子賣	Hei'an	1183	[Lady]
yoshi	F	Yoshime	吉賣	Nara	784	
yoshi	N	Hideyoshi	秀吉	Sengoku	1568	Extraordinary / Bountiful
yoshi	N	Mitsuyoshi	光吉	Kamakura	1332	Bright / Shining
yoshi	N	Sukeyoshi	佐吉	Kamakura	1332	Military Deputy
yoshi	N	Tadayoshi	忠吉	Sengoku	1568	Faithful / Loyal
yoshi	N	Takeyoshi	武吉	Nanboku	1392	Bravery / Military Force
yoshi	N	Yoshimasa	吉正	Uncertain	1600	Unerring / Genuine
yoshi	N	Yoshimitsu	吉光	Kamakura	1332	Bright / Shining
yoshi	N	Yoshitaka	吉隆	Kamakura	1332	Grow / Pile Up
yoshi	S	Yoshikawa	吉川	Sengoku	1568	River
yoshi	S	Yoshimi	吉見	Kamakura	1332	Vantage / View / Vista
yoshi	S	Yoshimizu	吉水	Nanboku	1392	Water

仁 Precious / Benevolence (Classical Chinese)

While this *kanji* is commonly found in the *nanori* of Japanese emperors, it is neither reserved to the imperial family nor do all emperors bear *nanori* incorporating this *kanji*. Satake Yoshihito 佐竹義仁 is an example of a *bushi* 武士 with such a *nanori*. His biographic entry in *Kamakura Muromachi Jinmei Jiten* does not indicate any relationship with the imperial family. Further, Go-Murakami Tennou 後村上天皇 was first known as Nori'naga 憲良 and later as Nagayoshi 良義. Finally, when this *kanji* takes its Chinese reading, it can form part of the *houmyou* 法名 of a monk or the *gagou* 雅号 of an artisan. Ka'ou Ninga 可翁仁賀 was a sumie artist with a *gagou* incorporating this character.

Reading	Type	Example	Kanji	Period	Date	Added Meaning
NI	F	Nikiko	仁善子	Hei'an	1183	Perform Well + [Lady]
NI	S	Niki	仁木	Kamakura	1332	Tree
NI	S	Nishi'na	仁科	Kamakura	1332	Quality / Type / Specialty
NIN	H	Ninga	仁賀	Nanboku	1392	Celebrate A Gain
NIN	Y	Ei'nin	永仁	Kamakura	1293	Forever
NIN	Y	Gennin	元仁	Kamakura	1224	Base / Original
NIN	Y	Kannin	寛仁	Hei'an	1017	Domestic Tranquility
NIN	Y	Kennin	建仁	Kamakura	1201	Found / Build / Construct
NIN	Y	Nin'an	仁安	Kamakura	1166	Gentle / Safe / Secure
NIN	Y	Ninji	仁治	Kamakura	1240	Govern / Rule
NIN	Y	Ninpei	仁平	Hei'an	1151	Peace / Tranquility
NIN	Y	Ou'nin	応仁	Sengoku	1467	Worthy / Suitable
NIN	Y	Ryaku'nin	歴仁	Kamakura	1238	Progress / Pass Through
NIN	Y	Tennin	天仁	Hei'an	1108	Sky / Heaven
hito	N	Arihito	有仁	Uncertain	1600	Exists
hito	N	Toshihito	利仁	Hei'an	1183	Produce Results
hito	N	Yoshihito	義仁	Muromachi	1572	Fealty

占 Misfortune

Reading	Type	Example	Kanji	Period	Date	Added Meaning
ura	F	Urako	占子	Hei'an	1183	[Lady]

信 Belief / Faith

Reading	Type	Example	Kanji	Period	Date	Added Meaning
SHIN	H	Shingen	信玄	Sengoku	1568	
makoto	N	Makoto	信	Uncertain	1600	
nobu	F	Nobuko	信子	Hei'an	1183	[Lady]
nobu	N	Aki'nobu	顕信	Nanboku	1392	High Status
nobu	N	Aki'nobu	朝信	Sengoku	1568	Morning
nobu	N	Ari'nobu	有信	Muromachi	1572	Exists
nobu	N	Chika'nobu	親信	Hei'an	1183	Intimate
nobu	N	Haru'nobu	晴信	Uncertain	1600	Clear (Sky)
nobu	N	Hisa'nobu	久信	Sengoku	1568	Longtime
nobu	N	Kage'nobu	景信	Muromachi	1572	Bright / Magnificent
nobu	N	Ka'ne'nobu	兼信	Kamakura	1332	Unite
nobu	N	Kore'nobu	惟信	Kamakura	1332	This / Here
nobu	N	Ku'ni'nobu	国信	Muromachi	1572	Country / Rural Area
nobu	N	Masa'nobu	正信	Muromachi	1572	Unerring / Genuine
nobu	N	Masa'nobu	昌信	Uncertain	1600	Clear / Bright
nobu	N	Michi'nobu	通信	Kamakura	1332	Pass Through
nobu	N	Michi'nobu	道信	Uncertain	1600	Road / Way
nobu	N	Mitsu'nobu	光信	Muromachi	1572	Bright / Shining
nobu	N	Mochi'nobu	持信	Muromachi	1572	Have / Possess
nobu	N	Mori'nobu	盛信	Uncertain	1600	Plentiful / Piled Up
nobu	N	Moro'nobu	師信	Kamakura	1332	Teacher / Expert
nobu	N	Moto'nobu	元信	Uncertain	1600	Base / Original
nobu	N	Mu'ne'nobu	宗信	Uncertain	1600	Master an Art
nobu	N	Nao'nobu	直信	Nanboku	1392	Adjust / Correct
nobu	N	Nobu'aki	信詮	Uncertain	1600	Explicit / Clear
nobu	N	Nobu'aki	信章	Hei'an	1183	Writing / Elucidate
nobu	N	Nobu'ari	信有	Muromachi	1572	Exists
nobu	N	Nobuchika	信親	Muromachi	1572	Intimate
nobu	N	Nobufusa	信房	Kamakura	1332	Monastic Cell
nobu	N	Nobuharu	信春	Nanboku	1392	Spring (Season)
nobu	N	Nobuhiro	信広	Muromachi	1572	Spacious / Expansive
nobu	N	Nobuhisa	信久	Sengoku	1568	Longtime
nobu	N	Nobukado	信廉	Uncertain	1600	Reason / Justification
nobu	N	Nobuka'ne	信兼	Hei'an	1183	Unite
nobu	N	Nobukata	信賢	Muromachi	1572	Genius
nobu	N	Nobukata	信方	Uncertain	1600	Direction / Method
nobu	N	Nobukimi	信君	Uncertain	1600	King / Emperor
nobu	N	Nobukiyo	信清	Kamakura	1332	Pure
nobu	N	Nobumasa	信政	Kamakura	1332	Govern / Rule
nobu	N	Nobumasa	信昌	Sengoku	1465	Clear / Bright
nobu	N	Nobumasu	信増	Nanboku	1392	Live Long / Prosper
nobu	N	Nobumitsu	信光	Kamakura	1248	Bright / Shining
nobu	N	Nobumitsu	信満	Muromachi	1417	Become Full / Abundant
nobu	N	Nobumoto	信元	Muromachi	1572	Base / Original
nobu	N	Nobu'naga	信長	Kamakura	1332	Long
nobu	N	Nobu'nari	信業	Uncertain	1600	Industry / Diligence
nobu	N	Nobu'nari	信成	Sengoku	1568	Become / Exist
nobu	N	Nobu'nori	信乗	Sengoku	1568	Mount / Multiply
nobu	N	Nobu'nori	信範	Hei'an	1183	Required Form / Pattern
nobu	N	Nobusada	信貞	Nanboku	1392	Correct Spirit
nobu	N	Nobusada	信定	Kamakura	1332	Determine
nobu	N	Nobusaka	信栄	Sengoku	1568	Bountiful / Fruitful
nobu	N	Nobusato	信達	Uncertain	1600	Carry / Deliver

Reading	Type	Example	Kanji	Period	Date	Added Meaning
nobu	N	Nobushige	信重	Muromachi	1450	Heavy / Serious
nobu	N	Nobushige	信繁	Uncertain	1600	Bloom / Bouquet
nobu	N	Nobushige	信茂	Uncertain	1600	Blossoming
nobu	N	Nobusuke	信資	Kamakura	1332	Raw Materials
nobu	N	Nobutada	信忠	Kamakura	1332	Faithful / Loyal
nobu	N	Nobutaka	信隆	Hei'an	1183	Grow / Pile Up
nobu	N	Nobutake	信武	Nanboku	1392	Bravery / Military Force
nobu	N	Nobuta'ne	信胤	Nanboku	1392	Blood Heir
nobu	N	Nobutatsu	信龍	Uncertain	1600	Dragon
nobu	N	Nobutoki	信時	Kamakura	1332	Time / Era
nobu	N	Nobutomo	信友	Uncertain	1600	Friend
nobu	N	Nobutoo	信遠	Hei'an	1183	Far
nobu	N	Nobutora	信虎	Sengoku	1519	Tiger
nobu	N	Nobutoshi	信俊	Uncertain	1600	Emotional
nobu	N	Nobutsugi	信次	Uncertain	1600	Next
nobu	N	Nobutsugu	信嗣	Kamakura	1332	Successor
nobu	N	Nobutsu'na	信綱	Kamakura	1332	Net
nobu	N	Nobutsura	信連	Hei'an	1183	Bring Along
nobu	N	Nobuyasu	信康	Uncertain	1600	Strong / Confident
nobu	N	Nobuyori	信頼	Hei'an	1183	Request / Ask
nobu	N	Nobuyoshi	信義	Kamakura	1332	Fealty
nobu	N	Nobuyoshi	信能	Hei'an	1183	Talent / Ability
nobu	N	Nobuyuki	信之	Sengoku	1568	Go / Depart
nobu	N	Nobuza'ne	信実	Kamakura	1332	Reality
nobu	N	Shige'nobu	重信	Kamakura	1332	Heavy / Serious
nobu	N	Suke'nobu	助信	Kamakura	1332	Deputy (Rescue / Assist)
nobu	N	Suke'nobu	祐信	Kamakura	1332	Divine Help
nobu	N	Tada'nobu	忠信	Kamakura	1332	Faithful / Loyal
nobu	N	Taka'nobu	高信	Kamakura	1332	Tall
nobu	N	Taka'nobu	隆信	Hei'an	1183	Grow / Pile Up
nobu	N	Tame'nobu	為信	Kamakura	1332	Purpose / Goal
nobu	N	Ta'ne'nobu	胤信	Kamakura	1332	Blood Heir
nobu	N	Toki'nobu	時信	Kamakura	1332	Time / Era
nobu	N	Tsugu'nobu	継信	Kamakura	1184	Connect / Adopt
nobu	N	Tsu'ne'nobu	経信	Muromachi	1572	True Path
nobu	N	Uji'nobu	氏信	Kamakura	1332	Family / Clan
nobu	N	Yasu'nobu	康信	Kamakura	1332	Strong / Confident
nobu	N	Yori'nobu	頼信	Kamakura	1332	Request / Ask
nobu	N	Yoshi'nobu	義信	Kamakura	1332	Fealty

教 Teaching / Dogma

Reading	Type	Example	Kanji	Period	Date	Added Meaning
nori	N	Ari'nori	有教	Kamakura	1332	Exists
nori	N	Chika'nori	親教	Muromachi	1572	Intimate
nori	N	Fuyu'nori	冬教	Kamakura	1332	Winter
nori	N	Ie'nori	家教	Kamakura	1332	Rural House / Family
nori	N	Ka'ne'nori	兼教	Kamakura	1332	Unite
nori	N	Kinnori	公教	Hei'an	1183	Noble / Official
nori	N	Kiyo'nori	清教	Uncertain	1600	Pure
nori	N	Michi'nori	道教	Nanboku	1392	Road / Way
nori	N	Mitsu'nori	満教	Muromachi	1572	Become Full / Abundant
nori	N	Moro'nori	師教	Kamakura	1332	Teacher / Expert
nori	N	Moto'nori	基教	Kamakura	1332	Foundation
nori	N	Mu'ne'nori	宗教	Kamakura	1332	Master an Art
nori	N	Norifuji	教藤	Nanboku	1392	Wisteria

Thematic Dictionary — Spiritual Traits 235

Reading	Type	Example	Kanji	Period	Date	Added Meaning
nori	N	Norifusa	教房	Muromachi	1572	Monastic Cell
nori	N	Norifuyu	教冬	Nanboku	1392	Winter
nori	N	Norihiro	教弘	Muromachi	1572	Draw / Stretch
nori	N	Norikage	教景	Muromachi	1572	Bright / Magnificent
nori	N	Norikiyo	教清	Muromachi	1572	Pure
nori	N	Norimasa	教政	Muromachi	1572	Govern / Rule
nori	N	Norimichi	教通	Uncertain	1600	Pass Through
nori	N	Norimori	教盛	Hei'an	1183	Plentiful / Piled Up
nori	N	Norimoto	教基	Muromachi	1572	Foundation
nori	N	Nori'oki	教興	Nanboku	1392	Happen / Begin
nori	N	Norisada	教定	Kamakura	1332	Determine
nori	N	Norishige	教成	Kamakura	1332	Become / Exist
nori	N	Noritaka	教高	Nanboku	1392	Tall
nori	N	Noritaka	教隆	Kamakura	1332	Grow / Pile Up
nori	N	Noritoki	教言	Nanboku	1392	Speak Truthfully
nori	N	Noritomo	教具	Muromachi	1572	Tool / Implement
nori	N	Noritomo	教朝	Muromachi	1572	Morning
nori	N	Noritoo	教遠	Nanboku	1392	Far
nori	N	Noritoyo	教豊	Muromachi	1572	Noble
nori	N	Noritsugu	教嗣	Muromachi	1572	Successor
nori	N	Noritsu'ne	教経	Hei'an	1183	True Path
nori	N	Noriyasu	教康	Muromachi	1572	Strong / Confident
nori	N	Noriyuki	教之	Muromachi	1572	Go / Depart
nori	N	Noriza'ne	教実	Kamakura	1332	Reality
nori	N	Sa'ne'nori	実教	Kamakura	1332	Reality
nori	N	Tame'nori	為教	Kamakura	1332	Purpose / Goal
nori	N	Tomo'nori	具教	Uncertain	1600	Tool / Implement
nori	N	Tsugu'nori	嗣教	Muromachi	1572	Successor
nori	N	Tsu'ne'nori	経教	Muromachi	1572	True Path
nori	N	Yoshi'nori	義教	Muromachi	1572	Fealty
nori	N	Yoshi'nori	良教	Kamakura	1332	Good / Superior

法 Law

Note that those names ending with Houshinnou 法親王 are generally the names of close relatives of the emperor or other higher nobility. For example. Kakukai Hosshinnou was the son of an emperor. As already noted, Shinnou 親王 is a titular element awarded by the emperor. In these names, 法 (HOU) appears to indicate the individual has taken the tonsure and entered into official retirement as a Buddhist lay monk. Eichuu Houshun was a Zen Buddhist monk.

Reading	Type	Example	Kanji	Period	Date	Added Meaning
HOU	B	Jirouhoujimaru	次郎法師丸	Muromachi	1572	Second Son + Teacher / Expert
HOU	H	En'e Houshinnou	円恵法親王	Hei'an	1152	Sanctify / Bless
HOU	H	Enjo Houshinnou	円助法親王	Kamakura	1332	Rescue
HOU	H	Eichuu Houshun	英仲法俊	Muromachi	1572	Gentle + Emotional / Second
HOU	H	Eijou Houshinnou	永助法親王	Muromachi	1572	Forever + Rescue
HOU	H	Houshi	法師	Muromachi	1374	Teacher / Expert
HOTSU	H	Kakukai Houshinnou	覚快法親王	Kamakura	1181	Insight + Pleasure / Agreement
nori	F	Nori	法	Uncertain	1600	

勢 Vigor / Spirit / Elan Vital

Reading	Type	Example	Kanji	Period	Date	Added Meaning
SE	S	Ise	伊勢	Nanboku	1392	This
SE	S	Nose	能勢	Kamakura	1332	Talent / Ability

倫 Obligatory Path

Reading	Type	Example	Kanji	Period	Date	Added Meaning
tomo	N	Tomo'naga	倫長	Kamakura	1332	Long
tomo	N	Tomoshige	倫重	Kamakura	1332	Heavy / Serious
tomo	N	Tomotsu'ne	倫経	Kamakura	1332	True Path

❖ Actions & Activities ❖

行 Going / Bound For / Bring

Reading	Type	Example	Kanji	Period	Date	Added Meaning
tsura	N	Masatsura	正行	Nanboku	1392	Unerring / Genuine
yuki	N	Chikayuki	親行	Kamakura	1332	Intimate
yuki	N	Hideyuki	秀行	Kamakura	1332	Extraordinary / Bountiful
yuki	N	Ieyuki	家行	Kamakura	1332	Rural House / Family
yuki	N	Kin'yuki	公行	Muromachi	1572	Noble / Official
yuki	N	Kiyoyuki	清行	Sengoku	1568	Pure
yuki	N	Masayuki	雅行	Kamakura	1332	High Quality
yuki	N	Masayuki	政行	Nanboku	1392	Govern / Rule
yuki	N	Masayuki	正行	Uncertain	1600	Unerring / Genuine
yuki	N	Michiyuki	通行	Muromachi	1572	Pass Through
yuki	N	Mitsuyuki	光行	Kamakura	1332	Bright / Shining
yuki	N	Moroyuki	師行	Nanboku	1392	Teacher / Expert
yuki	N	Motoyuki	基行	Kamakura	1332	Foundation
yuki	N	Mu'neyuki	宗行	Kamakura	1332	Master an Art
yuki	N	Nagayuki	永行	Muromachi	1572	Forever
yuki	N	Nagayuki	長行	Sengoku	1568	Long
yuki	N	Sadayuki	貞行	Muromachi	1572	Correct Spirit
yuki	N	Tadayuki	忠行	Muromachi	1572	Faithful / Loyal
yuki	N	Tameyuki	為行	Kamakura	1332	Purpose / Goal
yuki	N	Ta'neyuki	胤行	Kamakura	1332	Blood Heir
yuki	N	Tokiyuki	時行	Kamakura	1332	Time / Era
yuki	N	Tomoyuki	具行	Kamakura	1332	Tool / Implement
yuki	N	Tomoyuki	知行	Nanboku	1392	Knowledge
yuki	N	Toshiyuki	敏行	Uncertain	1600	Very Rapid Hard Work
yuki	N	Yasuyuki	頼行	Nanboku	1392	Request / Ask
yuki	N	Yoriyuki	頼行	Kamakura	1332	Request / Ask
yuki	N	Yoshiyuki	義行	Hei'an	1183	Fealty
yuki	N	Yuki'aki	行章	Kamakura	1332	Writing / Elucidate
yuki	N	Yuki'ari	行有	Kamakura	1332	Exists
yuki	N	Yukifuji	行藤	Kamakura	1332	Wisteria
yuki	N	Yukifusa	行房	Nanboku	1392	Monastic Cell
yuki	N	Yukihide	行秀	Nanboku	1392	Extraordinary / Bountiful
yuki	N	Yukihira	行平	Kamakura	1332	Tranquility
yuki	N	Yukihiro	行広	Muromachi	1572	Spacious / Expansive
yuki	N	Yukihisa	行久	Kamakura	1332	Longtime
yuki	N	Yuki'ie	行家	Kamakura	1332	Rural House / Family
yuki	N	Yukikata	行方	Kamakura	1332	Direction / Method
yuki	N	Yukikiyo	行清	Kamakura	1332	Pure
yuki	N	Yukimasa	行政	Kamakura	1332	Govern / Rule
yuki	N	Yukimichi	行通	Nanboku	1392	Pass Through
yuki	N	Yukimitsu	行光	Kamakura	1332	Bright / Shining
yuki	N	Yukimori	行盛	Kamakura	1332	Plentiful / Piled Up

Reading	Type	Example	Kanji	Period	Date	Added Meaning
yuki	N	Yukimu'ne	行宗	Hei'an	1183	Master an Art
yuki	N	Yukimura	行村	Kamakura	1332	Village
yuki	N	Yuki'naga	行長	Kamakura	1332	Long
yuki	N	Yuki'nao	行直	Nanboku	1392	Adjust / Correct
yuki	N	Yuki'nari	行成	Uncertain	1600	Become / Exist
yuki	N	Yuki'o	行雄	Kamakura	1332	Strength / Courage / Bravery
yuki	N	Yukisada	行貞	Kamakura	1332	Correct Spirit
yuki	N	Yukisuke	行佐	Kamakura	1332	Military Deputy
yuki	N	Yukitada	行忠	Muromachi	1572	Faithful / Loyal
yuki	N	Yukitaka	行高	Kamakura	1332	Tall
yuki	N	Yukitaka	行隆	Hei'an	1183	Grow / Pile Up
yuki	N	Yukitoki	行時	Nanboku	1392	Time / Era
yuki	N	Yukitomo	行朝	Nanboku	1392	Morning
yuki	N	Yukitsu'na	行綱	Hei'an	1183	Net
yuki	N	Yuki'uji	行氏	Kamakura	1332	Family / Clan
yuki	N	Yukiyasu	行康	Muromachi	1572	Strong / Confident
yuki	N	Yukiyasu	行泰	Kamakura	1332	Peace / Plenitude
yuki	N	Yukiyori	行頼	Kamakura	1332	Request / Ask
yuki	N	Yukiyoshi	行義	Kamakura	1332	Fealty
yuki	N	Yukiza'ne	行実	Kamakura	1332	Reality

之 Go / Depart

Reading	Type	Example	Kanji	Period	Date	Added Meaning
yuki	N	Masayuki	正之	Sengoku	1568	Unerring / Genuine
yuki	N	Masuyuki	益之	Muromachi	1572	Grow Numerous / Overflow
yuki	N	Michiyuki	通之	Muromachi	1572	Pass Through
yuki	N	Mochiyuki	持之	Muromachi	1572	Have / Possess
yuki	N	Nobuyuki	信之	Sengoku	1568	Belief / Faith
yuki	N	Noriyuki	教之	Muromachi	1572	Teaching / Dogma
yuki	N	Shigeyuki	重之	Muromachi	1572	Heavy / Serious
yuki	N	Tameyuki	為之	Muromachi	1572	Purpose / Goal
yuki	N	Ujiyuki	氏之	Muromachi	1572	Family / Clan
yuki	N	Yasuyuki	康之	Sengoku	1568	Strong / Confident
yuki	N	Yoriyuki	頼之	Nanboku	1392	Request / Ask

選 Follow After / Chosen

Reading	Type	Example	Kanji	Period	Date	Added Meaning
nobu	F	Nobuko	選子	Hei'an	1183	[Lady]

止 Stop / Desist

Repeated sound patterns and morphemes are rather common in feminine given names and rare in surnames. They appear to be practically nonexistent in masculine *nanori* and *houmyou*.

Reading	Type	Example	Kanji	Period	Date	Added Meaning
to	F	Totome	止々女	Hei'an	1183	[Woman]

Thematic Dictionary — **Actions & Activities**   239

取 Catch / Gather

This *kanji* is commonly found as the substantive element in occupational names. This is because Japanese is a verbal final language and the verb is nominalized to produce an occupational name.

Reading	Type	Example	Kanji	Period	Date	Added Meaning
tori	S	Takatori	鷹取	Nanboku	1392	Hawk

達 Carry / Deliver

Reading	Type	Example	Kanji	Period	Date	Added Meaning
DACHI	S	Adachi	安達	Kamakura	1332	Gentle / Safe / Secure
DACHI	S	Date	伊達	Nanboku	1392	This
sato	N	Nobusato	信達	Uncertain	1600	Belief / Faith

連 Bring Along

This *kanji* applies to animate beings who accompany somebody.

Reading	Type	Example	Kanji	Period	Date	Added Meaning
tsura	N	Ietsura	家連	Kamakura	1332	Rural House / Family
tsura	N	Ka'netsura	兼連	Nanboku	1392	Unite
tsura	N	Kintsura	公連	Muromachi	1572	Noble / Official
tsura	N	Moritsura	盛連	Kamakura	1332	Plentiful / Piled Up
tsura	N	Morotsura	師連	Kamakura	1332	Teacher / Expert
tsura	N	Mototsura	元連	Muromachi	1572	Base / Original
tsura	N	Naritsura	業連	Kamakura	1332	Industry / Diligence
tsura	N	Nobutsura	信連	Hei'an	1183	Belief / Faith
tsura	N	Sadatsura	貞連	Kamakura	1332	Correct Spirit
tsura	N	Takatsura	高連	Nanboku	1392	Tall
tsura	N	Tokitsura	時連	Kamakura	1332	Time / Era
tsura	N	Yasutsura	康連	Kamakura	1332	Strong / Confident
tsura	N	Yoshitsura	義連	Kamakura	1332	Fealty

提 Carry / Take Along

This *kanji* applies to objects which can be carried in the hand.

Reading	Type	Example	Kanji	Period	Date	Added Meaning
TEI	F	Uteme	宇提賣	Nara	784	

渡 Cross Over

Reading	Type	Example	Kanji	Period	Date	Added Meaning
TO	P	Sado	佐渡	Uncertain	1600	Military Deputy

歩 Walk

Reading	Type	Example	Kanji	Period	Date	Added Meaning
ayumi	F	Ayumime	歩女	Hei'an	1183	[Woman]

依 Follow

Reading	Type	Example	Kanji	Period	Date	Added Meaning
yori	F	Chiyorime	千依賣	Nara	784	Follow
yori	F	Teyorime	手依賣	Nara	784	Follow
yori	F	Yorime	依賣	Nara	784	
yori	N	Akiyori	秋依	Kamakura	1332	Autumn
[Special]	F	Yosamime	依羅賣	Nara	784	Fluff / Down

周 Tour / Travel / Bountiful Land

Reading	Type	Example	Kanji	Period	Date	Added Meaning
chika	F	Chikako	周子	Hei'an	1183	[Lady]
chika	N	Hirochika	広周	Muromachi	1572	Spacious / Expansive
chika	N	Korechika	伊周	Uncertain	1600	This

遊 Wander / Meander / Play

Reading	Type	Example	Kanji	Period	Date	Added Meaning
YU	S	Yusa	遊佐	Nanboku	1392	Military Deputy

訪 Visit

This *kanji* originally denoted consulting widely about something. Thus, someone travels to where other people live in order to discuss things with them.

Reading	Type	Example	Kanji	Period	Date	Added Meaning
[Special]	S	Suwa	諏訪	Nanboku	1392	Consult / Meet in Council

乗 Mount / Multiply / History Text

Originally, this *kanji* originally consisted of a man straddling a tree. Thus, its meaning was transferred to being born upon something. This character also appears in the *nanori* which is both the word for official given names and the practice of proclaiming ones lineage prior to personal combat on the battlefield.

Reading	Type	Example	Kanji	Period	Date	Added Meaning
nori	N	Nobu'nori	信乗	Sengoku	1568	Belief / Faith
taru	F	Shimatarume	島乗賣	Nara	784	Island

登 Climb / Ascend / Fly

Reading	Type	Example	Kanji	Period	Date	Added Meaning
TO	F	Totome	登々女	Muromachi	1572	[Woman]
TOU	F	Toushi	登子	Kamakura	1306	[Lady]
nari	F	Nariko	登子	Hei'an	1183	[Lady]

飛 Fly / Jump

Reading	Type	Example	Kanji	Period	Date	Added Meaning
[Special]	S	Asuka	飛鳥井	Kamakura	1332	

直　Adjust / Correct

Reading	Type	Example	Kanji	Period	Date	Added Meaning
nao	F	Nahoi	直子	Hei'an	1183	[Lady]
nao	N	Aki'nao	詮直	Nanboku	1392	Explicit / Clear
nao	N	Kinnao	公直	Kamakura	1332	Noble / Official
nao	N	Kore'nao	惟直	Kamakura	1332	This / Here
nao	N	Michi'nao	通直	Nanboku	1392	Pass Through
nao	N	Mitsu'nao	満直	Muromachi	1572	Become Full / Abundant
nao	N	Mori'nao	盛直	Hei'an	1183	Plentiful / Piled Up
nao	N	Moro'nao	師直	Hei'an	1183	Teacher / Expert
nao	N	Nahoza'ne	直実	Uncertain	1600	Reality
nao	N	Nao'aki	直顕	Kamakura	1332	High Status
nao	N	Nao'aki	直詮	Muromachi	1572	Explicit / Clear
nao	N	Nao'ie	直家	Kamakura	1332	Rural House / Family
nao	N	Naomitsu	直光	Hei'an	1183	Bright / Shining
nao	N	Naomochi	直持	Nanboku	1392	Have / Possess
nao	N	Nao'nobu	直信	Nanboku	1392	Belief / Faith
nao	N	Naosada	直貞	Nanboku	1392	Correct Spirit
nao	N	Naoshige	直重	Nanboku	1392	Heavy / Serious
nao	N	Naotoki	直時	Kamakura	1332	Time / Era
nao	N	Naotomo	直朝	Nanboku	1392	Morning
nao	N	Naotsu'ne	直経	Nanboku	1392	True Path
nao	N	Naotsu'ne	直常	Nanboku	1392	Permanent
nao	N	Nao'uji	直氏	Nanboku	1392	Family / Clan
nao	N	Naoyori	直頼	Nanboku	1392	Request / Ask
nao	N	Naoza'ne	直実	Hei'an	1183	Reality
nao	N	Sada'nao	貞直	Kamakura	1332	Correct Spirit
nao	N	Sa'ne'nao	実直	Nanboku	1392	Reality
nao	N	Taka'nao	高直	Hei'an	1183	Tall
nao	N	Ta'ne'nao	胤直	Hei'an	1183	Blood Heir
nao	N	Toki'nao	時直	Kamakura	1332	Time / Era
nao	N	Tomo'nao	朝直	Kamakura	1332	Morning
nao	N	Uji'nao	氏直	Nanboku	1392	Family / Clan
nao	N	Yori'nao	頼直	Kamakura	1332	Request / Ask
nao	N	Yoshi'nao	義直	Kamakura	1332	Fealty
nao	N	Yoshi'nao	能直	Kamakura	1332	Talent / Ability
nao	N	Yuki'nao	行直	Nanboku	1392	Going To / Bound For
nao	S	Nao'e	直江	Sengoku	1568	Inlet / Harbour / Cove
tada	N	Kazutada	一直	Sengoku	1568	One
tada	N	Mitsutada	満直	Muromachi	1572	Become Full / Abundant
tada	N	Tadafuyu	直冬	Nanboku	1392	Winter
tada	N	Tadashige	直茂	Sengoku	1568	Blossoming
tada	N	Tadatoshi	直俊	Nanboku	1392	Emotional
tada	N	Tadatsugi	直次	Sengoku	1568	Next
tada	N	Tadatsu'ne	直常	Uncertain	1600	Permanent
tada	N	Tadayasu	直保	Sengoku	1568	Guarantee
tada	N	Tadayoshi	直義	Nanboku	1392	Fealty
tada	N	Tadazumi	直澄	Sengoku	1568	Cleanse / Purify
tada	N	Yoshitada	義直	Uncertain	1600	Adjust / Correct Fealty

付 Attach / Arrive

This *kanji* has the nuance of permanence. Once attached, something is not separated.

Reading	Type	Example	Kanji	Period	Date	Added Meaning
tsuki	S	Kimotsuki	肝付	Nanboku	1392	Spirit / Courage

就 To Become / Arrive / Be Posted / Become Attached

Reading	Type	Example	Kanji	Period	Date	Added Meaning
nari	N	Moto'nari	元就	Uncertain	1600	Base / Original
nari	N	Yoshi'nari	義就	Muromachi	1572	Obligation / Fealty

使 Use

This *kanji* originally denoted using or employing a person. It was extended to mean making a person work and even using animals and inanimate objects.

Reading	Type	Example	Kanji	Period	Date	Added Meaning
[Special]	S	Teshigawara	勅使河原	Nanboku	1392	Decree + Meadow + Large River

用 Utilize / Employment / Service

This *kanji* originally denoted gathering together raw materials so that they could be made use of. This idea was extended to human service as well.

Reading	Type	Example	Kanji	Period	Date	Added Meaning
mochi	F	Mochime	用女	Hei'an	1183	[Woman]

任 Endure a Duty

Reading	Type	Example	Kanji	Period	Date	Added Meaning
TOU	N	Akitou	章任	Kamakura	1332	Writing / Elucidate
TOU	N	Ka'netou	兼任	Hei'an	1183	Unite
TOU	N	Michitou	通任	Nanboku	1392	Pass Through

勤 Daily Labour

Reading	Type	Example	Kanji	Period	Date	Added Meaning
iso	F	Isoko	勤子	Hei'an	1183	[Lady]

敏 Very Rapid Hard Work

Reading	Type	Example	Kanji	Period	Date	Added Meaning
toshi	N	Taketoshi	武敏	Nanboku	1392	Bravery / Military Force
toshi	N	Toshikage	敏景	Muromachi	1572	Bright / Magnificent
toshi	N	Toshiyuki	敏行	Uncertain	1600	Going To / Bound For
toshi	N	Yoshitoshi	義敏	Muromachi	1572	Fealty

Thematic Dictionary — **Actions & Activities**

蒔 Sow Seed / Paint

Reading	Type	Example	Kanji	Period	Date	Added Meaning
maku	S	Makuta	蒔田	Sengoku	1568	Rice Paddy

斉 Prepare / Gather

Reading	Type	Example	Kanji	Period	Date	Added Meaning
naru	N	Nariharu	斉晴	Nanboku	1392	Clear (Sky)

健 Build / Construct

Reading	Type	Example	Kanji	Period	Date	Added Meaning
KEN	M	Kentarou	健太郎	Modern	1983	First Son
take	N	Yoshitake	義健	Muromachi	1572	Fealty

堀 Dig / Carve / Excavation

Reading	Type	Example	Kanji	Period	Date	Added Meaning
hori	S	Fukahori	深堀	Kamakura	1332	Deep
hori	S	Hori	堀	Kamakura	1332	
hori	S	Horiguchi	堀口	Nanboku	1392	Mouth / Entrance
hori	S	Horikawa	堀川	Nanboku	1392	River
hori	S	Hori'o	堀尾	Sengoku	1568	Tail
hori	S	Horita	堀田	Sengoku	1568	Rice Paddy
hori	S	Hori'uchi	堀内	Sengoku	1568	Inside
hori	S	Hotta	堀田	Kamakura	1332	Rice Paddy

鎮 Quench / Immerse / Temper Steel

Reading	Type	Example	Kanji	Period	Date	Added Meaning
shige	N	Ujishige	氏鎮	Nanboku	1392	Family / Clan
shige	N	Yoshishige	義鎮	Uncertain	1600	Fealty

彩 Paint Colours

Reading	Type	Example	Kanji	Period	Date	Added Meaning
aya	F	Aya	彩	Uncertain	1600	

作 Make / Create

Reading	Type	Example	Kanji	Period	Date	Added Meaning
SAKU	S	Isaku	伊作	Kamakura	1332	This

造 Make / Manufacture

Reading	Type	Example	Kanji	Period	Date	Added Meaning
tsukuri	S	Kozukuri	木造	Nanboku	1392	Tree / Wooden

績 Spin (Thread)

This *kanji* and the reading appearing in the example are definitely vulgar.

Reading	Type	Example	Kanji	Period	Date	Added Meaning
[Special]	P	Omi	麻績	Modern	1983	Linen / Flax

結 Tie / Bind / Hold One's Breath

Reading	Type	Example	Kanji	Period	Date	Added Meaning
ui	S	Yuuki	結城	Kamakura	1332	Castle

綾 Knit / Entwine

Reading	Type	Example	Kanji	Period	Date	Added Meaning
aya	F	Aya	綾	Uncertain	1600	

織 Weave

Reading	Type	Example	Kanji	Period	Date	Added Meaning
o	S	Oda	織田	Sengoku	1568	Rice Paddy
ori	S	Nishigori	錦織	Kamakura	1332	Brocade

縫 Sew

Reading	Type	Example	Kanji	Period	Date	Added Meaning
nu	F	Ki'nu'nuhime	衣縫賣	Nara	784	Robe

干 Dry / Care For

Reading	Type	Example	Kanji	Period	Date	Added Meaning
yuki	N	Mu'neyuki	宗干	Uncertain	1600	Master an Art

支 Exchange Money

Reading	Type	Example	Kanji	Period	Date	Added Meaning
KI	F	Miyukime	御由支賣	Nara	784	Honourable + Purpose
hase	S	Hasekura	支倉	Uncertain	1600	Warehouse

富 Become Wealthy / Bountiful / Industrious

While Fuji 富士 means "industrious man," this name generally refers to the famous mountain.

Reading	Type	Example	Kanji	Period	Date	Added Meaning
FU	S	Fuji'na	富士名	Kamakura	1332	Warrior + Famous
FU	S	Obu	飯富	Uncertain	1600	Cooked Rice
to	S	Togashi	富樫	Muromachi	1572	Evergreen Oak
to	S	Toyama	富山	Uncertain	1600	Mountain
tomi	F	Tomiko	富子	Muromachi	1572	[Lady]
tomi	F	Tomime	富賣	Nara	784	
tomi	N	Yasutomi	康富	Muromachi	1572	Strong / Confident
tomi	S	Tomi'no	富野	Hei'an	1183	Wide Plain
tomi	S	Toyotomi	豊富	Uncertain	1600	Noble
tomi	S	Yasutomi	安富	Nanboku	1392	Gentle / Safe / Secure

賀 Celebrate A Gain

Reading	Type	Example	Kanji	Period	Date	Added Meaning
GA	S	Hiraga	平賀	Kamakura	1332	Tranquility
GA	S	Iga	伊賀	Kamakura	1332	This
GA	S	Kaga'i	加賀井	Sengoku	1568	Join Up / Enlist + Well
GA	S	Kagami	加賀美	Hei'an	1183	Enlist + Beauty
GA	S	Mega	目賀	Nanboku	1392	Eye
GA	S	Oosuga	大須賀	Kamakura	1332	Big + Necessity
GA	S	Shiga	志賀	Kamakura	1332	Determined
GA	S	Taga	多賀	Sengoku	1568	Many
KA	S	Hachisuka	蜂須賀	Sengoku	1568	Bee / Wasp + Small Necessity
KA	S	Takaya	高賀谷	Muromachi	1572	Tall + Valley
shige	F	Shigeko	賀子	Hei'an	1183	[Lady]

答 Answer / Reply

Reading	Type	Example	Kanji	Period	Date	Added Meaning
kotau	N	Kotau	答	Kamakura	1332	

頼 Request / Ask

Reading	Type	Example	Kanji	Period	Date	Added Meaning
yori	N	Atsuyori	敦頼	Hei'an	1183	Generous / Kind / Honest
yori	N	Fujiyori	藤頼	Muromachi	1572	Wisteria
yori	N	Kageyori	景頼	Kamakura	1332	Bright / Magnificent
yori	N	Ka'neyori	兼頼	Kamakura	1332	Unite
yori	N	Katsuyori	勝頼	Sengoku	1574	Conquer / Triumph
yori	N	Masayori	正頼	Sengoku	1568	Unerring / Genuine
yori	N	Michiyori	通頼	Kamakura	1332	Pass Through
yori	N	Mitsuyori	満頼	Hei'an	1183	Become Full / Abundant
yori	N	Mochiyori	持頼	Muromachi	1572	Have / Possess
yori	N	Moroyori	師頼	Uncertain	1600	Teacher / Expert
yori	N	Motoyori	基頼	Kamakura	1332	Foundation
yori	N	Mu'neyori	宗頼	Kamakura	1332	Master an Art
yori	N	Nagayori	長頼	Kamakura	1332	Long

yori	N	Nakayori	仲頼	Hei'an	1183	Middle of a Group
yori	N	Naoyori	直頼	Nanboku	1392	Adjust / Correct
yori	N	Nobuyori	信頼	Hei'an	1183	Belief / Faith
yori	N	Noriyori	憲頼	Hei'an	1183	Example / Pattern
yori	N	Noriyori	詮頼	Nanboku	1392	Explicit / Clear
yori	N	Noriyori	則頼	Sengoku	1568	Make an Example
yori	N	Noriyori	範頼	Hei'an	1183	Required Form / Pattern
yori	N	Sadayori	貞頼	Kamakura	1332	Correct Spirit
yori	N	Sadayori	定頼	Nanboku	1392	Determine
yori	N	Sakiyori	前頼	Nanboku	1392	Antecedent
yori	N	Sa'neyori	実頼	Uncertain	1600	Reality
yori	N	Shigeyori	重頼	Kamakura	1332	Heavy / Serious
yori	N	Sukeyori	資頼	Hei'an	1183	Raw Materials
yori	N	Tadayori	惟頼	Uncertain	1600	This / Here
yori	N	Tadayori	忠頼	Kamakura	1332	Faithful / Loyal
yori	N	Tameyori	為頼	Kamakura	1332	Purpose / Goal
yori	N	Ta'neyori	胤頼	Kamakura	1332	Blood Heir
yori	N	Tokiyori	時頼	Kamakura	1332	Time / Era
yori	N	Toshiyori	俊頼	Uncertain	1600	Emotional
yori	N	Tsu'neyori	経頼	Kamakura	1332	True Path
yori	N	Ujiyori	氏頼	Nanboku	1392	Family / Clan
yori	N	Yasuyori	康頼	Hei'an	1183	Strong / Confident
yori	N	Yasuyuki	頼行	Nanboku	1392	Going To / Bound For
yori	N	Yori'aki	頼章	Kamakura	1332	Writing / Elucidate
yori	N	Yori'aki	頼朝	Nanboku	1392	Morning
yori	N	Yori'aki	頼明	Sengoku	1568	Bright
yori	N	Yori'ari	頼有	Nanboku	1392	Exists
yori	N	Yorichika	頼親	Kamakura	1332	Intimate
yori	N	Yorifuji	頼藤	Nanboku	1392	Wisteria
yori	N	Yorifusa	頼房	Nanboku	1392	Monastic Cell
yori	N	Yoriharu	頼治	Nanboku	1392	Govern / Rule
yori	N	Yoriharu	頼春	Nanboku	1392	Spring (Season)
yori	N	Yorihide	頼秀	Kamakura	1332	Extraordinary / Bountiful
yori	N	Yorihira	頼平	Kamakura	1332	Tranquility
yori	N	Yorihisa	頼久	Muromachi	1572	Longtime
yori	N	Yorihisa	頼尚	Nanboku	1392	Excellence
yori	N	Yori'ie	頼家	Kamakura	1332	Rural House / Family
yori	N	Yorika'ne	頼兼	Hei'an	1183	Unite
yori	N	Yorikata	頼方	Hei'an	1183	Direction / Method
yori	N	Yorikawa	頼賢	Uncertain	1600	Genius
yori	N	Yorikazu	頼員	Kamakura	1332	Member
yori	N	Yorikiyo	頼清	Nanboku	1392	Pure
yori	N	Yorimasa	頼政	Hei'an	1183	Govern / Rule
yori	N	Yorimasu	頼益	Muromachi	1572	Grow Numerous / Overflow
yori	N	Yorimichi	頼通	Uncertain	1600	Pass Through
yori	N	Yorimitsu	頼光	Uncertain	1600	Bright / Shining
yori	N	Yorimori	頼盛	Hei'an	1183	Plentiful / Piled Up
yori	N	Yorimoto	頼基	Kamakura	1332	Foundation
yori	N	Yorimoto	頼元	Nanboku	1392	Base / Original
yori	N	Yorimu'ne	頼宗	Nanboku	1392	Master an Art
yori	N	Yori'naga	頼長	Uncertain	1600	Long
yori	N	Yori'nao	頼直	Kamakura	1332	Adjust / Correct
yori	N	Yori'nari	頼業	Hei'an	1183	Industry / Diligence
yori	N	Yori'nari	頼成	Uncertain	1600	Become / Exist
yori	N	Yori'nobu	頼信	Kamakura	1332	Belief / Faith
yori	N	Yorisada	頼貞	Kamakura	1332	Correct Spirit
yori	N	Yorishige	頼重	Kamakura	1332	Heavy / Serious

Thematic Dictionary — **Actions & Activities**   247

Reading	Type	Example	Kanji	Period	Date	Added Meaning
yori	N	Yorishige	頼茂	Kamakura	1332	Blossoming
yori	N	Yorisuke	頼助	Uncertain	1600	Deputy (Rescue / Assist)
yori	N	Yorisuke	頼輔	Hei'an	1183	Ministerial Deputy
yori	N	Yoritada	頼忠	Nanboku	1392	Faithful / Loyal
yori	N	Yoritaka	頼隆	Kamakura	1332	Grow / Pile Up
yori	N	Yorita'ne	頼胤	Kamakura	1332	Blood Heir
yori	N	Yoritoki	頼時	Nanboku	1392	Time / Era
yori	N	Yoritomo	頼朝	Kamakura	1332	Morning
yori	N	Yoritoo	頼遠	Nanboku	1392	Far
yori	N	Yoritoshi	頼俊	Kamakura	1332	Emotional
yori	N	Yoritsugu	頼嗣	Kamakura	1332	Successor
yori	N	Yoritsugu	頼次	Nanboku	1392	Next
yori	N	Yoritsu'na	頼綱	Kamakura	1332	Net
yori	N	Yoritsu'ne	頼経	Kamakura	1332	True Path
yori	N	Yori'uji	頼氏	Kamakura	1332	Family / Clan
yori	N	Yoriyasu	頼康	Nanboku	1392	Strong / Confident
yori	N	Yoriyasu	頼泰	Kamakura	1332	Peace / Plenitude
yori	N	Yoriyoshi	頼義	Uncertain	1600	Fealty
yori	N	Yoriyuki	頼行	Kamakura	1332	Going To / Bound For
yori	N	Yoriyuki	頼之	Nanboku	1392	Go / Depart
yori	N	Yoriza'ne	頼実	Kamakura	1332	Reality
yori	N	Yoshiyori	義頼	Uncertain	1600	Fealty
yori	N	Yukiyori	行頼	Kamakura	1332	Going To / Bound For

善 Perform Well

Reading	Type	Example	Kanji	Period	Date	Added Meaning
ZEN	M	Zengorou	善五郎	Uncertain	1600	Number Five Son
ZEN	M	Zenjirou	善次郎	Uncertain	1600	Second / Next + Son
yoshi	N	Koreyoshi	是善	Hei'an	880	Definite
yoshi	N	Yoshi'nari	善成	Nanboku	1392	Become / Exist
yoshi	S	Miyoshi	三善	Kamakura	1332	Three

卜 Divine / Foretell / Prophesy

Reading	Type	Example	Kanji	Period	Date	Added Meaning
ura	S	Urabe	卜部	Muromachi	1572	Monopoly Corporation

定 Fix / Specify / Determine

Reading	Type	Example	Kanji	Period	Date	Added Meaning
sada	N	Akisada	顕定	Muromachi	1572	High Status
sada	N	Arisada	有定	Muromachi	1572	Exists
sada	N	Hirosada	広定	Sengoku	1568	Spacious / Expansive
sada	N	Iesada	家定	Kamakura	1332	Rural House / Family
sada	N	Kinsada	公定	Kamakura	1332	Noble / Official
sada	N	Kiyosada	清定	Kamakura	1332	Pure
sada	N	Masasada	雅定	Hei'an	1183	High Quality
sada	N	Mitsusada	光定	Kamakura	1332	Bright / Shining
sada	N	Nagasada	長定	Kamakura	1332	Long
sada	N	Narisada	成定	Hei'an	1183	Become / Exist
sada	N	Nobusada	信定	Kamakura	1332	Belief / Faith
sada	N	Norisada	教定	Kamakura	1332	Teaching / Dogma

Reading	Type	Example	Kanji	Period	Date	Added Meaning
sada	N	Norisada	憲定	Muromachi	1572	Example / Pattern
sada	N	Sadachika	定親	Kamakura	1332	Intimate
sada	N	Sadafusa	定房	Kamakura	1332	Monastic Cell
sada	N	Sadahira	定平	Kamakura	1332	Tranquility
sada	N	Sada'ie	定家	Kamakura	1332	Rural House / Family
sada	N	Sadakage	定景	Kamakura	1332	Bright / Magnificent
sada	N	Sadakatsu	定勝	Sengoku	1568	Conquer / Triumph
sada	N	Sadakiyo	定清	Kamakura	1335	Pure
sada	N	Sadamasa	定雅	Kamakura	1332	High Quality
sada	N	Sadamasa	定正	Muromachi	1572	Unerring / Genuine
sada	N	Sadamichi	定通	Kamakura	1332	Pass Through
sada	N	Sadamu	定	Nanboku	1392	
sada	N	Sada'naga	定長	Kamakura	1332	Long
sada	N	Sada'nori	定範	Kamakura	1332	Required Form / Pattern
sada	N	Sadashige	定重	Kamakura	1332	Heavy / Serious
sada	N	Sadashige	定成	Hei'an	1183	Become / Exist
sada	N	Sadasuke	定輔	Hei'an	1183	Ministerial Deputy
sada	N	Sadataka	定高	Kamakura	1332	Tall
sada	N	Sadatoshi	定利	Kamakura	1332	Produce Results
sada	N	Sadatsugu	定継	Kamakura	1332	Connect / Adopt
sada	N	Sadatsugu	定嗣	Kamakura	1332	Successor
sada	N	Sadatsu'na	定綱	Hei'an	1183	Net
sada	N	Sadayasu	定康	Uncertain	1600	Strong / Confident
sada	N	Sadayori	定頼	Nanboku	1392	Request / Ask
sada	N	Sadayoshi	定能	Kamakura	1332	Talent / Ability
sada	N	Sadaza'ne	定実	Kamakura	1332	Reality
sada	N	Sa'nesada	実定	Hei'an	1183	Reality
sada	N	Shigesada	重定	Hei'an	1183	Heavy / Serious
sada	N	Sukesada	資定	Kamakura	1332	Raw Materials
sada	N	Tadasada	忠定	Nanboku	1392	Faithful / Loyal
sada	N	Tamesada	為定	Kamakura	1332	Purpose / Goal
sada	N	Teishi	定子	Uncertain	1600	Child
sada	N	Tokisada	時定	Hei'an	1183	Time / Era
sada	N	Tomosada	朝定	Nanboku	1392	Morning
sada	N	Yasusada	安定	Uncertain	1600	Gentle / Safe / Secure
sada	N	Yoshisada	義定	Hei'an	1183	Fealty
sada	N	Yoshisada	良定	Uncertain	1600	Good / Superior

閑 Leisure / Quiet

This *kanji* originally referred to confining horses and oxen in a barn or stable. Thus, the animals could not enter or leave the stable. This idea developed into the idea of quiet resulting from the absence of coming and going. Thus, it came to mean quiet or leisure.

Reading	Type	Example	Kanji	Period	Date	Added Meaning
shizu	F	Shizuko	閑子	Hei'an	1183	[Lady]

休 Rest / Leisure

This *kanji* evokes the image of a man resting under a tree.

Reading	Type	Example	Kanji	Period	Date	Added Meaning
KYUU	H	Rikyuu	利休	Sengoku	1568	Produce Results

坐 Sit Quietly

Reading	Type	Example	Kanji	Period	Date	Added Meaning
[Special]	F	Irimashime	入坐賣	Nara	784	Enter / Entrance

咋 Eat / Bite

Reading	Type	Example	Kanji	Period	Date	Added Meaning
kuhi	F	Kuhime	咋賣	Nara	784	

❖ Perceiving & Communicating ❖

得 Perceive / Understand

Reading	Type	Example	Kanji	Period	Date	Added Meaning
nari	F	Narime	得賣	Hei'an	1183	

監 Oversee / Inspect / See from Above

Reading	Type	Example	Kanji	Period	Date	Added Meaning
KEN	S	Kenmotsu	監物	Hei'an	1183	Thing / Artifact

観 Perceive / View / Spectacle / Appearance

Kannon 観音 is the Chinese name for an important Bhodisatva who is associated with Amida Butsu 阿弥陀仏 and is generally portrayed as androgynous. The Amida Buddha and Kannon Bosatsu 観音菩薩 are strongly associated with Pure Land Buddhism. In these sects, a merciful Buddha transports the dead to a "pure land" where it is easy to attain enlightenment. In one of these sects, merely wanting to believe in the power of the name of the Amida Buddha to assure this sort of salvation after death is considered sufficient. During the late Muromachi period, many teachers of the arts adopted names ending with -ami 阿弥 as in the name of the Amida Buddha.

Reading	Type	Example	Kanji	Period	Date	Added Meaning
KAN	F	Kannon	観音	Kamakura	1332	Sound
KAN	Y	Kan'ou	観応	Nanboku	1350	Worthy / Suitable

音 Sound

Kannon 観音 is the Chinese name for an important Bhodisatva who is associated with the Amida Buddha and is generally believed to be androgynous. The Amida Butsu and Kannon Bosatsu are strongly associated with Pure Land Buddhism. In these sects, a merciful Buddha transports the dead to a "pure land" where it is easy to attain enlightenment. In one of these sects, merely wanting to believe in the power of the name of the Buddha to assure this sort of salvation after death is considered sufficient.

Reading	Type	Example	Kanji	Period	Date	Added Meaning
ON	F	Kannon	観音	Kamakura	1332	Perceive / View

宣 Proclamation

Reading	Type	Example	Kanji	Period	Date	Added Meaning
nobu	F	Nobuko	宣子	Hei'an	1183	[Lady]
nobu	N	Ka'ne'nobu	兼宣	Muromachi	1572	Unite
nobu	N	Moto'nobu	基宣	Kamakura	1332	Foundation
nobu	N	Mu'ne'nobu	宗宣	Kamakura	1332	Master an Art

Thematic Dictionary — Perceiving & Communicating 251

Reading	Type	Example	Kanji	Period	Date	Added Meaning
nobu	N	Nobu'aki	宣明	Kamakura	1332	Bright
nobu	N	Nobufusa	宣房	Kamakura	1332	Monastic Cell
nobu	N	Nobuhide	宣栄	Nanboku	1392	Bountiful / Fruitful
nobu	N	Nobuhide	宣秀	Nanboku	1392	Extraordinary / Bountiful
nobu	N	Nobutoki	宣時	Kamakura	1332	Time / Era
nobu	N	Nobutoshi	宣俊	Muromachi	1572	Emotional
nobu	N	Tsu'ne'nobu	経宣	Kamakura	1332	True Path
nobu	N	Yoshi'nobu	義宣	Nanboku	1392	Fealty
nobu	N	Yoshi'nobu	能宣	Uncertain	1600	Talent / Ability
nobu	N	Yoshi'nobu	良宣	Muromachi	1572	Good / Superior

勅 Imperial Decree / Admonishment / Demand

Reading	Type	Example	Kanji	Period	Date	Added Meaning
[Special]	S	Teshigawara	勅使河原	Nanboku	1392	Meadow + Large River

諏 Confer / Consult / Meet in Council

Reading	Type	Example	Kanji	Period	Date	Added Meaning
SU	S	Suwa	諏訪	Nanboku	1392	Visit

❖ Feelings & Emotions ❖

俊 Emotional / Deep Feeling

Reading	Type	Example	Kanji	Period	Date	Added Meaning
toshi	F	Toshi'nari'nomusume	俊成女	Kamakura	1332	Become / Exist + [Woman]
toshi	N	Akitoshi	顕俊	Uncertain	1600	High Status
toshi	N	Chikatoshi	親俊	Muromachi	1572	Intimate
toshi	N	Katsutoshi	勝俊	Sengoku	1568	Conquer / Triumph
toshi	N	Kintoshi	公俊	Muromachi	1572	Noble / Official
toshi	N	Michitoshi	通俊	Uncertain	1600	Pass Through
toshi	N	Moritoshi	盛俊	Hei'an	1183	Plentiful / Piled Up
toshi	N	Nobutoshi	信俊	Uncertain	1600	Belief / Faith
toshi	N	Nobutoshi	宣俊	Muromachi	1572	Proclamation
toshi	N	Sa'netoshi	実俊	Nanboku	1392	Reality
toshi	N	Tadatoshi	直俊	Nanboku	1392	Adjust / Correct
toshi	N	Takatoshi	隆俊	Kamakura	1332	Grow / Pile Up
toshi	N	Tomotoshi	朝俊	Kamakura	1332	Morning
toshi	N	Toshihide	俊秀	Hei'an	1183	Extraordinary / Bountiful
toshi	N	Toshihira	俊衡	Hei'an	1183	A Yoke
toshi	N	Toshihira	俊平	Hei'an	1183	Tranquility
toshi	N	Toshika'ne	俊兼	Kamakura	1332	Unite
toshi	N	Toshiki	俊奇	Kamakura	1244	Strange / Unusual
toshi	N	Toshikiyo	俊清	Uncertain	1600	Pure
toshi	N	Toshimasa	俊政	Kamakura	1332	Govern / Rule
toshi	N	Toshimichi	俊通	Hei'an	1183	Pass Through
toshi	N	Toshimitsu	俊光	Kamakura	1332	Bright / Shining
toshi	N	Toshimoto	俊基	Kamakura	1332	Foundation
toshi	N	Toshi'naga	俊長	Kamakura	1332	Long
toshi	N	Toshi'nari	俊成	Hei'an	1183	Become / Exist
toshi	N	Toshisuke	俊輔	Muromachi	1572	Ministerial Deputy
toshi	N	Toshitsu'na	俊綱	Hei'an	1183	Net
toshi	N	Toshitsu'ne	俊経	Hei'an	1183	True Path
toshi	N	Toshiyasu	俊康	Muromachi	1572	Strong / Confident
toshi	N	Toshiyasu	俊泰	Muromachi	1572	Peace / Plenitude
toshi	N	Toshiyori	俊頼	Uncertain	1600	Request / Ask
toshi	N	Toshiza'ne	俊実	Kamakura	1332	Reality
toshi	N	Tsu'netoshi	経俊	Hei'an	1183	True Path
toshi	N	Ujitoshi	氏俊	Nanboku	1392	Family / Clan
toshi	N	Yasutoshi	安俊	Kamakura	1332	Gentle / Safe / Secure
toshi	N	Yasutoshi	康俊	Kamakura	1332	Strong / Confident
toshi	N	Yoritoshi	頼俊	Kamakura	1332	Request / Ask
toshi	N	Yoshitoshi	義俊	Kamakura	1332	Fealty

Thematic Dictionary — Feelings & Emotions   253

福　Happiness (Felicitude)

Reading	Type	Example	Kanji	Period	Date	Added Meaning
FUKU	P	Fukushima	福島	Modern	1881	Island
FUKU	Y	Tenpuku	天福	Kamakura	1233	Sky / Heaven

楽　Happiness (Joy)

Reading	Type	Example	Kanji	Period	Date	Added Meaning
RAKU	F	Raku	楽	Uncertain	1600	
yasu	F	Yasuko	楽子	Hei'an	1183	[Lady]

幸　Happy / Tattoo

Reading	Type	Example	Kanji	Period	Date	Added Meaning
sachi	F	Sachiko	幸子	Nanboku	1392	[Lady]
yoshi	N	Yoshi'naga	幸長	Sengoku	1568	Long
yoshi	N	Yoshiyuki	義幸	Nanboku	1392	Fealty
yuki	F	Yukiko	幸子	Hei'an	1183	[Lady]
yuki	N	Haruyuki	晴幸	Uncertain	1600	Clear (Sky)
yuki	N	Masayuki	雅幸	Nanboku	1390	High Quality
yuki	N	Masayuki	昌幸	Sengoku	1568	Clear / Bright
yuki	N	Mitsuyuki	満幸	Nanboku	1392	Become Full / Abundant
yuki	N	Nagayuki	永幸	Nanboku	1392	Forever
yuki	N	Nagayuki	長幸	Nanboku	1392	Long
yuki	N	Sadayuki	貞幸	Kamakura	1332	Correct Spirit
yuki	N	Tokiyuki	時幸	Kamakura	1332	Time / Era
yuki	N	Ujiyuki	氏幸	Nanboku	1392	Family / Clan
yuki	N	Yukimura	幸村	Sengoku	1568	Village
yuki	N	Yukitaka	幸隆	Uncertain	1600	Grow / Pile Up
yuki	N	Yuki'uji	幸氏	Kamakura	1332	Family / Clan

快　Pleasure / Enjoyment / Agreement / Good Health

This *kanji* and the reading appearing in the example are definitely vulgar.

Reading	Type	Example	Kanji	Period	Date	Added Meaning
KAI	H	Kakukai Hosshinnou	覚快法親王	Kamakura	1181	Revelation + Pleasure

慶　Rejoice / Deer Skin

In ancient Japan, there was a method of fortune telling which used a deer skin. Apparently, this method of divining the future was particularly propitious.

Reading	Type	Example	Kanji	Period	Date	Added Meaning
KEI	Y	Kakei	嘉慶	Nanboku	1387	Well Done
KEI	Y	Kei'an	慶安	Edo	1648	Gentle / Safe / Secure
KEI	Y	Keichou	慶長	Momoyama	1596	Long / Oldest / Senior
KEI	Y	Kei'ou	慶応	Edo	1865	Worthy / Suitable
KEI	Y	Shoukei	正慶	Hei'an	1332	Unerring / Genuine
KYOU	Y	Enkyou	延慶	Kamakura	1308	Prolong / Stretch Out
nori	N	Hisa'nori	尚慶	Sengoku	1568	Excellence

Reading	Type	Example	Kanji	Period	Date	Added Meaning
nori	N	Mitsu'nori	満慶	Muromachi	1572	Become Full / Abundant
yoshi	N	Nagayoshi	長慶	Sengoku	1568	Long
yoshi	N	Sadayoshi	貞慶	Muromachi	1572	Correct Spirit
yoshi	N	Yoshihide	慶秀	Kamakura	1332	Extraordinary / Bountiful

喜 Rejoice

Reading	Type	Example	Kanji	Period	Date	Added Meaning
KI	S	Ukita	宇喜多	Uncertain	1600	Large Roof + Many
KI	Y	Kanki	寛喜	Kamakura	1229	Domestic Tranquility
KI	Y	Tengi	天喜	Hei'an	1053	Sky / Heaven
yoshi	N	Motoyoshi	元喜	Uncertain	1600	Base / Original

懐 Nostalgic

Reading	Type	Example	Kanji	Period	Date	Added Meaning
yasu	F	Yasu	懐	Uncertain	1600	

弥 Nostalgic

Reading	Type	Example	Kanji	Period	Date	Added Meaning
MI	F	Mimi	弥々	Uncertain	1600	
ya	F	Yaya	弥々	Muromachi	1572	
ya	M	Yatarou	弥太郎	Momoyama	1438	First Son

希 Wish / Desire

Reading	Type	Example	Kanji	Period	Date	Added Meaning
tomare	N	Tomareyoshi	希義	Hei'an	1183	Fealty

望 Heartfelt Wish / Desire

This *kanji* denotes a heartfelt wish.

Reading	Type	Example	Kanji	Period	Date	Added Meaning
mochi	N	Hidemochi	秀望	Sengoku	1568	Extraordinary / Bountiful
mochi	N	Takamochi	高望	Uncertain	1600	Tall
mochi	N	Yoshimochi	良望	Uncertain	1600	Good / Superior

企 Long Term Desire / Plan

Reading	Type	Example	Kanji	Period	Date	Added Meaning
KI	S	Hiki	比企	Kamakura	1332	Measure Up / Strive

愛 Love

Reading	Type	Example	Kanji	Period	Date	Added Meaning
AI	F	Ai	愛	Uncertain	1600	
[Special]	F	Eme	愛賣	Nara	784	

好 Affection / Desire

Reading	Type	Example	Kanji	Period	Date	Added Meaning
yo	S	Yoshima	好島	Kamakura	1332	Island
yoshi	N	Ka'neyoshi	兼好	Uncertain	1600	Unite
yoshi	N	Yoshikata	好方	Hei'an	1183	Direction / Method
yoshi	N	Yoshitada	好忠	Uncertain	1600	Faithful / Loyal
yoshi	S	Miyoshi	三好	Sengoku	1568	Three

冷 Cold to the Touch / Unfeeling

Reading	Type	Example	Kanji	Period	Date	Added Meaning
suzushi	F	Suzushiko	冷子	Hei'an	1183	[Lady]

❖ Warfare ❖

保 Guarantee

Reading	Type	Example	Kanji	Period	Date	Added Meaning
HO	F	Nihofume	迩保布女	Nara	784	That + Cloth + [Woman]
HOU	Y	Bunpou	文保	Kamakura	1317	Literature / Culture
HOU	Y	Chouhou	長保	Hei'an	999	Long / Oldest / Senior
HOU	Y	Eihou	永保	Hei'an	1081	Forever
HOU	Y	Hou'an	保安	Hei'an	1120	Gentle / Safe / Secure
HOU	Y	Hou'ei	保永	Edo	1704	Forever
HOU	Y	Hou'en	保延	Hei'an	1135	Prolong / Stretch Out
HOU	Y	Hougen	保元	Kamakura	1156	Base / Original
HOU	Y	Houji	保治	Kamakura	1247	Govern / Rule
HOU	Y	Jouhou	承保	Hei'an	1074	Humbly Receive
HOU	Y	Kahou	嘉保	Hei'an	1094	Well Done
HOU	Y	Kanpou	寛保	Edo	1741	Domestic Tranquility
HOU	Y	Kenpou	建保	Kamakura	1213	Found / Build / Construct
HOU	Y	Kyouhou	享保	Edo	1716	Receive
HOU	Y	Ouhou	応保	Kamakura	1161	Worthy / Suitable
HOU	Y	Shouhou	正保	Edo	1644	Unerring / Genuine
HOU	Y	Tenpou	天保	Edo	1830	Sky / Heaven
yasu	F	Yasuko	保子	Hei'an	1183	[Lady]
yasu	N	Kin'yasu	公保	Hei'an	1183	Noble / Official
yasu	N	Sueyasu	季保	Muromachi	1572	Season
yasu	N	Tadayasu	直保	Sengoku	1568	Adjust / Correct
yasu	N	Ta'neyasu	種保	Kamakura	1332	Cause / Reason
yasu	N	Yasu'ie	保家	Hei'an	1183	Rural House / Family
yasu	N	Yasumasa	保昌	Uncertain	1600	Clear / Bright
yasu	N	Yasumori	保盛	Kamakura	1332	Plentiful / Piled Up
yasu	N	Yasu'nari	保業	Hei'an	1183	Industry / Diligence
yasu	N	Yasushige	保茂	Kamakura	1332	Blossoming
yasu	N	Yasutoo	保遠	Kamakura	1332	Far
yasu	N	Yoshiyasu	能保	Kamakura	1332	Talent / Ability
tamotsu	N	Tamotsu	保	Kamakura	1332	

衛 Protect / Defend

Note this character also appears in the thematic elements 衛門 (emon), 右衛門 (uemon) and 左衛門 (saemon). 右衛門 (uemon) and 左衛門 (saemon) refer to the Ministry of the Left and the Ministry of the right respectively and appear along with 衛門 (emon) in the section on Rank and Status.

Reading	Type	Example	Kanji	Period	Date	Added Meaning
E	N	Sada'e	貞衛	Muromachi	1572	Correct Spirit
hira	N	Tadahira	忠衛	Hei'an	1167	Faithful / Loyal

Thematic Dictionary — Warfare 257

勝 Win / Conquer / Triumph / Victory

Reading	Type	Example	Kanji	Period	Date	Added Meaning
kachi	F	Kachiko	勝子	Hei'an	1183	[Lady]
katsu	N	Kagekatsu	景勝	Uncertain	1600	Bright / Magnificent
katsu	N	Katsuhisa	勝久	Muromachi	1572	Longtime
katsu	N	Katsu'ie	勝家	Uncertain	1600	Rural House / Family
katsu	N	Katsumasa	勝正	Sengoku	1568	Unerring / Genuine
katsu	N	Katsumitsu	勝光	Muromachi	1572	Bright / Shining
katsu	N	Katsumoto	勝元	Muromachi	1572	Base / Original
katsu	N	Katsu'naga	勝永	Sengoku	1568	Forever
katsu	N	Katsutoshi	勝俊	Sengoku	1568	Emotional
katsu	N	Katsutoyo	勝豊	Muromachi	1572	Noble
katsu	N	Katsuyori	勝頼	Sengoku	1574	Request / Ask
katsu	N	Katsuyoshi	勝嘉	Sengoku	1568	Well Done
katsu	N	Masakatsu	正勝	Nanboku	1392	Unerring / Genuine
katsu	N	Nagakatsu	永勝	Sengoku	1568	Forever
katsu	N	Nagakatsu	長勝	Sengoku	1568	Long
katsu	N	Sadakatsu	定勝	Sengoku	1568	Determine
katsu	N	Sa'nekatsu	真勝	Sengoku	1568	Genuine
katsu	N	Shigekatsu	重勝	Nanboku	1392	Heavy / Serious
katsu	N	Shigekatsu	茂勝	Sengoku	1568	Blossoming
katsu	N	Tadakatsu	忠勝	Momoyama	1568	Faithful / Loyal
katsu	N	Yasukatsu	康勝	Sengoku	1568	Strong / Confident
katsu	N	Yoshikatsu	義勝	Muromachi	1572	Fealty
katsu	S	Kawakatsu	川勝	Sengoku	1568	River

武 Strong / Brave / Military Force

Reading	Type	Example	Kanji	Period	Date	Added Meaning
MU	P	Musashi	武蔵	Nara	784	Storehouse
MU	S	Mutou	武藤	Kamakura	1332	Wisteria
MU	Y	Kenmu	建武	Nanboku	1334	Found / Build / Construct
take	N	Koretake	惟武	Nanboku	1392	This / Here
take	N	Masatake	正武	Nanboku	1392	Unerring / Genuine
take	N	Nobutake	信武	Nanboku	1392	Belief / Faith
take	N	Shigetake	重武	Kamakura	1332	Heavy / Serious
take	N	Takefusa	武房	Kamakura	1332	Monastic Cell
take	N	Takemasa	武政	Nanboku	1392	Govern / Rule
take	N	Takemitsu	武光	Nanboku	1392	Bright / Shining
take	N	Take'o	武士	Nanboku	1392	Samurai / Warrior
take	N	Takeshige	武重	Nanboku	1392	Heavy / Serious
take	N	Taketoki	武時	Kamakura	1332	Time / Era
take	N	Taketomo	武朝	Nanboku	1392	Morning
take	N	Taketoshi	武敏	Nanboku	1392	Very Rapid Hard Work
take	N	Taketoshi	武朝	Nanboku	1392	Morning
take	N	Takeyoshi	武吉	Nanboku	1392	Lucky / Fortunate
take	N	Takeza'ne	武実	Nanboku	1392	Reality
take	N	Takezou	武蔵	Sengoku	1568	Storehouse
take	N	Takezumi	武澄	Nanboku	1392	Cleanse / Purify
take	S	Takeda	武田	Kamakura	1332	Rice Paddy
take	S	Take'no	武野	Sengoku	1568	Wide Plain

士 Samurai / Warrior

While Fuji 富士 means "industrious man" it generally refers to the famous mountain.

Reading	Type	Example	Kanji	Period	Date	Added Meaning
SHI	H	Shibutsu	士仏	Muromachi	1572	Buddah
SHI	P	Fujisan	富士山	Modern	1674	Industry
SHI	S	Fuji'na	富士名	Kamakura	1332	Industry + Famous
o	N	Take'o	武士	Nanboku	1392	Strong / Brave

❖ Art & Letters ❖

歌 Poem / Song

Reading	Type	Example	Kanji	Period	Date	Added Meaning
uta	F	Uta	歌	Uncertain	1600	

文 Literature / Culture = BUN / Writing = fumi / Colour Harmony = aya

While this *kanji* specifically refers to writing, it can also refer more generally to literature or culture as a whole.

Reading	Type	Example	Kanji	Period	Date	Added Meaning
BUN	S	Bun'ya	文屋	Uncertain	1600	Urban House / Artisan
BUN	Y	Bun'an	文安	Muromachi	1444	Gentle / Safe / Secure
BUN	Y	Bunchuu	文中	Nanboku	1372	Middle
BUN	Y	Bun'ei	文永	Kamakura	1264	Forever
BUN	Y	Bunji	文治	Kamakura	1185	Govern / Rule
BUN	Y	Bunka[37]	文化	Edo	1804	Change / Transformation
BUN	Y	Bunki	文亀	Sengoku	1501	Tortoise (Longevity)
BUN	Y	Bunkyuu	文久	Edo	1861	Longtime
BUN	Y	Bunmei	文明	Sengoku	1469	Bright
BUN	Y	Bunna	文和	Nanboku	1352	Peace / Tranquility / Harmony
BUN	Y	Bun'ou	文応	Kamakura	1260	Worthy / Suitable
BUN	Y	Bunpou	文保	Kamakura	1317	Guarantee
BUN	Y	Bunroku	文禄	Momoyama	1592	Gratitude / Beneficence
BUN	Y	Bunryaku	文歴	Kamakura	1234	Progress / Pass Through
BUN	Y	Bunsei	文政	Edo	1818	Govern / Rule
BUN	Y	Bunshou	文正	Muromachi	1466	Unerring / Genuine
BUN	Y	Enbun	延文	Nanboku	1356	Prolong / Stretch Out
BUN	Y	Genbun	元文	Edo	1736	Base / Original
BUN	Y	Kanbun	寛文	Edo	1661	Domestic Tranquility
BUN	Y	Tenbun	天文	Sengoku	1532	Sky / Heaven
MON	S	Ichimonji	一文字	Hei'an	1183	One + Letter
aya	F	Aya	文	Uncertain	1600	
aya	F	Ayame	文女	Kamakura	1332	[Woman]
fumi	N	Fumitoki	文時	Hei'an	981	Time / Era
fumi	N	Ka'nefumi	兼文	Kamakura	1266	Unite
fumi	N	Nakabumi	仲文	Uncertain	1600	Middle of a Group
fumi	N	Sadabumi	貞文	Uncertain	1600	Correct Spirit
fumi	N	Tadafumi	忠文	Uncertain	1600	Faithful / Loyal

[37] Bunka is an actual word in Japanese which means "culture" or "civilization".

章 Symbol / Writing / Elucidate

Reading	Type	Example	Kanji	Period	Date	Added Meaning
aki	N	Akifusa	章房	Kamakura	1332	Monastic Cell
aki	N	Akika'ne	章兼	Nanboku	1392	Unite
aki	N	Akitou	章任	Kamakura	1332	Endure a Duty
aki	N	Nobu'aki	信章	Hei'an	1183	Belief / Faith
aki	N	Taka'aki	隆章	Kamakura	1332	Grow / Pile Up
aki	N	Tomo'aki	知章	Hei'an	1183	Knowledge
aki	N	Yori'aki	頼章	Kamakura	1332	Request / Ask
aki	N	Yuki'aki	行章	Kamakura	1332	Going To / Bound For
akira	N	Toki'akira	時章	Kamakura	1332	Time / Era

述 State / Speak / Declare / Proclaim

This *kanji* originally denoted the act of sending an emissary.

Reading	Type	Example	Kanji	Period	Date	Added Meaning
nobu	F	Nobuko	述子	Hei'an	1183	[Lady]

言 Word / Speak Truthfully

Reading	Type	Example	Kanji	Period	Date	Added Meaning
koto	N	Hirokoto	広言	Kamakura	1332	Spacious / Expansive
toki	N	Michitoki	通言	Nanboku	1392	Pass Through
toki	N	Noritoki	教言	Nanboku	1392	Teaching / Dogma
toki	N	Tokiku'ni	言国	Muromachi	1572	Country / Rural Area

字 Letter / Character / Symbol

Reading	Type	Example	Kanji	Period	Date	Added Meaning
JI	S	Ichimonji	一文字	Hei'an	1183	One + Writing

典 Text Book

Reading	Type	Example	Kanji	Period	Date	Added Meaning
nori	F	Noriko	典子	Hei'an	1183	[Lady]

経 Sutra / True Path / Travel Straight

Reading	Type	Example	Kanji	Period	Date	Added Meaning
tsune	N	Chikatsu'ne	親経	Kamakura	1332	Intimate
tsune	N	Hisatsu'ne	久経	Kamakura	1332	Longtime
tsune	N	Ietsu'ne	家経	Kamakura	1332	Rural House / Family
tsune	N	Kagetsu'ne	景経	Hei'an	1183	Bright / Magnificent
tsune	N	Ka'netsu'ne	兼経	Kamakura	1332	Unite
tsune	N	Kintsu'ne	公経	Hei'an	1183	Noble / Official
tsune	N	Kiyotsu'ne	清経	Hei'an	1183	Pure
tsune	N	Masatsu'ne	雅経	Kamakura	1332	High Quality

tsune	N	Masatsu'ne	政経	Muromachi	1572	Govern / Rule
tsune	N	Michitsu'ne	通経	Kamakura	1332	Pass Through
tsune	N	Michitsu'ne	道経	Kamakura	1332	Road / Way
tsune	N	Mitsutsu'ne	光経	Kamakura	1332	Bright / Shining
tsune	N	Mitsutsu'ne	満経	Muromachi	1572	Become Full / Abundant
tsune	N	Morotsu'ne	師経	Kamakura	1332	Teacher / Expert
tsune	N	Mototsu'ne	基経	Uncertain	1600	Foundation
tsune	N	Mu'netsu'ne	宗経	Kamakura	1332	Master an Art
tsune	N	Naotsu'ne	直経	Nanboku	1392	Adjust / Correct
tsune	N	Naritsu'ne	成経	Hei'an	1183	Become / Exist
tsune	N	Noritsu'ne	教経	Hei'an	1183	Teaching / Dogma
tsune	N	Sadatsu'ne	貞経	Kamakura	1332	Correct Spirit
tsune	N	Sa'netsu'ne	実経	Kamakura	1332	Reality
tsune	N	Shigetsu'ne	重経	Uncertain	1600	Heavy / Serious
tsune	N	Suetsu'ne	季経	Hei'an	1183	Season
tsune	N	Suketsu'ne	資経	Kamakura	1332	Raw Materials
tsune	N	Suketsu'ne	祐経	Kamakura	1332	Divine Help
tsune	N	Tadatsu'ne	忠経	Kamakura	1332	Faithful / Loyal
tsune	N	Takatsu'ne	高経	Kamakura	1332	Tall
tsune	N	Takatsu'ne	隆経	Uncertain	1600	Grow / Pile Up
tsune	N	Tomotsu'ne	朝経	Kamakura	1332	Morning
tsune	N	Tomotsu'ne	倫経	Kamakura	1332	Obligatory Path
tsune	N	Toshitsu'ne	俊経	Hei'an	1183	Emotional
tsune	N	Tsu'ne'aki	経顕	Nanboku	1392	High Status
tsune	N	Tsu'nechika	経親	Kamakura	1332	Intimate
tsune	N	Tsu'nefusa	経房	Hei'an	1183	Monastic Cell
tsune	N	Tsu'nega'ne	経兼	Uncertain	1600	Unite
tsune	N	Tsu'nehira	経平	Kamakura	1332	Tranquility
tsune	N	Tsu'nehisa	経久	Sengoku	1568	Longtime
tsune	N	Tsu'ne'ie	経家	Kamakura	1332	Rural House / Family
tsune	N	Tsu'nekage	経景	Uncertain	1600	Bright / Magnificent
tsune	N	Tsu'neka'ne	経兼	Nanboku	1392	Unite
tsune	N	Tsu'neku'ni	経国	Kamakura	1332	Country / Rural Area
tsune	N	Tsu'nemasa	経政	Kamakura	1332	Govern / Rule
tsune	N	Tsu'nemasa	経正	Hei'an	1183	Unerring / Genuine
tsune	N	Tsu'nemi	経見	Nanboku	1392	Vantage / View / Vista
tsune	N	Tsu'nemichi	経通	Nanboku	1392	Pass Through
tsune	N	Tsu'nemitsu	経光	Kamakura	1332	Bright / Shining
tsune	N	Tsu'nemori	経盛	Hei'an	1183	Plentiful / Piled Up
tsune	N	Tsu'nemu'ne	経宗	Hei'an	1183	Master an Art
tsune	N	Tsu'ne'naga	経永	Kamakura	1332	Forever
tsune	N	Tsu'ne'naka	経仲	Kamakura	1332	Middle of a Group
tsune	N	Tsu'ne'nari	経成	Uncertain	1600	Become / Exist
tsune	N	Tsu'ne'nobu	経信	Muromachi	1572	Belief / Faith
tsune	N	Tsu'ne'nobu	経宣	Kamakura	1332	Proclamation
tsune	N	Tsu'ne'nori	経教	Muromachi	1572	Teaching / Dogma
tsune	N	Tsu'neshige	経茂	Nanboku	1392	Blossoming
tsune	N	Tsu'nesue	経季	Kamakura	1332	Season
tsune	N	Tsu'nesuke	経資	Kamakura	1332	Raw Materials
tsune	N	Tsu'netada	経忠	Kamakura	1332	Faithful / Loyal
tsune	N	Tsu'netaka	経高	Hei'an	1183	Tall
tsune	N	Tsu'netaka	経隆	Kamakura	1332	Grow / Pile Up
tsune	N	Tsu'netoki	経時	Kamakura	1332	Time / Era
tsune	N	Tsu'netoshi	経俊	Hei'an	1183	Emotional
tsune	N	Tsu'netsugu	経嗣	Nanboku	1392	Successor
tsune	N	Tsu'ne'uji	経氏	Kamakura	1332	Family / Clan
tsune	N	Tsu'neyasu	経康	Nanboku	1392	Strong / Confident

Reading	Type	Example	Kanji	Period	Date	Added Meaning
tsune	N	Tsu'neyasu	経泰	Nanboku	1392	Peace / Plenitude
tsune	N	Tsu'neyori	経頼	Kamakura	1332	Request / Ask
tsune	N	Uchitsu'ne	内経	Kamakura	1332	Inside
tsune	N	Ujitsu'ne	氏経	Kamakura	1332	Family / Clan
tsune	N	Yasutsu'ne	泰経	Hei'an	1183	Peace / Plenitude
tsune	N	Yoritsu'ne	頼経	Kamakura	1332	Request / Ask
tsune	N	Yoshitsu'ne	義経	Hei'an	1183	Fealty
tsune	N	Yoshitsu'ne	良経	Kamakura	1332	Good / Superior

詮 Explicit / Clear

Reading	Type	Example	Kanji	Period	Date	Added Meaning
aki	F	Akiko	詮子	Hei'an	1183	[Lady]
aki	N	Aki'nao	詮直	Nanboku	1392	Adjust / Correct
aki	N	Aki'nori	詮範	Muromachi	1572	Required Form / Pattern
aki	N	Hide'aki	秀詮	Nanboku	1392	Extraordinary / Bountiful
aki	N	Mitsu'aki	満詮	Muromachi	1572	Become Full / Abundant
aki	N	Nao'aki	直詮	Muromachi	1572	Adjust / Correct
aki	N	Nobu'aki	信詮	Uncertain	1600	Belief / Faith
aki	N	Taka'aki	高詮	Nanboku	1392	Tall
aki	N	Uji'aki	氏詮	Nanboku	1392	Family / Clan
akira	N	Mori'akira	盛詮	Muromachi	1572	Plentiful / Piled Up
akira	N	Moro'akira	師詮	Nanboku	1392	Teacher / Expert
akira	N	Yoshi'akira	義詮	Nanboku	1367	Fealty
nori	N	Noriyori	詮頼	Nanboku	1392	Request / Ask
nori	N	Taka'nori	高詮	Nanboku	1392	Tall

宗 Master an Art

Like Sen 千, Sou 宗 is an unusual family name, because it is a single character family name which takes its Sino-Japanese *onyomi* reading.

Reading	Type	Example	Kanji	Period	Date	Added Meaning
SOU	H	Soutan	宗湛	Uncertain	1600	Fill Up / Become Abundant
SOU	M	Sou'ichirou	宗一郎	Modern	1983	First Son
SOU	M	Soujirou	宗次郎	Uncertain	1600	Second / Next + Son
SOU	S	Sou	宗	Nanboku	1392	
mune	F	Mu'neko	宗子	Hei'an	1183	[Lady]
mune	M	Mu'nesa'emon	宗左衛門	Uncertain	1600	Ministry of the Left
mune	N	Akimu'ne	明宗	Nanboku	1392	Bright
mune	N	Chikamu'ne	親宗	Hei'an	1183	Intimate
mune	N	Kagemu'ne	景宗	Nanboku	1392	Bright / Magnificent
mune	N	Ka'nemu'ne	兼宗	Kamakura	1332	Unite
mune	N	Kinmu'ne	公宗	Kamakura	1332	Noble / Official
mune	N	Kiyomu'ne	清宗	Hei'an	1183	Pure
mune	N	Masamu'ne	政宗	Nanboku	1392	Govern / Rule
mune	N	Mitsumu'ne	光宗	Kamakura	1332	Bright / Shining
mune	N	Mochimu'ne	持宗	Muromachi	1572	Have / Possess
mune	N	Motomu'ne	基宗	Kamakura	1332	Foundation
mune	N	Mu'ne'atsu	宗敦	Uncertain	1600	Generous / Kind / Honest
mune	N	Mu'nechika	宗親	Kamakura	1332	Intimate
mune	N	Mu'nefuji	宗藤	Kamakura	1332	Wisteria
mune	N	Mu'nehide	宗秀	Kamakura	1332	Extraordinary / Bountiful
mune	N	Mu'nehira	宗衡	Kamakura	1332	A Yoke
mune	N	Mu'nehira	宗平	Nanboku	1392	Tranquility
mune	N	Mu'nehiro	宗広	Kamakura	1332	Spacious / Expansive

Thematic Dictionary — Arts & Letters

mune	N	Mu'nehiro	宗弘	Kamakura	1332	Draw / Stretch
mune	N	Mu'nehisa	宗久	Kamakura	1332	Longtime
mune	N	Mu'ne'ie	宗家	Kamakura	1332	Rural House / Family
mune	N	Mu'nekage	宗景	Muromachi	1572	Bright / Magnificent
mune	N	Mu'nekata	宗賢	Kamakura	1332	Genius
mune	N	Mu'nekata	宗方	Kamakura	1332	Direction / Method
mune	N	Mu'nekiyo	宗清	Hei'an	1183	Pure
mune	N	Mu'nemasa	宗政	Kamakura	1332	Govern / Rule
mune	N	Mu'nemitsu	宗光	Kamakura	1332	Bright / Shining
mune	N	Mu'nemori	宗盛	Hei'an	1183	Plentiful / Piled Up
mune	N	Mu'nemoto	宗元	Nanboku	1392	Base / Original
mune	N	Mu'ne'naga	宗長	Kamakura	1332	Long
mune	N	Mu'ne'nari	宗業	Kamakura	1332	Industry / Diligence
mune	N	Mu'ne'nobu	宗宣	Kamakura	1332	Proclamation
mune	N	Mu'ne'nobu	宗信	Uncertain	1600	Belief / Faith
mune	N	Mu'ne'nori	宗矩	Kamakura	1332	Quadrant / Regulated
mune	N	Mu'ne'nori	宗教	Kamakura	1332	Teaching / Dogma
mune	N	Mu'neshige	宗重	Hei'an	1183	Heavy / Serious
mune	N	Mu'neshige	宗茂	Sengoku	1568	Blossoming
mune	N	Mu'nesuke	宗介	Kamakura	1332	Regional Deputy
mune	N	Mu'nesuke	宗輔	Hei'an	1183	Ministerial Deputy
mune	N	Mu'nesuke	宗祐	Nanboku	1392	Divine Help
mune	N	Mu'neta	宗太	Uncertain	1600	Fat
mune	N	Mu'netada	宗忠	Nanboku	1392	Faithful / Loyal
mune	N	Mu'netaka	宗隆	Hei'an	1183	Grow / Pile Up
mune	N	Mu'neta'ne	宗胤	Kamakura	1332	Blood Heir
mune	N	Mu'netoki	宗時	Uncertain	1600	Time / Era
mune	N	Mu'netoo	宗遠	Hei'an	1183	Far
mune	N	Mu'netsu'na	宗綱	Kamakura	1332	Net
mune	N	Mu'netsu'ne	宗経	Kamakura	1332	True Path
mune	N	Mu'ne'uji	宗氏	Kamakura	1332	Family / Clan
mune	N	Mu'neyasu	宗泰	Kamakura	1332	Peace / Plenitude
mune	N	Mu'neyori	宗頼	Kamakura	1332	Request / Ask
mune	N	Mu'neyoshi	宗能	Hei'an	1183	Talent / Ability
mune	N	Mu'neyoshi	宗良経	Kamakura	1332	Good / Superior
mune	N	Mu'neyuki	宗干	Uncertain	1600	Dry / Care For
mune	N	Mu'neyuki	宗行	Kamakura	1332	Going To / Bound For
mune	N	Mu'neza'ne	宗実	Hei'an	1183	Reality
mune	N	Nakamu'ne	仲宗	Hei'an	1183	Middle of a Group
mune	N	Norimu'ne	則宗	Hei'an	1183	Make an Example
mune	N	Norimu'ne	範宗	Muromachi	1572	Required Form / Pattern
mune	N	Sadamu'ne	貞宗	Kamakura	1332	Correct Spirit
mune	N	Sa'nemu'ne	実宗	Kamakura	1332	Reality
mune	N	Tadamu'ne	忠宗	Kamakura	1332	Faithful / Loyal
mune	N	Takamu'ne	高宗	Nanboku	1392	Tall
mune	N	Takamu'ne	孝宗	Nanboku	1392	Filial Loyalty
mune	N	Ta'nemu'ne	胤宗	Kamakura	1332	Blood Heir
mune	N	Tokimu'ne	時宗	Kamakura	1332	Time / Era
mune	N	Tomomu'ne	知宗	Kamakura	1184	Knowledge
mune	N	Tomomu'ne	朝宗	Nanboku	1392	Morning
mune	N	Tsu'nemu'ne	経宗	Hei'an	1183	True Path
mune	N	Ujimu'ne	氏宗	Sengoku	1568	Family / Clan
mune	N	Yasumu'ne	康宗	Kamakura	1332	Strong / Confident
mune	N	Yorimu'ne	頼宗	Nanboku	1392	Request / Ask
mune	N	Yoshimu'ne	義宗	Kamakura	1332	Fealty
mune	N	Yukimu'ne	行宗	Hei'an	1183	Going To / Bound For
mune	S	Mu'nawoka	宗岳	Hei'an	1183	Peak

修 Polish / Refine / Practice (An Art)

Reading	Type	Example	Kanji	Period	Date	Added Meaning
naka	F	Nakako	修子	Hei'an	1183	[Lady]
naka	N	Nagahiro	修弘	Sengoku	1568	Draw / Stretch

賢 Genius

Note that there are two different native *kunyomi* readings given for this character. Of these, "kata" is both more numerous than "kawa" and documented by superior sources. Further, one source reads Morokata 師賢 as "Morokawa." Unfortunately, we do not know whether both sources refer to the same individual. However, this character should probably be read as "kata" and not as "kawa". This is true even for those combinations listed in the tables where the alternate reading is given. This is done solely to retain fidelity to the sources and is not a recommendation for actual use. Finally, neither "kata" nor "kawa" are modern ways of reading 賢. Currently, the Japanese Ministry of Education only lists "KEN", "sato" and "satoshi" for use in names.

Reading	Type	Example	Kanji	Period	Date	Added Meaning
kata	N	Iekata	家賢	Nanboku	1392	Rural House / Family
kata	N	Kinkata	公賢	Kamakura	1332	Noble / Official
kata	N	Masakata	雅賢	Hei'an	1183	High Quality
kata	N	Mochikata	持賢	Muromachi	1572	Have / Possess
kata	N	Morokata	師賢	Kamakura	1332	Teacher / Expert
kata	N	Mu'nekata	宗賢	Kamakura	1332	Master an Art
kata	N	Nobukata	信賢	Muromachi	1572	Belief / Faith
kata	N	Sukekata	資賢	Hei'an	1183	Raw Materials
kawa	N	Kawahide	賢秀	Sengoku	1568	Extraordinary / Bountiful
kawa	N	Morokawa	師賢	Uncertain	1600	Teacher / Expert
kawa	N	Yorikawa	頼賢	Uncertain	1600	Request / Ask

理 Reason / Logic

Reading	Type	Example	Kanji	Period	Date	Added Meaning
RI	F	Riri	理々	Momoyama	1438	
masa	F	Masako	理子	Hei'an	1183	[Lady]
masa	N	Sukemasa	佐理	Uncertain	1600	Military Deputy
tada	N	Yoshitada	義理	Nanboku	1392	Fealty

分 Divide / Partition / Understand

This *kanji* evokes the image of something being cut in two with a knife.

Reading	Type	Example	Kanji	Period	Date	Added Meaning
wake	F	Wakeme	分女	Hei'an	1183	[Woman]
	S	Kokubu	国分	Kamakura	1332	Country / Rural Area

智 Intelligent

Reading	Type	Example	Kanji	Period	Date	Added Meaning
CHI	N	Yoshichi	義智	Sengoku	1568	Fealty
CHI	S	Akechi	明智	Uncertain	1600	Bright

知 Knowledge

Reading	Type	Example	Kanji	Period	Date	Added Meaning
CHI	S	Ochi	越知	Muromachi	1572	Surpass
tomo	F	Tomotsume	知都賣	Nara	784	Beautiful (Cultured)
tomo	N	Masatomo	政知	Muromachi	1572	Govern / Rule
tomo	N	Moritomo	守知	Sengoku	1568	Protect / Defend
tomo	N	Takatomo	高知	Kamakura	1332	Tall
tomo	N	Tomo'aki	知章	Hei'an	1183	Writing / Elucidate
tomo	N	Tomohisa	知尚	Kamakura	1332	Excellence
tomo	N	Tomo'ie	知家	Kamakura	1332	Rural House / Family
tomo	N	Tomomori	知盛	Hei'an	1183	Plentiful / Piled Up
tomo	N	Tomomu'ne	知宗	Kamakura	1184	Master an Art
tomo	N	Tomo'nori	知度	Hei'an	1183	Event / Consult / Confer
tomo	N	Tomosada	知貞	Nanboku	1392	Correct Spirit
tomo	N	Tomo'uji	知氏	Nanboku	1392	Family / Clan
tomo	N	Tomoyasu	知康	Hei'an	1183	Strong / Confident
tomo	N	Tomoyuki	知行	Nanboku	1392	Going To / Bound For

伎 Artisan / Artistry / Craft / Skill

Reading	Type	Example	Kanji	Period	Date	Added Meaning
KI	F	Ki'nume	伎怒賣	Nara	784	Valor / Anger / Rage
KI	F	Yukime	由伎賣	Nara	784	Origin / Purpose

能 Talent / Ability

Reading	Type	Example	Kanji	Period	Date	Added Meaning
NO	S	Nose	能勢	Kamakura	1332	Vigor / Spirit / Elan Vital
yoshi	N	Akiyoshi	顕能	Nanboku	1392	High Status
yoshi	N	Chikayoshi	親能	Kamakura	1332	Intimate
yoshi	N	Hideyoshi	秀能	Kamakura	1332	Extraordinary / Bountiful
yoshi	N	Koreyoshi	惟能	Hei'an	1183	This / Here
yoshi	N	Masayoshi	昌能	Nanboku	1392	Clear / Bright
yoshi	N	Michiyoshi	通能	Nanboku	1392	Pass Through
yoshi	N	Mitsuyoshi	光能	Hei'an	1183	Bright / Shining
yoshi	N	Motoyoshi	基能	Nanboku	1392	Foundation
yoshi	N	Mu'neyoshi	宗能	Hei'an	1183	Master an Art
yoshi	N	Nobuyoshi	信能	Hei'an	1183	Belief / Faith
yoshi	N	Sadayoshi	貞能	Hei'an	1183	Correct Spirit
yoshi	N	Sadayoshi	定能	Kamakura	1332	Determine
yoshi	N	Shigeyoshi	重能	Nanboku	1392	Heavy / Serious
yoshi	N	Shigeyoshi	成能	Hei'an	1183	Become / Exist
yoshi	N	Sueyoshi	季能	Kamakura	1332	Season
yoshi	N	Sukeyoshi	資能	Kamakura	1332	Raw Materials
yoshi	N	Sukeyoshi	助能	Kamakura	1332	Deputy (Rescue / Assist)
yoshi	N	Tadayoshi	忠能	Kamakura	1332	Faithful / Loyal
yoshi	N	Takayoshi	隆能	Hei'an	1183	Grow / Pile Up
yoshi	N	Tokiyoshi	時能	Nanboku	1392	Time / Era
yoshi	N	Ujiyoshi	氏能	Nanboku	1392	Family / Clan
yoshi	N	Yoshihide	能秀	Kamakura	1332	Extraordinary / Bountiful
yoshi	N	Yoshihisa	能久	Kamakura	1332	Longtime

Reading	Type	Example	Kanji	Period	Date	Added Meaning
yoshi	N	Yoshikazu	能員	Kamakura	1332	Member
yoshi	N	Yoshimori	能盛	Hei'an	1183	Plentiful / Piled Up
yoshi	N	Yoshi'naka	能仲	Kamakura	1332	Middle of a Group
yoshi	N	Yoshi'nao	能直	Kamakura	1332	Adjust / Correct
yoshi	N	Yoshi'nari	能成	Kamakura	1332	Become / Exist
yoshi	N	Yoshi'nobu	能宣	Uncertain	1600	Proclamation
yoshi	N	Yoshi'nori	能憲	Nanboku	1392	Example / Pattern
yoshi	N	Yoshisato	能郷	Kamakura	1332	Hometown
yoshi	N	Yoshitaka	能隆	Kamakura	1332	Grow / Pile Up
yoshi	N	Yoshi'uji	能氏	Kamakura	1332	Family / Clan
yoshi	N	Yoshiyasu	能保	Kamakura	1332	Guarantee

慧 Wise

Reading	Type	Example	Kanji	Period	Date	Added Meaning
[Special]	F	Akirakeiko	慧子	Hei'an	1183	[Lady]

博 Well Traveled / Learned

Reading	Type	Example	Kanji	Period	Date	Added Meaning
hiro	N	Hiro'ie	博家	Kamakura	1332	Rural House / Family
hiro	N	Hiromasa	博雅	Uncertain	1600	High Quality
hiro	N	Michihiro	通博	Muromachi	1572	Pass Through
hiro	N	Sa'nehiro	実博	Muromachi	1572	Reality
hiro	N	Takahiro	隆博	Kamakura	1332	Grow / Pile Up

意 Idea / Opinion

Reading	Type	Example	Kanji	Period	Date	Added Meaning
wo	F	Wobitome	意比等賣	Nara	784	Strive + Rank / Level

❖ BEING & EXISTING ❖

成 Become / Exist

Reading	Type	Example	Kanji	Period	Date	Added Meaning
SEI	Y	Heisei	平成	Modern	1989	Tranquility
nari	F	Narime	成女	Nara	784	[Woman]
nari	N	Fusa'nari	房成	Hei'an	1183	Monastic Cell
nari	N	Hama'nari	浜成	Uncertain	1600	Beach
nari	N	Ie'nari	家成	Uncertain	1600	Rural House / Family
nari	N	Masa'nari	正成	Uncertain	1600	Unerring / Genuine
nari	N	Masa'nari	昌成	Hei'an	1183	Clear / Bright
nari	N	Michi'nari	通成	Kamakura	1332	Pass Through
nari	N	Mitsu'nari	光成	Sengoku	1568	Bright / Shining
nari	N	Mitsu'nari	三成	Uncertain	1600	Three
nari	N	Mitsu'nari	満成	Muromachi	1572	Become Full / Abundant
nari	N	Moto'nari	基成	Kamakura	1332	Foundation
nari	N	Naga'nari	長成	Uncertain	1600	Long
nari	N	Naka'nari	仲成	Uncertain	1600	Middle of a Group
nari	N	Narichika	成親	Hei'an	1183	Intimate
nari	N	Nari'ie	成家	Kamakura	1332	Rural House / Family
nari	N	Narimasa	成雅	Uncertain	1600	High Quality
nari	N	Nari'nori	成範	Hei'an	1183	Required Form / Pattern
nari	N	Narisada	成定	Hei'an	1183	Determine
nari	N	Narishige	成重	Kamakura	1332	Heavy / Serious
nari	N	Narisue	成季	Kamakura	1332	Season
nari	N	Narisuke	成輔	Kamakura	1332	Ministerial Deputy
nari	N	Narita'ne	成胤	Kamakura	1332	Blood Heir
nari	N	Naritsu'na	成綱	Hei'an	1183	Net
nari	N	Naritsu'ne	成経	Hei'an	1183	True Path
nari	N	Nari'uji	成氏	Uncertain	1600	Family / Clan
nari	N	Nariyoshi	成義	Muromachi	1572	Fealty
nari	N	Nobu'nari	信成	Sengoku	1568	Belief / Faith
nari	N	Shige'nari	重成	Kamakura	1332	Heavy / Serious
nari	N	Suke'nari	資成	Uncertain	1600	Raw Materials
nari	N	Suke'nari	祐成	Kamakura	1332	Divine Help
nari	N	Toki'nari	時成	Kamakura	1332	Time / Era
nari	N	Toshi'nari	俊成	Hei'an	1183	Emotional
nari	N	Tsu'ne'nari	経成	Uncertain	1600	True Path
nari	N	Uji'nari	氏成	Uncertain	1600	Family / Clan
nari	N	Yori'nari	頼成	Uncertain	1600	Request / Ask
nari	N	Yoshi'nari	義成	Kamakura	1332	Fealty
nari	N	Yoshi'nari	善成	Nanboku	1392	Perform Well
nari	N	Yoshi'nari	能成	Kamakura	1332	Talent / Ability
nari	N	Yuki'nari	行成	Uncertain	1600	Going To / Bound For
nari	S	Narita	成田	Kamakura	1332	Rice Paddy
shige	F	Shigeko	成子	Hei'an	1183	[Lady]

Reading	Type	Example	Kanji	Period	Date	Added Meaning
shige	N	Kiyoshige	清成	Kamakura	1332	Pure
shige	N	Masashige	正成	Nanboku	1392	Unerring / Genuine
shige	N	Norishige	教成	Kamakura	1332	Teaching / Dogma
shige	N	Sadashige	定成	Hei'an	1183	Determine
shige	N	Shigemoto	成職	Muromachi	1572	Employment / Occupation
shige	N	Shigetomo	成朝	Muromachi	1572	Morning
shige	N	Shige'uji	成氏	Muromachi	1572	Family / Clan
shige	N	Shigeyoshi	成能	Hei'an	1183	Talent / Ability
shige	N	Tadashige	忠成	Kamakura	1332	Faithful / Loyal

生 Life / Live / Living

Reading	Type	Example	Kanji	Period	Date	Added Meaning
iku	S	Ikoma	生駒	Sengoku	1568	Pony
nari	F	Narime	生女	Muromachi	1572	[Woman]
[Special]	S	Gamou	蒲生	Sengoku	1568	The Mace Plant
[Special]	S	Mifu	壬生	Uncertain	1600	Ninth
[Special]	S	Uryuu	瓜生	Kamakura	1332	Melon / Cucumber
[Special]	S	Yagyuu	柳生	Sengoku	1568	Willow Tree

在 Lives / Exists (Animate)

Reading	Type	Example	Kanji	Period	Date	Added Meaning
ari	N	Arihiro	在弘	Nanboku	1392	Draw / Stretch

有 Exists (Inanimate)

Reading	Type	Example	Kanji	Period	Date	Added Meaning
ari	N	Arichika	有親	Kamakura	1332	Intimate
ari	N	Arifusa	有房	Kamakura	1332	Monastic Cell
ari	N	Arihito	有仁	Uncertain	1600	Precious
ari	N	Ari'ie	有家	Kamakura	1332	Rural House / Family
ari	N	Arimasa	有雅	Kamakura	1332	High Quality
ari	N	Arimitsu	有光	Muromachi	1572	Bright / Shining
ari	N	Arimori	有盛	Hei'an	1183	Plentiful / Piled Up
ari	N	Ari'naga	有長	Kamakura	1332	Long
ari	N	Ari'nobu	有信	Muromachi	1572	Belief / Faith
ari	N	Ari'nori	有教	Kamakura	1332	Teaching / Dogma
ari	N	Ari'nori	有範	Kamakura	1332	Required Form / Pattern
ari	N	Arisada	有定	Muromachi	1572	Determine
ari	N	Arishige	有重	Kamakura	1332	Heavy / Serious
ari	N	Aritoki	有時	Kamakura	1332	Time / Era
ari	N	Ariyasu	有安	Hei'an	1183	Gentle / Safe / Secure
ari	N	Ariyo	有世	Nanboku	1392	Generation / Life
ari	N	Ariyoshi	有義	Kamakura	1332	Fealty
ari	N	Atsu'ari	敦有	Nanboku	1392	Generous / Kind / Honest
ari	N	Kin'ari	公有	Muromachi	1572	Noble / Official
ari	N	Masa'ari	雅有	Kamakura	1241	High Quality
ari	N	Michi'ari	通有	Kamakura	1332	Pass Through
ari	N	Nobu'ari	信有	Muromachi	1572	Belief / Faith
ari	N	Yasu'ari	康有	Kamakura	1332	Strong / Confident
ari	N	Yori'ari	頼有	Nanboku	1392	Request / Ask

Thematic Dictionary — Being & Existing

Reading	Type	Example	Kanji	Period	Date	Added Meaning
ari	N	Yoshi'ari	義有	Uncertain	1600	Fealty
ari	N	Yuki'ari	行有	Kamakura	1332	Going To / Bound For
ari	S	Arima	有馬	Sengoku	1568	Horse
ari	S	Arimoto	有元	Kamakura	1332	Base / Original
tomo	N	Tomohisa	有久	Kamakura	1332	Longtime
tomo	N	Tomoyasu	有康	Kamakura	1332	Strong / Confident

是 This / Decide / Choose / Definite

Reading	Type	Example	Kanji	Period	Date	Added Meaning
ZE	F	Zezeme	是々女	Nanboku	1392	[Woman]
kore	N	Kore'nori	是則	Uncertain	1600	Make an Example
kore	N	Koreyoshi	是善	Hei'an	880	Perform Well

伊 This / Him / Her / Rule / Conquer

Note that "Rule" and "Conquer" are older meanings. "This" is a fairly faithful translation of "kore".

Reading	Type	Example	Kanji	Period	Date	Added Meaning
I	F	Ikuheme	伊久倍賣	Nara	784	Longtime + Propagate
I	F	I'nishime	伊尼斯賣	Nara	784	Buddhist Nun + This Way
I	F	Ise	伊勢	Uncertain	1600	Vigor / Spirit / Elan Vital
I	F	Itome	伊刀賣	Nara	784	Sword
I	S	Iga	伊賀	Kamakura	1332	Celebrate A Gain
I	S	I'i	井伊	Nanboku	1392	Well
I	S	Ijuu'in	伊集院	Nanboku	1392	Gather Together + Mansion
I	S	Isaku	伊作	Kamakura	1332	Make / Create
I	S	Isawa	伊澤	Kamakura	1332	Glen / Run
I	S	Ise	伊勢	Nanboku	1392	Vigor / Spirit / Elan Vital
I	S	Itou	伊東	Hei'an	1183	East
I	S	Itou	伊藤	Sengoku	1568	Wisteria
kore	N	Korechika	伊周	Uncertain	1600	Tour / Travel / Bountiful Land
kore	N	Korefusa	伊房	Uncertain	1600	Monastic Cell
kore	N	Korehisa	伊久	Nanboku	1392	Longtime
kore	N	Koretada	伊忠	Muromachi	1572	Faithful / Loyal
[Special]	N	Tadatsu'na	伊綱	Nanboku	1392	Net
[Special]	S	Date	伊達	Nanboku	1392	Carry / Deliver

乃 There

Reading	Type	Example	Kanji	Period	Date	Added Meaning
no	S	Oo'no	大乃	Hei'an	1183	Big

持 Have / Possess

Reading	Type	Example	Kanji	Period	Date	Added Meaning
mochi	N	Mochifusa	持房	Muromachi	1572	Monastic Cell
mochi	N	Mochiharu	持春	Muromachi	1572	Spring (Season)
mochi	N	Mochi'ie	持家	Muromachi	1572	Rural House / Family
mochi	N	Mochikata	持賢	Muromachi	1572	Genius
mochi	N	Mochikiyo	持清	Muromachi	1572	Pure
mochi	N	Mochiku'ni	持国	Muromachi	1572	Country / Rural Area

Reading	Type	Example	Kanji	Period	Date	Added Meaning
mochi	N	Mochimasu	持益	Muromachi	1572	Grow Numerous / Overflow
mochi	N	Mochimichi	持通	Muromachi	1572	Pass Through
mochi	N	Mochimitsu	持光	Muromachi	1572	Bright / Shining
mochi	N	Mochimoto	持基	Muromachi	1572	Foundation
mochi	N	Mochimu'ne	持宗	Muromachi	1572	Master an Art
mochi	N	Mochi'naga	持長	Muromachi	1572	Long
mochi	N	Mochi'naka	持仲	Muromachi	1572	Middle of a Group
mochi	N	Mochi'nobu	持信	Muromachi	1572	Belief / Faith
mochi	N	Mochi'nori	持憲	Muromachi	1440	Example / Pattern
mochi	N	Mochisada	持貞	Muromachi	1572	Correct Spirit
mochi	N	Mochitame	持為	Muromachi	1572	Purpose / Goal
mochi	N	Mochitomo	持朝	Muromachi	1572	Morning
mochi	N	Mochitoyo	持豊	Muromachi	1572	Noble
mochi	N	Mochi'uji	持氏	Muromachi	1572	Family / Clan
mochi	N	Mochiyo	持世	Muromachi	1572	Generation / Life
mochi	N	Mochiyori	持頼	Muromachi	1572	Request / Ask
mochi	N	Mochiyuki	持之	Muromachi	1572	Go / Depart
mochi	N	Naomochi	直持	Nanboku	1392	Adjust / Correct
mochi	N	Yasumochi	康持	Kamakura	1332	Strong / Confident
mochi	N	Yoshimochi	義持	Muromachi	1572	Fealty

惟 This / Here / Now / Ponder

Reading	Type	Example	Kanji	Period	Date	Added Meaning
kore	N	Korechika	惟親	Kamakura	1332	Intimate
kore	N	Korehisa	惟久	Kamakura	1332	Longtime
kore	N	Korekata	惟方	Hei'an	1183	Direction / Method
kore	N	Koremasa	惟政	Nanboku	1392	Govern / Rule
kore	N	Koremasa	惟正	Nanboku	1392	Unerring / Genuine
kore	N	Koremura	惟村	Nanboku	1392	Village
kore	N	Kore'nao	惟直	Kamakura	1332	Adjust / Correct
kore	N	Kore'nobu	惟信	Kamakura	1332	Belief / Faith
kore	N	Koresato	惟郷	Muromachi	1572	Hometown
kore	N	Koreshige	惟重	Kamakura	1332	Heavy / Serious
kore	N	Koretaka	惟孝	Nanboku	1392	Filial Loyalty
kore	N	Koretaka	惟隆	Hei'an	1183	Grow / Pile Up
kore	N	Koretake	惟武	Nanboku	1392	Bravery / Military Force
kore	N	Koretoki	惟時	Nanboku	1392	Time / Era
kore	N	Koretsugu	惟継	Kamakura	1332	Connect / Adopt
kore	N	Koreyoshi	惟義	Kamakura	1332	Fealty
kore	N	Koreyoshi	惟能	Hei'an	1183	Talent / Ability
kore	N	Korezumi	惟澄	Nanboku	1392	Cleanse / Purify
tada	N	Tadayori	惟頼	Uncertain	1600	Request / Ask

斯 This / This Way

Reading	Type	Example	Kanji	Period	Date	Added Meaning
SHI	F	I'nishi	伊尼斯	Uncertain	1600	This
SHI	S	Shiba	斯波	Kamakura	1332	Wave

❖ Artifacts ❖

物 Thing / Artifact

Those familiar with Japanese will recognize that this *kanji* is the substantive element for the generic words for plants and animals.

Reading	Type	Example	Kanji	Period	Date	Added Meaning
MOTSU	S	Kenmotsu	監物	Hei'an	1183	Oversee / Inspect
mono	U	Mo'no'nobe	物部	Nara	710	Monopoly Corporation

琴 Koto (Harp)

Reading	Type	Example	Kanji	Period	Date	Added Meaning
koto	P	Kotohira	琴平	Modern	1983	Tranquility
koto	P	Koto'oka	琴丘	Modern	1983	Hillock

金 Gold / Metal / Money

Reading	Type	Example	Kanji	Period	Date	Added Meaning
kana	S	Ka'namori	金森	Sengoku	1568	Woods
kana	S	Ka'naya	金谷	Nanboku	1392	Valley
kana	S	Ka'nazawa	金澤	Uncertain	1600	Glen / Run
kane	P	Ka'neyama	金山	Modern	1983	Mountain
kane	S	Ka'neko	金子	Kamakura	1332	[Lady]
kane	S	Ka'nezawa	金澤	Uncertain	1600	Glen / Run

鉄 Iron

Reading	Type	Example	Kanji	Period	Date	Added Meaning
[Special]	P	Chichibu	秩父	Modern	1983	

鞠 Toy Ball

Reading	Type	Example	Kanji	Period	Date	Added Meaning
mari	F	Mari	鞠	Uncertain	1600	

玉 Jewel / Sphere

A jewel was one of the three sacred treasures presented to the emperor at. There is some controversy surrounding the nature of this artifact.

Reading	Type	Example	Kanji	Period	Date	Added Meaning
tama	F	Tama	玉	Momoyama	1438	
tama	F	Tamame	玉賣	Nara	784	
tama	F	Tamamushime	玉虫賣	Nara	784	Bug / Insect / Snake
tama	F	Tamatarime	玉足女	Nara	784	Foot / Sufficient + [Woman]
tama	F	Tamateme	玉手	Modern	1983	Hand
tama	F	Tamatsume	玉津賣	Nara	784	Harbour
tama	S	Tama'i	玉井	Nanboku	1392	Well

珂 Gem

These are second in beauty only to true jewels. Suzuki, Takebe and Mizukami specifically mention the crystals found in a geode.

Reading	Type	Example	Kanji	Period	Date	Added Meaning
KA	S	Naka	那珂	Nanboku	1392	What / Whither / How

宝 Treasure

Reading	Type	Example	Kanji	Period	Date	Added Meaning
HOU	Y	Houreki	宝歴	Edo	1751	Progress / Pass Through
HOU	Y	Houtoku	宝徳	Muromachi	1449	Righteous / Just
HOU	Y	Tenpou	延宝	Edo	1673	Prolong / Stretch Out
ku	B	Chikumaru	千宝丸	Kamakura	1332	Thousand + [Boy]
ku	F	Kubome	宝門賣	Hei'an	1183	Gate

鐘 Bell

Buddhist temples in Japan usually have one or more gates, a main hall, a large bell, and one or more pagodas which are reliquaries descended from Indian *stupah* style tombs. The main temple bell is used to announce the hours and smaller bells and chimes are sounded during various ceremonies. A *mokugyo* 木魚 is another noisemaker which is often shaped like a wooden fish. Some sects keep time to chanting sutras by striking a small *mokugyo*. In Zen temples, a large *mokugyo* is often use to summon the monks to meals and other assemblies. *Heike Monogatari* begins with a description of a temple bell tolling the futility of human desire.

Reading	Type	Example	Kanji	Period	Date	Added Meaning
kane	N	Yoshika'ne	義鐘	Muromachi	1572	Obligation / Fealty

鈴 Small Bell

These are very typically very small rattle like bells.

Reading	Type	Example	Kanji	Period	Date	Added Meaning
suzu	F	Suzu	鈴	Uncertain	1600	
suzu	S	Suzuki	鈴木	Uncertain	1600	Tree

幡 Flag / Banner

Reading	Type	Example	Kanji	Period	Date	Added Meaning
hata	F	Hatako	幡子	Hei'an	1183	[Lady]
hata	S	Obata	小幡	Uncertain	1600	Small

紙 Paper

Reading	Type	Example	Kanji	Period	Date	Added Meaning
kami	F	Kamime	紙賣	Nara	784	

香 Incense

Like many other items appearing in Japanese names, incense is strongly associated with Buddhism. Further, the incense ceremonially was a popular pastime dating from the Hei'an period. As such, it is strongly associated with *Genji Monogatari*.

Reading	Type	Example	Kanji	Period	Date	Added Meaning
KOU	S	Kouzai	香西	Kamakura	1332	West
ka	N	Ku'nika	国香	Uncertain	1600	Country / Rural Area
kaori	F	Kaorime	香賣	Nara	784	
[Special]	F	Takako	香子	Hei'an	1183	[Lady]

笠 Umbrella

Reading	Type	Example	Kanji	Period	Date	Added Meaning
kasa	S	Kasawara	笠原	Uncertain	1600	Meadow
kasa	S	Ogasawara	小笠原	Nanboku	1392	Small + Meadow

薬 Drugs

Reading	Type	Example	Kanji	Period	Date	Added Meaning
kusu	F	Kusuko	薬子	Hei'an	1183	[Lady]
kusu	F	Yakushime	薬師女	Kamakura	1332	Teacher / Expert + [Woman]

塩 Salt

Reading	Type	Example	Kanji	Period	Date	Added Meaning
EN	P	Enzan	塩山	Modern	1983	Mountain
shio	F	Shiome	塩賣	Nara	784	
shio	S	Shiozaki	塩崎	Uncertain	1600	Slope

米 Uncooked Rice

Reading	Type	Example	Kanji	Period	Date	Added Meaning
ME	F	Mehirume	米比留賣	Nara	784	Strive + Stay Over / Camp
ME	F	Mememe	米々女	Muromachi	1572	[Woman]
yone	F	Yoneme	米女	Hei'an	1183	[Woman]

酒 Sake / Rice Wine / Alcohol

Reading	Type	Example	Kanji	Period	Date	Added Meaning
saka	S	Sakabe	酒部	Hei'an	1183	Monopoly Corporation
saka	S	Saka'i	酒井	Sengoku	1568	Well

鍋 Cook Pot

Reading	Type	Example	Kanji	Period	Date	Added Meaning
nabe	F	Nabe	鍋	Uncertain	1600	
nabe	S	Nabeshima	鍋島	Uncertain	1600	Island

飯 Cooked Rice

Reading	Type	Example	Kanji	Period	Date	Added Meaning
ii	S	Aihara	栗飯原	Nanboku	1392	Chestnut + Meadow
ii	S	I'i	飯井	Uncertain	1600	Well
ii	S	Iida	飯田	Kamakura	1332	Rice Paddy
ii	S	Ii'no	飯野	Nanboku	1392	Wide Plain
ii	S	I'no'o	飯尾	Muromachi	1572	Tail
[Special]	S	Obu	飯富	Uncertain	1600	Industry

板 Board / Plank

Reading	Type	Example	Kanji	Period	Date	Added Meaning
ita	S	Itagaki	板垣	Kamakura	1332	Fence / Hedge

箱 Box

Reading	Type	Example	Kanji	Period	Date	Added Meaning
hako	P	Hako'ne	箱根	Modern	1983	Root / Base

函 Letter Box

A box in which letters are stored or carried.

Reading	Type	Example	Kanji	Period	Date	Added Meaning
hako	P	Hakodate	函館	Modern	1983	Mansion / Hall

桶 Barrel

Reading	Type	Example	Kanji	Period	Date	Added Meaning
oke	S	Okeguchi	桶口	Uncertain	1600	Mouth / Entrance

筒 Tubular Box

These containers are usually made out of bamboo and are usually closed with a wooden plug.

Reading	Type	Example	Kanji	Period	Date	Added Meaning
tsutsu	S	Tsutsu'i	筒井	Muromachi	1572	Well

鏡 Mirror

Early Japanese mirrors were made out of polished metal such as bronze. A mirror was one of the three sacred treasures presented to the emperor at.

Reading	Type	Example	Kanji	Period	Date	Added Meaning
kagami	S	Kagami	鏡	Kamakura	1332	

船 Boat / Ship

Reading	Type	Example	Kanji	Period	Date	Added Meaning
funa	P	Fu'nabashi	船橋	Modern	1983	Bridge
funa	S	Fu'nada	船田	Kamakura	1332	Rice Paddy
fune	S	Osafu'ne	長船	Kamakura	1332	Long

梶 Rudder

Reading	Type	Example	Kanji	Period	Date	Added Meaning
kaji	S	Kajiwara	梶原	Kamakura	1332	Meadow

糸 Thread

Reading	Type	Example	Kanji	Period	Date	Added Meaning
ito	F	Ito	糸	Momoyama	1590	
ito	F	Ito'ito	糸々	Uncertain	1600	
ito	S	Itoda	糸田	Kamakura	1332	Rice Paddy

維 Cable / Rope

Reading	Type	Example	Kanji	Period	Date	Added Meaning
kore	N	Korehira	維衡	Uncertain	1600	A Yoke
kore	N	Korehira	維平	Kamakura	1332	Tranquility
kore	N	Koremichi	維道	Muromachi	1572	Road / Way
kore	N	Koremochi	維茂	Uncertain	1600	Blossoming
kore	N	Koremori	維盛	Hei'an	1183	Plentiful / Piled Up
kore	N	Koresada	維貞	Kamakura	1332	Correct Spirit

緒 Rope / Cord / Strap / Thong / Functional Beginning

Reading	Type	Example	Kanji	Period	Date	Added Meaning
o	N	Moro'o	師緒	Kamakura	1332	Teacher / Expert
o	S	Ogata	緒方	Hei'an	1183	Direction / Method

糾 Twist / Braid / Rope

Reading	Type	Example	Kanji	Period	Date	Added Meaning
tada	F	Tadasu	糾子	Hei'an	1183	[Lady]

綱 Net

Reading	Type	Example	Kanji	Period	Date	Added Meaning
tsuna	N	Akitsu'na	顕綱	Nanboku	1392	High Status
tsuna	N	Hidetsu'na	秀綱	Nanboku	1392	Extraordinary / Bountiful
tsuna	N	Hirotsu'na	広綱	Kamakura	1332	Spacious / Expansive
tsuna	N	Hirotsu'na	広綱	Kamakura	1332	Spacious / Expansive
tsuna	N	Hisatsu'na	久綱	Kamakura	1332	Longtime
tsuna	N	Hisatsu'na	比綱	Kamakura	1332	Measure Up / Strive
tsuna	N	Kagetsu'na	景綱	Kamakura	1332	Bright / Magnificent
tsuna	N	Ka'netsu'na	兼綱	Hei'an	1183	Unite
tsuna	N	Kintsu'na	公綱	Kamakura	1332	Noble / Official
tsuna	N	Kiyotsu'na	清綱	Hei'an	1183	Pure
tsuna	N	Ku'nitsu'na	国綱	Hei'an	1183	Country / Rural Area
tsuna	N	Ku'nitsu'na	邦綱	Hei'an	1183	Big Country
tsuna	N	Masatsu'na	雅綱	Uncertain	1600	High Quality
tsuna	N	Masatsu'na	政綱	Kamakura	1328	Govern / Rule
tsuna	N	Masatsu'na	正綱	Kamakura	1332	Unerring / Genuine
tsuna	N	Michitsu'na	道綱	Nanboku	1392	Road / Way
tsuna	N	Mitsutsu'na	満綱	Muromachi	1572	Become Full / Abundant
tsuna	N	Moritsu'na	盛綱	Hei'an	1183	Plentiful / Piled Up
tsuna	N	Morotsu'na	師綱	Nanboku	1392	Teacher / Expert
tsuna	N	Mototsu'na	基綱	Kamakura	1332	Foundation
tsuna	N	Mototsu'na	元綱	Sengoku	1568	Base / Original
tsuna	N	Mu'netsu'na	宗綱	Kamakura	1332	Master an Art
tsuna	N	Nakatsu'na	仲綱	Hei'an	1183	Middle of a Group
tsuna	N	Naritsu'na	成綱	Hei'an	1183	Become / Exist
tsuna	N	Nobutsu'na	信綱	Kamakura	1332	Belief / Faith
tsuna	N	Sadatsu'na	貞綱	Kamakura	1332	Correct Spirit
tsuna	N	Sadatsu'na	定綱	Hei'an	1183	Determine
tsuna	N	Sa'netsu'na	実綱	Hei'an	1183	Reality
tsuna	N	Shigetsu'na	重綱	Kamakura	1332	Heavy / Serious
tsuna	N	Suetsu'na	季綱	Muromachi	1572	Season
tsuna	N	Suketsu'na	助綱	Kamakura	1332	Deputy (Rescue / Assist)
tsuna	N	Tadatsu'na	伊綱	Nanboku	1392	This
tsuna	N	Tadatsu'na	忠綱	Hei'an	1183	Faithful / Loyal
tsuna	N	Takatsu'na	高綱	Hei'an	1183	Tall
tsuna	N	Ta'netsu'na	胤綱	Kamakura	1332	Blood Heir
tsuna	N	Tokitsu'na	時綱	Kamakura	1332	Time / Era
tsuna	N	Tomotsu'na	朝綱	Kamakura	1332	Morning
tsuna	N	Tomotsu'na	等綱	Muromachi	1572	Rank / Level
tsuna	N	Toshitsu'na	俊綱	Hei'an	1183	Emotional
tsuna	N	Toshitsu'na	利綱	Muromachi	1572	Produce Results
tsuna	N	Tsunamitsu	綱光	Muromachi	1572	Bright / Shining
tsuna	N	Ujitsu'na	氏綱	Nanboku	1392	Family / Clan
tsuna	N	Yasutsu'na	泰綱	Kamakura	1332	Peace / Plenitude
tsuna	N	Yoritsu'na	頼綱	Kamakura	1332	Request / Ask
tsuna	N	Yoshitsu'na	義綱	Kamakura	1332	Fealty
tsuna	N	Yukitsu'na	行綱	Hei'an	1183	Going To / Bound For

Thematic Dictionary — Artifacts

品 Goods

Reading	Type	Example	Kanji	Period	Date	Added Meaning
shina	S	Shi'nagawa	品河	Kamakura	1332	Large River

彰 Showpiece / Masterpiece

Reading	Type	Example	Kanji	Period	Date	Added Meaning
aki	F	Aki	彰	Uncertain	1600	

台 Pedestal / Dais

Reading	Type	Example	Kanji	Period	Date	Added Meaning
DAI	P	Sendai	仙台	Modern	1983	Hermit / Adept

❖ Textiles & Clothing ❖

絹 Silk

Reading	Type	Example	Kanji	Period	Date	Added Meaning
kinu	F	Ki'nu	絹	Uncertain	1600	

麻 Linen / Flax

Reading	Type	Example	Kanji	Period	Date	Added Meaning
asa	P	Azabu	麻布	Modern	1983	Cloth
asa	P	Asou	麻生	Modern	1983	Life / Live / Living
[Special]	P	Omi	麻績	Modern	1983	Spin (Thread)

布 Cloth

Reading	Type	Example	Kanji	Period	Date	Added Meaning
FU	F	Nihofume	尔保布女	Nara	784	That + Guarantee + [Woman]
FU	F	Shitafume	志多布賣	Nara	784	Many + Cloth
FU	P	Azabu	麻布	Modern	1983	Flax / Linen

錦 Brocade

Note that the final syllable of "nishiki" is coarticulated with the first syllable of "ori" in Nishigori.

Reading	Type	Example	Kanji	Period	Date	Added Meaning
nishiki	S	Nishigori	錦織	Kamakura	1332	Weave

絢 Pretty Cloth

Reading	Type	Example	Kanji	Period	Date	Added Meaning
aya	F	Aya	絢	Uncertain	1600	

総 Tuft / Fringe / Tassel

This *kanji* also denotes the entirety of something. You may think of this as meaning "to the tassels."

Reading	Type	Example	Kanji	Period	Date	Added Meaning
fusa	S	Kazusa	上総	Kamakura	1332	Superior

衣 Robe

Reading	Type	Example	Kanji	Period	Date	Added Meaning
kinu	F	Ki'nume	衣女	Nara	784	[Woman]
kinu	F	Ki'nume	衣賣	Nara	784	
kinu	F	Ki'nu'nuhime	衣縫賣	Nara	784	Sew

蓑 Rain or Snow Cape

These rain or snow capes are made out of rushes.

Reading	Type	Example	Kanji	Period	Date	Added Meaning
mino	F	Omi'nome	小蓑賣	Nara	784	Small
mino	F	Womi'nome	小蓑賣	Nara	784	Small

❖ Tools & Implements ❖

工   Tool / Artisan

Reading	Type	Example	Kanji	Period	Date	Added Meaning
KU	S	Kudou	工藤	Kamakura	1332	Wisteria

具   Tool / Implement

Reading	Type	Example	Kanji	Period	Date	Added Meaning
tomo	F	Tomoko	具子	Nanboku	1392	[Lady]
tomo	F	Tomotarime	具足女	Nara	784	Foot / Sufficient + [Woman]
tomo	N	Harutomo	晴具	Uncertain	1600	Clear (Sky)
tomo	N	Masatomo	政具	Uncertain	1600	Govern / Rule
tomo	N	Michitomo	通具	Kamakura	1332	Pass Through
tomo	N	Noritomo	教具	Muromachi	1572	Teaching / Dogma
tomo	N	Tomomichi	具通	Nanboku	1392	Pass Through
tomo	N	Tomomori	具守	Kamakura	1332	Protect / Defend
tomo	N	Tomo'nori	具教	Uncertain	1600	Teaching / Dogma
tomo	N	Tomoshige	具滋	Kamakura	1332	Grow / Blossom
tomo	N	Tomoyuki	具行	Kamakura	1332	Going To / Bound For

爾   Bobbin / Distaff / Spool

While this *kanji* originally represented a bobbin or spool, it was later used as a second person pronoun. This is how it is used in modern Japanese.

Reading	Type	Example	Kanji	Period	Date	Added Meaning
JI	H	Shouji	章爾	Uncertain	1600	Writing / Elucidate
JI	H	Shouji	晶爾	Uncertain	1600	Star Light / Pure Light
NI	F	Ku'nime	久爾賣	Nara	784	Longtime
NI	F	Na'nimo	奈爾毛	Uncertain	1600	Why? / How? + Wool
NI	F	Na'nimome	奈爾毛賣	Nara	784	Why? / How? + Wool
NI	F	Nihime	爾比賣	Nara	784	Measure Up / Strive
NI	F	Nikoyame	爾古屋賣	Nara	784	Old Artisan

針   Needle

Reading	Type	Example	Kanji	Period	Date	Added Meaning
hari	F	Harime	針賣	Nara	784	
hari	S	Hariya	針屋	Uncertain	1600	Urban House / Artisan

Thematic Dictionary — Tools & Implements

臼 Grindstone / Mortar (Implement)

Reading	Type	Example	Kanji	Period	Date	Added Meaning
usu	S	Usu'i	臼井	Nanboku	1392	Well
usu	S	Usuki	臼杵	Hei'an	1183	Pestle

杵 Pestle

Note that the final syllable of "kine" is dropped in Usuki.

Reading	Type	Example	Kanji	Period	Date	Added Meaning
kine	S	Usuki	臼杵	Hei'an	1183	Mortar (Implement)

砥 Whetstone / Grindstone / Flat

Reading	Type	Example	Kanji	Period	Date	Added Meaning
to	S	Aoto	青砥	Kamakura	1332	Blue / Green

鎌 Scythe

Reading	Type	Example	Kanji	Period	Date	Added Meaning
kama	N	Kamatari	鎌足	Uncertain	1600	Foot / Sufficient
kama	S	Kamata	鎌田	Hei'an	1183	Rice Paddy

刀 Sword

Early Japanese swords were long and straight and were suspended from a belt about the waist by two cords. A sword was one of the three sacred treasures presented to the emperor at.

Reading	Type	Example	Kanji	Period	Date	Added Meaning
TO	F	Itome	伊刀賣	Nara	784	This / Him / Her / Conquer
TO	F	Tojime	刀自賣	Nara	784	Independent
TO	F	Tome	刀賣	Nara	784	
TO	F	Tomime	刀美賣	Nara	784	Beauty
TO	F	Torame	刀良賣	Nara	784	Good / Superior
TO	F	Wotojime	乎刀自賣	Nara	784	Destination + Indenpent
[Special]	F	Hakashime	刀賣	Nara	784	

矢 Arrow

Reading	Type	Example	Kanji	Period	Date	Added Meaning
ya	S	Ooya'no	大矢野	Kamakura	1332	Big + Wide Plain
ya	S	Yagi	矢木	Kamakura	1332	Tree
ya	P	Yaguchi	矢口	Modern	1983	Mouth / Entrance

弓 Bow

This *kanji* represents the weapon and those things which resemble it.

Reading	Type	Example	Kanji	Period	Date	Added Meaning
TE	F	Soteme	蘇弓賣	Nara	784	Dark Crimson

輪 Cart Wheel

Wheels are particularly associated with karma in Buddhism and with the *Genji Monogatari*.

Reading	Type	Example	Kanji	Period	Date	Added Meaning
nawa	S	Tannawa	淡輪	Nanboku	1392	Thin / Pale / Weak

衡 A Yoke

Reading	Type	Example	Kanji	Period	Date	Added Meaning
hira	N	Akihira	明衡	Uncertain	1600	Bright
hira	N	Chikahira	親衡	Kamakura	1213	Intimate
hira	N	Hidehira	秀衡	Hei'an	1183	Extraordinary / Bountiful
hira	N	Ka'nehira	兼衡	Hei'an	1183	Unite
hira	N	Kinhira	公衡	Kamakura	1332	Noble / Official
hira	N	Kiyohira	清衡	Uncertain	1600	Pure
hira	N	Korehira	維衡	Uncertain	1600	Cable / Rope
hira	N	Ku'nihira	国衡	Kamakura	1189	Country / Rural Area
hira	N	Masahira	正衡	Uncertain	1600	Unerring / Genuine
hira	N	Motohira	基衡	Uncertain	1600	Foundation
hira	N	Mu'nehira	宗衡	Kamakura	1332	Master an Art
hira	N	Sadahira	貞衡	Kamakura	1332	Correct Spirit
hira	N	Shigehira	重衡	Hei'an	1183	Heavy / Serious
hira	N	Sukehira	資衡	Muromachi	1572	Raw Materials
hira	N	Takahira	高衡	Kamakura	1332	Tall
hira	N	Takahira	隆衡	Kamakura	1332	Grow / Pile Up
hira	N	Toshihira	俊衡	Hei'an	1183	Emotional
hira	N	Yasuhira	泰衡	Hei'an	1155	Peace / Plenitude

❖ Purity ❖

清 Pure

Names containing an element associated with water are especially propitious for these people. Kiyofusa 清房 contains 清(purity) as a descriptive element. Like many older religions, Shintoh is a purity cult. Shintohists purified themselves by bathing in a manner similar to the god Izanagi. Consequently, water is an auspicious symbol of purity in Japan. The first four *kanji* in this section share a common ideographic water radical.

Reading	Type	Example	Kanji	Period	Date	Added Meaning
SEI	F	Seishi	清子	Kamakura	1332	[Lady]
kiyo	F	Kiyoko	清子	Nanboku	1392	[Lady]
kiyo	N	Chikakiyo	親清	Kamakura	1332	Intimate
kiyo	N	Hidekiyo	秀清	Kamakura	1332	Extraordinary / Bountiful
kiyo	N	Kagekiyo	景清	Hei'an	1183	Bright / Magnificent
kiyo	N	Kinkiyo	公清	Nanboku	1392	Noble / Official
kiyo	N	Kiyofusa	清房	Hei'an	1183	Monastic Cell
kiyo	N	Kiyohide	清秀	Uncertain	1600	Extraordinary / Bountiful
kiyo	N	Kiyohira	清衡	Uncertain	1600	A Yoke
kiyo	N	Kiyohira	清平	Muromachi	1572	Tranquility
kiyo	N	Kiyokata	清方	Muromachi	1572	Direction / Method
kiyo	N	Kiyoku'ni	清邦	Hei'an	1183	Big Country
kiyo	N	Kiyomasa	清正	Uncertain	1600	Unerring / Genuine
kiyo	N	Kiyomitsu	清光	Hei'an	1183	Bright / Shining
kiyo	N	Kiyomori	清盛	Hei'an	1183	Plentiful / Piled Up
kiyo	N	Kiyomu'ne	清宗	Hei'an	1183	Master an Art
kiyo	N	Kiyo'naga	清長	Kamakura	1332	Long
kiyo	N	Kiyo'nari	清業	Hei'an	1183	Industry / Diligence
kiyo	N	Kiyo'nori	清教	Uncertain	1600	Teaching / Dogma
kiyo	N	Kiyosada	清貞	Nanboku	1392	Correct Spirit
kiyo	N	Kiyosada	清定	Kamakura	1332	Determine
kiyo	N	Kiyoshige	清重	Hei'an	1183	Heavy / Serious
kiyo	N	Kiyoshige	清成	Kamakura	1332	Become / Exist
kiyo	N	Kiyosuke	清輔	Uncertain	1600	Ministerial Deputy
kiyo	N	Kiyotada	清忠	Kamakura	1332	Faithful / Loyal
kiyo	N	Kiyotaka	清高	Kamakura	1332	Tall
kiyo	N	Kiyota'ne	清胤	Nanboku	1392	Blood Heir
kiyo	N	Kiyota'ne	清種	Kamakura	1332	Cause / Reason
kiyo	N	Kiyotoki	清時	Kamakura	1332	Time / Era
kiyo	N	Kiyotomo	清公	Hei'an	842	Noble / Official
kiyo	N	Kiyotsu'na	清綱	Hei'an	1183	Net
kiyo	N	Kiyotsu'ne	清経	Hei'an	1183	True Path
kiyo	N	Kiyo'uji	清氏	Nanboku	1392	Family / Clan
kiyo	N	Kiyo'uji	清氏	Nanboku	1392	Family / Clan
kiyo	N	Kiyoyuki	清行	Sengoku	1568	Going To / Bound For
kiyo	N	Ku'nikiyo	国清	Nanboku	1392	Country / Rural Area
kiyo	N	Masakiyo	雅清	Nanboku	1390	High Quality
kiyo	N	Masakiyo	政清	Muromachi	1572	Govern / Rule

Reading	Type	Example	Kanji	Period	Date	Added Meaning
kiyo	N	Masakiyo	正清	Hei'an	1183	Unerring / Genuine
kiyo	N	Michikiyo	通清	Kamakura	1332	Pass Through
kiyo	N	Mochikiyo	持清	Muromachi	1572	Have / Possess
kiyo	N	Motokiyo	基清	Kamakura	1332	Foundation
kiyo	N	Motokiyo	元清	Nanboku	1392	Base / Original
kiyo	N	Mu'nekiyo	宗清	Hei'an	1183	Master an Art
kiyo	N	Nagakiyo	長清	Kamakura	1332	Long
kiyo	N	Nobukiyo	信清	Kamakura	1332	Belief / Faith
kiyo	N	Norikiyo	憲清	Muromachi	1397	Example / Pattern
kiyo	N	Norikiyo	教清	Muromachi	1572	Teaching / Dogma
kiyo	N	Norikiyo	則清	Hei'an	1183	Make an Example
kiyo	N	Sadakiyo	貞清	Kamakura	1332	Correct Spirit
kiyo	N	Sadakiyo	定清	Nanboku	1335	Determine
kiyo	N	Shigekiyo	重清	Nanboku	1392	Heavy / Serious
kiyo	N	Sukekiyo	資清	Muromachi	1572	Raw Materials
kiyo	N	Sukekiyo	祐清	Kamakura	1332	Divine Help
kiyo	N	Tadakiyo	忠清	Kamakura	1332	Faithful / Loyal
kiyo	N	Takakiyo	高清	Hei'an	1183	Tall
kiyo	N	Takakiyo	隆清	Kamakura	1332	Grow / Pile Up
kiyo	N	Tokikiyo	時清	Kamakura	1332	Time / Era
kiyo	N	Toshikiyo	俊清	Uncertain	1600	Emotional
kiyo	N	Ujikiyo	氏清	Nanboku	1392	Family / Clan
kiyo	N	Yasukiyo	泰清	Kamakura	1332	Peace / Plenitude
kiyo	N	Yorikiyo	頼清	Nanboku	1392	Request / Ask
kiyo	N	Yoshikiyo	義清	Hei'an	1163	Fealty
kiyo	N	Yukikiyo	行清	Kamakura	1332	Going To / Bound For
kiyo	P	Kiyomizudera	清水寺	Modern	1983	Water + Temple
kiyo	S	Kiyohara	清原	Kamakura	1332	Meadow

潔 Purity

Reading	Type	Example	Kanji	Period	Date	Added Meaning
[Special]	F	Kiyoi	潔子	Hei'an	1183	[Lady]

澄 Cleanse / Purify

Reading	Type	Example	Kanji	Period	Date	Added Meaning
sumi	N	Hirozumi	広澄	Sengoku	1568	Spacious / Expansive
sumi	N	Korezumi	惟澄	Nanboku	1392	This / Here
sumi	N	Shigezumi	重澄	Hei'an	1183	Heavy / Serious
sumi	N	Tadazumi	忠澄	Kamakura	1332	Faithful / Loyal
sumi	N	Tadazumi	直澄	Sengoku	1568	Adjust / Correct
sumi	N	Takezumi	武澄	Nanboku	1392	Bravery / Military Force
sumi	N	Tsu'nezumi	常澄	Hei'an	1183	Permanent
sumi	N	Yoshizumi	義澄	Kamakura	1332	Fealty

淑 Clean / Beautiful

Reading	Type	Example	Kanji	Period	Date	Added Meaning
yoshi	F	Yoshihime	淑姫	Hei'an	1183	Princess
yoshi	F	Yoshiko	淑子	Hei'an	1183	[Lady]

性 Nature / Attributes / Purity

While this *kanji* normally only takes the meaning "purity" when it takes 'SHOU" as its *onyomi*, it seems likely that this is the intended meaning in the *houmyou* given below.

Reading	Type	Example	Kanji	Period	Date	Added Meaning
SEI	H	Sosei	素性	Uncertain	1600	White / Unused / Virgin

乎 Simple / Pure (Strong Image) / Destination / Objective / Simple / Easy

Reading	Type	Example	Kanji	Period	Date	Added Meaning
wo	F	Tawo	多乎	Uncertain	1600	Many
wo	F	Tawome	多乎賣	Nara	784	Destination
wo	F	Wobame	乎婆賣	Nara	784	Old Woman / Hag
wo	F	Womame	乎麻賣	Nara	784	Flax / Linen
wo	F	Woshime	乎姿賣	Nara	784	Form / Shape / Figure
wo	F	Wotojime	乎刀自賣	Nara	784	Sword + Independent
wo	F	Woyame	乎夜賣	Nara	784	Evening

純 Natural / Pure / Uncontaminated

Reading	Type	Example	Kanji	Period	Date	Added Meaning
sumi	N	Akizumi	明純	Muromachi	1572	Bright
sumi	N	Iezumi	家純	Muromachi	1572	Rural House / Family
sumi	N	Masazumi	正純	Momoyama	1585	Unerring / Genuine
sumi	N	Mitsuzumi	満純	Muromachi	1572	Become Full / Abundant
sumi	N	Naozumi	尚純	Muromachi	1572	Excellence
sumi	N	Sumitomo	純友	Uncertain	1600	Friend
sumi	N	Yoshizumi	義純	Hei'an	1183	Fealty

嘉 Well Done

Reading	Type	Example	Kanji	Period	Date	Added Meaning
KA	Y	Ka'ei	嘉永	Edo	1848	Forever
KA	Y	Kagen	嘉元	Kamakura	1303	Base / Original
KA	Y	Kahou	嘉保	Hei'an	1094	Guarantee
KA	Y	Kakei	嘉慶	Nanboku	1387	Rejoice / Deer Skin
KA	Y	Kakitsu	嘉吉	Muromachi	1441	Lucky / Fortunate
KA	Y	Ku'ou	嘉応	Kamakura	1169	Worthy / Suitable
KA	Y	Karoku	嘉禄	Kamakura	1225	Gratitude / Beneficence
KA	Y	Karyaku	嘉歴	Kamakura	1326	Progress / Pass Through
KA	Y	Kashou	嘉承	Hei'an	1106	Humbly Receive
KA	Y	Katei	嘉禎	Kamakura	1235	Divine Fortune / Happy
KA	Y	Shouka	正嘉	Kamakura	1257	Unerring / Genuine
yoshi	N	Katsuyoshi	勝嘉	Sengoku	1568	Conquer / Triumph
yoshi	N	Mitsuyoshi	光嘉	Sengoku	1568	Bright / Shining
yoshi	N	Yoshihiro	嘉広	Higashiyama	1575	Spacious / Expansive

範 Required Form / Example

Reading	Type	Example	Kanji	Period	Date	Added Meaning
HAN	F	Hanshi	範子	Kamakura	1200	[Lady]
nori	N	Aki'nori	詮範	Muromachi	1572	Explicit / Clear
nori	N	Ari'nori	有範	Kamakura	1332	Exists
nori	N	Chika'nori	親範	Hei'an	1183	Intimate
nori	N	Mitsu'nori	光範	Nanboku	1392	Bright / Shining
nori	N	Mitsu'nori	満範	Muromachi	1572	Become Full / Abundant
nori	N	Moto'nori	基範	Hei'an	1183	Foundation
nori	N	Nari'nori	成範	Hei'an	1183	Become / Exist
nori	N	Nobu'nori	信範	Hei'an	1183	Belief / Faith
nori	N	Norihiro	範広	Nanboku	1392	Spacious / Expansive
nori	N	Nori'ie	範家	Hei'an	1183	Rural House / Family
nori	N	Norika'ne	範兼	Uncertain	1600	Unite
nori	N	Noriku'ni	範国	Nanboku	1392	Country / Rural Area
nori	N	Norimasa	範政	Muromachi	1572	Govern / Rule
nori	N	Norimitsu	範光	Nanboku	1392	Bright / Shining
nori	N	Norimu'ne	範宗	Muromachi	1572	Master an Art
nori	N	Nori'naga	範長	Nanboku	1392	Long
nori	N	Norishige	範茂	Kamakura	1332	Blossoming
nori	N	Norisue	範季	Kamakura	1332	Season
nori	N	Norisuke	範資	Nanboku	1392	Raw Materials
nori	N	Norisuke	範輔	Kamakura	1332	Ministerial Deputy
nori	N	Noritada	範忠	Muromachi	1572	Faithful / Loyal
nori	N	Noritomo	範朝	Kamakura	1332	Morning
nori	N	Nori'uji	範氏	Nanboku	1392	Family / Clan
nori	N	Noriyori	範頼	Hei'an	1183	Request / Ask
nori	N	Noriza'ne	範実	Nanboku	1392	Reality
nori	N	Sada'nori	定範	Kamakura	1332	Determine
nori	N	Shige'nori	重範	Kamakura	1332	Heavy / Serious
nori	N	Tomo'nori	朝範	Nanboku	1392	Morning
nori	N	Uji'nori	氏範	Nanboku	1392	Family / Clan
nori	N	Yasu'nori	泰範	Nanboku	1392	Peace / Plenitude
nori	N	Yoshi'nori	義範	Kamakura	1332	Fealty

模 Model / Example / Guide

Originally, this *kanji* was more specific and referred to making wooden models.

Reading	Type	Example	Kanji	Period	Date	Added Meaning
sa	F	Sakami	相模	Uncertain	1600	Togeterh / Team Work

憲 Example / Pattern

Reading	Type	Example	Kanji	Period	Date	Added Meaning
nori	N	Michi'nori	通憲	Hei'an	1183	Pass Through
nori	N	Mochi'nori	持憲	Muromachi	1440	Have / Possess
nori	N	Nori'aki	憲顕	Nanboku	1392	High Status
nori	N	Nori'aki	憲秋	Nanboku	1392	Autumn
nori	N	Norifuji	憲藤	Nanboku	1392	Wisteria
nori	N	Norifusa	憲房	Nanboku	1392	Monastic Cell
nori	N	Noriharu	憲春	Nanboku	1392	Spring (Season)
nori	N	Norikata	憲方	Nanboku	1392	Direction / Method

Thematic Dictionary — **Purity**   287

Reading	Type	Example	Kanji	Period	Date	Added Meaning
nori	N	Norikiyo	憲清	Muromachi	1397	Pure
nori	N	Norimasa	憲将	Uncertain	1600	Commander
nori	N	Norimoto	憲幹	Kamakura	1332	Trunk / Stalk
nori	N	Norimoto	憲基	Muromachi	1572	Foundation
nori	N	Norisada	憲定	Muromachi	1572	Determine
nori	N	Norisaka	憲栄	Uncertain	1600	Bountiful / Fruitful
nori	N	Noritada	憲忠	Nanboku	1392	Faithful / Loyal
nori	N	Noritaka	憲孝	Nanboku	1392	Filial Loyalty
nori	N	Norita'ne	憲胤	Nanboku	1392	Blood Heir
nori	N	Noriyori	憲頼	Hei'an	1183	Request / Ask
nori	N	Noriza'ne	憲実	Muromachi	1572	Reality
nori	N	Tame'nori	為憲	Uncertain	1600	Purpose / Goal
nori	N	Uji'nori	氏憲	Muromachi	1572	Family / Clan
nori	N	Yoshi'nori	能憲	Nanboku	1392	Talent / Ability

則 Make an Example

This is yet another character which means "example" or guide in some sense. This particular character means to decide upon an example.

Reading	Type	Example	Kanji	Period	Date	Added Meaning
nori	N	Chika'nori	近則	Kamakura	1332	Near
nori	N	Kore'nori	是則	Uncertain	1600	Definite
nori	N	Masa'nori	政則	Muromachi	1572	Govern / Rule
nori	N	Masa'nori	正則	Sengoku	1568	Unerring / Genuine
nori	N	Mitsu'nori	満則	Muromachi	1572	Become Full / Abundant
nori	N	Norikiyo	則清	Hei'an	1183	Pure
nori	N	Norimu'ne	則宗	Hei'an	1183	Master an Art
nori	N	Norimura	則村	Kamakura	1332	Village
nori	N	Nori'nao	則尚	Muromachi	1572	Excellence
nori	N	Norishige	則繁	Muromachi	1572	Bloom / Bouquet
nori	N	Norisuke	則祐	Nanboku	1392	Divine Help
nori	N	Noriyori	則頼	Sengoku	1568	Request / Ask
nori	N	Suke'nori	祐則	Muromachi	1572	Divine Help
nori	N	Tomo'nori	友則	Uncertain	1600	Friend
nori	N	Yoshi'nori	義則	Nanboku	1392	Fealty

❖ Ethics ❖

秀 Produce Good / Extraordinary / Bountiful

Reading	Type	Example	Kanji	Period	Date	Added Meaning
hide	F	Hideko	秀子	Nanboku	1392	[Lady]
hide	N	Akihide	顕秀	Kamakura	1332	High Status
hide	N	Chikahide	親秀	Kamakura	1332	Intimate
hide	N	Hide'aki	秀詮	Nanboku	1392	Explicit / Clear
hide	N	Hidehira	秀衡	Hei'an	1183	A Yoke
hide	N	Hide'ie	秀家	Uncertain	1600	Rural House / Family
hide	N	Hidekazu	秀一	Sengoku	1568	One
hide	N	Hidekiyo	秀清原	Kamakura	1332	Pure
hide	N	Hidemasa	秀政	Sengoku	1568	Govern / Rule
hide	N	Hidemochi	秀望	Sengoku	1568	Heartfelt Wish
hide	N	Hidemoto	秀幹	Muromachi	1572	Trunk / Stalk
hide	N	Hidemoto	秀元	Sengoku	1568	Base / Original
hide	N	Hide'naga	秀永	Uncertain	1600	Forever
hide	N	Hidesato	秀郷	Uncertain	1600	Hometown
hide	N	Hidetada	秀忠	Uncertain	1600	Faithful / Loyal
hide	N	Hideta'ne	秀胤	Kamakura	1332	Blood Heir
hide	N	Hidetomo	秀朝	Kamakura	1332	Morning
hide	N	Hidetsugu	秀次	Uncertain	1600	Next
hide	N	Hidetsu'na	秀綱	Nanboku	1392	Net
hide	N	Hide'uji	秀氏	Sengoku	1568	Family / Clan
hide	N	Hideyasu	秀康	Kamakura	1332	Strong / Confident
hide	N	Hideyoshi	秀義	Hei'an	1183	Fealty
hide	N	Hideyoshi	秀吉	Sengoku	1568	Lucky / Fortunate
hide	N	Hideyoshi	秀能	Kamakura	1332	Talent / Ability
hide	N	Hideyuki	秀行	Kamakura	1332	Going To / Bound For
hide	N	Hisahide	久秀	Uncertain	1600	Longtime
hide	N	Kawahide	賢秀	Sengoku	1568	Genius
hide	N	Kinhide	公秀	Kamakura	1332	Noble / Official
hide	N	Kiyohide	清秀	Uncertain	1600	Pure
hide	N	Masahide	正秀	Uncertain	1600	Unerring / Genuine
hide	N	Michihide	通秀	Muromachi	1572	Pass Through
hide	N	Mitsuhide	光秀	Sengoku	1568	Bright / Shining
hide	N	Mitsuhide	満秀	Muromachi	1572	Become Full / Abundant
hide	N	Morihide	盛秀	Uncertain	1600	Plentiful / Piled Up
hide	N	Morohide	師秀	Nanboku	1392	Teacher / Expert
hide	N	Motohide	基秀	Muromachi	1572	Foundation
hide	N	Mu'nehide	宗秀	Kamakura	1332	Master an Art
hide	N	Nagahide	長秀	Muromachi	1572	Long
hide	N	Nobuhide	宣秀	Nanboku	1392	Proclamation
hide	N	Sadahide	貞秀	Nanboku	1392	Correct Spirit
hide	N	Sa'nehide	実秀	Muromachi	1572	Reality
hide	N	Sukehide	佐秀	Nanboku	1392	Military Deputy

Thematic Dictionary — Ethics   289

Reading	Type	Example	Kanji	Period	Date	Added Meaning
hide	N	Takahide	高秀	Nanboku	1392	Tall
hide	N	Tamehide	為秀	Nanboku	1392	Purpose / Goal
hide	N	Tokihide	時秀	Kamakura	1332	Time / Era
hide	N	Toshihide	俊秀	Hei'an	1183	Emotional
hide	N	Tsu'nehide	常秀	Kamakura	1332	Permanent
hide	N	Ujihide	氏秀	Nanboku	1392	Family / Clan
hide	N	Yasuhide	康秀	Uncertain	1600	Strong / Confident
hide	N	Yasuhide	泰秀	Kamakura	1332	Peace / Plenitude
hide	N	Yorihide	頼秀	Kamakura	1332	Request / Ask
hide	N	Yoshihide	慶秀	Kamakura	1332	Rejoice / Deer Skin
hide	N	Yoshihide	義秀	Kamakura	1332	Fealty
hide	N	Yoshihide	能秀	Kamakura	1332	Talent / Ability
hide	N	Yukihide	行秀	Nanboku	1392	Going To / Bound For

良 Good / Superior

Reading	Type	Example	Kanji	Period	Date	Added Meaning
RA	F	Tora	刀良	Uncertain	1600	Sword
RA	P	Nara	奈良	Hei'an	800	Why? / How?
yoshi	N	Hikoyoshi	彦良	Nanboku	1392	Boy / Young Scholar
yoshi	N	Ieyoshi	家良	Kamakura	1332	Rural House / Family
yoshi	N	Ka'nera	兼良	Muromachi	1572	Unite
yoshi	N	Michi'naga	道良	Kamakura	1332	Road / Way
yoshi	N	Moroyoshi	師良	Nanboku	1392	Teacher / Expert
yoshi	N	Motoyoshi	元良	Uncertain	1600	Base / Original
yoshi	N	Mu'neyoshi	宗良	Kamakura	1332	Master an Art
yoshi	N	Nagayoshi	長良	Uncertain	1600	Long
yoshi	N	Tadayoshi	忠良	Kamakura	1332	Faithful / Loyal
yoshi	N	Yoshi'ai	良相	Uncertain	1600	Together / Team Work
yoshi	N	Yoshifusa	良房	Uncertain	1600	Monastic Cell
yoshi	N	Yoshihira	良平	Kamakura	1332	Tranquility
yoshi	N	Yoshikado	良門	Uncertain	1600	Gate
yoshi	N	Yoshimasa	良将	Uncertain	1600	Commander
yoshi	N	Yoshimichi	良通	Hei'an	1183	Pass Through
yoshi	N	Yoshimochi	良望	Uncertain	1600	Heartfelt Wish
yoshi	N	Yoshimoto	良基	Nanboku	1392	Foundation
yoshi	N	Yoshi'nari	良業	Kamakura	1332	Industry / Diligence
yoshi	N	Yoshi'nobu	良宣	Muromachi	1572	Proclamation
yoshi	N	Yoshi'nori	良教	Kamakura	1332	Teaching / Dogma
yoshi	N	Yoshisada	良定	Uncertain	1600	Determine
yoshi	N	Yoshisuke	良相	Uncertain	1600	Together / Team Work
yoshi	N	Yoshisuke	良輔	Kamakura	1332	Ministerial Deputy
yoshi	N	Yoshitsugu	良嗣	Muromachi	1572	Successor
yoshi	N	Yoshitsu'ne	良経	Kamakura	1332	True Path
yoshi	N	Yoshiza'ne	良実	Kamakura	1332	Reality
yoshi	S	Era	恵良	Nanboku	1392	Sanctify / Bless
yoshi	S	Kira	吉良	Kamakura	1332	Lucky / Fortunate
yoshi	S	Sagara	相良	Kamakura	1332	Together / Team Work
yoshi	S	Serada	世良田	Kamakura	1332	Generation + Rice Paddy
yoshi	S	Tatara	多々良	Kamakura	1332	Many
yoshi	S	Yura	由良	Kamakura	1332	Purpose

廉 Reason / Justification

Reading	Type	Example	Kanji	Period	Date	Added Meaning
kado	N	Kagekado	景廉	Kamakura	1332	Bright / Magnificent
kado	N	Nobukado	信廉	Uncertain	1600	Belief / Faith
kado	N	Yoshikado	義廉	Muromachi	1572	Obligation / Fealty
yasu	F	Yasuko	廉子	Nanboku	1392	[Lady]
yasu	N	Yoshiyasu	義廉	Uncertain	1600	Obligation / Fealty

為 Purpose / Goal

Reading	Type	Example	Kanji	Period	Date	Added Meaning
tame	N	Mochitame	持為	Muromachi	1572	Have / Possess
tame	N	Tame'aki	為明	Nanboku	1392	Bright
tame	N	Tamefuyu	為冬	Kamakura	1332	Winter
tame	N	Tamehide	為秀	Nanboku	1392	Extraordinary / Bountiful
tame	N	Tamehiro	為広	Sengoku	1568	Spacious / Expansive
tame	N	Tamehisa	為久	Kamakura	1332	Longtime
tame	N	Tame'ie	為家	Kamakura	1332	Rural House / Family
tame	N	Tameka'ne	為兼	Kamakura	1332	Unite
tame	N	Tamekazu	為数	Muromachi	1572	Fate / Determined Amount
tame	N	Tamemitsu	為光	Uncertain	1600	Bright / Shining
tame	N	Tamemori	為守	Kamakura	1332	Protect / Defend
tame	N	Tamemoto	為基	Hei'an	1183	Foundation
tame	N	Tame'naga	為長	Kamakura	1332	Long
tame	N	Tame'nobu	為信	Kamakura	1332	Belief / Faith
tame	N	Tame'nori	為教	Kamakura	1332	Teaching / Dogma
tame	N	Tame'nori	為憲	Uncertain	1600	Example / Pattern
tame	N	Tamesada	為貞	Kamakura	1332	Correct Spirit
tame	N	Tamesada	為定	Kamakura	1332	Determine
tame	N	Tameshige	為重	Kamakura	1332	Heavy / Serious
tame	N	Tamesuke	為相	Kamakura	1332	Together / Team Work
tame	N	Tameta'ne	為種	Muromachi	1572	Cause / Reason
tame	N	Tametoki	為時	Uncertain	1600	Time / Era
tame	N	Tametomo	為朝	Uncertain	1600	Morning
tame	N	Tame'uji	為氏	Kamakura	1332	Family / Clan
tame	N	Tameyo	為世	Kamakura	1332	Generation / Life
tame	N	Tameyori	為頼	Kamakura	1332	Request / Ask
tame	N	Tameyoshi	為義	Uncertain	1600	Fealty
tame	N	Tameyuki	為行	Kamakura	1332	Going To / Bound For
tame	N	Tameyuki	為之	Muromachi	1572	Go / Depart
tame	N	Tameza'ne	為実	Kamakura	1332	Reality
[Special]	F	Raishi	為子	Kamakura	1332	[Lady]

真 Genuine

Reading	Type	Example	Kanji	Period	Date	Added Meaning
ma	S	Makabe	真壁	Nanboku	1392	Wall
masa	N	Masata'ne	真種	Nanboku	1392	Cause / Reason
sana	S	Sa'nada	真田	Uncertain	1600	Rice Paddy
sane	N	Michiza'ne	道真	Hei'an	903	Road / Way
sane	N	Sa'nekatsu	真勝	Sengoku	1568	Conquer / Triumph

正 Unerring / Genuine / Correct / True

Reading	Type	Example	Kanji	Period	Date	Added Meaning
SHOU	Y	Bunshou	文正	Muromachi	1466	Literature / Culture
SHOU	Y	Eishou	永正	Sengoku	1504	Forever
SHOU	Y	Kanshou	寛正	Muromachi	1460	Domestic Tranquility
SHOU	Y	Koushou	康正	Muromachi	1455	Strong / Confident
SHOU	Y	Shou'an	正安	Kamakura	1299	Gentle / Safe / Secure
SHOU	Y	Shouchou	正長	Muromachi	1428	Long / Oldest / Senior
SHOU	Y	Shouchuu	正中	Kamakura	1324	Middle
SHOU	Y	Shougen	正元	Kamakura	1259	Base / Original
SHOU	Y	Shouhei	正平	Nanboku	1346	Peace / Tranquility
SHOU	Y	Shouhou	正保	Edo	1644	Guarantee
SHOU	Y	Shouji	正治	Kamakura	1199	Govern / Rule
SHOU	Y	Shouka	正嘉	Kamakura	1257	Well Done
SHOU	Y	Shoukei	正慶	Hei'an	1332	Rejoice / Deer Skin
SHOU	Y	Shou'ou	正応	Kamakura	1288	Worthy / Suitable
SHOU	Y	Shouryaku	正歴	Hei'an	990	Progress / Pass Through
SHOU	Y	Shoutoku	正徳	Edo	1711	Righteous / Just
SHOU	Y	Shouwa	正和	Kamakura	1312	Peace / Tranquility / Harmony
SHOU	Y	Taishou	大正	Modern	1912	Big
SHOU	Y	Tenshou	天正	Momoyama	1573	Sky / Heaven
masa	F	Masahime	正妃	Hei'an	1183	Queen / Princess / Consort
masa	F	Masako	正子	Nanboku	1392	[Lady]
masa	N	Kagemasa	景正	Kamakura	1332	Bright / Magnificent
masa	N	Katsumasa	勝正	Sengoku	1568	Conquer / Triumph
masa	N	Kiyomasa	清正	Uncertain	1600	Pure
masa	N	Koremasa	惟正	Nanboku	1392	This / Here
masa	N	Masahide	正秀	Uncertain	1600	Extraordinary / Bountiful
masa	N	Masahira	正衡	Uncertain	1600	A Yoke
masa	N	Masahira	正平	Uncertain	1600	Tranquility
masa	N	Masa'ie	正家	Nanboku	1392	Rural House / Family
masa	N	Masakatsu	正勝	Nanboku	1392	Conquer / Triumph
masa	N	Masakiyo	正清	Hei'an	1183	Pure
masa	N	Masamori	正盛	Uncertain	1600	Plentiful / Piled Up
masa	N	Masa'nari	正成	Uncertain	1600	Become / Exist
masa	N	Masa'nobu	正信	Muromachi	1572	Belief / Faith
masa	N	Masa'nori	正儀	Nanboku	1392	Precept
masa	N	Masa'nori	正則	Sengoku	1568	Make an Example
masa	N	Masa'nori	正度	Uncertain	1600	Event / Consult / Confer
masa	N	Masashige	正成	Nanboku	1392	Become / Exist
masa	N	Masasue	正季	Nanboku	1392	Season
masa	N	Masatada	正忠	Nanboku	1392	Faithful / Loyal
masa	N	Masatake	正武	Nanboku	1392	Bravery / Military Force
masa	N	Masatoki	正時	Nanboku	1392	Time / Era
masa	N	Masatoo	正遠	Nanboku	1392	Far
masa	N	Masatora	正虎	Uncertain	1600	Tiger
masa	N	Masatsugu	正次	Muromachi	1572	Next
masa	N	Masatsu'na	正綱	Kamakura	1332	Net
masa	N	Masatsura	正行	Nanboku	1392	Going To / Bound For
masa	N	Masa'uji	正氏	Uncertain	1600	Family / Clan
masa	N	Masayasu	正泰	Kamakura	1332	Peace / Plenitude
masa	N	Masayori	正頼	Sengoku	1568	Request / Ask
masa	N	Masayuki	正行	Uncertain	1600	Going To / Bound For
masa	N	Masayuki	正之	Sengoku	1568	Go / Depart
masa	N	Masazumi	正純	Momoyama	1585	Natural / Pure

Reading	Type	Example	Kanji	Period	Date	Added Meaning
masa	N	Mitsumasa	光正	Nanboku	1392	Bright / Shining
masa	N	Mitsumasa	充正	Muromachi	1572	Satisfy / Fill
masa	N	Morimasa	守正	Kamakura	1332	Protect / Defend
masa	N	Sadamasa	定正	Muromachi	1572	Determine
masa	N	Sadatoshi	正利	Kamakura	1332	Produce Results
masa	N	Tadamasa	忠正	Hei'an	1183	Faithful / Loyal
masa	N	Ta'nemasa	胤正	Kamakura	1332	Blood Heir
masa	N	Tsu'nemasa	経正	Hei'an	1183	True Path
masa	N	Yoshimasa	吉正	Uncertain	1600	Lucky / Fortunate

貞 Correct Spirit / Composure / Modesty / Tranquility / Equanimity

Doing the correct thing is important in Japanese society. Thus, there is a rich vocabulary for how one comports himself. This particular variation on correct behavior concerns itself with the inner nature of what is being done. This is viewed as being particularly important for women. Thus, this is a common character in women's names. Specifically, a woman should be modest and not become angry or aggressive.

Reading	Type	Example	Kanji	Period	Date	Added Meaning
JOU	Y	Jou'ei	貞永	Kamakura	1232	Forever
JOU	Y	Jouji	貞治	Nanboku	1362	Govern / Rule
JOU	Y	Joukyou	貞享	Edo	1684	Receive
JOU	Y	Jou'ou	貞応	Kamakura	1222	Worthy / Suitable
JOU	Y	Jouwa	貞和	Nanboku	1345	Peace / Tranquility / Harmony
TEI	Y	Antei	安貞	Kamakura	1227	Gentle / Safe / Secure
sada	F	Sadako	貞子	Hei'an	1183	[Lady]
sada	N	Iesada	家貞	Hei'an	1183	Rural House / Family
sada	N	Kiyosada	清貞	Nanboku	1392	Pure
sada	N	Koresada	維貞	Kamakura	1332	Cable / Robe
sada	N	Michisada	通貞	Nanboku	1392	Pass Through
sada	N	Mitsusada	満貞	Nanboku	1392	Become Full / Abundant
sada	N	Mochisada	持貞	Muromachi	1572	Have / Possess
sada	N	Nakasada	仲貞	Nanboku	1392	Middle of a Group
sada	N	Naosada	直貞	Nanboku	1392	Adjust / Correct
sada	N	Nobusada	信貞	Nanboku	1392	Belief / Faith
sada	N	Sada'aki	貞顕	Kamakura	1332	High Status
sada	N	Sadabumi	貞文	Uncertain	1600	Writing
sada	N	Sadachika	貞親	Kamakura	1332	Intimate
sada	N	Sada'e	貞衛	Uncertain	1600	Protect / Defend
sada	N	Sadafuji	貞藤	Kamakura	1332	Wisteria
sada	N	Sadafusa	貞房	Kamakura	1332	Monastic Cell
sada	N	Sadahide	貞秀	Nanboku	1392	Extraordinary / Bountiful
sada	N	Sadahira	貞衡	Kamakura	1332	A Yoke
sada	N	Sadahiro	貞広	Nanboku	1392	Spacious / Expansive
sada	N	Sadahisa	貞久	Kamakura	1332	Longtime
sada	N	Sada'ie	貞家	Nanboku	1392	Rural House / Family
sada	N	Sadakata	貞方	Nanboku	1392	Direction / Method
sada	N	Sadakiyo	貞清	Kamakura	1332	Pure
sada	N	Sadaku'ni	貞国	Muromachi	1572	Country / Rural Area
sada	N	Sadamasa	貞縁	Kamakura	1332	Edge
sada	N	Sadamasa	貞将	Kamakura	1332	Commander
sada	N	Sadamasa	貞政	Kamakura	1332	Govern / Rule
sada	N	Sadamichi	貞通	Sengoku	1568	Pass Through
sada	N	Sadamitsu	貞光	Uncertain	1600	Bright / Shining
sada	N	Sadamitsu	貞満	Nanboku	1392	Become Full / Abundant
sada	N	Sadamori	貞盛	Muromachi	1572	Plentiful / Piled Up
sada	N	Sadamu'ne	貞宗	Kamakura	1332	Master an Art
sada	N	Sadamura	貞村	Muromachi	1572	Village

Reading	Type	Example	Kanji	Period	Date	Added Meaning
sada	N	Sada'naga	貞長	Nanboku	1392	Long
sada	N	Sada'nao	貞直	Kamakura	1332	Adjust / Correct
sada	N	Sada'nori	貞載	Nanboku	1392	Year (Loading Cargo)
sada	N	Sadashige	貞重	Kamakura	1332	Heavy / Serious
sada	N	Sadashige	貞茂	Muromachi	1572	Blossoming
sada	N	Sadasue	貞季	Kamakura	1332	Season
sada	N	Sadataka	貞高	Muromachi	1572	Tall
sada	N	Sadata'ne	貞胤	Kamakura	1332	Blood Heir
sada	N	Sadatoki	貞時	Kamakura	1332	Time / Era
sada	N	Sadatomo	貞朝	Kamakura	1332	Morning
sada	N	Sadatsugu	貞継	Nanboku	1392	Connect / Adopt
sada	N	Sadatsu'na	貞綱	Kamakura	1332	Net
sada	N	Sadatsu'ne	貞経	Kamakura	1332	True Path
sada	N	Sadatsura	貞連	Kamakura	1332	Bring Along
sada	N	Sada'uji	貞氏	Kamakura	1332	Family / Clan
sada	N	Sadayasu	貞泰	Kamakura	1332	Peace / Plenitude
sada	N	Sadayo	貞世	Nanboku	1392	Generation / Life
sada	N	Sadayori	貞頼	Kamakura	1332	Request / Ask
sada	N	Sadayoshi	貞義	Kamakura	1332	Fealty
sada	N	Sadayoshi	貞慶	Muromachi	1572	Rejoice / Deer Skin
sada	N	Sadayoshi	貞能	Hei'an	1183	Talent / Ability
sada	N	Sadayuki	貞幸	Kamakura	1332	Happy / Tattoo
sada	N	Sadayuki	貞行	Muromachi	1572	Going To / Bound For
sada	N	Takasada	高貞	Nanboku	1392	Tall
sada	N	Tamesada	為貞	Kamakura	1332	Purpose / Goal
sada	N	Tokisada	時貞	Nanboku	1392	Time / Era
sada	N	Tomosada	知貞	Nanboku	1392	Knowledge
sada	N	Yasusada	泰貞	Nanboku	1392	Peace / Plenitude
sada	N	Yorisada	頼貞	Kamakura	1332	Request / Ask
sada	N	Yoshisada	義貞	Kamakura	1332	Fealty
sada	N	Yukisada	行貞	Kamakura	1332	Going To / Bound For

匡 Make Correct

Reading	Type	Example	Kanji	Period	Date	Added Meaning
masa	N	Masafusa	匡房	Uncertain	1600	Monastic Cell
tada	N	Tadatoo	匡遠	Nanboku	1392	Far

利 Produce Results / Work Well

Please note that Toshihito 利仁 was a member of the *buke* 部家 or warrior class and not a member of the imperial family. In fact, he is described in *Kamakura Muromachi Jinmei Jiten* 鎌倉室町人名辞典 as a *bushi* 武士 or soldier and not even as a *bushou* 武将 or Knight. Also, please note that Sen no Rikyuu 千 利休 was the principal founder of the tea cult in Japan.

Reading	Type	Example	Kanji	Period	Date	Added Meaning
RI	S	Amari	甘利	Uncertain	1600	Sweet
RI	S	Mouri	毛利	Kamakura	1332	Wool
RI	S	Yuri	由利	Kamakura	1332	Purpose
RI	H	Rikyuu	利休	Momoyama	1438	Rest / Leisure
kaga	S	Ashikaga	足利	Kamakura	1332	Foot / Sufficient
toshi	N	Hirotoshi	普利	Sengoku	1568	Wide Spread / Typical
toshi	N	Sadatoshi	正利	Kamakura	1332	Unerring / Genuine
toshi	N	Sadatoshi	定利	Kamakura	1332	Determine
toshi	N	Toshihito	利仁	Hei'an	1183	Precious

Reading	Type	Example	Kanji	Period	Date	Added Meaning
toshi	N	Toshi'ie	利家	Sengoku	1568	Rural House / Family
toshi	N	Toshi'naga	利長	Sengoku	1568	Long
toshi	N	Toshitsu'na	利綱	Muromachi	1572	Net
toshi	N	Toshiyasu	利康	Kamakura	1332	Strong / Confident
toshi	N	Ujitoshi	氏利	Muromachi	1572	Family / Clan

比 Measure Up / Strive

Reading	Type	Example	Kanji	Period	Date	Added Meaning
HI	F	Hikome	比古賣	Nara	784	Old
HI	F	Hime	比賣	Nara	784	
HI	F	Hime	比女	Nara	784	[Woman]
HI	F	Himetarime	比女足女	Nara	784	Woman + Sufficient + [Woman]
HI	F	Hisatsume	比佐豆賣	Nara	784	Military Deputy
HI	F	Hisatsume	比佐津女	Nara	784	Deputy + Harbour + [Woman]
HI	N	Hisatsu'na	比綱	Kamakura	1332	Net
HI	N	Mitsuhiko	光比己	Uncertain	1600	Bright / Shining
HI	S	Abiru	阿比留	Kamakura	1332	Crevice + Stay Over / Camp
HI	S	Asahi'na	朝比奈	Uncertain	1600	Morning
HI	S	Hiki	比企	Kamakura	1332	Long Term Desire / Plan
HI	S	Kehi	気比	Nanboku	1392	Spirit / Breath

競 Emulate / Compete

Reading	Type	Example	Kanji	Period	Date	Added Meaning
kisoi	N	Kisoi	競	Kamakura	1234	

越 Surpass

Reading	Type	Example	Kanji	Period	Date	Added Meaning
ETSU	P	Jou'etsu	上越	Modern	1983	Upper
OTSU	S	Ochi	越知	Muromachi	1572	Knowledge
koe	S	Kawagoe	河越	Kamakura	1332	Large River

❖ VIRTUES ❖

義 Obligation / Fealty / Foster Child

This character is used to write *giri* 義理 which represents the obligation to serve another person. Further, *Giri* represents adoption by someone who is not a blood relative. By itself, 義 (GI) stands for a clearly defined difficult path which people are required to follow. The Japanese reading "yoshi" refers to adopted sons or anyone who assumes a subordinate relationship with someone who is not a blood relative. Finally, this character represents any substitute or proxy.

Reading	Type	Example	Kanji	Period	Date	Added Meaning
yoshi	N	Ariyoshi	有義	Kamakura	1332	Exists
yoshi	N	Hideyoshi	秀義	Hei'an	1183	Extraordinary / Bountiful
yoshi	N	Hisayoshi	久義	Nanboku	1392	Longtime
yoshi	N	Ieyoshi	家義	Kamakura	1332	Rural House / Family
yoshi	N	Kageyoshi	景義	Kamakura	1332	Bright / Magnificent
yoshi	N	Kazuyoshi	和義	Nanboku	1392	Peace / Tranquility
yoshi	N	Koreyoshi	惟義	Kamakura	1332	This / Here
yoshi	N	Masayoshi	政義	Kamakura	1332	Govern / Rule
yoshi	N	Moriyoshi	盛義	Uncertain	1600	Plentiful / Piled Up
yoshi	N	Moroyoshi	師義	Nanboku	1392	Teacher / Expert
yoshi	N	Motoyoshi	基義	Uncertain	1600	Foundation
yoshi	N	Nariyoshi	成義	Muromachi	1572	Become / Exist
yoshi	N	Nobuyoshi	信義	Kamakura	1332	Belief / Faith
yoshi	N	Sadayoshi	貞義	Kamakura	1332	Correct Spirit
yoshi	N	Shigeyoshi	重義	Kamakura	1332	Heavy / Serious
yoshi	N	Tadayoshi	忠義	Hei'an	1183	Faithful / Loyal
yoshi	N	Tadayoshi	直義	Nanboku	1392	Adjust / Correct
yoshi	N	Takayoshi	隆義	Hei'an	1183	Grow / Pile Up
yoshi	N	Tameyoshi	為義	Uncertain	1600	Purpose / Goal
yoshi	N	Ta'neyoshi	胤義	Kamakura	1332	Blood Heir
yoshi	N	Tomareyoshi	希義	Hei'an	1183	Wish / Desire
yoshi	N	Yoriyoshi	頼義	Uncertain	1600	Request / Ask
yoshi	N	Yoshi	義	Muromachi	1572	
yoshi	N	Yoshi'aki	義顕	Hei'an	1183	High Status
yoshi	N	Yoshi'aki	義昭	Uncertain	1600	Bright
yoshi	N	Yoshi'aki	義朝	Hei'an	1183	Morning
yoshi	N	Yoshi'akira	義詮	Nanboku	1367	Explicit / Clear
yoshi	N	Yoshi'ari	義有	Uncertain	1600	Exists
yoshi	N	Yoshi'atsu	義淳	Muromachi	1572	Steadfast / Honest / Natural
yoshi	N	Yoshi'atsu	義篤	Nanboku	1392	Deep Resolve / Perseverence
yoshi	N	Yoshichi	義智	Sengoku	1568	Intelligent
yoshi	N	Yoshichika	義親	Uncertain	1600	Intimate
yoshi	N	Yoshifusa	義房	Nanboku	1392	Monastic Cell
yoshi	N	Yoshifuyu	義冬	Nanboku	1392	Winter
yoshi	N	Yoshiharu	義治	Nanboku	1392	Govern / Rule
yoshi	N	Yoshihide	義秀	Kamakura	1332	Extraordinary / Bountiful
yoshi	N	Yoshihira	義平	Hei'an	1183	Tranquility

yoshi	N	Yoshihiro	義弘	Kamakura	1332	Draw / Stretch
yoshi	N	Yoshihisa	義久	Uncertain	1600	Longtime
yoshi	N	Yoshihisa	義尚	Muromachi	1465	Excellence
yoshi	N	Yoshihito	義人	Muromachi	1572	Person / Human
yoshi	N	Yoshihito	義仁	Muromachi	1572	Precious
yoshi	N	Yoshi'ie	義家	Uncertain	1600	Rural House / Family
yoshi	N	Yoshikado	義廉	Muromachi	1572	Reason / Justification
yoshi	N	Yoshikage	義景	Kamakura	1332	Bright / Magnificent
yoshi	N	Yoshika'ne	義兼	Kamakura	1332	Unite
yoshi	N	Yoshika'ne	義鐘	Muromachi	1572	Bell
yoshi	N	Yoshikatsu	義勝	Muromachi	1572	Conquer / Triumph
yoshi	N	Yoshikazu	義量	Muromachi	1572	Generosity ./ Spirit
yoshi	N	Yoshikiyo	義清	Hei'an	1163	Pure
yoshi	N	Yoshiku'ni	義国	Hei'an	1183	Country / Rural Area
yoshi	N	Yoshimasa	義将	Muromachi	1572	Commander
yoshi	N	Yoshimasa	義政	Kamakura	1332	Govern / Rule
yoshi	N	Yoshimasa	義昌	Kamakura	1332	Clear / Bright
yoshi	N	Yoshimi	義視	Muromachi	1439	Be Careful / Look Out
yoshi	N	Yoshimitsu	義満	Muromachi	1572	Become Full / Abundant
yoshi	N	Yoshimochi	義持	Muromachi	1572	Have / Possess
yoshi	N	Yoshimochi	義茂	Kamakura	1332	Blossoming
yoshi	N	Yoshimori	義盛	Hei'an	1183	Plentiful / Piled Up
yoshi	N	Yoshimoto	義基	Uncertain	1600	Foundation
yoshi	N	Yoshimoto	義幹	Kamakura	1332	Trunk / Stalk
yoshi	N	Yoshimoto	義元	Uncertain	1600	Base / Original
yoshi	N	Yoshimu'ne	義宗	Kamakura	1332	Master an Art
yoshi	N	Yoshimu'ne	義統	Muromachi	1572	Lineage / Govern
yoshi	N	Yoshimura	義村	Kamakura	1332	Village
yoshi	N	Yoshi'naga	義長	Nanboku	1392	Long
yoshi	N	Yoshi'naka	義仲	Muromachi	1572	Middle of a Group
yoshi	N	Yoshi'nao	義直	Kamakura	1332	Adjust / Correct
yoshi	N	Yoshi'nari	義就	Muromachi	1572	To Become / Be Posted
yoshi	N	Yoshi'nari	義成	Kamakura	1332	Become / Exist
yoshi	N	Yoshi'natsu	義夏	Muromachi	1572	Summer
yoshi	N	Yoshi'nobu	義宣	Nanboku	1392	Proclamation
yoshi	N	Yoshi'nobu	義信	Kamakura	1332	Belief / Faith
yoshi	N	Yoshi'nori	義教	Muromachi	1572	Teaching / Dogma
yoshi	N	Yoshi'nori	義則	Nanboku	1392	Make an Example
yoshi	N	Yoshi'nori	義範	Kamakura	1332	Required Form / Pattern
yoshi	N	Yoshi'oki	義興	Nanboku	1392	Happen / Begin
yoshi	N	Yoshisada	義貞	Kamakura	1332	Correct Spirit
yoshi	N	Yoshisada	義定	Hei'an	1183	Determine
yoshi	N	Yoshisata	義郷	Muromachi	1572	Hometown
yoshi	N	Yoshishige	義重	Hei'an	1183	Heavy / Serious
yoshi	N	Yoshishige	義鎮	Uncertain	1600	Quench / Immerse / Temper
yoshi	N	Yoshishige	義繁	Nanboku	1392	Bloom / Bouquet
yoshi	N	Yoshisue	義季	Nanboku	1392	Season
yoshi	N	Yoshisuke	義資	Kamakura	1332	Raw Materials
yoshi	N	Yoshisuke	義助	Nanboku	1392	Deputy (Rescue / Assist)
yoshi	N	Yoshitada	義忠	Hei'an	1183	Faithful / Loyal
yoshi	N	Yoshitada	義直	Uncertain	1600	Adjust / Correct
yoshi	N	Yoshitada	義理	Nanboku	1392	Reason / Logic
yoshi	N	Yoshitaka	義高	Hei'an	1183	Tall
yoshi	N	Yoshitaka	義孝	Uncertain	1600	Filial Loyalty
yoshi	N	Yoshitaka	義隆	Kamakura	1332	Grow / Pile Up
yoshi	N	Yoshitake	義健	Muromachi	1572	Build / Construct
yoshi	N	Yoshita'ne	義胤	Kamakura	1332	Blood Heir

Thematic Dictionary — **Virtues**   297

Reading	Type	Example	Kanji	Period	Date	Added Meaning
yoshi	N	Yoshita'ne	義植	Uncertain	1600	Rooted / Planted
yoshi	N	Yoshita'ne	義種	Nanboku	1392	Cause / Reason
yoshi	N	Yoshitatsu	義龍	Uncertain	1600	Dragon
yoshi	N	Yoshiteru	義光	Kamakura	1332	Bright / Shining
yoshi	N	Yoshitoki	義時	Kamakura	1332	Time / Era
yoshi	N	Yoshitomo	義朝	Hei'an	1183	Morning
yoshi	N	Yoshitoo	義深	Nanboku	1392	Deep
yoshi	N	Yoshitoshi	義俊	Kamakura	1332	Emotional
yoshi	N	Yoshitoshi	義敏	Muromachi	1572	Very Rapid Hard Work
yoshi	N	Yoshitoyo	義豊	Muromachi	1572	Noble
yoshi	N	Yoshitsugu	義継	Kamakura	1332	Connect / Adopt
yoshi	N	Yoshitsugu	義嗣	Muromachi	1572	Successor
yoshi	N	Yoshitsuke	義助	Uncertain	1600	Deputy (Rescue / Assist)
yoshi	N	Yoshitsu'na	義綱	Kamakura	1332	Net
yoshi	N	Yoshitsu'ne	義経	Hei'an	1183	True Path
yoshi	N	Yoshitsu'ne	義常	Hei'an	1183	Permanent
yoshi	N	Yoshitsura	義貫	Muromachi	1572	Perseverance
yoshi	N	Yoshitsura	義連	Kamakura	1332	Bring Along
yoshi	N	Yoshi'uji	義氏	Kamakura	1332	Family / Clan
yoshi	N	Yoshiyasu	義康	Hei'an	1183	Strong / Confident
yoshi	N	Yoshiyasu	義廉	Uncertain	1600	Reason / Justification
yoshi	N	Yoshiyori	義頼	Uncertain	1600	Request / Ask
yoshi	N	Yoshiyuki	義幸	Nanboku	1392	Happy / Tattoo
yoshi	N	Yoshiyuki	義行	Hei'an	1183	Going To / Bound For
yoshi	N	Yoshiza'ne	義実	Hei'an	1183	Reality
yoshi	N	Yoshizumi	義純	Hei'an	1183	Natural / Pure
yoshi	N	Yoshizumi	義澄	Kamakura	1332	Cleanse / Purify
yoshi	N	Yukiyoshi	行義	Kamakura	1332	Going To / Bound For

英 Produce Good / Kind / Gentle / Male Flower

Reading	Type	Example	Kanji	Period	Date	Added Meaning
EI	F	Eishi	英子	Uncertain	1600	[Lady]
hide	F	Hideko	英子	Hei'an	1183	[Lady]
hide	N	Hide'aki	英秋	Nanboku	1392	Autumn
hide	N	Hidetoki	英時	Kamakura	1332	Time / Era
hide	N	Hisahide	久英	Uncertain	1600	Longtime
hide	N	Morohide	師英	Muromachi	1572	Teacher / Expert

恭 Respectful / Reverent

Reading	Type	Example	Kanji	Period	Date	Added Meaning
taka	F	Takako	恭子	Hei'an	1183	[Lady]

裕 Reverent / Serene

Reading	Type	Example	Kanji	Period	Date	Added Meaning
hiro	F	Hiroko	裕子	Hei'an	1183	[Lady]

淳 Steadfast / Honest / Natural

Reading	Type	Example	Kanji	Period	Date	Added Meaning
atsu	N	Atsutaka	淳高	Kamakura	1332	Tall
atsu	N	Michi'atsu	通淳	Muromachi	1572	Pass Through
atsu	N	Sa'ne'atsu	実淳	Muromachi	1572	Reality
atsu	N	Yoshi'atsu	義淳	Muromachi	1572	Fealty

貫 Perseverance

Reading	Type	Example	Kanji	Period	Date	Added Meaning
tsura	N	Tsura'uji	貫氏	Muromachi	1572	Family / Clan
tsura	N	Yoshitsura	義貫	Muromachi	1572	Fealty
nuki	S	Sa'nuki	佐貫	Kamakura	1332	Military Deputy

続 Continue / Perpetuate / Persist

Persistence, endurance and effort are highly valued virtues in Japan.

Reading	Type	Example	Kanji	Period	Date	Added Meaning
tsugu	N	Ka'netsugu	兼続	Sengoku	1568	Unite / Heavy Service

忍 Endurance

Reading	Type	Example	Kanji	Period	Date	Added Meaning
[Special]	F	Oshime	忍賣	Nara	784	

篤 Deep Resolve / Perseverance

Reading	Type	Example	Kanji	Period	Date	Added Meaning
atsu	F	Atsuko	篤子	Hei'an	1183	[Lady]
atsu	N	Yoshi'atsu	義篤	Nanboku	1392	Fealty

業 Industry / Diligence

Reading	Type	Example	Kanji	Period	Date	Added Meaning
nari	F	Nariko	業子	Nanboku	1392	[Lady]
nari	N	Kimi'nari	公業	Kamakura	1332	Noble / Official
nari	N	Kiyo'nari	清業	Hei'an	1183	Pure
nari	N	Ku'ni'nari	邦業	Kamakura	1332	Big Country
nari	N	Mu'ne'nari	宗業	Kamakura	1332	Master an Art
nari	N	Naka'nari	仲業	Kamakura	1332	Middle of a Group
nari	N	Narifusa	業房	Hei'an	1183	Monastic Cell
nari	N	Narika'ne	業兼	Kamakura	1332	Unite
nari	N	Narimori	業盛	Hei'an	1183	Plentiful / Piled Up
nari	N	Naritada	業忠	Hei'an	1183	Faithful / Loyal
nari	N	Naritoki	業時	Kamakura	1332	Time / Era
nari	N	Naritsura	業連	Kamakura	1332	Bring Along
nari	N	Nobu'nari	信業	Uncertain	1600	Belief / Faith

Reading	Type	Example	Kanji	Period	Date	Added Meaning
nari	N	Toki'nari	時業	Kamakura	1332	Time / Era
nari	N	Tomo'nari	朝業	Kamakura	1332	Morning
nari	N	Yasu'nari	保業	Hei'an	1183	Guarantee
nari	N	Yori'nari	頼業	Hei'an	1183	Request / Ask
nari	N	Yoshi'nari	良業	Kamakura	1332	Good / Superior

寧 Gentle

Reading	Type	Example	Kanji	Period	Date	Added Meaning
NEI	F	Nei	寧	Uncertain	1600	

量 Generosity / Intelligence / Spirit

This *kanji* primarily denotes measurement by weight and is sometimes used for measurement of area or volume as well. This concept is extended to gauging the spiritual capacity of other people.

Reading	Type	Example	Kanji	Period	Date	Added Meaning
kazu	N	Sa'nekazu	実量	Muromachi	1572	Plentiful / Reality
kazu	N	Yoshikazu	義量	Muromachi	1572	Obligation / Fealty

敦 Generous / Kind / Honest

Reading	Type	Example	Kanji	Period	Date	Added Meaning
atsu	N	Atsu'ari	敦有	Nanboku	1392	Exists
atsu	N	Atsumori	敦盛	Hei'an	1183	Plentiful / Piled Up
atsu	N	Atsutada	敦忠	Uncertain	1600	Faithful / Loyal
atsu	N	Atsuyori	敦頼	Hei'an	1183	Request / Ask
atsu	N	Ka'ne'atsu	兼敦	Nanboku	1392	Unite
atsu	N	Mu'ne'atsu	宗敦	Uncertain	1600	Master an Art
atsu	N	Taka'atsu	隆敦	Muromachi	1572	Grow / Pile Up

堅 Tough / Strong

Reading	Type	Example	Kanji	Period	Date	Added Meaning
kata	S	Katata	堅田	Sengoku	1568	Rice Paddy

忠 Faithful / Loyal

Reading	Type	Example	Kanji	Period	Date	Added Meaning
tada	F	Tadako	忠子	Hei'an	1183	[Lady]
tada	N	Akitada	朝忠	Uncertain	1600	Morning
tada	N	Atsutada	敦忠	Uncertain	1600	Generous / Kind / Honest
tada	N	Harutada	治忠	Sengoku	1568	Govern / Rule
tada	N	Hidetada	秀忠	Uncertain	1600	Extraordinary / Bountiful
tada	N	Ietada	家忠	Kamakura	1332	Rural House / Family
tada	N	Kagetada	景忠	Kamakura	1332	Bright / Magnificent
tada	N	Ka'netada	兼忠	Kamakura	1332	Unite
tada	N	Kintada	公忠	Nanboku	1392	Noble / Official
tada	N	Kiyotada	清忠	Kamakura	1332	Pure
tada	N	Koretada	伊忠	Muromachi	1572	This

tada	N	Masatada	雅忠	Kamakura	1332	High Quality
tada	N	Masatada	正忠	Nanboku	1392	Unerring / Genuine
tada	N	Michitada	通忠	Kamakura	1332	Pass Through
tada	N	Morotada	師忠	Kamakura	1332	Teacher / Expert
tada	N	Mototada	基忠	Kamakura	1332	Foundation
tada	N	Mu'netada	宗忠	Nanboku	1392	Master an Art
tada	N	Naritada	業忠	Hei'an	1183	Industry / Diligence
tada	N	Nobutada	信忠	Kamakura	1332	Belief / Faith
tada	N	Noritada	憲忠	Nanboku	1392	Example / Pattern
tada	N	Noritada	範忠	Muromachi	1572	Required Form / Pattern
tada	N	Sa'netada	実忠	Kamakura	1332	Reality
tada	N	Shigetada	重忠	Kamakura	1332	Heavy / Serious
tada	N	Suetada	末忠	Nanboku	1392	Last
tada	N	Suketada	資忠	Kamakura	1332	Raw Materials
tada	N	Tada'aki	忠顕	Nanboku	1392	High Status
tada	N	Tadachika	忠親	Hei'an	1183	Intimate
tada	N	Tadafumi	忠文	Uncertain	1600	Writing
tada	N	Tadafusa	忠房	Hei'an	1183	Monastic Cell
tada	N	Tadahira	忠衛	Hei'an	1167	Protect / Defend
tada	N	Tadahira	忠平	Uncertain	1600	Tranquility
tada	N	Tadahisa	忠久	Kamakura	1332	Longtime
tada	N	Tada'ie	忠家	Kamakura	1332	Rural House / Family
tada	N	Tadaka'ne	忠兼	Nanboku	1392	Unite
tada	N	Tadakatsu	忠勝	Momoyama	1568	Conquer / Triumph
tada	N	Tadakiyo	忠清	Kamakura	1332	Pure
tada	N	Tadaku'ni	忠国	Nanboku	1392	Country / Rural Area
tada	N	Tadamasa	忠雅	Hei'an	1183	High Quality
tada	N	Tadamasa	忠政	Sengoku	1568	Govern / Rule
tada	N	Tadamasa	忠正	Hei'an	1183	Unerring / Genuine
tada	N	Tadamichi	忠通	Hei'an	1183	Pass Through
tada	N	Tadamichi	忠道	Uncertain	1600	Road / Way
tada	N	Tadamitsu	忠光	Hei'an	1183	Bright / Shining
tada	N	Tadamori	忠盛	Hei'an	1183	Plentiful / Piled Up
tada	N	Tadamoto	忠幹	Kamakura	1332	Trunk / Stalk
tada	N	Tadamu'ne	忠宗	Kamakura	1332	Master an Art
tada	N	Tadamu'ne	忠致	Hei'an	1183	Taste / Elegance / Grand Effect
tada	N	Tada'nobu	忠信	Kamakura	1332	Belief / Faith
tada	N	Tada'nori	忠度	Hei'an	1183	Event / Consult / Confer
tada	N	Tada'oki	忠興	Sengoku	1568	Happen / Begin
tada	N	Tadasada	忠定	Nanboku	1392	Determine
tada	N	Tadashige	忠成	Kamakura	1332	Become / Exist
tada	N	Tadasue	忠季	Kamakura	1332	Season
tada	N	Tadatoki	忠時	Kamakura	1332	Time / Era
tada	N	Tadatoki	忠節	Hei'an	1183	Season
tada	N	Tadatsugu	忠嗣	Muromachi	1572	Successor
tada	N	Tadatsu'na	忠綱	Hei'an	1183	Net
tada	N	Tadatsu'ne	忠経	Kamakura	1332	True Path
tada	N	Tadatsu'ne	忠常	Kamakura	1332	Permanent
tada	N	Tada'uji	忠氏	Sengoku	1568	Family / Clan
tada	N	Tadayori	忠頼	Kamakura	1332	Request / Ask
tada	N	Tadayoshi	忠義	Hei'an	1183	Fealty
tada	N	Tadayoshi	忠吉	Sengoku	1568	Lucky / Fortunate
tada	N	Tadayoshi	忠能	Kamakura	1332	Talent / Ability
tada	N	Tadayoshi	忠良	Kamakura	1332	Good / Superior
tada	N	Tadayuki	忠行	Muromachi	1572	Going To / Bound For
tada	N	Tadaza'ne	忠実	Hei'an	1183	Reality
tada	N	Tadazumi	忠澄	Kamakura	1332	Cleanse / Purify

Thematic Dictionary — Virtues   301

Reading	Type	Example	Kanji	Period	Date	Added Meaning
tada	N	Takatada	隆忠	Kamakura	1332	Grow / Pile Up
tada	N	Tokitada	時忠	Hei'an	1183	Time / Era
tada	N	Tomotada	朝忠	Nanboku	1392	Morning
tada	N	Tsu'netada	経忠	Kamakura	1332	True Path
tada	N	Yoritada	頼忠	Nanboku	1392	Request / Ask
tada	N	Yoshitada	義忠	Hei'an	1183	Fealty
tada	N	Yoshitada	好忠	Uncertain	1600	Affection / Desire
tada	N	Yukitada	行忠	Muromachi	1572	Going To / Bound For

重 Heavy / Weighty / Serious

Reading	Type	Example	Kanji	Period	Date	Added Meaning
shige	F	Shigeko	重子	Nanboku	1392	[Lady]
shige	F	Shigeme	重女	Kamakura	1332	[Woman]
shige	N	Arishige	有重	Kamakura	1332	Exists
shige	N	Ka'neshige	兼重	Nanboku	1392	Unite
shige	N	Kazushige	一重	Sengoku	1568	One
shige	N	Kiyoshige	清重	Hei'an	1183	Pure
shige	N	Koreshige	惟重	Kamakura	1332	This / Here
shige	N	Ku'nishige	国重	Kamakura	1332	Country / Rural Area
shige	N	Michishige	通重	Kamakura	1332	Pass Through
shige	N	Mitsushige	光重	Kamakura	1332	Bright / Shining
shige	N	Mitsushige	満重	Muromachi	1572	Become Full / Abundant
shige	N	Moroshige	師重	Kamakura	1332	Teacher / Expert
shige	N	Motoshige	幹重	Nanboku	1392	Trunk / Stalk
shige	N	Motoshige	基重	Hei'an	1183	Foundation
shige	N	Motoshige	元重	Muromachi	1572	Base / Original
shige	N	Mu'neshige	宗重	Hei'an	1183	Master an Art
shige	N	Murashige	村重	Uncertain	1600	Village
shige	N	Nagashige	長重	Nanboku	1392	Long
shige	N	Naoshige	直重	Nanboku	1392	Adjust / Correct
shige	N	Narishige	成重	Kamakura	1332	Become / Exist
shige	N	Nobushige	信重	Muromachi	1450	Belief / Faith
shige	N	Sadashige	貞重	Kamakura	1332	Correct Spirit
shige	N	Sadashige	定重	Kamakura	1332	Determine
shige	N	Sa'neshige	実重	Kamakura	1332	Reality
shige	N	Shigechika	重親	Uncertain	1600	Intimate
shige	N	Shigefusa	重房	Kamakura	1332	Monastic Cell
shige	N	Shigehira	重衡	Hei'an	1183	A Yoke
shige	N	Shigehiro	重広	Kamakura	1332	Spacious / Expansive
shige	N	Shigehisa	重尚	Kamakura	1246	Excellence
shige	N	Shigekatsu	重勝	Nanboku	1392	Conquer / Triumph
shige	N	Shigekiyo	重清	Nanboku	1392	Pure
shige	N	Shigeku'ni	重国	Kamakura	1332	Country / Rural Area
shige	N	Shigemasa	重政	Sengoku	1568	Govern / Rule
shige	N	Shigemitsu	重光	Muromachi	1572	Bright / Shining
shige	N	Shigemochi	重茂	Nanboku	1392	Blossoming
shige	N	Shigemori	重盛	Hei'an	1183	Plentiful / Piled Up
shige	N	Shigemoto	重元	Sengoku	1568	Base / Original
shige	N	Shige'naga	重長	Kamakura	1332	Long
shige	N	Shige'nari	重成	Kamakura	1332	Become / Exist
shige	N	Shige'nobu	重信	Kamakura	1332	Belief / Faith
shige	N	Shige'nori	重範	Kamakura	1332	Required Form / Pattern
shige	N	Shigesada	重定	Hei'an	1183	Determine
shige	N	Shigetada	重忠	Kamakura	1332	Faithful / Loyal
shige	N	Shigetaka	重高	Hei'an	1183	Tall

Reading	Type	Example	Kanji	Period	Date	Added Meaning
shige	N	Shigetaka	重隆	Kamakura	1332	Grow / Pile Up
shige	N	Shigetake	重武	Kamakura	1332	Bravery / Military Force
shige	N	Shigeta'ne	重胤	Kamakura	1332	Blood Heir
shige	N	Shigetoki	重時	Kamakura	1332	Time / Era
shige	N	Shigetomo	重朝	Muromachi	1572	Morning
shige	N	Shigetsugu	重継	Kamakura	1332	Connect / Adopt
shige	N	Shigetsugu	重次	Momoyama	1549	Next
shige	N	Shigetsu'na	重綱	Kamakura	1332	Net
shige	N	Shigetsu'ne	重経	Uncertain	1600	True Path
shige	N	Shige'uji	重氏	Kamakura	1332	Family / Clan
shige	N	Shigeyasu	重安	Sengoku	1568	Gentle / Safe / Secure
shige	N	Shigeyori	重頼	Kamakura	1332	Request / Ask
shige	N	Shigeyoshi	重義	Kamakura	1332	Fealty
shige	N	Shigeyoshi	重能	Nanboku	1392	Talent / Ability
shige	N	Shigeyuki	重之	Muromachi	1572	Go / Depart
shige	N	Shigezumi	重澄	Hei'an	1183	Cleanse / Purify
shige	N	Sukeshige	助重	Nanboku	1392	Deputy (Rescue / Assist)
shige	N	Takashige	高重	Kamakura	1332	Tall
shige	N	Takashige	隆重	Sengoku	1568	Grow / Pile Up
shige	N	Takeshige	武重	Nanboku	1392	Bravery / Military Force
shige	N	Tameshige	為重	Kamakura	1332	Purpose / Goal
shige	N	Ta'neshige	種重	Kamakura	1332	Cause / Reason
shige	N	Tokishige	時重	Nanboku	1392	Time / Era
shige	N	Tomoshige	倫重	Kamakura	1332	Obligatory Path
shige	N	Tsu'neshige	常重	Hei'an	1183	Permanent
shige	N	Yasushige	泰重	Kamakura	1332	Peace / Plenitude
shige	N	Yorishige	頼重	Kamakura	1332	Request / Ask
shige	N	Yoshishige	義重	Hei'an	1183	Fealty

志 Determined

Reading	Type	Example	Kanji	Period	Date	Added Meaning
SHI	F	Shikitame	志祁多女	Nara	784	Many + [Woman]
SHI	F	Shitafume	志多布賣	Nara	784	Many + Cloth
SHI	S	Shiga	志賀	Kamakura	1332	Celebrate A Gain

孝 Filial Loyalty

Reading	Type	Example	Kanji	Period	Date	Added Meaning
taka	N	Koretaka	惟孝	Nanboku	1392	This / Here
taka	N	Noritaka	憲孝	Nanboku	1392	Example / Pattern
taka	N	Takakage	孝景	Nanboku	1392	Bright / Magnificent
taka	N	Takamu'ne	孝宗	Nanboku	1392	Master an Art
taka	N	Takasue	孝標	Hei'an	1008	Tree Top (Display)
taka	N	Takatomo	孝朝	Nanboku	1392	Morning
taka	N	Yoshitaka	義孝	Uncertain	1600	Fealty

勇 Bravery / Courage

Reading	Type	Example	Kanji	Period	Date	Added Meaning
isa	F	Isame	勇賣	Nara	784	

雄 Strength / Courage / Bravery

Reading	Type	Example	Kanji	Period	Date	Added Meaning
YUU	F	Yuuko	雄子	Hei'an	1183	[Lady]
o	N	Kin'o	公雄	Kamakura	1332	Noble / Official
o	N	Michi'o	通雄	Kamakura	1332	Pass Through
o	N	Sa'ne'o	実雄	Kamakura	1332	Reality
o	N	Yuki'o	行雄	Kamakura	1332	Going To / Bound For

肝 Spirit / Courage / Bravery / Valour / Liver

Reading	Type	Example	Kanji	Period	Date	Added Meaning
kimo	S	Kimotsuki	肝付	Nanboku	1392	Attach / Arrive

怒 Valour / Intrepid / Anger / Rage / Furor

The image of this *kanji* is one of true feeling combined with great strength. While it is being included with the virtues, it may actually be seen more as a vice. Thus, it could be thought of as "shrewish" or with other negative connotations. This is particularly likely as 女 (the radical for woman) appears in this *kanji* which is used in early-period names for women. Such names are frequently highly uncomplimentary.

Reading	Type	Example	Kanji	Period	Date	Added Meaning
NU	F	E'nume	恵怒賣	Nara	784	Sanctify / Bless
NU	F	Ki'nume	伎怒賣	Nara	784	Artisan / Artistry

康 Strong / Confident

Reading	Type	Example	Kanji	Period	Date	Added Meaning
KOU	Y	Gekou	元康	Kamakura	1331	Base / Original
KOU	Y	Kou'an	康安	Nanboku	1361	Gentle / Safe / Secure
KOU	Y	Kou'ei	康永	Nanboku	1342	Forever
KOU	Y	Kougen	康元	Kamakura	1256	Base / Original
KOU	Y	Kouhei	康平	Hei'an	1058	Peace / Tranquility
KOU	Y	Kouji	康治	Hei'an	1142	Govern / Rule
KOU	Y	Kou'ou	康応	Nanboku	1389	Worthy / Suitable
KOU	Y	Kouryaku	康歴	Nanboku	1379	Progress / Pass Through
KOU	Y	Koushou	康正	Muromachi	1455	Unerring / Genuine
KOU	Y	Kouwa	康和	Hei'an	1099	Peace / Tranquility / Harmony
yasu	N	Akiyasu	朝康	Uncertain	1600	Morning
yasu	N	Chikayasu	親康	Kamakura	1332	Intimate
yasu	N	Fuyuyasu	冬康	Kamakura	1332	Winter
yasu	N	Hideyasu	秀康	Kamakura	1332	Extraordinary / Bountiful
yasu	N	Ieyasu	家康	Hei'an	1183	Rural House / Family
yasu	N	Ka'neyasu	兼康	Hei'an	1183	Unite
yasu	N	Masayasu	政康	Muromachi	1572	Govern / Rule
yasu	N	Motoyasu	基康	Uncertain	1600	Foundation
yasu	N	Nobuyasu	信康	Uncertain	1600	Belief / Faith
yasu	N	Noriyasu	教康	Muromachi	1572	Teaching / Dogma
yasu	N	Sadayasu	定康	Uncertain	1600	Determine
yasu	N	Sa'neyasu	実康	Uncertain	1600	Reality
yasu	N	Tomoyasu	知康	Hei'an	1183	Knowledge
yasu	N	Tomoyasu	有康	Kamakura	1332	Exists

yasu	N	Toshiyasu	俊康	Muromachi	1572	Emotional
yasu	N	Toshiyasu	利康	Kamakura	1332	Produce Results
yasu	N	Tsu'neyasu	経康	Nanboku	1392	True Path
yasu	N	Yasu'ari	康有	Kamakura	1332	Exists
yasu	N	Yasuchika	康親	Sengoku	1568	Intimate
yasu	N	Yasuhide	康秀	Uncertain	1600	Extraordinary / Bountiful
yasu	N	Yasukatsu	康勝	Sengoku	1568	Conquer / Triumph
yasu	N	Yasumasa	康政	Sengoku	1568	Govern / Rule
yasu	N	Yasumichi	康通	Sengoku	1568	Pass Through
yasu	N	Yasumochi	康持	Kamakura	1332	Have / Possess
yasu	N	Yasumori	康盛	Hei'an	1183	Plentiful / Piled Up
yasu	N	Yasumoto	康基	Uncertain	1600	Foundation
yasu	N	Yasmu'ne	康宗	Kamakura	1332	Master an Art
yasu	N	Yasu'naga	康長	Uncertain	1600	Long
yasu	N	Yasu'nobu	康信	Kamakura	1332	Belief / Faith
yasu	N	Yasutomi	康富	Muromachi	1572	Industry
yasu	N	Yasutoshi	康俊	Kamakura	1332	Emotional
yasu	N	Yasutsura	康連	Kamakura	1332	Bring Along
yasu	N	Yasuyori	康頼	Hei'an	1183	Request / Ask
yasu	N	Yasuyuki	康之	Sengoku	1568	Go / Depart
yasu	N	Yoriyasu	頼康	Nanboku	1392	Request / Ask
yasu	N	Yoshiyasu	義康	Hei'an	1183	Fealty
yasu	N	Yukiyasu	行康	Muromachi	1572	Going To / Bound For

徳 Righteous / Just

Reading	Type	Example	Kanji	Period	Date	Added Meaning
TOKU	F	Toku	徳	Momoyama	1438	
TOKU	F	Tokutoshime	徳寿女	Kamakura	1332	Longevity + [Woman]
TOKU	P	Dai'toku'ji	大徳寺	Uncertain	1600	Big + Temple
TOKU	P	Tokushima	徳島	Hei'an	1183	Island
TOKU	S	Tokuda	徳田	Nanboku	1392	Rice Paddy
TOKU	S	Tokugawa	徳川	Uncertain	1600	River
TOKU	S	Toku'naga	徳永	Sengoku	1568	Forever
TOKU	Y	Choutoku	長徳	Hei'an	995	Long / Oldest / Senior
TOKU	Y	Eitoku	永徳	Nanboku	1381	Forever
TOKU	Y	Entoku	延徳	Sengoku	1489	Prolong / Stretch Out
TOKU	Y	Gentoku	元徳	Kamakura	1329	Base / Original
TOKU	Y	Houtoku	宝徳	Muromachi	1449	Treasure
TOKU	Y	Joutoku	承徳	Hei'an	1097	Humbly Receive
TOKU	Y	Kantoku	寛徳	Hei'an	1044	Domestic Tranquility
TOKU	Y	Kentoku	建徳	Nanboku	1370	Found / Build / Construct
TOKU	Y	Kyoutoku	享徳	Muromachi	1452	Receive
TOKU	Y	Meitoku	明徳	Nanboku	1390	Bright
TOKU	Y	Outoku	応徳	Hei'an	1084	Worthy / Suitable
TOKU	Y	Shitoku	至徳	Nanboku	1384	Hit the Mark / Reach / Arrive
TOKU	Y	Shoutoku	正徳	Edo	1711	Unerring / Genuine
TOKU	Y	Tokuji	徳治	Kamakura	1306	Govern / Rule
nori	N	Taka'nori	高徳	Nanboku	1392	Tall
[Special]	F	Tokome	徳賣	Nara	784	

❖ Miscellaneous ❖

且 Moreover

Reading	Type	Example	Kanji	Period	Date	Added Meaning
katsu	N	Katsumoto	且元	Sengoku	1568	Base / Original

材 Log / Timber / Lumber / Wood / Raw Matterial / Talent

Reading	Type	Example	Kanji	Period	Date	Added Meaning
ki	N	Nakaki	仲材	Sengoku	1568	Middle of a Group

資 Raw Matterial / Talent

Reading	Type	Example	Kanji	Period	Date	Added Meaning
suke	F	Sukeko	資子	Nanboku	1384	[Lady]
suke	N	Fuyusuke	冬資	Nanboku	1392	Winter
suke	N	Kagesuke	景資	Kamakura	1332	Bright / Magnificent
suke	N	Michisuke	通資	Kamakura	1332	Pass Through
suke	N	Motosuke	元資	Muromachi	1572	Base / Original
suke	N	Nobusuke	信資	Kamakura	1332	Belief / Faith
suke	N	Norisuke	範資	Nanboku	1392	Required Form / Pattern
suke	N	Suke'aki	資明	Nanboku	1392	Bright
suke	N	Sukechika	資親	Nanboku	1392	Intimate
suke	N	Sukefuji	資藤	Nanboku	1392	Wisteria
suke	N	Sukefusa	資房	Muromachi	1572	Monastic Cell
suke	N	Sukehira	資衡	Muromachi	1572	A Yoke
suke	N	Sukehira	資平	Kamakura	1332	Tranquility
suke	N	Suke'ie	資家	Muromachi	1572	Rural House / Family
suke	N	Sukekata	資賢	Hei'an	1183	Genius
suke	N	Sukekiyo	資清	Muromachi	1572	Pure
suke	N	Sukeku'ni	資国	Kamakura	1332	Country / Rural Area
suke	N	Sukemori	資盛	Hei'an	1183	Plentiful / Piled Up
suke	N	Sukemoto	資基	Kamakura	1332	Foundation
suke	N	Sukemura	資村	Kamakura	1332	Village
suke	N	Suke'na	資名	Kamakura	1332	Famous / Admirable
suke	N	Suke'naga	資永	Kamakura	1332	Forever
suke	N	Suke'naga	資長	Nanboku	1392	Long
suke	N	Suke'nari	資成	Uncertain	1600	Become / Exist
suke	N	Sukesada	資定	Kamakura	1332	Determine
suke	N	Sukesue	資季	Kamakura	1332	Season
suke	N	Suketada	資忠	Kamakura	1332	Faithful / Loyal
suke	N	Suketaka	資隆	Hei'an	1183	Grow / Pile Up
suke	N	Suketoki	資時	Kamakura	1332	Time / Era

Reading	Type	Example	Kanji	Period	Date	Added Meaning
suke	N	Suketomo	資朝	Kamakura	1332	Morning
suke	N	Suketsu'ne	資経	Kamakura	1332	True Path
suke	N	Sukeyasu	資泰	Hei'an	1183	Peace / Plenitude
suke	N	Sukeyori	資頼	Hei'an	1183	Request / Ask
suke	N	Sukeyoshi	資能	Kamakura	1332	Talent / Ability
suke	N	Sukeza'ne	資実	Kamakura	1332	Reality
suke	N	Takasuke	高資	Kamakura	1332	Tall
suke	N	Takasuke	隆資	Nanboku	1392	Grow / Pile Up
suke	N	Tsu'nesuke	経資	Kamakura	1332	True Path
suke	N	Yoshisuke	義資	Kamakura	1332	Fealty

奈 Why? / How?

Reading	Type	Example	Kanji	Period	Date	Added Meaning
na	F	Namime	奈見賣	Nara	784	Vantage / View / Vista
na	F	Na'na	奈々	Uncertain	1600	
na	F	Na'nimome	奈爾毛賣	Nara	784	Bobbin / Distaff + Wool
na	F	Natsu	奈津	Uncertain	1600	Harbour
na	P	Nara	奈良	Hei'an	800	Why? / How?
na	S	Asahi'na	朝比奈	Uncertain	1600	Morning + Measure Up / Strive
na	S	Sa'nada	佐奈田	Nara	784	Military Deputy + Rice Paddy

可 Do this

Reading	Type	Example	Kanji	Period	Date	Added Meaning
yoshi	N	Nagayoshi	長可	Sengoku	1568	Long
yoshi	N	Yoshiharu	可晴	Sengoku	1568	Clear (Sky)

須 Necessity (Small)

Reading	Type	Example	Kanji	Period	Date	Added Meaning
SU	F	Sukoteme	須古提賣	Nara	784	Old
SU	S	Hachisuka	蜂須賀	Sengoku	1568	Bee / Wap + Celebrate A Gain
SU	S	Nasu	那須	Kamakura	1332	What / Whither / How
SU	S	Oosuga	大須賀	Kamakura	1332	Celebrate A Gain Big
SU	S	Yasu	夜須	Hei'an	1183	Evening

充 Satisfy / Fill

Reading	Type	Example	Kanji	Period	Date	Added Meaning
mitsu	N	Mitsumasa	充正	Muromachi	1572	Unerring / Genuine
mitsu	N	Nagamitsu	長充	Muromachi	1572	Long

融 Melt

Reading	Type	Example	Kanji	Period	Date	Added Meaning
too	N	Tooru	融	Uncertain	1600	

牟 Mooing of a Cow

Reading	Type	Example	Kanji	Period	Date	Added Meaning
MU	F	Musubime	牟須比賣	Nara	784	Necessity + Strive
MU	N	Otomuro	乙牟漏	Uncertain	1600	Second (Cute)

束 Grasp / Span / Hand's Breadth

Reading	Type	Example	Kanji	Period	Date	Added Meaning
tsuka	S	Nagatsuka	長束	Sengoku	1568	Long / Oldest / Senior

科 Quality / Type / Specialty

Reading	Type	Example	Kanji	Period	Date	Added Meaning
shina	S	Nishi'na	仁科	Kamakura	1332	Precious

逆 Contrary / Disobedient / Obstinant / Backwards

Reading	Type	Example	Kanji	Period	Date	Added Meaning
saka	F	Sakame	逆賣	Nara	784	

朽 Decay / Rot

Reading	Type	Example	Kanji	Period	Date	Added Meaning
suki	S	Kutsuki	朽木	Kamakura	1332	Tree

極 Summit / Pinnacle

Reading	Type	Example	Kanji	Period	Date	Added Meaning
GOKU	S	Kyougoku	京極	Kamakura	1332	Capital City

計 Plan / Scheme / Trick / Total / Gauge

Reading	Type	Example	Kanji	Period	Date	Added Meaning
kazu	F	Kazuko	計子	Hei'an	1183	[Lady]

産 Childbirth / Native / Produce / Yield Up

Reading	Type	Example	Kanji	Period	Date	Added Meaning
nari	F	Nariko	産子	Nara	784	[Lady]

視 Be Careful / Look Out

Reading	Type	Example	Kanji	Period	Date	Added Meaning
mi	N	Yoshimi	義視	Muromachi	1439	Obligation / Fealty

宍 Meat / Flesh

This *kanji* is rather vulgar.

Reading	Type	Example	Kanji	Period	Date	Added Meaning
shishi	S	Shishido	宍戸	Kamakura	1332	Door

数 Fate / Determined Amount

Reading	Type	Example	Kanji	Period	Date	Added Meaning
kazu	N	Takakazu	高数	Muromachi	1572	Tall / High
	N	Tamekazu	為数	Muromachi	1572	Purpose / Goal

栖 Bird Nest / Play / Rest

Reading	Type	Example	Kanji	Period	Date	Added Meaning
nara	F	Narame	栖賣	Nara	784	

他 Other / Foreign

This *kanji* originally denoted a poisonous snake. It's meaning was later transferred and the written form somewhat simplified. This *kanji* appears to be substituted for 小 in the one name where it appears. Further, note the antique pronunciation of the initial syllable. This syllable becomes "o" in Modern Japanese. Essentially, classical Japanese appears to have avoided syllable consisting of naked vowels preceding them with either a "w" or an "f" sound. The "w" sound appears to be characteristic of initial syllables while the "f" sound appears in case endings for verbs. Regardless, this antique reading does not appear to be related to any of the modern readings for this character which takes "TA" as it *onyomi* and "hoka" as its *kunyomi*.

Reading	Type	Example	Kanji	Period	Date	Added Meaning
wo	S	Wosada	他田	Hei'an	1183	Rice Paddy / Flooded Field

那 What / Whither / How

Reading	Type	Example	Kanji	Period	Date	Added Meaning
NA	S	Kutsu'na	忽那	Kamakura	1332	In a Twinkling
	S	Naka	那珂	Nanboku	1392	Gem
	S	Nasu	那須	Kamakura	1332	Necessity

迩 That

Reading	Type	Example	Kanji	Period	Date	Added Meaning
NI	F	Nihofume	迩保布女	Nara	784	Guarantee + Cloth + [Woman]

Thematic Dictionary — Miscellaneous

倍 Propagate / Multiply

Although this *kanji* takes "masu" as a *kunyomi* in modern Japanese names, its single occurrence in a premodern name suggests that it was actually used as an orthographic and semantic variant of 部 (BE) which was used to form the names of monopoly corporations.

Reading	Type	Example	Kanji	Period	Date	Added Meaning
hito	S	Abe	安倍	Hei'an	1183	Gentle / Safe / Secure

肥 Grow Fat / Grow Muscle / Fertile

Reading	Type	Example	Kanji	Period	Date	Added Meaning
HI	F	Hime	肥賣	Nara	784	
	S	Dohi	土肥	Kamakura	1332	Dirt / Earth

備 Prepare

This *kanji* evokes the image of a warrior gathering arrows in preparation for battle. Bizen is one of the ancient Japanese provinces.

Reading	Type	Example	Kanji	Period	Date	Added Meaning
BI	S	Bizen	備前	Hei'an	1183	Antecedent

包 Wrap / Bundle

Reading	Type	Example	Kanji	Period	Date	Added Meaning
kane	N	Ka'ne'naga	包永	Kamakura	1332	Forever

来 Come Here / Immediate Future

Reading	Type	Example	Kanji	Period	Date	Added Meaning
kuru	S	Kurushima	来島	Sengoku	1568	Island

覚 Revelation / Insight / Learn / Memorize

Originally, this *kanji* evoked an image of sudden enlightenment obtained by the thing itself being suddenly revealed or placed before an individual. In the example, this *kanji* appears in the name of an imperial prince.

Reading	Type	Example	Kanji	Period	Date	Added Meaning
KAKUn	H	Kakukai Hosshinnou	覚快法親王	Kamakura	1181	Pleasure + Law + [Prince]

自 Independent / Self / By One's Self

Originally, this *kanji* evoked an image of a human nose.

Reading	Type	Example	Kanji	Period	Date	Added Meaning
JI	F	Kajime	加自賣	Nara	784	Join Up / Enlist
JI	F	Tojime	刀自賣	Nara	784	Sword
JI	F	Wotojime	乎刀自賣	Nara	784	Destination + Sword

職 Employment / Occupation
The image evoked by this *kanji* is hearing and faithfully performing orders.

Reading	Type	Example	Kanji	Period	Date	Added Meaning
moto	N	Chikamoto	親職	Kamakura	1332	Intimate
moto	N	Shigemoto	成職	Muromachi	1572	Become / Exist
moto	N	Sukemoto	助職	Kamakura	1332	Deputy (Rescue / Assist)
moto	N	Takamoto	隆職	Hei'an	1183	Grow / Pile Up

甚 Terrible
This *kanji* evokes an image of domestic conflict. More specifically, it relates to "the war between the sexes" or marital problems.

Reading	Type	Example	Kanji	Period	Date	Added Meaning
KU	M	Jinkurou	甚九郎	Sengoku	1568	Nine + Son

頭 Head / First / Zenith

Reading	Type	Example	Kanji	Period	Date	Added Meaning
ZU	P	Senzu	千頭	Modern	1983	One Thousand

位 Level / Status / Station
This *kanji* evokes an image of a person standing in their designated place.

Reading	Type	Example	Kanji	Period	Date	Added Meaning
I	F	Itsu'i	五位	Muromachi	1572	Fifth

也 Exists (Archaic)
This *kanji* represents an auxiliary form which indicates a definite or determined state of affairs. It is commonly found at the end of declarative sentences. Oddly enough, this *kanji* evokes the image of a snake slithering through the grass.

Reading	Type	Example	Kanji	Period	Date	Added Meaning
kazu	M	Kazu'nari	一也	Modern	1983	One

歴 Progress / Pass Through
Oddly enough, this *kanji* evokes the image of a snake slithering through the grass.

Reading	Type	Example	Kanji	Period	Date	Added Meaning
REKI	Y	Houreki	宝歴	Edo	1751	Treasure
REKI	Y	Meireki	明歴	Edo	1655	Bright
RYAKU	Y	Bunryaku	文歴	Kamakura	1234	Literature / Culture
RYAKU	Y	Chouryaku	長歴	Hei'an	1037	Long / Oldest / Senior
RYAKU	Y	Eiryaku	永歴	Kamakura	1160	Forever
RYAKU	Y	Genryaku	元歴	Kamakura	1184	Base / Original
RYAKU	Y	Jiryaku	治歴	Hei'an	1065	Govern / Rule
RYAKU	Y	Jouryaku	承歴	Hei'an	1077	Humbly Receive
RYAKU	Y	Karyaku	嘉歴	Kamakura	1326	Well Done
RYAKU	Y	Kenryaku	建歴	Kamakura	1211	Found / Build / Construct

Thematic Dictionary — Miscellaneous   311

Reading	Type	Example	Kanji	Period	Date	Added Meaning
RYAKU	Y	Kouryaku	康歴	Nanboku	1379	Strong / Confident
RYAKU	Y	Ryaku'nin	歴仁	Kamakura	1238	Precious
RYAKU	Y	Ryaku'ou	歴応	Nanboku	1338	Worthy / Suitable
RYAKU	Y	Shouryaku	正歴	Hei'an	990	Unerring / Genuine / Correct

寛 Domestic Tranquility

Reading	Type	Example	Kanji	Period	Date	Added Meaning
KAN	Y	Choukan	長寛	Kamakura	1163	Long / Oldest / Senior
KAN	Y	Kanbun	寛文	Edo	1661	Literature / Culture
KAN	Y	Kan'ei	寛永	Edo	1624	Forever
KAN	Y	Kan'en	寛延	Edo	1748	Prolong / Stretch Out
KAN	Y	Kangen	寛元	Kamakura	1243	Base / Original
KAN	Y	Kanji	寛治	Hei'an	1087	Govern / Rule
KAN	Y	Kanki	寛喜	Kamakura	1229	Rejoice
KAN	Y	Kankou	寛弘	Hei'an	1004	Draw / Stretch / Spread Out
KAN	Y	Kannin	寛仁	Hei'an	1017	Precious
KAN	Y	Kanpou	寛保	Edo	1741	Guarantee
KAN	Y	Kansei	寛政	Edo	1789	Govern / Rule
KAN	Y	Kanshou	寛正	Muromachi	1460	Unerring / Genuine
KAN	Y	Kantoku	寛徳	Hei'an	1044	Righteous / Just

承 Humbly Receive

This *kanji* evokes the image of a kneeling person receiving something with both hands.

Reading	Type	Example	Kanji	Period	Date	Added Meaning
JOU	Y	Jou'an	承安	Kamakura	1171	Gentle / Safe / Secure
JOU	Y	Jouhou	承保	Hei'an	1074	Guarantee
JOU	Y	Jouryaku	承歴	Hei'an	1077	Progress / Pass Through
JOU	Y	Joutoku	承徳	Hei'an	1097	Righteous / Just
SHOU	Y	Choushou	長承	Hei'an	1132	Long / Oldest / Senior
SHOU	Y	Eishou	永承	Hei'an	1046	Forever
SHOU	Y	Jishou	治承	Kamakura	1177	Govern / Rule
SHOU	Y	Kashou	嘉承	Hei'an	1106	Well Done
SHOU	Y	Tenshou	天承	Hei'an	1131	Sky / Heaven

応 Worthy / Suitable

Reading	Type	Example	Kanji	Period	Date	Added Meaning
OU	Y	Bun'ou	文応	Kamakura	1260	Literature / Culture
OU	Y	En'ou	延応	Kamakura	1239	Prolong / Stretch Out
OU	Y	Gen'ou	元応	Kamakura	1319	Base / Original
OU	Y	Jou'ou	丞応	Edo	1652	Rescue from a Pit
OU	Y	Jou'ou	貞応	Kamakura	1222	Correct Spirit
OU	Y	Kan'ou	観応	Nanboku	1350	Perceive / View
OU	Y	Ku'ou	嘉応	Kamakura	1169	Well Done
OU	Y	Kei'ou	慶応	Edo	1865	Rejoice / Deer Skin
OU	Y	Kou'ou	康応	Nanboku	1389	Strong / Confident
OU	Y	Mei'ou	明応	Sengoku	1492	Bright
OU	Y	Ou'an	応安	Nanboku	1368	Gentle / Safe / Secure
OU	Y	Ouchou	応長	Kamakura	1311	Long / Oldest / Senior
OU	Y	Ou'ei	応永	Muromachi	1394	Forever

OU	Y	Ouhou	応保	Kamakura	1161	Guarantee
OU	Y	Ou'nin	応仁	Sengoku	1467	Precious
OU	Y	Outoku	応徳	Hei'an	1084	Righteous / Just
OU	Y	Ryaku'ou	歴応	Nanboku	1338	Progress / Pass Through
OU	Y	Shou'ou	正応	Kamakura	1288	Unerring / Genuine

享 Receive

While this *kanji* originally evoked the image of a watchtower on a castle wall, it was transferred to mean receiving something which was sought after.

Reading	Type	Example	Kanji	Period	Date	Added Meaning
KYOU	Y	Eikyou	永享	Muromachi	1429	Forever
KYOU	Y	Joukyou	貞享	Edo	1684	Correct Spirit
KYOU	Y	Kyouhou	享保	Edo	1716	Guarantee
KYOU	Y	Kyouroku	享禄	Sengoku	1528	Gratitude / Beneficence
KYOU	Y	Kyoutoku	享徳	Muromachi	1452	Righteous / Just
KYOU	Y	Kyouwa	享和	Edo	1801	Peace / Tranquility / Harmony
KYOU	Y	Choukyou	長享	Sengoku	1487	Long / Oldest / Senior
KYOU	Y	Eikyou	永享	Muromachi	1429	Forever
KYOU	Y	Enkyou	延享	Edo	1744	Prolong / Stretch Out

亨 Receive Smoothly

This *kanji* is actually derived from 享 it differs only in the sense of comparative ease with which things are passed over.

Reading	Type	Example	Kanji	Period	Date	Added Meaning
KOU	Y	Genkou	元亨	Kamakura	1321	Base / Original

乾 High Heaven / Ancient Times

Reading	Type	Example	Kanji	Period	Date	Added Meaning
KEN	Y	Kengen	乾元	Kamakura	1302	Base / Original

建 Found / Build / Construct

Specifically, this *kanji* refers to starting something new from the beginning. It also carries the meaning to speak or offer one's opinion or belief.

Reading	Type	Example	Kanji	Period	Date	Added Meaning
KEN	Y	Kenchou	建長	Kamakura	1249	Long / Oldest / Senior
KEN	Y	Ken'ei	建永	Kamakura	1206	Forever
KEN	Y	Kenji	建治	Kamakura	1275	Govern / Rule
KEN	Y	Kenkyuu	建久	Kamakura	1190	Longtime
KEN	Y	Kenmu	建武	Nanboku	1334	Bravery / Military Force
KEN	Y	Kennin	建仁	Kamakura	1201	Precious
KEN	Y	Kenpou	建保	Kamakura	1213	Guarantee
KEN	Y	Kenryaku	建歴	Kamakura	1211	Progress / Pass Through
KEN	Y	Kentoku	建徳	Nanboku	1370	Righteous / Just
take	S	Takebe	建部	Kamakura	1332	Monopoly Corporation

至　Hit the Mark / Reach / Arrive

This *kanji* evokes the image of an arrow standing upright in the ground.

Reading	Type	Example	Kanji	Period	Date	Added Meaning
SHI	Y	Shitoku	至徳	Nanboku	1384	Righteous / Just

丞　Rescue from a Pit

Reading	Type	Example	Kanji	Period	Date	Added Meaning
JOU	Y	Jougen	丞元	Kamakura	1207	Base / Original
JOU	Y	Joukyuu	丞久	Kamakura	1219	Longtime
JOU	Y	Jou'ou	丞応	Edo	1652	Worthy / Suitable

養　Rear / Raise / Nourish

The root idea of this *kanji* is providing food. The meaning is extended to the raising of a family or a nation.

Reading	Type	Example	Kanji	Period	Date	Added Meaning
YOU	Y	Ten'you	天養	Hei'an	1144	Sky / Heaven
YOU	Y	Youwa	養和	Kamakura	1181	Peace / Tranquility / Harmony

化　Change / Transformation

Reading	Type	Example	Kanji	Period	Date	Added Meaning
KA	Y	Bunka[38]	文化	Edo	1804	Literature / Culture
KA	Y	Kouka	弘化	Edo	1844	Draw / Stretch / Spread Out

授　Grant / Bestow

Reading	Type	Example	Kanji	Period	Date	Added Meaning
JU	Y	Tenju	天授	Nanboku	1375	Sky / Heaven

禄　Gratitude / Blessing / Beneficence

This *kanji* evokes the image of hearing the voice of god beside an alter. Upon receiving aid from the god, one's heart is filled with well being and gratitude.

Reading	Type	Example	Kanji	Period	Date	Added Meaning
ROKU	Y	Bunroku	文禄	Momoyama	1592	Literature / Culture
ROKU	Y	Chouroku	長禄	Muromachi	1457	Long / Oldest / Senior
ROKU	Y	Eiroku	永禄	Sengoku	1558	Forever
ROKU	Y	Genroku	元禄	Edo	1688	Base / Original
ROKU	Y	Karoku	嘉禄	Kamakura	1225	Well Done
ROKU	Y	Kyouroku	享禄	Sengoku	1528	Receive

---

[38] Bunka is an actual word in Japanese which means "culture" or "civilization".

禎 Divine Fortune / Happy

Reading	Type	Example	Kanji	Period	Date	Added Meaning
TEI	Y	Katei	嘉禎	Kamakura	1235	Well Done

Japanese Names From Historical Sources

Historical Surnames	315
Historical Masculine Nanori	331
Historical Masculine Yobina	370
Historical Feminine Names	374
Ancient & Mediæval Clans	390
Historical Occupational Lineages	399
Figures from History & Literature	403
Japanese Emperors	405
Historical Nengou Since 990 CE	409

❖ Historical Surnames ❖

あ ❖❖❖❖❖ A

Surname	Kanji	Period	Date	Notes
Abe	安倍	Hei'an 平安	1147	
Abiru	阿比留	Kamakura 鎌倉	1332	
Adachi	安達	Kamakura 鎌倉	1332	
Adachi	足立	Kamakura 鎌倉	1332	
Aeba	饗場	Nanboku 南北	1392	
A'ihara	栗飯原	Nanboku 南北	1392	
Aikawa	淡河	Kamakura 鎌倉	1332	
Akahashi	赤橋	Uncertain 不詳	1600	(Houjou)
Akamatsu	赤松	Nanboku 南北	1392	Red Pine Tree
Akashi	赤石	Nanboku 南北	1371	
Akechi	明智	Uncertain 不詳	1600	
Akimatsu	秋松	Uncertain 不詳	1600	Autumn Pine Tree
Akita	秋田	Uncertain 不詳	1600	Autumn Rice Paddy
Akiyama	秋山	Uncertain 不詳	1600	Autumn Mountain
Akizuki	秋月	Nanboku 南北	1392	Autumn Moon
Amako	尼子	Sengoku 戦国	1568	
Ama'no	天野	Kamakura 鎌倉	1332	Heavenly Meadow
Amari	甘利	Uncertain 不詳	1600	
Anayama	穴山	Uncertain 不詳	1600	Cleft Mountain
Andou	安東	Kamakura 鎌倉	1332	
Aoki	青木	Sengoku 戦国	1568	Blue/Green Tree
Aoto	青砥	Kamakura 鎌倉	1332	
Arakawa	荒川	Nanboku 南北	1392	
Araki	荒木	Muromachi 室町	1572	
Arima	有馬	Sengoku 戦国	1568	
Arimoto	有元	Kamakura 鎌倉	1332	
Asahara	浅原	Kamakura 鎌倉	1332	
Asahi'na	朝比奈	Uncertain 不詳	1600	(Wada Yoshihida)
Asa'i	浅井	Uncertain 不詳	1600	Shallow Well
Asakura	朝倉	Muromachi 室町	1572	Morning Storehouse
Asa'no	浅野	Sengoku 戦国	1568	Shallow Meadow
Asayama	朝山	Nanboku 南北	1392	
Ashikaga	足利	Kamakura 鎌倉	1332	
Ashi'na	蘆名	Kamakura 鎌倉	1332	
Aso	阿蘇	Nanboku 南北	1392	
Aso'numa	阿曾沼	Nanboku 南北	1392	
Asuka'i	飛鳥井	Kamakura 鎌倉	1332	Flying Bird Well
Asuke	足助	Kamakura 鎌倉	1332	
Atagi	安宅	Nanboku 南北	1392	
Awata	粟田	Hei'an 平安	1147	
Awataguchi	粟田口	Kamakura 鎌倉	1332	

ば ❖❖❖❖❖ Ba

Surname	Kanji	Period	Date		Notes
Baba	馬場	Uncertain	不詳	1600	Horse Place

べ ❖❖❖❖❖ Be

Surname	Kanji	Period	Date		Notes
Bessho	別所	Sengoku	戦国	1568	Another Place

び ❖❖❖❖❖ Bi

Surname	Kanji	Period	Date		Notes
Bitou	尾藤	Kamakura	鎌倉	1332	
Bizen	備前	Hei'an	平安	1147	

ぼ ❖❖❖❖❖ Bo

Surname	Kanji	Period	Date		Notes
Boumon	坊門	Kamakura	鎌倉	1332	[unusual]
Bun'ya	文屋	Uncertain	不詳	1600	Scribal/Literary House
Bunzou	豊三	Hei'an	平安	1147	[unusual]

ち ❖❖❖❖❖ Chi

Surname	Kanji	Period	Date		Notes
Chiba	千葉	Kamakura	鎌倉	1332	
Chikamatsu	近松	Uncertain	不詳	1600	Near Pine Tree

ちょ ❖❖❖❖❖ Cho

Surname	Kanji	Period	Date		Notes
Chousokabe	長宗我部	Uncertain	不詳	1600	

だ ❖❖❖❖❖ Da

Surname	Kanji	Period	Date		Notes
Date	伊達	Nanboku	南北	1392	

ど ❖❖❖❖❖ Do

Surname	Kanji	Period		Date	Notes
Dohi	土肥	Kamakura	鎌倉	1332	
Doi	土居	Nanboku	南北	1392	

え ❖❖❖❖❖ E

Surname	Kanji	Period		Date	Notes
Eda	江田	Nanboku	南北	1392	
Edo	江戸	Kamakura	鎌倉	1332	
Endou	遠藤	Sengoku	戦国	1568	Distant Wysteria
Era	恵良	Nanboku	南北	1392	

ふ ❖❖❖❖❖ Fu

Surname	Kanji	Period		Date	Notes
Fuji'i	藤井	Hei'an	平安	1147	Wysteria Well
Fuji'na	富士名	Kamakura	鎌倉	1332	[unusual]
Fujiwara	藤原	Nara	奈良	784	Wysteria Plain
Fukahori	深堀	Kamakura	鎌倉	1332	Deep Hole
Fukuhara	福原	Sengoku	戦国	1568	Fortunate Plain
Fukumitsu	福光	Kamakura	鎌倉	1332	
Fukushima	福島	Sengoku	戦国	1568	Fortunate Island
Fu'nada	船田	Kamakura	鎌倉	1332	
Furuda	古田	Sengoku	戦国	1568	Old Rice Paddy
Furuta	古田	Sengoku	戦国	1568	Old Rice Paddy

が ❖❖❖❖❖ Ga

Surname	Kanji	Period		Date	Notes
Gamou	蒲生	Sengoku	戦国	1568	
Goshima	五島	Sengoku	戦国	1568	Fifth Island
Gotou	後藤	Kamakura	鎌倉	1332	

は ❖❖❖❖❖ Ha

Surname	Kanji	Period		Date	Notes
Hachisuka	蜂須賀	Sengoku	戦国	1568	
Haki'i	波木井	Kamakura	鎌倉	1332	
Ha'nawa	塙	Sengoku	戦国	1568	
Ha'nebuchi	羽淵	Higashiyama	東山	1482	
Ha'neda	羽田	Higashiyama	東山	1482	
Hara	原	Hei'an	平安	1147	Plain
Harada	原田	Nanboku	南北	1392	
Hariya	針屋	Uncertain	不詳	1600	Needle Maker
Harumichi	春道	Uncertain	不詳	1600	
Hasebe	長谷部	Hei'an	平安	1147	

Surname	Kanji	Period	Date	Notes
Hasegawa	長谷川	Sengoku	戦国	1568	
Hasekura	支倉	Uncertain	不詳	1600	
Hata	秦	Nanboku	南北	1392	
Hatakeyama	畠山	Kamakura	鎌倉	1332	
Hata'no	波多野	Kamakura	鎌倉	1332	
Hatta	八田	Hei'an	平安	1147	
Hayakawa	早川	Uncertain	不詳	1600	Rapid River
Hayashi	林	Uncertain	不詳	1600	Forrest

ひ ❖❖❖❖❖ Hi

Surname	Kanji	Period	Date	Notes
Higuchi	樋口	Hei'an	平安	1147	
Hiki	比企	Kamakura	鎌倉	1332	
Hi'ne'no	日根野	Nanboku	南北	1392	
Hiraga	平賀	Kamakura	鎌倉	1332	
Hira'iwa	平岩	Sengoku	戦国	1568	Flat Boulder
Hira'no	平野	Momoyama	桃山	1428	Flat Meadow
Hirata	平田	Hei'an	平安	1147	Flat Rice Paddy
Hiratsuka	平塚	Sengoku	戦国	1568	Flat Tomb
Hirayama	平山	Kamakura	鎌倉	1332	
Hisada	久田	Sengoku	戦国	1568	
Hizume	樋爪	Hei'an	平安	1147	

ほ ❖❖❖❖❖ Ho

Surname	Kanji	Period	Date	Notes
Honda	本多	Uncertain	不詳	1600	Original Multitudes
Honjou	本庄	Kamakura	鎌倉	1332	
Honma	本間	Kamakura	鎌倉	1332	Original Space
Hori	堀	Kamakura	鎌倉	1332	Irrigation Ditch
Horiguchi	堀口	Nanboku	南北	1392	Mouth of Ditch
Horikawa	堀川	Nanboku	南北	1392	Irrigation River
Hori'o	堀尾	Sengoku	戦国	1568	End of the Ditch
Horita	堀田	Sengoku	戦国	1568	Irrigated Rice Paddy
Hori'uchi	堀内	Sengoku	戦国	1568	Inside the Ditch
Hosokawa	細川	Nanboku	南北	1392	Narrow River
Hotta	堀田	Kamakura	鎌倉	1332	
Houjou	北条	Kamakura	鎌倉	1332	

い ❖❖❖❖❖ I

Surname	Kanji	Period	Date	Notes
Ichijou	一条	Kamakura	鎌倉	1332	
Ichikawa	市河	Nanboku	南北	1392	
Ichimonji	一文字	Hei'an	平安	1147	
Ichi'no'i	一井	Kamakura	鎌倉	1332	
Ida	井田	Kamakura	鎌倉	1332	
Iga	伊賀	Kamakura	鎌倉	1332	
Ihohara	蘆原	Hei'an	平安	1147	
I'i	井伊	Nanboku	南北	1392	

Surname	Kanji	Period		Date	Notes
I'i	飯井	Uncertain	不詳	1600	Rice Well
Iida	飯田	Kamakura	鎌倉	1332	
Ii'no	飯野	Nanboku	南北	1392	
Ijuu'in	伊集院	Nanboku	南北	1392	
Ike	池	Uncertain	不詳	1600	Pond
Ikeda	池田	Hei'an	平安	1147	Pond Rice Paddy
Ikoma	生駒	Sengoku	戦国	1568	Live Ponies
Imagawa	今川	Nanboku	南北	1392	
Ima'i	今井	Hei'an	平安	1147	Current Well
Imakawa	今川	Uncertain	不詳	1600	Current River
Ima'nishi	今西	Uncertain	不詳	1600	Current West
Ima'oka	今岡	Nanboku	南北	1392	
I'naba	稲葉	Sengoku	戦国	1568	Rice Leaves
I'nage	稲毛	Kamakura	鎌倉	1332	
I'no'o	飯尾	Muromachi	室町	1572	
Inuhara	犬原	Hei'an	平安	1147	Dog Plain
Irobe	色部	Uncertain	不詳	1600	
Isaku	伊作	Kamakura	鎌倉	1332	
Isawa	伊澤	Kamakura	鎌倉	1332	
Ise	伊勢	Nanboku	南北	1392	
Ishibashi	石橋	Nanboku	南北	1392	Stone Bridge
Ishida	石田	Sengoku	戦国	1568	Rocky Rice Paddy
Ishidou	石塔	Nanboku	南北	1392	
Ishi'i	石井	Nanboku	南北	1392	
Ishikawa	石川	Hei'an	平安	1147	Rocky River
Ishizaki	石崎	Muromachi	室町	1572	
Isshiki	一色	Nanboku	南北	1392	
Itagaki	板垣	Kamakura	鎌倉	1332	
Itoda	糸田	Kamakura	鎌倉	1332	Thread Rice Paddy
Itou	伊東	Hei'an	平安	1147	
Itou	伊藤	Sengoku	戦国	1568	
Iwamatsu	岩松	Muromachi	室町	1572	
Iwami	石見	Muromachi	室町	1572	
Iwase	岩瀬	Hei'an	平安	1147	
Izumi	泉	(Kamakura)	鎌倉	1213	

か ❖❖❖❖❖ Ka

Surname	Kanji	Period		Date	Notes
Kaga'i	加賀井	Sengoku	戦国	1568	Well in Kaga
Kagami	加賀美	Hei'an	平安	1147	
Kagami	鏡	Kamakura	鎌倉	1332	
Kai	甲斐	Muromachi	室町	1572	
Kaitou	海東	Kamakura	鎌倉	1332	
Kaji	加地	Uncertain	不詳	1600	
Kajiwara	梶原	Kamakura	鎌倉	1332	
Kakimoto	柿本	Uncertain	不詳	1600	
Kamata	鎌田	Hei'an	平安	1147	
Kame'i	亀井	Sengoku	戦国	1568	Turtle Well
Kameyama	亀山	Kamakura	鎌倉	1332	Turtle Mountain
Kamiya	神谷	Uncertain	不詳	1600	Valley of the Gods
Kamiyama	上山	Nanboku	南北	1392	
Ka'namori	金森	Sengoku	戦国	1568	Golden Woods
Ka'naya	金谷	Nanboku	南北	1392	Gold Valley
Ka'nazawa	金澤	Uncertain	不詳	1600	

Surname	Kanji	Period	Date	Notes
Ka'neko	金子	Kamakura 鎌倉	1332	
Ka'nezawa	金澤	Uncertain 不詳	1600	(Houjou Tokonori)
Kasai	葛西	Kamakura 鎌倉	1332	
Kasawara	笠原	Uncertain 不詳	1600	Umberella Plain
Kashima	鹿島	Muromachi 室町	1572	Deer Island
Kasuga	春日	Nanboku 南北	1392	
Katagiri	片桐	Sengoku 戦国	1568	
Kata'oka	片岡	Kamakura 鎌倉	1332	
Katata	堅田	Sengoku 戦国	1568	
Katou	加東	Uncertain 不詳	1600	
Katou	加藤	Kamakura 鎌倉	1332	
Kawachi	河内	Uncertain 不詳	1600	Inside a River
Kawagoe	河越	Kamakura 鎌倉	1332	
Kawakatsu	川勝	Sengoku 戦国	1568	River Victory
Kawamura	河村	Kamakura 鎌倉	1332	River Village
Kawa'no	河野	Uncertain 不詳	1600	River Meadow
Kawara	河原	Hei'an 平安	1147	
Kawashima	河嶋	Uncertain 不詳	1600	River Island
Kawashiri	川尻	Sengoku 戦国	1568	
Kawa'uchihara	河内原	Uncertain 不詳	1600	Plain inside a River
Kazusa	上総	Kamakura 鎌倉	1332	

け ❖❖❖❖❖ Ke

Surname	Kanji	Period	Date	Notes
Kehi	気比	Nanboku 南北	1392	
Kenmotsu	監物	Hei'an 平安	1147	

き ❖❖❖❖❖ Ki

Surname	Kanji	Period	Date	Notes
Kido	木戸	Muromachi 室町	1572	
Kikkawa	吉川	Nanboku 南北	1392	
Kikuchi	菊池	Kamakura 鎌倉	1332	
Kikusui	菊水	Uncertain 不詳	1600	Chrysanthumum Water
Kimoto	木本	Nanboku 南北	1392	
Kimotsuki	肝付	Nanboku 南北	1392	
Kimura	木村	Sengoku 戦国	1568	Tree Village
Ki'noshita	木下	Sengoku 戦国	1568	Bellow the Tree
Kira	吉良	Kamakura 鎌倉	1332	
Kishi'ta	岸田	Sengoku 戦国	1568	
Kiso	木曾	Uncertain 不詳	1600	
Kita	木田	Uncertain 不詳	1600	Tree Rice Paddy
Kitabatake	北畠	Nanboku 南北	1392	
Kiyohara	清原	Kamakura 鎌倉	1332	Pure Plain

こ ❖❖❖❖❖ Ko

Surname	Kanji	Period		Date	Notes
Kobayakawa	小早川	Kamakura	鎌倉	1332	Small Rapid River
Kojima	児島	Nanboku	南北	1392	
Kokubu	国分	Kamakura	鎌倉	1332	
Kondou	近藤	Kamakura	鎌倉	1332	Near Wysteria
Ko'nishi	小西	Sengoku	戦国	1568	Small West
Ko'uchi	河内	Uncertain	不詳	1600	
Kou'no	河野	Kamakura	鎌倉	1332	
Kousaka	高坂	Nanboku	南北	1392	
Koutou	厚東	Nanboku	南北	1392	
Kouzai	香西	Kamakura	鎌倉	1332	
Koyama	小山	Uncertain	不詳	1600	Small Mountain
Kozukuri	木造	Nanboku	南北	1392	

く ❖❖❖❖❖ Ku

Surname	Kanji	Period		Date	Notes
Kudou	工藤	Kamakura	鎌倉	1332	
Kuga	久我	Uncertain	不詳	1600	
Kuge	久下	Hei'an	平安	1147	
Kujou	九条	Kamakura	鎌倉	1219	Ninth Avenue in Hei'ankyou
Kumagai	熊谷	Hei'an	平安	1147	
Kumagaya	熊谷	Sengoku	戦国	1568	Bear Valley
Kuroda	黒田	Sengoku	戦国	1568	Black Rice Paddy
Kurushima	来島	Sengoku	戦国	1568	
Kusa'no	草野	Kamakura	鎌倉	1332	
Kusu'noki	楠木	Nanboku	南北	1392	Camphor Tree
Kutsu'na	忽那	Kamakura	鎌倉	1332	
Kutsuki	朽木	Kamakura	鎌倉	1332	
Kuwayama	桑山	Sengoku	戦国	1568	
Kuzurahara	葛原	Uncertain	不詳	1600	

きょ ❖❖❖❖❖ Kyo

Surname	Kanji	Period		Date	Notes
Kyougoku	京極	Kamakura	鎌倉	1332	

ま ❖❖❖❖❖ Ma

Surname	Kanji	Period		Date	Notes
Maeba	前波	Sengoku	戦国	1568	Front Wave
Maeda	前田	Sengoku	戦国	1568	Front Rice Paddy
Makabe	真壁	Nanboku	南北	1392	
Maki	牧	Kamakura	鎌倉	1332	
Makuta	蒔田	Sengoku	戦国	1568	
Masuda	益田	Nanboku	南北	1392	
Masuda	増田	Uncertain	不詳	1600	Expanded Rice Paddy
Matsuda	松田	Nanboku	南北	1392	

Surname	Kanji	Period		Date	Notes
Matsudaira	松平	Muromachi	室町	1572	Pine Tree (Taira Clan)
Matsumoto	松本	Sengoku	戦国	1468	[松本備前守政信]
Matsu'i	松井	Sengoku	戦国	1568	Pine Tree Well
Matsu'naga	松永	Uncertain	不詳	1600	
Matsushita	松下	Sengoku	戦国	1568	Bellow the Pine Tree
Matsu'ura	松浦	Muromachi	室町	1572	

め ❖❖❖❖❖ Me

Surname	Kanji	Period		Date	Notes
Mega	目賀	Nanboku	南北	1392	

み ❖❖❖❖❖ Mi

Surname	Kanji	Period		Date	Notes
Mifu	壬生	Uncertain	不詳	1600	
Miki	三木	Kamakura	鎌倉	1332	Three Trees
Mi'nakawa	皆川	Uncertain	不詳	1600	Common River
Mi'namoto	源	Hei'an	平安	1147	
Misumi	三隅	Nanboku	南北	1392	
Mito	三戸	Nanboku	南北	1392	
Mi'ura	三浦	Kamakura	鎌倉	1332	
Miyabe	宮部	Uncertain	不詳	1600	
Miyamoto	宮本	Sengoku	戦国	1568	Base of the Palace
Miyazaki	宮崎	Kamakura	鎌倉	1332	
Miyoshi	三好	Sengoku	戦国	1568	
Miyoshi	三善	Kamakura	鎌倉	1332	
Mizoguchi	溝口	Sengoku	戦国	1568	
Mizu'no	水野	Sengoku	戦国	1568	Water Meadow
Mizuta'ni	水谷	Sengoku	戦国	1568	Water Valley

も ❖❖❖❖❖ Mo

Surname	Kanji	Period		Date	Notes
Mogami	最上	Uncertain	不詳	1600	
Momo'no'i	桃井	Nanboku	南北	1392	Peach Well
Mori	森	Uncertain	不詳	1600	Woods
Morita	森田	Momoyama	桃山	1428	Paddy in the Woods
Moriyama	守山	Nanboku	南北	1392	
Moro	毛呂	Kamakura	鎌倉	1332	
Motegi	茂木	Nanboku	南北	1392	
Mouri	毛利	Kamakura	鎌倉	1332	

む ❖❖❖❖❖ Mu

Surname	Kanji	Period		Date	Notes
Mu'nawoka	宗岳	Hei'an	平安	1147	
Mura'i	村井	Uncertain	不詳	1600	Village Well
Murakami	村上	Kamakura	鎌倉	1332	Above the Village
Murata	村田	Uncertain	不詳	1600	Village Rice Paddy
Murayama	村山	Nanboku	南北	1392	Village Mountain
Mutou	武藤	Kamakura	鎌倉	1332	

な ❖❖❖❖❖ Na

Surname	Kanji	Period		Date	Notes
Nabeshima	鍋島	Uncertain	不詳	1600	Pot Island
Naga'i	長井	Kamakura	鎌倉	1332	Long Well
Naga'numa	長沼	Kamakura	鎌倉	1332	
Naga'o	長尾	Kamakura	鎌倉	1332	
Naga'oka	長岡	Kamakura	鎌倉	1332	
Nagasa	長狭	Hei'an	平安	1147	
Nagasaki	長崎	Kamakura	鎌倉	1332	
Nagase	長瀬	Nanboku	南北	1392	
Nagatsuka	長束	Sengoku	戦国	1568	
Nagazawa	中澤	Muromachi	室町	1572	
Naitou	内藤	Kamakura	鎌倉	1332	
Naka	那珂	Nanboku	南北	1392	
Naka'e	中江	Sengoku	戦国	1568	Middle Large River
Nakagawa	中川	Sengoku	戦国	1568	Middle River
Nakahara	中原	Hei'an	平安	1147	Middle Plain
Naka'i	中井	Sengoku	戦国	1568	Middle Well
Nakajou	中条	Kamakura	鎌倉	1332	
Nakamura	中村	Kamakura	鎌倉	1332	Middle Village
Naka'no	中野	Kamakura	鎌倉	1332	
Nanbu	南部	Kamakura	鎌倉	1332	Sothern Section
Nao'e	直江	Sengoku	戦国	1568	
Narita	成田	Kamakura	鎌倉	1332	
Nasu	那須	Kamakura	鎌倉	1332	
Nawa	名和	Kamakura	鎌倉	1332	

に ❖❖❖❖❖ Ni

Surname	Kanji	Period		Date	Notes
Nigita	和田	Nanboku	南北	1392	[reading in book but]
Nikaidou	二階堂	Kamakura	鎌倉	1332	
Niki	仁木	Kamakura	鎌倉	1332	
Nishigori	錦織	Kamakura	鎌倉	1332	
Nishimura	西村	Sengoku	戦国	1568	West Village
Nishi'na	仁科	Kamakura	鎌倉	1332	
Nishi'o	西尾	Sengoku	戦国	1568	Western Limit
Nishiyama	西山	Sengoku	戦国	1568	
Nitta	新田	Kamakura	鎌倉	1332	New Rice Paddy

の ❖❖❖❖❖ No

Surname	Kanji	Period		Date	Notes
Nogami	野上	Nanboku	南北	1392	
Noma	野間	Momoyama	桃山	1428	Meadow Space
Nose	能勢	Kamakura	鎌倉	1332	

ぬ ❖❖❖❖❖ Nu

Surname	Kanji	Period		Date	Notes
Numada	沼田	Muromachi	室町	1572	Swampy Rice Paddy

お ❖❖❖❖❖ O

Surname	Kanji	Period		Date	Notes
Obata	小幡	Uncertain	不詳	1600	
Obu	飯富	Uncertain	不詳	1600	(Reading: as in book)
Ochi	越知	Muromachi	室町	1572	
Oda	御田	Uncertain	不詳	1600	Honourable Rice Paddy
Oda	小田	Nanboku	南北	1392	Small Rice Paddy
Oda	織田	Sengoku	戦国	1568	Braided Rice Paddy
Ogasawara	小笠原	Nanboku	南北	1392	
Ogashima	小鹿島	Kamakura	鎌倉	1332	Small Deer Island
Ogata	緒方	Hei'an	平安	1147	Near the Beginning
Ogawa	小川	Uncertain	不詳	1600	Brook
Ogi'no	荻野	Nanboku	南北	1392	
Ogura	小倉	Kamakura	鎌倉	1332	Small Storehouse
Oguri	小栗	Muromachi	室町	1572	Small Chestnut Tree
Ohoshika	凡河	Uncertain	不詳	1600	
Okabe	岡部	Kamakura	鎌倉	1332	
Okamoto	岡本	Sengoku	戦国	1568	
Okazaki	岡崎	Hei'an	平安	1147	
Okeguchi	桶口	Uncertain	不詳	1600	Barrel Mouth
Oku'ni	小国	Uncertain	不詳	1600	Small Country
Okuyama	奥山	Sengoku	戦国	1568	Inner Mountain
O'no	小野	Hei'an	平安	1147	Small Meadow
O'nodera	小野寺	Uncertain	不詳	1600	Small Meadow Temple
Ooba	大庭	Hei'an	平安	1147	Large Garden
Oobatake	大畠	Uncertain	不詳	1600	
Oobayashi	大林	Uncertain	不詳	1600	Large Forest
Ooda	大田	Kamakura	鎌倉	1332	Large Rice Paddy
Oodachi	大館	Nanboku	南北	1392	
Oo'e	大江	Hei'an	平安	1147	Large River
Oogimachi	大親町	Nanboku	南北	1392	
Oohara	大原	Kamakura	鎌倉	1332	Large Plain
Oo'i	大井	Uncertain	不詳	1600	Large Well
Oo'i'da	大井田	Kamakura	鎌倉	1332	Large Well Paddy
Oomiya	大宮	Nanboku	南北	1392	Large Shrine or Palace
Oomori	大森	Nanboku	南北	1392	Large Woods
Oomura	大村	Sengoku	戦国	1568	Large Village
Oo'naka	大中	Hei'an	平安	1147	Large Middle
Oo'nakatomi	大中友	Hei'an	平安	1147	

Surname	Kanji	Period		Date	Notes
Oo'no	大乃	Hei'an	平安	1147	Large
Oo'no	大野	Sengoku	戦国	1568	Large Meadow
Oosaki	大崎	Uncertain	不詳	1600	
Ooshima	大島	Uncertain	不詳	1600	Big Island
Oosuga	大須賀	Kamakura	鎌倉	1332	
Oota	太田	Muromachi	室町	1572	
Ootaka	大高	Nanboku	南北	1392	Large High
Oota'ni	大谷	Sengoku	戦国	1568	Big Valley
Ootomo	大友	Kamakura	鎌倉	1332	
Ootsubo	大坪	Kamakura	鎌倉	1332	
Ootsuka	大塚	Nanboku	南北	1392	
Oo'uchi	大内	Kamakura	鎌倉	1332	
Ooyama	大山	Sengoku	戦国	1568	Large Mountain
Ooya'no	大矢野	Kamakura	鎌倉	1332	
Oozeki	大関	Sengoku	戦国	1568	Big Barrier
Osada	長田	Hei'an	平安	1147	Long Rice Paddy
Osafu'ne	長船	Kamakura	鎌倉	1332	Long Boat
Oyama	小山	Kamakura	鎌倉	1332	
Oyamada	小山田	Nanboku	南北	1392	Small Mountain Paddy
Ozuki	小槻	Kamakura	鎌倉	1332	

りゅ ❖❖❖❖❖ Ryu

Surname	Kanji	Period		Date	Notes
Ryuu'zou'ji	竜造寺	Nanboku	南北	1392	[unusual]

さ ❖❖❖❖❖ Sa

Surname	Kanji	Period		Date	Notes
Sagara	相良	Kamakura	鎌倉	1332	
Sahara	佐原	Hei'an	平安	1147	
Saigusa	三枝	Uncertain	不詳	1600	(Note: Name=Kamon)
Saitou	斎藤	Kamakura	鎌倉	1332	
Sakabe	酒部	Hei'an	平安	1147	
Sakagami	坂上	Nanboku	南北	1392	
Saka'i	酒井	Sengoku	戦国	1568	Sake Well
Sakakibara	榊原	Sengoku	戦国	1568	
Saka'no'ue	坂上	Kamakura	鎌倉	1332	
Saka'uchi	坂内	Uncertain	不詳	1600	
Sakuma	佐久間	Sengoku	戦国	1568	
Sakurada	桜田	Uncertain	不詳	1600	Cherry Rice Paddy
Sakura'i	桜井	Higashiyama	東山	1482	Cherry Well
Sakurayama	桜山	Uncertain	不詳	1600	Cherry Mountain
Samejima	鮫島	Kamakura	鎌倉	1332	
Samukawa	寒河	Muromachi	室町	1572	Cold River
Sa'nada	佐奈田	Hei'an	平安	1147	
Sa'nada	真田	Uncertain	不詳	1600	Real Rice Paddy
Sa'no	佐野	Kamakura	鎌倉	1332	
Sa'nuki	佐貫	Kamakura	鎌倉	1332	
Sasabe	雀部	Hei'an	平安	1147	
Sasaki	佐々木	Kamakura	鎌倉	1332	
Sata	佐田	Muromachi	室町	1572	
Satake	佐竹	Kamakura	鎌倉	1332	

Surname	Kanji	Period		Date	Notes
Satomi	里見	Kamakura	鎌倉	1332	View of one's Native Home
Satomura	里村	Sengoku	戦国	1568	Native Village
Satou	佐藤	Kamakura	鎌倉	1332	
Sawa	澤	Nanboku	南北	1392	
Sawamura	澤村	Kamakura	鎌倉	1332	

せ ❖❖❖❖❖ Se

Surname	Kanji	Period		Date	Notes
Seki	関	Sengoku	戦国	1568	Barrier
Sen	千	Uncertain	不詳	1600	One Thousand
Se'no'o	妹尾	Hei'an	平安	1147	
Senseki	仙石	Sengoku	戦国	1568	Hermit / Adept Rock
Serada	世良田	Kamakura	鎌倉	1332	
Seto'i	瀬戸井	Kamakura	鎌倉	1332	

し ❖❖❖❖❖ Shi

Surname	Kanji	Period		Date	Notes
Shiba	斯波	Kamakura	鎌倉	1332	
Shiba	芝	Kamakura	鎌倉	1332	
Shibata	柴田	Uncertain	不詳	1600	
Shibukawa	渋川	Nanboku	南北	1392	
Shibuya	渋谷	Kamakura	鎌倉	1332	
Shiga	志賀	Kamakura	鎌倉	1332	
Shige'no	滋野	Hei'an	平安	1147	
Shijou	四条	Kamakura	鎌倉	1332	
Shima	島	Sengoku	戦国	1568	Island
Shimada	島田	Muromachi	室町	1572	
Shima'i	島井	Uncertain	不詳	1600	Island Well
Shimazu	島津	Kamakura	鎌倉	1332	
Shimotsuma	下妻	Kamakura	鎌倉	1332	
Shi'nagawa	品河	Kamakura	鎌倉	1332	
Shiozaki	塩崎	Uncertain	不詳	1600	
Shishido	宍戸	Kamakura	鎌倉	1332	

そ ❖❖❖❖❖ So

Surname	Kanji	Period		Date	Notes
Soga	曽我	Uncertain	不詳	1600	
So'ne	曾禰	Uncertain	不詳	1600	
So'noda	園田	Kamakura	鎌倉	1332	
Sou	宗	Nanboku	南北	1392	
Souma	相馬	Kamakura	鎌倉	1332	

た ❖❖❖❖❖ Ta

Surname	Kanji	Period		Date	Notes
Tabara	田原	Nanboku	南北	1392	
Tachiba'na	橘	Hei'an	平安	1147	Tangerine
Tachiba'na	立花	Uncertain	不詳	1600	
Tada	多田	Hei'an	平安	1147	Many Rice Paddies
Taga	多賀	Sengoku	戦国	1568	
Taguchi	田口	Hei'an	平安	1147	Mouth of the Rice Paddy
Taira	平	Hei'an	平安	1147	Flat
Tajimi	多治見	Kamakura	鎌倉	1332	
Tajiri	田尻	Kamakura	鎌倉	1332	
Takahashi	高橋	Sengoku	戦国	1568	Tall Bridge
Taka'i	高井	Kamakura	鎌倉	1332	Tall/High Well
Taka'ishi	高石	Kamakura	鎌倉	1332	
Takaki	高木	Sengoku	戦国	1568	Tall Tree
Takama	高間	Nanboku	南北	1392	
Takamatsu	高松	Nanboku	南北	1392	
Taka'nashi	高梨	Uncertain	不詳	1600	Tall Pear Tree
Takashi'na	高階	Kamakura	鎌倉	1332	
Takata	高田	Sengoku	戦国	1568	Tall Rice Paddy
Takatori	鷹取	Nanboku	南北	1392	
Takatsu	高津	Nanboku	南北	1392	
Takaya	高賀谷	Muromachi	室町	1572	
Takebe	建部	Kamakura	鎌倉	1332	
Takeda	武田	Kamakura	鎌倉	1332	
Take'naka	竹中	Sengoku	戦国	1568	Middle of the Bamboo
Take'no	武野	Sengoku	戦国	1568	Strong Meadow
Takezaki	竹崎	Kamakura	鎌倉	1332	
Takikawa	瀧川	Uncertain	不詳	1600	Waterfall River
Tama'i	玉井	Nanboku	南北	1392	
Tamaru	田丸	Sengoku	戦国	1568	
Tamura	田村	Nanboku	南北	1392	
Ta'naka	田中	Hei'an	平安	1147	Middle of the Paddy
Tanba	丹羽	Uncertain	不詳	1600	
Ta'ni	谷	Sengoku	戦国	1568	Valley
Tannawa	淡輪	Nanboku	南北	1392	
Tashiro	田代	Nanboku	南北	1392	
Tatara	多々良	Kamakura	鎌倉	1332	
Tatsukawa	龍川	Uncertain	不詳	1600	Dragon River

て ❖❖❖❖❖ Te

Surname	Kanji	Period		Date	Notes
Terada	寺田	Kamakura	鎌倉	1332	Temple Rice Paddy
Tera'nishi	寺西	Sengoku	戦国	1568	West of the Temple
Terazawa	寺澤	Sengoku	戦国	1568	
Teshigawara	勅使河原	Nanboku	南北	1392	

と ❖❖❖❖❖ To

Surname	Kanji	Period		Date	Notes
Toda	戸田	Sengoku	戦国	1568	
Togashi	富樫	Muromachi	室町	1572	
Tokawa	戸川	Sengoku	戦国	1568	
Toki	土岐	Kamakura	鎌倉	1332	
Tokuda	徳田	Nanboku	南北	1392	
Tokugawa	徳川	Uncertain	不詳	1600	
Toku'naga	徳永	Sengoku	戦国	1568	
Tomi'no	富野	Hei'an	平安	1147	Pleantiful Meadow
Toriyama	鳥山	Uncertain	不詳	1600	Bird Island
Toshima	豊島	Hei'an	平安	1147	
Toyama	富山	Uncertain	不詳	1600	
Toyoda	豊田	Sengoku	戦国	1568	
Toyotomi	豊富	Uncertain	不詳	1600	
Tozawa	戸澤	Sengoku	戦国	1568	

つ ❖❖❖❖❖ Tsu

Surname	Kanji	Period		Date	Notes
Tsuchiya	土屋	Hei'an	平安	1147	
Tsuda	津田	Sengoku	戦国	1568	
Tsugaru	津軽	Sengoku	戦国	1568	
Tsutsu'i	筒井	Muromachi	室町	1572	
Tsutsumi	堤	Hei'an	平安	1147	

う ❖❖❖❖❖ U

Surname	Kanji	Period		Date	Notes
Uda	宇多	Sengoku	戦国	1568	
Ue'no	上野	Nanboku	南北	1392	
Uesugi	上杉	Kamakura	鎌倉	1332	Upper Cedar Tree
Ueta	上田	Sengoku	戦国	1568	Upper Rice Paddy
Ukita	宇喜多	Uncertain	不詳	1600	
Umewaka	梅若	Muromachi	室町	1572	
Unno	海野	Kamakura	鎌倉	1332	
Urabe	卜部	Muromachi	室町	1572	
Uragami	浦上	Muromachi	室町	1572	
Urakami	浦上	Uncertain	不詳	1600	
Uryuu	瓜生	Kamakura	鎌倉	1332	
Usa	宇佐	Hei'an	平安	1147	
Usu'i	臼井	Nanboku	南北	1392	
Usuki	臼杵	Hei'an	平安	1147	
Utsu'nomiya	宇都宮	Kamakura	鎌倉	1332	

わ ❖❖❖❖❖ Wa

Surname	Kanji	Period		Date	Notes
Wada	和田	Kamakura	鎌倉	1332	Peaceful Rice Paddy
Wakasa	若狭	Kamakura	鎌倉	1332	
Waki	和気	Nanboku	南北	1392	Peaceful Spirit
Wakisaka	脇坂	Sengoku	戦国	1568	
Wakiya	脇屋	Nanboku	南北	1392	
Wosada	他田	Hei'an	平安	1147	Another Rice Paddy

や ❖❖❖❖❖ Ya

Surname	Kanji	Period		Date	Notes
Yabu'no'uchi	薮内	Sengoku	戦国	1568	
Yagi	矢木	Kamakura	鎌倉	1332	
Yagyuu	柳生	Sengoku	戦国	1568	
Yamada	山田	Hei'an	平安	1147	Mountain Rice Paddy
Yamagata	山形	Uncertain	不詳	1600	Mountanous
Yamagata	山県	Uncertain	不詳	1600	
Yamagi	山木	Hei'an	平安	1147	
Yamaguchi	山口	Sengoku	戦国	1568	Mountain Entrance
Yamakawa	山川	Sengoku	戦国	1568	Mountain River
Yamamoto	山本	Hei'an	平安	1147	Base of the Mountain
Yama'na	山名	Kamakura	鎌倉	1332	Mountain Name
Yama'nobe	山辺	Uncertain	不詳	1600	Near the Mountain
Yama'no'uchi	山内	Hei'an	平安	1147	Inside the Mountain
Yama'no'ue	山上	Nanboku	南北	1392	Top of the Mountain
Yama'oka	山岡	Uncertain	不詳	1600	
Yamashiro	山城	Uncertain	不詳	1600	Mountian Fortress
Yamato	大和	Hei'an	平安	1147	Great Peace
Yama'uchi	山内	Muromachi	室町	1572	Inside the Mountain
Yamazaki	山崎	Momoyama	桃山	1428	
Yasu	夜須	Hei'an	平安	1147	
Yasuda	安田	Hei'an	平安	1147	Peaceful Rice Paddy
Yasutomi	安富	Nanboku	南北	1392	

よ ❖❖❖❖❖ Yo

Surname	Kanji	Period		Date	Notes
Yokose	横瀬	Muromachi	室町	1572	
Yokota	横田	Uncertain	不詳	1600	Flat Rice Paddy
Yokoyama	横山	Kamakura	鎌倉	1332	
Yoshikawa	吉川	Sengoku	戦国	1568	Happy River
Yoshima	好島	Kamakura	鎌倉	1332	
Yoshimi	吉見	Kamakura	鎌倉	1332	
Yoshimizu	吉水	Nanboku	南北	1392	Happy Water

ゆ ❖❖❖❖❖ Yu

Surname	Kanji	Period		Date	Notes
Yu'asa	湯浅	Kamakura	鎌倉	1332	Hot Water Shallow
Yu'i	由井	Kamakura	鎌倉	1332	
Yura	由良	Kamakura	鎌倉	1332	
Yuri	由利	Kamakura	鎌倉	1332	
Yusa	遊佐	Nanboku	南北	1392	
Yuuki	結城	Kamakura	鎌倉	1332	

❖ Historical Masculine Nanori ❖

あ ❖❖❖❖❖ A

Nanori	Kanji	Period	Date	Notes	
Akahito	赤人	Uncertain	不詳	1600	
Akifusa	顕房	Muromachi	室町	1572	
Akifusa	章房	Kamakura	鎌倉	1332	*Myoubouka*	Chinese Legal Expert
Akihide	顕秀	Kamakura	鎌倉	1332	
Akihira	明衡	Uncertain	不詳	1600	
Akihiro	顕広	Hei'an	平安	1147	*kajin*	Poet
Aki'ie	顕家	Kamakura	鎌倉	1332	*kizoku*	Ancient Nobility
Aki'ie	秋家	Kamakura	鎌倉	1332	
Akika'ne	顕兼	Kamakura	鎌倉	1332	*kizoku*	Ancient Nobility
Akika'ne	章兼	Nanboku	南北	1392	*kizoku*	Ancient Nobility
Akikuni	顕国	Nanboku	南北	1392	
Akimasa	顕雅	Kamakura	鎌倉	1332	
Akimori	顕盛	Kamakura	鎌倉	1332	
Akimoto	顕幹	Nanboku	南北	1392	
Akimoto	秋元	Kamakura	鎌倉	1332	
Akimoto	明基	Hei'an	平安	1147	*Myoubouka*	Chinese Legal Expert
Akimu'ne	明宗	Nanboku	南北	1392	
Aki'naga	顕長	Hei'an	平安	1147	儒者	
Aki'nao	詮直	Nanboku	南北	1392	*Samakurai dokorotoujin*	
Aki'nobu	顕信	Nanboku	南北	1392	
Aki'nobu	朝信	Sengoku	戦国	1568	Morning Faith	
Aki'nori	詮範	Muromachi	室町	1572	
Aki'oki	顕興	Nanboku	南北	1392	
Akisada	顕定	Muromachi	室町	1572	
Akisuke	顕輔	Uncertain	不詳	1600	
Akitada	朝忠	Uncertain	不詳	1600	Morning Loyalty	
Akita'ne	明胤	Kamakura	鎌倉	1332	*jitou*	Estate Steward
Akitoki	顕時	Kamakura	鎌倉	1332	
Akitomo	顕友	Nanboku	南北	1392	
Akitoshi	顕俊	Uncertain	不詳	1600	
Akitou	章任	Kamakura	鎌倉	1332	*Myoubouka*	Chinese Legal Expert
Akitsu'na	顕綱	Nanboku	南北	1392	
Aki'uji	顕氏	Nanboku	南北	1392	
Aki'uji	朝氏	Uncertain	不詳	1600	Morning Clan/Family	
Akiyasu	顕泰	Nanboku	南北	1392	
Akiyasu	朝康	Uncertain	不詳	1600	Morning Trustworthiness	
Akiyori	秋依	Kamakura	鎌倉	1332	
Akiyoshi	顕能	Nanboku	南北	1392	
Akizumi	明純	Muromachi	室町	1572	
Arichika	有親	Kamakura	鎌倉	1332	*kugyou*	High Courtier Official
Arifusa	有房	Kamakura	鎌倉	1332	*kizoku*	Ancient Nobility

Nanori	Kanji	Period	Date	Notes	
Arihiro	在弘	Nanboku	南北	1392		
Arihito	有仁	Uncertain	不詳	1600		
Ari'ie	有家	Kamakura	鎌倉	1332	*gaka*	Graphic Artist
Arimasa	有雅	Kamakura	鎌倉	1332		
Arimitsu	有光	Muromachi	室町	1572	*kugyou*	High Courtier Official
Arimori	有盛	Hei'an	平安	1147		
Ari'naga	有長	Kamakura	鎌倉	1332	*kugyou*	High Courtier Official
Ari'nobu	有信	Muromachi	室町	1572	仏画家	Buddhist Artist
Ari'nori	有教	Kamakura	鎌倉	1332	*kugyou*	High Courtier Official
Ari'nori	有範	Kamakura	鎌倉	1332		
Arisada	有定	Muromachi	室町	1572	*kizoku*	Ancient Nobility
Arishige	有重	Kamakura	鎌倉	1332		
Aritoki	有時	Kamakura	鎌倉	1332		
Ariyasu	有安	Hei'an	平安	1147	廷臣	
Ariyo	有世	Nanboku	南北	1392		
Ariyoshi	有義	Kamakura	鎌倉	1332		
Atsu'ari	敦有	Nanboku	南北	1392	*kuge*	
Atsumori	敦盛	Hei'an	平安	1147		
Atsutada	敦忠	Uncertain	不詳	1600		
Atsutaka	淳高	Kamakura	鎌倉	1332	*kannin*	Government Official
Atsuyori	敦頼	Hei'an	平安	1147	*kajin*	Poet

ち ❖❖❖❖❖ Chi

Nanori	Kanji	Period	Date	Notes	
Chika'aki	親顕	Nanboku	南北	1392	*kugyou*	High Courtier Official
Chikafusa	親房	Kamakura	鎌倉	1332	*kizoku*	Ancient Nobility
Chikaharu	親治	Hei'an	平安	1147		
Chikahide	親秀	Kamakura	鎌倉	1332		
Chikahira	親衡	Kamakura	鎌倉	1213		
Chikahiro	親広	Kamakura	鎌倉	1332		
Chika'ie	親家	Hei'an	平安	1147		
Chikakage	親景	Muromachi	室町	1572		
Chikakatsu	近葛	Kamakura	鎌倉	1332	*mairakushi*	Dance Master
Chikakiyo	親清	Kamakura	鎌倉	1332		
Chikakuni	親国	Hei'an	平安	1147	*kugyou*	High Courtier Official
Chikamasa	親雅	Kamakura	鎌倉	1332	*kugyou*	High Courtier Official
Chikamasa	親政	Uncertain	不詳	1600		
Chikamasa	親昌	Nanboku	南北	1392	*jinkan*	Shintoh Official
Chikamitsu	親光	Kamakura	鎌倉	1332		
Chikamoto	親元	Muromachi	室町	1572		
Chikamoto	親職	Kamakura	鎌倉	1332		
Chikamu'ne	親宗	Hei'an	平安	1147	*kugyou*	High Courtier Official
Chikamu'ne	親致	Kamakura	鎌倉	1332		
Chika'naga	親長	Kamakura	鎌倉	1332		
Chika'nobu	親信	Hei'an	平安	1147	*kugyou*	High Courtier Official
Chika'nori	近則	Kamakura	鎌倉	1332	*gokenin*	Shogunal Vassal
Chika'nori	親教	Muromachi	室町	1572		
Chika'nori	親範	Hei'an	平安	1147	*kugyou*	High Courtier Official
Chikasue	親季	Kamakura	鎌倉	1332	*kugyou*	High Courtier Official
Chikasuke	親輔	Kamakura	鎌倉	1332	*kizoku*	Ancient Nobility
Chikataka	親隆	Hei'an	平安	1147		
Chikata'ne	親胤	Nanboku	南北	1392		
Chikatomo	親朝	Nanboku	南北	1392		
Chikatoshi	親俊	Muromachi	室町	1572		

Nanori	Kanji	Period		Date	Notes	
Chikatsugu	親継	Kamakura	鎌倉	1332	*kannin*	Government Official
Chikatsu'ne	親経	Kamakura	鎌倉	1332	*kugyou*	High Courtier Official
Chikayasu	親康	Kamakura	鎌倉	1332	*kuge*	
Chikayo	親世	Muromachi	室町	1572	*shugo*	Provincial Constable
Chikayoshi	親能	Kamakura	鎌倉	1332	*Myoubouhakushi*	Chinese Legal Professor
Chikayuki	親行	Kamakura	鎌倉	1332	*kagakusha*	Literary Scholar
Chikaza'ne	近実	Kamakura	鎌倉	1332	*mairakushi*	Dance Master
Chikaza'ne	親実	Kamakura	鎌倉	1332	*kugyou*	High Courtier Official
Chisato	千里	Uncertain	不詳	1600	1000 Native Homes	

ふ ❖❖❖❖❖ Fu

Nanori	Kanji	Period		Date	Notes	
Fujifusa	藤房	Kamakura	鎌倉	1332	*kugyou*	High Courtier Official
Fujihiro	藤広	Sengoku	戦国	1568		
Fujiyori	藤頼	Muromachi	室町	1572		
Fumitoki	文時	Hei'an	平安	981		
Fusa'aki	房顕	Muromachi	室町	1572		
Fusahira	房平	Muromachi	室町	1572		
Fusakage	房景	Muromachi	室町	1572		
Fusamasa	房昌	Hei'an	平安	1147		
Fusa'nari	房成	Hei'an	平安	1147		
Fusasaki	房前	Uncertain	不詳	1600		
Fusashige	房繁	Muromachi	室町	1572	馬術家	Horse Soldier
Fusatsugu	房嗣	Muromachi	室町	1572	*kugyou*	High Courtier Official
Fusaza'ne	房実	Kamakura	鎌倉	1332	*kugyou*	High Courtier Official
Fuyufusa	冬房	Muromachi	室町	1572	*kugyou*	High Courtier Official
Fuyuhira	冬平	Kamakura	鎌倉	1332	*kugyou*	High Courtier Official
Fuyu'ie	冬家	Nanboku	南北	1392	*kugyou*	High Courtier Official
Fuyumichi	冬通	Nanboku	南北	1392	*kugyou*	High Courtier Official
Fuyu'nori	冬教	Kamakura	鎌倉	1332	*kugyou*	High Courtier Official
Fuyusuke	冬資	Nanboku	南北	1392		
Fuyutsugu	冬嗣	Uncertain	不詳	1600		
Fuyu'uji	冬氏	Kamakura	鎌倉	1332	*kugyou*	High Courtier Official
Fuyuyasu	冬康	Kamakura	鎌倉	1332	*ishi*	physician

は ❖❖❖❖❖ Ha

Nanori	Kanji	Period		Date	Notes	
Hama'nari	浜成	Uncertain	不詳	1600		
Harufusa	春房	Muromachi	室町	1572	*kugyou*	High Courtier Official
Haruhisa	治久	Kamakura	鎌倉	1332		
Haruhisa	晴久	Sengoku	戦国	1568		
Haru'naga	治長	Sengoku	戦国	1568		
Haru'nobu	晴信	Uncertain	不詳	1600		
Harutada	治忠	Sengoku	戦国	1568		
Harutomo	晴具	Uncertain	不詳	1600		
Haruyuki	晴幸	Uncertain	不詳	1600		

ち ❖❖❖❖❖ Chi

Nanori	Kanji	Period	Date	Notes	
Hide'aki	英秋	Nanboku	南北	1392	*gakujin* Musician
Hideaki	秀詮	Nanboku	南北	1392	
Hidehira	秀衡	Hei'an	平安	1147	
Hide'ie	秀家	Uncertain	不詳	1600	Superior House/Family
Hidekazu	秀一	Sengoku	戦国	1568	Superior First Born
Hidekiyo	秀清	Kamakura	鎌倉	1332	
Hidemasa	秀政	Sengoku	戦国	1568	Superior Correctness
Hidemochi	秀望	Sengoku	戦国	1568	Superior Wishes
Hidemoto	秀幹	Muromachi	室町	1572	
Hidemoto	秀元	Sengoku	戦国	1568	Superior Origin
Hide'naga	秀永	Uncertain	不詳	1600	Superior Longevity
Hidesato	秀郷	Uncertain	不詳	1600	Superior Native Town
Hidetada	秀忠	Uncertain	不詳	1600	Superior Faithfulness
Hideta'ne	秀胤	Kamakura	鎌倉	1332	
Hidetoki	英時	Kamakura	鎌倉	1332	Successful Time
Hidetomo	秀朝	Kamakura	鎌倉	1332	
Hidetsugu	秀次	Uncertain	不詳	1600	Superior Second Born
Hidetsu'na	秀綱	Nanboku	南北	1392	
Hide'uji	秀氏	Sengoku	戦国	1568	Superior Family/Clan
Hideyasu	秀康	Kamakura	鎌倉	1332	
Hideyoshi	秀吉	Sengoku	戦国	1568	Superior Fortune
Hideyoshi	秀義	Hei'an	平安	1147	
Hideyoshi	秀能	Kamakura	鎌倉	1332	
Hideyuki	秀行	Kamakura	鎌倉	1332	
Hikaru	光	Uncertain	不詳	1600	
Hikoyoshi	彦良	Nanboku	南北	1392	*kugyou* High Courtier Official
Hiro'aki	広明	Kamakura	鎌倉	1332	
Hirochika	広周	Muromachi	室町	1572	*gaka* Graphic Artist
Hirofusa	広房	Kamakura	鎌倉	1332	*kannin* Government Official
Hiro'ie	博家	Kamakura	鎌倉	1332	*kajin* Poet
Hirokado	広門	Sengoku	戦国	1568	
Hirokoto	広言	Kamakura	鎌倉	1332	*kajin* Poet
Hiromasa	博雅	Uncertain	不詳	1600	
Hiromoto	広元	Kamakura	鎌倉	1332	*bakufukanryou* Bakufu Bureaucrat
Hirosada	広定	Sengoku	戦国	1568	
Hiroshige	弘茂	Muromachi	室町	1572	
Hirotoshi	普利	Sengoku	戦国	1568	
Hirotsugu	広嗣	Uncertain	不詳	1600	
Hirotsu'na	広綱	Kamakura	鎌倉	1332	
Hirotsu'ne	広常	Hei'an	平安	1147	
Hiroyo	弘世	Nanboku	南北	1392	
Hirozumi	広澄	Sengoku	戦国	1568	
Hisahide	久英	Uncertain	不詳	1600	
Hisahide	久秀	Uncertain	不詳	1600	Ancient Superiority
Hisaka'ne	久兼	Kamakura	鎌倉	1332	
Hisakuni	久国	Muromachi	室町	1572	*eishi* Graphic Artist
Hisa'naga	久長	Muromachi	室町	1572	*kizoku* Ancient Nobility
Hisa'nobu	久信	Sengoku	戦国	1568	
Hisa'nori	尚慶	Sengoku	戦国	1568	
Hisatoki	久時	Kamakura	鎌倉	1332	
Hisatoyo	久豊	Muromachi	室町	1572	
Hisatsu'na	久綱	Kamakura	鎌倉	1332	
Hisatsu'na	比綱	Kamakura	鎌倉	1332	

Historical Masculine Nanori 335

Nanori	Kanji	Period		Date
Hisatsu'ne	久経	Kamakura	鎌倉	1332
Hisa'uji	尚氏	Muromachi	室町	1572
Hisayoshi	久義	Nanboku	南北	1392
Hisayoshi	尚順	Sengoku	戦国	1568
Hitoshi	等	Uncertain	不詳	1600

い ❖❖❖❖❖ I

Nanori	Kanji	Period		Date	Notes	
Iefusa	家房	Kamakura	鎌倉	1332	*kugyou*	High Courtier Official
Iehide	家栄	Muromachi	室町	1572		
Iehira	家平	Kamakura	鎌倉	1332		
Iekage	家景	Kamakura	鎌倉	1187		
Ieka'ne	家兼	Nanboku	南北	1392		
Iekata	家賢	Nanboku	南北	1392	*kuge*	
Iemasa	家政	Kamakura	鎌倉	1332		
Iemichi	家通	Hei'an	平安	1147	*kugyou*	High Courtier Official
Iemitsu	家光	Kamakura	鎌倉	1332	*kugyou*	High Courtier Official
Iemoto	家基	Kamakura	鎌倉	1332	*kugyou*	High Courtier Official
Ie'naga	家永	Kamakura	鎌倉	1332	*Sumougyoushi*	Sumou Referee
Ie'naga	家長	Hei'an	平安	1147		
Ie'nari	家成	Uncertain	不詳	1600		
Ie'nori	家教	Kamakura	鎌倉	1332	*kugyou*	High Courtier Official
Iesada	家貞	Hei'an	平安	1147		
Iesada	家定	Kamakura	鎌倉	1332	*kugyou*	High Courtier Official
Ietada	家忠	Kamakura	鎌倉	1332		
Ietaka	家高	Kamakura	鎌倉	1332	*gokenin*	Shogunal Vassal
Ietaka	家隆	Kamakura	鎌倉	1332	*kajin*	Poet
Ietoki	家時	Kamakura	鎌倉	1332		
Ietoyo	家豊	Muromachi	室町	1572	*kizoku*	Ancient Nobility
Ietsugu	家継	Hei'an	平安	1147		
Ietsugu	家嗣	Uncertain	不詳	1600	*kugyou*	High Courtier Official
Ietsu'ne	家経	Kamakura	鎌倉	1332	*kugyou*	High Courtier Official
Ietsu'ne	家常	Kamakura	鎌倉	1332		
Ietsura	家連	Kamakura	鎌倉	1332	*gokenin*	Shogunal Vassal
Ie'uji	家氏	Kamakura	鎌倉	1332		
Ieyasu	家康	Hei'an	平安	1147		
Ieyasu	家泰	Nanboku	南北	1392		
Ieyoshi	家義	Kamakura	鎌倉	1332		
Ieyoshi	家良	Kamakura	鎌倉	1332	*kajin*	Poet
Ieyuki	家行	Kamakura	鎌倉	1332	*kugyou*	High Courtier Official
Ieza'ne	家実	Kamakura	鎌倉	1332	*kugyou*	High Courtier Official
Iezumi	家純	Muromachi	室町	1572		

か ❖❖❖❖❖ Ka

Nanori	Kanji	Period		Date	Notes	
Kagechika	景親	Hei'an	平安	1147		
Kageharu	景春	Muromachi	室町	1572		
Kagehira	景平	Kamakura	鎌倉	1332		
Kagehiro	景弘	Hei'an	平安	1147	*jinkan*	Shintoh Official
Kagehisa	景久	Kamakura	鎌倉	1332		
Kage'ie	景家	Hei'an	平安	1147		

Kagekado	景廉	Kamakura	鎌倉	1332		
Kagekatsu	景勝	Uncertain	不詳	1600		
Kagekazu	景員	Hei'an	平安	1147		
Kagekiyo	景清	Hei'an	平安	1147		
Kagemasa	景正	Kamakura	鎌倉	1332	*toukou*	Potter
Kagemasu	景益	Kamakura	鎌倉	1332		
Kagemitsu	景光	Kamakura	鎌倉	1332		
Kagemochi	景茂	Kamakura	鎌倉	1332		
Kagemori	景盛	Kamakura	鎌倉	1332		
Kagemu'ne	景宗	Nanboku	南北	1392		
Kage'naga	景長	Kamakura	鎌倉	1332		
Kage'naka	景仲	Muromachi	室町	1572		
Kage'nobu	景信	Muromachi	室町	1572		
Kageshige	景繁	Kamakura	鎌倉	1332		
Kagesue	景季	Kamakura	鎌倉	1332		
Kagesuke	景資	Kamakura	鎌倉	1332		
Kagetada	景忠	Kamakura	鎌倉	1332		
Kagetaka	景高	Hei'an	平安	1147		
Kagetaka	景隆	Kamakura	鎌倉	1332		
Kagetoki	景時	Kamakura	鎌倉	1332		
Kagetomo	景朝	Kamakura	鎌倉	1332		
Kagetora	景虎	Uncertain	不詳	1600		
Kagetsugu	景継	Kamakura	鎌倉	1332		
Kagetsu'na	景綱	Kamakura	鎌倉	1332		
Kagetsu'ne	景経	Hei'an	平安	1147		
Kagetsu'ne	景恒	Nanboku	南北	1392		
Kageyasu	景泰	Kamakura	鎌倉	1332		
Kageyori	景頼	Kamakura	鎌倉	1332		
Kageyoshi	景義	Kamakura	鎌倉	1332		
Kamatari	鎌足	Uncertain	不詳	1600		
Ka'ne'aki	兼秋	Kamakura	鎌倉	1332	*gakujin*	Musician
Ka'ne'atsu	兼敦	Nanboku	南北	1392	*jinshuu*	Shintoh Priest
Ka'nechika	兼親	Kamakura	鎌倉	1332	*kugyou*	High Courtier Official
Ka'nefumi	兼文	Kamakura	鎌倉	1266	神祇権大副に在任	
Ka'nefusa	兼房	Kamakura	鎌倉	1332	*kugyou*	High Courtier Official
Ka'nehira	兼衡	Hei'an	平安	1147		
Ka'nehira	兼平	Hei'an	平安	1147		
Ka'ne'ie	兼家	Muromachi	室町	1572		
Ka'nekata	兼方	Kamakura	鎌倉	1250		
Ka'neku'ni	兼邦	Nanboku	南北	1392	*kugyou*	High Courtier Official
Ka'nemasa	兼雅	Hei'an	平安	1147	*kugyou*	High Courtier Official
Ka'nemasa	兼昌	Uncertain	不詳	1600		
Ka'nemichi	兼通	Uncertain	不詳	1600		
Ka'nemitsu	兼光	Kamakura	鎌倉	1332	*toukou*	Swordmaker
Ka'nemori	兼盛	Uncertain	不詳	1600		
Ka'nemoto	兼基	Kamakura	鎌倉	1332	*kugyou*	High Courtier Official
Ka'nemoto	兼元	Muromachi	室町	1572	*toukou*	Swordmaker
Ka'nemu'ne	兼宗	Kamakura	鎌倉	1332	*kugyou*	High Courtier Official
Ka'ne'naga	兼永	Muromachi	室町	1572	*shintouka*	Shintouist
Ka'ne'naga	包永	Kamakura	鎌倉	1332	*toukou*	Swordmaker
Ka'ne'naka	兼仲	Kamakura	鎌倉	1332	*kugyou*	High Courtier Official
Ka'ne'nobu	兼宣	Muromachi	室町	1572	*kizoku*	Ancient Nobility
Ka'ne'nobu	兼信	Kamakura	鎌倉	1332		
Ka'ne'nori	兼教	Kamakura	鎌倉	1332	*kugyou*	High Courtier Official
Ka'nera	兼良	Muromachi	室町	1572	*kugyou*	High Courtier Official
Ka'neshige	兼重	Nanboku	南北	1392		
Ka'nesue	兼季	Kamakura	鎌倉	1332	*kugyou*	High Courtier Official

Nanori	Kanji	Period	Date		Notes
Ka'nesuke	兼輔	Sengoku	戦国	1568	*kugyou*	High Courtier Official
Ka'netada	兼忠	Kamakura	鎌倉	1332	*kugyou*	High Courtier Official
Ka'netaka	兼隆	Hei'an	平安	1147		
Ka'neta'ne	兼胤	Muromachi	室町	1572		
Ka'netoki	兼時	Kamakura	鎌倉	1332		
Ka'netomo	兼倶	Muromachi	室町	1572	*shintouka*	Shintouist
Ka'netomo	兼朝	Muromachi	室町	1572		
Ka'netou	兼任	Hei'an	平安	1147	*gouzoku*	
Ka'netsugu	兼嗣	Nanboku	南北	1392	*kugyou*	High Courtier Official
Ka'netsugu	兼続	Sengoku	戦国	1568		
Ka'netsu'na	兼綱	Hei'an	平安	1147		
Ka'netsu'ne	兼経	Kamakura	鎌倉	1332	*kugyou*	High Courtier Official
Ka'netsura	兼連	Nanboku	南北	1392		
Ka'ne'uji	兼氏	Kamakura	鎌倉	1332	*toukou*	Swordmaker
Ka'neyasu	兼康	Hei'an	平安	1147		
Ka'neyo	兼世	Nanboku	南北	1392		
Ka'neyori	兼頼	Kamakura	鎌倉	1332	*gokenin*	Shogunal Vassal
Ka'neyoshi	兼好	Uncertain	不詳	1600	業能	
Ka'neza'ne	兼実	Hei'an	平安	1147	*kugyou*	High Courtier Official
Kata'ie	片家	Uncertain	不詳	1600		
Katsuhisa	勝久	Muromachi	室町	1572		
Katsu'ie	勝家	Uncertain	不詳	1600		
Katsumasa	勝正	Sengoku	戦国	1568		
Katsumitsu	勝光	Muromachi	室町	1572	*kugyou*	High Courtier Official
Katsumoto	旦元	Sengoku	戦国	1568		
Katsumoto	勝元	Muromachi	室町	1572		
Katsu'naga	勝永	Sengoku	戦国	1568		
Katsutoshi	勝俊	Sengoku	戦国	1568		
Katsutoyo	勝豊	Muromachi	室町	1572		
Katsuyori	勝頼	Uncertain	不詳	1600		
Katsuyoshi	勝嘉	Sengoku	戦国	1568		
Kawahide	賢秀	Sengoku	戦国	1568		Exceedingly Superior
Kazumasa	員昌	Uncertain	不詳	1600		
Kazushige	一重	Sengoku	戦国	1568		
Kazutada	一直	Sengoku	戦国	1568		
Kazutoyo	一豊	Sengoku	戦国	1568		
Kazu'uji	和氏	Nanboku	南北	1392		
Kazuyoshi	和義	Nanboku	南北	1392		

き ❖❖❖❖❖ Ki

Nanori	Kanji	Period	Date	Notes	
Kimimichi	公通	Hei'an	平安	1147	*jinkan*	Shintoh Official [宇佐]
Kimi'nari	公業	Kamakura	鎌倉	1332	男鹿島公業	
Kimitomo	公朝	Kamakura	鎌倉	1332		
Kin'aki	公明	Kamakura	鎌倉	1332	*kugyou*	High Courtier Official
Kin'ari	公有	Muromachi	室町	1572	*kugyou*	High Courtier Official
Kinchika	公親	Kamakura	鎌倉	1332	*kugyou*	High Courtier Official
Kinfusa	公房	Kamakura	鎌倉	1332	*kugyou*	High Courtier Official
Kinfuyu	公冬	Muromachi	室町	1572	*kugyou*	High Courtier Official
Kinhide	公秀	Kamakura	鎌倉	1332	*kugyou*	High Courtier Official
Kinhira	公衡	Kamakura	鎌倉	1332	*kugyou*	High Courtier Official
Kinkata	公賢	Kamakura	鎌倉	1332	*kizoku*	Ancient Nobility
Kinkiyo	公清	Nanboku	南北	1392	*kugyou*	High Courtier Official
Kinmasa	公雅	Kamakura	鎌倉	1332	*kugyou*	High Courtier Official

Kinmichi	公通	Hei'an	平安	1147	*kugyou*	High Courtier Official
Kinmitsu	公光	Hei'an	平安	1147	*kugyou*	High Courtier Official
Kinmori	公守	Kamakura	鎌倉	1332	*kugyou*	High Courtier Official
Kinmoto	公基	Kamakura	鎌倉	1332	*kugyou*	High Courtier Official
Kinmu'ne	公宗	Kamakura	鎌倉	1332	*kugyou*	High Courtier Official
Kinnaga	公長	Kamakura	鎌倉	1332	*kugyou*	High Courtier Official
Kinnao	公直	Kamakura	鎌倉	1332	*kugyou*	High Courtier Official
Kinnori	公教	Hei'an	平安	1147	*kugyou*	High Courtier Official
Kin'o	公雄	Kamakura	鎌倉	1332	*kugyou*	High Courtier Official
Kinsada	公定	Kamakura	鎌倉	1332	*kkizoku*	Ancient Nobility
Kinshige	公茂	Kamakura	鎌倉	1332	*kugyou*	High Courtier Official
Kinsue	公季	Uncertain	不詳	1600		
Kinsuke	公相	Kamakura	鎌倉	1332	*kugyou*	High Courtier Official
Kintada	公忠	Nanboku	南北	1392	*kugyou*	High Courtier Official
Kintoki	公時	Nanboku	南北	1392	*kugyou*	High Courtier Official
Kintoshi	公俊	Muromachi	室町	1572	*kugyou*	High Courtier Official
Kintsugu	公継	Kamakura	鎌倉	1332	*kugyou*	High Courtier Official
Kintsu'na	公綱	Kamakura	鎌倉	1332		
Kintsu'ne	公経	Hei'an	平安	1147	*kugyou*	High Courtier Official
Kintsura	公連	Muromachi	室町	1572	*kizoku*	Ancient Nobility
Kin'yasu	公保	Hei'an	平安	1147	*kugyou*	High Courtier Official
Kin'yuki	公行	Muromachi	室町	1572	*kugyou*	High Courtier Official
Kisoi	競	Kamakura	鎌倉	1234		
Kiyofusa	清房	Hei'an	平安	1147		
Kiyohide	清秀	Uncertain	不詳	1600		Pure Superiority
Kiyohira	清衡	Uncertain	不詳	1600		
Kiyohira	清平	Muromachi	室町	1572	*jitou*	Estate Steward
Kiyokata	清方	Muromachi	室町	1572		
Kiyokuni	清邦	Hei'an	平安	1147	*kokushi*	
Kiyomasa	清正	Uncertain	不詳	1600		
Kiyomitsu	清光	Hei'an	平安	1147		
Kiyomori	清盛	Hei'an	平安	1147		
Kiyomu'ne	清宗	Hei'an	平安	1147	*kugyou*	High Courtier Official
Kiyo'naga	清長	Kamakura	鎌倉	1332	*kizoku*	Ancient Nobility
Kiyo'nari	清業	Hei'an	平安	1147	*kekyuukannin*	bureaucrat
Kiyo'nori	清教	Uncertain	不詳	1600		
Kiyosada	清貞	Nanboku	南北	1392		
Kiyosada	清定	Kamakura	鎌倉	1332		
Kiyoshige	清重	Hei'an	平安	1147		
Kiyoshige	清成	Kamakura	鎌倉	1332	*ishi*	physician
Kiyosuke	清輔	Uncertain	不詳	1600		
Kiyotada	清忠	Kamakura	鎌倉	1332	*kugyou*	High Courtier Official
Kiyotaka	清高	Kamakura	鎌倉	1332		
Kiyota'ne	清胤	Nanboku	南北	1392		
Kiyota'ne	清種	Kamakura	鎌倉	1332	*jitou*	Estate Steward
Kiyotoki	清時	Kamakura	鎌倉	1332		
Kiyotomo	清公	Hei'an	平安	842		
Kiyotsu'na	清綱	Hei'an	平安	1147		
Kiyotsu'ne	清経	Hei'an	平安	1147		
Kiyo'uji	清氏	Nanboku	南北	1392		
Kiyoyuki	清行	Sengoku	戦国	1568		

こ ❖❖❖❖❖ Ko

Nanori	Kanji	Period	Date	Notes	
Korechika	惟親	Kamakura	鎌倉	1332	
Korechika	伊周	Uncertain	不詳	1600	
Korefusa	伊房	Uncertain	不詳	1600	
Korehira	維衡	Uncertain	不詳	1600	
Korehira	維平	Kamakura	鎌倉	1332	
Korehisa	惟久	Kamakura	鎌倉	1332	*gaka*	Graphic Artist
Korehisa	伊久	Nanboku	南北	1392	
Korekata	惟方	Hei'an	平安	1147	*kizoku*	Ancient Nobility
Koremasa	惟政	Nanboku	南北	1392	
Koremasa	惟正	Nanboku	南北	1392	
Koremichi	維道	Muromachi	室町	1572	
Koremochi	維茂	Uncertain	不詳	1600	
Koremori	維盛	Hei'an	平安	1147	
Koremura	惟村	Nanboku	南北	1392	
Kore'nao	惟直	Kamakura	鎌倉	1332	
Kore'nobu	惟信	Kamakura	鎌倉	1332	
Kore'nori	是則	Uncertain	不詳	1600	
Koresada	維貞	Kamakura	鎌倉	1332	
Koresato	惟郷	Muromachi	室町	1572	
Koreshige	惟重	Kamakura	鎌倉	1332	
Koretada	伊忠	Muromachi	室町	1572	*kugyou*	High Courtier Official
Koretaka	惟孝	Nanboku	南北	1392	
Koretaka	惟隆	Hei'an	平安	1147	
Koretake	惟武	Nanboku	南北	1392	
Koretoki	惟時	Nanboku	南北	1392	
Koretsugu	惟継	Kamakura	鎌倉	1332	*kugyou*	High Courtier Official
Koreyoshi	惟義	Kamakura	鎌倉	1332	
Koreyoshi	惟能	Hei'an	平安	1147	
Koreyoshi	是善	Hei'an	平安	880	
Korezumi	惟澄	Nanboku	南北	1392	
Kotau	答	Kamakura	鎌倉	1332	

く ❖❖❖❖❖ Ku

Nanori	Kanji	Period	Date	Notes	
Ku'nihira	国衡	Kamakura	鎌倉	1189	
Ku'nihira	国平	Kamakura	鎌倉	1332	
Ku'nika	国香	Uncertain	不詳	1600	
Ku'nikiyo	国清	Nanboku	南北	1392	National Purity	
Ku'nimichi	邦通	Kamakura	鎌倉	1332	*bunkan*	Librarian
Ku'nimichi	邦道	Hei'an	平安	1147	
Ku'nimitsu	邦光	Nanboku	南北	1392	廷臣	
Ku'nimoto	国基	Kamakura	鎌倉	1332	
Ku'ni'naga	国長	Nanboku	南北	1392	
Ku'ni'nari	邦業	Kamakura	鎌倉	1332	
Ku'ni'nobu	国信	Muromachi	室町	1572	
Ku'nishige	国重	Kamakura	鎌倉	1332	
Ku'nitoki	邦時	Uncertain	不詳	1600	
Ku'nitsu'na	国綱	Hei'an	平安	1147	*toukou*	Swordmaker
Ku'nitsu'na	邦綱	Hei'an	平安	1147	*kizoku*	Ancient Nobility
Ku'niyasu	国泰	Nanboku	南北	1392	

きゅ ◆◆◆◆◆ Kyu

Nanori	Kanji	Period		Date	Notes	
Kyuuzou	久蔵	Sengoku	戦国	1568	type	

ま ◆◆◆◆◆ Ma

Nanori	Kanji	Period		Date	Notes	
Makoto	信	Uncertain	不詳	1600		
Masa'ari	雅有	Kamakura	鎌倉	1241	*kajin*	Poet
Masachika	雅親	Sengoku	戦国	1490	*kajin*	Poet
Masachika	政親	Kamakura	鎌倉	1332	*jinkan*	Shintoh Official/武将
Masafusa	匡房	Uncertain	不詳	1600		
Masahide	正秀	Uncertain	不詳	1600	Correct Superiority	
Masahira	政平	Kamakura	鎌倉	1332		
Masahira	正衡	Uncertain	不詳	1600		
Masahira	正平	Uncertain	不詳	1600		
Masahiro	政弘	Sengoku	戦国	1568		
Masa'ie	雅家	Kamakura	鎌倉	1332	*kizoku*	Ancient Nobility
Masa'ie	政家	Muromachi	室町	1572	*kugyou*	High Courtier Official
Masa'ie	正家	Nanboku	南北	1392		
Masa'ie	昌家	Nanboku	南北	1392		
Masakado	将門	Uncertain	不詳	1600		
Masakage	昌景	Uncertain	不詳	1600		
Masakata	雅賢	Hei'an	平安	1147	*kugyou*	High Courtier Official
Masakatsu	正勝	Nanboku	南北	1392		
Masakiyo	雅清	Muromachi	室町	1390	*kajin*	Poet
Masakiyo	政清	Muromachi	室町	1572		
Masakiyo	正清	Hei'an	平安	1147		
Masakuni	政国	Muromachi	室町	1572		
Masamichi	雅通	Uncertain	不詳	1600		
Masamitsu	政光	Hei'an	平安	1147		
Masamori	正盛	Uncertain	不詳	1600		
Masamori	昌盛	Uncertain	不詳	1600		
Masamoto	政基	Muromachi	室町	1572	*kugyou*	High Courtier Official
Masamoto	政幹	Nanboku	南北	1392		
Masamoto	政元	Nanboku	南北	1392		
Masamu'ne	政宗	Nanboku	南北	1392		
Masamura	政村	Kamakura	鎌倉	1332		
Masa'naga	雅長	Hei'an	平安	1147	*kugyou*	High Courtier Official
Masa'naga	政長	Nanboku	南北	1392		
Masa'nari	正成	Uncertain	不詳	1600		
Masa'nari	昌成	Hei'an	平安	1147		
Masa'nobu	正信	Muromachi	室町	1572		
Masa'nobu	昌信	Uncertain	不詳	1600		
Masa'nori	政則	Muromachi	室町	1572		
Masa'nori	正儀	Nanboku	南北	1392		
Masa'nori	正則	Sengoku	戦国	1568		
Masa'nori	正度	Uncertain	不詳	1600		
Masasada	雅定	Hei'an	平安	1147	廷臣	
Masashige	政茂	Kamakura	鎌倉	1332		
Masashige	正成	Nanboku	南北	1392		
Masasue	正季	Nanboku	南北	1392		
Masasuke	雅助	Muromachi	室町	1572		

Nanori	Kanji	Period	Date	Notes	
Masasuke	政助	Uncertain	不詳	1600	
Masasuke	政祐	Nanboku	南北	1392	
Masatada	雅忠	Kamakura	鎌倉	1332	任臣
Masatada	正忠	Nanboku	南北	1392	
Masataka	雅隆	Kamakura	鎌倉	1332	*kajin* Poet
Masataka	政高	Muromachi	室町	1572	
Masatake	正武	Nanboku	南北	1392	
Masata'ne	真種	Nanboku	南北	1392	
Masata'ne	昌胤	Uncertain	不詳	1600	
Masatoki	正時	Nanboku	南北	1392	
Masatomo	政具	Uncertain	不詳	1600	
Masatomo	政知	Muromachi	室町	1572	
Masatoo	正遠	Nanboku	南北	1392	
Masatora	正虎	Uncertain	不詳	1600	
Masatoyo	政豊	Muromachi	室町	1572	
Masatoyo	昌豊	Uncertain	不詳	1600	
Masatsugu	政嗣	Kamakura	鎌倉	1332	
Masatsugu	正次	Muromachi	室町	1572	射術家
Masatsugu	昌次	Uncertain	不詳	1600	
Masatsu'na	雅綱	Uncertain	不詳	1600	
Masatsu'na	政綱	Kamakura	鎌倉	1328	*jitou* Estate Steward
Masatsu'na	正綱	Kamakura	鎌倉	1332	
Masatsu'ne	雅経	Kamakura	鎌倉	1332	
Masatsu'ne	政経	Muromachi	室町	1572	
Masatsura	正行	Nanboku	南北	1392	
Masa'uji	雅氏	Muromachi	室町	1390	
Masa'uji	政氏	Sengoku	戦国	1568	
Masa'uji	正氏	Uncertain	不詳	1600	
Masayasu	政康	Muromachi	室町	1572	
Masayasu	政泰	Kamakura	鎌倉	1332	
Masayasu	正泰	Kamakura	鎌倉	1332	
Masayo	雅世	Muromachi	室町	1390	
Masayori	正頼	Sengoku	戦国	1568	
Masayoshi	政義	Kamakura	鎌倉	1332	
Masayoshi	昌能	Nanboku	南北	1392	*jinkan* Shintoh Official
Masayuki	雅幸	Muromachi	室町	1390	
Masayuki	雅行	Kamakura	鎌倉	1332	
Masayuki	政行	Nanboku	南北	1392	
Masayuki	正行	Uncertain	不詳	1600	
Masayuki	正之	Sengoku	戦国	1568	
Masayuki	昌幸	Sengoku	戦国	1568	
Masaza'ne	雅実	Uncertain	不詳	1600	
Masuyuki	益之	Muromachi	室町	1572	*Kajin* Poet

み ❖❖❖❖❖ Mi

Nanori	Kanji	Period	Date	Notes	
Michi'aki	通顕	Kamakura	鎌倉	1332	*kugyou* High Courtier Official
Michi'aki	通昭	Kamakura	鎌倉	1332	
Michi'ari	通有	Kamakura	鎌倉	1332	
Michi'atsu	通淳	Muromachi	室町	1572	*kugyou* High Courtier Official
Michichika	通親	Hei'an	平安	1147	*kugyou* High Courtier Official
Michifuyu	通冬	Nanboku	南北	1392	*kugyou* High Courtier Official
Michigane	道兼	Uncertain	不詳	1600	
Michiharu	通春	Muromachi	室町	1572	

Michiharu	通治	Kamakura	鎌倉	1332		
Michihide	通秀	Muromachi	室町	1572	*kugyou*	High Courtier Official
Michihira	道平	Kamakura	鎌倉	1332	*kugyou*	High Courtier Official
Michihiro	通博	Muromachi	室町	1572	*kugyou*	High Courtier Official
Michihisa	通久	Kamakura	鎌倉	1332		
Michi'ie	道家	Kamakura	鎌倉	1332	*kugyou*	High Courtier Official
Michikata	通方	Kamakura	鎌倉	1332	廷臣	
Michikiyo	通清	Kamakura	鎌倉	1332		
Michimasa	道雅	Uncertain	不詳	1600		
Michimasa	道政	Nanboku	南北	1392		
Michimasu	通増	Nanboku	南北	1392		
Michimitsu	通光	Kamakura	鎌倉	1332	*kugyou*	High Courtier Official
Michimori	通守	Muromachi	室町	1572	*kugyou*	High Courtier Official
Michimori	通盛	Kamakura	鎌倉	1332		
Michi'naga	道長	Uncertain	不詳	1600		
Michi'naga	道良	Kamakura	鎌倉	1332	*kugyou*	High Courtier Official
Michi'nao	通直	Nanboku	南北	1392		
Michi'nari	通成	Kamakura	鎌倉	1332	*kugyou*	High Courtier Official
Michi'nobu	通信	Kamakura	鎌倉	1332		
Michi'nobu	道信	Uncertain	不詳	1600		
Michi'nori	通憲	Hei'an	平安	1147	政治家	
Michi'nori	道教	Nanboku	南北	1392	*kugyou*	High Courtier Official
Michi'o	通雄	Kamakura	鎌倉	1332	*kugyou*	High Courtier Official
Michisada	通貞	Nanboku	南北	1392		
Michishige	通重	Kamakura	鎌倉	1332	*kugyou*	High Courtier Official
Michisuke	通相	Nanboku	南北	1392	*kugyou*	High Courtier Official
Michisuke	通資	Kamakura	鎌倉	1332		
Michitada	通忠	Kamakura	鎌倉	1332		
Michitaka	通尭	Nanboku	南北	1392		
Michitaka	道隆	Uncertain	不詳	1600		
Michita'ne	通種	Nanboku	南北	1392		
Michitoki	通言	Nanboku	南北	1392		
Michitoki	通時	Kamakura	鎌倉	1332		
Michitoki	道辰	Nanboku	南北	1392		
Michitomo	通具	Kamakura	鎌倉	1332	*kugyou*	High Courtier Official
Michitomo	通朝	Nanboku	南北	1392		
Michitoshi	通俊	Uncertain	不詳	1600		
Michitou	通任	Nanboku	南北	1392		
Michitsugu	通継	Kamakura	鎌倉	1332		
Michitsugu	道嗣	Kamakura	鎌倉	1332	*kugyou*	High Courtier Official
Michitsu'na	道綱	Nanboku	南北	1392		
Michitsu'ne	通経	Kamakura	鎌倉	1332		
Michitsu'ne	道経	Kamakura	鎌倉	1332	*kugyou*	High Courtier Official
Michi'uji	通氏	Nanboku	南北	1392	*kugyou*	High Courtier Official
Michiyori	通頼	Kamakura	鎌倉	1332	*kugyou*	High Courtier Official
Michiyoshi	通能	Nanboku	南北	1392		
Michiyuki	通行	Muromachi	室町	1572	*kugyou*	High Courtier Official
Michiyuki	通之	Muromachi	室町	1572		
Michiza'ne	道真	Hei'an	平安	903		
Mitsu'aki	満詮	Muromachi	室町	1572		
Mitsuchika	光親	Kamakura	鎌倉	1332	*kugyou*	High Courtier Official
Mitsuchika	満親	Nanboku	南北	1392	*kugyou*	High Courtier Official
Mitsufuji	満藤	Muromachi	室町	1572		
Mitsuhide	光秀	Sengoku	戦国	1568	Bright/Shining Superiority	
Mitsuhide	満秀	Muromachi	室町	1572		
Mitsuhiko	光比己	Uncertain	不詳	1600		
Mitsu'ie	光家	Kamakura	鎌倉	1332		

Historical Masculine Nanori   343

Mitsu'ie	満家	Muromachi	室町	1572		
Mitsuka'ne	満兼	Muromachi	室町	1572		
Mitsukazu	光員	Kamakura	鎌倉	1332		
Mitsukuni	光国	Kamakura	鎌倉	1332	kugyou	High Courtier Official
Mitsumasa	光政	Hei'an	平安	1147		
Mitsumasa	光正	Nanboku	南北	1392		
Mitsumasa	充正	Muromachi	室町	1572		
Mitsumasa	満雅	Muromachi	室町	1572	Abundant	
Mitsumasa	満政	Muromachi	室町	1572		
Mitsumori	光盛	Kamakura	鎌倉	1332	kugyou	High Courtier Official
Mitsumoto	満元	Muromachi	室町	1572		
Mitsumu'ne	光宗	Kamakura	鎌倉	1332	伊賀次郎	
Mitsumura	光村	Kamakura	鎌倉	1332		
Mitsu'naga	光長	Hei'an	平安	1147	gaka	Graphic Artist
Mitsu'naka	満仲	Uncertain	不詳	1600	Abundant	
Mitsu'nao	満直	Muromachi	室町	1572		
Mitsu'nari	光成	Sengoku	戦国	1568		
Mitsu'nari	三成	Uncertain	不詳	1600		
Mitsu'nari	満成	Muromachi	室町	1572		
Mitsu'nobu	光信	Muromachi	室町	1572	gaka	Graphic Artist
Mitsu'nori	光範	Nanboku	南北	1392		
Mitsu'nori	満慶	Muromachi	室町	1572		
Mitsu'nori	満教	Muromachi	室町	1572	kugyou	High Courtier Official
Mitsu'nori	満則	Muromachi	室町	1572		
Mitsu'nori	満範	Muromachi	室町	1572		
Mitsusada	光定	Kamakura	鎌倉	1332	ason	
Mitsusada	満貞	Nanboku	南北	1392	Abundant	
Mitsusato	光郷	Nanboku	南北	1392		
Mitsushige	光重	Kamakura	鎌倉	1332		
Mitsushige	光茂	Muromachi	室町	1572	gaka	Graphic Artist
Mitsushige	満重	Muromachi	室町	1572		
Mitsusue	光季	Kamakura	鎌倉	1332		
Mitsusue	満季	Muromachi	室町	1572	kizoku	Ancient Nobility
Mitsusuke	満祐	Muromachi	室町	1572	Abundant	
Mitsutada	満直	Muromachi	室町	1572		
Mitsutaka	満高	Nanboku	南北	1392		
Mitsutaka	満隆	Muromachi	室町	1572		
Mitsuta'ne	光胤	Nanboku	南北	1392		
Mitsuta'ne	満胤	Muromachi	室町	1572		
Mitsutoki	光時	Kamakura	鎌倉	1332		
Mitsutomo	満朝	Muromachi	室町	1572		
Mitsutsugu	光継	Nanboku	南北	1392	kizoku	Ancient Nobility
Mitsutsu'na	満綱	Muromachi	室町	1572		
Mitsutsu'ne	光経	Kamakura	鎌倉	1332	kajin	Poet
Mitsutsu'ne	満経	Muromachi	室町	1572		
Mitsu'uji	満氏	Muromachi	室町	1572		
Mitsuyasu	光泰	Nanboku	南北	1392		
Mitsuyori	満頼	Hei'an	平安	1147	kugyou	High Courtier Official
Mitsuyoshi	光吉	Kamakura	鎌倉	1332	kajin	Poet
Mitsuyoshi	光嘉	Sengoku	戦国	1568		
Mitsuyoshi	光能	Hei'an	平安	1147	kugyou	High Courtier Official
Mitsuyuki	光行	Kamakura	鎌倉	1332		
Mitsuyuki	満幸	Nanboku	南北	1392		
Mitsuzumi	満純	Muromachi	室町	1572		

も ❖❖❖❖❖ Mo

Nanori	Kanji	Period	Date	Notes	
Mochifusa	持房	Muromachi	室町	1572	
Mochiharu	持春	Muromachi	室町	1572	
Mochi'ie	持家	Muromachi	室町	1572	
Mochikata	持賢	Muromachi	室町	1572	
Mochikiyo	持清	Muromachi	室町	1572	
Mochikuni	持国	Muromachi	室町	1572	
Mochimasa	以政	Hei'an	平安	1147	
Mochimasu	持益	Muromachi	室町	1572	
Mochimichi	持通	Muromachi	室町	1572	*kugyou* — High Courtier Official
Mochimitsu	以光	Muromachi	室町	1572	*gajin* — Artist
Mochimitsu	持光	Muromachi	室町	1572	
Mochimori	以盛	Muromachi	室町	1572	*gajin* — Artist
Mochimoto	持基	Muromachi	室町	1572	*kugyou* — High Courtier Official
Mochimu'ne	持宗	Muromachi	室町	1572	
Mochi'naga	持長	Muromachi	室町	1572	
Mochi'naka	持仲	Muromachi	室町	1572	
Mochi'nobu	持信	Muromachi	室町	1572	Hold Faith
Mochi'nori	持憲	Muromachi	室町	1440	
Mochisada	持貞	Muromachi	室町	1572	
Mochitame	持為	Muromachi	室町	1572	*kugyou* — High Courtier Official
Mochitomo	持朝	Muromachi	室町	1572	
Mochitoyo	持豊	Muromachi	室町	1572	
Mochi'uji	持氏	Muromachi	室町	1572	
Mochiyo	持世	Muromachi	室町	1572	
Mochiyori	持頼	Muromachi	室町	1572	
Mochiyuki	持之	Muromachi	室町	1572	
Mochiza'ne	茂実	Uncertain	不詳	1600	
Momokawa	百川	Uncertain	不詳	1600	
Mori'akira	盛詮	Muromachi	室町	1572	
Mori'akira	盛明	Kamakura	鎌倉	1332	
Morichika	守親	Uncertain	不詳	1600	
Morigane	盛兼	Sengoku	戦国	1568	
Morihide	盛秀	Uncertain	不詳	1600	Plentiful Superiority
Morihiro	盛弘	Muromachi	室町	1572	
Morihisa	盛久	Muromachi	室町	1572	
Mori'ie	盛家	Kamakura	鎌倉	1332	*gokenin* — Shogunal Vassal
Morikage	盛景	Kamakura	鎌倉	1332	
Morika'ne	盛兼	Kamakura	鎌倉	1332	*kugyou* — High Courtier Official
Morikazu	盛員	Kamakura	鎌倉	1332	
Morikuni	盛国	Hei'an	平安	1147	
Morimasa	守正	Kamakura	鎌倉	1332	*gakujin* — Musician
Morimasa	盛政	Kamakura	鎌倉	1332	
Morimi	盛見	Muromachi	室町	1572	
Morimitsu	盛光	Nanboku	南北	1392	
Morimori	盛守	Uncertain	不詳	1600	
Mori'naga	盛長	Hei'an	平安	1147	
Mori'naka	盛仲	Uncertain	不詳	1600	
Mori'nao	盛直	Hei'an	平安	1147	
Mori'nobu	守延	Kamakura	鎌倉	1332	
Mori'nobu	盛信	Uncertain	不詳	1600	
Moritaka	盛高	Muromachi	室町	1572	
Moritaka	盛隆	Kamakura	鎌倉	1332	
Moritoki	守時	Kamakura	鎌倉	1332	

Moritoki	盛時	Kamakura	鎌倉	1332			
Moritomo	守知	Sengoku	戦国	1568			
Moritomo	守友	Uncertain	不詳	1600			
Moritoo	盛遠	Kamakura	鎌倉	1332			
Moritoshi	盛俊	Hei'an	平安	1147			
Moritsugu	盛継	Uncertain	不詳	1600			
Moritsugu	盛嗣	Hei'an	平安	1147			
Moritsu'na	盛綱	Hei'an	平安	1147			
Moritsura	盛連	Kamakura	鎌倉	1332			
Mori'uji	盛氏	Kamakura	鎌倉	1332			
Moriyoshi	盛義	Uncertain	不詳	1600			
Moro'aki	師顕	Kamakura	鎌倉	1332			
Moro'aki	師秋	Nanboku	南北	1392			
Moro'akira	師詮	Nanboku	南北	1392			
Morochika	師親	Kamakura	鎌倉	1332			
Morofusa	師房	Uncertain	不詳	1600			
Morofuyu	師冬	Nanboku	南北	1392			
Morohide	師英	Muromachi	室町	1572			
Morohide	師秀	Nanboku	南北	1392			
Morohira	師平	Kamakura	鎌倉	1332	*kugyou*	High Courtier Official	
Morohisa	師久	Nanboku	南北	1392			
Morohisa	師尚	Hei'an	平安	1147	*Myoubouka*	Chinese Legal Expert	
Moro'ie	師家	Hei'an	平安	1147	*kugyou*	High Courtier Official	
Morokage	師景	Nanboku	南北	1392			
Moroka'ne	師兼	Kamakura	鎌倉	1332	*Myoubouka*	Chinese Legal Expert	
Morokata	師賢	Kamakura	鎌倉	1332	*kugyou*	High Courtier Official	
Morokawa	師賢	Uncertain	不詳	1600			
Morokazu	師員	Kamakura	鎌倉	1332	*Myoubouka*	Chinese Legal Expert	
Moromichi	師通	Uncertain	不詳	1600			
Moromitsu	師光	Hei'an	平安	1177	近臣		
Moromochi	師茂	Nanboku	南北	1392			
Moromori	師守	Nanboku	南北	1392	明経博士		
Moromori	師盛	Hei'an	平安	1147			
Moromoto	師基	Nanboku	南北	1392	*kugyou*	High Courtier Official	
Moro'naga	師長	Hei'an	平安	1147	*kizoku*	Ancient Nobility	
Moro'naka	師仲	Hei'an	平安	1147	*kugyou*	High Courtier Official	
Moro'nao	師直	Hei'an	平安	1147	*Myoubouka*	Chinese Legal Expert	
Moro'natsu	師夏	Nanboku	南北	1392			
Moro'nobu	師信	Kamakura	鎌倉	1332	*kugyou*	High Courtier Official	
Moro'nori	師教	Kamakura	鎌倉	1332	*kugyou*	High Courtier Official	
Moro'o	師緒	Kamakura	鎌倉	1332	*Myoubouka*	Chinese Legal Expert	
Moroshige	師重	Kamakura	鎌倉	1332	*kugyou*	High Courtier Official	
Moroshige	師茂	Nanboku	南北	1392	*Myoubouka*	Chinese Legal Expert	
Morosuke	師助	Nanboku	南北	1392			
Morosuke	師輔	Uncertain	不詳	1600			
Morotada	師忠	Kamakura	鎌倉	1332	*kugyou*	High Courtier Official	
Morotoki	師時	Kamakura	鎌倉	1332			
Morotsugu	師嗣	Muromachi	室町	1572	*kugyou*	High Courtier Official	
Morotsu'na	師綱	Nanboku	南北	1392	*kajin*	Poet	
Morotsu'ne	師経	Kamakura	鎌倉	1332	*kugyou*	High Courtier Official	
Morotsu'ne	師常	Kamakura	鎌倉	1332			
Morotsura	師連	Kamakura	鎌倉	1332	評定衆		
Moro'uji	師氏	Nanboku	南北	1392			
Moroyasu	師泰	Nanboku	南北	1392			
Moroyori	師頼	Uncertain	不詳	1600			
Moroyoshi	師義	Nanboku	南北	1392			
Moroyoshi	師良	Nanboku	南北	1392	*kugyou*	High Courtier Official	

Moroyuki	師行	Nanboku	南北	1392		
Moroza'ne	師実	Uncertain	不詳	1600		
Motochika	基親	Kamakura	鎌倉	1332	kugyou	High Courtier Official
Motochika	元親	Uncertain	不詳	1600		
Motofusa	基房	Hei'an	平安	1147	kugyou	High Courtier Official
Motoharu	元春	Nanboku	南北	1392		
Motoharu	元治	Hei'an	平安	1147	gouzoku	
Motohide	基秀	Muromachi	室町	1572	kugyou	High Courtier Official
Motohira	基衡	Uncertain	不詳	1600		
Motohira	基平	Kamakura	鎌倉	1332	kugyou	High Courtier Official
Motohisa	元久	Nanboku	南北	1392		
Moto'ie	基家	Kamakura	鎌倉	1332	kugyou	High Courtier Official
Motoka'ne	基兼	Hei'an	平安	1147	gekyuukannin	Bureaucrat
Motokiyo	基清	Kamakura	鎌倉	1332		
Motokiyo	元清	Nanboku	南北	1392		
Motokuni	基国	Nanboku	南北	1392		
Motokuni	元国	Muromachi	室町	1572		
Motomasa	基政	Kamakura	鎌倉	1332		
Motomasa	元雅	Muromachi	室町	1572	謡曲作者	
Motomichi	基通	Hei'an	平安	1147	kugyou	High Courtier Official
Motomitsu	元光	Muromachi	室町	1572		
Motomori	基盛	Hei'an	平安	1147		
Motomu'ne	基宗	Kamakura	鎌倉	1332		
Moto'naga	基長	Nanboku	南北	1392		
Moto'naga	元長	Muromachi	室町	1572	kugyou	High Courtier Official
Moto'nari	基成	Kamakura	鎌倉	1332	kugyou	High Courtier Official
Moto'nari	元就	Uncertain	不詳	1600		
Moto'nobu	基宣	Kamakura	鎌倉	1332	kugyou	High Courtier Official
Moto'nobu	元信	Uncertain	不詳	1600		
Moto'nori	基教	Kamakura	鎌倉	1332	kugyou	High Courtier Official
Moto'nori	基範	Hei'an	平安	1147	kugyou	High Courtier Official
Motoshige	基重	Hei'an	平安	1147	kugyou	High Courtier Official
Motoshige	幹重	Nanboku	南北	1392		
Motoshige	元重	Muromachi	室町	1572		
Motosuke	基佐	Higashiyama	東山	1482		
Motosuke	基輔	Kamakura	鎌倉	1332	kugyou	High Courtier Official
Motosuke	元資	Muromachi	室町	1572		
Motosuke	元輔	Uncertain	不詳	1600		
Mototada	基忠	Kamakura	鎌倉	1332	kugyou	High Courtier Official
Mototaka	基隆	Kamakura	鎌倉	1332	kugyou	High Courtier Official
Motota'ne	元胤	Muromachi	室町	1572		
Mototoki	基時	Kamakura	鎌倉	1332		
Mototsugu	基嗣	Kamakura	鎌倉	1332	kugyou	High Courtier Official
Mototsu'na	基綱	Kamakura	鎌倉	1332		
Mototsu'na	元綱	Sengoku	戦国	1568		
Mototsu'ne	基経	Uncertain	不詳	1600		
Mototsu'ne	基恒	Muromachi	室町	1572		
Mototsura	元連	Muromachi	室町	1572		
Moto'uji	基氏	Kamakura	鎌倉	1332		
Moto'uji	元氏	Nanboku	南北	1392		
Moto'uji	源氏	Kamakura	鎌倉	1332		
Motoyasu	基康	Uncertain	不詳	1600		
Motoyori	基頼	Kamakura	鎌倉	1332		
Motoyoshi	基義	Uncertain	不詳	1600		
Motoyoshi	基能	Nanboku	南北	1392		
Motoyoshi	元喜	Uncertain	不詳	1600	36 ancient poets	
Motoyoshi	元良	Uncertain	不詳	1600		

Nanori	Kanji	Period		Date	Notes	
Motoyuki	基行	Kamakura	鎌倉	1332		
Motoza'ne	基実	Hei'an	平安	1147	kugyou	High Courtier Official
Motsuza'ne	以実	Momoyama	桃山	1480		

む ❖❖❖❖❖ Mu

Nanori	Kanji	Period		Date	Notes	
Mu'ne'aki	統秋	Muromachi	室町	1572	gakujin	Musician
Mu'ne'atsu	宗敦	Uncertain	不詳	1600		
Mu'nechika	宗親	Kamakura	鎌倉	1332		
Mu'nef'uji	宗藤	Kamakura	鎌倉	1332		
Mu'nehide	宗秀	Kamakura	鎌倉	1332		
Mu'nehira	宗衡	Kamakura	鎌倉	1332		
Mu'nehira	宗平	Nanboku	南北	1392		
Mu'nehiro	宗広	Kamakura	鎌倉	1332		
Mu'nehiro	宗弘	Kamakura	鎌倉	1332		
Mu'nehisa	宗久	Kamakura	鎌倉	1332		
Mu'ne'ie	宗家	Kamakura	鎌倉	1332		
Mu'nekage	宗景	Muromachi	室町	1572		
Mu'nekata	宗賢	Kamakura	鎌倉	1332		
Mu'nekata	宗方	Kamakura	鎌倉	1332		
Mu'nekiyo	宗清	Hei'an	平安	1147		
Mu'nemasa	宗政	Kamakura	鎌倉	1332		
Mu'nemitsu	宗光	Kamakura	鎌倉	1332		
Mu'nemori	宗盛	Hei'an	平安	1147		
Mu'nemoto	宗元	Nanboku	南北	1392		
Mu'ne'naga	宗長	Kamakura	鎌倉	1332	kugyou	High Courtier Official
Mu'ne'nari	宗業	Kamakura	鎌倉	1332		
Mu'ne'nobu	宗宣	Kamakura	鎌倉	1332		
Mu'ne'nobu	宗信	Uncertain	不詳	1600		
Mu'ne'nori	宗矩	Kamakura	鎌倉	1332	kannin	Government Official
Mu'ne'nori	宗教	Kamakura	鎌倉	1332	kugyou	High Courtier Official
Mu'neshige	宗重	Hei'an	平安	1147		
Mu'neshige	宗茂	Sengoku	戦国	1568		
Mu'nesuke	宗介	Kamakura	鎌倉	1332		Armorer
Mu'nesuke	宗輔	Hei'an	平安	1147	kugyou	High Courtier Official
Mu'nesuke	宗祐	Nanboku	南北	1392		
Mu'neta	宗太	Uncertain	不詳	1600		
Mu'netada	宗忠	Nanboku	南北	1392	jinkan	Shintoh Official
Mu'netaka	宗隆	Hei'an	平安	1147		
Mu'neta'ne	宗胤	Kamakura	鎌倉	1332		
Mu'netoki	宗時	Uncertain	不詳	1600		
Mu'netoo	宗遠	Hei'an	平安	1147		
Mu'netsu'na	宗綱	Kamakura	鎌倉	1332		
Mu'netsu'ne	宗経	Kamakura	鎌倉	1332	kugyou	High Courtier Official
Mu'ne'uji	宗氏	Kamakura	鎌倉	1332		
Mu'neyasu	宗泰	Kamakura	鎌倉	1332		
Mu'neyori	宗頼	Kamakura	鎌倉	1332		
Mu'neyoshi	宗能	Hei'an	平安	1147	kugyou	High Courtier Official
Mu'neyoshi	宗良	Kamakura	鎌倉	1332		
Mu'neyuki	宗干	Uncertain	不詳	1600		
Mu'neyuki	宗行	Kamakura	鎌倉	1332	kugyou	High Courtier Official
Mu'neza'ne	宗実	Hei'an	平安	1147	kannin	Government Official
Murashige	村重	Uncertain	不詳	1600		

な ❖❖❖❖❖ Na

Nanori	Kanji	Period	Date	Notes	
Nagachika	長親	Hei'an	平安	1147	廷臣
Nagafuji	永藤	Muromachi	室町	1572	*kugyou*	High Courtier Official
Nagafusa	長房	Kamakura	鎌倉	1332	*kugyou*	High Courtier Official
Nagahide	長秀	Muromachi	室町	1572		
Nagahira	永平	Hei'an	平安	1147		
Nagahiro	修弘	Sengoku	戦国	1568		
Nagahisa	長久	Uncertain	不詳	1600		
Nagaka'ne	長兼	Kamakura	鎌倉	1332	*kugyou*	High Courtier Official
Nagakata	長方	Hei'an	平安	1147	*kugyou*	High Courtier Official
Nagakatsu	永勝	Sengoku	戦国	1568		
Nagakatsu	長勝	Sengoku	戦国	1568		
Nagakiyo	長清	Kamakura	鎌倉	1332		
Nagamasa	永昌	Kamakura	鎌倉	1332	刀鍛治	
Nagamasa	長政	Kamakura	鎌倉	1332		
Nagamichi	長通	Kamakura	鎌倉	1332	*kugyou*	High Courtier Official
Nagamitsu	長光	Kamakura	鎌倉	1332	*toukou*	Swordmaker
Nagamitsu	長充	Muromachi	室町	1572		Lacquerware Maker
Nagamochi	長茂	Kamakura	鎌倉	1332		
Nagamori	長守	Kamakura	鎌倉	1332	*kugyou*	High Courtier Official
Nagamori	長盛	Uncertain	不詳	1600		
Nagamoto	長基	Nanboku	南北	1392		
Nagamoto	長幹	Kamakura	鎌倉	1332		
Naga'nari	長成	Uncertain	不詳	1600		
Naga'oki	長興	Muromachi	室町	1572	*kannin*	Government Official
Nagasada	長定	Kamakura	鎌倉	1332		
Nagashige	長重	Nanboku	南北	1392		
Nagasue	永季	Nanboku	南北	1392	*kugyou*	High Courtier Official
Nagataka	長隆	Kamakura	鎌倉	1332	*kugyou*	High Courtier Official
Nagateru	長輝	Sengoku	戦国	1568		
Nagatoki	長時	Kamakura	鎌倉	1332		
Nagatoshi	長年	Kamakura	鎌倉	1332		Long Years
Naga'uji	長氏	Kamakura	鎌倉	1332		
Nagayo	長世	Kamakura	鎌倉	1332	*ishi*	physician
Nagayori	長頼	Kamakura	鎌倉	1332		
Nagayoshi	長慶	Sengoku	戦国	1568		
Nagayoshi	長可	Sengoku	戦国	1568		
Nagayoshi	長良	Uncertain	不詳	1600		
Nagayuki	永幸	Nanboku	南北	1392		Long/Eternal Happiness
Nagayuki	永行	Muromachi	室町	1572	*kugyou*	High Courtier Official
Nagayuki	長幸	Nanboku	南北	1392		
Nagayuki	長行	Sengoku	戦国	1568		
Nageta'ne	長胤	Nanboku	南北	1392		
Nahoza'ne	直実	Uncertain	不詳	1600		
Naka'aki	仲秋	Nanboku	南北	1392		
Nakabumi	仲文	Uncertain	不詳	1600		36 ancient poets
Nakachika	仲親	Kamakura	鎌倉	1332		
Nakafusa	仲房	Nanboku	南北	1392	*kugyou*	High Courtier Official
Nakahira	仲平	Uncertain	不詳	1600		
Naka'ie	仲家	Kamakura	鎌倉	1332	*kajin*	Poet
Naka'ki	仲材	Sengoku	戦国	1568		
Nakakuni	仲国	Kamakura	鎌倉	1332	*kuge*	
Nakamaro	仲麻呂	Uncertain	不詳	1600		
Nakamaro	仲麿	Uncertain	不詳	1600		

Nanori	Kanji	Period		Date	Notes	
Nakamitsu	仲光	Muromachi	室町	1572	*kizoku*	Ancient Nobility
Nakamoto	仲基	Hei'an	平安	1147	廷臣	
Nakamu'ne	仲宗	Hei'an	平安	1147		
Naka'nari	仲業	Kamakura	鎌倉	1332	*gokenin*	Shogunal Vassal
Naka'nari	仲成	Uncertain	不詳	1600		
Nakasada	仲貞	Nanboku	南北	1392		
Nakatoki	仲時	Kamakura	鎌倉	1332		
Nakatsu'na	仲綱	Hei'an	平安	1147		
Nakayori	仲頼	Hei'an	平安	1147		
Nao'aki	直顕	Kamakura	鎌倉	1332		
Nao'aki	直詮	Muromachi	室町	1572		
Nao'ie	直家	Kamakura	鎌倉	1332		
Naomitsu	直光	Hei'an	平安	1147		
Naomochi	直持	Nanboku	南北	1392		
Nao'nobu	直信	Nanboku	南北	1392		
Naosada	直貞	Nanboku	南北	1392		
Naoshige	直重	Nanboku	南北	1392		
Naotoki	直時	Kamakura	鎌倉	1332		
Naotomo	直朝	Nanboku	南北	1392		
Naotsu'ne	直経	Nanboku	南北	1392		
Naotsu'ne	直常	Nanboku	南北	1392		
Nao'uji	直氏	Nanboku	南北	1392	侍所頭人	
Naoyori	直頼	Nanboku	南北	1392		
Naoza'ne	直実	Hei'an	平安	1147		
Naozumi	尚純	Muromachi	室町	1572		
Narichika	成親	Hei'an	平安	1147	*kizoku*	Ancient Nobility
Narifusa	業房	Hei'an	平安	1147	廷臣	
Nariharu	斉晴	Nanboku	南北	1392		
Nari'ie	成家	Kamakura	鎌倉	1332	*kugyou*	High Courtier Official
Narika'ne	業兼	Kamakura	鎌倉	1332	廷臣	
Narimasa	成雅	Uncertain	不詳	1600	*kugyou*	High Courtier Official
Narimori	業盛	Hei'an	平安	1147		
Nari'nori	成範	Hei'an	平安	1147	*kizoku*	Ancient Nobility
Narisada	成定	Hei'an	平安	1147	廷臣	
Narishige	成重	Kamakura	鎌倉	1332		
Narisue	成季	Kamakura	鎌倉	1332		
Narisuke	成輔	Kamakura	鎌倉	1332	*kugyou*	High Courtier Official
Naritada	業忠	Hei'an	平安	1147	*kannin*	Government Official
Narita'ne	成胤	Kamakura	鎌倉	1332		
Naritoki	業時	Kamakura	鎌倉	1332	評定衆	
Naritsu'na	成綱	Hei'an	平安	1147		
Naritsu'ne	成経	Hei'an	平安	1147	*kizoku*	Ancient Nobility
Naritsura	業連	Kamakura	鎌倉	1332	評定衆	
Nari'uji	成氏	Uncertain	不詳	1600		
Nariyoshi	成義	Muromachi	室町	1572		

に ❖❖❖❖❖ Ni

Nanori	Kanji	Period		Date	Notes	
Nishikintoki	西公時	Nanboku	南北	1392	*kugyou*	High Courtier Official
Nishikin'yasu	西公保	Muromachi	室町	1572	*kugyou*	High Courtier Official
Nishisanetaka	西実隆	Muromachi	室町	1572	*kugyou*	High Courtier Official

の ❖❖❖❖❖ No

Nanori	Kanji	Period	Date	Notes	
Nobu'aki	宣明	Kamakura	鎌倉	1332	*kugyou*	High Courtier Official
Nobu'aki	信詮	Uncertain	不詳	1600	36 ancient poets
Nobu'aki	信章	Hei'an	平安	1147	国司
Nobu'ari	信有	Muromachi	室町	1572	
Nobuchika	信親	Muromachi	室町	1572	
Nobufusa	宣房	Kamakura	鎌倉	1332	廷臣/地頭
Nobufusa	信房	Kamakura	鎌倉	1332	
Nobuharu	信春	Nanboku	南北	1392	
Nobuhide	宣栄	Nanboku	南北	1392	
Nobuhide	宣秀	Nanboku	南北	1392	*kugyou*	High Courtier Official
Nobuhiro	信広	Muromachi	室町	1572	
Nobuhisa	信久	Sengoku	戦国	1568	
Nobukado	信廉	Uncertain	不詳	1600	
Nobuka'ne	信兼	Hei'an	平安	1147	*kannin*	Government Official
Nobukata	信賢	Muromachi	室町	1572	
Nobukata	信方	Uncertain	不詳	1600	
Nobukimi	信君	Uncertain	不詳	1600	
Nobukiyo	信清	Kamakura	鎌倉	1332	*kugyou*	High Courtier Official
Nobumasa	信政	Kamakura	鎌倉	1332	
Nobumasu	信増	Nanboku	南北	1392	
Nobumitsu	信光	Kamakura	鎌倉	1332	
Nobumitsu	信満	Muromachi	室町	1572	
Nobumoto	信元	Muromachi	室町	1572	
Nobu'naga	信長	Kamakura	鎌倉	1332	
Nobu'nari	信業	Uncertain	不詳	1600	
Nobu'nari	信成	Sengoku	戦国	1568	
Nobu'nori	延礼	Muromachi	室町	1572	*ishi*	physician
Nobu'nori	信乗	Sengoku	戦国	1568	
Nobu'nori	信範	Hei'an	平安	1147	*kannin*	Government Official
Nobusada	信貞	Nanboku	南北	1392	
Nobusada	信定	Kamakura	鎌倉	1332	*kugyou*	High Courtier Official
Nobusaka	信栄	Sengoku	戦国	1568	
Nobusato	信達	Uncertain	不詳	1600	
Nobushige	信重	Muromachi	室町	1572	
Nobushige	信繁	Uncertain	不詳	1600	
Nobushige	信茂	Uncertain	不詳	1600	
Nobusuke	信資	Kamakura	鎌倉	1332	
Nobutada	信忠	Kamakura	鎌倉	1332	
Nobutaka	信隆	Hei'an	平安	1147	*kuge*
Nobutake	信武	Nanboku	南北	1392	
Nobuta'ne	信胤	Nanboku	南北	1392	
Nobutatsu	信龍	Uncertain	不詳	1600	
Nobutoki	宣時	Kamakura	鎌倉	1332	
Nobutoki	信時	Kamakura	鎌倉	1332	
Nobutomo	信友	Uncertain	不詳	1600	
Nobutoo	信遠	Hei'an	平安	1147	
Nobutoshi	宣俊	Muromachi	室町	1572	*kugyou*	High Courtier Official
Nobutoshi	信俊	Uncertain	不詳	1600	
Nobutsugi	信次	Uncertain	不詳	1600	
Nobutsugu	信嗣	Kamakura	鎌倉	1332	*kugyou*	High Courtier Official
Nobutsu'na	信綱	Kamakura	鎌倉	1332	
Nobutsura	信連	Hei'an	平安	1147	
Nobuyasu	信康	Uncertain	不詳	1600	

Historical Masculine Nanori 351

Nobuyori	信頼	Hei'an	平安	1147	kizoku	Ancient Nobility
Nobuyoshi	信義	Kamakura	鎌倉	1332		
Nobuyoshi	信能	Hei'an	平安	1147	kugyou	High Courtier Official
Nobuyuki	信之	Sengoku	戦国	1568		
Nobuza'ne	信実	Kamakura	鎌倉	1332		
Nori'aki	憲顕	Nanboku	南北	1392		
Nori'aki	憲秋	Nanboku	南北	1392		
Norifuji	憲藤	Nanboku	南北	1392		
Norifuji	教藤	Nanboku	南北	1392	kizoku	Ancient Nobility
Norifusa	憲房	Nanboku	南北	1392		
Norifusa	教房	Muromachi	室町	1572	kugyou	High Courtier Official
Norifuyu	教冬	Nanboku	南北	1392	kizoku	Ancient Nobility
Noriharu	憲春	Nanboku	南北	1392		
Norihiro	教弘	Muromachi	室町	1572		
Norihiro	範広	Nanboku	南北	1392		
Nori'ie	範家	Hei'an	平安	1147	kugyou	High Courtier Official
Norikage	教景	Muromachi	室町	1572		
Norika'ne	範兼	Uncertain	不詳	1600		
Norikata	憲方	Nanboku	南北	1392		
Norikiyo	憲清	Muromachi	室町	1397		
Norikiyo	教清	Muromachi	室町	1572		
Norikiyo	則清	Hei'an	平安	1147	kokushi	Provincial Governor
Norikuni	範国	Nanboku	南北	1392		
Norimasa	憲将	Uncertain	不詳	1600		
Norimasa	教政	Muromachi	室町	1572		
Norimasa	範政	Muromachi	室町	1572		
Norimichi	教通	Uncertain	不詳	1600		
Norimitsu	範光	Nanboku	南北	1392		
Norimori	教盛	Hei'an	平安	1147		
Norimoto	憲基	Muromachi	室町	1572		
Norimoto	憲幹	Kamakura	鎌倉	1332		
Norimoto	教基	Muromachi	室町	1572	kugyou	High Courtier Official
Norimu'ne	則宗	Hei'an	平安	1147	toukou	Swordmaker
Norimu'ne	範宗	Muromachi	室町	1572	kizoku	Ancient Nobility
Norimura	則村	Kamakura	鎌倉	1332		
Nori'naga	範長	Nanboku	南北	1392		
Nori'nao	則尚	Muromachi	室町	1572		
Nori'oki	教興	Nanboku	南北	1392		
Norisada	憲定	Muromachi	室町	1572		
Norisada	教定	Kamakura	鎌倉	1332	kugyou	High Courtier Official
Norisaka	憲栄	Uncertain	不詳	1600		
Norishige	教成	Kamakura	鎌倉	1332	kizoku	Ancient Nobility
Norishige	則繁	Muromachi	室町	1572		
Norishige	範茂	Kamakura	鎌倉	1332	kugyou	High Courtier Official
Norisue	範季	Kamakura	鎌倉	1332	kugyou	High Courtier Official
Norisuke	則祐	Nanboku	南北	1392		
Norisuke	範資	Nanboku	南北	1392		
Norisuke	範輔	Kamakura	鎌倉	1332	kugyou	High Courtier Official
Noritada	憲忠	Nanboku	南北	1392		
Noritada	範忠	Muromachi	室町	1572		
Noritaka	憲孝	Nanboku	南北	1392		
Noritaka	教高	Nanboku	南北	1392		
Noritaka	教隆	Kamakura	鎌倉	1332	儒者	
Norita'ne	憲胤	Nanboku	南北	1392		
Noritoki	季時	Kamakura	鎌倉	1332		
Noritoki	教言	Nanboku	南北	1392	kizoku	Ancient Nobility
Noritomo	教具	Muromachi	室町	1572	kugyou	High Courtier Official

Nanori	Kanji	Period		Date	Notes	
Noritomo	教朝	Muromachi	室町	1572		
Noritomo	範朝	Kamakura	鎌倉	1332	*kugyou*	High Courtier Official
Noritoo	教遠	Nanboku	南北	1392	*kizoku*	Ancient Nobility
Noritoyo	教豊	Muromachi	室町	1572		
Noritsugu	教嗣	Muromachi	室町	1572	*kugyou*	High Courtier Official
Noritsu'ne	教経	Hei'an	平安	1147		
Nori'uji	紀氏	Muromachi	室町	1572		
Nori'uji	範氏	Nanboku	南北	1392		
Noriyasu	教康	Muromachi	室町	1572		
Noriyori	憲頼	Hei'an	平安	1147		
Noriyori	詮頼	Nanboku	南北	1392		
Noriyori	則頼	Sengoku	戦国	1568		
Noriyori	範頼	Hei'an	平安	1147		
Noriyuki	教之	Muromachi	室町	1572		
Noriza'ne	憲実	Muromachi	室町	1572		
Noriza'ne	教実	Kamakura	鎌倉	1332	*kugyou*	High Courtier Official
Noriza'ne	範実	Nanboku	南北	1392		

お ❖❖❖❖❖ O

Nanori	Kanji	Period		Date	Notes
Okikaze	興風	Uncertain	不詳	1600	
Okita'ne	興胤	Nanboku	南北	1392	
Okitsu'ne	興常	Muromachi	室町	1572	
Otomuro	乙牟漏	Uncertain	不詳	1600	

さ ❖❖❖❖❖ Sa

Nanori	Kanji	Period		Date	Notes	
Sada'aki	貞顕	Kamakura	鎌倉	1332		
Sadabumi	貞文	Uncertain	不詳	1600	36 medieval poets	
Sadachika	貞親	Kamakura	鎌倉	1332		
Sadachika	定親	Kamakura	鎌倉	1332	廷臣	
Sada'e	貞衛	Uncertain	不詳	1600		
Sadafuji	貞藤	Kamakura	鎌倉	1332		
Sadafusa	貞房	Kamakura	鎌倉	1332		
Sadafusa	定房	Kamakura	鎌倉	1332	*kugyou*	High Courtier Official
Sadahide	貞秀	Nanboku	南北	1392		
Sadahira	貞衡	Kamakura	鎌倉	1332		
Sadahira	定平	Kamakura	鎌倉	1332	*kugyou*	High Courtier Official
Sadahiro	貞広	Nanboku	南北	1392		
Sadahisa	貞久	Kamakura	鎌倉	1332		
Sada'ie	貞家	Nanboku	南北	1392		
Sada'ie	定家	Kamakura	鎌倉	1332	*kajin*	Poet
Sadakage	定景	Kamakura	鎌倉	1332		
Sadakata	貞方	Nanboku	南北	1392		
Sadakatsu	定勝	Sengoku	戦国	1568		
Sadakiyo	貞清	Kamakura	鎌倉	1332		
Sadakiyo	定清	Nanboku	南北	1335		
Sadakuni	貞国	Muromachi	室町	1572		
Sadamasa	貞縁	Kamakura	鎌倉	1332		
Sadamasa	貞将	Kamakura	鎌倉	1332		
Sadamasa	貞政	Kamakura	鎌倉	1332		

Sadamasa	定雅	Kamakura	鎌倉	1332	*kugyou*	High Courtier Official
Sadamasa	定正	Muromachi	室町	1572		
Sadamichi	貞通	Sengoku	戦国	1568		
Sadamichi	定通	Kamakura	鎌倉	1332	*kugyou*	High Courtier Official
Sadamitsu	貞光	Uncertain	不詳	1600		
Sadamitsu	貞満	Nanboku	南北	1392		
Sadamori	貞盛	Muromachi	室町	1572		
Sadamu	定	Nanboku	南北	1392		
Sadamu'ne	貞宗	Kamakura	鎌倉	1332		
Sadamura	貞村	Muromachi	室町	1572		
Sada'naga	貞長	Nanboku	南北	1392		
Sada'naga	定長	Kamakura	鎌倉	1332	*kajin*	Poet
Sada'nao	貞直	Kamakura	鎌倉	1332		
Sada'nori	貞載	Nanboku	南北	1392		
Sada'nori	定範	Kamakura	鎌倉	1332		
Sadashige	貞重	Kamakura	鎌倉	1332	*gokenin*	Shogunal Vassal
Sadashige	貞茂	Muromachi	室町	1572		
Sadashige	定重	Kamakura	鎌倉	1332		
Sadashige	定成	Hei'an	平安	1147	*ishi*	physician
Sadasue	貞季	Kamakura	鎌倉	1332		
Sadasuke	定輔	Hei'an	平安	1147	*kuge*	
Sadataka	貞高	Muromachi	室町	1572		
Sadataka	定高	Kamakura	鎌倉	1332	*kugyou*	High Courtier Official
Sadata'ne	貞胤	Kamakura	鎌倉	1332		
Sadatoki	貞時	Kamakura	鎌倉	1332		
Sadatomo	貞朝	Kamakura	鎌倉	1332		
Sadatoshi	正利	Kamakura	鎌倉	1332		
Sadatoshi	定利	Kamakura	鎌倉	1332		Sword Polisher
Sadatsugu	貞継	Nanboku	南北	1392		
Sadatsugu	定継	Kamakura	鎌倉	1332	*kugyou*	High Courtier Official
Sadatsugu	定嗣	Kamakura	鎌倉	1332	*kugyou*	High Courtier Official
Sadatsu'na	貞綱	Kamakura	鎌倉	1332		
Sadatsu'na	定綱	Hei'an	平安	1147		
Sadatsu'ne	貞経	Kamakura	鎌倉	1332		
Sadatsura	貞連	Kamakura	鎌倉	1332		
Sada'uji	貞氏	Kamakura	鎌倉	1332		
Sadayasu	貞泰	Kamakura	鎌倉	1332		
Sadayasu	定康	Uncertain	不詳	1600		
Sadayo	貞世	Nanboku	南北	1392		
Sadayori	貞頼	Kamakura	鎌倉	1332		
Sadayori	定頼	Nanboku	南北	1392		
Sadayoshi	貞慶	Muromachi	室町	1572		
Sadayoshi	貞義	Kamakura	鎌倉	1332		
Sadayoshi	貞能	Hei'an	平安	1147		
Sadayoshi	定能	Kamakura	鎌倉	1332		
Sadayuki	貞幸	Kamakura	鎌倉	1332		
Sadayuki	貞行	Muromachi	室町	1572		
Sadaza'ne	定実	Kamakura	鎌倉	1332	*kugyou*	High Courtier Official
Sakiyori	前頼	Nanboku	南北	1392		
Sa'ne'atsu	実淳	Muromachi	室町	1572	*kugyou*	High Courtier Official
Sa'nechika	実親	Kamakura	鎌倉	1332	*kugyou*	High Courtier Official
Sa'nefusa	実房	Hei'an	平安	1147	*kugyou*	High Courtier Official
Sa'nefuyu	実冬	Nanboku	南北	1392	*kugyou*	High Courtier Official
Sa'nehide	実秀	Muromachi	室町	1572	*kugyou*	High Courtier Official
Sa'nehira	実平	Kamakura	鎌倉	1332	*gokenin*	Shogunal Vassal
Sa'nehiro	実博	Muromachi	室町	1572	*kizoku*	Ancient Nobility
Sa'neka'ne	実兼	Kamakura	鎌倉	1332	*kugyou*	High Courtier Official

Nanori	Kanji	Period	Date		Notes
Sa'nekatsu	真勝	Sengoku 戦国	1568		
Sa'nekazu	実員	Kamakura 鎌倉	1332		
Sa'nekazu	実量	Muromachi 室町	1572	*kugyou*	High Courtier Official
Sa'neku'ni	実国	Hei'an 平安	1147	*kugyou*	High Courtier Official
Sa'nemasa	実雅	Kamakura 鎌倉	1332	*kugyou*	High Courtier Official
Sa'nemasa	実政	Kamakura 鎌倉	1332		
Sa'nemitsu	実光	Kamakura 鎌倉	1332	*kugyou*	High Courtier Official
Sa'nemori	実盛	Hei'an 平安	1147		
Sa'nemoto	実基	Kamakura 鎌倉	1332		
Sa'nemu'ne	実宗	Kamakura 鎌倉	1332	*kugyou*	High Courtier Official
Sa'ne'naga	実永	Muromachi 室町	1572	*kugyou*	High Courtier Official
Sa'ne'naga	実長	Kamakura 鎌倉	1332		
Sa'ne'naka	実仲	Kamakura 鎌倉	1332	*kugyou*	High Courtier Official
Sa'ne'nao	実直	Nanboku 南北	1392	*kugyou*	High Courtier Official
Sa'ne'natsu	実夏	Nanboku 南北	1392	*kugyou*	High Courtier Official
Sa'ne'nori	実教	Kamakura 鎌倉	1332	*kugyou*	High Courtier Official
Sa'ne'o	実雄	Kamakura 鎌倉	1332	*kugyou*	High Courtier Official
Sa'nesada	実定	Hei'an 平安	1147	*kugyou*	High Courtier Official
Sa'neshige	実重	Kamakura 鎌倉	1332	*kugyou*	High Courtier Official
Sa'neshige	実茂	Muromachi 室町	1572	*kugyou*	High Courtier Official
Sa'netada	実忠	Kamakura 鎌倉	1332	*kugyou*	High Courtier Official
Sa'netaka	実隆	Muromachi 室町	1572	*kugyou*	High Courtier Official
Sa'netoki	実時	Kamakura 鎌倉	1332		
Sa'netomo	実朝	Kamakura 鎌倉	1332		
Sa'netoshi	実俊	Nanboku 南北	1392	*kugyou*	High Courtier Official
Sa'netsugu	実継	Kamakura 鎌倉	1332	*kugyou*	High Courtier Official
Sa'netsu'na	実綱	Hei'an 平安	1147	*kugyou*	High Courtier Official
Sa'netsu'ne	実経	Kamakura 鎌倉	1332	*kugyou*	High Courtier Official
Sa'ne'uji	実氏	Kamakura 鎌倉	1332	*kugyou*	High Courtier Official
Sa'neyasu	実康	Uncertain 不詳	1600		
Sa'neyasu	実泰	Kamakura 鎌倉	1332	*kizoku*	Ancient Nobility
Sa'neyo	実世	Kamakura 鎌倉	1332	*kizoku*	Ancient Nobility
Sa'neyori	実頼	Uncertain 不詳	1600		

し ❖❖❖❖❖ Shi

Nanori	Kanji	Period	Date		Notes
Shigechika	重親	Uncertain 不詳	1600		
Shigefusa	重房	Kamakura 鎌倉	1332		
Shigeharu	滋春	Hei'an 平安	1147		
Shigehira	重衡	Hei'an 平安	1147		
Shigehira	茂平	Kamakura 鎌倉	1332	地頭御家人	
Shigehiro	重広	Kamakura 鎌倉	1332		
Shigehisa	重尚	Kamakura 鎌倉	1246		
Shigekatsu	重勝	Nanboku 南北	1392		
Shigekatsu	茂勝	Sengoku 戦国	1568		
Shigekiyo	重清	Nanboku 南北	1392		
Shigekuni	重国	Kamakura 鎌倉	1332		
Shigemasa	重政	Sengoku 戦国	1568		
Shigemasa	繁昌	Kamakura 鎌倉	1332	在地領主	
Shigemitsu	重光	Muromachi 室町	1572	*kugyou*	High Courtier Official
Shigemitsu	茂光	Hei'an 平安	1147		
Shigemochi	重茂	Nanboku 南北	1392		
Shigemori	重盛	Hei'an 平安	1147		
Shigemoto	重元	Sengoku 戦国	1568		

Nanori	Kanji	Period		Date	Notes	
Shigemoto	成職	Muromachi	室町	1572		
Shige'naga	重長	Kamakura	鎌倉	1332		
Shige'naga	茂長	Kamakura	鎌倉	1332	kizoku	Ancient Nobility
Shige'nari	重成	Kamakura	鎌倉	1332		
Shige'nobu	重信	Kamakura	鎌倉	1332		
Shige'nori	重範	Kamakura	鎌倉	1332		
Shigesada	重定	Hei'an	平安	1147		
Shigetada	重忠	Kamakura	鎌倉	1332		
Shigetaka	重高	Hei'an	平安	1147		
Shigetaka	重隆	Kamakura	鎌倉	1332		
Shigetake	重武	Kamakura	鎌倉	1332	足助三郎重武	
Shigeta'ne	重胤	Kamakura	鎌倉	1332	kajin	Poet
Shigetoki	重時	Kamakura	鎌倉	1332		
Shigetoki	茂時	Kamakura	鎌倉	1332		
Shigetomo	重朝	Muromachi	室町	1572		
Shigetomo	成朝	Muromachi	室町	1572		
Shigetsugu	重継	Kamakura	鎌倉	1332		
Shigetsu'na	重綱	Kamakura	鎌倉	1332		
Shigetsu'ne	重経	Uncertain	不詳	1600		
Shige'uji	重氏	Kamakura	鎌倉	1332		
Shige'uji	成氏	Muromachi	室町	1572		
Shige'uji	繁氏	Nanboku	南北	1392		
Shigeyasu	重安	Sengoku	戦国	1568		
Shigeyori	重頼	Kamakura	鎌倉	1332		
Shigeyoshi	重義	Kamakura	鎌倉	1332		
Shigeyoshi	重能	Nanboku	南北	1392		
Shigeyoshi	成能	Hei'an	平安	1147		
Shigeyuki	重之	Muromachi	室町	1572		
Shigeza'ne	茂実	Nanboku	南北	1392		
Shigezumi	重澄	Hei'an	平安	1147		
Shitagau	順	Uncertain	不詳	1600	36 ancient poets	

す Su

Nanori	Kanji	Period		Date	Notes	
Suefusa	季房	Kamakura	鎌倉	1332	kugyou	High Courtier Official
Sueka'ne	季兼	Kamakura	鎌倉	1332	悪党	
Suemitsu	季光	Kamakura	鎌倉	1332		
Sue'naga	季長	Kamakura	鎌倉	1332		
Suetada	末忠	Nanboku	南北	1392		
Suetoki	季時	Kamakura	鎌倉	1332		
Suetsugu	季継	Kamakura	鎌倉	1332	kannin	Government Official
Suetsu'na	季綱	Muromachi	室町	1572		
Suetsu'ne	季経	Hei'an	平安	1147	kugyou	High Courtier Official
Sueyasu	季保	Muromachi	室町	1572	kugyou	High Courtier Official
Sueyoshi	季能	Kamakura	鎌倉	1332	kugyou	High Courtier Official
Suke'aki	資明	Nanboku	南北	1392	kugyou	High Courtier Official
Suke'aki	祐明	Kamakura	鎌倉	1332	kajin	Poet
Sukechika	資親	Nanboku	南北	1392		
Sukechika	祐親	Hei'an	平安	1147		
Sukefuji	資藤	Nanboku	南北	1392	kugyou	High Courtier Official
Sukefusa	資房	Muromachi	室町	1572		
Sukeharu	祐春	Kamakura	鎌倉	1332	kajin	Poet
Sukehide	佐秀	Nanboku	南北	1392		
Sukehira	資衡	Muromachi	室町	1572	kugyou	High Courtier Official

Sukehira	資平	Kamakura	鎌倉	1332	*kugyou*	High Courtier Official
Sukehiro	佐弘	Kamakura	鎌倉	1332		
Suke'ie	資家	Muromachi	室町	1572	*kugyou*	High Courtier Official
Suke'ie	助家	Nanboku	南北	1392		
Sukekage	輔景	Kamakura	鎌倉	1332		
Sukekata	資賢	Hei'an	平安	1147	*kugyou*	High Courtier Official
Sukekazu	助員	Kamakura	鎌倉	1332		
Sukekiyo	資清	Muromachi	室町	1572		
Sukekiyo	祐清	Kamakura	鎌倉	1332		
Sukekuni	資国	Kamakura	鎌倉	1332		
Sukekuni	助国	Kamakura	鎌倉	1332		
Sukemasa	佐理	Uncertain	不詳	1600		
Sukemitsu	佐光	Kamakura	鎌倉	1332		
Sukemochi	祐茂	Kamakura	鎌倉	1332		
Sukemori	資盛	Hei'an	平安	1147		
Sukemoto	資基	Kamakura	鎌倉	1332		
Sukemoto	助職	Kamakura	鎌倉	1332		
Sukemura	資村	Kamakura	鎌倉	1332		
Suke'na	資名	Kamakura	鎌倉	1332	*kugyou*	High Courtier Official
Suke'naga	佐長	Kamakura	鎌倉	1332		
Suke'naga	資永	Kamakura	鎌倉	1332		
Suke'naga	資長	Nanboku	南北	1392		
Suke'nari	資成	Uncertain	不詳	1600		
Suke'nari	祐成	Kamakura	鎌倉	1332		
Suke'nobu	助信	Kamakura	鎌倉	1332		
Suke'nobu	祐信	Kamakura	鎌倉	1332		
Suke'nori	祐則	Muromachi	室町	1572		
Suke'omi	祐臣	Kamakura	鎌倉	1332	*kajin*	Poet
Sukesada	資定	Kamakura	鎌倉	1332		
Sukeshige	助重	Nanboku	南北	1392		
Sukeshige	祐茂	Kamakura	鎌倉	1332	*jinkan*	Shintoh Official
Sukesue	資季	Kamakura	鎌倉	1332	任臣	
Suketada	資忠	Kamakura	鎌倉	1332		
Suketaka	資隆	Hei'an	平安	1147	*kajin*	Poet
Suketa'ne	輔胤	Muromachi	室町	1572		
Suketoki	資時	Kamakura	鎌倉	1332		
Suketoki	祐時	Kamakura	鎌倉	1332		
Suketomo	資朝	Kamakura	鎌倉	1332	*kugyou*	High Courtier Official
Suketomo	助朝	Nanboku	南北	1392		
Suketsu'na	助綱	Kamakura	鎌倉	1332		
Suketsu'ne	資経	Kamakura	鎌倉	1332	*kugyou*	High Courtier Official
Suketsu'ne	祐経	Kamakura	鎌倉	1332		
Suke'uji	助氏	Nanboku	南北	1392		
Sukeyasu	資泰	Hei'an	平安	1147	家司	
Sukeyasu	祐泰	Hei'an	平安	1147		
Sukeyori	資頼	Hei'an	平安	1147		
Sukeyoshi	佐吉	Kamakura	鎌倉	1332		
Sukeyoshi	資能	Kamakura	鎌倉	1332		
Sukeyoshi	助能	Kamakura	鎌倉	1332		
Sukeza'ne	資実	Kamakura	鎌倉	1332	*kugyou*	High Courtier Official
Sumitomo	純友	Uncertain	不詳	1600		
Susumu	進	Kamakura	鎌倉	1234		

た ❖❖❖❖❖ Ta

Nanori	Kanji	Period		Date	Notes	
Tada'aki	忠顕	Nanboku	南北	1392	*kizoku*	Ancient Nobility
Tadachika	忠親	Hei'an	平安	1147	*kugyou*	High Courtier Official
Tadafumi	忠文	Uncertain	不詳	1600	Loyal Culture	
Tadafusa	忠房	Hei'an	平安	1147		
Tadafuyu	直冬	Nanboku	南北	1392		
Tadahira	忠衛	Hei'an	平安	1167		
Tadahira	忠平	Uncertain	不詳	1600		
Tadahisa	忠久	Kamakura	鎌倉	1332		
Tada'ie	忠家	Kamakura	鎌倉	1332	*kugyou*	High Courtier Official
Tadaka'ne	忠兼	Nanboku	南北	1392		
Tadakiyo	忠清	Kamakura	鎌倉	1332		
Tadakuni	忠国	Nanboku	南北	1392		
Tadamasa	忠雅	Hei'an	平安	1147	*kugyou*	High Courtier Official
Tadamasa	忠政	Sengoku	戦国	1568		
Tadamasa	忠正	Hei'an	平安	1147		
Tadamichi	忠通	Hei'an	平安	1147	政治家	
Tadamichi	忠道	Uncertain	不詳	1600		
Tadamitsu	忠光	Hei'an	平安	1147		
Tadamori	忠盛	Hei'an	平安	1147		
Tadamoto	忠幹	Kamakura	鎌倉	1332		
Tadamu'ne	忠宗	Kamakura	鎌倉	1332		
Tadamu'ne	忠致	Hei'an	平安	1147		
Tada'nobu	忠信	Kamakura	鎌倉	1332	*kugyou*	High Courtier Official
Tada'nori	忠度	Hei'an	平安	1147		
Tada'oki	忠興	Sengoku	戦国	1568		
Tadasada	忠定	Nanboku	南北	1392	*kugyou*	High Courtier Official
Tadashige	忠成	Kamakura	鎌倉	1332	関東評定衆	
Tadashige	直茂	Sengoku	戦国	1568		
Tadasue	忠季	Kamakura	鎌倉	1332		
Tadatoki	忠節	Hei'an	平安	1147	*gakujin*	Musician
Tadatoki	忠時	Kamakura	鎌倉	1332		
Tadatoo	匡遠	Nanboku	南北	1392	*kannin*	Government Official
Tadatoshi	直俊	Nanboku	南北	1392		
Tadatsugi	直次	Sengoku	戦国	1568		
Tadatsugu	忠嗣	Muromachi	室町	1572	*kugyou*	High Courtier Official
Tadatsu'na	伊綱	Nanboku	南北	1392		
Tadatsu'na	忠綱	Hei'an	平安	1147		
Tadatsu'ne	忠経	Kamakura	鎌倉	1332	*kugyou*	High Courtier Official
Tadatsu'ne	忠常	Kamakura	鎌倉	1332		
Tadatsu'ne	直常	Uncertain	不詳	1600		
Tada'uji	忠氏	Sengoku	戦国	1568		
Tadayasu	直保	Sengoku	戦国	1568		
Tadayori	惟頼	Uncertain	不詳	1600		
Tadayori	忠頼	Kamakura	鎌倉	1332		
Tadayoshi	忠吉	Sengoku	戦国	1568		
Tadayoshi	忠義	Hei'an	平安	1147		
Tadayoshi	忠能	Kamakura	鎌倉	1332		
Tadayoshi	忠良	Kamakura	鎌倉	1332	*kugyou*	High Courtier Official
Tadayoshi	直義	Nanboku	南北	1392		
Tadayuki	忠行	Muromachi	室町	1572		
Tadaza'ne	忠実	Hei'an	平安	1147	*kugyou*	High Courtier Official
Tadazumi	忠澄	Kamakura	鎌倉	1332		
Tadazumi	直澄	Sengoku	戦国	1568		

Taka'aki	高顕	Nanboku	南北	1392		
Taka'aki	高詮	Nanboku	南北	1392		
Taka'aki	高明	Uncertain	不詳	1600		
Taka'aki	隆顕	Kamakura	鎌倉	1332	kugyou	High Courtier Official
Taka'aki	隆章	Kamakura	鎌倉	1332	gaka	Graphic Artist
Taka'atsu	隆敦	Muromachi	室町	1572	kugyou	High Courtier Official
Takachika	高親	Muromachi	室町	1572		
Takachika	隆親	Hei'an	平安	1147	ugyou	High Courtier Official
Takafusa	隆房	Kamakura	鎌倉	1332	kugyou	High Courtier Official
Takahide	高秀	Nanboku	南北	1392		
Takahira	高衡	Kamakura	鎌倉	1332	kugyou	High Courtier Official
Takahira	隆衡	Kamakura	鎌倉	1332	kugyou	High Courtier Official
Takahiro	隆博	Kamakura	鎌倉	1332	kajin	Poet
Takahisa	高久	Uncertain	不詳	1600		
Taka'ie	高家	Kamakura	鎌倉	1332		
Taka'ie	隆家	Uncertain	不詳	1600		
Takakage	高景	Kamakura	鎌倉	1332		
Takakage	孝景	Nanboku	南北	1392		
Takakage	隆蔭	Nanboku	南北	1392	kugyou	High Courtier Official
Takaka'ne	隆兼	Kamakura	鎌倉	1332	eishi	Graphic Artist
Takakazu	高数	Muromachi	室町	1572		
Takakiyo	高清	Hei'an	平安	1147		
Takakiyo	隆清	Kamakura	鎌倉	1332	kugyou	High Courtier Official
Takakuni	隆国	Uncertain	不詳	1600		
Takamasa	高政	Sengoku	戦国	1568		
Takamasa	隆政	Nanboku	南北	1392		
Takamichi	隆通	Uncertain	不詳	1600		
Takamitsu	高光	Muromachi	室町	1572		
Takamochi	高望	Uncertain	不詳	1600		
Takamori	隆盛	Uncertain	不詳	1600		
Takamoto	高幹	Nanboku	南北	1392		
Takamoto	高元	Nanboku	南北	1392		
Takamoto	隆職	Hei'an	平安	1147	kannin	Government Official
Takamu'ne	高宗	Nanboku	南北	1392		
Takamu'ne	孝宗	Nanboku	南北	1392	gouzoku	
Taka'naga	高長	Uncertain	不詳	1600		
Taka'naka	隆仲	Nanboku	南北	1392	kizoku	Ancient Nobility
Taka'nao	高直	Hei'an	平安	1147		
Taka'nobu	高信	Kamakura	鎌倉	1332		
Taka'nobu	隆信	Hei'an	平安	1147		
Taka'nori	高詮	Nanboku	南北	1392		
Taka'nori	高徳	Nanboku	南北	1392		
Takasada	高貞	Nanboku	南北	1392		
Takashige	高重	Kamakura	鎌倉	1332		
Takashige	隆重	Sengoku	戦国	1568		
Takasue	孝標	Hei'an	平安	1008		
Takasue	隆季	Hei'an	平安	1147	kugyou	High Courtier Official
Takasuke	高資	Kamakura	鎌倉	1332		
Takasuke	高祐	Sengoku	戦国	1568		
Takasuke	隆右	Nanboku	南北	1392	kugyou	High Courtier Official
Takasuke	隆資	Nanboku	南北	1392	kugyou	High Courtier Official
Takasuke	隆祐	Kamakura	鎌倉	1332	kajin	Poet
Takatada	隆忠	Kamakura	鎌倉	1332	kugyou	High Courtier Official
Takatoki	高時	Kamakura	鎌倉	1332		
Takatomo	高知	Kamakura	鎌倉	1332		
Takatomo	孝朝	Nanboku	南北	1392		
Takatora	高虎	Sengoku	戦国	1568		

Takatoshi	高松	Uncertain	不詳	1600	Tall Pine Tree	
Takatoshi	隆俊	Kamakura	鎌倉	1332	任臣	
Takatsu'na	高綱	Hei'an	平安	1147		
Takatsu'ne	高経	Kamakura	鎌倉	1332	*ason*	
Takatsu'ne	隆経	Uncertain	不詳	1600		
Takatsura	高連	Nanboku	南北	1392		
Taka'uji	高氏	Kamakura	鎌倉	1332		
Taka'uji	尊氏	Kamakura	鎌倉	1305		
Takayoshi	隆義	Hei'an	平安	1147		
Takayoshi	隆能	Hei'an	平安	1147	任臣	
Takefusa	武房	Kamakura	鎌倉	1332		
Takemasa	武政	Nanboku	南北	1392		
Takemitsu	武光	Nanboku	南北	1392		
Take'o	武士	Nanboku	南北	1392		
Takeshige	武重	Nanboku	南北	1392		
Taketoki	武時	Kamakura	鎌倉	1332		
Taketomo	武朝	Nanboku	南北	1392		
Taketoshi	武敏	Nanboku	南北	1392		
Taketoshi	武朝	Nanboku	南北	1392		
Takeyoshi	武吉	Nanboku	南北	1392		
Takeza'ne	武実	Nanboku	南北	1392		
Takezou	武蔵	Sengoku	戦国	1568		
Takezumi	武澄	Nanboku	南北	1392		
Tame'aki	為明	Nanboku	南北	1392	*kugyou*	High Courtier Official
Tamefuyu	為冬	Kamakura	鎌倉	1332	*kuge*	
Tamehide	為秀	Nanboku	南北	1392	*kugyou*	High Courtier Official
Tamehiro	為広	Sengoku	戦国	1568		
Tamehisa	為久	Kamakura	鎌倉	1332	*gaka*	Graphic Artist
Tame'ie	為家	Kamakura	鎌倉	1332	*kajin*	Poet
Tameka'ne	為兼	Kamakura	鎌倉	1332	*kugyou*	High Courtier Official
Tamekazu	為数	Muromachi	室町	1572		
Tamemitsu	為光	Uncertain	不詳	1600		
Tamemori	為守	Kamakura	鎌倉	1332	*okenin*	Shogunal Vassal
Tamemoto	為基	Hei'an	平安	1147	*gaka*	Graphic Artist
Tame'naga	為長	Kamakura	鎌倉	1332	*kugyou*	High Courtier Official
Tame'nobu	為信	Kamakura	鎌倉	1332	*gaka*	Graphic Artist
Tame'nori	為憲	Uncertain	不詳	1600		
Tame'nori	為教	Kamakura	鎌倉	1332	廷臣	
Tamesada	為貞	Kamakura	鎌倉	1332		
Tamesada	為定	Kamakura	鎌倉	1332	*gokenin*	Shogunal Vassal
Tameshige	為重	Kamakura	鎌倉	1332	*kuge*	
Tamesuke	為相	Kamakura	鎌倉	1332	*kajin*	Poet
Tameta'ne	為種	Muromachi	室町	1572		
Tametoki	為時	Uncertain	不詳	1600		
Tametomo	為朝	Uncertain	不詳	1600		
Tame'uji	為氏	Kamakura	鎌倉	1332	*kajin*	Poet
Tameyo	為世	Kamakura	鎌倉	1332	*kajin*	Poet
Tameyori	為頼	Kamakura	鎌倉	1332		
Tameyoshi	為義	Uncertain	不詳	1600		
Tameyuki	為行	Kamakura	鎌倉	1332	*gaka*	Graphic Artist
Tameyuki	為之	Muromachi	室町	1572	*kajin*	Poet
Tameza'ne	為実	Kamakura	鎌倉	1332	*kugyou*	High Courtier Official
Tamotsu	保	Kamakura	鎌倉	1332		
Ta'nefusa	胤房	Muromachi	室町	1572		
Ta'ne'ie	胤家	Kamakura	鎌倉	1332		
Ta'nemasa	胤正	Kamakura	鎌倉	1332		
Ta'nemichi	胤通	Kamakura	鎌倉	1332		

Nanori	Kanji	Period	Date		Notes
Ta'nemichi	種道	Nanboku	南北	1392	
Ta'nemori	胤盛	Kamakura	鎌倉	1332	
Ta'nemu'ne	胤宗	Kamakura	鎌倉	1332	
Ta'nemura	種村	Kamakura	鎌倉	1332	
Ta'ne'naga	胤長	Kamakura	鎌倉	1332	
Ta'ne'naga	種長	Sengoku	戦国	1568	
Ta'ne'nao	胤直	Hei'an	平安	1147	
Ta'ne'nobu	胤信	Kamakura	鎌倉	1332	
Ta'neshige	種重	Kamakura	鎌倉	1332	
Ta'nesuke	種佐	Nanboku	南北	1392	
Ta'netomo	胤朝	Muromachi	室町	1572	
Ta'netsugu	種継	Uncertain	不詳	1600	
Ta'netsu'na	胤綱	Kamakura	鎌倉	1332	
Ta'neyasu	種保	Kamakura	鎌倉	1332	
Ta'neyori	胤頼	Kamakura	鎌倉	1332	
Ta'neyoshi	胤義	Kamakura	鎌倉	1332	
Ta'neyuki	胤行	Kamakura	鎌倉	1332	
Tatsu'aki	竜秋	Kamakura	鎌倉	1332	*gakujin* Musician
Tatsuhisa	立久	Muromachi	室町	1572	
Teishi	定子	Uncertain	不詳	1600	
Terasu	照	Nanboku	南北	1392	
Teru'aki	輝顕	Nanboku	南北	1392	
Terumoto	輝元	Sengoku	戦国	1568	

と ❖❖❖❖❖ To

Nanori	Kanji	Period	Date		Notes
Toki'aki	時顕	Kamakura	鎌倉	1332	
Toki'akira	時章	Kamakura	鎌倉	1332	
Tokifusa	時房	Kamakura	鎌倉	1332	
Tokiharu	時治	Kamakura	鎌倉	1332	
Tokihide	時秀	Kamakura	鎌倉	1332	
Tokihira	時平	Uncertain	不詳	1600	
Tokihiro	時広	Kamakura	鎌倉	1332	*gokenin* Shogunal Vassal
Toki'ie	時家	Hei'an	平安	1147	廷臣
Tokika'ne	時兼	Kamakura	鎌倉	1332	
Tokikiyo	時清	Kamakura	鎌倉	1332	
Tokikuni	言国	Muromachi	室町	1572	*kizoku* Ancient Nobility
Tokimasa	時政	Hei'an	平安	1147	
Tokimasu	時益	Kamakura	鎌倉	1332	
Tokimichi	時通	Nanboku	南北	1392	
Tokimochi	時茂	Kamakura	鎌倉	1332	
Tokimori	時盛	Kamakura	鎌倉	1332	
Tokimoto	時基	Kamakura	鎌倉	1332	
Tokimu'ne	時宗	Kamakura	鎌倉	1332	
Tokimu'ne	時致	Kamakura	鎌倉	1332	
Tokimura	時村	Kamakura	鎌倉	1332	
Toki'naga	時長	Kamakura	鎌倉	1332	
Toki'nao	時直	Kamakura	鎌倉	1332	
Toki'nari	時業	Kamakura	鎌倉	1332	
Toki'nari	時成	Kamakura	鎌倉	1332	
Toki'nobu	時信	Kamakura	鎌倉	1332	
Tokisada	時貞	Nanboku	南北	1392	
Tokisada	時定	Hei'an	平安	1147	
Tokishige	時重	Nanboku	南北	1392	

Historical Masculine Nanori 361

Tokishige	時茂	Kamakura	鎌倉	1332		
Tokisuke	時輔	Kamakura	鎌倉	1332		
Tokitada	時忠	Hei'an	平安	1147	*kugyou*	High Courtier Official
Tokitaka	時高	Kamakura	鎌倉	1332	*kugyou*	High Courtier Official
Tokitaka	時隆	Uncertain	不詳	1600		
Tokitsugu	時継	Kamakura	鎌倉	1332	*kugyou*	High Courtier Official
Tokitsu'na	時綱	Kamakura	鎌倉	1332		
Tokitsura	時連	Kamakura	鎌倉	1332		
Toki'uji	時氏	Kamakura	鎌倉	1332		
Tokiyori	時頼	Kamakura	鎌倉	1332		
Tokiyoshi	時能	Nanboku	南北	1392		
Tokiyuki	時幸	Kamakura	鎌倉	1332		
Tokiyuki	時行	Kamakura	鎌倉	1332		
Tokiza'ne	時実	Kamakura	鎌倉	1332	*kugyou*	High Courtier Official
Tomareyoshi	希義	Hei'an	平安	1147		
Tomo'aki	知章	Hei'an	平安	1147		
Tomofusa	朝房	Nanboku	南北	1392		
Tomohiro	朝広	Kamakura	鎌倉	1332		
Tomohisa	知尚	Kamakura	鎌倉	1332		
Tomohisa	朝久	Muromachi	室町	1572		
Tomohisa	有久	Kamakura	鎌倉	1332	*gaka*	Graphic Artist
Tomo'ie	知家	Kamakura	鎌倉	1332		
Tomokage	朝景	Kamakura	鎌倉	1332		
Tomokage	友景	Kamakura	鎌倉	1332		
Tomokata	朝方	Hei'an	平安	1147	*kugyou*	High Courtier Official
Tomokata	友方	Uncertain	不詳	1600		
Tomokatsu	朝葛	Kamakura	鎌倉	1332	*mairakushi*	Dance Master
Tomomasa	朝雅	Kamakura	鎌倉	1332		
Tomomasa	朝政	Kamakura	鎌倉	1332		
Tomomichi	具通	Nanboku	南北	1392	*kugyou*	High Courtier Official
Tomomitsu	朝光	Kamakura	鎌倉	1332		
Tomomori	具守	Kamakura	鎌倉	1332	*kugyou*	High Courtier Official
Tomomori	知盛	Hei'an	平安	1147		
Tomomori	朝盛	Kamakura	鎌倉	1332		
Tomomu'ne	知宗	Kamakura	鎌倉	1184		
Tomomu'ne	朝宗	Nanboku	南北	1392		
Tomomu'ne	朝棟	Nanboku	南北	1392		
Tomomura	朝村	Kamakura	鎌倉	1332		
Tomo'naga	朝長	Hei'an	平安	1147		
Tomo'naga	倫長	Kamakura	鎌倉	1332	評定衆	
Tomo'nao	朝直	Kamakura	鎌倉	1332		
Tomo'nari	朝業	Kamakura	鎌倉	1332		
Tomo'nori	具教	Uncertain	不詳	1600		
Tomo'nori	知度	Hei'an	平安	1147		
Tomo'nori	朝範	Nanboku	南北	1392		
Tomo'nori	友則	Uncertain	不詳	1600		
Tomo'oki	朝興	Uncertain	不詳	1600		
Tomosada	知貞	Nanboku	南北	1392		
Tomosada	朝定	Nanboku	南北	1392		
Tomoshige	具滋	Kamakura	鎌倉	1332		
Tomoshige	倫重	Kamakura	鎌倉	1332	評定衆	
Tomotada	朝忠	Nanboku	南北	1392		
Tomotoki	朝時	Kamakura	鎌倉	1332		
Tomotoshi	朝俊	Kamakura	鎌倉	1332		
Tomotsu'na	等綱	Muromachi	室町	1572		
Tomotsu'na	朝綱	Kamakura	鎌倉	1332		
Tomotsu'ne	朝経	Kamakura	鎌倉	1332	*kizoku*	Ancient Nobility

Tomotsu'ne	朝常	Nanboku	南北	1392		
Tomotsu'ne	倫経	Kamakura	鎌倉	1332		
Tomo'uji	知氏	Nanboku	南北	1392		
Tomoyasu	知康	Hei'an	平安	1147	kannin	Government Official
Tomoyasu	有康	Kamakura	鎌倉	1332	gaka	Graphic Artist
Tomoyuki	具行	Kamakura	鎌倉	1332	kugyou	High Courtier Official
Tomoyuki	知行	Nanboku	南北	1392	gakusha	Scholar
Toochika	遠親	Kamakura	鎌倉	1332		
Toohira	遠平	Kamakura	鎌倉	1332		
Tookage	遠景	Kamakura	鎌倉	1332		
Toomitsu	遠光	Hei'an	平安	1147		
Toomochi	遠茂	Hei'an	平安	1147		
Toomoto	遠元	Kamakura	鎌倉	1332		
Tooru	融	Uncertain	不詳	1600		
Toramasa	虎昌	Uncertain	不詳	1600		
Toramori	虎盛	Uncertain	不詳	1600		
Torata'ne	虎胤	Uncertain	不詳	1600		
Torayasu	虎泰	Uncertain	不詳	1600		
Toshihide	俊秀	Hei'an	平安	1147		
Toshihira	俊衡	Hei'an	平安	1147		
Toshihira	俊平	Hei'an	平安	1147		
Toshihito	利仁	Hei'an	平安	1147		
Toshi'ie	利家	Sengoku	戦国	1568		
Toshikage	敏景	Muromachi	室町	1572		
Toshika'ne	俊兼	Kamakura	鎌倉	1332		
Toshiki	俊奇	Kamakura	鎌倉	1244		
Toshikiyo	俊清	Uncertain	不詳	1600		
Toshimasa	俊政	Kamakura	鎌倉	1332		
Toshimichi	俊通	Hei'an	平安	1147		
Toshimitsu	俊光	Kamakura	鎌倉	1332	kugyou	High Courtier Official
Toshimoto	俊基	Kamakura	鎌倉	1332	kugyou	High Courtier Official
Toshi'naga	俊長	Kamakura	鎌倉	1332		Sword Polisher
Toshi'naga	利長	Sengoku	戦国	1568		
Toshi'nari	俊成	Hei'an	平安	1147	kajin	Poet
Toshisuke	俊輔	Muromachi	室町	1572	kugyou	High Courtier Official
Toshitsu'na	俊綱	Hei'an	平安	1147		
Toshitsu'na	利綱	Muromachi	室町	1572		
Toshitsu'ne	俊経	Hei'an	平安	1147	kugyou	High Courtier Official
Toshiyasu	俊康	Muromachi	室町	1572		
Toshiyasu	俊泰	Muromachi	室町	1572		
Toshiyasu	利康	Kamakura	鎌倉	1332	ishi	physician
Toshiyori	俊頼	Uncertain	不詳	1600		
Toshiyuki	敏行	Uncertain	不詳	1600		
Toshiza'ne	俊実	Kamakura	鎌倉	1332	kugyou	High Courtier Official
Toyofusa	豊房	Muromachi	室町	1572	kugyou	High Courtier Official
Toyomichi	豊通	Muromachi	室町	1572	kugyou	High Courtier Official
Toyomitsu	豊光	Muromachi	室町	1572	kizoku	Ancient Nobility

つ ❖❖❖❖❖ Tsu

Nanori	Kanji	Period	Date	Notes	
Tsugufusa	嗣房	Nanboku	南北	1392	*kugyou*	High Courtier Official
Tsugu'nobu	継信	Kamakura	鎌倉	1184	佐藤継信	
Tsugu'nori	嗣教	Muromachi	室町	1572		
Tsunamitsu	綱光	Muromachi	室町	1572	*kizoku*	Ancient Nobility
Tsu'ne'aki	経顕	Nanboku	南北	1392	*kugyou*	High Courtier Official
Tsu'nechika	経親	Kamakura	鎌倉	1332	*kugyou*	High Courtier Official
Tsu'nefusa	経房	Hei'an	平安	1147	*kugyou*	High Courtier Official
Tsu'neharu	常治	Kamakura	鎌倉	1332		
Tsu'nehide	常秀	Kamakura	鎌倉	1332		
Tsu'nehira	経平	Kamakura	鎌倉	1332	*kugyou*	High Courtier Official
Tsu'nehisa	経久	Sengoku	戦国	1568		
Tsu'ne'ie	経家	Kamakura	鎌倉	1332		
Tsu'nekage	経景	Uncertain	不詳	1600		
Tsu'neka'ne	経兼	Nanboku	南北	1392		
Tsu'neku'ni	経国	Kamakura	鎌倉	1332	*jinkan*	Shintoh Official
Tsu'nemasa	経政	Kamakura	鎌倉	1332		
Tsu'nemasa	経正	Hei'an	平安	1147		
Tsu'nemi	経見	Nanboku	南北	1392		
Tsu'nemichi	経通	Nanboku	南北	1392	*kugyou*	High Courtier Official
Tsu'nemitsu	経光	Kamakura	鎌倉	1332		
Tsu'nemori	経盛	Hei'an	平安	1147		
Tsu'nemori	常盛	Kamakura	鎌倉	1332		
Tsu'nemoto	常基	Hei'an	平安	1147		
Tsu'nemu'ne	経宗	Hei'an	平安	1147	*kugyou*	High Courtier Official
Tsu'ne'naga	経永	Kamakura	鎌倉	1332	*jinkan*	Shintoh Official
Tsu'ne'naga	常長	Uncertain	不詳	1600		
Tsu'ne'naka	経仲	Kamakura	鎌倉	1332	*kugyou*	High Courtier Official
Tsu'ne'nari	経成	Uncertain	不詳	1600		
Tsu'ne'nobu	経宣	Kamakura	鎌倉	1332	*kugyou*	High Courtier Official
Tsu'ne'nobu	経信	Muromachi	室町	1572		
Tsu'ne'nori	経教	Muromachi	室町	1572	*kugyou*	High Courtier Official
Tsu'neshige	経茂	Nanboku	南北	1392		
Tsu'neshige	常重	Hei'an	平安	1147		
Tsu'nesue	経季	Kamakura	鎌倉	1332	*kugyou*	High Courtier Official
Tsu'nesuke	経資	Kamakura	鎌倉	1332		
Tsu'netada	経忠	Kamakura	鎌倉	1332	*kugyou*	High Courtier Official
Tsu'netaka	経高	Hei'an	平安	1147		
Tsu'netaka	経隆	Kamakura	鎌倉	1332		
Tsu'neta'ne	常胤	Hei'an	平安	1147		
Tsu'netoki	経時	Kamakura	鎌倉	1332		
Tsu'netomo	常伴	Hei'an	平安	1147		
Tsu'netoshi	経俊	Hei'an	平安	1147		
Tsu'netsugu	経嗣	Nanboku	南北	1392	*kugyou*	High Courtier Official
Tsu'ne'uji	経氏	Kamakura	鎌倉	1332		
Tsu'neyasu	経康	Nanboku	南北	1392	*ishi*	physician
Tsu'neyasu	経泰	Nanboku	南北	1392		
Tsu'neyasu	常安	Kamakura	鎌倉	1332		
Tsu'neyori	経頼	Kamakura	鎌倉	1332		
Tsu'neyori	常縁	Muromachi	室町	1572	*kajin*	Poet
Tsu'neyoshi	常昌	Nanboku	南北	1392		
Tsu'nezumi	常澄	Hei'an	平安	1147		
Tsura'uji	貫氏	Muromachi	室町	1572		

う ❖❖❖❖❖ U

Nanori	Kanji	Period	Date	Notes	
Uchitsu'ne	内経	Kamakura	鎌倉	1332	*kugyou*	High Courtier Official
Uchiza'ne	内実	Kamakura	鎌倉	1332	*kugyou*	High Courtier Official
Uji'aki	氏詮	Nanboku	南北	1392		
Uji'aki	氏朝	Nanboku	南北	1392		
Uji'aki	氏明	Nanboku	南北	1392		
Ujifuyu	氏冬	Nanboku	南北	1392		
Ujiharu	氏春	Nanboku	南北	1392		
Ujiharu	氏治	Nanboku	南北	1392		
Ujihide	氏秀	Nanboku	南北	1392		
Ujihiro	氏弘	Muromachi	室町	1572		
Ujihisa	氏久	Nanboku	南北	1392		
Uji'ie	氏家	Muromachi	室町	1572		
Ujikiyo	氏清	Nanboku	南北	1392		
Ujiku'ni	氏国	Kamakura	鎌倉	1332	*jinkan*	Shintoh Official
Ujimitsu	氏光	Nanboku	南北	1392		
Ujimitsu	氏満	Nanboku	南北	1392		
Ujimori	氏盛	Sengoku	戦国	1568		
Ujimu'ne	氏宗	Sengoku	戦国	1568		
Uji'nao	氏直	Nanboku	南北	1392		
Uji'nari	氏成	Uncertain	不詳	1600		
Uji'nobu	氏信	Kamakura	鎌倉	1332		
Uji'nori	氏憲	Muromachi	室町	1572		
Uji'nori	氏範	Nanboku	南北	1392		
Ujisato	氏郷	Sengoku	戦国	1568		
Ujishige	氏鎮	Nanboku	南北	1392		
Ujita'ne	氏胤	Nanboku	南北	1392		
Ujitoki	氏時	Nanboku	南北	1392		
Ujitomo	氏朝	Muromachi	室町	1572		
Ujitoshi	氏俊	Nanboku	南北	1392	*jinkan*	Shintoh Official
Ujitoshi	氏利	Muromachi	室町	1572		
Ujitsu'na	氏綱	Nanboku	南北	1392		
Ujitsu'ne	氏経	Kamakura	鎌倉	1332	*jinkan*	Shintoh Official [南北]
Ujitzugu	氏継	Uncertain	不詳	1600		
Ujiyasu	氏泰	Nanboku	南北	1392		
Ujiyori	氏頼	Nanboku	南北	1392		
Ujiyoshi	氏能	Nanboku	南北	1392		
Ujiyuki	氏幸	Nanboku	南北	1392		
Ujiyuki	氏之	Muromachi	室町	1572		
Umakai	宇合	Uncertain	不詳	1600		

や  Ya

Nanori	Kanji	Period	Date	Notes	
Yasu'ari	康有	Kamakura	鎌倉	1332	評定衆	
Yasuchika	康親	Sengoku	戦国	1568		
Yasuchika	泰親	Hei'an	平安	1147		
Yasuharu	泰治	Nanboku	南北	1392		
Yasuhide	康秀	Uncertain	不詳	1600		
Yasuhide	泰秀	Kamakura	鎌倉	1332	*gokenin*	Shogunal Vassal
Yasuhira	泰衡	Hei'an	平安	1155		
Yasu'ie	泰家	Kamakura	鎌倉	1332		

Nanori	Kanji	Period		Date	Notes	
Yasu'ie	保家	Hei'an	平安	1147	*kugyou*	High Courtier Official
Yasukatsu	康勝	Sengoku	戦国	1568		
Yasukiyo	泰清	Kamakura	鎌倉	1332		
Yasumasa	康政	Sengoku	戦国	1568		
Yasumasa	保昌	Uncertain	不詳	1600		
Yasumichi	康通	Sengoku	戦国	1568		
Yasumichi	泰通	Hei'an	平安	1147	*kugyou*	High Courtier Official
Yasumochi	康持	Kamakura	鎌倉	1332	評定衆	
Yasumori	康盛	Hei'an	平安	1147		
Yasumori	泰盛	Kamakura	鎌倉	1332		
Yasumori	保盛	Kamakura	鎌倉	1332	*kugyou*	High Courtier Official
Yasumoto	康基	Uncertain	不詳	1600		
Yasumu'ne	康宗	Kamakura	鎌倉	1332		
Yasumura	泰村	Kamakura	鎌倉	1332		
Yasu'naga	康長	Uncertain	不詳	1600		
Yasu'nari	保業	Hei'an	平安	1147	廷臣	
Yasu'nobu	康信	Kamakura	鎌倉	1332		
Yasu'nori	泰範	Nanboku	南北	1392		
Yasusada	安定	Uncertain	不詳	1600		
Yasusada	泰貞	Nanboku	南北	1392		
Yasushige	泰重	Nanboku	南北	1392	*gokenin*	Shogunal Vassal
Yasushige	保茂	Kamakura	鎌倉	1332		
Yasutaka	泰高	Muromachi	室町	1572		
Yasuta'ne	泰胤	Kamakura	鎌倉	1332		
Yasutoki	泰時	Kamakura	鎌倉	1332		
Yasutomi	康富	Muromachi	室町	1572	*Myoubouka*	Chinese Legal Expert
Yasutomo	泰朝	Kamakura	鎌倉	1332	*gokenin*	Shogunal Vassal
Yasutoo	保遠	Kamakura	鎌倉	1332		
Yasutoshi	安俊	Kamakura	鎌倉	1332	*jinkan*	Shintoh Official
Yasutoshi	康俊	Kamakura	鎌倉	1332	評定衆	
Yasutsugi	安次	Sengoku	戦国	1568		
Yasutsu'na	泰綱	Kamakura	鎌倉	1332		
Yasutsu'ne	泰経	Hei'an	平安	1147	*kugyou*	High Courtier Official
Yasutsura	康連	Kamakura	鎌倉	1332	評定衆	
Yasu'uji	泰氏	Uncertain	不詳	1600		
Yasuyori	康頼	Hei'an	平安	1147		
Yasuyuki	康之	Sengoku	戦国	1568		
Yasuyuki	頼行	Nanboku	南北	1392		

よ ❖❖❖❖❖ Yo

Nanori	Kanji	Period		Date	Notes	
Yori'aki	頼章	Kamakura	鎌倉	1332		
Yori'aki	頼朝	Nanboku	南北	1392		
Yori'aki	頼明	Sengoku	戦国	1568		
Yori'ari	頼有	Nanboku	南北	1392		
Yorichika	頼親	Kamakura	鎌倉	1332		
Yorifuji	頼藤	Nanboku	南北	1392		
Yorifusa	頼房	Nanboku	南北	1392		
Yoriharu	頼春	Nanboku	南北	1392		
Yoriharu	頼治	Nanboku	南北	1392	*kannin*	Government Official
Yorihide	頼秀	Kamakura	鎌倉	1332		
Yorihira	頼平	Kamakura	鎌倉	1332		
Yorihisa	頼久	Muromachi	室町	1572		
Yorihisa	頼尚	Nanboku	南北	1392		

Yori'ie	頼家	Kamakura	鎌倉	1332		
Yorika'ne	頼兼	Hei'an	平安	1147		
Yorikata	頼方	Hei'an	平安	1147		
Yorikawa	頼賢	Uncertain	不詳	1600		
Yorikazu	頼員	Kamakura	鎌倉	1332		
Yorikiyo	頼清	Nanboku	南北	1392		
Yorimasa	頼政	Hei'an	平安	1147		
Yorimasu	頼益	Muromachi	室町	1572		
Yorimichi	頼通	Uncertain	不詳	1600		
Yorimitsu	頼光	Uncertain	不詳	1600		
Yorimori	頼盛	Hei'an	平安	1147		
Yorimoto	頼基	Kamakura	鎌倉	1332		
Yorimoto	頼元	Nanboku	南北	1392		
Yorimu'ne	頼宗	Nanboku	南北	1392		
Yori'naga	頼長	Uncertain	不詳	1600		
Yori'nao	頼直	Kamakura	鎌倉	1332		
Yori'nari	頼業	Hei'an	平安	1147	儒者	
Yori'nari	頼成	Uncertain	不詳	1600		
Yori'nobu	頼信	Kamakura	鎌倉	1332		
Yorisada	頼貞	Kamakura	鎌倉	1332		
Yorishige	頼重	Kamakura	鎌倉	1332		
Yorishige	頼茂	Kamakura	鎌倉	1332		
Yorisuke	頼助	Uncertain	不詳	1600		
Yorisuke	頼輔	Hei'an	平安	1147	*kugyou*	High Courtier Official
Yoritada	頼忠	Nanboku	南北	1392		
Yoritaka	頼隆	Kamakura	鎌倉	1332	*kugyou*	High Courtier Official
Yorita'ne	頼胤	Kamakura	鎌倉	1332		
Yoritoki	頼時	Nanboku	南北	1392		
Yoritomo	頼朝	Kamakura	鎌倉	1332		
Yoritoo	頼遠	Nanboku	南北	1392		
Yoritoshi	頼俊	Kamakura	鎌倉	1332		
Yoritsugu	頼嗣	Kamakura	鎌倉	1332	*shougun*	
Yoritsugu	頼次	Nanboku	南北	1392		
Yoritsu'na	頼綱	Kamakura	鎌倉	1332		
Yoritsu'ne	頼経	Kamakura	鎌倉	1332	*shougun*	
Yori'uji	頼氏	Kamakura	鎌倉	1332		
Yoriyasu	頼康	Nanboku	南北	1392		
Yoriyasu	頼泰	Kamakura	鎌倉	1332		
Yoriyoshi	頼義	Uncertain	不詳	1600		
Yoriyuki	頼行	Kamakura	鎌倉	1332	*gokenin*	Shogunal Vassal
Yoriyuki	頼之	Nanboku	南北	1392		
Yoriza'ne	頼実	Kamakura	鎌倉	1332	*kugyou*	High Courtier Official
Yoshi	義	Muromachi	室町	1572		
Yoshi'ai	良相	Uncertain	不詳	1600		
Yoshi'aki	義顕	Hei'an	平安	1147		
Yoshi'aki	義昭	Uncertain	不詳	1600		
Yoshi'aki	義朝	Hei'an	平安	1147		
Yoshi'akira	義詮	Nanboku	南北	1367		
Yoshi'ari	義有	Uncertain	不詳	1600		
Yoshi'atsu	義淳	Muromachi	室町	1572		
Yoshi'atsu	義篤	Nanboku	南北	1392		
Yoshichi	義智	Sengoku	戦国	1568		
Yoshichika	義親	Uncertain	不詳	1600		
Yoshifusa	義房	Nanboku	南北	1392		
Yoshifusa	良房	Uncertain	不詳	1600		
Yoshifuyu	義冬	Nanboku	南北	1392		
Yoshiharu	義治	Nanboku	南北	1392		

Historical Masculine Nanori 367

Yoshiharu	可晴	Sengoku	戦国	1568		
Yoshihide	慶秀	Kamakura	鎌倉	1332		
Yoshihide	義秀	Kamakura	鎌倉	1332		
Yoshihide	能秀	Kamakura	鎌倉	1332		
Yoshihira	義弘	Nanboku	南北	1392		
Yoshihira	義平	Hei'an	平安	1147		
Yoshihira	良平	Kamakura	鎌倉	1332	kugyou	High Courtier Official
Yoshihiro	義弘	Kamakura	鎌倉	1332	toukou	Swordmaker
Yoshihiro	嘉広	Momoyama	桃山	1428		
Yoshihisa	義久	Uncertain	不詳	1600		
Yoshihisa	義尚	Muromachi	室町	1465		
Yoshihisa	能久	Kamakura	鎌倉	1332	jinkan	Shintoh Official
Yoshihito	義人	Muromachi	室町	1572		
Yoshihito	義仁	Muromachi	室町	1572		
Yoshi'ie	義家	Uncertain	不詳	1600		
Yoshikado	義廉	Muromachi	室町	1572		
Yoshikado	良門	Uncertain	不詳	1600		
Yoshikage	義景	Kamakura	鎌倉	1332		
Yoshika'ne	義兼	Kamakura	鎌倉	1332		
Yoshika'ne	義鐘	Muromachi	室町	1572		
Yoshikata	好方	Hei'an	平安	1147	gakujin	Musician
Yoshikatsu	義勝	Muromachi	室町	1572		
Yoshikazu	義量	Muromachi	室町	1572		
Yoshikazu	能員	Kamakura	鎌倉	1332		
Yoshikiyo	義清	Hei'an	平安	1147		
Yoshikuni	義国	Hei'an	平安	1147		
Yoshimasa	吉正	Uncertain	不詳	1600		
Yoshimasa	義将	Muromachi	室町	1572		
Yoshimasa	義政	Kamakura	鎌倉	1332		
Yoshimasa	義昌	Kamakura	鎌倉	1332		
Yoshimasa	良将	Uncertain	不詳	1600		
Yoshimi	義視	Nanboku	南北	1439		
Yoshimichi	良通	Hei'an	平安	1147	kugyou	High Courtier Official
Yoshimitsu	吉光	Kamakura	鎌倉	1332	Sword Maker / Painter	
Yoshimitsu	義満	Muromachi	室町	1572		
Yoshimochi	義持	Muromachi	室町	1572		
Yoshimochi	義茂	Kamakura	鎌倉	1332		
Yoshimochi	良望	Uncertain	不詳	1600		
Yoshimori	義盛	Hei'an	平安	1147		
Yoshimori	能盛	Hei'an	平安	1147	kizoku	Ancient Nobility
Yoshimoto	義基	Uncertain	不詳	1600		
Yoshimoto	義幹	Kamakura	鎌倉	1332		
Yoshimoto	義元	Uncertain	不詳	1600		
Yoshimoto	良基	Nanboku	南北	1392	kugyou	High Courtier Official
Yoshimu'ne	義宗	Kamakura	鎌倉	1332		
Yoshimu'ne	義統	Muromachi	室町	1572		
Yoshimura	義村	Kamakura	鎌倉	1332		
Yoshi'naga	義長	Nanboku	南北	1392		
Yoshi'naga	幸長	Sengoku	戦国	1568		
Yoshi'naga	芳長	Uncertain	不詳	1600		
Yoshi'naka	義仲	Muromachi	室町	1572		
Yoshi'naka	能仲	Kamakura	鎌倉	1332		
Yoshi'nao	義直	Kamakura	鎌倉	1332		
Yoshi'nao	能直	Kamakura	鎌倉	1332		
Yoshi'nari	義就	Muromachi	室町	1572		
Yoshi'nari	義成	Kamakura	鎌倉	1332		
Yoshi'nari	善成	Nanboku	南北	1392	kugyou	High Courtier Official

Yoshi'nari	能成	Kamakura	鎌倉	1332		
Yoshi'nari	良業	Kamakura	鎌倉	1332	儒者	
Yoshi'natsu	義夏	Muromachi	室町	1572		
Yoshi'nobu	義宣	Nanboku	南北	1392		
Yoshi'nobu	義信	Kamakura	鎌倉	1332		
Yoshi'nobu	能宣	Uncertain	不詳	1600		
Yoshi'nobu	良宣	Muromachi	室町	1572		
Yoshi'nori	義教	Muromachi	室町	1572		
Yoshi'nori	義則	Nanboku	南北	1392		
Yoshi'nori	義範	Kamakura	鎌倉	1332		
Yoshi'nori	能憲	Nanboku	南北	1392		
Yoshi'nori	良教	Kamakura	鎌倉	1332	kugyou	High Courtier Official
Yoshi'oki	義興	Nanboku	南北	1392		
Yoshisada	義貞	Kamakura	鎌倉	1332		
Yoshisada	義定	Hei'an	平安	1147		
Yoshisada	良定	Uncertain	不詳	1600		
Yoshisato	義郷	Muromachi	室町	1572		
Yoshisato	能郷	Kamakura	鎌倉	1332		
Yoshishige	義重	Hei'an	平安	1147		
Yoshishige	義鎮	Uncertain	不詳	1600		
Yoshishige	義繁	Nanboku	南北	1392		
Yoshisue	義季	Nanboku	南北	1392		
Yoshisuke	義資	Kamakura	鎌倉	1332		
Yoshisuke	義助	Nanboku	南北	1392		
Yoshisuke	良相	Uncertain	不詳	1600		
Yoshisuke	良輔	Kamakura	鎌倉	1332	kugyou	High Courtier Official
Yoshitada	義忠	Hei'an	平安	1147		
Yoshitada	義直	Uncertain	不詳	1600		
Yoshitada	義理	Nanboku	南北	1392		
Yoshitada	好忠	Uncertain	不詳	1600		
Yoshitaka	吉隆	Kamakura	鎌倉	1332		
Yoshitaka	義高	Hei'an	平安	1147		
Yoshitaka	義孝	Uncertain	不詳	1600		
Yoshitaka	義隆	Kamakura	鎌倉	1332		
Yoshitaka	能隆	Kamakura	鎌倉	1332	伊勢神宮祭主	
Yoshitake	義健	Muromachi	室町	1572		
Yoshita'ne	義胤	Kamakura	鎌倉	1332		
Yoshita'ne	義植	Uncertain	不詳	1600		
Yoshita'ne	義種	Nanboku	南北	1392		
Yoshitatsu	義龍	Uncertain	不詳	1600		
Yoshiteru	義光	Kamakura	鎌倉	1332		
Yoshitoki	義時	Kamakura	鎌倉	1332		
Yoshitomo	義朝	Hei'an	平安	1147		
Yoshitoo	義深	Nanboku	南北	1392		
Yoshitoshi	義俊	Kamakura	鎌倉	1332		
Yoshitoshi	義敏	Muromachi	室町	1572		
Yoshitoyo	義豊	Muromachi	室町	1572		
Yoshitsugu	義継	Kamakura	鎌倉	1332		
Yoshitsugu	義嗣	Muromachi	室町	1572		
Yoshitsugu	良嗣	Muromachi	室町	1572	kugyou	High Courtier Official
Yoshitsuke	義助	Uncertain	不詳	1600		
Yoshitsu'na	義綱	Kamakura	鎌倉	1332		
Yoshitsu'ne	義経	Hei'an	平安	1147		
Yoshitsu'ne	義常	Hei'an	平安	1147		
Yoshitsu'ne	良経	Kamakura	鎌倉	1332	kugyou	High Courtier Official
Yoshitsura	義貫	Muromachi	室町	1572	Reach an end Fullfillment	
Yoshitsura	義連	Kamakura	鎌倉	1332		

Nanori	Kanji	Period		Date	Notes	
Yoshi'uji	義氏	Kamakura	鎌倉	1332		
Yoshi'uji	能氏	Kamakura	鎌倉	1332		
Yoshiyasu	義康	Hei'an	平安	1147		
Yoshiyasu	義廉	Uncertain	不詳	1600		
Yoshiyasu	能保	Kamakura	鎌倉	1332	*kugyou*	High Courtier Official
Yoshiyori	義頼	Uncertain	不詳	1600		
Yoshiyuki	義幸	Nanboku	南北	1392		
Yoshiyuki	義行	Hei'an	平安	1147		
Yoshiza'ne	義実	Hei'an	平安	1147		
Yoshiza'ne	良実	Kamakura	鎌倉	1332	*kugyou*	High Courtier Official
Yoshizumi	義純	Hei'an	平安	1147		
Yoshizumi	義澄	Kamakura	鎌倉	1332		

ゆ  Yu

Nanori	Kanji	Period		Date	Notes	
Yuki'aki	行章	Kamakura	鎌倉	1332		
Yuki'ari	行有	Kamakura	鎌倉	1332		
Yukifuji	行藤	Kamakura	鎌倉	1332	Nikaidou	
Yukifusa	行房	Nanboku	南北	1392	任臣	
Yukihide	行秀	Nanboku	南北	1392		
Yukihira	行平	Kamakura	鎌倉	1332		
Yukihiro	行広	Muromachi	室町	1572	*gaka*	Graphic Artist
Yukihisa	行久	Kamakura	鎌倉	1332		
Yuki'ie	行家	Kamakura	鎌倉	1332		
Yukikata	行方	Kamakura	鎌倉	1332		
Yukikiyo	行清	Kamakura	鎌倉	1332		
Yukimasa	行政	Kamakura	鎌倉	1332	*kizoku*	Ancient Nobility
Yukimichi	行通	Nanboku	南北	1392		
Yukimitsu	行光	Kamakura	鎌倉	1332		
Yukimori	行盛	Kamakura	鎌倉	1332		
Yukimu'ne	行宗	Hei'an	平安	1147		
Yukimura	幸村	Sengoku	戦国	1568		
Yukimura	行村	Kamakura	鎌倉	1332	Nikaidou	
Yuki'naga	行長	Kamakura	鎌倉	1332	*kuge*	
Yuki'nao	行直	Nanboku	南北	1392		
Yuki'nari	行成	Uncertain	不詳	1600		
Yuki'o	行雄	Kamakura	鎌倉	1332		
Yukisada	行貞	Kamakura	鎌倉	1332		
Yukisuke	行佐	Kamakura	鎌倉	1332		
Yukitada	行忠	Muromachi	室町	1572	*gaka*	Graphic Artist
Yukitaka	幸隆	Uncertain	不詳	1600		
Yukitaka	行高	Kamakura	鎌倉	1332	*kizoku*	Ancient Nobility
Yukitaka	行隆	Hei'an	平安	1147	*kuge*	
Yukitoki	行時	Nanboku	南北	1392	*kugyou*	High Courtier Official
Yukitomo	行朝	Nanboku	南北	1392		
Yukitsu'na	行綱	Hei'an	平安	1147		
Yuki'uji	幸氏	Kamakura	鎌倉	1332		
Yuki'uji	行氏	Kamakura	鎌倉	1332		
Yukiyasu	行康	Muromachi	室町	1572	*kugyou*	High Courtier Official
Yukiyasu	行泰	Kamakura	鎌倉	1332		
Yukiyori	行頼	Kamakura	鎌倉	1332		
Yukiyoshi	行義	Kamakura	鎌倉	1332		
Yukiza'ne	行実	Kamakura	鎌倉	1332		

❖ Historical Masculine Yobina ❖

あ ❖❖❖❖❖ A

Yobina	Kanji	Period	Date	Notes
Ajirou	悪四郎	Nanboku	南北 1392	自読
Akasaburou	丹三郎	Nanboku	南北 1392	自読

ちょ ❖❖❖❖❖ Cho

Yobina	Kanji	Period	Date	Notes
Cho'u'emon	猪右衛門	Sengoku	戦国 1568	

ふ ❖❖❖❖❖ Fu

Yobina	Kanji	Period	Date	Notes
Fujigorou	藤五郎	Uncertain	不詳 1600	Wysteria Fifth Son

げ ❖❖❖❖❖ Ge

Yobina	Kanji	Period	Date	Notes
Gengorou	源五郎	Uncertain	不詳 1600	
Genjirou	源次郎	Uncertain	不詳 1600	
Genjirou	源六郎	Muromachi	室町 1572	自読
Genkutarou	彦九太郎	Uncertain	不詳 1600	
Gensaburou	源三郎	Momoyama	桃山 1428	
Genta	源太	Uncertain	不詳 1600	
Genza'emon	源左衛門	Kamakura	鎌倉 1332	

ご ❖❖❖❖❖ Go

Yobina	Kanji	Period	Date	Notes
Gorou	五郎	Higashiyama	東山 1482	Fifth Son
Gorousa'emon	五郎左衛門	Uncertain	不詳 1600	

は ❖❖❖❖❖ Ha

Yobina	Kanji	Period	Date	Notes
Hachirou	八郎	Uncertain	不詳	1600	Eighth Son

ひ ❖❖❖❖❖ Hi

Yobina	Kanji	Period	Date	Notes
Hikosaburou	彦三郎	Muromachi	室町	1572	
Hirasaburou	平三郎	Kamakura	鎌倉	1332	自読 / 刀工

い ❖❖❖❖❖ I

Yobina	Kanji	Period	Date	Notes
Izumisaburou	泉三郎	Hei'an	平安	1167	自読

じ ❖❖❖❖❖ Ji

Yobina	Kanji	Period	Date	Notes
Jinkurou	甚九郎	Sengoku	戦国	1568	
Jirou	次郎	Uncertain	不詳	1600	Next Son

じょ ❖❖❖❖❖ Jo

Yobina	Kanji	Period	Date	Notes
Jogorou	助五郎	Uncertain	不詳	1600	

じゅ ❖❖❖❖❖ Ju

Yobina	Kanji	Period	Date	Notes
Juurou	十郎	Kamakura	鎌倉	1332	Tenth Son

こ ❖❖❖❖❖ Ko

Yobina	Kanji	Period	Date	Notes
Koshirou	小四郎	Kamakura	鎌倉	1332	

く ❖❖❖❖❖ Ku

Yobina	Kanji	Period	Date	Notes
Kurou	九郎	Kamakura	鎌倉	1332	Nineth Son
Kutarou	久太郎	Sengoku	戦国	1568	

ま ❖❖❖❖❖ Ma

Yobina	Kanji	Period	Date	Notes
Masatsugu	正次	Sengoku	戦国	1568
Matajirou	又次郎	Uncertain	不詳	1600
Matashirou	又四郎	Sengoku	戦国	1568
Matatarou	又太郎	Nanboku	南北	1392

も ❖❖❖❖❖ Mo

Yobina	Kanji	Period	Date	Notes
Moto'u'emon	源右衛門	Uncertain	不詳	1600

む ❖❖❖❖❖ Mu

Yobina	Kanji	Period	Date	Notes
Mu'nesa'emon	宗左衛門	Uncertain	不詳	1600

ろ ❖❖❖❖❖ Ro

Yobina	Kanji	Period	Date	Notes
Rokurou	六郎	Kamakura	鎌倉	1332
Rokurou	六郎	Kamakura	鎌倉	1332

さ ❖❖❖❖❖ Sa

Yobina	Kanji	Period	Date	Notes
Saburou	三郎	Muromachi	室町	1572	通称

し ❖❖❖❖❖ Shi

Yobina	Kanji	Period	Date	Notes
Shige'nosuke	茂助	Sengoku	戦国	1568	
Shirou	四郎	Nanboku	南北	1392	Fourth Son
Shirou Hyou'e'nojou[39]	四郎兵衛尉	Kamakura	鎌倉	1332	自読 / Note the Title

そ ❖❖❖❖❖ So

Yobina	Kanji	Period	Date	Notes
Songorou	孫五郎	Uncertain	不詳	1600	
Sonjirou	孫次郎	Uncertain	不詳	1600	
Soujirou	宗次郎	Uncertain	不詳	1600	Perfect Second Son

---

[39] Hyou'e'nojou 兵衛尉 may have still been a title at this point and not a freely assumable name element. However, it belongs to a class of imperial titles which progressively moved down the social ladder.

す ❖❖❖❖❖ Su

Yobina	Kanji	Period	Date	Notes
Sukesa'emon	助左衛門	Uncertain	不詳	1600

た ❖❖❖❖❖ Ta

Yobina	Kanji	Period	Date	Notes
Tarou	太郎	Uncertain	不詳	1600	First Son
Tarousa'emon	太郎左衛門	Uncertain	不詳	1600

わ ❖❖❖❖❖ Wa

Yobina	Kanji	Period	Date	Notes
Watasaburou	弥三郎	Kamakura	鎌倉	1332	自読

や ❖❖❖❖❖ Ya

Yobina	Kanji	Period	Date	Notes
Yatarou	弥太郎	Momoyama	桃山	1428

よ ❖❖❖❖❖ Yo

Yobina	Kanji	Period	Date	Notes
Yogotarou	与五太郎	Uncertain	不詳	1600
Yo'ichirou	与一郎	Uncertain	不詳	1600
Yo'ichitarou	与一太郎	Hei'an	平安	1147
Yokurou	与九郎	Uncertain	不詳	1600
Yoshirou	義郎	Uncertain	不詳	1600
Yotarou	与太郎	Uncertain	不詳	1600

ぜ ❖❖❖❖❖ Ze

Yobina	Kanji	Period	Date	Notes
Zengorou	善五郎	Sengoku	戦国	1568
Zenjirou	善次郎	Uncertain	不詳	1600

❖ Historical Feminine Names ❖

あ ❖❖❖❖❖ A

Name	Kanji	Period		Date	Notes	
Acha	阿茶	Muromachi	室町	1572		
Achacha	阿茶茶	Uncertain	不詳	1600		
Achame	阿茶女	Nanboku	南北	1392		
Aguri	阿久里	Nanboku	南北	1392		
Ai	愛	Uncertain	不詳	1600	Love	
Akaka	あかか	Nanboku	南北	1392		
Akame	赤賣	Nara	奈良	793	Red / Bright / Happy	
Akameko	赤目子	Yamato	大和	710	Red + Eyes	
Aki	彰	Uncertain	不詳	1600		
Akiko	見子	Nanboku	南北	1392		
Akiko	詮子	Hei'an	平安	1147		
Akime	秋女	Nara	奈良	793	shoumin	Commoner
Akirakeiko	明子	Hei'an	平安	1147		
Akirakeiko Naishinnou	慧子内親王	Hei'an	平安	1147	Imperial Princess	
Akiyamame	秋山賣	Nara	奈良	793		
Ako	阿子	Muromachi	室町	1572		
Akome	阿古女	Nara	奈良	793		
Akome	阿子女	Nanboku	南北	1392		
Akome	阿小女	Nanboku	南北	1392		
Akome	あこめ	Hei'an	平安	1147		
Akume	阿久女	Nanboku	南北	1392		
Amako	安万子	Hei'an	平安	1147		
Ama'neiko	普子	Hei'an	平安	1147		
A'ne	阿泥	Uncertain	不詳	1600		
A'ne'noko	姉子	Hei'an	平安	1147		
A'netsume	姉都賣	Nara	奈良	793		
Arame	安良女	Hei'an	平安	1147		
Areme	吾女	Nara	奈良	793		
Arime	阿里賣	Nara	奈良	793		
Ariteme	在手賣	Nara	奈良	793		
Arukame	阿流加賣	Nara	奈良	793		
Asahi	朝日	Uncertain	不詳	1600	Morning Sun	
Asu	あす	Hei'an	平安	1147	shoumin	Commoner
Atsuko	京子	Hei'an	平安	1147	kizoku	Noble
Atsuko	篤子	Hei'an	平安	1147		
Atsuko Naishinnou	濃子内親王	Hei'an	平安	1147	Imperial Princess	
Aya	絢	Uncertain	不詳	1600		
Aya	綾	Uncertain	不詳	1600		
Aya	彩	Uncertain	不詳	1600		
Ayako	郁子	Hei'an	平安	1147		
Ayame	漢賣	Nara	奈良	793		
Ayame	文女	Kamakura	鎌倉	1332	Literary Composition	

Name	Kanji	Period		Date	Notes
Ayumime	歩女	Hei'an	平安	1147	
Ayuteme	阿由提賣	Nara	奈良	793	
Azumame	東女	Nara	奈良	793	East
Azumame	東方賣	Nara	奈良	793	Eastern

ちゃ ❖❖❖❖❖ Cha

Name	Kanji	Period		Date	Notes
Chako	茶子	Muromachi	室町	1572	Tea

ち ❖❖❖❖❖ Chi

Name	Kanji	Period		Date	Notes
Chikako	親子	Nanboku	南北	1392	
Chikako	周子	Hei'an	平安	1147	
Chikako Naishinnou	親子内親王	Hei'an	平安	1147	Imperial Princess
Chime	千賣	Nara	奈良	793	
Chime	千賣	Nara	奈良	793	One Thousand
Chiyo	千代	Momoyama	桃山	1428	Thousand Generations
Chiyo'i'nu	千代犬	Momoyama	桃山	1428	1000 Generation Dog
Chiyorime	千依賣	Nara	奈良	793	
Chiyotsurume	千世鶴女	Nanboku	南北	1392	1000 Generation Crane

え ❖❖❖❖❖ E

Name	Kanji	Period		Date	Notes
Eishi	栄子	Kamakura	鎌倉	1332	Married to Kameyama Tennou
Eishi	英子	Uncertain	不詳	1600	(状態伏見天皇の妃)
Eme	愛賣	Nara	奈良	793	Love
Emishime	毛女	Nara	奈良	793	
E'nume	恵怒賣	Nara	奈良	793	

ふ ❖❖❖❖❖ Fu

Name	Kanji	Period		Date	Notes	
Fujiko	藤子	Hei'an	平安	1147	Wysteria	
Fujime	藤賣	Hei'an	平安	1147	shoumin	Commoner
Furuamame	古阿麻賣	Nara	奈良	793		
Furume	古賣	Nara	奈良	793	Old	
Fusako	房子	Hei'an	平安	1147	kizoku	Noble
Fuyume	冬女	Hei'an	平安	1147	shoumin	Commoner

は ❖❖❖❖❖ Ha

Name	Kanji	Period		Date	Notes
Hajime	初	Muromachi	室町	1572	Beginning
Hajimeme	初女	Muromachi	室町	1572	Beginning
Hakashime	刀賣	Nara	奈良	793	Sword
Hakome	波古賣	Nara	奈良	793	
Hamame	浜女	Nara	奈良	793	

Name	Kanji	Period		Date	Notes	
Ha'nako	花子	Nanboku	南北	1392	Flower / Blossom	
Ha'name	花賣	Hei'an	平安	1147	shoumin	Commoner
Ha'netsume	羽津賣	Nara	奈良	793		
Hanshi	範子	Kamakura	鎌倉	1200		
Harime	針賣	Nara	奈良	793	Needle	
Haru	はる	Haru	鎌倉	1332	shoumin	Commoner
Haruhime	春日女	Nara	奈良	793	Spring Day	
Harukiri	春霧	Muromachi	室町	1572	Spring Mist	
Haruko	春子	Kamakura	鎌倉	1332	Spring	
Haruko	治子	Nanboku	南北	1392		
Haruko Jo'ou	春子女王	Hei'an	平安	1147	Spring	
Harumatsu	春松	Kamakura	鎌倉	1332	Spring Pine	
Harutoshime	春寿女	Kamakura	鎌倉	1332		
Hatako	幡子	Hei'an	平安	1147	kizoku	Noble
Hatame	波太賣	Nara	奈良	793		

ひ ❖❖❖❖❖ Hi

Name	Kanji	Period		Date	Notes	
Hideko	英子	Hei'an	平安	1147		
Hideko	秀子	Nanboku	南北	1392		
Hikome	比古賣	Nara	奈良	793		
Hime	肥賣	Nara	奈良	793		
Hime	比賣	Nara	奈良	793		
Hime	比女	Nara	奈良	793		
Hime	日賣	Nara	奈良	793	Sun	
Himekurome	姫黒女	Nanboku	南北	1392		
Himeme	姫賣	Nara	奈良	793		
Himeshirome	姫代女	Nanboku	南北	1392		
Himetarime	比女足女	Nara	奈良	793		
Himewakame	姫若女	Nanboku	南北	1392		
Hirame	平女	Hei'an	平安	1147	shoumin	Commoner
Hirame	枚賣	Nara	奈良	793		
Hiroko	弘子	Hei'an	平安	1147	kizoku	Noble
Hiroko	普子	Hei'an	平安	1147	kizoku	Noble
Hiroko	裕子	Hei'an	平安	1147		
Hisako	尚子	Hei'an	平安	1147		
Hisako	寿子	Kamakura	鎌倉	1332		
Hisako Naishinnou	久子内親王	Hei'an	平安	1147	Imperial Princess	
Hisame	日佐賣	Nara	奈良	793		
Hisatsume	比佐豆賣	Nara	奈良	793		
Hisatsume	比佐津女	Nara	奈良	793		
Hisa'uji	尚氏	Muromachi	室町	1572		
Hishimame	日嶋女	Nara	奈良	793		
Hitoshi Naishinnou	同子内親王	Hei'an	平安	1147		
Hitsujime	羊賣	Nara	奈良	793	Goat	

ほ ❖❖❖❖❖ Ho

Name	Kanji	Period		Date	Notes
Hokurome	黒子賣	Hei'an	平安	1147	
Hoshi	輔子	Hei'an	平安	1182	
Hosomeme	細目賣	Nara	奈良	793	
Hoteme	法提賣	Nara	奈良	793	

い ❖❖❖❖❖ I

Name	Kanji	Period		Date	Notes	
Ichi	市	Momoyama	桃山	1428		
Iha	岩	Muromachi	室町	1572		
Ihamime	石身賣	Nara	奈良	793		
Ihosume	五百寸賣	Nara	奈良	793		
Ikeko	池子	Nanboku	南北	1392		
Ikuheme	伊久倍賣	Nara	奈良	793		
Ima	今	Muromachi	室町	1572		
Imako	今子	Nanboku	南北	1392		
I'nako	稲子	Hei'an	平安	1147		
I'name	稲賣	Nara	奈良	793		
I'nishime	伊尼斯賣	Nara	奈良	793		
Inu	いぬ	Hei'an	平安	1147	shoumin	Commoner
Inuko	犬子	Hei'an	平安	1147	shoumin	Commoner
Inume	犬賣	Nara	奈良	793	Dog	
Inume	犬女	Hei'an	平安	1147	shoumin	Commoner
Inuwaka	犬若	Uncertain	不詳	1600	Dog Youth	
Irimashime	入坐賣	Nara	奈良	793		
Isakome	功子賣	Nara	奈良	793		
Isame	勇賣	Nara	奈良	793		
Ise	伊勢	Uncertain	不詳	1600		
Ishi	石	Muromachi	室町	1572	Rock	
Ishime	石女	Kamakura	鎌倉	1332	shoumin	Commoner
Isogamime	十五上女	Nara	奈良	793		
Isoko	勤子	Hei'an	平安	1147		
Iteme	井手賣	Nara	奈良	793		
Ito	糸	Momoyama	桃山	1428		
Ito'ito	糸々	Uncertain	不詳	1600	Thread	
Itome	伊刀賣	Nara	奈良	793		
Itsu'i	五位	Muromachi	室町	1572		
Itsu'itsu	五々	Muromachi	室町	1572		
Iwa	岩	Uncertain	不詳	1600	Boulder	
Iwatsurume	岩鶴女	Nanboku	南北	1392	Boulder Crane	
Iwokome	魚子賣	Hei'an	平安	1147		
Iwome	魚賣	Nara	奈良	793	shoumin	Commoner

じ ❖❖❖❖❖ Ji

Name	Kanji	Period		Date	Notes
Jizoumae	地蔵前	Kamakura	鎌倉	1332	
Jizoume	地蔵女	Kamakura	鎌倉	1332	

か ❖❖❖❖❖ Ka

Name	Kanji	Period		Date	Notes
Kachiko	勝子	Hei'an	平安	1147	
Kahime	加比賣	Nara	奈良	793	
Kajime	加自賣	Nara	奈良	793	
Kakame	加々女	Hei'an	平安	1147	
Kame	亀	Kamakura	鎌倉	1332	Turtle
Kamematsu	亀松	Kamakura	鎌倉	1332	Turtle Pine

Name	Kanji	Period		Date	Notes	
Kametsuru	亀鶴	Nanboku	南北	1392	Turtle Crane	
Kameyo	亀夜	Momoyama	桃山	1428	Turtle Evening	
Kamime	紙賣	Nara	奈良	793		
Ka'neko	封子	Hei'an	平安	1147		
Ka'neko Jo'ou	兼子女王	Hei'an	平安	1155		
Ka'neme	金女	Kamakura	鎌倉	1132	shoumin	Commoner
Kannon	観音	Kamakura	鎌倉	1332		
Kaorime	香賣	Nara	奈良	793		
Karime	加利賣	Nara	奈良	793		
Kasugame	春日女	Nanboku	南北	1392	Spring Sun	
Kazuko	員子	Nanboku	南北	1392		
Kazuko	計子	Hei'an	平安	1147		
Kazuko	和子	Hei'an	平安	1147		

け ❖❖❖❖❖ Ke

Name	Kanji	Period		Date	Notes
Kesame	介佐賣	Hei'an	平安	1147	

き ❖❖❖❖❖ Ki

Name	Kanji	Period		Date	Notes	
Kiku	菊	Muromachi	室町	1572	Chrysanthemum	
Kikumatsu	菊松	Kamakura	鎌倉	1332	Chrysanthemum Pine	
Kikume	菊女	Kamakura	鎌倉	1332	shoumin	Commoner
Kimorime	己母里賣	Nara	奈良	793		
Ki'neko Naishinnou	真子内親王	Hei'an	平安	1147		
Ki'nu	絹	Uncertain	不詳	1600	Silk	
Ki'nume	衣賣	Nara	奈良	793	Robe	
Ki'nume	衣女	Nara	奈良	793	shoumin	Commoner
Ki'nume	伎怒賣	Nara	奈良	793		
Ki'numurame	衣村賣	Nara	奈良	793		
Ki'nu'nuhime	衣縫賣	Nara	奈良	793		
Kita	北	Momoyama	桃山	1428	North	
Kitsume	橘賣	Nara	奈良	793	Tangerine	
Kiyoi	潔子	Hei'an	平安	1147		
Kiyoko	清子	Nanboku	南北	1392	Purity	
Kiyoko Jo'ou	清子女王	Hei'an	平安	1147	Purity	

こ ❖❖❖❖❖ Ko

Name	Kanji	Period		Date	Notes
Kodamame	小玉賣	Nara	奈良	793	
Kohime	古比賣	Nara	奈良	793	
Ko'imome	小妹賣	Nara	奈良	793	
Ko'i'name	小稲賣	Nara	奈良	793	
Kojimame	小嶋賣	Nara	奈良	793	
Kokurome	小黒女	Nara	奈良	793	
Koma	駒	Muromachi	室町	1572	
Komame	駒賣	Nara	奈良	793	
Komame	古麻賣	Nara	奈良	793	
Ko'ne'neme	小子々女	Muromachi	室町	1572	
Kosasa	小笹	Kamakura	鎌倉	1332	

Name	Kanji	Period	Date	Notes	
Kosoko	巨曾子	Nara	奈良	793	
Kotame	古多賣	Nara	奈良	793	
Kotaroume	小太郎女	Nara	奈良	793	shoumin Commoner
Kotekome	古手子賣	Nara	奈良	793	
Kotori	小鳥	Kamakura	鎌倉	1332	Small Bird
Kotsume	古都賣	Nara	奈良	793	
Koyakatoyome	小宅豊賣	Nara	奈良	793	

く ❖❖❖❖❖ Ku

Name	Kanji	Period	Date	Notes	
Kubome	宝門賣	Hei'an	平安	1147	
Kuhime	咋賣	Nara	奈良	793	
Kuhime	咋女	Hei'an	平安	1147	shoumin Commoner
Kujirako	鯨子	Hei'an	平安	1147	Whale
Kumako Jo'ou	阿子女王	Hei'an	平安	1147	Imperial Princess
Kumoko	雲子	Hei'an	平安	1147	Cloud
Kumome	雲女	Nara	奈良	793	Cloud
Ku'niko	国子	Hei'an	平安	1147	Country/Nation
Ku'niko	都子	Hei'an	平安	1147	
Ku'nime	久爾賣	Nara	奈良	793	
Kurame	椋賣	Nara	奈良	793	
Kurateme	椋手賣	Nara	奈良	793	
Kure	呉	Uncertain	不詳	1600	
Kuri	栗	Uncertain	不詳	1600	Chestnut
Kuriya	厨子	Hei'an	平安	1147	
Kuriyame	厨賣	Nara	奈良	793	
Kuroko	玄子	Hei'an	平安	1147	kizoku Noble
Kurome	黒賣	Nara	奈良	793	
Kurome	黒女	Nara	奈良	793	
Kusome	久曾賣	Nara	奈良	793	
Kusuko	薬子	Hei'an	平安	1147	kizoku Noble
Kusuri'no'ue	薬上	kamakura	鎌倉	1332	shoumin Commoner
Kuzuko	葛子	Yamato	大和	710	

ま ❖❖❖❖❖ Ma

Name	Kanji	Period	Date	Notes
Ma	麻	Uncertain	不詳	1600	Flax / Linen
Machime	町女	Hei'an	平安	1147	Town
Maeme	麻得女	Nara	奈良	793	
Makayame	麻何夜賣	Nara	奈良	793	
Makime	牧賣	Nara	奈良	793	
Maki'nokata	牧方	Kamakura	鎌倉	1332	
Mama	まゝ	Muromachi	室町	1572	
Mamime	馬身賣	Nara	奈良	793	
Manme	万女	Hei'an	平安	1147	Ten Tousand
Mari	鞠	Uncertain	不詳	1600	
Marime	麻里賣	Nara	奈良	793	
Masahime	正妃	Hei'an	平安	1147	
Masako	雅子	Hei'an	平安	1147	
Masako	政子	Kamakura	鎌倉	1332	
Masako	正子	Nanboku	南北	1392	Correct
Masako	理子	Hei'an	平安	1147	

Name	Kanji	Period		Date	Notes	
Masaru	多子	Hei'an	平安	1147	Numerous	
Mashime	麻志女	Nara	奈良	793		
Matatsuguko	全継子	Hei'an	平安	1147		
Mateme	馬手賣	Nara	奈良	793		
Matsu	松	Kamakura	平安	1147	shoumin	Commoner
Matsume	松賣	Hei'an	平安	1147	shoumin	Commoner
Matsume	松女	Hei'an	平安	1147	shoumin	Commoner
Matsu'nomae	松前	Kamakura	鎌倉	1332	shoumin	Commoner
Mawayame	麻我夜賣	Nara	奈良	793		

め ❖❖❖❖❖ Me

Name	Kanji	Period		Date	Notes	
Mehirume	米比留賣	Nara	奈良	793		
Mekusuwau	女楠王	Kamakura	鎌倉	1332	shoumin	Commoner
Meme	女々	Uncertain	不詳	1600	Woman	
Mememe	米々女	Muromachi	室町	1572	Rice Rice	
Mememe	目々女	Hei'an	平安	1147	shoumin	Commoner
Mezurame	目都良賣	Nara	奈良	793		

み ❖❖❖❖❖ Mi

Name	Kanji	Period		Date	Notes	
Michime	道女	Nara	奈良	793	Road/Path	
Midori	ミドリ	Kamakura	鎌倉	1332	shoumin	Commoner
Mihime	御比賣	Nara	奈良	793		
Mikeshime	御衣賣	Nara	奈良	793		
Mikime	美気女	Nara	奈良	793	shoumin	Commoner
Mime	身賣	Nara	奈良	793		
Mimi	弥々	Uncertain	不詳	1600		
Mimime	御々女	Nanboku	南北	1392		
Mi'namime	南賣	Nara	奈良	793		
Mi'nazuki	六月賣	Hei'an	平安	1147		
Mi'nome	蓑賣	Hei'an	平安	1147	shoumin	Commoner
Mitomime	御富賣	Nara	奈良	793		
Mitoshime	参歳賣	Nara	奈良	793		
Mitsu	味津	Uncertain	不詳	1600		
Mitsuko	光子	Hei'an	平安	1147		
Mitsu'nyo	満女	Kamakura	鎌倉	1332	shoumin	Commoner
Miwame	神賣	Nara	奈良	793		
Miyame	宮賣	Nara	奈良	793		
Miyome	未代女	Kamakura	鎌倉	1332	shoumin	Commoner
Miyukime	御由支賣	Nara	奈良	793		
Miyukime	三雪女	Nara	奈良	793	Three Snows	

も ❖❖❖❖❖ Mo

Name	Kanji	Period		Date	Notes	
Mochime	毛知賣	Nara	奈良	793		
Mochime	用女	Hei'an	平安	1147	shoumin	Commoner
Momo	桃	Uncertain	不詳	1600	Peach	
Momoe	百恵	Uncertain	不詳	1600		
Momoko	百子	Hei'an	平安	1147	izoku	Noble

Name	Kanji	Period		Date	Notes	
Momome	百賣	Nara	奈良	793	One Hundred	
Momoteme	百手賣	Nara	奈良	793	One Hundred Hands	
Moriko	森子	Nanboku	南北	1392		
Morime	母里賣	Nara	奈良	783		
Morime	毛里賣	Nara	奈良	793		
Morome	師女	Hei'an	平安	1147		
Motoko	基子	Hei'an	平安	1147	kizoku	Noble
Motoko	元子	Nanboku	南北	1392	Origin	

む ❖❖❖❖❖ Mu

Name	Kanji	Period		Date	Notes
Mumatsume	馬都賣	Nara	奈良	793	
Mume	梅	Nanboku	南北	1392	plum
Mu'neko	宗子	Hei'an	平安	1147	
Mu'neko	棟子	Kamakura	鎌倉	1332	Married to a shougun
Murasaki	紫	Muromachi	室町	1572	
Mushime	虫賣	Nara	奈良	793	
Musu	蒸	Uncertain	不詳	1600	
Musubime	牟須比賣	Nara	奈良	793	
Mutsu	六	Uncertain	不詳	1600	Six

みよ ❖❖❖❖❖ Myo

Name	Kanji	Period		Date	Notes
Myouhoume	妙法女	Kamakura	鎌倉	1332	

な ❖❖❖❖❖ Na

Name	Kanji	Period		Date	Notes	
Nabe	鍋	Uncertain	不詳	1600	A Pot	
Naeme	苗女	Hei'an	平安	1147		
Nagako	永子	Hei'an	平安	1147	kizoku	Noble
Nagako	長子	Hei'an	平安	1147	shoumin	Commoner
Nagatoshime	長寿女	Kamakura	鎌倉	1332		
Nagokome	和子賣	Nara	奈良	793		
Nahoi	直子	Hei'an	平安	1147		
Nakachiko	仲子	Yamato	大和	710		
Nakako	修子	Hei'an	平安	1147		
Nakako	名子	Nanboku	南北	1392	Name	
Naka'noko	仲子	Hei'an	平安	1147		
Namime	奈見賣	Nara	奈良	793		
Na'na	奈々	Uncertain	不詳	1600		
Na'na	名々	Nanboku	南北	1392	Name	
Na'naheme	漆重賣	Nara	奈良	793	Lacquer + Heavy	
Na'name	漆女	Hei'an	平安	1147	shoumin	Commoner
Na'nimome	奈爾毛賣	Nara	奈良	793		
Narame	栖賣	Nara	奈良	793		
Nariko	業子	Nanboku	南北	1392		
Nariko	産子	Nara	奈良	793		
Nariko	登子	Hei'an	平安	1147		
Narime	成女	Nara	奈良	793		
Narime	生女	Muromachi	室町	1572	Fruitful / Pregnant	

Name	Kanji	Period	Date	Notes	
Narime	得賣	Hei'an	平安	1147	
Narime	得女	Hei'an	平安	1147	shoumin Commoner
Natoko	名門子	Hei'an	平安	1147	
Natsu	夏	Momoyama	桃山	1428	Summer
Natsu	夏女	Hei'an	平安	1147	Summer
Natsu	奈津	Uncertain	不詳	1600	

ね ❖❖❖❖❖ Ne

Name	Kanji	Period	Date	Notes
Nebame	泥婆賣	Nara	奈良	793
Nei	寧	Uncertain	不詳	1600
Neko	襧子	Nanboku	南北	1392
Neme	根賣	Nara	奈良	793
Nemushime	根虫賣	Nara	奈良	793
Ne'ne	襧々	Momoyama	桃山	1428
Ne'neme	子々女	Muromachi	室町	1572
Ne'neme	襧々女	Nanboku	南北	1392
Neshime	泥姿賣	Nara	奈良	793

に ❖❖❖❖❖ Ni

Name	Kanji	Period	Date	Notes
Nifuko	凡生子	Hei'an	平安	1147	
Nihiko Naishinnou	新子内親王	Hei'an	平安	1147	Note Classical Pronunciation
Nihime	爾比賣	Nara	奈良	793	
Nihofume	迩保布女	Nara	奈良	793	
Nikiko	仁善子	Hei'an	平安	1147	
Nikkouhime	日光姫	Kamakura	鎌倉	1332	
Nikoyame	爾古屋賣	Nara	奈良	793	
Nishi	西	Momoyama	桃山	1428	West

の ❖❖❖❖❖ No

Name	Kanji	Period	Date	Notes	
Nobuko	宣子	Hei'an	平安	1147	
Nobuko	選子	Hei'an	平安	1147	
Nobuko	信子	Hei'an	平安	1147	kizoku Noble
Nobuko	述子	Hei'an	平安	1147	
Nobuko	尊子	Hei'an	平安	1147	
Noriko	式子	Hei'an	平安	1147	
Noriko	式子	Hei'an	平安	1147	kizoku Noble
Noriko	德子	Hei'an	平安	1147	kizoku Noble
Noriko	範子	Hei'an	平安	1147	kizoku Noble
Noriko	典子	Hei'an	平安	1147	
Norime	法賣	Nara	奈良	793	Law

ぬ ❖❖❖❖❖ Nu

Name	Kanji	Period	Date	Notes
Nume	泥賣	Nara	奈良	793

お ❖❖❖❖❖ O

Name	Kanji	Period	Date	Notes	
Obame	乎婆賣	Nara	奈良	793	
Ohirame	小比良賣	Nara	奈良	793	
Oho'neme	大根賣	Nara	奈良	793	
Ohotsume	大津女	Nara	奈良	793	
Ohoyame	大家女	Nara	奈良	793	
Okiko	息子	Hei'an	平安	1147	
Omi'nako	婦子	Kamakura	鎌倉	1332	
Omi'nome	小蓑賣	Nara	奈良	793	
Omiyame	小宮賣	Nara	奈良	793	
Onitaroume	鬼太郎女	Kamakura	鎌倉	1332	
Oohime	大姫	Kamakura	鎌倉	1197	
Ooshiamame	大海賣	Nara	奈良	793	
Ootakume	大宅賣	Nara	奈良	793	
Ootakume	大宅女	Nara	奈良	793	
Ootsume	大津賣	Nara	奈良	793	
Ooyakeme	大屋賣	Nara	奈良	793	
Oshime	忍賣	Nara	奈良	793	
Ou'name	老女	Nara	奈良	793	
Owime	小猪賣	Nara	奈良	793	
Oyako	祖子	Nara	奈良	793	

ら ❖❖❖❖❖ Ra

Name	Kanji	Period	Date	Notes	
Raishi	為子	Kamakura	鎌倉	1332	
Raku	楽	Uncertain	不詳	1600	Happiness
Riri	理々	Momoyama	桃山	1428	Reason
Ryuu'nomae	龍前	Kamakura	鎌倉	1332	shoumin	Commoner

さ ❖❖❖❖❖ Sa

Name	Kanji	Period	Date	Notes	
Sabame	沙婆賣	Nara	奈良	793	
Sabame	鯖賣	Nara	奈良	793	
Sachiko	幸子	Nanboku	南北	1392	
Sachiko	祥子	Nanboku	南北	1392	
Sadako	貞子	Hei'an	平安	1147	
Sadako	貞子	Kamakura	鎌倉	1296	kuge	Courtier
Sakame	逆賣	Nara	奈良	793	shoumin	Commoner
Sakame	逆女	Kamakura	鎌倉	1332	shoumin	Commoner
Sakami	相模	Uncertain	不詳	1600	
Saka'nyou	尺女	Kamakura	鎌倉	1332	shoumin	Commoner
Sakiko	前子	Momoyama	桃山	1428	
Sakuma	茶阿	Uncertain	不詳	1600	
Samiko	佐美子	Hei'an	平安	1147	
Samime	佐美賣	Nara	奈良	793	
Sanko	佐子	Muromachi	室町	1455	
Sanno'ko	三子	Kamakura	鎌倉	1332	shoumin	Commoner
Sarume	申賣	Nara	奈良	793	
Sasame	佐々賣	Nara	奈良	793	

Name	Kanji	Period	Date	Notes	
Sashime	沙姿賣	Nara	奈良	793	
Satoko	郷子	Nanboku	南北	1392	
Satsukime	五月賣	Hei'an	平安	1147	Fifth Month
Sayo	小夜	Uncertain	不詳	1600	Small Evening
Sayome	佐夜賣	Nara	奈良	793	

せ ❖❖❖❖❖ Se

Name	Kanji	Period	Date	Notes	
Seishi	清子	Kamakura	鎌倉	1332	
Sen	仙	Uncertain	不詳	1600	Adept/Exemplar
Senchiyo	千千代	Momoyama	桃山	1428	

し ❖❖❖❖❖ Shi

Name	Kanji	Period	Date	Notes	
Shidzuko	閑子	Hei'an	平安	1147		
Shigeko	賀子	Hei'an	平安	1147	kizoku	Noble
Shigeko	賀子	Hei'an	平安	1147	kizoku	Noble
Shigeko	重子	Nanboku	南北	1392		
Shigeko	成子	Hei'an	平安	1147		
Shigeko Jo'ou	重子女王	Hei'an	平安	1147	Imperial Princess	
Shigeko Naishinnou	重子内親王	Hei'an	平安	1147	Imperial Princess	
Shigeme	重女	Kamakura	鎌倉	1332	shoumin	Commoner
Shikitame	志祁多女	Nara	奈良	793		
Shimame	嶋賣	Nara	奈良	793		
Shima'nushime	嶋主女	Nara	奈良	793		
Shimatarume	島乘賣	Nara	奈良	793		
Shinshi	親子	Kamakura	鎌倉	1332		
Shiome	塩賣	Nara	奈良	793		
Shirakamime	白髪賣	Nara	奈良	793		
Shirimachime	後町女	Hei'an	平安	1147		
Shiro	白	Muromachi	室町	1572	White	
Shitafume	志多布賣	Nara	奈良	793		
Shizuko	静子	Hei'an	平安	1147	kizoku	Noble

そ ❖❖❖❖❖ So

Name	Kanji	Period	Date	Notes
Soteme	蘇弓賣	Nara	奈良	793

す ❖❖❖❖❖ Su

Name	Kanji	Period	Date	Notes
Sue	寿恵	Uncertain	不詳	1600
Sueko	末子	Nanboku	南北	1392
Sugurime	勝賣	Nara	奈良	793	Conquer / Triumph
Sukeko	資子	Kamakura	鎌倉	1332
Sukoteme	須古提賣	Nara	奈良	793
Suku'name	宿奈女	Nara	奈良	793
Sukutame	宿太賣	Nara	奈良	793

Name	Kanji	Period	Date	Notes	
Suzu	鈴	Uncertain	不詳	1600	Small Rattle
Suzushiko	冷子	Hei'an	平安	1147	

た ❖❖❖❖❖ Ta

Name	Kanji	Period	Date	Notes	
Nagakoshinnou	揭子内親王	Hei'an	平安	1147	Imperial Princess
Tadako	忠子	Hei'an	平安	1147	kizoku	Noble
Tadako	田子	Hei'an	平安	1147	Rice Paddy
Tadasu	紀子	Hei'an	平安	1147	
Tahe	妙	Muromachi	室町	1572	Mysterious
Taheme	妙賣	Nara	奈良	793	
Taifu	大輔	Kamakura	鎌倉	1332	
Taime	鯛女	Nara	奈良	793	Carp
Tairakeiko Naishinnou	平子内親王	Hei'an	平安	1147	Imperial Princess
Takaharu	乙春	Hei'an	平安	1147	
Takai	高子	Hei'an	平安	1147	Tall
Takai Naishinnou	高子内親王	Hei'an	平安	1147	Imperial Princess
Takako	貴子	Hei'an	平安	1147	
Takako	恭子	Hei'an	平安	1147	
Takako	香子	Hei'an	平安	1147	kizoku	Noble
Takako	高子	Hei'an	平安	1147	
Takako	鳳子	Hei'an	平安	1147	kizoku	Noble
Takako	命子	Hei'an	平安	1147	shoumin	Commoner
Takako Naishinnou	崇子内親王	Hei'an	平安	1147	
Takame	乙女	Hei'an	平安	1147	shoumin	Commoner
Take	竹	Momoyama	桃山	1428	Bamboo
Takeme	竹女	Kamakura	鎌倉	1332	shoumin	Commoner
Takemo'no'me	武物女	Nara	奈良	793	shoumin	Commoner
Taki	たき	Hei'an	平安	1147	shoumin	Commoner
Taki	多喜	Hei'an	平安	1147	
Takime	瀧女	Kamakura	鎌倉	1332	shoumin	Commoner
Takume	宅賣	Nara	奈良	793	Residence
Tama	玉	Momoyama	桃山	1428	Treasure
Tamame	玉賣	Nara	奈良	793	Treasure
Tamamushime	玉虫賣	Nara	奈良	793	
Tamatarime	玉足女	Nara	奈良	793	
Tamateme	玉手賣	Nara	奈良	793	
Tamatsume	玉津賣	Nara	奈良	793	
Tamiko	多美子	Hei'an	平安	1147	Many Beauty
Tamochime	手持賣	Nara	奈良	793	
Ta'nushime	田主女	Nara	奈良	793	
Tarime	太利賣	Nara	奈良	793	
Tarime	足賣	Nara	奈良	793	Sufficient
Tarumime	多流美賣	Nara	奈良	793	
Tasukime	田次女	Nara	奈良	793	
Tata	多々	Nanboku	南北	1392	
Tatsuko	辰子	Muromachi	室町	1572	Dragon (Zodiac)
Tatsume	立賣	Nara	奈良	793	Arise
Tatsume	龍賣	Nara	奈良	793	Dragon
Tatsutoshime	龍寿女	Kamakura	鎌倉	1332	
Tawome	多乎賣	Nara	奈良	793	

て ❖❖❖❖❖ Te

Name	Kanji	Period	Date	Notes
Tei	丁	Uncertain	不詳	1600
Terame	寺賣	Nara	奈良	793	Temple
Teyorime	手依賣	Nara	奈良	793

と ❖❖❖❖❖ To

Name	Kanji	Period	Date	Notes	
To'ime	等伊賣	Nara	奈良	793	
Tojime	刀自賣	Nara	奈良	793	
Tokiko	時子	Hei'an	平安	1147	(平清盛の妻)
Tokime	時賣	Nara	奈良	793	Time
Tokime	時賣	Nara	奈良	793	Time
Tokiwagozen	常盤御前	Hei'an	平安	1138	
Tokome	徳賣	Nara	奈良	793	
Tokome	徳賣	Nara	奈良	793	
Tokoyome	床世賣	Nara	奈良	793	
Toku	徳	Momoyama	桃山	1428	
Toku'nyo	徳女	Kamakura	鎌倉	1332	shoumin	Commoner
Tokutoshime	徳寿女	Kamakura	鎌倉	1332	
Tome	刀賣	Nara	奈良	793	
Tome	刀賣	Nara	奈良	793	Sword
Tomiko	富子	Muromachi	室町	1572	
Tomime	刀美賣	Nara	奈良	793	
Tomime	富賣	Nara	奈良	793	
Tomoe	巴	Uncertain	不詳	1600	
Tomoko	具子	Nanboku	南北	1392	
Tomoko	興子	Hei'an	平安	1147	kizoku	Noble
Tomoko	度茂子	Hei'an	平安	1147	
Tomoko	類子	Hei'an	平安	1147	
Tomotarime	具足女	Nara	奈良	793	
Tomotsume	知都賣	Nara	奈良	793	
To'no'ko	等能子	Nara	奈良	793	
Tora	虎	Uncertain	不詳	1600	Tiger
Tora	寅	Muromachi	室町	1572	Tiger
Tora'i'nume	寅犬女	Nanboku	南北	1392	Tiger-Dog
Torako	十良子	Hei'an	平安	1147	shoumin	Commoner
Toramatsume	虎松女	Nanboku	南北	1392	Tiger Pine
Torame	刀良賣	Nara	奈良	793	
Torame	刀良賣	Nara	奈良	793	
Torame	寅女	Hei'an	平安	1147	Tiger
Torikime	鳥木賣	Nara	奈良	793	Bird + Tree
Torime	鳥賣	Nara	奈良	793	Bird
Torime	鳥女	Nara	奈良	793	Bird
Toshimame	豊島賣	Nara	奈良	793	
Toshi'nari'nomusume	俊成女	Kamakura	鎌倉	1332	Poet
Toto	戸々	Uncertain	不詳	1600	
Totome	止々女	Hei'an	平安	1147	
Totome	登々女	Muromachi	室町	1572	
Toushi	登子	Kamakura	鎌倉	1332	
Toyome	兎世女	Muromachi	室町	1572	
Toyome	豊女	Hei'an	平安	1147	

つ ❖❖❖❖❖ Tu

Name	Kanji	Period		Date	Notes	
Tsuchi	土	Momoyama	桃山	1428	Dirt/Soil	
Tsuchime	土賣	Nara	奈良	793	Dirt/Soil	
Tsugume	次女	Nara	奈良	793	Next	
Tsukime	月賣	Hei'an	平安	1147	Moon	
Tsuma	妻	Uncertain	不詳	1600	Wife	
Tsume	都女	Nara	奈良	793		
Tsu'nume	角女	Nara	奈良	793	Horn	
Tsurako	通子	Nanboku	南北	1392		
Tsuru	鶴	Kamakura	鎌倉	1332	shoumin	Commoner
Tsurukome	鶴子女	Kamakura	鎌倉	1332	Crane Child	
Tsurume	鶴女	Nanboku	南北	1332	shoumin	Commoner
Tsutomeme	都刀米賣	Nara	奈良	793		

う ❖❖❖❖❖ U

Name	Kanji	Period		Date	Notes	
Ujiko	氏子	Nanboku	南北	1392		
Uji'noko	氏子	Kamakura	鎌倉	1332	shoumin	Commoner
Uji'no'nyo	氏女	Kamakura	鎌倉	1332	shoumin	Commoner
Ukon	右近	Uncertain	不詳	1600		
Uma	馬	Muromachi	室町	1572	Horse	
Umagome	宇麻古賣	Nara	奈良	793		
Umame	馬女	Nara	奈良	793	Horse	
Umatsume	馬都賣	Nara	奈良	793		
Umatsume	馬津賣	Nara	奈良	793		
Umeme	梅女	Kamakura	鎌倉	1332	Plum (Wifely Devotion)	
Umishime	毛女	Nara	奈良	793	Hair	
Urako	占子	Hei'an	平安	1147		
Urime	宇利賣	Nara	奈良	793		
Ushi	牛	Nara	奈良	793	Ox	
Ushime	牛賣	Nara	奈良	793	Ox	
Uta	歌	Uncertain	不詳	1600	Song/Poem	
Uteme	宇提賣	Nara	奈良	793		

わ ❖❖❖❖❖ Wa

Name	Kanji	Period		Date	Notes	
Wagimome	我妹賣	Nara	奈良	793		
Wakagozen	若御前	Kamakura	鎌倉	1332	shoumin	Commoner
Wakako	和香子	Hei'an	平安	1147	Peaceful Aroma	
Wakame	若賣	Nara	奈良	793	Youth	
Wakeme	分女	Hei'an	平安	1147	shoumin	Commoner
Wakigeme	和岐毛賣	Nara	奈良	793		
Wakugo	若子	Nara	奈良	793	Youth	
Wakugome	若子賣	Nara	奈良	793	Youth	
Wakume	和賣	Nara	奈良	793	Peaceful	
Warahagozen	童子御前	Kamakura	鎌倉	1332	shoumin	Commoner
Warahako	童子	Hei'an	平安	1147	Child	

を ❖❖❖❖❖ Wo

Name	Kanji	Period	Date	Notes	
Wobame	乎婆賣	Nara	奈良	793	
Wobitome	意比等賣	Nara	奈良	793	
Wogusome	小屎賣	Nara	奈良	793	
Wohirame	小比良賣	Nara	奈良	793	
Womame	乎麻賣	Nara	奈良	793	
Womi'nako	婦子	Kamakura	鎌倉	1332	shoumin Commoner
Womi'nome	小蓑賣	Nara	奈良	793	
Wonnako	婦子	Hei'an	平安	1147	shoumin Commoner
Wosame	長賣	Nara	奈良	793	Long
Woshime	乎姿賣	Nara	奈良	793	
Woto	乙	Kamakura	鎌倉	1332	shoumin Commoner
Wotojime	乎刀自賣	Nara	奈良	793	
Wotome	小女	Hei'an	平安	1147	shoumin Commoner
Wotome	少女	Nara	奈良	793	
Wou'name	老女	Nara	奈良	793	Aged
Woyame	乎夜賣	Nara	奈良	793	

や ❖❖❖❖❖ Ya

Name	Kanji	Period	Date	Notes	
Yabushime	夜夫志賣	Nara	奈良	793	
Yakako	家児	Nara	奈良	793	
Yakame	家女	Nara	奈良	793	
Yakame	宅賣	Nara	奈良	793	
Yaka'narime	家成賣	Nara	奈良	793	
Yakushime	薬師女	Kamakura	鎌倉	1332	
Yamabukime	山吹女	Muromachi	室町	1572	Yellow Rose Tree
Yasu	懐	Uncertain	不詳	1600	
Yasuko	楽子	Hei'an	平安	1147	kizoku Noble
Yasuko	安子	Hei'an	平安	1147	
Yasuko	保子	Hei'an	平安	1147	
Yasuko	廉子	Nanboku	南北	1392	
Yasukome	安子賣	Hei'an	平安	1147	
Yasuko Naishinnou	柔子内親王	Hei'an	平安	1147	Imperial Princess
Yasume	安女	Hei'an	平安	1147	shoumin Commoner
Yasuurame	安占賣	Nara	奈良	793	
Yawako	やわこ	Hei'an	平安	1147	
Yaweme	夜恵賣	Nara	奈良	793	
Yaya	弥々	Muromachi	室町	1572	
Yaya	稍	Muromachi	室町	1572	
Yayorime	屋依賣	Nara	奈良	793	

よ ❖❖❖❖❖ Yo

Name	Kanji	Period	Date	Notes	
Yochiko	四千子	Hei'an	平安	1147	
Yo'neme	米女	Hei'an	平安	1147	shoumin Commoner
Yo'ne'nyo	米女	Kamakura	鎌倉	1332	shoumin Commoner
Yorime	依賣	Nara	奈良	793	
Yosamime	依羅賣	Nara	奈良	793	

Name	Kanji	Period		Date	Notes	
Yoshihime	淑姫	Hei'an	平安	1147		
Yoshiko	温子	Hei'an	平安	1147		
Yoshiko	淑子	Hei'an	平安	1147		
Yoshiko	鮮子	Hei'an	平安	1147		
Yoshikome	吉子賣	Hei'an	平安	1147		
Yoshiko Naishinnou	儀子内親王	Hei'an	平安	1147	Imperial Princess	
Yoshiko Naishinnou	珍子内親王	Hei'an	平安	1147	Imperial Princess	
Yoshime	吉賣	Nara	奈良	793		
Yoshime	芳賣	Nara	奈良	793		

ゆ ❖❖❖❖❖ Yu

Name	Kanji	Period		Date	Notes	
Yukiko	幸子	Hei'an	平安	1147		
Yukiko	雪子	Nanboku	南北	1392	Snow Child	
Yukime	如女	Hei'an	平安	1147	shoumin	Commoner
Yukime	由伎賣	Nara	奈良	793		
Yuuko	雄子	Hei'an	平安	1147		
Yuume	有女	Hei'an	平安	1147	shoumin	Commoner

ぜ ❖❖❖❖❖ Ze

Name	Kanji	Period		Date	Notes	
Zenni	禅尼	Kamakura	鎌倉	1332		
Zennyo	善女	Kamakura	鎌倉	1332	shoumin	Commoner
Zezeme	是々女	Nanboku	南北	1392	Chosen	

❖ Ancient & Mediæval Clans[40] ❖

あ ❖❖❖❖❖ A

Clan Name	Kanji	Reference	Kabane	Kanji	Extant	Notes
Abe[41]	阿倍	GR 89	Omi	臣		Ancient
Abe	安倍				◎	
Agata no Inukai	県犬養	GR 165	Muraji	連		Ancient
Ahe	阿閉	GR 128	Omi	臣		Ancient
Amabe	海部		Obito	首		Ancient
Ama no Inukai	海犬養	GR 183	Muraji	連		Ancient
Anahobe	穴掘部	GR 50	Miyatsuko	造		Ancient
Ariwara	在原				◎	
Ato	阿刀	GR 176	Muraji	連		Ancient
Atoki	阿直	GR 68	Fubjito	史		Ancient
Awata	粟田	GR 99	Omi	臣		Ancient
Aya	綾	GR 125	Kimi	君		Ancient
Azumi	阿曇	GR 141	Muraji	連		Ancient

ち ❖❖❖❖❖ Chi

Clan Name	Kanji	Reference	Kabane	Kanji	Extant	Notes
Chiisakobe	少小部	GR 179	Muraji	連		Ancient
Chimori	道守	GR 133	Omi	臣		Ancient

[40]Prior to the Taika Reform in 645, Japanese government consisted of a collection of more or less autonomous kinship groups called *uji* which are collectively known as the *shisei* system. Although clan chiefs called *ujigami* were often males, clan membership appears to have followed the female line. While men went on to found families, women retained their original *uji* membership up through the early Kamakura period. The Taika Reform established an imperial government which stripped the *kuge* families of their extended kinship groups. The new *ujizoku* 氏続 consisted only of direct descendants from the former *ujigami* or clan heads. Later the *uji* reacquired propriety holdings and the *uji* re-emerged as clans with hereditary holdings which did not necessarily claim common ancestry.

Entries in the **Reference** section of the table give some idea of where to locate source material for annotated entries. Dated entries are generally drawn from *Nihon Kodai Shizoku Jinmeijiten* by Sakamoto and Hirano (1990) while GR entries are references to the *Shinsen Shoujiroku* using the annotation scheme of Miller (1974) in *Ancient Japanese Nobility: The Kabane Ranking System*.

The **Kabane** is as listed by Miller (1974) in *Ancient Japanese Nobility: The Kabane Ranking System*. The Heguri, Kazuraki, Kose, and Soga were later appointed *oomi* 大臣. While the Ootomo and Mo'no'nobe were later appointed *oomuraji* 大連.

An entry is noted as **Extant** if it appears as an *uji* in *Kamon Kakei Jiten* by Yoshida (1979). This generally means that modern families are claiming descent from this lineage.

[41]This is an *uji* with an occupational name. In some cases clans may have emerged from essentially occupational rather than agrarian lineages. In other cases, a member of the *kuge* acquired an existing occupational lineage and established a new *uji* named after the occupational group.

ちょ ❖❖❖❖❖ Cho

Clan Name	Kanji	Reference	Kabane	Kanji	Extant	Notes
Chou	張				◎	

ふ ❖❖❖❖❖ Fu

Clan Name	Kanji	Reference	Kabane	Kanji	Extant	Notes
Fujiwara[42]	藤原	669 CE			◎	Classical
Fujiwarabe	藤原部	GR 24	Miyatsuko	造		Ancient
Fumi	書	GR 199	Muraji	連		Ancient
Fumi	文	GR 54	Obito	首		Ancient
Fu'ne	船	GR 61	Fubjito	史		Ancient
Furu	布留	GR 188	Muraji	連		Ancient

は ❖❖❖❖❖ Ha

Clan Name	Kanji	Reference	Kabane	Kanji	Extant	Notes
Hada	秦	GR 197	Muraji	連		Ancient
Hada	秦	GR 40	Miyatsuko	造		Ancient
Hahaki	伯耆	GR 60	Miyatsuko	造		Ancient
Haji	土師	GR 146	Muraji	連		Ancient
Hami	波彌	GR 130	Omi	臣		Ancient
Hashihito	間人	GR 186	Muraji	連		Ancient
Hata	羽田	GR 83	Kimi	君		Ancient
Hata	波多	GR 93	Omi	臣		Ancient
Hata	秦				◎	
Hatakumi	爪工	GR 175	Muraji	連		Ancient
Hatsukashi	羽束	GR 53	Miyatsuko	造		Ancient
Hattori	服部				◎	
Hayashi	林	GR 129	Omi	臣		Ancient
Hazukashibe	泥部	GR 49	Miyatsuko	造		Ancient

へ ❖❖❖❖❖ He

Clan Name	Kanji	Reference	Kabane	Kanji	Extant	Notes
Heguri	平群	GR 95	Omi	臣		Ancient

ひ ❖❖❖❖❖ Hi

Clan Name	Kanji	Reference	Kabane	Kanji	Extant	Notes
Hi	氷	GR 170	Muraji	連		Ancient
Hi'nokumo no To'neri	檜隈舍人	GR 38	Muraji	連		Ancient

---

[42] An offshoot of the Nakatomi 中臣 *uji* established by Nakatomi Kamatari 中臣鎌足 in 645 following the imperial coup which overthrew the Soga 蘇我 *uji* and the *shizoku* system of autonomous *uji*. One branch of the Fujiwara *uji* eventually took control of the government by marrying the daughters of the clan chief to the emperor and securing the office of imperial regent for each of the imperial heirs.

ほ ❖❖❖❖❖ Ho

Clan Name	Kanji	Reference	Kabane	Kanji	Extant	Notes
Hoshikawa	星川	GR 121	Omi	臣		Ancient
Hozumi	穂積	GR 105	Omi	臣	◎	Ancient

い ❖❖❖❖❖ I

Clan Name	Kanji	Reference	Kabane	Kanji	Extant	Notes
Ichi'i	櫟井	GR 110	Omi	臣		Ancient
Iga	伊賀	GR 127	Omi	臣		Ancient
Ikeda	池田	GR 136	Kimi	君		Ancient
Iki	壹伎	GR 62	Fubjito	史		Ancient
Imibe	忌部	GR 142	Muraji	連		Ancient
I'na	猪名	GR 81	Kimi	君		Ancient
Inukami	犬上	GR 118	Kimi	君		Ancient
Ioki'be	伊福部	GR 150	Muraji	連		Ancient
Ishikawa	石川	GR 100	Omi	臣		Ancient
Iso'no'kamibe	石上部	GR 47	Miyatsuko	造		Ancient
Itsukushi	猪使	GR 182	Muraji	連		Ancient
Izumo	出雲		臣	Omi		Ancient

か ❖❖❖❖❖ Ka

Clan Name	Kanji	Reference	Kabane	Kanji	Extant	Notes
Kadobe	門部	GR 33	Atae	直		Ancient
Kaf'uchi	川内	GR 7	Atae Agata	直		Ancient
Kafuchi no Aya	川内漢	GR 196	Muraji	連		Ancient
Kafuchi no Umakai	川内馬養	GR 43	Miyatsuko	造		Ancient
Kagami Tsukuri	鏡作	GR 71	Miyatsuko	造		Ancient
Kaki'nomoto	柿本	GR 111	Omi	臣		Ancient
Kamitsuke'no	上毛野	GR 119	Kimi	君		Ancient
Kamo	鴨	GR 107	Kimi	君		Ancient
Kamo	賀茂				◎	
Kamuhatori	神服	GR 162	Muraji	連		Ancient
Kamu'nakibe	巫部	GR 151	Muraji	連		Ancient
Ka'nimori	掃部	GR 147	Muraji	連		Ancient
Karube	軽部	GR 112	Omi	臣		Ancient
Kasa	笠	GR 138	Omi	臣	◎	Ancient
Kashiwade	膳	GR 91	Omi	臣		Ancient
Katari	語	GR 57	Miyatsuko	造		Ancient
Kawachi'nofumi	西文	S 36	Obito	首		Ancient
Kawahe	川邊	GR 109	Omi	臣		Ancient
Kawase	川瀬	GR 41	Miyatsuko	造		Ancient
Kazura	縵	GR 35	Miyatsuko	造		Ancient
Kazura'ki	葛城		Omi	臣		Ancient

け ❖❖❖❖❖ Ke

Clan Name	Kanji	Reference	Kabane	Kanji	Extant	Notes
Ke'nu	毛野	GR 92	Kimi	君		Ancient

き ❖❖❖❖❖ Ki

Clan Name	Kanji	Reference	Kabane	Kanji	Extant	Notes
Ki	紀	GR 92	Omi	臣	◎	Ancient
Ki no Sakahito	紀酒人	GR 94	Muraji	連		Ancient
Kifumi	黄文	GR 44	Miyatsuko	造		Ancient
Ki'nu'nui	衣縫		Miyatsuko	造		Ancient
Kishi'ta	岸田	GR 114	Omi	臣		Ancient
Kibi	吉備	695 CE	Omi	臣		Ancient
Kiyohara	清原				◎	

こ ❖❖❖❖❖ Ko

Clan Name	Kanji	Reference	Kabane	Kanji	Extant	Notes
Kobe	兒部	GR 155	Muraji	連		Ancient
Koremu'ne	惟宗				◎	
Kose	巨勢	GR 90	Omi	臣		Ancient
Kou	高				◎	

く ❖❖❖❖❖ Ku

Clan Name	Kanji	Reference	Kabane	Kanji	Extant	Notes
Kudara	百済	GR 56	Miyatsuko	造		Ancient
Kume	來目	GR 117	Omi	臣		Ancient
Kura	倉	GR 144	Muraji	連		Ancient
Kura no Ki'nu'nui	内蔵衣縫	GR 73	Miyatsuko	造		Ancient
Kurukuma	栗隈	GR 21	Obito	首		Ancient
Kurumochi	車持	GR 124	Kimi	君		Ancient
Kusakabe	草壁	GR 153	Muraji	連	◎	Ancient
Kusakabe	日下部					
Kuwahara	桑原	GR 200				Ancient

ま ❖❖❖❖❖ Ma

Clan Name	Kanji	Reference	Kabane	Kanji	Extant	Notes
Magari no Hakozukuri	勾筥作	GR 46	Miyatsuko	造		Ancient
Mamuta	茨田	GR 177	Muraji	連		Ancient

み ❖❖❖❖❖ Mi

Clan Name	Kanji	Reference	Kabane	Kanji	Extant	Notes
Michi	路	GR 75	Kimi	君		Ancient
Miku'ni	三国	GR 77	Kimi	君		Ancient
Mi'namoto[43]	源	Yoshida 14			◎	Classical
Mi'no	三野	GR 186	Agata'nushi	県主		Ancient
Mi'no no Yatsume	三野矢集	GR 186	Muraji	連		Ancient
Miyaji	宮道				◎	
Miyake	三宅	GR 154	Muraji	連	◎	Ancient
Miyake	三宅	GR 58	Kishi	吉士	◎	Ancient
Miyoshi	三善				◎	

も ❖❖❖❖❖ Mo

Clan Name	Kanji	Reference	Kabane	Kanji	Extant	Notes
Mohitori	水取	GR 22	Miyatsuko	造		Ancient
Mo'no'nobe[44]	物部	GR 29	Obito	首	◎	Ancient
Mo'no'nobe	物部	GR 94	Muraji	連		Ancient
Moriyama	守山	GR 74	Kimi	君		Ancient
Moroai	諸會	GR 187	Omi	臣		Ancient

む ❖❖❖❖❖ Mu

Clan Name	Kanji	Reference	Kabane	Kanji	Extant	Notes
Mu'nakata	胸方	GR 123	Kimi	君		Ancient

な ❖❖❖❖❖ Na

Clan Name	Kanji	Reference	Kabane	Kanji	Extant	Notes
Nakahara	中原				◎	
Nakatomi[45]	中臣	GR 97	Muraji	連		Ancient
Nakatomi no Sakahito	中臣酒人	GR 145	Muraji	連		Ancient
Na'niwa	難波	GR 193	Muraji	連		Ancient

---

[43] An *uji* established in 814 by Emperor Saga 嵯峨天皇 (810–823) for rusticated imperial princes. Princes who were not given either the title of 親王 *shinnou* or 王 *ou* frequently became members of the *kuge* class and took an *uji* name reserved for that purpose. The Seiwa-genji 清和源氏 are a particularly famous and important branch of this *uji* whose members claimed descent from Emperor Seiwa 清和天皇 (859–876). Other important branches claim descent from Emperor Murakami 村上天皇 (947–967), Emperor Daigo 醍醐天皇 (898–930), and Emperor Uda 宇田天皇 (889–897).

[44] Although the name for this *uji* takes the form of names used by groups of labourers, it is an early *uji* and was part of the *shisei* system. Some authorities attribute the origin of this *uji* to a pre-sixth century and therefore pre-historic corps of imperial palace guards. The Mo'no'nobe were deposed by the Soga in 587.

[45] The Nakatomi are an ancient clan which is generally believed to have been in charge of religious affairs prior to introduction of Chinese style government. The Soga were deposed by the Nakatomi in 645. The identity of the imperial *uji* is obscure. It may be that the imperial family was a branch of the Nakatomi *uji*. Regardless, the Nakatomi effectively absorbed the Imperial family by marrying their daughters into the imperial family.

に ❖❖❖❖❖ Ni

Clan Name	Kanji	Reference	Kabane	Kanji	Extant	Notes
Niitabe	新田部	GR 168	Muraji	連		Ancient
Nishikori	錦織	GR 34	Miyatsuko	造		Ancient

ぬ ❖❖❖❖❖ Nu

Clan Name	Kanji	Reference	Kabane	Kanji	Extant	Notes
Nukatabe	額田部	GR 163	Muraji	連		Ancient
Nuribe	漆部	GR 158	Muraji	連		Ancient

お ❖❖❖❖❖ O

Clan Name	Kanji	Reference	Kabane	Kanji	Extant	Notes
Ochi	越智				◎	
Ohari	尾張	GR 143	Muraji	連		Ancient
Oharida	小墾田	GR 104	Omi	臣		Ancient
Oharida	小治田	GR 181	Muraji	連		Ancient
Ohatsuse	小泊瀬	GR 55	Miyatsuko	造		Ancient
Oki'naga	息長	GR 84	Kimi	君		Ancient
O'no	小野	GR 108	Omi	臣	◎	Ancient
Oo	多	GR 122	Omi	臣		Ancient
Oo'e	大江	Yoshida 14			◎	
Ookasuga	大春日	GR 88	Omi	臣		Ancient
Ookoma	大狛	GR 39	Miyatsuko	造		Ancient
Ookura	大蔵				◎	
Oomiwa	大三輪	GR 87	Kimi	君		Ancient
Oomiwa	大神				◎	
Oo'no	大野	GR 134	Kimi	君		Ancient
Ooshiko'uchi	凡河内	GR 191	Atae	直		Ancient
Ooshiko'uchi	凡川内	GR 191	Muraji	連		Ancient
Ooshiama	凡海	GR 171	Muraji	連		Ancient
Oosumi	大隈	GR 198	Atae	直		Ancient
Ootomo	大伴	GR 139	Muraji	連		Ancient
Ooyake	大宅	GR 98	Omi	臣		Ancient
Ooyue	大湯人	GR 139	Muraji	連		Ancient
Osakabe	刑部	GR 152	Miyatsuko	造		Ancient
Osakabe	忍壁	GR 152	Muraji	連		Ancient
Oshi'numi	忍海	GR 52	Miyatsuko	造		Ancient

さ ❖❖❖❖❖ Sa

Clan Name	Kanji	Reference	Kabane	Kanji	Extant	Notes
Saheki	佐伯	GR 140	Muraji	連		Ancient
Sa'i	狭井	GR 174	Muraji	連		Ancient
Saigusa	三枝				◎	
Sakahito	酒人	GR 85	Kimi	君		Ancient
Sakaibe	境部	GR 148	Muraji	連		Ancient
Sakamoto	坂本	GR 135	Omi	臣		Ancient

Clan Name	Kanji	Reference	Kabane	Kanji	Extant	Notes
Saka'no'ue	坂上	758 CE			◎	Ancient
Sakata	坂田	GR 82	Kimi	君		Ancient
Sakikusabe	福草部	GR 26	Miyatsuko	造		Ancient
Sakura'i	桜井	GR 101	Omi	臣		Ancient
Sakurai no Tabe	桜井田部	GR 149	Miyatsuko	造		Ancient
Sami	佐味	GR 132	Kimi	君		Ancient
Sarara no Umakai	娑羅羅馬飼	GR 63	Miyatsuko	造		Ancient
Sazakibe	雀部	GR 96	Omi	臣		Ancient

し ❖❖❖❖❖ Shi

Clan Name	Kanji	Reference	Kabane	Kanji	Extant	Notes
Shibi	磯城	GR 70	Agata'nushi	県主		Ancient
Shige'no	滋野				◎	
Shiki	志紀		Obito	首		Ancient
Shimotsuke'no	下毛野	GR 131	Kimi	君		Ancient
Shimotsumichi	下道	GR 126	Omi	臣		Ancient
Shirakabe	白髪部	GR 51	Miyatsuko	造		Ancient
Shishihito	宍人	GR 116	Omi	臣		Ancient
Shitsuori	倭文	GR 169	Muraji	連		Ancient

そ ❖❖❖❖❖ So

Clan Name	Kanji	Reference	Kabane	Kanji	Extant	Notes
Soga[46]	蘇我		Omi	臣		Ancient

す ❖❖❖❖❖ Su

Clan Name	Kanji	Reference	Kabane	Kanji	Extant	Notes
Sugawara	菅原	845 CE			◎	Ancient
Sukita no Kurahito	次田倉人	GR 5	Mukutari	椋足		Ancient

た ❖❖❖❖❖ Ta

Clan Name	Kanji	Reference	Kabane	Kanji	Extant	Notes
Tachiba'na	橘	684 CE			◎	Ancient
Tagima	當麻	GR 78	Kimi	君		Ancient
Ta'i	田井	GR 4	Atae	直		Ancient
Taira[47]	平	Yoshida 14			◎	Classical
Tajii	丹比	GR 80	Kimi	君		Ancient
Takahashi	高橋	GR 76	Kimi	君		Ancient
Takamuku	高向	GR 115	Omi	臣		Ancient
Takara no Himatsuri	財日奉	GR 48	Miyatsuko	造		Ancient

[46]The Soga were a powerful *uji* which overthrew the Mo'no'nobe in 587 and were instrumental in introducing Chinese style government and Buddhism into Japan and promoted Buddhism as a new state religion. The Soga were overthrown by the Nakatomi in 645.

[47]An *uji* established for rusticated imperial princes. Princes who were not given either the title of 親王 *shinnou* or 王 *ou* frequently became members of the *kuge* class and took an *uji* name reserved for that purpose. This *uji* was founded by Prince Takamune 高棟王, a grandson of Emperor Kammu 桓武天皇 (781–806) who was rusticated in 825 and given the name Taira.

Ancient & Mediæval Clans

Clan Name	Kanji	Reference	Kabane	Kanji	Extant	Notes
Takashi'na	高階				◎	
Takechi	高市	GR 69	Agata'nushi	県主		Ancient
Tama'noya	玉祖	GR 167	Muraji	連		Ancient
Tamate	玉手	GR 137	Omi	臣		Ancient
Tame	田目	GR 178	Muraji	連		Ancient
Ta'naka	田中	GR 103	Omi	臣		Ancient
Tanji	丹治				◎	
Tasuki	手繦丹比	GR 156	Muraji	連		Ancient
Tatara	多々良				◎	

と ❖❖❖❖❖ To

Clan Name	Kanji	Reference	Kabane	Kanji	Extant	Notes
Totori	鳥取	GR 36	Miyatsuko	造		Ancient
Tomo	伴				◎	
Toyotomi[48]	豊臣	Yoshida 14			◎	Mediæveal

つ ❖❖❖❖❖ Tsu

Clan Name	Kanji	Reference	Kabane	Kanji	Extant	Notes
Tsuki'nomoto	槻本	GR 201	Suguri			Ancient
Tsukiyo'ne	春米	GR 185	Muraji	連		Ancient
Tsukushi	筑紫		Kimi	君		Ancient
Tsumori	津守	GR 164	Muraji	連		Ancient
Tsu'no	角	GR 120	Omi	臣		Ancient

う ❖❖❖❖❖ U

Clan Name	Kanji	Reference	Kabane	Kanji	Extant	Notes
Uji	菟道	GR 180	Muraji	連		Ancient
Umaraki	茨城	GR 79	Kimi	君		Ancient
Uneme	采女	GR 102	Omi	臣		Ancient
Uneme	采女	GR 67	Miyatsuko	造		Ancient
U'no no Umakai	菟野馬飼	GR 64	Miyatsuko	造		Ancient

わ ❖❖❖❖❖ Wa

Clan Name	Kanji	Reference	Kabane	Kanji	Extant	Notes
Waka'i'nukai	若犬養	GR 166	Muraji	連		Ancient
Wakasakurabe	若櫻部	GR 113	Omi	臣		Ancient
Wakayue	若湯人	GR 160	Muraji	連		Ancient
Wake	和気				◎	

---

[48]This was the line founded by Hideyoshi in the late sixteenth century. While today there are numerous people claiming descent from Hideyoshi, this is a post mediæval development.

や Ya

Clan Name	Kanji	Reference	Kabane	Kanji	Extant	Notes
Yamabe	山部	GR 172	Muraji	連		Ancient
Yamaji	山道	GR 86	Kimi	君		Ancient
Yama'no	山野				◎	
Yamashiro	山背	GR 106	Omi	臣		Ancient
Yamashiro	山背	GR 192	Atae	直		Ancient
Yamashiro	山背	GR 192	Muraji	連		Ancient
Yamato	大倭	GR 189	Muraji	連		Ancient
Yamato	倭	GR 189	Atae	直		Ancient
Yamato no Aya	倭漢	GR 195	Atae	直		Ancient
Yamato no Aya	倭漢	GR 195	Muraji	連		Ancient
Yamato no Umakai	倭馬飼	GR 42	Miyatsuko	造		Ancient
Yatabe	矢田部	GR 23	Miyatsuko	造		Ancient
Yatsume	矢集	GR 173	Muraji	連		Ancient

よ Yo

Clan Name	Kanji	Reference	Kabane	Kanji	Extant	Notes
Yoshimi'ne	良峰				◎	
Yoshi'no	吉野	GR 65	Obito	首		Ancient

ゆ Yu

Clan Name	Kanji	Reference	Kabane	Kanji	Extant	Notes
Yuge	弓削	GR 161	Muraji	連	◎	Ancient
Yuki no Tajihi	靫丹比	GR 157	Muraji	連		Ancient

❖ Historical Occupational Lineages[49] ❖

あ ❖❖❖❖❖ A

Occupational Lineage	Kanji	Reference	Type	Notes
Abe	安倍	Sakamoto		
Abe	阿倍	Sakamoto		
Amabe	海部	Sakamoto:877	Occupational	Sea Fishermen
Anahobe	孔王部	69:16	Minashiro	
Asobibe	遊部	Sakamoto		May be an *uji*

え ❖❖❖❖❖ E

Occupational Lineage	Kanji	Reference	Type	Notes
Ekakibe	画部		Occupational	Artists

ふ ❖❖❖❖❖ Fu

Occupational Lineage	Kanji	Reference	Type	Notes
Fuhitobe	史部	Sakamoto:36	Occupational	Scribes & Historians

は ❖❖❖❖❖ Ha

Occupational Lineage	Kanji	Reference	Type	Notes
Hajibe	土師部	76:10	Occupational	Potters
Ha'ni'shibe	土師部	76:10	Occupational	Potters
Hasebe	長谷部	62:12/127:5	Regional	
Hatori	服部			Weavers
Hatsusebe		62:12/127:5	Regional	

ほ ❖❖❖❖❖ Ho

Occupational Lineage	Kanji	Reference	Type	Notes
Homujibe		63:16/74:12	Mikoshiro	

[49] These were occupational groups of labourers. These groups can be divided into several types including: workers on imperial estates, workers on private estate or *shouen* 荘園 which belonged to an *uji*, and members of occupational groups established to support specialists in such things as pottery and brocade weaving and various service groups in the imperial court such as the court ladies.

Entries in the **Reference** section of the table give some idea of where to locate source material for annotated entries. Numerical references such as 76:10 refer to chapter and verse numbers in the *Kojiki*. Entries such as S:19 drawn from *Nihon Kodai Shizoku Jinmeijiten* by Sakamoto and Hirano are indicated by page number.

い ❖❖❖❖❖ I

Occupational Lineage	Kanji	Reference	Type	Notes
Ibe	伊部	Sakamoto:753		753 CE
Imube	忌部	30:9	Occupational	Abstainers
I'nabe	猪名部	Sakamoto:758		758 CE
Inbe	忌部	30:9	Occupational	Abstainers
Inbe	斎部	Sakamoto:653		653 CE
Inukaibe	犬養部		Occupational	Houndsmen
Ioki'be	伊福部	Sakamoto:710		710 CE
Isebe	伊勢部	104:1	Regional	
Isobe	磯部	Sakamoto:711	Occupational	Seaweed Gatherers
Itobe		69:20	Regional	
Iwarebe		119:27	Regional	

か ❖❖❖❖❖ Ka

Occupational Lineage	Kanji	Reference	Type	Notes
Kadobe	門部	Sakamoto		683 CE
Kannagibe	巫部	Sakamoto		845 CE
Ka'nuchibe	鍛冶部			Blacksmiths
Karatan'uchibe	韓鍛治部	Sakamoto:35	Occupational	Korean Smiths
Karube	軽部	62:13/121:12	Minashiro	
Kashiwadebe	膳部			Oak Leaf Gatherers
Kasugabe	春日部	69:19	Regional	
Kataribe	語部	Sakamoto		683 CE
Kawabe		121:14	Minashiro	
Kawabe		62:14	Regional	
Kawabitobe			Occupational	River Folk
Kawakamibe		69:13	Minashiro	
Kawa'nobe		62:14	Regional	
Kazurakibe	葛城部	109:11	Minashiro	

き ❖❖❖❖❖ Ki

Occupational Lineage	Kanji	Reference	Type	Notes
Ki'nu'nuibe	衣縫部		Occupational	Court Tailors
Kishibe		96:8	Korean	

く ❖❖❖❖❖ Ku

Occupational Lineage	Kanji	Reference	Type	Notes
Kuratsukuribe	鞍作部	Sakamoto:35		Saddle Makers
Kusakabe		109:14	Minashiro	

み ❖❖❖❖❖ Mi

Occupational Lineage	Kanji	Reference	Type	Notes
Mibube	壬生部	109:12	Mikoshiro	
Mi'nabe		63:33	Minashiro	
Miwabe	神部	Sakamoto		708 CE
Miwahitobe	神人部	Sakamoto		755 CE
Miyabe	宮部	Sakamoto		

Historical Occupational Lineages

も Mo

Occupational Lineage	Kanji	Reference	Type	Notes
Mo'no'nobe[50]	物部	Sakamoto	Occupational	Imperial Guards

に Ni

Occupational Lineage	Kanji	Reference	Type	Notes
Nishigoribe	錦織部	Sakamoto:35	Occupational	Brocade Weavers

ぬ Nu

Occupational Lineage	Kanji	Reference	Type	Notes
Nukatabe		15:22	Imperial	

お O

Occupational Lineage	Kanji	Reference	Type	Notes
Ohasebe	小長谷部			
Ooe	大枝			Medieval
Oribe	織部			Weavers
Ootomobe	大伴部		Private	
Osakabe	刑部	121:13	Minashiro	
Oshi'numibe		63:33	Regional	

さ Sa

Occupational Lineage	Kanji	Reference	Type	Notes
Saigusabe	三枝部	15:22	Minashiro	
Sakabe	酒部	77:15	Occupational	Winemakers
Sakaibe		55:22	Regional	
Sakikusabe		15:22	Minashiro	
Sazakibe		55:22/62:13	Minashiro	

し Shi

Occupational Lineage	Kanji	Reference	Type	Notes
Shi'nabe	品部		Occupational	General Labourer
Shiragabe		127:4/135:3	Minashiro	

そ So

Occupational Lineage	Kanji	Reference	Type	Notes
Sogabe	蘇我部		Private	Soga
So'nobe	園部	125:13	Occupational	Gardeners
So'nobito	園人部	125:13	Occupational	Gardeners

---

[50]Mo'no'nobe is constructed as an occupational byname. This is the source of much speculation including the theory that they were an imperial guard unit. However, they were more likely an independent military *uji*. Other references give page numbers in *Nihon Kodai Shizoku Jinmeijiten* by Sakamoto and Hirano (1990).

す ❖❖❖❖❖ Su

Occupational Lineage	Kanji	Reference	Type	Notes
Suetsukuribe	陶作部	Sakamoto:35	Occupational	Potters

た ❖❖❖❖❖ Ta

Occupational Lineage	Kanji	Reference	Type	Notes
Tabe	田部	78:7/99:10	Miyake	Imperial Serfs
Takakai	鷹飼		Occupational	Falconers
Takebe	建部	89:9	Minashiro	
Tamatsukuribe	玉造部		Occupational	Jewlers
Tate'nuibe	楯縫部		Occupational	Shield Stitchers

と ❖❖❖❖❖ To

Occupational Lineage	Kanji	Reference	Type	Notes
Tomobe	品部		Occupational	General Labourer
Torikaibe	鳥飼部	74:12	Occupational	Bird Feeders
Totoribe	鳥取部		Occupational	Bird Catchers

う ❖❖❖❖❖ U

Occupational Lineage	Kanji	Reference	Type	Notes
Ukaibe	鵜甘部		Occupational	Cormoranters
Ujibe	宇治部		Regional	
Umakaibe	馬飼部		Occupational	Horsemen
Unebe	采女		Imperial	Imperial Waitresses
Urabe	卜部		Occupational	Diviners

や ❖❖❖❖❖ Ya

Occupational Lineage	Kanji	Reference	Type	Notes
Yahagibe	矢矧部			Fletchers
Yamabe	山部	136:2	Occupational	Foresters
Yamamoribe	山盛部	104:1	Occupational	Wountain Wardens
Yatabe		114:17	Minashiro	

ゆ ❖❖❖❖❖ Yu

Occupational Lineage	Kanji	Reference	Type	Notes
Yuebe	湯坐部		Occupational	Bathing-Nurses
Yugebe	弓削部		Occupational	Boyers

❖ Figures From History & Literature ❖

Kamakura Shougun

Mi'namoto Yoritomo	源頼朝	1147 – 1199	Mu'netaka Shinnou[51]	宗尊親王	1242 – 1274
Mi'namoto Yori'ie	源頼家	1182 – 1204	Koreyasu Shinnou	惟康親王	1264 – 1326
Mi'namoto Sa'netomo	源実朝	1192 – 1219	Hisa'aki Shinnou	久明親王	1276 – 1328
Kujou Yoritsu'ne	九条頼経	1219 – 1244	Kujou Yoritsugu	九条頼嗣	1239 – 1256
Kujou Yoritsugu	九条頼嗣	1239 – 1256			

Muromachi Shougun

Ashikaga Taka'uji	足利尊氏	1305 – 1358	Ashikaga Yoshihisa	足利義尚	1465 – 1489
Ashikaga Yoshi'akira	足利義詮	1330 – 1367	Ashikaga Yoshita'ne	足利義種	1466 – 1523
Ashikaga Yoshimitsu	足利義満	1358 – 1408	Ashikaga Yoshizumi	足利義澄	1480 – 1511
Ashikaga Yoshimochi	足利義持	1386 – 1428	Ashikaga Yoshikiyo	足利義清	n/a – 1183
Ashikaga Yoshikazu	足利義量	1407 – 1425	Ashikaga Yoshiteru	足利義輝	1546 – 1565
Ashikaga Yoshi'nori	足利義教	1394 – 1441	Ashikaga Yoshihide	足利義栄	1538 – 1568
Ashikaga Yoshikatsu	足利義勝	1434 – 1443	Ashikaga Yoshi'aki	足利義昭	1537 – 1597
Ashikaga Yoshimasa	足利義政	1436 – 1490			

Edo Shougun

Tokugawa Ieyasu	徳川家康	1542 – 1616	Tokugawa Ieshige	徳川家重	1711 – 1761
Tokugawa Hidetada	徳川秀忠	1579 – 1632	Tokugawa Ieharu	徳川家治	1737 – 1786
Tokugawa Iemitsu	徳川家光	1604 – 1651	Tokugawa Ie'nari	徳川家斉	1773 – 1841
Tokugawa Ietsuna	徳川家綱	1641 – 1680	Tokugawa Ieyoshi	徳川家慶	1793 – 1853
Tokugawa Tsunayoshi	徳川綱吉	1646 – 1709	Tokugawa Iesada	徳川家定	1824 – 1858
Tokugawa Ie'nobu	徳川家宣	1662 – 1712	Tokugawa Iemochi	徳川家茂	1846 – 1866
Tokugawa Ietsugu	徳川家継	1709 – 1716	Tokugawa Yoshi'nobu	徳川慶喜	1837 – 1913
Tokugawa Yoshimu'ne	徳川吉宗	1684 – 1751			

Historical Taikou

Toyotomi Hideyoshi   豊臣秀吉   1536 – 1598

Historical Daijoudaijin

Taira Kiyomori   平清盛   1118 – 1181

---

[51] The three *shougun* whose names end in *shinou* were imperial princes. As previously noted, *shinou* is a distinctive titular element found in the names of high court nobility.

Historical Shikken

Houjou Tokimasa	北条時政	1305 – 1358	Houjou Sadatoki	北条貞時	1271 – 1311
Houjou Yoshitoki	北条義時	1163 – 1224	Houjou Morotoki	北条師時	1275 – 1311
Houjou Yasutoki	北条泰時	1183 – 1242	Houjou Mu'ne'nobu	北条宗宣	1259 – 1312
Houjou Tsu'netoki	北条経持	1224 – 1246	Houjou Hirotoki	北条熙時	1279 – 1315
Houjou Tokiyori	北条時頼	1227 – 1263	Houjou Mototoki	北条基時	n/a – 1333
Houjou Nagatoki	北条長時	1227 – 1264	Houjou Takatoki	北条高時	1303 – 1333
Houjou Masamura	北条政村	1205 – 1273	Houjou Sada'aki	北条貞顕	1278 – 1333
Houjou Tokimu'ne	北条時宗	1251 – 1284			

Names Of Other Important Figures

Akechi Mitsuhide	明智光秀	1526 – 1582	Miyamoto Musashi[52]	宮本武蔵	1584 – 1645
Asa'i Nagamasa	浅井長政	ca 1570	Mizoguchi Hidekatsu	溝口秀勝	ca 1581
Asakura Yoshikage	朝倉義景	ca 1566	Mouri Motonari	毛利元就	ca 1523
Asa'no Naga'nori	浅野長矩	ca 1674	Nabeshima Tadashige	鍋島直茂	1573 – 1591
Benkei	弁慶	n/a – 1189	Nakagawa Kiyohide	中川清秀	ca 1578
Chousokabe	長宗我倍	ca 1560	Nakamura Katsuuji	中村勝氏	ca 1582
Date Masamu'ne	伊達政宗	1567 – 1636	Nanbu Nobutada	南部信直	ca 1435
Dougen	道元	1200 – 1253	Nichiren	日蓮	1222 – 1282
Fujidou Takatora	藤堂高虎	ca 1680	Nitta Yoshisada	新田義貞	ca 1333
Fukushima Masa'nori	福島正則	ca 1595	Oda Nobu'naga	織田信長	1534 – 1582
Gamou Ujisato	蒲生氏郷	ca 1580	Ogasawara Nagatoki	小笠原長時	ca 1539
Hachisuka Masakatsu	蜂須賀正勝	ca 1582	Ootomo Yoshishige	大友義鎮	1530 – 1587
Honda Tadakatsu	本多忠勝	ca 1601	Oo'uchi Yoshitaka	大内義隆	ca 1532
Hori Hidemasa	堀秀政	ca 1573	Sakai Tadatsugu	酒井忠次	1527 – 1596
Horida Masamori	堀田正盛	ca 1620	Sasaki Kojirou[53]	佐々木小次郎	n/a – 1612
Hosokawa Yuusai	細川幽斎	ca 1568	Shibata Katsu'ie	柴田勝家	1522 – 1583
Houjou Naga'uji	北条長氏	1432 – 1519	Shimazu Yoshihiro	島津義弘	ca 1598
Houjou Sou'un	北条早雲	1432 – 1519	Shinran	親鸞	1173 – 1262
I'i Naosuke	井伊直弼	ca 1850	Sou Yoshitomo	宗義智	ca 1587
Ikeda Nobuteru	池田信輝	ca 1562	Tachiba'na Mu'neshige	立花宗茂	ca 1581
I'naba Ittetsu	稲葉一鉄	1515 – 1588	Takeda Haru'nobu	武田晴信	1521 – 1573
Ishida Mitsunari	石田三成	ca 1595	Takeda Shingen	武田信玄	1521 – 1573
Katou Kiyoma	加藤清正	ca 1598	Take'naka Shigeharu	竹中重治	ca 1580
Kikkawa Motoharu	吉川元春	ca 1582	Taku'an Souhou	澤庵宗彭	1573 – 1645
Kuki Yoshitaka	九鬼義隆	ca 1568	Tanba Nagahide	丹羽長秀	ca 1568
Kuroda Yoshitaka	黒田義高	ca 1577	Tomoegozen	巴御前	ca 1184
Maeda Toshi'ie	前田利家	ca 1570	Tooyama Kagemoto	遠山景元	ca 1835
Matsudaira Nobutsuna	松平信綱	ca 1604	Tori'i Mototada	鳥居元忠	ca 1582
Matsu'naga Hisahide	松永久秀	ca 1563	Tsugaru Tame'nobu	津軽為信	ca 1571
Matsura Shige'nobu	松浦鎮信	ca 1609	Uesugi Ka'ne'nobu	上杉兼信	ca 1561
Miyamoto Masa'na	宮本政名	1584 – 1645	Yama'uchi Katsutoyo	山内一豊	ca 1600

---

[52] You must understand that the name by which a historical individual is known is not always their "official" name and in particular does not necessarily represent normative Japanese naming practices. Shingen 信玄 is in fact the *houmyou* 法名 and Harunobu 晴信 the *nanori* 名乗 for the same individual. Similarly, Musashi 武蔵 is a special name and not a normative *nanori* 名乗.

[53] Kojirou appears to be an *azana* and not a *nanori*. However, no other names are given for this individual in *Kamakura Muromachi Jinmei Jiten*.

❖ Japanese Emperors & Empresses[54] ❖

Posthumous Name	Kanji	Reign	Dates	Nanori	Kanji	Line	Notes
Jinmu[55]	神武	1					Mythological
Suizei	綏靖	2					Legendary
Annei	安寧	3					Legendary
Itoku	懿徳	4					Legendary
Koushou	孝昭	5					Legendary
Kou'an	孝安	6					Legendary
Kourei	孝霊	7					Legendary
Kougen	孝元	8					Legendary
Kaika	開化	9					Legendary
Sujin[56]	崇神	10					Attributed[57]
Sui'nin	垂仁	11					Attributed
Keikou	景行	12					Attributed
Seimu	成務	13					Attributed
Chuu'ai	仲哀	14					Attributed
Jinguu[58]	神功						Attributed — Empress
Oujin[59]	応神	15					Attributed
Nintoku	仁徳	16					Attributed
Richuu	履中	17					Attributed
Hanzei	反正	18					Attributed[54]
Ingyou	允恭	19					Attributed

[54]Currently, Japanese emperors are known by their *nanori* until they are enthroned after which they are referred to only by their title. After death, emperors are customarily referred to by their Chinese style posthumous name. Currently, the era name and the posthumous name are proclaimed at the inception of the emperor's reign. The very early emperors are clearly mythological. Regnal dates are given for those emperors for whom the dates of their reign appear reliable.

[55]Jinmu is the mythological founder of the imperial family. His mother was a daughter of the sea god. The *Nihongi* records that his father was buried in a monumental tomb called a *misasagi* and that he was descended from the "heavenly child" who was sent from high heaven to rule the Central Land of the Reed Plains. The *Nihongi* states that Jimmu was the fourth son of his father. This reflects the appointive nature of the imperial line and other Japanese offices.

[56]Generally regarded to be the first historical emperor. Although extant records are more recent, writing was introduced to Japan ca 400, and recorded history begins at this time. Fifth century Chinese records mention a number of Japanese *ou* 王 or kings. Suijin is the first Japanese emperor to appear in these records. During this early period, Japanese emperors were often confirmed as kings by the Chinese emperor.

[57]Originally, Japan was not Buddhist and did not use Chinese style Buddhist posthumous names. After the imperial court adopted this practice, the chroniclers attributed Chinese style posthumous names to earlier emperors. Regardless, *Daijirin* distinguishes between earlier posthumous names and the Chinese style names of subsequent emperors.

[58]Empress Jinguu Kougou 神功皇后 is not assigned a reign as she was the consort of Emperor Chuu'ai 仲哀天皇. Both the *Nihongi* and the *Kojiki* relate that she dispatched an army to conquer Korea which defeated the disunited Korean kingdoms. Although she ruled Japan, she did not receive the imperial title *tennou* 天皇 and is not counted in the lineage of Japanese emperors.

[59]Some hold that Oujin is the first historical emperor. Regardless, scholars generally agree that Japan was involved in Korean politics during this period. While the *Nihongi* and the *Kojiki* describe Japanese conquest of Korea, at least part of the Japanese court was itself of Korean origin. Consequently, the relationship may have resembled that between England and France following the conquest.

406 Name Construction in Mediæval Japan

Posthumous Name	Kanji	Reign	Dates	Nanori	Kanji	Line	Notes
Ankou	安康	20					Attributed
Yuuryaku	雄略	21					Attributed
Sei'nei	清寧	22					Attributed
Kenzou	顕宗	23					Attributed
Ninken	仁賢	24					Attributed
Buretsu	武烈	25					Attributed
Keitai[60]	継体	26	507–531				Attributed
Ankan	安閑	27	531–535				Attributed
Senka	宣化	28	536–539				Attributed
Kinmei[61]	欽明	29	539–571				Attributed
Bidatsu	敏達	30	572–585				Attributed
Youmei[62]	用明	31	586–587				Attributed
Sushun	崇峻	32	588–592	Hassebe[63]	泊瀬部		Attributed
Suiko[64]	推古	33	592–628	Nukatabe	額田部		Attributed — Empress
Joumei[65]	舒明	34	628–642				Attributed
Kougyoku	皇極	35	642–645	Tomi no Koujo	宝皇女		Empress — Later (37)
Koutoku[66]	孝徳	36	645–655	Karu no Ouji	軽皇子		First Absolute Monarch
Saimei	斉明	37	655–661	Tomi no Koujo	宝皇女		Empress — Earlier (35)
Tenji	天智	38	668–671	Kazuraki no Ouji	葛城皇子		Attributed
Koubun[67]	弘文	39	671–672	Ootomo no Ouji	大友皇子		Attributed
				Iga no Ouji	伊賀皇子		Emperor Koubun
Temmu	天武	40	673–686	Oo'ama no Ouji	大海人皇子		Attributed
Jitou	持統	41	687–697	U'no no Sarara			Empress
Monmu[68]	文武	42	697–707	Karu	珂瑠		
Genmei	元明	43	707–715	Abe	安閑		
Genshou	元正	44	715–724	Hidaka	氷高		
Shoumu	聖武	45	724–749	Obito	首		

[60]In 507, Ootomo Ka'namura 大伴金村 controls the succession, and gains effective control of the government.

[61]The Mo'no'nobe 物部 *uji* deposed the Ootomo 大伴 *uji* in 540.

[62]Youmei declared his support for Buddhism, but was opposed by the Mo'no'nobe and the Nakatomi *uji*. Soga no Umako 蘇我馬子 deposed the Mo'no'nobe 物部 *uji* in 587. Subsequently, the Soga 蘇我 *uji* controlled imperial succession and the imperial government.

[63]Shoutoku Taishi 聖徳太子(574–622), the second son of Emperor Youmei, 用明天皇 was appointed regent for Empress Suiko. Shoutoku Taishi is credited for the *Constitution of Seventeen Articles*, establishing the first system of court ranks, taking the first steps toward forming an imperial bureaucracy, sending students to China, and promoting Buddhism. He is one of the most highly respected figures of Japanese history.

[64]Early imperial personal names appear to associate emperors with specific regions, *uji*, or occupational corporations. We need to understand that the early Japanese concept of family and lineage was quite different from that of contemporary America. While lines of descent may be recorded as passing from father to son or from one brother to another, this does not mean that this was their birth relationship. This potentially allows for a great deal of fluidity in the imperial family.

[65]Recorded Japanese history begins with the *Kojiki no Kiji* 古事記の記事 which recorded matters up to 626.

[66]Koutoku was the first true emperor of Japan. Nakatomi Kamatari along with Prince Naka no Ooe no Ouji 中大兄皇子 overthrew the Soga and proclaimed the Taika Reform which nationalized the clan holdings. The prince was proclaimed emperor and Kamatari was appointed imperial regent and founded the Fujiwara *ujizoku*. The *uji* were abolished and *ujizoku* families were compensated by receiving positions in the new imperial government.

[67]Two names are listed in *Daijrin* for Emperor Koubun Tennou 弘文天皇.

[68]Monmu is the first emperor for whom *Daijrin* does not specially gloss their Chinese style name. Monmu is the first emperor whose reign follows the period covered by the *Nihongi*. Following Monmu, emperors definitely acquired Chinese style names by which they and their reigns are generally known.

Japanese Emperors & Empresses

Posthumous Name	Kanji	Reign	Dates	Nanori	Kanji	Line Notes
Kouken	孝謙	46	749–758	Abe	阿倍	Reascention
Junnin	淳仁	47	758–764	Oo'i	大炊	
Shoutoku	称徳	48	764–770	Chiyo'uso	重祚	
Kou'nin[69]	光仁	49	770–781	Shirakabe	白壁	
Kanmu	桓武	50	781–806	Yamabe	山部	Kanmu Heishi
Heizei	平城	51	806–809	Ate	安殿	
Saga	嵯峨	52	809–823	Kami'no	神野	Saga Genji
Junna	諄和	53	823–833	Ootomo	大伴	
Ninmyou	仁明	54	833–850	Masara	正良	Ninmyou Genji / Heishi
Montoku	文徳	55	850–858	Michiyasu	道康	Montoku Genji / Heishi
Seiwa	清和	56	858–876	Korehito	惟仁	Seiwa Genji
Youzei	陽成	57	876–884	Sada'akira	貞明	
Koukou	光孝	58	884-887	Tokiyasu	時康	Koukou Heishi
Uda	宇多	59	887–897	Sadami	定省	Uda Genji
Daigo	醍醐	60	897–930	Atsugimi	敦仁	Daigo Genji
Suzaku	朱雀	61	930–946	Yuta'akira	寛明	
Murakami	村上	62	946–967	Nariakira	成明	Murakami Genji
Reizei	冷泉	63	967–969	Norihira	憲平	
En'yuu	円融	64	969–984	Morihira	守平	
Kazan	花山	65	984–986	Morosada	師貞	Kazan Genji
Ichijou	一条	66	986–1011	Yasuhito	懐仁	
Sanjou	三条	67	1011–1016	Okisada	居貞	
Go-Ichijou	後一条	68	1016–1036	Atsuhira	敦成	
Go-Suzaku	後朱雀	69	1036–1045	Atsu'naga	敦良	
Go-Reizei	後冷泉	70	1045–1068	Takahito	親仁	
Go-Sanjou[70]	後三条	71	1068–1072	Takahito	尊仁	
Shirakawa	白河	72	1072–1086	Sadahito	貞仁	Joukou (1086–1129)
Horikawa	堀河	73	1086–1107	Taruhito	善仁	
Toba	鳥羽	74	1107–1123	Mu'nehito	宗仁	Joukou (1129–1156)
Sutoku	崇徳	75	1123–1141	Akihito	顕仁	
Ko'noe	近衛	76	1141–1155	Narihito	体仁	
Go-Shirakawa	後白河	77	1155–1158	Wakahito	稚仁	Joukou (1158–1192)
Nijou	二条	78	1158–1165	Morihito	守仁	
Rokujou	六条	79	1165–1168	Nobuhito	順仁	
Takakura[71]	高倉	80	1168–1180	Norihito	憲仁	Joukou (1180–1181)
Antoku[72]	安徳	81	1180–1185	Tokihito	言仁	
Go-Toba	後鳥羽	82	1183–1198	Takahira	尊成	Joukou (1198–1221)
Tsuchimikado	土御門	83	1198–1210	Tamehito	為仁	
Juntoku	順徳	84	1210–1221	Morihira	守成	
Chuukyou[73]	仲恭	85	1221–1221	Ka'ne'nari	懐仁	

[69]Following the death of Emperor Kounin in 781, the council of state refused to place a woman on the throne. George Sansom argues that this was in response to the influence exerted by the monk Doukyou 道鏡 on Empress Shoutoku (718–770). The primary issue was the potential loss of Fujiwara influence over female emperors. Not only did the Fujiwara prevent ascension of female emperors, they arranged to move the capital out of Heijoukyou 平城京(Nara).

[70]Sanjou instituted the *insei* cloistered government. Earlier emperors frequently retired and took the tonsure. These retired emperors took the title *hou'ou* 法皇 translated by George Sansom as "sacred ruler". Following abdication, Go-Sanjou moved to acquire *shou'en* for the imperial family and established a private court patterned after those of the Fujiwara and *kuge* families. The *joukou* 上皇 or senior retired emperor exercised authority similar to that which had been exercised by the Fujiwara regents. He was both head of a great household and controlled a variety of government appointments.

[71]Taira no Kiyomori 平清盛 wed his daughter Tokuko 徳子 to Takakura. Later, he placed their two year old son Antoku on the throne. The following Genpei War deposed the Heike and ended in the death of Emperor Antoku at Dan no Ura 壇の浦.

[72]Go-toba was the son of Takakura by Shichijou'in Nakako 七条院殖子.

Posthumous Name	Kanji	Reign	Dates	Nanori	Kanji	Line	Notes
Go-Horikawa	後堀河	86	1221–1232	Yutahito	茂仁		Joukou (1232–1234)
Shijou	四条	87	1232–1242	Mitsuhito	秀仁		
Go-Saga	後嵯峨	88	1242–1246	Ku'nihito	邦仁		Joukou (1246–1272)
Go-Fukakusa[74]	後深草	89	1246–1259	Hisahito	久仁	S	Joukou (1287–1301)
Kameyama[75]	亀山	90	1259–1274	Tsu'nehito	恒仁	J	Joukou (1274–1287)
Go-Uda	後宇多	91	1274–1287	Yohito	世仁	J	Joukou (1301–1308)
Fushimi	伏見	92	1287–1298	Hirohito	熙仁	S	
Go-Fushimi	後伏見	93	1298–1301	Ta'nehito	胤仁	S	
Go-Nijou	後二条	94	1301–1308	Ku'niharu	邦治	J	
Ha'nazo'no	花園	95	1308–1318	Tomihito	富仁	S	
Go-Daigo[76]	後醍醐	96	1318–1339	Takaharu	尊治	J	(Deposed in North)
Go-Murakami	後村上	97	1339–1368	Nori'naga	義良	J	Southern Court
Choukei	長慶	98	1368–1383	Hirohira	寛成	J	Southern Court
Go-Kameyama	後亀山	99	1383–1392	Teruhito	照仁	J	(Deposed in South)
Kougon	光厳	97	1331–1333	Kazuhito	量仁	S	Northern Court
Koumyou	光明	98	1336–1348	Toyohito	豊仁	S	Northern Court
Sukou	崇光	99	1348–1351	Okihito	興仁	S	Northern Court
Go-Kougon	後厳	100	1352–1371	Iyahito	弥仁	S	Northern Court
Go-En'yuu	後円融	101	1371–1382	Ohito	緒仁	S	Northern Court
Go-Komatsu	後小松	102	1382–1412	Motohito	幹仁	S	Northern Court
Shoukou	称光	103	1412–1428	Mihito	美仁	S	
Go-Ha'nazo'no	後花園	102	1428–1464	Hikohito	彦仁	S	
Go-Tsuchimikado	後土御門	103	1465–1500	Fusahito	成仁	S	
Go-Kashiwabara	後柏原	104	1500–1526	Katsuhito	勝仁	S	
Go-Nara	後奈良	105	1526–1557	Tomohito	知仁	S	
Ogimachi	正親町	106	1560–1586	Shigehito	方仁	S	
Go-Youzei	後陽成	107	1586–1611	Kazuhito	和仁	S	
Go-Mizu'no'o	後水尾	108	1611–1629	Kotohito	政仁	S	
Meishou	明正	109	1629–1643	Kyouko	興子	S	Empress
Go-Koumyou	後光明	110	1643–1654	Tsuguhito	紹仁	S	
Go-Sai	後西	111	1654–1663	Nagahito	良仁	S	
Reigen	霊元	112	1663–1687	Satohito	識仁	S	
Higashiyama	東山	113	1687–1709	Asahito	朝仁	S	
Nakamikado	中御門	114	1709–1735	Yasuhito	慶仁	S	
Sakuramachi	櫻町	115	1735–1747	Teruhito	昭仁	S	
Momozo'no	桃園	116	1747–1762	Toohito	遐仁	S	
Go-Sakuramachi	後櫻町	117	1762–1770	Toshiko	智子	S	Empress
Go-Momozo'no	後桃園	118	1770–1779	Hidehito	英仁	S	
Koukaku	光格	119	1780–1817	Tomohito	兼仁	S	
Ninkou	仁孝	120	1817–1846	Ayahito	恵仁	S	
Koumei	孝明	121	1847–1866	Osahito	統仁	S	
Meiji	明治	122	1967–1912	Mutsuhito	睦仁	S	
Taishou	大正	123	1912–1926	Yoshihito	嘉仁	S	
Shouwa	昭和	124	1925–1989	Hirohito	裕仁	S	
Heisei	平成	125	1989–	Akihito	明仁	S	Currently reigning

[73]Chuukyou was deposed after only seventy days. Pre-modern histories do not recognize his reign.

[74]Ancestor of the "senior line" of empeors descended from Go-Saga. Emperors belonging to this line are denoted by an S.

[75]Ancestor of the "junior line" of empeors descended from Go-Saga. Emperors belonging to this line are denoted by an J. Kameyama was the favorite son of Go-Saga. Go-Saga first placed his son Go-Fukakusa on the throne and then forced his abdication in favour of Kameyama so that the imperial line would continue from Kameyama. This resulted in a dynastic dispute following Go-Saga's death. It was temporarily resolved by alternating the throne between the two lines. The attempt by Kenmu to consolidate the lines resulted in the Nanboku Period.

[76]Go-Daigo abolished the *insei* cloistered government in 1321 and proclaimed the short-lived Kenmu Restoration in 1334.

❖ Historical Nengou[77] Since 990 CE ❖

	Alphabetical	
安永	An'ei	1772 – 1781
安元	Angen	1175 – 1177
安貞	Antei	1227 – 1229
文安	Bun'an	1444 – 1449
文中	Bunchuu[南]	1372 – 1375
文永	Bun'ei	1264 – 1275
文治	Bunji	1185 – 1190
文化	Bunka	1804 – 1818
文亀	Bunki	1501 – 1504
文久	Bunkyuu	1861 – 1864
文明	Bunmei	1469 – 1487
文和	Bunna[北]	1352 – 1356
文応	Bun'ou	1260 – 1261
文保	Bunpou	1317 – 1319
文禄	Bunroku	1592 – 1596
文歴	Bunryaku	1234 – 1235
文政	Bunsei	1818 – 1830
文正	Bunshou	1466 – 1467
長元	Chougen	1028 – 1037
長保	Chouhou	999 – 1004
長治	Chouji	1104 – 1106
長寛	Choukan	1163 – 1165
長享	Choukyou	1487 – 1489
長久	Choukyuu	1040 – 1044
長禄	Chouroku	1457 – 1460
長歴	Chouryaku	1037 – 1040
長承	Choushou	1132 – 1135
長徳	Choutoku	995 – 999
長和	Chouwa	1012 – 1017
大治	Daiji	1126 – 1131
永長	Eichou	1096 – 1097
永保	Eihou	1081 – 1084
永治	Eiji	1141 – 1142
永享	Eikyou	1429 – 1441
永久	Eikyuu	1113 – 1118
永万	Eiman	1165 – 1166
永仁	Ei'nin	1293 – 1299
永禄	Eiroku	1558 – 1570
永歴	Eiryaku	1160 – 1161
永承	Eishou	1046 – 1053
永正	Eishou	1504 – 1521
永徳	Eitoku[北]	1381 – 1384
永和	Eiwa[北]	1375 – 1389
延文	Enbun[北]	1356 – 1361
延元	Engen[南]	1336 – 1340
延慶	Enkyou	1308 – 1311
延享	Enkyou	1744 – 1748
延久	Enkyuu	1069 – 1074
延応	En'ou	1239 – 1240
応安	Ouan[北]	1368 – 1375
延徳	Entoku	1489 – 1492
元康	Gekou[南]	1331 – 1334
元文	Genbun	1736 – 1741
元中	Genchuu[南]	1384 – 1392
元永	Gen'ei	1118 – 1120
元治	Genji	1864 – 1865
元亀	Genki	1570 – 1573
元弘	Genkou	1321 – 1324
元久	Genkyuu	1204 – 1206
元和	Genna	1615 – 1624
元仁	Gennin	1224 – 1225
元応	Gen'ou	1319 – 1321
元禄	Genroku	1688 – 1704
元歴	Genryaku	1184 – 1185
元徳	Gentoku	1329 – 1331
平治	Heiji	1159 – 1160
平成	Heisei	1989 –
保安	Hou'an	1120 – 1124
保永	Hou'ei	1704 – 1711
保延	Houen	1135 – 1141
保元	Hougen	1156 – 1159
保治	Houji	1247 – 1249
宝歴	Houreki	1751 – 1764
宝徳	Houtoku	1449 – 1452
治安	Ji'an	1021 – 1024
治歴	Jiryaku	1065 – 1069
治承	Jishou	1177 – 1181
承安	Jou'an	1171 – 1175
貞永	Jou'ei	1232 – 1233
丞元	Jougen	1207 – 1211
承保	Jouhou	1074 – 1077
貞治	Jouji[北]	1362 – 1368
貞享	Joukyou	1684 – 1688
丞久	Joukyuu	1219 – 1222
丞応	Jou'ou	1652 – 1655
貞応	Jou'ou	1222 – 1224
承歴	Jouryaku	1077 – 1081
承徳	Joutoku	1097 – 1099
貞和	Jouwa[北]	1345 – 1350
寿永	Ju'ei	1182 – 1184
嘉永	Ka'ei	1848 – 1854
嘉元	Kagen	1303 – 1306
嘉保	Kahou	1094 – 1096
嘉慶	Kakei[北]	1387 – 1389
嘉吉	Kakitsu	1441 – 1444
寛文	Kanbun	1661 – 1673
寛永	Kan'ei	1624 – 1644
寛延	Kan'en	1748 – 1751
寛元	Kangen	1243 – 1247
寛治	Kanji	1087 – 1094
寛喜	Kanki	1229 – 1232
寛弘	Kankou	1004 – 1012
寛仁	Kannin	1017 – 1021
観応	Kan'ou[北]	1350 – 1352
寛保	Kanpou	1741 – 1744
寛政	Kansei	1789 – 1801
寛正	Kanshou	1460 – 1466
寛徳	Kantoku	1044 – 1046
嘉応	Ka'ou	1169 – 1171
嘉禄	Karoku	1225 – 1227
嘉歴	Karyaku	1326 – 1329

---

[77]Emperor Koutoku[1] Tennou 孝徳天皇 proclaimed the Taika 大化 *nengou* or era name in 645 establishing a tradition of era names which is still in use. Under this system, year numbers are reset to one at the beginning of each era. Thus the same year can be both the last year of one era and the first year of the next era. Dates before the beginning of the new era are given in terms of the old era. The first year of an era is customarily called *gan-nen* 元年 and the second year is called *ni-nen* 二年. For example, 2003 is Heisei juu-go-nen 平静十五年. In general, *nengou* did not coincide with reigns until the Meiji Restoration in the nineteenth century.

[南] Era names adopted by the Southern Court.

[北] Era names adopted by the Northern Court.

410 NAME CONSTRUCTION IN MEDIÆVAL JAPAN

嘉承	Kashou	1106 – 1108	歴仁	Ryaku'nin	1238 – 1239	延久	Enkyuu	1069 – 1074
嘉禎	Katei	1235 – 1238	歴応	Ryaku'ou北	1338 – 1342	承保	Jouhou	1074 – 1077
慶安	Kei'an	1648 – 1652	至徳	Shitoku北	1384 – 1387	承歴	Jouryaku	1077 – 1081
慶長	Keichou	1596 – 1615	正安	Shou'an	1299 – 1302	永保	Eihou	1081 – 1084
慶応	Keiou	1865 – 1868	正長	Shouchou	1428 – 1429	応徳	Outoku	1084 – 1087
建長	Kenchou	1249 – 1256	正中	Shouchuu	1324 – 1326	寛治	Kanji	1087 – 1094
建永	Ken'ei	1206 – 1207	正元	Shougen	1259 – 1260	嘉保	Kahou	1094 – 1096
乾元	Kengen	1302 – 1303	正平	Shouhei南	1346 – 1370	永長	Eichou	1096 – 1097
建治	Kenji	1275 – 1278	正保	Shouhou	1644 – 1648	承徳	Joutoku	1097 – 1099
建久	Kenkyuu	1190 – 1199	正治	Shouji	1199 – 1201	康和	Kouwa	1099 – 1104
建武	Kenmu南	1334 – 1336	正嘉	Shouka	1257 – 1259	長治	Chouji	1104 – 1106
建武	Kenmu北	1334 – 1338	正慶	Shoukei北	1332 – 1333	嘉承	Kashou	1106 – 1108
建仁	Kennin	1201 – 1204	正応	Shou'ou	1288 – 1293	天仁	Tennin	1108 – 1110
建保	Kenpou	1213 – 1219	正歴	Shouryaku	990 – 995	天永	Ten'ei	1110 – 1113
建歴	Kenryaku	1211 – 1213	正徳	Shoutoku	1711 – 1716	永久	Eikyuu	1113 – 1118
建徳	Kentoku南	1370 – 1372	正和	Shouwa	1312 – 1317	元永	Gen'ei	1118 – 1120
康安	Kou'an北	1361 – 1362	昭和	Shouwa	1926 – 1989	保安	Hou'an	1120 – 1124
弘安	Kou'an	1278 – 1288	大永	Tai'ei	1521 – 1528	天治	Tenji	1124 – 1126
弘長	Kouchou	1261 – 1264	大正	Taishou	1912 – 1926	大治	Daiji	1126 – 1131
康永	Kou'ei北	1342 – 1345	天文	Tenbun	1532 – 1555	天承	Tenshou	1131 – 1132
康元	Kougen	1256 – 1257	天永	Ten'ei	1110 – 1113	長承	Choushou	1132 – 1135
康平	Kouhei	1058 – 1065	天喜	Tengi	1053 – 1058	保延	Hou'en	1135 – 1141
康治	Kouji	1142 – 1144	天治	Tenji	1124 – 1126	永治	Eiji	1141 – 1142
弘治	Kouji	1555 – 1558	天授	Tenju南	1375 – 1381	康治	Kouji	1142 – 1144
弘化	Kouka	1844 – 1848	天明	Tenmei	1781 – 1789	天養	Tenyou	1144 – 1145
興国	Koukoku南	1340 – 1346	天和	Tenna	1681 – 1684	久安	Kyuu'an	1145 – 1151
康応	Kou'ou北	1389 – 1390	天仁	Tennin	1108 – 1110	仁平	Ninpei	1151 – 1154
康歴	Kouryaku北	1379 – 1381	天保	Tenpou	1830 – 1844	久寿	Kyuuju	1154 – 1156
康正	Koushou	1455 – 1457	天福	Tenpuku	1233 – 1234	保元	Hougen	1156 – 1159
康和	Kouwa	1099 – 1104	天承	Tenshou	1131 – 1132	平治	Heiji	1159 – 1160
弘和	Kouwa南	1381 – 1384	天正	Tenshou	1573 – 1592	永歴	Eiryaku	1160 – 1161
享保	Kyouhou	1716 – 1736	天養	Ten'you	1144 – 1145	応保	Ouhou	1161 – 1163
享禄	Kyouroku	1528 – 1532	徳治	Tokuji	1306 – 1308	長寛	Choukan	1163 – 1165
享徳	Kyoutoku	1452 – 1455	養和	Youwa	1181 – 1182	永万	Eiman	1165 – 1166
享和	Kyouwa	1801 – 1804				仁安	Nin'an	1166 – 1169
久安	Kyuu'an	1145 – 1151	**CHRONOLOGICAL**			嘉応	Ka'ou	1169 – 1171
久寿	Kyuuju	1154 – 1156				承安	Jou'an	1171 – 1175
万延	Man'en	1860 – 1861	正歴	Shouryaku	990 – 995	安元	Angen	1175 – 1177
万治	Manji	1658 – 1661	長徳	Choutoku	995 – 999	治承	Jishou	1177 – 1181
万寿	Manju	1024 – 2028	長保	Chouhou	999 – 1004	養和	Youwa	1181 – 1182
明治	Meiji	1868 – 1912	寛弘	Kankou	1004 – 1012	寿永	Ju'ei	1182 – 1184
明応	Mei'ou	1492 – 1501	長和	Chouwa	1012 – 1017	元歴	Genryaku	1184 – 1185
明歴	Meireki	1655 – 1658	寛仁	Kannin	1017 – 1021	文治	Bunji	1185 – 1190
明徳	Meitoku北	1390 – 1394	治安	Ji'an	1021 – 1024	建久	Kenkyuu	1190 – 1199
明和	Meiwa	1764 – 1772	万寿	Manju	1024 – 2028	正治	Shouji	1199 – 1201
仁安	Nin'an	1166 – 1169	長元	Chougen	1028 – 1037	建仁	Kennin	1201 – 1204
仁治	Ninji	1240 – 1243	長歴	Chouryaku	1037 – 1040	元久	Genkyuu	1204 – 1206
仁平	Ninpei	1151 – 1154	長久	Choukyuu	1040 – 1044	建永	Ken'ei	1206 – 1207
応長	Ouchou	1311 – 1312	寛徳	Kantoku	1044 – 1046	丞元	Jougen	1207 – 1211
応永	Ou'ei	1394 – 1428	永承	Eishou	1046 – 1053	建歴	Kenryaku	1211 – 1213
応保	Ouhou	1161 – 1163	天喜	Tengi	1053 – 1058	建保	Kenpou	1213 – 1219
応仁	Ou'nin	1467 – 1487	康平	Kouhei	1058 – 1065	丞久	Joukyuu	1219 – 1222
応徳	Outoku	1084 – 1087	治歴	Jiryaku	1065 – 1069	貞応	Jou'ou	1222 – 1224

南 Era names adopted by the Southern Court.

北 Era names adopted by the Northern Court.

Historical Nengou Since 990 CE

元仁	Gennin	1224 – 1225	永和	Eiwa^北	1375 – 1389	享保	Kyouhou	1716 – 1736
嘉禄	Karoku	1225 – 1227	天授	Tenju^南	1375 – 1381	元文	Genbun	1736 – 1741
安貞	Antei	1227 – 1229	文中	Bunchuu^南	1375 – 1375	寛保	Kanpou	1741 – 1744
寛喜	Kanki	1229 – 1232	文和	Bunna^北	1375 – 1356	延享	Enkyou	1744 – 1748
貞永	Jou'ei	1232 – 1233	康暦	Kouryaku^北	1379 – 1381	寛延	Kan'en	1748 – 1751
天福	Tenpuku	1233 – 1234	永徳	Eitoku^北	1381 – 1384	宝暦	Houreki	1751 – 1764
文暦	Bunryaku	1234 – 1235	弘和	Kouwa^南	1381 – 1384	明和	Meiwa	1764 – 1772
嘉禎	Katei	1235 – 1238	元中	Genchuu^南	1384 – 1392	安永	An'ei	1772 – 1781
暦仁	Ryaku'nin	1238 – 1239	至徳	Shitoku^北	1384 – 1387	天明	Tenmei	1781 – 1789
延応	En'ou	1239 – 1240	嘉慶	Kakei^北	1387 – 1389	寛政	Kansei	1789 – 1801
仁治	Ninji	1240 – 1243	康応	Kou'ou^北	1389 – 1390	享和	Kyouwa	1801 – 1804
寛元	Kangen	1243 – 1247	明徳	Meitoku^北	1390 – 1394	文化	Bunka	1804 – 1818
保治	Houji	1247 – 1249	応永	Ou'ei	1394 – 1428	文政	Bunsei	1818 – 1830
建長	Kenchou	1249 – 1256	正長	Shouchou	1428 – 1429	天保	Tenpou	1830 – 1844
康元	Kougen	1256 – 1257	永享	Eikyou	1429 – 1441	弘化	Kouka	1844 – 1848
正嘉	Shouka	1257 – 1259	嘉吉	Kakitsu	1441 – 1444	嘉永	Ka'ei	1848 – 1854
正元	Shougen	1259 – 1260	文安	Bun'an	1444 – 1449	万延	Man'en	1860 – 1861
文応	Bun'ou	1260 – 1261	宝徳	Houtoku	1449 – 1452	文久	Bunkyuu	1861 – 1864
弘長	Kouchou	1261 – 1264	享徳	Kyoutoku	1452 – 1455	元治	Genji	1864 – 1865
文永	Bun'ei	1264 – 1275	康正	Koushou	1455 – 1457	慶応	Kei'ou	1865 – 1868
建治	Kenji	1275 – 1278	長禄	Chouroku	1457 – 1460	明治	Meiji	1868 – 1912
弘安	Kou'an	1278 – 1288	寛正	Kanshou	1460 – 1466	大正	Taishou	1912 – 1926
正応	Shou'ou	1288 – 1293	文正	Bunshou	1466 – 1467	昭和	Shouwa	1926 – 1989
永仁	Ei'nin	1293 – 1299	応仁	Ou'nin	1467 – 1487	平成	Heisei	1989 –
正安	Shou'an	1299 – 1302	文明	Bunmei	1469 – 1487			
乾元	Kengen	1302 – 1303	長享	Choukyou	1487 – 1489			
嘉元	Kagen	1303 – 1306	延徳	Entoku	1489 – 1492			
徳治	Tokuji	1306 – 1308	明応	Meiou	1492 – 1501			
延慶	Enkyou	1308 – 1311	文亀	Bunki	1501 – 1504			
応長	Ouchou	1311 – 1312	永正	Eishou	1504 – 1521			
正和	Shouwa	1312 – 1317	大永	Tai'ei	1521 – 1528			
文保	Bunpou	1317 – 1319	享禄	Kyouroku	1528 – 1532			
元応	Gen'ou	1319 – 1321	天文	Tenbun	1532 – 1555			
元亨	Genkou	1321 – 1324	弘治	Kouji	1555 – 1558			
正中	Shouchuu	1324 – 1326	永禄	Eiroku	1558 – 1570			
嘉暦	Karyaku	1326 – 1329	元亀	Genki	1570 – 1573			
元徳	Gentoku	1329 – 1331	天正	Tenshou	1573 – 1592			
元弘	Gekou^南	1331 – 1334	文禄	Bunroku	1592 – 1596			
正慶	Shoukei^北	1332 – 1333	慶長	Keichou	1596 – 1615			
建武	Kenmu^南	1334 – 1336	元和	Genna	1615 – 1624			
建武	Kenmu^北	1334 – 1338	寛永	Kan'ei	1624 – 1644			
延元	Engen^南	1336 – 1340	正保	Shouhou	1644 – 1648			
暦応	Ryaku'ou^北	1338 – 1342	慶安	Kei'an	1648 – 1652			
興国	Koukoku^南	1340 – 1346	承応	Jou'ou	1652 – 1655			
康永	Kou'ei^北	1342 – 1345	明暦	Meireki	1655 – 1658			
貞和	Jouwa^北	1345 – 1350	万治	Manji	1658 – 1661			
正平	Shouhei^南	1346 – 1370	寛文	Kanbun	1661 – 1673			
観応	Kan'ou^北	1350 – 1352	延宝	Enpou	1673 – 1681			
延文	Enbun^北	1356 – 1361	天和	Tenna	1681 – 1684			
康安	Kou'an^北	1361 – 1362	貞享	Joukyou	1684 – 1688			
貞治	Jouji^北	1362 – 1368	元禄	Genroku	1688 – 1704			
応安	Ou'an^北	1368 – 1375	宝永	Hou'ei	1704 – 1711			
建徳	Kentoku^南	1370 – 1372	正徳	Shoutoku	1711 – 1716			

^南 Era names adopted by the Southern Court.

^北 Era names adopted by the Northern Court.

Research Aids

Glossary	413
Bibliography	427
Name Index	437
General Index	459

Glossary

agata 県
Imperial estates populated by the guild of agricultural workers.

agata no miyatsuko 県造
Before the Taika Reform, these were residential governors of imperial estates. Later, this title became a *kabane*.

agatanushi 県主
Before the Taika Reform, these were residential governors of districts belonging to imperial estates. They were immediately subordinate to the *agata no miyatsuko*. Later, this title became a *kabane*.

ako 阿古
A titular suffix used for forming women's names during the Heian period.

akome 阿古女
A titular suffix used for forming women's names during the Heian period.

ama 天
Literally "heaven", this element commonly appears as the first element in the names of Japanese goddesses.

amatsu 天
This element is equivalent to *amano*.

andojou 安堵状
A document confirming land tenure.

anzu 安主
An administrator belonging to the *mandokoro* of a noble house.

ashigaru 足軽
A light foot soldier used for urban warfare during the Muromachi period. The *ashigaru* were trained to use a single weapon such as the bow or matchlock and organized into platoons.

Ashikaga 足利
A branch of the Seiwa-Genji which governed Japan from Muromachi following the failure of the imperial restoration by Emperor Go-Daigo.

Ashikaga Bakufu 足利幕府
A modern term for the military government established in 1338 CE by Ashikaga Takauji.

asomi 朝臣
The second highest of the eight *kabane* established in 684 CE by Emperor Tenmu.

ason 朝臣
An alternate and generally later reading of *asomi*.

azana 字
Originally a scholarly name adopted by Confucian scholars in China. In Japan, students often adopted an *azana* when they matriculated in a school.

azukari dokoro 預所
The office responsible for managing a *shouen* estate. Sometimes used to refer to the chief manager of an estate.

bakufu 幕府
(1) During ancient and medieval times, *bakufu* referred to the residence of a military commander.
(2) A modern term for a medieval military government.

be 部
In early Japan, these were monopoly corporations or guilds together with their dependent agricultural holdings and peasants.

be-no-miyatsuko 部造
In ancient Japan, these were heads of monopoly corporations. These titles were suppressed following the Taika Reform, and replaced by ministerial titles. For example, the Yamabe no Miyatsuko 山部の部造 of the foresters.

bettou 別當
Director of the administrative office of a noble house or religious order.

bugyou 奉行
Local chief administrative officer or magistrate. During the Kamakura period, complete titles were formed by affixing *bugyou* as a suffix to the domain of authority. Thus, the Jishabugyou 寺社奉行 had responsibility for temples and shrines. The Chinzei bugyou 鎭西奉行 were commissions for Kyuushuu appointed by the Kamakura Bakufu before 1290.

buke 武家
The warrior class. A person need not have actually been a warrior to have belonged to this class.

bushi 武士
A warrior.

chamei 茶名
A *gagou* assumed by a tea master.

chigyou koku 知行国
A province held by a noble house or religious order as distinct from imperial lands or lands held in local hands.

chiji 知事
Administrators responsible for the land holdings and other property of a Zen monastery.

Chinzei 鎮西
The military government of Kyuushuu. By extension, this name also referred to the island itself.

Chinzei tandai 鎮西探題
After 1290, these were viceregal deputies for Kyuushuu appointed by the Kamakura Bakufu.

Chinzei hyoujoushuu 鎮西評定衆
Officials charged with dispensing justice in Kyuushuu from 1299 CE till the office was abolished by the Muromachi Bakufu.

chou 町
Unit of land equal to 2.94 acres until it was reduced to 2.45 acres by Hideyoshi.

choudouin 朝堂院
Governmental offices located in the precincts of the imperial palace.

chokushiden 勅旨田
Lands held directly by the emperor. Within the Society for Creative Anachronism, these could be used for lands outside of the current Known World or for lands held directly by a kingdom.

choushu 頭首
Religious officials of a Zen monastery.

daidairi 大内裏
Imperial palace compound. As in China, the Japanese imperial palace and its official buildings was surrounded by a wall to form a "forbidden city".

daikanjin 大勧進
An imperial title given to the chief monk of a large temple. These officials were usually responsible for temple construction. This title continued in use from 1180 CE through the Tokugawa period.

daigokuden 大極殿
The main audience hall of the emperor.

dairi 内裏
The imperial palace.

daijou 大乗
Mahâyâna or "Great Vehicle" Buddhism. This later form of Buddhism opens the possibility of *satori* (Buddhist enlightenment) to the masses.

dajoudaijin 太政大臣
The "prime minister" and head of the council of state. Within the Society for Creative Anachronism, this title is appropriate for the Society Steward or possibly the Society Seneschal.

dajoukan 太政官
Imperial Council of State established in 702 CE. The council consisted of the *dajoudaijin* 太政大臣 prime minister, the *sadaijin* 左大臣 minister of the left, the *udaijin* 右大臣 minister of the right, the *naidaijin* 内大臣 assistant minister of operations, the four *dainagon* 大納言 grand counselors, and the three *shounagon* 小納言 lesser counselors.

daimyou 大名
Originally, the holder of any large private estate. Later constables called *shugo daimyou* 守護大名 held whole districts and provinces as parts of their estates.

dairyou 大領
District magistrate, see *gunji*.

daijoutennou 太上天皇
An honourifc title for retired emperors instituted in 697 CE. Also *joukoutennou*. See *joukou*.

daijouhou'ou 太上法皇
An honourific title for a retired emperor who has taken religious orders and left the family compound of the imperial family.

daijoukan 太政官
A member of the *sangi* or Imperial Council of State.

dazaifu 大宰府
Imperial governor general of Kyuushuu.

daizen no daibu 大膳大夫
The imperial title held by Takeda Shingen. This title was held by the minister of the imperial household.

Dazaifu 太宰府
Ministry charged with coastal defense and the military government of Kyuushuu.

densou 伝奏
Official solicitors who transmitted petitions from imperial princes, courtiers, temple officials and members of the buke class either to the emperor or the principal retired emperor.

dono 殿
This is an honourific which means "lord". It can be used both following a name and independently as a pronoun. When used as a pronoun, it is sometimes rendered as "tono".

dougou 道号
A "path name" commonly adopted by Zen monks in addition to their other more official names. These names commonly expressed their own vision of enlightenment.

doushu 堂衆
Local monks who sometimes took up arms.

eboshi 烏帽子
A ceremonial hat of any of a variety of styles placed on the head of a young man at his coming of age ceremony. These hats were often made of lacquered silk.

eboshi'na 烏帽子名
A name conferred on a young man at his coming of age ceremony by combining an element of the name born by his *eboshi'oya* (sponsor) with his childhood name.

eboshi'oya 烏帽子親
The official sponsor who places the *eboshi* on the head of a young man at his *genfuku no shiki*.ceremony.

Edo Bakufu 江戸幕府
The military government established in Edo by Tokugawa Ieyasu early in the seventeenth century.

eifu 衛府
The Taihou Code established five division of imperial guards:

左衛士	Saweji	右衛士	Uweji
左兵衛	Sahyauwe	右兵衛	Uhyauwe
衛門	Eimon		

Following 811 CE, there were six divisions:

左近衛	Sakonwe	右近衛	Ukonwe
左衛門	Saeimon	右衛門	Ueimon
左兵衛	Sahyauwe	右兵衛	Uhyauwe

Appointment to one of these guard units became very popular among members of the *buke* class. Eventually, the titles associated with these appointments became independent name elements.

fudoki 風土記
Provincial reports commissioned by Empress Genmei in 713 CE.

fudono 文殿
Archives. A secretariat within the court of the retired emperor responsible for examining and preserving documents. Later, this office assumed independent judicial authority. During the Kamakura period, this office issued summary judgements based upon documentary evidence.

fugo 封戸
The number of serf house households allocated to a noble under the Taihou Code according to their court rank and governmental office.

fujin 婦人
A married woman.

Fujiwara 藤原
A courtier family which controlled the imperial government during parts of the Heian period. Later, Fujiwara princes served in the Kamakura Bakufu.

fumie 踏絵
A Christian icon produced by the Edo Bakufu for subjects to step on.

furigana 振り仮名
Kana written beside *kanji* to explicate the correct reading.

ga ヶ
An abbreviation for 箇, this element is found conjoining descriptions with locatives. Typically, both the description and the locative are either Japanese *kun'yomi* words or proper names. Essentially, the descriptive element modifies the substantive element in these names.

ga 箇
The original *kanji* for which ヶ is an abbreviation. Normally, the abbreviation is used in forming names.

gagou 雅号
An artistic pseudonym.

ge 解
A petition submitted to a higher authority. Also, *gesho* 解書, *gebumi* 解文, and *moushibumi* 申文.

gechi 下知
An order or command issued by the Kamakura or Muromachi Bakufu. The Kamakura Bakufu issued decrees beginning,「鎌倉殿、御下知を添へて遣はさる」.

genfuku no shiki 元服の式
A coming of age ceremony. Literally, first clothing ceremony.

Genji 源氏
The clan established by rusticated imperial princes who took the name Minamoto. Later, this clan was greatly expanded by Minamoto no Yoritomo who granted clan membership to warriors in exchange for fealty and homage.

gesu 下司
Resident manager of a *shouen* estate.

giyouden 宜陽殿
An office building for the *kugyou* located in the imperial compound.

go 後
A prefix used in creating regnal names for emperors who choose a previously used regnal name. (e.g. Go-Murakami Tennou followed Murakami. Tenno)

goin 後院
The palace of a retired emperor.

goke'nin 御家人
A direct vassal of the *shougun*. Originally, these were the *shugo* and *jitou*, during the Tokugawa Bakufu, the *gokenin* were vassals inferior to the *hatamoto*. Within the context of the Society for Creative Anachronism, these people correspond to the peers, court barons and barons holding lands directly from the crown.

goshi 五師
The five "rectors" or senior monks of a monastery.

gouka 豪家
The ancient *uji* (clan) nobility.

gozen 御前
A suffix found in women's names of the late Heian and early Kamakura periods.

gun 郡
Rural administrative district similar to a county.

gunji 郡司
The imperial administrator of a rural district.

guuji 宮司
The head of a Shintoh shrine.

han 藩
The domain held by a daimyou during the Tokugawa period. This period is considered post-mediæval by Japanese historians.

hanashikotoba 話言葉
A word or phrase used in spoken Japanese.

hanchou 藩庁
Imperial official charged with managing the former domain of a *daimyou* immediately following the Meiji Restoration.

hanzei 半済
These were allocations of half the agricultural output of *shouen* estates to feudal vassals during the Muromachi period. They quickly became effective partitions of the original estates.

haru no miya 春の宮
crown prince.

hatamoto 旗本
During the Sengoku period, these "banner men" lead subdivisions of the military *ikki* called *kumi*. During the Tokugawa Bakufu, the *hatamoto* were direct vassals of the *shougun* and often were specialists of one sort or another. This was the sort of position held by Will Adams, who is known in Japan as Miura Anjin 三浦按針.

Heian-jidai 平安時代
The period during which effective government was located in Heiankyou 平安京 now called Kyôto. This period may be further divided into periods of rule by the emperor, the Fujiwara family and the *insei*.

Heiankyou 平安京
The classical name for Kyouto. Today, it is known simply as Kyôto 京都. The capital was established here in 794 CE following its removal from Heijoukyou 平城京 (Nara) to Nagaokakyô 長岡京 in 784 CE.

Heijoukyou 平城京
First successful imperial capital established at Nara. Later, this city was known as Nara 奈良 and the period during which Heijoukyou was the capital is known as the Nara period.

heika 陛下
Your majesty. Used when addressing or referring to the emperor.

Heike 平家
The Taira family. HEI is the Chinese reading and taira the Japanese reading of the initial *kanji*.

Heike Monogatari 平家物語
A popular account of the Genpei War compiled during the middle ages. Aside from battles and intrigue, this work has a rather moral tone and opens with a temple bell announcing the futility of political ambition.

Heishi 平氏
The Taira *uji* or family. Heishi is preferred when combining the family name with the posthumous name of the imperial progenitor of a specific branch.

hikan 被官
A man at arms or any other personal follower or retainer of low rank.

hikitsukeshuu 引付衆
Judicial agency of the Kamakura Bakufu.

hime 姫
Princess. Appears as a titular final element in women's names.

hime 媛
Princess. Appears as a titular final element in women's names.

himenomikoto 媛命
A suffix found in the names of goddesses.

hiragana 平仮名
One of the two syllabic writing systems used to transcribe Japanese. It is supposed to have a more feminine aesthetic than does *katakana*.

hito 仁
A *tsuuji* commonly appearing in *nanori* born by male members of the imperial family. While there are instances of this element appearing as the substantive element of *nanori* born by *shomin*, such use is comparatively rare.

hokumen 北面
Northern palace guards. A guard unit serving the *insei* established by Shirakawa.

honjo 本所
General management office of a *shouen* estate. Generally the names of private or regional offices are formed by 所 (sho) which is simply a place where some prescribed activity is performed. Thus, 本 (hon) which means either "main" or "central" is used to form the word for a "main office" of a privately held estate.

honke 本家
Proprietor of a *shouen* estate. This was the highest level of *shiki* rights or land tenure. This title actually refers to a family and its head rather than to an individual proprietor.

honmyou 本名
True or "legal" name.

houmyou 法名
A Buddhist name. The 法 (hou) in *houmyou* is a reference to the Buddhist law. This is not law in a judicial sense, but in a causative sense.

hyougi 評議
The governing council of the Kamakura Bakufu. Within the Society for Creative Anachronism, this is equivalent to *Curia Regis*. This term might also be used to designate any royal court. However, the term properly refers to a collegial meeting of peers.

hyoujou 評定
Similar in meaning to *hyougi*, but referring specifically to a meeting of the *hyoujoushuu* or Supreme Council.

hyoujoushuu 評定衆
Supreme council of the Kamakura Bakufu established in 1225 CE.

ie 家
Literally a house, it also refers to a household.

iemoto 家元
The holder of the primary license of a school or more correctly tradition *ryuuha* 流派 of some art form. The *iemoto* system was primarily instituted early in the Tokugawa period to control the spread and practice of various art forms. Only those obtaining a license could study or practice one of these restricted forms. Students received licences either from the *iemoto* or indirectly through their own teacher.

ikai 位階
Court Rank. The system of court ranks (distinct from *kabane*) was imported from China by Emperor Monmu. A modified system of ranks was promulgated as part of the Taihou Code in 702 CE. Court rank was distinguished by sumptuary laws regulating hats and colour of court costume.

ikishiki 位記式
A solemn ceremony of elevation to higher rank at the imperial court.

ikki 一揆
Originally, a military organization organized for a single purpose. Later, a general term for any revolt.

imiki 忌寸
A *kabane* of the fourth rank established in 684 CE.

imi'na 諱
The *houmyou* born by a Buddhist monk. Technically, it is a posthumous name.

in 院
A retired emperor. Usually, this term refers to the senior retired emperor at the head of the *insei*.

inaki 稲置
Before the Taika Reform, the *inaki* administered rural districts.

inbe 忌部
A monopoly corporation of ritual abstainers.

inbe 斎部
A noble family of ritualists descended from the monopoly corporation of ritual abstainers.

ingou 院号
Honourific palace names awarded by the emperor.

inkan 印鑑
A legal signature seal.

in no chou 院朝
Administrative headquarters of a retired emperor. (See *insei*.)

in no hyoujoushuu 院平定衆
A judicial body formally attached to the imperial court, but answering to the Kamakura Bakufu. This body primarily adjudicated boundary disputes.

insei 院政
Cloistered government. Traditional term for government by retired emperors. The effective power of this government varied quite a bit. It was generally most powerful from the establishment of the *in* until the ascendancy of the Taira family preceding the Genpei war. The *insei* was finally abolished by Emperor Go-Daigo at the end of the Kamakura period.

inshi 院司
An official of the *insei* cloistered government.

inzen 院宣
Edict issued by the *in* which was the title awarded to the principal retired emperor.

ippon 一品
The highest of court ranks. This rank was one of four court ranks reserved for imperial princes and princesses.

irashime 郎女
One of several titular suffixes found in feminine names dating from the Yamato Period.

iratsume 郎
An honourifc suffix found in Japanese women's names dating from the Yamato period. The same *kanji* was used to write men's names, but it took a different reading.

jika gyouji 寺家行事
Bakufu officials assigned to oversee Rinzai Zen monasteries.

jin no sadame 陣定
An official meeting of the *kugyou* or council of state. During the Kamakura period, representatives of the *bakufu* obtained appointments to this council.

jishu 寺衆
The monk responsible for administering temple finances.

jitou 地頭
A steward of a *shouen* estate appointed by the *bakufu* and responsible for tax collection.

jitsumei 実名
A real or genuine name as opposed to an assumed name.

jo'ou 女王
Titular suffix used by imperial princes who had not received *naishinnousenge*.

Joudou Shinshuu 浄道真宗
The pure land school of Buddhism established by Shinran.

jou'ingou 女院号
An honourific name awarded to women by the emperor. The elevation ceremony is called *moninsenge*.

Joukou 上皇
The *joukou* or *daijou tennou* 太上天皇 was a senior retired emperors who exercised authority similar to that exercised by the Fujiwara regents. He was both head of a great household and controlled a variety of government appointments.

Joukyuu no hen 丞久の変
    The Joukyuu Disturbance. In 1221 CE, the emperor mustered his palace guards and other followers in an attempt to overthrow the *bakufu*. This failure of the imperial armies marks the end of the relative autonomy previously enjoyed by women.

joushi 上司
    Superintendents who oversaw the geshu and relayed orders from the *mandokoro* of the *shouen* proprietor.

jouza 上座
    The head of the governing council or *sangou* of a large temple.

kabane 姓
    These are a source of great confusion. In China, a SHI 氏 was a clan and a SEI 姓 was a family name. However, the Japanese used *kabane* 姓 to refer to certain hereditary titles within the clans. Originally, there were at least thirty different *kabane*. The Taika Reform (645) absorbed these titles into the imperial government. Following Emperor Temmu 天武天皇(672–686), Japanese emperors regulated the *kabane* and reduced their number. Thus, some of the old *kabane* with new additions became the substantive elements in new imperial titles. These titles were frequently formed by combining a locative with the titular element. After the new imperial offices became hereditary, these titles were abbreviated an were treated as family.

kaimyou 戒名
    A posthumous name.

Kamakura 鎌倉
    A town located in the Kantou region which was home to the military government established by Minamoto no Yoritomo.

Kamakaura Bakufu 鎌倉幕府
    A modern term for the military "tent government" established by Minamoto no Yoritomo at Kamakura.

Kamakura-jidai 鎌倉時代
    The period from 1148 CE to 1333 CE when Japan was ruled by the military government at Kamakura. This period is generally characterized as being a period of "consular government" in which power was shared by the court and the *bakufu*. Following the Joukyuu disturbance, the power of the court was greatly reduced.

kamei 家名
    A house or family name.

kami 上
    A generic title for chief. This title was in common use before the Taika Reform. This title was attached as a suffix to the domain controlled by the chief. In the verbal form of the title, a possessive "no" was inserted between the domain and the titular element.

kami 神
    A god.

kamon 家紋
    A family heraldic design.

kan 貫
    A monetary unit equal to 1000 *mon*.

kan 官
    Position, Title or Office. The Taihou Code allotted stipends on the basis of 位 (i) court rank and 官 (kan) office.

Kan 漢
    The Han dynasty of China and the dialect thereof. Most *on'yomi* are derived from this dialect.

kana 仮名
    Syllabic writing.

kanji 漢字
    Pictographic or ideographic writing. Literally "Chinese letters". The Japanese invented novel *kanji* which are unknown in China as well as importing thousands of Chinese *kanji*.

kanshoufu 官省符
    Certificate of tax immunity for a *shouen* estate.

kanpaku 関白
    The imperial regent for an adult emperor.

kanwajiten 漢和辞典
    Literally a Chinese-Japanese dictionary. These are Japanese dictionaries arranged by the initial *kanji* appearing an a word.

ka'ou 花押
    Signature or autograph. Court aristocrats commonly transformed their two kanji names into single character quasi-pictorial calligraphic designs. These signatures are closely related to "grass script" which they resemble. The word *kaou* 花押 literally means "flower impression" because of the resemblance of these autographs to pressed flowers.

katakana 片仮名
    One of two syllabaries used for writing Japanese phonetically. This syllabary is characterized by its upright or "proper" form. This form supposably evidences a "masculine" aesthetic.

kazoku 家族
    A family or group of people living together.

kebi'idokoro 検非違所
    A provincial police office

kebi'ishichou 検非違使庁
    Provincial ministries of justice created in 839 CE. They comprised three departments: *eifu* 衛府 enforcement, *danjôdai* 弾正台 adjudication, and *gyôbushô* 刑部省 execution.

keishi 家司
    Household officials. Originally, officials serving *shinnô* and *kanpaku*.

Kemyou 仮名
    Names attached to the *eboshi* at the *genfuku* ceremony

Kenmu Shinsei 建武新政
Imperial restoration by Go-Daigo Tennou.

ke'nin 家人
Direct vassal.

kenza 件座
An audience. Specifically, an employment interview during the Heian period.

kime 屎女
A vulgar suffix found in the names of female commoners during the Heian period.

kimi 君
An honourific showing greater respect than *dono* but less than *kami*. Generally, the lowest honourific appropriate for the emperor. This title was often appended to the names of juvenile imperial princes.

kin 公
An initial element found as the initial element in the *nanori* of certain high ranking courtiers.

kishin 寄進
Commendation of alodial lands to an overlord. This might be done either for simple tax relief or in exchange for a feudal relationship. Lands commended in this way were combined to form the *shouen* estates.

ko 子
An honourific suffix originally found in men's names, but later characteristic of high ranking women.

kokubunji 国分寺
Government supported provincial temple.

kokuga 国衙
Imperial provincial headquarters.

kokugaryou 国衙領
Public lands subject to taxation by the imperial government.

kokujin 国人
During the Muromachi period, a generic term for local warriors.

Kofun-jidai 古墳時代
The tumulus period. 100 – 562 CE.

Kojiki 古事記
"Annals of Old Affairs" commissioned in 682 CE by Emperor Tenmu.

Kokuki 国記
The "National Annals" portion of the *Kyuujiki* which was saved from destruction.

kokushi 国司
Officers of the imperial provincial government. These officers were responsible for the census, taxation and maintaining order. The term was also used to designate provisional provincial governors dispatched from the capital to handle emergencies.

kokushu 国守
Provincial governor.

kome 子賣
Feminine titular suffix appearing in the Heian and Kamakura periods.

koseki 戸籍
A residential certificate. These certificates maintained at the citizen's bureau of the municipal government record the members of every Japanese household and affirm citizenship.

kouji 公示
A public announcement or proclamation.

koutaishi 皇太子
Crown prince. Papinot reports that Emperor Keitai was the first to appoint his own successor by imperial decree in 531 CE.

koutei 皇帝
The emperor or empress.

koutou 勾当
A superintendent either within an imperial agency or within a private chancellery.

koutou no naishi 勾当内侍
Female superintendent of all of the women in the imperial court. She resided in the *Nagahashi no Tsubone* 長橋の局 within the imperial palace and was commonly called *Nagahashi dono* 長橋殿.

kubunden 口分田
Fields allotted to individual cultivators under the Taihou Code.

kudashibumi 下文
A permanent edict or decree.

kuge 公家
The ancient court nobility claiming descent from the gods.

kugyou 公卿
The highest rank of courtier officials. During the Heian period, these officials constituted a council of state.

kumi 組
A military subdivision of a *kuni ikki*.

kumon 公文
A deputy of the gesu.

kuni 国
A province.

kuni no miyatsuko 国造
A provincial governor before the Taika Reform.

kun'yomi 訓読
Native Japanese "reading" for a *kanji*.

kuraudo no kami 蔵人頭
Imperial chief of staff.

Kyuujiki 旧事記
An early chronicle of Japanese history compiled in 621 CE and later destroyed.

machime 町賣
A feminine suffix found in the names of commoners during the Heian period, and in the names of noble women during the Nara period.

magatama 曲玉
A stone hand scythe.

mahito 真人
A *kabane* of the first rank established in 684 CE.

mandokoro 政所
The chancellery of the *bakufu* or an aristocratic family. This body functioned as the civil arm of the *bakufu*.

manzai 漫才
A comic sketch or dialogue.

maro 麿
A suffix originally found in the names of adult men and later found in the names of boys and male infants. This kanji was invented in Japan by combining two phonetic elements. Later, 麿 was replaced by 丸 which eventually took the reading "maru".

maru 丸
An affection suffix found in the names of male infants and young boys. In ordinary speech and writing, this is a word meaning "round". While this appears to be the intended meaning in the names of ships and boats, in human names it appears to connote good health.

mashi まし
A second person personal pronoun best reserved for subordinates held in low esteem.

me 女
A suffix commonly found in female names from the Nara and Heian periods which remained in use throughout the Muromachi period. This suffix simply means woman.

me 賣
The predominant suffix in women's names from the Nara period, this element was gradually replace by 女 (me) and both were superseded by 子 (ko). 賣 literally means to sell or send forth.

michi no shi 道師
A *kabane* of the fifth rank established in 684 CE.

mikado 帝
The emperor.

mikoto 命
An honourific suffix found in the names of gods and goddesses.

migyousho 御教書
A written order or directive of temporary duration.

Mima'na 屯倉
In ancient times, a Japanese colony on the Korean peninsula.

Minamoto 源
A family name sometimes adopted by rusticated imperial princes. Together, the various Minamoto houses formed the basis for the Genji 源氏 clan. Each lineage within the clan is known by the emperor from which it is descended. The Seiwa Genji 清和源氏 are decendents of Emperor Seiwa 清和天皇.

miya 宮
A shrine or palace. Also, a titular suffix sometimes found in the names of imperial princes sent into exile. Hokurikunomiya 北陸宮 was a grandson of Go-Shirakawa Tennnou and was sent into exile in Hoku-riku, hence his name.

miyake 屯倉
Literally a granary. Imperial estates were also known as *miyake*.

Miyako 都
Originally the name for the palace or court, the imperial city was often known simply as *miyako* during the middle ages.

miyatsuko 造
A *kabane* used by local governors before the Taika Reform. This element can be placed after any pre-Classical political division. Papinot claims that it can be placed after Island to form Shima no Miyatsuko. 島造. Such a title would be used by the overlord of an entire island.

mokudai 目代
Residential Lieutenant Governor, the titular governor residing after the 11th century in Kyouto.

mon 文
A monetary unit. Specifically, a bronze coin.

monin 門院
An honourific suffix attached to women's names by imperial decree.

mon'in senge 門院宣下
An imperial proclamation granting *monin* as an augmentation to a woman's name.

mora
The smallest suprasegmental unit in Japanese speech. These are usually represented by a single *kana* letter and always correspond to a single rhythmic unit.

moushitsugi 申次
An official courier who acted as liaison between the imperial court and the *bakufu*.

muraji 連
Originally ranking second after *omi* 臣, this *kabane* was effectively degraded following the Taika Reform to occupy the seventh rank.

Muromachi Bakufu 室町幕府
The military government established by Ashikaga Takauji.

Musashi 武蔵
A province formerly located in the Kantou region of central Kyuushuu containing Kamakura and Edo.

mushime 虫賣
A suffix found in women's names of the Nara and Heian periods.

myou 名
A unit of land tenure for private estates used during the middle ages. These units appear to correspond to individual tenant allotments. A local land owner was called a *myôju* 名主. The owner of a smaller holding was known as a *shômyou* 小名, and the owner of a larger holding was known as a *daimyô* 大名.

myoubu 名簿
During the Nara and Heian periods, a name card detailing the rank and station of a supplicant seeking employment with either the government or a noble family.

myouden 名田
An estate consisting of rice fields newly cleared after the Taika Reform. These holdings were registered under the name of the land holder.

myouji 苗字
A family name.

myoujigomen 苗字御免
Official permission to assume a family name.

myoushu 名主
A holder of proprietary land tenure.

Nagaokakyou 長岡京
Location of the imperial capital between its removal from Nara and the construction of Heiankyou.

nagaya 長屋
Long urban tenements often with multiple entrances.

naginata 薙刀
A Japanese halberd. Japanese sword technique generally employed thrusts and vertical strokes. The *naginata* was designed for horizontal strokes. Although the *naginata* is sometimes mistakenly thought of as a women's weapon, it was widely used by imperial forces during the Heian period and was a military weapon in the sixteenth century.

naishinnou 内親王
A title originally assumed by imperial princesses closely related to the emperor. Later, use of this title was restricted to those who received by imperial decree. Like their brothers, not all imperial princesses would receive the accolade.

naishinnou senge 内親王宣下
An imperial decree conferring the title of *naishinnou* upon an imperial princess.

nanbokuchou 南北朝
The period (1336 CE—1392 CE) during which there were two rival imperial courts. The legitimate southern court eventually surrendered to the illegitimate norther court which was supported by the *bakufu*.

nanori 名乗
An official given name. *Nanori* appear on formal documents and were proclaimed before giving combat on the battlefield. Bearing these names was a privilege reserved to the *kuge* and the *buke* classes. These names appear to have originated in Japanese assuming Chinese names and then applying Japanese readings to them.

Nara 奈良
Location of Heijoukyou, the first successful attempt to found a permanent capital. During the middle ages, this town somewhat reduced from its imperial splendour was known as Nara.

Nara-jidai 奈良時代
The period (710 CE — 794 CE) between the founding of Heijoukyou and the founding of Heiankyou. This includes the ten year period when the capital was located at Nagaokakyou.

nengou 年号
Era names. During the middle ages, the imperial court would occasionally declare a new era. All subsequent dates were dated from that era. Thus, the year in which a new era was proclaimed frequently had two *nengou* with dates using the era name in force when it occurred.

Nihongi 日本記
Chronicles of Japan from the age of the gods till 697.

nengu 年貢
An annual land tax paid to the proprietor of a *shouen* estate. Originally, these taxes were assessed and paid in produce derived from the land holding. Beginning in the middle of the Kamakura period, these payments in kind were commuted into monetary payments.

nenyosho 年預所
The *mandokoro* attached to large temples.

no mikoto 命
A titular suffix found in the names of gods and goddesses.

nomae 前
A suffix used during the Kamakura period to form feminine names from the names of flora and fauna.

nushi 主
Lord or master.

nyo 女
A suffix found in women's names of the Kamakura and Muromachi periods. While *me* is a native Japanese reading, NYOU is a Chinese reading of this *kanji*.

nyou 女
An alternate Chinese reading of 女 found in women's names.

nyuudou 入道
Literally "entered the path". This is a prefix sometimes found attached to the *houmyou* of lay monks.

o 御
Beginning in the Muromachi period, an honourific prefix used to form feminine names. This construction eventually supplanted names formed using honourific suffixes.

o 阿
Beginning in the Muromachi period, an honourific prefix used to form feminine names. This construction eventually supplanted names formed using honourific suffixes.

o 於
Beginning in the Muromachi period, an honourific prefix used to form feminine names. This construction eventually supplanted names formed using honourific suffixes.

ooban yaku 大番役
Guards stationed in the imperial capital by the Kamakura Bakufu.

obito 首
The *kabane* for the executive officer of a monopoly corporation.

okami 御上
A pronoun used to refer either to the emperor, the *shougun* or a head of government.

omi 臣
Originally the highest *kabane*, this title occupied the sixth rank after Taika Reform.

onchi 恩地
A land grant given to a vassal during the Kamakura or Muromachi period as a token of gratitude.

onshou 恩賞
A general term for largess. The gift could take the form of a bequest of land, *shiki* rights or money.

on'yomi 音読
Chinese "reading" for a *kanji*.

oo-muraji 大連
The great *muraji*. One of the two prime ministers before the Taika reform.

oo-omi 大臣
The great *omi*. One of the two prime ministers before the Taika reform.

ookimi 王
A title used by imperial princes.

osanana 幼名
A name born by an infant or young child.

ou 王
A titular element attached to the names of imperial princes who have not received *shinnousenge*.

ouji 皇子
An imperial prince.

Ounin Ran 応仁乱
The Onin Rebellion began over several contested successions among ranking families of the Muromachi Bakufu. The Onin Ran lead to the age of battles in which the *shugo daimyou* sought to expand their personal holdings and competed for national supremacy.

Rakuchuu 洛中
Mediæval name for the imperial city.

reiben 隷弁
Original pictographic and ideographic Chinese characters adapted for engraving in stone.

reimei 霊名
A baptismal or "spirit" name.

reisho 隷書
A style of writing based on *reiben* or any text written in *reiben*.

rensho 連署
Multiple signatures. During the Houjou regency, *bakufu* documents carried two signatures. One signature belonged to the *shikken* and another belonged to the Houjou family council of elders.

rinji 綸旨
An imperial decree personally issued by the emperor. These edicts were actually written by the *geki* 外記 or external secretary.

Rokuhara tandai 六波羅探題
Viceregal deputies appointed by the Kamakura Bakufu to oversee central and western Japan. The title derives from the location of their official residence in the Rokuhara district of Kyouto. Other regional officials held similar titles.

ryou 領
A suffix used to indicate proprietary land tenure or other land rights.

ryouji 令旨
Decrees or warrants issued by an imperial prince.

ryouke 領家
The proprietor of a *shouen* estate.

ryoushu 領主
Any land lord.

sa'emon 右衛門
Originally a detachment of palace guards, sa'emon became an *honourific* title and eventually an independent name element.

sa'emonnodaibu 左衛門大夫
A low ranking member of the left hand detachment of palace guards. Within the Society for Creative Anachronism, this title has been used to ennoble subjects of the East Kingdom upon being awarded arms for service in the arts and sciences.

saimen 西面
Western palace guards. A guard unit serving the *insei* established by Shirakawa.

samurai 侍
Literally a servant. The samurai were warriors in service to noble houses. Eventually, the military class formed military governments in which the samurai were in fealty to other members of the military class. However, imperial appointments and titles remained the imprimatur of legitimacy and status for the military.

samuraidokoro 侍所
Originally the name for any private military organization attached to a temple or noble family. During the Kamakura

period, the *samuraidokoro* was the military arm of the *bakufu*. The head of the *samuraidokoro* was called the *bettou*. The Houjou regent held both this title and the title of *shikken*.

sangi 参議
Imperial Council of State. In the Heian period, membership was fixed at eight.

satodairi 里内裏
An unofficial imperial residence. Specifically a country estate.

satori 悟り
Awakening or perceiving. Buddhist enlightenment.

seiitaishougun 征夷大将軍
Barbarian suppressing generalissimo. Originally a provisional title for leaders of expeditionary forces, this became the imperial title born by the titular head of the military government.

seishi 姓氏
The *kabane* followed by the clan name. Later, the family name followed by the clan name. In modern Japan, this word is synonymous with *myouji* or family name.

Seiwa Genji 清和源氏
Rusticated descendents of the Seiwa emperor.

Sengoku-jidai 戦国時代
The "warring states" period from the Onin Ran to national reunification in the sixteenth century.

senji 宣旨
A formal imperial edict issued during the Heian and Kamakura periods.

senpai 先輩
An honourific pronoun used by junior students when addressing senior students.

sensei 先生
An honourific pronoun used by students when addressing or talking about their teachers. It is also generally used as a title of respect for learned experts.

shigou 諡号
Posthumous names used by the imperial family.

shiki 職
Originally this term applied to a specific office or occupation. However, as the offices became hereditary and actual administration was transferred into private hands, this term came to represent land tenure and other revenues and prerogatives attached to a title.

shikibu 式部
The ritual department of the imperial government.

Shikibu Kyau 部卿
Head of the imperial ritual ministry.

shikken 執権
Originally the head of the *mandokoro* or civil arm of the Kamakura Bakufu, this title came to designate the shougunal regent.

shinji 信士
A titular element commonly found in masculine posthumous names.

shinka 臣下
A subject.

shinnou 親王
An honourific title granted by special decree to imperial princes. Generally, the sons of imperial princes who do not receive this title are rusticated while the sons of those who do remain in the imperial family for another generation.

shinnou senge 親王宣下
The imperial decree which confers the title *shinnou* upon an imperial prince.

shinnyou 信女
A titular element commonly found in feminine posthumous names.

shinshi 進止
Transfer of legal jurisdiction over land to a resident military vassal. These transfers were often effective partition or expropriation of land

shisei 氏姓
Literally uji and kabane. A tribal system of government which preceded the Taika Reform (645). The *uji* were extended kinship groups and the *kabane* were titles such as *ason* and *muraji* assumed by clan chiefs.

shitsuji 執事
The deputy chief of the mandokoro. Papinot notes that the shitsuji acted as the first minister of the shikken.

Shintoh 神道
Here we have opted for a traditional spelling rather than following the systematic romanization rules used for other Japanese words. Under that system, this word would be rendered as *shintou*. Regardless, this is the indigenous religion of Japan. It is essentially a purity cult which worships anthropomorphic gods and goddesses who are thought to be the progenitors of the Japanese nobility.

shiryou 私領
Private land tenure. A legal term during the Heian and Kamakura periods designating heritable land holdings.

Shishinden 紫宸殿
The central audience chamber of the imperial palace.

shomin 庶民
Commoners. Japanese historians group rusticated nobility and the entire *buke* class together with peasants, merchants and artisans into this category.

shou'en 荘園
A private estate. Many of these estates were originally given only as bequests of tax-exempt *shiki* rights from the emperor. These were converted into private holdings by the holders of these rights claiming to exercise judicial authority within these allotments. As some *shiki* rights derived from judicial appointments, not all of these claims

were without merit. However, most of them very simply presumptive. Also, many fraudulent claims to land tenure were made which were never adequately adjudicated. Many holders of these rights did not actually live on or directly manage their estates. Rather, they appointed *jitou* as resident estate stewards. The *jitou* often acquired their own *shiki* rights and emerged as rustic nobility.

shou'en 庄園
An alternate way of writing *shouen*. This rendering evokes an image of the fields surrounding a farmers hut. By comparison, 荘 expresses more the idea of a rural villa owned by an urban noble.

shougun 将軍
Often an abbreviated for *seiitaishougun*. Actually, other titles can be formed which incorporate *shougun*.

shouji 荘司
The proprietor of a *shouen* estate.

shoujou 小乗
Hînayâna or "small vehicle" Buddhism. This form of Buddhism emphasized the difficulty of attaining *satori* and the consequent uniqueness of the Buddha.

shoukan 荘官
Any *shouen* official.

shouke 荘家
A family holding land primary tenure or *shiki* rights. Properly, this term refers to a family enjoying private land tenure.

shoumin 荘民
Generic term for *shouen* residents.

shouryou 所領
A private *shouen* estate. This is a legal term specifying heritable and transferable proprietary rights over a particular place.

shoushi 荘司
Any *shouen* officer.

shugo 守護
Provincial constables originally dispatched by the Kamakura Bakufu. Later, these constables acquired effective title to their provinces to become the *shugo daimyou*.

shugodai 守護代
A deputy *shugo*. These appointments were generally made by the *shugo* himself and not by the central authority.

shugo daimyou 守護大名
A *shugou* who has converted his province into a vast personal estate.

shugo ryougoku 守護護国
The process by which the *shugo* took possession of the provinces they were appointed to govern and converted them into private holdings. This might involve nominal joint tenure with the original proprietors and the *jitou*.

shugoshi 守護使
An inspector dispatched annually by the *shugo* to inspect rice fields and fix taxation.

shujin 主人
Lord. During the Heian period, a title of respect used by a vassal when addressing his employer. In modern Japanese, this is a word for "husband".

shukuryou 宿老
Elders who met in council to determine *bakufu* policy.

shuu 州
The second element in the "Chinese" names of Japanese provinces.

songou 尊号
An honourific name.

souryou 惣領
The head of a warrior household.

soutsuibushi 総追捕使
In 1183 CE, Minamoto no Yoritomo dispatched provincial governors called *soutsuibushi*. Later, these officers were called *shugo*. Papinot reports that Minamoto no Yoritomo was sometimes referred to as Nihon Sôtsuibushi 日本総追捕使 or governor general of Japan.

suke 介
A suffix used to form the titles of certain deputies.

suku'ne 宿禰
The third highest of the eight *kabane* established in 684 CE by Emperor Tenmu. While the *kabane* was most often added to the family name, there are instances in *Heike Monogatari* of *kabane* being added to *nanori* when the family name is not given.

tadokoro 田所
A *shouen* official responsible for land surveying and tax collection.

Taihouritsuryou 大宝律令
The Taihou Code was originally promulgated by Emperor Monmu in 701 CE and remained the fundamental source of imperial law throughout the middle ages. 律 (ritsu) comprises the criminal code and 令 (ryô) the civil law. Later, additional ordinances called *kaku* 格 and rituals called *shiki* 式 were added to complete the Japanese legal code. The Taihô Code established a system of state controlled land tenure wherein courtiers received allotments due both to rank and office.

Taika 大化
The first imperial era or *nengou*. The system of named eras was imported from China during the reign of Emperor Koutoku.

Taika no Kaishin 大化の改新
See Taika Reform

Taika Reform
Abolition of *shisei* tribal government in 645. The Taika Reform replaced the old clan centered government of Japan with a central imperial government patterned after the Chinese imperial system. Effectively, the old government was replaced with a wholly new one. For this reason, on writer calls the Taika Reform a coup d'etat.

Taikou 太閤
A retirement title assumed by a *kanpaku* (imperial regent) who has passed the office of *taikou* to his son. This title is especially associated with Hideyoshi.

Taira 平
A family name sometimes assumed by rusticated members of the imperial family. The Taira and their supporters fought the Genpei War with their Minamoto cousins.

taiseidaijin 大政大臣
Modern reading for *dajoudaijin*. The "prime minister" and head of the council of state. Within the Society for Creative Anachronism, this title is appropriate for the Society Steward or possibly the Society Seneschal.

taishi 太子
Crown Prince.

tandai 探題
A deputy dispatched by the Kamakura Bakufu to oversee the government of large regions of Japan. One pair of deputies was charged with governing the entire Island of Kyuushuu and another pair was charged with governing the remainder of western Japan. This is probably the office within the Kamakura Bakufu which most close approximates the role of a territorial prince in the Society for Creative Anachronism.

teihatsu 剃髪
Shave one's head and become a monk. Upon the death of his father in 1180 CE, Hokurikumiya 北陸宮 was compelled to shave his head and become a monk. He was then sent into exile.

teme 手賣
A suffix found in women's names during the Nara period.

Tendaishuu 天台宗
A Buddhist sect originating in China which practices Zen meditation. Tendai Buddhists try to live by the three precepts of shunning evil, doing good works and kindness toward existing beings.

tennou 天皇
The most common title for the emperor. It is almost always used together with their posthumous name when speaking of deceased emperors. It is commonly used in life in conjunction with honourific appellations such as *heika* 陛下 in phrases such as *tennou heika* 天皇陛下 which roughly translates as "his majesty the emperor." Tennou literally means "lord of high heaven". This reflects the priestly origin of the imperial family.

tenshi 天子
Another title for the emperor. This title expresses the heavenly mandate for the earthly sovereignty of the emperor.

tobe 戸邊
A suffix appearing in feminine names dating from the Yamato period.

Tokugawa 徳川
A cadet branch of the Seiwa Genji which gained control of Japan at the Battle of Sekigahara in 1600 CE.

Tokugawa Bakufu 徳川幕府
The military government established by Tokugawa Ieyasu in Edo at the close of the Japanese middle ages.

tomo 伴
In ancient Japan, an agricultural collective.

tomo-no-miyatsuko 伴造
The chief of or local nobility of an ancient agricultural collective.

toneri 舎人
Low placed retainers of great families. As such, they might perform a variety of tasks. During the Heian period, these retainers included the footmen who accompanied the extorts bearing the great nobles. Generally, these servants were housed in barracks, hence their name.

Tou 唐
The T'ang dynasty of China and the dialect thereof. A common source of *on'yomi*.

touguu 東宮
Palace occupied by the crown prince. Also an honourific pronoun referring to the crown prince. Here we see an example of the name of a place being transferred to an individual. The names of rooms in the imperial palace assigned to court ladies were often similarly transferred to their occupants.

touryou 棟梁
The leader of a warrior band.

tsubokiri no ken 壺切剣
A sword ceremoniously presented to the newly elected crown prince by the emperor.

tsubone 局
A final element sometimes found in honourific women's names since the early Kamakura period. This element is found in the name born by Tangou no Tsubone 丹後局 who was a contemporary of Minamoto no Yoritomo. She was also known as Takashina Eishi 高階栄子. A *tsubone* is the private quarters of a female courtier inside the imperial palace. Tangou no Tsubone was actually a unique office created by the emperor for Takashina Eishi.

tsuuji 通字
A *kanji* shared in the *nanori* of members of a lineage. We have also seen an example where the Chinese reading of the *tsuuji* was taken when forming a Buddhist name.

tsuushou 通称
A common use name, not a nickname. Masculine *tsuushou* were typically formed from a very restricted repertoire of name elements and had a well defined construction. While these names primarily appear to signify birth order, because of the fluid nature of mediæval Japanese kinship patterns, they may actually indicate primacy with a jurisdiction and not actual birth order.

ue 上
An honourific suffix added to a name as a sign of respect.

u'emon 右衛門
Originally a detachment of palace guards, uaemon became an *honourific* title and eventually an independent name element.

u'emonnodaibu 右衛門大夫
A low ranking member of the right hand detachment of palace guards. Within the Society for Creative Anachronism, this title has been used to ennoble subjects of the East Kingdom upon being awarded arms for service in the martial activities.

uhe 上
An older variant of *ue*.

uji 氏
A clan. The large kinship group in ancient Japan. This was also an element in constructing certain mediæval feminine names.

ujigami 氏神
A clan god.

uji no chouja 氏長者
A clan chief appointed or confirmed by the emperor.

uji no kami 氏上
In ancient Japan, a title born by a clan chief.

ujizoku 氏族
Direct descendants of the pre-Taika Reform (645) *uji no kami* or clan chiefs.

Urasenke 裏千家
One of several "schools" of tea claiming descent from Sen no Rikyuu.

utaishau 右大将
Commander of the *ukonwe* 右近衛 division of inner palace guards. This is the highest imperial appointment ever received by Minamoto Yoritomo. This is another reason for adopting the *eifu* ranks for granting rank within the Society for Creative Anachronism. *Utaishou* is a more modern reading for this title.

waka 若
Literally young. This element was a common component in suffixes used to form feminine names from the Nara period through the Kamakura period. It also appeared along with *maru* in the names of Japanese boys.

warawana 童名
A childhood name.

Yamamori 山守
Mountain Wardens. The *yamamori* were guild or monopoly corporation in ancient Japan renowned for the ferocity of its warriors.

Yamato 大和
A region in central Honshuu which was the center of much of the early history of Japan. The name of this province appears in the Japanese style posthumous name of Jinmu Tennou. The literal meaning of the *kanji* used to write this name is "great peace". Indeed "peace" is a common theme in Japanese era names. Originally, the name of the province was Yamato 倭, at which time its Chinese style name was Wakoku 倭国. Its name was changed in 737 CE to Yamato 大和.

Yamato-jidai 大和時代
A period preceding the Nara Period during which the imperial court was located at different places in the province of Yamato.

yasa 夜叉
A suffix found in women's names during the Nanboku period.

yasame 夜叉女
A suffix found in women's names during the Nanboku period.

yobina 呼び名
A name commonly used to in conversation or to "call" someone.

yomikotoba 読言葉
A literary word or phrase which is not normally spoken. This distinction between the written and spoken languages is generally more acute in Japanese than it is in English. This is partly due to the relatively free way in which kanji can be agglutinated in the written language and a restricted phonetic system which results in many homonyms being produced.

yoriai 寄合
A general term for any council or meeting. During the Kamakura period, the Houjou adopted this term for meetings of their council of elders. This term was also applied to meetings held by leaders of warrior bands and can be generally applied to clan councils.

za 座
During the Kamakura and Muromachi periods, a chartered guild of independent artisans licensed to produce and sell specified products. These guilds are quite distinct from the earlier monopoly corporations.

zokumyou 俗名
Any common use name.

Bibliography

While many of the Japanese works listed have *furigana* indicating the preferred reading the title and author, many do not. Consequently, the readings of Japanese titles and authors given in this bibliography may not agree with bibliographic entries found in library catalogues or other bibliographies. Transliteration of titles and authors in this bibliography follows the Hepburn system unless another transliteration is preferred by the source or the name has entered the English language. City of publication is omitted for works published in Tokyo.

Most of the books listed in this bibliography are held in the collections of various East Asian libraries. Harvard Yenching Library, the Cheng Yu Tung Library of the University of Toronto, the East Asia Collection of the Theodore R. McKeldin Library of the University of Maryland College Park, and the Kroch-Asia Collection at Cornell University greatly helped research for this monograph. The University of Hawaii at Manoa, the University of Washington, Stanford University, the University of California at Berkeley, and the Pennsylvania State University also have valuable collections.

Abe and Nishimura 1990
> Abe Takeshi 阿部猛 and Nishimura Keiko 西村圭子. *Sengoku Jinmeijiten Compact Edition.* 戦国人名辞典コンパクト版. Shinjinbutsu Ôraisha, 1990.
>
> This book is a *Who's Who in Japan* during the warring states period. It includes articles about many prominent individuals from the late Muromachi period through the early Edo Period. Each of these articles details the names of the individual and when they lived in Western calendar dates. Although partially duplicated by *Kamakura Muromachi Jinmei Jiten,* this book is a valuable source for Japanese names during the *sengoku* period. Unfortunately, this book does not provide as much detail concerning name usage as the other volume.

Araki 1959
> Araki Ryôzô 荒木良造. *Nanorijiten.* 名乗辞典. Tôkyôdô Shuppansha, 1959.
>
> This book appears to be primarily a list of modern Japanese given names. While it is very large and rather useful for general scholarship, it is not a particularly useful source for understanding pre-modern Japanese names.

Aston 1972
> Aston, William George (trans.). *Nihongi.* Rutland, C. E. Tuttle Co., 1972.
>
> This is a fine translation of one of the classics of Japanese antiquity which was patterned after similar chronicles found in China. There are many names from the classical period in this book and it has ample footnotes. However, while the translator includes occasional *kanji*, he does not adequately explain issues of onomastic interest. Further, as all of the names are given in translation without accompanying *kanji*, this book is not as useful as it could have been. While translations may not hinder use of this book for many other purposes, the quasi-titular and descriptive naming practices of early Japan make this book of somewhat limited use.

Benedict 1946
> Benedict, Ruth. *The Chrysanthemum and the Sword.* Boston, Houghton Mifflin Company, 1946.
>
> This is a charming, informative, and very readable introduction to Japanese Society.

Bijutsu Kôronsha 1989

Bijutsu Kôronsha. 美術公論社. *Haijintechô*. 俳人手帳. Bijutsu Kôronsha. 美術公論社, 1989.

> This book is useful for research about the *gago* of modern haiku poets. It also contains the lineage of several schools of haiku poetry going as far back as the early modern period. While this book is not a source for pre-modern names, it is none the less an interesting source for understanding *gago*.

Bryant 1993

Bryant, Anthony. *A Japanese Miscellany*. The Complete Anachronist Volume 65. Milpitas, Society for Creative Anachronism, 1993.

> This pamphlet in the *Complete Anachronist* series is a JTB travel guide to medieval Japan. It presents short informative essays on a variety of subjects. The onomastic section of this pamphlet is largely derived from the introduction to *Japanese Names and How to Read Them* by Koop and Inada.

Chen 1972

Chen Cheng-chi. *A Standard Romanized Dictionary of Chinese and Japanese Popular Surnames*. Oriental Society, 1972.

> As suggested by the title, this book is a list of contemporary surnames found in both China and Japan. While many of these surnames were extant during mediæval times, this book does not concern itself with onomastic history.

Chamberlain 1971

Chamberlain, Basil Hall. *Japanese Things*. Rutland, C. E. Tuttle Co., 1971.

> This book is one of the best miscellanies of Japanese culture available. This book is a valuable addition to the library of any person interested in recreating Japanese culture.

Chamberlain 1932

Chamberlain, Basil Hall (trans). *Ko-ji-ki*. Kobe, J. L. Thompson & Co., 1932.

> The *Kojiki* largely parallels the *Nihongi*. It ends with lengthy genealogies which provide more names than does the *Nihongi*. Serious students should obtain Japanese copies of both the *Kojiki* and the *Nihongi* and use the translations as study guides.

Chao 2000

Chao, Sheau-yueh J. *In Search of Your Asian Roots: Genealogical Research on Chinese Surnames*. Baltimore, Clearfield Company, Inc., 2000.

> An historical introduction to Chinese surnames including a genealogical analysis of Chinese surnames found in *Pai Chia Hsing* 百家姓 and an annotated bibliography.

Farris 1995

Farris, William Wayne. *Heavenly Warriors: The Evolution of Japan's Military, 500-1300*. Cambridge, Harvard University Press, 1995.

> In some respects, Prof. Farris is the intellectual successor of Jeffrey P. Mass. While Mass emphasized the continuation of imperial institutions during the Kamakura period, Farris uncovers the antecedents of warrior rule in the Heian period. This book is invaluable in understanding the stake holders of political power in mediæval Japan. As with many Japanese history books, this book is graced with genealogical tables and other data of interest to onomastic inquirey.

Frederic 1972

Frederic, Louis. Eileen M. Lowe (Trans.) *Daily Life in Japan at the Time of the Samurai: 118–1603*. New York, Praeger Publishers, 1972.

> This book is an accessible cultural history of mediæval Japan. It concerns itself with matters of daily life and provides insights into the name culture of mediæval Japan.

Frederic 2002
: Frederic, Louis. Käthe Roth (Trans.) *Japan Encyclopedia.* Cambridge, Belknap-Harvard, 2002.

    In some respects this fine volume is the intellectual heir to Papinot's *Historical and Geographical Dictionary of Japan.* It has many biographical and geographic entries. Unlike Papinot, this work does not include Japanese orthography with its entries. This makes it less valuable as an onomastic reference than it otherwise would be.

Gomi, Takano, and Toriumi 1998
: Gomi Fumihiko 五味文彦, Takano Toshihiko 高埜利彦, Toriumi Yasushi 鳥海靖. Shôsetsu Nihonshhi Kenkyû 詳説日本史研究. Yamakawa Shuppan, 1998.

    This is a recent and handsomely produced Japanese high school history textbook. It features a wealth of photographs and figures. As with other Japanese history textbooks, this book holds a wealth of dated historical figures and genealogical charts.

Hall and Brown 1993
: Hall, John Whitney and Delmer M. Brown. (Ed.) *The Cambridge History of Japan: Ancient Japan.* Cambridge, Cambridge University Press, 1993.

    This is the initial volume in the *Cambridge History of Japan.* The books is organized as a collection of chapters written by experts in the field. This series is currently the definitive Japanese history text available in English.

Hall and Mass 1974
: Hall, John W. and Jeffrey P. Mass. *Medieval Japan: Essays in Institutional History.* New Haven, Yale University Press, 1974.

    This is a highly informative collection of essays on mediæval Japanese political institutions. Further, it lends insight into questions about *uji, kabane,* and *kamyou.*

Hashimoto 1965
: Hashimoto Hiroshi. 橋本博. *Daibukan* 大武鑑. Tokyo, Meicho Kenkyûkai, 1965.

    This is a three volume registry of major military men including their lineages and heraldry. This registry is organized by historical periods with the period up to 1600 covered in the first volume.

Hawley 1974
: Hawley, W. M. *Honorary Titles used by Swordsmiths.* Hollywood, W. M. Hawley, 1974.

    This remarkable pamphlet catalogues swordsmiths by the honourary titles that appear in their sword inscriptions. It also contains facsimiles of rubbings taken from various Japanese swords.

Hawley 1976
: Hawley, W. M. *Japanese Sword Inscriptions.* Hollywood, W. M. Hawley, 1976.

    This thirteen page pamphlet concerns itself with teaching the reader how to decipher the inscriptions on Japanese swords. Thus it begins with a brief article on Japanese personal names and includes tables of provincial names and era names. It also discusses honourary titles found in sword inscriptions. While this pamphlet is highly useful for studying the names of Japanese swordsmiths, Hawley appears to have neglected comparing these names with the names of other artisans.

Hawley 1978
: Hawley, W. M. *Japanese Swordsmith Groups.* Hollywood, W. M. Hawley, 1978.

    Many of the group names appearing in this pamphlet, such as Awataguchi 粟田口, were in use by 1600 CE. Fortunately, not only does Hawley provide dates for the various schools listed, but their names can be independently verified by using articles in Japanese dictionaries.

Hawley 1967
: Hawley, W. M. *Japanese Swordsmith*. Hollywood, W. M. Hawley, 1967.

    At the time of publication, this two volume 750 page book was the largest list of Japanese swordsmiths ever compiled. It contains over 18,000 names and many tables.

Hawley 1976
: Hawley, W. M. *Koto Sword Scrapbook from an Appraiser's Manuscript of about 1550*. Hollywood, W. M. Hawley, 1976.

    This 64 page pamphlet reproduces sketches of many sword inscriptions.

Hearn 1900
: Hearn, Lafcadio. "Japanese Female Names" in *Shadowings*. Boston, Little Brown, 1900.

    This is a relatively famous article written during the Meiji period. Hearn documents what were then contemporary name distributions and changes in the way girls were being named in Japan. He cites a study by a Japanese academic in this article which has never been properly attributed. I suspect that this study was actually conducted by Hearn himself and that this attribution to an unnamed academic is simply anonymous pseudodeparagrapha. I believe that he did this in order to add credence to his study.

Hori 1952
: Hori Nikkô 掘日亨. *Shinpen Nichiren Daishônin Goshô Zenshû* 新編日蓮大聖人御書全集. Seikyo Shinbunsha, 1952.

    This is a collection of letters and religious tracts written during the Kamakura period by the founder of a Buddhist sect. It contains numerous names and is a readily available primary source for forms of address in Japanese letters from this period.

Iguchi 1979
: Iguchi Kaisen 井口海仙 Nagashima Fukutarô 長島福太郎. *Sadôjiten* 茶道辞典. Tankôsha, 1979.

    This is the comprehensive source for short articles on the tea ceremony and contains brief biographies of many prominent people who lived during the sixteenth century. It also reproduces the *kao* (signatures) of several of these people.

Inadaira, Kawamura, and Amakasu 1973
: Inadaira Yasuhiko 稲坦泰彦, Kawamura Zenjirô 川村善二郎, and Amakasu Takeshi 甘粕健. *Nipponshi San Teiban* 日本史三訂版. Sanseidô, 1973.

    This is a history textbook for Japanese high school students. Consequently, it contains the names of many Japanese and brief articles about Japanese government and culture.

Katagiri 1983
: Katagiri Yôichi 片桐洋一. *Kashinka Kotoba Jiten* 歌枕歌ことば辞典. Kadokawa Shoten, 1983.

    This book is primarily useful as an aid for understanding literary Japanese.

Kiyomizu 1989
: Kiyomizu Osamu 清水治. 1989 *Nenpan Bijutsuka Meigan* １９８９年版美術家名鑑. Bijutsu Gurakubu, 1989.

    This book is essentially a *Who's Who* in Japanese arts. While this book is published annually and is intended as a directory of contemporary artists, it is useful for understanding *gago* or artistic pseudonyms. Further, many Japanese artists belong to lineages extending back to the sixteenth century. In some cases their name is inherited and often the lineage of names for a particular school is carefully documented.

Koop and Inada 1923

Koop, Alert James and Inada Hogitaro. *Japanese Names and How to Read Them*. Routledge, 1923.

This book remains the definitive work on Japanese names available in English.

Kuno 1973

Kuno Susumu. *The Structure of the Japanese Language*. Cambridge, MIT Press, 1973.

This classic text remains a useful reference for students of Japanese linguistics.

Lang 1973

Lang, Roland A. *The Phonology of Eighth-Century Japanese*. Sophia University, 1973.

Lang's original work was submitted as his doctoral dissertation to the University of Michigan in 1968. This book is a revised version of the original dissertation and is intended for a more general audience. Lang used selected poems from the *Mân'jôshu* which are attributed to the Nara region as the basis for his reconstruction of early classical Japanese phonology.

Lin 1988

Lin, Shan. *Name Your Baby in Chinese*. Union City, Calif., Heian International, 1988

While not as scholarly as the book by Chao (2000), this book does provide an introduction to *kanji* used in Chinese names along with their meanings and both Pin-Yin and Wade-Giles romanization. It also discusses the influence of the Chinese calendar and zodiac on name selection.

Mass 1982

Mass, Jeffrey. *Court and Bakufu in Japan*. New Haven, Yale University Press, 1982.

This book is an extensive study of Japanese polity during the Kamakura period. It contains many names faithfully transliterated into English. Unfortunately, the authors do not supply the corresponding *kanji*. This problem is alleviated by the fact that most of the individuals named are listed in *Kamakura Muromachi Jinmei Jiten*. This book does much to elucidate ranks, offices, and titles used during the Kamakura period and has a useful glossary.

Mass 1992

Mass, Jeffrey. "Identity, Personal Names, and Kamakura Society" in *Antiquity and Anachronism in Japanese History*. Stanford, Stanford University Press, 1992.

This is a highly useful essay on Japanese onomastic by one of the leading authorities on the Kamakura period. Of special note is the section devoted to women's names.

Matsui 1989

Matsui Yashiko 松井泰彦. *Sen Rikyû no Seigai* 千利休の生涯. Tankôsha, 1989.

This book is a facsimile reproduction with accompanying verbatim transcriptions of over a dozen late sixteenth century documents. These documents contain lists of individuals with attached honorifics.

Matsumura 1988

Matsumura Akira. *Sanseidô Daijirin* 三省堂大辞林. Sanseidô, 1988.

This book, with 2616 pages of main text and 26 pages of appendices, is the entry by Sanseidô into the comprehensive and unabridged Japanese dictionary market. It is a very modern dictionary with many excellent articles in addition to the main text. It contains biographical entries for all major figures in Japanese history. Sanseidô is a major academic publisher in Japan and this book lives up to both the reputation of the company and its press releases prior to publication. It contains many tables and illustrations.

McCullough 1988
: McCullough, Helen Craig. *Bungo Manual.* Cornell East Asia Series. Ithaca, Cornell University, 1988.

    This manual is a compendium of grammar notes for Classical Japanese derived from a variety of sources. The author has translated these notes along with illustrative examples and collected them together into a compact handbook. This book renders complete conjugations tables for classical and modern Japanese verbs in romaji.

Miller 1974
: Miller, Richard J. *Ancient Japanese Nobility: The Kabane Ranking System.* Berkeley, University of California Press, 1974.

    The only generally available English language monograph on *kabane* and the *Shinsen Shojiroku*. It includes detailed breakdowns of early clans recorded by *uji* and *kabane*.

Miller 1967
: Miller, Roy Andrew. *The Japanese Language.* Chicago, University of Chicago Press, 1967.

    This seminal work is still considered by many scholars to be the standard reference work for the Japanese language.

Milner, Odagiri, and Morrell 1985
: Milner, Earl, Odagiri Hiroko, and Robert Morrell. *The Princeton Companion to Classical Japanese Literature.* Princeton, 1985.

    This book guides the reader through the mountain of Japanese literature beginning with classical works and continuing through contemporary Japanese literature.

Miyakoshi 1989
: Miyakoshi Satoshi 宮腰賢. *Kiso kara Yoku Wakaru Koten* 基礎からよくわかる古典. Obunsha, 1989.

    This is a Japanese preparatory school textbook for mediæval Japanese literature written in both Classical Japanese and Chinese. As such, it explicates mediæval Japanese grammar and contains many classical and mediæval readings.

Morimoto 1988
: Morimoto Koryu, Cynthia Fitz Collins von Schlussel, Tamsin of the Raven Tresses, and Kensuki Kobori. *Japanese Names and Related Topics.* Kirkland, Anthony Ferrucci, 1988.

    This little known pamphlet appears to be based largely on the work of Koop and Inada. It contains a number of useful tables on thematic elements in Japanese names and their statistical distribution. It also contains a description of the title system instituted during the Meiji restoration in the nineteenth century.

Murabayashi 1942
: Murabayashi Magoshirô 村林孫四郎. *Kojikijiten* 古事記辞典. Kinseisha, 1942.

    A *kana*-order dictionary of the *Kojiki* with entries for people, deities, and places.

Murdoch 1964
: Murdoch, James. *A History of Japan Vol. 1.* New York, Frederick Ungar Publishing Co, 1964.

    This book, which is actually published in two volumes, is a detailed history of Japan from antiquity to the arrival of the Portuguese in 1542. This book has the virtue of a reliable romanization system which breaks names into fragments corresponding to individual *kanji* by inserting hyphens. This facilitates not only understanding, but correct pronunciation. As with English, Japanese words are best broken at thematic transitions. This book also contains much useful material on clans, the feudal structure of clans and ennoblement. Unfortunately, Murdoch translates titles instead of transliterating them which limits the usefulness of this book for onomastic research.

Nakada 1963
　　Nakada Norio 中田祝夫. *Shinsen Kogojiten*. Shogakukan, 1963.

　　　This 1338 page book is the entry by Shogakukan into the classical Japanese dictionary market. Its appendices contain tables of ranks, offices,titles, honourifics, and formal speech for classical and mediæval Japan. Although it does not contain any biographic entries, it does explain onomastic concepts which have disappeared from modern Japanese

Nakayama 1969
　　Nakayama Shigeru. *A History of Japanese Astronomy: History of Japanese Astronomy: Chinese Background and Western Impact*. Cambridge, Harvard University, 1969.

　　　This book is a detailed study of Japanese astronomy and calendric science. It includes a fine exposition on the organization of these departments in the Japanese imperial government. Further, it discusses the development of the equal fields system, the examination system, and the role that family membership played in these things.

Nishitani 1985a
　　Nishitani Moto'o 西谷元夫. *Konjaku Monogatari - Uji Shûi Monogatari* 今昔物語・宇治拾遺物語. Jûtenkoji Vol. 5. Yûmeidô, 1985.

　　　This book contains transcriptions of two works from Japanese literature with accompanying translations into modern Japanese, marginal notes, and explanatory articles. This book together with *Ôkane - Heike Monogatari* constitute the principal source for the pattern of Japanese name construction advocated in this monograph.

Nishitani 1985b
　　Nishitani Moto'o 西谷元夫. *Ôkane - Heike Monogatari* 大鐘・平家物語. Obunsha, 1985.

　　　This book contains transcriptions of two works from Japanese literature with accompanying translations into modern Japanese, marginal notes, and explanatory articles. This book together with *Konjaku Monogatari - Uji Shûi Monogatari* constitute the principal source for the pattern of Japanese name construction advocated in this monograph.

O'Neil 1972
　　O'Neil, Patrick Geoffrey. *Japanese Names*. Wetherhill, 1972.

　　　This book is the most widely available source book for Japanese names. O'Neil and his wife collected names from every possible source on index cards which were then assembled into a book. Thus, this book contains names derived from telephone books, novels, casual conversations, and other non-attested sources. While O'Neil does indicate whether a name is a masculine name, a feminine name, a surname, or a palace name, he makes no other distinctions between them. Further, this book lacks the ideographic analysis and the expository material found in the book by Koop and Inada. Consequently, this book is of limited use in constructing or analyzing a mediæval Japanese name.

Papinot 1972
　　Papinot, E. *Historical and Geographical Dictionary of Japan*. Rutland, C. E. Tuttle Co., 1972.

　　　This is the best single English language book available to society heralds today. This valuable book contains many bibliographic entries for both Japanese and historically important western residents of Japan. When known by the author, this book includes an illustration of the *kamon* used by each of these individuals. Fortunately, it renders Japanese names with both Japanese and English orthography. Further, it provides a handy cross-reference between the *nanori* and family name of famous Japanese. Finally, it includes brief articles on Japanese name elements.

Philippi 1969

Philippi, Donald. *Kojiki: Translated with and Introduction and Notes*. Tokyo, University of Tokyo Press, 1969.

> This is a modern translation of the *Kojiki* and includes an extensive glossary and notes about the evolution of Japanese phonology. Although generally neglected by historians, the *Kojiki* concludes with extensive genealogies and is a more extensive source for names than is the *Nihongi*. This translation is based on the critical edition published in Heibonsha in 1958 as volume 7 of the *Kojiki Taisei*.

Piggott 1977

Piggott, Joan R. *The Emergence of Japanese Kingship*. Stanford, Stanford University Press, 1977.

> This is an excellent study of early Japanese history and social organization. The author organizes her work chronologically with chapters named after seven pivotal figures in the emergence of imperial authority: Himiko, Yûryaku, Suiko, Tenji, Temmu, Jitô, and Shômu.

Plutschow 1995

Plutschow, Herbert E. *Japan's Name Culture: The Significance of Names in a Religious, Political and Social Context*. Richmond, Surrey, England, Curzon Press, 1995.

> This book approaches the cultural and historical significance of Japanese names in light of the work of Derida and others. While this book provides invaluable information about the history and culture of Japanese names, it is not an onomastic reference book. However, it provides much useful information about the significance of names.

Sakamonto and Hirano 1990

Sakamoto Tarô 坂本太郎 and Hirono Kunio 平野邦雄. *Nihon Kodai Shizoku Jinmeijiten*. 日本古代氏族人名辞典. Yoshikawa Kôbunkan, 1990.

> This book is an excellent source for early Japanese names. It is especially useful in that it cites specific ancient manuscripts. It also lists the *kabane* associated with the individual *uji*.

Sansom 1963

Sansom, George. *A History of Japan. Vol. 1-3*. Stanford, Stanford University Press, 1958-1963.

> Every student of Japanese history should own copies of these books. Unfortunately, Japanese orthography is entirely absent from the text. This is only partially remedied by the inclusion of Japanese orthography in the index.

Shibatani 1990

Shibatani Masayoshi. *The Languages of Japan. Cambridge Language Surveys*. Cambridge, Cambridge University Press, 1990.

> This particularly interesting linguistics text has useful discussions of the origin and early phonology of the Japanese language. Despite the fact that Japanese and the Ryukyu languages are mutually incomprehensible, the author treats the Ryukyu language as a dialect of Japanese. This book also covers the Utari (Ainu) language.

Shively and McCullough 1999

Shively, Donald H. and William H. McCullough. (Ed.) *The Cambridge History of Japan: Heian Japan*. Cambridge, Cambridge University Press, 1999.

> This volume in the *Cambridge History of Japan* concerns itself with classical Japan. The books is organized as a collection of chapters written by experts in the field. This series is currently the definitive Japanese history text available in English.

Suzuki, Takebe, and Mizukami 1982

Suzuki Shûji 鈴木修次, Takebe Yoshiaki 武部良明, and Mizukami Shizuo 水上静夫. *Dainipan Kadokawa Saishin Kanwajiten* 第二版角川最新漢和辞典. Kadokawa, 1982.

> With the exception of highly abridged dictionaries intended for elementary school students, this is the most easy to use *kanji* dictionary on the market. *Kanji* dictionaries are highly useful in Japanese onomastic research. They give readings, etymology, and meanings for thousands of *kanji*. They explain the nuances of the different readings for individual *kanji* and correct usage of *kanji* with related sound and meaning. They also note when *kanji* assume special meanings when they appear in names. Unfortunately, these tables include only those *kanji* officially approved by the Japanese Ministry of Education. Further, some names use now obsolete readings which do not appear in this dictionary. However, it remains the first stop when determining the reading for an unfamiliar name.

Takagi and Tomiyama 1958

Takagi Ichinotsuke 高木市之助 and Tomiyama Tamizô. *Kojiki Taisei.* 古事記大成. Heibonsha, 1958.

> This original critical edition of the *Kojiki* has been reprinted many times with expanded glosses.

Takamaru 1989

Takamaru Shinjô 太丸神章. *Rekishi Bessatsu Series* 歴史別冊シリーズ. Vol. 1-11. Gakken, 1988-1989.

> These "Mooks" were issued monthly and were extended collections of articles on related historical subjects from the Japanese middle ages. One issue might cover the life of Tokugawa Ieyasu and another the battle of Sekigahara. Although very popular in nature, they do contain many facsimiles of documents and paintings from the period of interest. As Japanese artists frequently labeled their figures, these constitute primary sources for onomastic research. Further, these publications contain many genealogical trees which are generally more accessible than the genealogical references in *Kamakura Muromachi Jinmei Jiten*.

Takebayashi and Nakao 1983

Takebayashi Shigeru 竹林滋 and Nakao Toshio 中尾俊夫. *Kenkyusha's New Little English-Japanese Dictionary.* Kenkyusha, Ltd., 1983.

> This little dictionary was my constant companion during my early years in Japan. While I am citing it here, it was in storage during all but the final days of working on the first edition of this book.

Tanaka 1996

Tanaka Takashi 田中卓. *Shinsen Shojiroku no Kenkyû* 新撰姓氏録の研究. Kokusho Kankokai, 1996.

> This book is a one-volume study of the *Shinsen Shojiroku* which is a record of almost 1182 *uji* or imperially recognized lineages along with *kabane* compiled in 815. This valuable source was discovered too late for inclusion in the present work.

Taniguchi 1983

Taniguchi Gyoku 谷口玉泉. *Sekigahara Kassen ni Manabu* 関ヶ原合戦に学ぶ. Hôzôji, 1983.

> This book gives the names and *kamon* of the principal participants in the battle of Sekigahara.

Tanioka and Yamaguchi 1987

Tanioka Takeo 谷岡武雄 and Yamaguchi Eichirô 山口恵一郎 *Concise Nippon Chimeijiten* コンサイス日本地名辞典. Sanseidô, 1987.

> This book contains 20,500 geographic entries many of them containing historical notes which give the name in use during the middle ages.

Tsunoda 1988
: Tsunoda Bunei 角田文衛. *Nippon Joseimei* 日本女性名. Vol. 1-3. Kyôikusha, 1980-1988.

    Published over a ten year period, these three volumes are an invaluable source for Japanese female names. The author includes reproductions of ancient census records and memorial inscriptions.

Varley and Kumakura 1989
: Varley, Paul and Kumakura Isao. *Tea in Japan*. University of Hawaii Press, 1989.

    This may be the best historical study of Japanese tea culture available in English. Japanese tea culture developed during the Muromachi period and is epitomized by Sen no Rikyu who was an advisor to Toyotomi Hideyoshi who later ordered him to commit *seppuku*. This book is useful for onomastic research because it describes the names used by certain adepts during the sixteenth century.

Withycombe 1977
: Withycombe, E. G. *The Oxford Dictionary of English Christian Names*. 3rd Ed. Oxford University Press, 1977.

    While this is not a source book for Japanese naming practice, it does provide a nice exposition on Greek and Roman naming practices. In particular, both Withycombe and Tsunoda analyze the name *Publius Cornelius Scipio*. This book also provides a handy source for comparative studies concerning the adaptation of masculine names for use by women.

Yamamura 1990
: Yamamura Kozo. *The Cambridge History of Japan: Medieval Japan*. Cambridge, Cambridge University Press, 1990.

    This long awaited volume in the *Cambridge History of Japan* concerns itself with the Japanese middle ages. The books is organized as a collection of chapters written by experts in the field. This series is currently the definitive Japanese history text available in English.

Yasuda 1990
: Yasuda Motohisa 安田元久. *Kamakura - Muromachi Jinmeijiten* 鎌倉・室町人名事典. Shinjinbutsu, 1990.

    This book is a *Who's Who in Japan* during the Kamakura and Muromachi periods. It also includes many prominent individuals from the Heian period through the early Edo period. It was compiled by a staff of scholars who contributed individual articles for the people included in the book. Each of these properly attributed articles begins with their official name, when they lived in Western calendar dates, the period during which they lived, and their principal occupation. It continues with discussions of other names they used during their lives and their relationships with other people. These articles conclude with a brief biography.

Yokoyama 1987
: Yokoyama Sumio 横山住雄. *Inuyamajô Zuroku* 犬山城図録. Gifu, Kyôiku Shûpan Bunkakai, 1987.

    This book is available from the museum store at Inuyama castle. It contains glossy photogravure reproductions of official documents relating to Inuyama castle along with the names of various individuals associated with the castle. Unfortunately, most of these people were born after 1600.

Yoshida 1986
: Yoshida Taiyô 吉田大洋. *Kamon Kakei Jiten*. Shômonsha, 1986.

    Although a popular pocket book of the sort purchased at train stations, this book contains many genealogical notes.

Name Index

A

Abe N (E); O; S; U	406, 406; 399; 208, 309, 315; 390
Abiru S	115, 137, 294, 315
Acha F	115, 166, 374
Achacha F	115, 166, 374
Achame F	115, 199, 374
Adachi S	114, 176, 208, 239, 315
Aeba S	97, 228, 315
Afui F	160
Agata no I'nukai U	390
Aguri F	115, 374
Ahe U	390
Ai F	255, 374
Aizawa	150, 168,
A'ihara S	152, 161, 274, 315
Aikawa S	151, 226, 315
Ajirou M	370
Akahashi S	144, 184, 315
Akahito N	171, 184, 331
Akaka F	374
Akamatsu S	159, 184, 315
Akame F	184, 374
Akameko F	374
Akasaburou M	370
Akashi S	153, 184, 315
Akechi S	179, 264, 315, 404
Akemi F	227
Aki F	277, 374
Akifusa N	133, 202, 260, 331
Akihide N	202, 288, 331
Akihira N	179, 282, 331
Akihiro N	100, 202, 331
Akihito N (E)	407-408
Aki'ie N	127, 135, 202, 331
Akika'ne N	202, 205, 260, 331
Akiko F	129, 197, 262, 374
Akiku'ni N	98, 202, 331
Akimasa N	202, 230, 331
Akimatsu S	128, 159, 315
Akime F	127, 199, 374
Akimori N	202, 222, 331
Akimoto N	127, 139, 167, 179, 202, 217, 331
Akimu'ne N	179, 262, 331
Aki'naga N	111, 202, 331
Aki'nao N	241, 262, 331
Aki'nobu N	125, 202, 233, 331
Aki'nori N	262, 286, 331
Aki'oki N	116, 202, 331
Akirakeiko F	179, 197, 266, 374
Akisada N	202, 247, 331
Akisuke N	194, 202, 331
Akita S	128, 143, 315
Akitada N	125, 299, 331
Akita'ne N	179, 206, 331
Akitoki N	122, 202, 331
Akitomo N	201-202, 331
Akitoshi N	202, 252, 331
Akitou N	242, 260, 331
Akitsu'na N	202, 276, 331
Aki'uji N	125, 187, 202, 331
Akiyama S	128, 145, 315
Akiyamame F	127, 374
Akiyasu N	125, 202, 209, 303, 331
Akiyori N	127, 240, 331
Akiyoshi N	202, 265, 331
Akizuki S	128, 155, 315
Akizumi N	179, 285, 331
Ako F	115, 197, 374
Akome F	115, 199, 374
Akume F	115, 199, 374
Ama no I'nukai U	390
Amabe O; U	37, 399; 390
Amako F; S	208, 374; 97, 203, 315
Ama'neiko F	220, 374
Ama'no S	152, 155, 315
Amari S	225, 293, 315
A'nahobe O; U	399; 390
a'nayama S	145, 147, 315
Andou S	104, 208, 315
A'ne F	115, 374
An'ei Y	117, 208, 409, 411
A'ne'noko F	198, 374
A'netsume F	198, 374
Angen Y	208, 216, 409-410
Ankan H (E)	406
Ankou H (E)	406
Annei H (E)	405
Antei Y	208, 292, 409, 411
Antoku H (E)	407
Aoi F	160
Aoki S	159, 184, 315
Aoto S	184, 281, 315
Aoyama P	184
Arakawa S	150, 154, 315
Araki S	154, 159, 315
Arame F	199, 208, 374
Areme F	187, 199, 374
Arichika N	203, 268, 331
Arifusa N	133, 268, 331
Arihiro N	106, 268, 332
Arihito N	232, 268, 332
Ari'ie N	135, 268, 332
Arima S	172, 269, 315
Arimasa N	230, 268, 332
Arime F	115, 374
Arimitsu N	180, 268, 332
Arimori N	222, 268, 332
Arimoto S	217, 269, 315
Ari'naga N	111, 268, 332
Ari'nobu N	233, 268, 332
Ari'nori N	234, 268, 286, 332
Arisada N	247, 268, 332
Arishige N	268, 301, 332
Ariteme F	374
Aritoki N	122, 268, 332
Ariwara U	390
Ariyasu N	208, 268, 332
Ariyo N	124, 268, 332
Ariyoshi N	268, 295, 332
Arukame F	374
Asahara S	109, 152, 315
Asahi F	125, 374
Asahi'na S	125, 294, 306, 315
Asahito N (E)	408
Asa'i S	109, 131, 315, 404
Asakura S	125, 137, 315, 404
Asa'no S	109, 152, 315, 404
Asayama S	125, 145, 315
Ashikaga S	176, 293, 315, 403
Ashi'na S	164, 203, 315
Aso S	115, 184, 315
Asobibe O	399
Aso'numa S	115, 117, 150, 315
Asou P	278
Asu F	374
Asuka P	173
Asuka'i S	131, 173, 315
Asuke S	176, 195, 315
Atagi S	135, 208, 315
Ate N (E)	407

B	Infants & Children	**F**	Female Names	**M**	Male Yobina
E	Emperors	**H**	Chinese Style Names	**N**	Male Nanori

S	Surname	**U**	Uji
Y	Era Names	**O**	Be

Ato U	390	Chiga'no'ura P	216	Chouryaku Y	111, 310, 409-410
Atoki U	390	Chiisakobe U	390	Choushou Y	111, 311, 409-410
Atsu'ari N	268, 299, 332	Chika'aki N	202-203, 332	Chousokabe S	185, 316
Atsugimi N (E)	407	Chikafusa N	133, 203, 332	Choutoku Y	111, 304, 409-410
Atsuhira N (E)	407	Chikaharu N	191, 203, 332	Chouwa Y	111, 209, 409-410
Atsuko F	142, 298, 374	Chikahide N	203, 288, 332	Chuu'ai H (E)	405
Atsumori N	222, 299, 332	Chikahira N	203, 282, 332	Chuuka P	168
Atsu'naga N (E)	407	Chikahiro N	100, 204, 332	Chuukyou H (E)	407
Atsu'naga N (E)	407	Chika'ie N	135, 204, 332		
Atsutada N	299, 332	Chikakage N	182, 204, 332	**D**	
Atsutaka N	107, 298, 332	Chikakatsu N	113, 165, 332		
Atsuyori N	245, 299, 332	Chikakiyo N	204, 283, 332	Daigo H (E)	407
Augo P	226	Chikako F	203, 240, 375	Daiji Y	101, 191, 409-410
Awata S; U	143, 166, 315; 390	Chikaku'ni N	98, 204, 332	Dai'toku'ji P	138, 304
Awataguchi S	100, 143, 166, 315	Chikamasa N	180, 189, 204, 230, 332	Date S	239, 269, 316, 404
Aya F; U	243-244, 259, 278, 374; 390	Chikamatsu S	113, 159, 316	Dohi S	153, 309, 317
Ayahito N (E)	408	Chikamitsu N	180, 204, 332	Do'i S	135, 153, 317
Ayako F	225, 374	Chikamoto N	204, 217, 310, 332	Dou'an H	208
Ayame F	99, 199, 259, 374	Chikamu'ne N	204, 226, 262, 332	Dougen H	404
Ayumime F	199, 239, 375	Chika'naga N	111, 204, 332		
Ayuteme F	115, 375	Chika'nobu N	204, 233, 332	**E**	
Azabu P	278	Chika'nori N	113, 204, 234, 286-7, 332		
Azuma F	104			Eda S	143, 151, 317
Azumame F	104, 375	Chikasue N	126, 204, 332	Edo S	133, 151, 317
Azumi U	390	Chikasuke N	194, 204, 332	Eichou Y	111, 117, 409-410
		Chikataka N	108, 204, 332	Eichuu H	235
B		Chikata'ne N	204, 206, 332	Eihou Y	117, 256, 409-410
		Chikatomo N	125, 204, 332	Eiji Y	117, 19, 409-410
Baba S	97, 172, 316	Chikatoshi N	204, 252, 332	Eijou H	235
Benkei H	404	Chikatsugu N	187, 204, 333	Eikyou Y	117, 312, 409, 411
Bessho S	97, 221, 316	Chikatsu'ne N	204, 260, 333	Eikyuu Y	117, 119, 409-410
Bidatsu H (E)	406	Chikayasu N	204, 303, 333	Eiman Y	117, 216, 409-410
Bitou S	163, 176, 316	Chikayo N	124, 204, 333	Ei'nin Y	117, 232, 409, 411
Bizen S	104, 309, 316	Chikayoshi N	204, 265, 333	Eiroku Y	117, 313, 409, 411
Boumon S	132, 141, 316	Chikayuki N	204, 237, 333	Eiryaku Y	117, 310, 409-410
Bun'an Y	208, 259, 409, 411	Chikaza'ne N	113, 168, 204, 333	Eishi F	222, 297, 375
Bunchuu Y	103, 259, 409, 411	Chikumaru B	121, 216, 272	Eishou Y	117, 291, 311, 409-411
Bun'ei Y	117, 259, 409, 411	Chime F	216, 375	Eitoku Y	117, 304, 409, 411
Bunji Y	191, 259, 409-410	Chimori U	390	Eiwa Y	117, 209, 409, 411
Bunka Y	259, 313, 409, 411	Chisato N	140, 216, 333	Ekakibe O	37, 399
Bunki Y	175, 259, 409, 411	Chitakamaru B	121	Eme F	255, 375
Bunkyuu Y	119, 259, 409, 411	Chiyo F	216, 375	Emishime F	375
Bunmei Y	179, 259, 409, 411	Chiyo'i'nu F	124, 216, 375	Enbun Y	105, 259, 409, 411
Bunna Y	209, 259, 409, 411	Chiyokumamaru B	121, 124	Endou S	113, 163, 317
Bun'ou Y	259, 311, 409, 411	Chiyorime F	216, 240, 375	En'e H	235
Bunpou Y	256, 259, 409, 411	Chiyotsurume F	199, 216, 375	Engen Y	105, 216, 409, 411
Bunroku Y	259, 313, 409, 411	Chiyo'uso N (E)	407	Enjo H	235
Bunryaku Y	259, 310, 409, 411	Chiyo'uso N (E)	407	Enkyou Y	105, 253, 312, 409, 411
Bunsei Y	189, 259, 409, 411	Chou U	391	Enkyuu Y	105, 119, 409-410
Bunshou Y	259, 291, 409, 411	Cho'u'emon M	370	En'ou Y	105, 311, 409, 411
Bun'ya S	137, 259, 316	Chougen Y	111, 216, 409-410	Enpou Y	105, 411
Bunzou S	213, 231, 316	Chouhou Y	111, 256, 409-410	Enshi F	193
Buretsu H (E)	406	Chouji Y	111	Entoku Y	105, 304, 409, 411
		Chouji Y	191, 409-410	E'nume F	229, 303, 375
C		Choukan Y	111, 311, 409-410	En'yuu H (E)	407
		Choukei H (E)	408	Enzan P	145, 273
Chako F	166, 375	Choukyou Y	111, 312, 409, 411	Era S	229, 289, 317
Chiba S	168, 216, 316	Choukyuu Y	111, 119, 409-410	Etsushi F	193
Chichibu P	271	Chouroku Y	111, 313, 409, 411		

B	Infants & Children	**F**	Female Names	**M**	Male Yobina	**S**	Surname	**U**	Uji
E	Emperors	**H**	Chinese Style Names	**N**	Male Nanori	**Y**	Era Names	**O**	Be

Name Index

F

Fuhitobe O	37, 399
Fujidou S	404
Fujifusa N	133, 163, 333
Fujigorou M	214, 370
Fujihiro N	100, 163, 333
Fuji'i S	131, 163, 317
Fujiko F	163, 375
Fujime F	163, 375
Fuji'na S	203, 245, 258, 317
Fuji'san P	145, 258
Fujiwara S; U	152, 163, 317; 391
Fujiwarabe U	391
Fujiyori N	163, 245, 333
Fukahori S	109, 243, 317
Fukuhara S	152, 231, 317
Fukumitsu S	181, 231, 317
Fukushima P; S	253; 146, 231, 317, 404
Fumi U	391
Fumitoki N	122, 259, 333
Fu'nabashi P	275
Fu'nada S	143, 275, 317
Fu'ne U	391
Furu U	391
Furuamame F	375
Furuda S	120, 143, 317
Furume F	120, 375
Furuta S	120, 143, 317
Fusa'aki N	133, 202, 333
Fusahira N	110, 133, 333
Fusahito N (E)	408
Fusakage N	134, 182, 333
Fusako F	133, 375
Fusamasa N	134, 180, 333
Fusa'nari N	134, 267, 333
Fusasaki N	104, 134, 333
Fusashige N	134, 166, 333
Fusatsugu N	134, 207, 333
Fusaza'ne N	134, 168, 333
Fushimi H (E)	408
Futaba P	213
Futagawa P	213
Futama P	213
Futami S	213
Fuyufusa N	128, 134, 333
Fuyuhira N	110, 128, 333
Fuyu'ie N	128, 135, 333
Fuyume F	128, 199, 375
Fuyumichi N	128-129, 333
Fuyu'nori N	128, 234, 333
Fuyusuke N	128, 305, 333
Fuyutsugu N	128, 207, 333
Fuyu'uji N	128, 187, 333
Fuyuyasu N	128, 303, 333

G

Gamou S	165, 268, 317, 404
Gekou Y	303, 409, 411
Genbun Y	216, 259, 409, 411
Genchuu Y	103, 216, 409, 411
Gen'ei Y	117, 216, 409-410
Gengorou M	214, 370
Genji Y	191, 216, 409, 411
Genjirou M	97, 212, 370
Genki Y	175, 216, 409, 411
Genkou Y	216, 312, 409, 411
Genkutarou M	200, 211, 215, 370
Genkyuu Y	119, 216, 409-410
Genmei H (E)	406
Genna Y	210, 216, 409, 411
Gennin Y	216, 232, 409, 411
Gen'ou Y	216, 311, 409, 411
Genroku Y	216, 313, 409, 411
Genryaku Y	217, 310, 409-410
Gensaburou M	212, 370
Genshou H (E)	406
Genta M	370
Gentoku Y	217, 304, 409, 411
Genza'emon M	105, 370
Gesan P	168
Giman H	223
Gishin H	203
Go-Daigo H (E)	408
Go-En'yuu H (E)	408
Go-Fukakusa H (E)	408
Go-Fushimi H (E)	408
Go-Ha'nazo'no H (E)	408
Go-Horikawa H (E)	408
Go-Ichijou H (E)	407
Go-Kameyama H (E)	408
Go-Kashiwabara H (E)	408
Go-Komatsu H (E)	408
Go-Kougon H (E)	408
Go-Koumyou H (E)	408
Go-Mizu'no'o H (E)	408
Go-Momozo'no H (E)	408
Go-Murakami H (E)	408
Go-Nara H (E)	408
Go-Nijou H (E)	408
Go-Reizei H (E)	407
Go-Saga H (E)	408
Go-Sai H (E)	408
Go-Sakuramachi H (E)	408
Go-Sanjou H (E)	407
Go-Shirakawa H (E)	407
Go-Suzaku H (E)	407
Go-Toba H (E)	407
Go-Tsuchimikado H (E)	408
Go-Uda H (E)	408
Go-Youzei H (E)	408
Gorou M	214, 370
Gorousa'emon M	196, 214, 370
Goshima S	146, 214, 317
Gotou S	117, 163, 317
Gou'toku'ji P	138

H

Hachirou M	215, 371
Hachisuka S	174, 245, 306, 317, 404
Hada U	391
Hagi P	164
Hagihara P	164
Hagi'no P	164
Hagiyama P	164
Hahaki U	391
Haji U	391
Hajibe O	399
Hajime F	116, 213, 375
Hajimeme F	116, 199, 375
Hakashime F	281, 375
Haki'i S	131, 149, 159, 317
Hakodate P	137, 274
Hakome F	149, 375
Hako'ne P	274
Hamame F	149, 375
Hama'nari N	149, 267, 333
Hami U	391
Hamoda S	132, 143, 177
Ha'nako F	168, 376
Ha'name F	168, 198, 376
Ha'nawa S	147, 317
Ha'nazo'no H (E)	408
Handa S	212
Ha'nebuchi S	149, 177, 317
Ha'neda S	143, 177, 317
Ha'netsume F	177, 198, 376
Ha'ni'shibe O	399
Hanshi F	193, 286, 376
Hanzei H (E)	405
Hara S	152, 317
Harada S	143, 152, 317
Harime F	198, 280, 376
Hariya S	137, 280, 317
Haru F	127, 376
Harufusa N	127, 134, 333
Haruhime F	127, 376
Haruhisa N	119, 157, 191, 333
Harukiri F	127, 158, 376
Haruko F	191, 376
Harumatsu F	127, 376
Harumichi S	127, 131, 317
Haru'naga N	111, 191, 333
Haru'nobu N	157, 233, 333, 404
Harutada N	191, 299, 333
Harutomo N	157, 280, 333
Harutoshime F	127, 376
Haruwaramaru B	121
Haruyuki N	157, 253, 333
Hasebe O; S	399; 113, 147, 185, 317
Hasegawa S	113, 147, 150, 318

B	Infants & Children
E	Emperors
F	Female Names
H	Chinese Style Names
M	Male Yobina
N	Male Nanori
S	Surname
Y	Era Names
U	Uji
O	Be

Hasekura S	137, 244, 318	Hime F	155, 197-199, 294, 309, 376	Hitomaru B	171
Hashihito U	391	Himekurome F	197, 376	Hitoshi F; M; N	220; 213; 206, 335
Hassebe N (E)	406	Himeme F	197, 199, 376	Hitoshi Naishinnou F	376
Hata S; U	99, 318; 391	Himeshirome F	197, 376	Hitsujime F	157, 173, 199, 376
Hatakeyama S	142, 145, 318	Himetarime F	294, 376	Hizume S	144, 178, 318
Hatako F	273, 376	Himewakame F	197, 376	Hokurome F	183, 199, 376
Hatakumi U	391	Hi'ne'no S	152, 155, 318	Homujibe O	399
Hatame F	149, 198, 376	Hi'noe M	219	Honda S	97, 221, 318, 404
Hata'no S	149, 152, 221, 318	Hi'nokumo no To'neri U	391	Honjou S	97, 141, 318
Hatori O	37	Hiraga S	110, 245, 318	Honma S	97, 133, 318
Hatsukashi U	391	Hira'iwa S	110, 154, 318	Hori S	243, 318, 404
Hatsusebe O	399	Hirame F	109-110, 199, 376	Horida S	404
Hatta S	143, 215, 318	Hira'no S	110, 152, 318	Horiguchi S	100, 243, 318
Hattori U; O	391; 399	Hirasaburou M	371	Horikawa H (E); S	407; 150, 243, 318
Hayakawa S	122, 150, 318	Hirata S	110, 143, 318	Hori'o S	176, 243, 318
Hayashi S; U	148, 318; 391	Hiratsuka S	110, 139, 318	Horita S	143, 243, 318
Hazukashibe U	391	Hirayama S	110, 145, 318	Hori'uchi S	103, 243, 318
Heguri U	36, 391	Hiro'aki N	100, 179, 334	Hoshi F	194, 197, 376
Hei'ankyou P	110, 142	Hirochika N	100, 240, 334	Hoshikawa U	392
Heigo M	157, 219	Hirofusa N	100, 134, 334	Hosokawa S	106, 150, 318, 404
Heiji Y	110, 191, 409-410	Hirohira N (E)	408	Hosomeme F	106, 199, 376
Heijoukyou P	110, 137	Hirohito N (E)	408	Hoteme F	376
Heisei H (E) Y;	408; 110, 267; 409, 411	Hiro'ie N	135, 266, 334	Hotta S	143, 243, 318
		Hirokado N	100, 132, 334	Hou'an Y	208, 256, 409-410
Heizei H (E)	407	Hirokatamaru B	121	Hou'ei Y	117, 256, 409, 411
Hi U	391	Hiroko F	220, 297, 376	Hou'en Y	105, 256, 409-410
Hidaka N (E)	406	Hirokoto N	100, 260, 334	Hougen Y	217, 256, 409-410
Hide'aki N	127, 262, 288, 297, 334	Hiromasa N	230, 266, 334	Houji Y	191, 256, 409, 411
Hidehira N	282, 288, 334	Hiromoto N	100, 217, 334	Houjou S	105, 189
Hidehito N (E)	408	Hirosada N	100, 247, 334	Houjou S	318, 404
Hide'ie N	135, 288, 334	Hirosasamaru B	121	Houreki Y	272, 310, 409, 411
Hidekatsu N	404	Hiroshige N	106, 167, 334	Houshi H	235
Hidekazu N	213, 288, 334	Hirotoki N	404	Houtoku Y	272, 304, 409, 411
Hidekiyo N	283, 288, 334	Hirotoshi N	220, 293, 334	Hozumi U	392
Hideko F	288, 297, 376	Hirotsugu N	100, 207, 334		
Hidemasa N	189, 288, 334, 404	Hirotsu'na N	100, 276, 334	**I**	
Hidemochi N	254, 288, 334	Hirotsu'ne N	100, 118, 334		
Hidemoto N	167, 217, 288, 334	Hiroyo N	106, 124, 334	Ibe O	400
Hide'naga N	117, 288, 334	Hirozumi N	100, 284, 334	Ichi F	142, 377
Hidesato N	140, 288, 334	Hisa'aki S	403	Ichi'i U	392
Hidetada N	288, 299, 334, 403	Hisada S	119, 143, 318	Ichijou H (E); S	407; 189, 212, 318
Hideta'ne N	206, 288, 334	Hisahide N	119, 288, 297, 334, 404	Ichikawa S	142, 151, 318
Hidetoki N	122, 297, 334	Hisahito N (E)	408	Ichimonji S	213, 259-260, 318
Hidetomo N	125, 288, 334	Hisaka'ne N	119, 205, 334	Ichi'no'i S	131, 213, 318
Hidetsugu N	218, 288, 334	Hisako F	120, 231, 376	Ichirou M	211-213
Hidetsu'na N	276, 288, 334	Hisako Naishinnou F	376	Ida S	131, 143, 318
Hide'uji N	187, 288, 334	Hisaku'ni N	98, 119, 334	Iefusa N	134-135, 335
Hideyasu N	288, 303, 334	Hisame F	155, 199, 376	Ieharu N	403
Hideyoshi N	232, 265, 288, 295, 334, 403	Hisa'naga N	111, 119, 334	Iehide N	135, 222, 335
		Hisa'nobu N	119, 233, 334	Iehira N	110, 135, 335
Hideyuki N	237, 288, 334	Hisa'nori N	231, 253, 334	Iekage N	135, 102, 335
Higashiyama H (E)	408	Hisatoki N	119, 122, 334	Ieka'ne N	135, 205, 335
Higuchi S	100, 144, 318	Hisatoyo N	119, 231, 334	Iekata N	135, 264, 335
Hikaru N	180, 334	Hisatsume F	199, 294, 376	Iemasa N	135, 190, 335
Hiki S	254, 294, 318	Hisatsu'na N	119, 276, 294, 334	Iemichi N	129, 135, 335
Hikohito N (E)	408	Hisatsu'ne N	119, 260, 335	Iemitsu N	135, 180, 335, 403
Hikome F	198, 294, 376	Hisa'uji F; N	231, 376; 187, 231, 335	Iemochi N	403
Hikosaburou M	200, 212, 371	Hisayoshi N	119, 216, 231, 295, 335	Iemoto N	135, 139, 335
Hikoyoshi N	200, 289, 334	Hishimame F	155, 376	Ie'naga N	111, 117, 135, 335

B	Infants & Children	F	Female Names	M	Male Yobina	S	Surname	U	Uji
E	Emperors	H	Chinese Style Names	N	Male Nanori	Y	Era Names	O	Be

Ie'nari N	135, 267, 335, 403	I'nukami U	392	Jinguu H (E)	405
Ie'nobu N	403	I'nuko F	377	Jin'ichi M	220
Ie'nori N	135, 234, 335	I'nume F	173, 377	Jinkurou M	215, 310, 371
Iesada N	135, 247, 292, 335, 403	I'nuwaka F	173, 377	Jinmu H (E)	405
Ieshige N	403	I'nuyama P	173	Jirou M	211-212, 371
Ietada N	135, 299, 335	Ioki'be O	400, 392	Jirouhoujimaru B	121, 235
Ietaka N	107-108, 135, 335	Irimashime F	100, 249, 377	Jiryaku Y	191, 310, 409-410
Ietoki N	122, 135, 335	Irobe S	183, 185, 319	Jishou Y	191, 311, 409-410
Ietoyo N	135, 231, 335	Isakome F	185, 377	Jitou H (E)	406
Ietsugu N	135, 187, 207, 335, 403	Isaku S	243, 269, 319	Jizoumae F	99, 377
Ietsu'na N	403	Isame F	302, 377	Jizoume F	99, 377
Ietsu'ne N	118, 135-136, 260, 335	Isawa S	150, 269, 319	Jogorou M	214, 371
Ietsura N	136, 239, 335	Ise F; S	269, 377; 235, 269, 319	Jou'an Y	208, 311, 409-410
Ie'uji N	136, 187, 335	Isebe O	400	Jou'ei Y	117, 292, 409, 411
Ieyasu N	136, 209, 303, 335, 403	Ishi F	153, 377	Jou'etsu P	294
Ieyoshi N	136, 289, 295, 335, 403	Ishibashi S	144, 153, 319	Jougen Y	217, 313, 409-410
Ieyuki N	136, 237, 335	Ishida S	143, 153, 319, 404	Jouhou Y	256, 311, 409-410
Ieza'ne N	136, 168, 335	Ishidou S	139, 153, 319	Jou'ichi H	137
Iezumi N	136, 285, 335	Ishi'i S	131, 153, 319	Jouji Y	191, 292, 409, 411
Iga S; U	245, 269, 318; 392	Ishikawa S; U	150, 153, 319; 392	Joukyou Y	292, 312, 409, 411
Iga no Ouji N (E)	406	Ishime F	153, 377	Joukyuu Y	119, 313 409-410
Iha F	154, 377	Ishizaki S	146, 153, 319	Joumei H (E)	406
Ihamime F	153, 176, 199, 377	Isobe O	37, 400	Jou'ou Y	292, 311, 313, 409, 411
Ihohara S	153, 164, 318	Isogamime F	214-215, 377	Jouryaku Y	310-311, 409-410
Ihosume F	113, 199, 214, 377	Isoko F	242, 377	Joutoku Y	304, 311, 409-410
I'i S	131, 269, 274, 318-319, 404	Iso'no'kamibe U	392	Jouwa Y	210, 292, 409, 411
Iida S	143, 274, 319	Isshiki S	183, 213, 319	Ju'ei Y	117, 120, 409-410
Ii'no S	152, 274, 319	Itagaki S	132, 274, 319	Junna H (E)	407
Ijuu'in S	139, 186, 269, 319	Iteme F	131, 377	Junnin H (E)	406
Ike S	149, 319	Ito F	275, 377	Juntoku H (E)	407
Ikeda S; U	143, 149, 319, 404, 392	Itobe O	400	Juubutsu H	215, 228
Ikeko F	149, 377	Itoda S	143, 275, 319	Juurou M	215, 371
Iki U	392	Ito'ito F	275, 377		
Ikoma S	172, 268, 319	Itoku H (E)	405	**K**	
Ikuheme F	199, 269, 377	Itome F	269, 281, 377		
Ima F	122, 377	Itou S	104, 163, 269, 319	Kachiko F	257, 377
Imagawa S	122, 150, 319	Itsu'i F	214, 310, 377	Kadobe O; U	400; 392
Ima'i S	122, 131, 319	Itsu'itsu F	214	Ka'ei Y	117, 285, 409, 411
Imakawa S	122, 150, 319	Itsu'itsu F	377	Kafuchi U	392
Imako F	122, 377	Itsukushi U	392	Kafuchi no Aya U	392
Ima'nishi S	104, 122, 319	Ittetsu N	404	Kafuchi no Umakai U	392
Ima'oka S	122, 147, 319	Iwa F	154, 377	Kaga'i S	131, 186, 245, 319
Imibe U	392	Iwamatsu S	154, 159, 319	Kagami S	186, 227, 245, 275, 319
Imube O	400	Iwami N; S	129; 153, 319	Kagami Tsukuri U	392
I'na U	392	Iwarebe O	400	Kagechika N	182, 204, 335
I'naba S	165, 168, 319, 404	Iwase S	151, 154, 319	Kageharu N	127, 182, 335
I'nabe O	400	Iwate P	176	Kagehira N	110, 182, 335
I'nage S	165, 177, 319	Iwatsurume F	154, 377	Kagehiro N	106, 182, 335
I'nako F	165, 377	Iwokome F	175, 377	Kagehisa N	119, 182, 335
I'name F	165, 377	Iwome F	175, 377	Kage'ie N	136, 182, 335
Inbe O; U	400; 36	Iyahito N (E)	408	Kagekado N	182, 290, 336
Ingyou H (E)	405	Izumi S	152, 319	Kagekatsu N	182, 257, 336
I'nishi F	203, 270	Izumisaburou M	371	Kagekazu N	182, 203, 336
I'nishime F	269, 377	Izumo U	392	Kagekiyo N	182, 283, 336
I'noha'na P	172, 176			Kagemasa N	182, 291, 336
I'no'o S	176, 274, 319	**J**		Kagemasu N	182, 221, 336
I'nu F	173, 377			Kagemitsu N	180, 182, 336
I'nuhara S	153, 173, 319	Ji'an Y	191, 208, 409-410	Kagemochi N	166, 182, 336
I'nukaibe O	400	Jihei M	213	Kagemori N	182, 222, 336

B	Infants & Children	F	Female Names	M	Male Yobina	S	Surname	U	Uji
E	Emperors	H	Chinese Style Names	N	Male Nanori	Y	Era Names	O	Be

Kagemoto N	404	Ka'ne'aki N	127, 205, 336	Kansei Y	189, 311, 409, 411
Kagemu'ne N	182, 262, 336	Ka'ne'atsu N	205, 299, 336	Kanshou Y	291, 311, 409, 411
Kagen Y	217, 285, 409, 411	Ka'nechika N	204-205, 336	Kantoku Y	304, 311, 409-410
Kage'naga N	111, 182, 336	Ka'nefumi N	205, 259, 336	Ka'nuchibe O	37
Kage'naka N	182, 217, 336	Ka'nefusa N	134, 205, 336		
Kage'nobu N	182, 233, 336	Ka'negimimaru B	121	Kaorime F	273, 378
Kageshige N	166, 182, 336	Ka'nehira N	110, 205, 282, 336	Ka'ou Y	409-410
Kagesue N	126, 182, 336	Kan'ei Y	117, 311, 409, 411	Karatan'uchibe O	400
Kagesuke N	182, 305, 336	Ka'ne'ie N	136, 205, 336	Karime F	186, 378
Kagetada N	182, 299, 336	Ka'nekata N	114, 205, 336	Karoku Y	285, 313, 409, 411
Kagetaka N	107-108, 182, 336	Ka'neko F; S	132, 205, 378; 197, 271, 320, 378	Karu N (E)	406
Kagetoki N	122, 182, 336			Karu no Ouji N (E)	406
Kagetomo N	125, 182, 336	Ka'neku'ni N	99, 205, 336	Karube O; U	400; 392
Kagetora N	171, 182, 336	Ka'nemasa N	180, 205, 230, 336	Karuizawa P	226
Kagetsugu N	182, 187, 336	Ka'neme F	378	Karyaku Y	285, 310, 410-411
Kagetsu'na N	182, 276, 336	Ka'nemichi N	129, 205, 336	Kasa U	392
Kagetsu'ne N	118, 182, 260, 336	Ka'nemitsu N	180, 205, 336	Kasai S	104, 165, 320
Kageyasu N	182, 209, 336	Ka'nemori N	205, 222, 336	Kasawara S	153, 273, 320
Kageyori N	182, 245, 336	Ka'nemoto N	139, 205, 217, 336	Kashima S	146, 173, 320
Kageyoshi N	182, 295, 336	Ka'nemu'ne N	205, 262, 336	Kashiwade U	392
Kagoshima P	146, 173, 200	Kan'en Y	105, 311, 409, 411	Kashiwadebe O	15, 37, 400
Kahime F	186, 377	Ka'ne'naga N	118, 205, 309, 336	Kashou Y	285, 311, 410
Kahou Y	256, 285, 409-410	Ka'ne'naka N	205, 217, 336	Kasuga S	127, 155, 320
Kai S	219, 227, 319	Ka'ne'nari N (E)	407	Kasugabe O	400
Kaika H (E)	405	Ka'ne'nobu N	205, 233, 250, 336, 404	Kasugame F	127, 378
Kaitou S	104, 148, 319	Ka'ne'nori N	205, 234, 336	Katagiri S	162, 212, 320
Kaji S	99, 186, 319	Ka'nera N	205, 289, 336	Kata'ie N	136, 212, 337
Kajime F	186, 309, 377	Ka'neshige N	205, 301, 336	Kata'oka S	147, 212, 320
Kajiwara S	153, 275, 319	Ka'nesue N	126, 205, 336	Katari U	392
Kakame F	186, 377	Ka'nesuke N	194, 205, 337	Kataribe O	400
Kakei Y	253, 285, 409, 411	Ka'netada N	205, 299, 337	Katata S	143, 299, 320
Kakimoto S	97, 161, 319	Ka'netaka N	108, 205, 337	Katei Y	285, 314, 410-411
Kaki'nomoto U	392	Ka'neta'ne N	205-206, 337	Katou S	104, 163, 186, 320, 404
Kakitsu Y	232, 285, 409, 411	Ka'netoki N	122, 206, 337	Katsuhiko M	200, 219
Kakukai H	235, 253, 309	Ka'netomo N	125, 186, 206, 337	Katsuhisa N	119, 257, 337
Kamata P; S	165; 143, 281, 319	Ka'netou N	206, 242, 337	Katsuhito N (E)	408
Kamatari N	176, 281, 336, 391	Ka'netsugu N	206-207, 298, 337	Katsu'ie N	136, 257, 337, 404
Kame F	175, 377	Ka'netsu'na N	206, 276, 337	Katsumasa N	257, 291, 337
Kame'i S	131, 175, 319	Ka'netsu'ne N	206, 260, 337	Katsumitsu N	180, 257, 337
Kamematsu F	175, 377	Ka'netsura N	206, 239, 337	Katsumoto N	217, 257, 305, 337
Kametsuru F	175, 378	Ka'ne'uji N	188, 206, 337	Katsu'naga N	118, 257, 337
Kamewakamaru B	120-121	Ka'neyama P	271	Katsuragawa P	161
Kameyama H (E)	408	Ka'neyasu N	206, 303, 337	Katsutoshi N	252, 257, 337
Kameyama S	145, 175, 319	Ka'neyo N	124, 206, 337	Katsutoyo N	231, 257, 337, 404
Kameyo F	175, 378	Ka'neyori N	206, 245, 337	Katsuuji N	404
Kamime F	273, 378	Ka'neyoshi N	206, 255, 337	Katsuyori N	245, 257, 337
Kami'no N (E)	407	Ka'neza'ne N	168, 206, 337	Katsuyoshi N	257, 285, 337
Kami'no N (E)	407	Ka'nezawa S	150, 271, 320	Kawabe O	400
Kamitsuke'no U	392	Kangen Y	217, 311, 409, 411	Kawabitobe O	400
Kamiya S	147, 228, 319	Ka'nimori U	392	Kawachi S	103, 151, 320
Kamiyama S	102, 145, 319	Kanji Y	191, 311, 409-410	Kawachi'nofumi U	392
Kamo U	392	Kanki Y	254, 311, 409, 411	Kawagoe S	151, 294, 320
Kamuhatori U	392	Kankou Y	106, 311, 409-410	Kawahe U	392
Kamu'nakibe U	392	Kanmu H (E)	407	Kawahide N	264, 288, 337
Ka'namori S	148, 271, 319	Kannagibe O	400	Kawakamibe O	400
Ka'naya S	147, 271, 319	Kannin Y	232, 311, 409-410	Kawakatsu S	150, 257, 320
Ka'nazawa S	150, 271, 319	Kannon F	250, 378	Kawamura S	141, 151, 320
Kanbun Y	259, 311, 409, 411	Kan'ou Y	250, 311, 409, 411	Kawa'no S	151-152, 320
Kanda P	228	Kanpou Y	256, 311, 409, 411	Kawa'nobe O	400

B	Infants & Children	F	Female Names	M	Male Yobina	S	Surname	U	Uji
E	Emperors	H	Chinese Style Names	N	Male Nanori	Y	Era Names	O	Be

Name Index   443

Name	Pages	Name	Pages	Name	Pages
Kawara S	151, 153, 320	Kin'aki N	179, 192, 337	Kiyoko Jo'ou F	378
Kawase U	392	Kin'ari N	192, 268, 337	Kiyoko F	283, 378
Kawashima S	146, 151, 320	Kinchika N	192, 204, 337	Kiyoku'ni N	99, 283, 338
Kawashiri S	150, 178, 320	Ki'ne'o M	219	Kiyoma N	404
Kawa'uchihara S	103, 151, 153, 320	Ki'neko F	378	Kiyomasa N	283, 291, 338
Kazan H (E)	407	Kinfusa N	134, 192, 337	Kiyomitsu N	180, 283, 338
Kazuhito N (E)	408	Kinfuyu N	128, 192, 337	Kiyomizudera P	284
Kazuko F	203, 210, 307, 378	Kinhide N	192, 288, 337	Kiyomori N	222, 283, 338, 403
Kazumasa N	180, 203, 337	Kinhira N	192, 282, 337	Kiyomu'ne N	262, 283, 338
Kazu'nari M	213, 310	Kinkata N	192, 264, 337	Kiyo'naga N	111, 283, 338
Kazura U	392	Kinkiyo N	192, 283, 337	Kiyo'nari N	283, 298, 338
Kazuraki U	36, 392	Kinmasa N	192, 230, 337	Kiyo'nori N	234, 283, 338
Kazuraki no Ouji N (E)	406	Kinmei H (E)	406	Kiyosada N	247, 283, 292, 338
Kazurakibe O	400	Kinmichi N	129, 192, 338	Kiyoshige N	268, 283, 301, 338
Kazusa S	102, 278, 320	Kinmitsu N	180, 192, 338	Kiyosuke N	194, 283, 338
Kazushige N	213, 301, 337	Kinmori N	192-193, 338	Kiyotada N	283, 299, 338
Kazutada N	213, 241, 337	Kinmoto N	139, 192, 338	Kiyotaka N	107, 283, 338
Kazutoyo N	213, 231, 337	Kinmu'ne N	192, 262, 338	Kiyota'ne N	170, 206, 283, 338
Kazu'uji N	188, 210, 337	Kinnaga N	111, 192, 338	Kiyotoki N	122, 283, 338
Kazuyoshi N	210, 295, 337	Kinnao N	192, 241, 338	Kiyotomo N	192, 283, 338
Kehi S	229, 294, 320	Kinnori N	192, 234, 338	Kiyotsu'na N	276, 283, 338
Kei'an Y	208, 253, 410-411	Kin'o N	192, 303, 338	Kiyotsu'ne N	260, 283, 338
Keichou Y	111, 253, 410-411	Ki no Sakahito U	393	Kiyo'uji N	188, 283, 338
Keikou H (E)	405	Ki'noshita S	103, 159, 320	Kiyoyuki N	237, 283, 338
Kei'ou Y	253, 311, 410-411	Kinsada N	192, 247, 338	Kobayakawa S	102, 150, 321
Keitai H (E)	406	Kinshige N	167, 192, 338	Kobe U	393
Kenchou Y	111, 312, 410-411	Kinsue N	126, 192, 338	Kodamame F	102, 378
Ken'ei Y	117, 312, 410	Kinsuke N	186, 192, 338	Kohime F	120, 378
Kengen Y	217, 312, 410-411	Kintada N	192, 299, 338	Ko'imome F	102, 378
Kenji Y	191, 312, 410-411	Kintoki N	122, 192, 338	Ko'i'name F	102, 378
Kenkyuu Y	119, 312, 410	Kintoshi N	192, 252, 338	Kojima S	146, 200, 321
Kenmotsu S	250, 271, 320	Kintsugu N	187, 192, 338	Kojimame F	102, 378
Kenmu Y	257, 312, 410-411	Kintsu'na N	192, 276, 338	Kojirou M	212, 404
Kennin Y	232, 312, 410	Kintsu'ne N	192, 260, 338	Kokasahara S	102, 153
Kenpou Y	256, 312, 410	Kintsura N	192, 239, 338	Kokubu S	98, 212, 264, 321
Kenryaku Y	310, 312, 410	Ki'nu F	278, 378	Kokurome F	102, 378
Kentarou M	211, 243	Ki'nume F	265, 279, 303, 378	Koma F	172, 378
Kentoku Y	304, 312, 410-411	Ki'numurame F	378	Komame F	120, 172, 378
Ke'nu U	393	Ki'nu'nui	393	Kondou S	113, 163, 321
Kenzou H (E)	406	Ki'nu'nuhime F	244, 279, 378	Ko'ne'neme F	102
Kesame F	194, 378	Ki'nu'nui O; U	400; 393	Ko'ne'neme F	378
Kesatsurumaru B	121	Ki'nu'nui be O	37	Ko'nishi S	102, 104, 321
Ki U	393	Kin'yasu N	192, 256, 338	Ko'noe H (E)	407
Kibi U	393	Kin'yuki N	192, 237, 338	Korechika N	204, 240, 269-270, 339
Kido S	133, 159, 320	Kira S	232, 289, 320	Korefusa N	134, 269, 339
Kifumi U	393	Kirishima P	158	Korehira N	110, 275, 282, 339
Kikkawa S	150, 232, 320, 404	Kishibe O	400	Korehisa N	119, 269-270, 339
Kiku F	164, 378	Kishi'ta S; U	143, 149, 320; 393	Korehito N (E)	407
Kikuchi S	149, 164, 320	Kiso S	117, 159, 320	Korekata N	114, 270, 339
Kikumatsu F	164, 378	Kisoi N	294, 338	Koremasa N	190, 270, 291, 339
Kikume F	164, 378	Kita F; S	105, 378; 143, 159, 320	Koremichi N	131, 275, 339
Kikusui S	148, 164, 320	Kitabatake S	105, 142, 320	Koremochi N	166, 275, 339
Kimimichi N	129, 192, 337	Kitsume F	161, 378	Koremori N	222, 275, 339
Kimi'nari N	192, 298, 337	Kiyofusa N	134, 283, 338	Koremu'ne U	393
Kimitomo N	125, 192, 337	Kiyohara S; U	153, 284, 320; 393	Koremura N	141, 270, 339
Kimorime F	219, 378	Kiyohide N	283, 288, 338, 404	Kore'nao N	241, 270, 339
Kimoto S	97, 159, 320	Kiyohira N	110, 282-283, 338	Kore'nobu N	233, 270, 339
Kimotsuki S	242, 303, 320	Kiyoi F	284, 378	Kore'nori N	269, 287, 339
Kimura S	141, 159, 320	Kiyokata N	114, 283, 338	Koresada N	275, 292, 339

B	Infants & Children	F	Female Names	M	Male Yobina	S	Surname	U	Uji
E	Emperors	H	Chinese Style Names	N	Male Nanori	Y	Era Names	O	Be

Koresato N	140, 270, 339	
Koreshige N	270, 301, 339	
Koretada N	269, 299, 339	
Koretaka N	108, 270, 302, 339	
Koretake N	257, 270, 339	
Koretoki N	122, 270, 339	
Koretsugu N	187, 270, 339	
Koreyasu S	403	
Koreyoshi N	247, 265, 269-270, 295, 339	
Korezumi N	270, 284, 339	
Kosasa F	102, 163, 379	
Kose U	393	
Koshirou M	371	
Kosoko F	117, 221, 379	
Kotame F	120, 379	
Kotaroume F	379	
Kotau N	245, 339	
Kotekome F	120, 379	
Kotohira P	271	
Kotohito N (E)	408	
Koto'oka P	147, 271	
Kotori F	102, 379	
Kotsume F	120, 379	
Kou U	393	
Kou'an H (E); Y	405; 106, 208, 303, 410-411	
Koubun H (E)	406	
Ko'uchi S	103, 151, 321	
Kouchou Y	106, 111, 410-411	
Kou'ei Y	117, 303, 410-411	
Kougen H (E); Y	405; 217, 303, 410-411	
Kougon H (E)	408	
Kougyoku H (E)	406	
Kouhei Y	110, 303, 410	
Kouji Y	191, 303, 106, 410-411	
Koujirou M	219	
Kouka Y	106, 313, 410-411	
Koukaku H (E)	408	
Kouken H (E)	406	
Koukoku Y	98, 116, 410-411	
Koukou H (E)	407	
Koumei H (E)	408	
Koumyou H (E)	408	
Kou'nin H (E)	407	
Kou'no S	151-152, 321	
Kou'ou Y	303, 311, 410-411	
Kourei H (E)	405	
Kouryaku Y	303, 311, 410-411	
Kousa H	180, 195	
Kousaka S	107, 129, 321	
Koushou H (E); Y	405; 291, 303, 410-411	
Koutoku H (E)	406	
Koutou S	104, 106, 321	
Kouwa Y	106, 210, 303, 410-411	
Kouzai S	104, 273, 321	
Koyakatoyome F	102, 379	
Koyama S	102, 145, 321
Kozukuri S	159, 244, 321
Kubome F	272, 379
Kubutsu H	228, 215
Kudara U	393
Kudou S	163, 280, 321
Kuga S	119, 187, 321
Kuge S	103, 119, 321
Kuhime F	249, 379
Kujirako F	175, 379
Kujou S	189, 215, 321, 403
Kuki S	404
Kumagai S	147, 172, 321
Kumagaya S	147, 172, 321
Kumako Jo'ou F	379
Kume U	393
Kumoko F	158, 379
Kumome F	158, 379
Ku'niharu N (E)	408
Ku'nihira N	98, 110, 282, 339
Ku'nihito N (E)	408
Ku'nika N	98, 273, 339
Ku'nikiyo N	98, 283, 339
Ku'niko F	98, 142, 379
Ku'nime F	119, 280, 379
Ku'nimichi N	99, 129, 131, 339
Ku'nimitsu N	99, 180, 339
Ku'nimoto N	98, 139, 339
Ku'ni'naga N	98, 111, 339
Ku'ni'nari N	99, 298, 339
Ku'ni'nobu N	98, 233, 339
Ku'nishige N	98, 301, 339
Ku'nitoki N	99, 122, 339
Ku'nitsu'na N	98-99, 276, 339
Ku'niyasu N	98, 209, 340
Ku'ou N	285, 311
Kura U	393
Kura no Ki'nu'nui U	393
Kurame F	161, 379
Kurateme F	161, 176, 379
Kuratsukuribe O	37, 400
Kure F	126, 379
Kuri F	161, 379
Kuriya F	379
Kuriyako F	133
Kuriyame F	133, 379
Kuroda S	143, 183, 321, 404
Kuroko F	183, 379
Kurome F	183, 379
Kurou M	215, 371
Kurukuma U	393
Kurumochi U	393
Kurushima S	146, 309, 321
Kusakabe O; U	400; 393
Kusa'no S	152, 165, 321
Kusome F	119, 379
Kusuko F	273, 379
Kusu'noki S	159, 162, 321
Kusuri'no'ue F	379
Kutarou M	211, 371
Kutsuki S	159, 307, 321
Kutsu'na S	120, 308, 321
Kuuju Y	120
Kuwahara U	393
Kuwayama S	145, 162, 321
Kuzuko F	379
Kuzurahara S	153, 165, 321
Kyougoku S	142, 307, 321
Kyouhou Y	256, 312, 410-411
Kyoujirou M	211
Kyouko N (E)	408
Kyouroku Y	304, 312-313, 410-411
Kyouwa Y	210, 312, 410-411
Kyuu'an Y	119, 208, 410
Kyuuju Y	119, 410
Kyuushi F	193
Kyuuzou N	119, 138, 340

M

Ma F	165, 379
Machime F	141, 379
Maeba S	104, 149, 321
Maeda S	104, 143, 321, 404
Maeme F	165, 379
Magari no Hakozukuri U	393
Mahisamaru B	121
Makabe S	133, 290, 321
Makayame F	165, 379
Maki S	153, 321
Makime F	153, 379
Maki'nokata F	114, 153, 379
Makoto N	233, 340
Makuta S	143, 243, 321
Mama F	379
Mamime F	172, 176, 379
Mamuta U	393
Man'en Y	105, 216, 410-411
Manji Y	191, 216, 410-411
Manju Y	120, 216, 410
Manme F	216, 379
Mari F	271, 379
Marime F	165, 379
Masa'ari N	230, 268, 340
Masachika N	190, 204, 230, 340
Masafusa N	134, 293, 340
Masahide N	288, 291, 340
Masahime F	197, 291, 379
Masahira N	110, 190, 282, 291, 340
Masahiro N	106, 190, 340
Masa'ie N	136, 180, 190, 230, 291, 340
Masakado N	132, 194, 340
Masakage N	180, 182, 340
Masakata N	230, 264, 340
Masakatsu N	257, 291, 340, 404
Masakiyo N	190, 230, 283-284, 291, 340

B	Infants & Children	F	Female Names	M	Male Yobina	S	Surname	U Uji
E	Emperors	H	Chinese Style Names	N	Male Nanori	Y	Era Names	O Be

Name Index 445

Masako F	189, 230, 264, 291, 379	
Masaku'ni N	98, 190, 340	
Masami M	219	
Masamichi N	129, 230, 340	
Masamitsu N	180, 190, 340	
Masamori N	180, 222, 291, 340, 404	
Masamoto N	139, 167, 190, 217, 340	
Masamu'ne N	190, 262, 340, 404	
Masamura N	141, 190, 340, 404	
Masa'na N	404	
Masa'naga N	111, 190, 230, 340, 340	
Masa'nari N	180, 267, 291	
Masa'nobu N	180, 233, 291, 340	
Masa'nori N	190-11, 216, 287, 291, 340, 404	
Masara N (E)	407	
Masaru F	221, 380	
Masasada N	230, 247, 340	
Masashige N	167, 190, 268, 291, 340	
Masasue N	126, 291, 340	
Masasuke N	190, 195, 229-230, 340-341	
Masatada N	230, 291, 300, 341	
Masataka N	107-108, 190, 230, 341	
Masatake N	257, 291, 341	
Masata'ne N	170, 180, 206, 290, 341	
Masatoki N	122, 291, 341	
Masatomo N	190, 265, 280, 341	
Masatoo N	113, 291, 341	
Masatora N	171, 291, 341	
Masatoyo N	180, 190, 231, 341	
Masatsugu M; N	372; 180, 190, 207, 218, 291, 341	
Masatsuguko F	212	
Masatsu'na N	190, 230, 276, 291, 341	
Masatsu'ne N	190, 230, 260-261, 341	
Masatsura N	237, 291, 341	
Masa'uji N	188, 190, 230, 291, 341	
Masayasu N	190, 209, 291, 303, 341	
Masayo N	124, 230, 341	
Masayori N	245, 291, 341	
Masayoshi N	180, 190, 265, 295, 341	
Masayuki N	180, 190, 230, 237-238, 253, 291, 341	
Masaza'ne N	168, 230, 341	
Masazumi N	285, 291	
Mashime F	165, 380	
Masuda S	143, 221-222, 321	
Masuharu N	191	
Masuyuki N	221, 238, 341	
Matajirou M	212, 218, 372	
Matashirou M	372	
Matatarou M	211, 372	
Matatsuguko F	380	
Mateme F	172, 380	
Matsu F	159, 380	
Matsuda S	143, 159, 321	
Matsudaira S	110, 159, 322, 404	
Matsugimimaru B	121	
Matsu'i S	131, 159, 322	
Matsumaru B	121	
Matsume F	159, 380	
Matsumoto S	97, 160, 322	
Matsu'naga S	118, 160, 322, 404	
Matsu'nomae F	380	
Matsura S	404	
Matsushita S	103, 160, 322	
Matsu'ura S	149, 160, 322	
Mawayame F	165, 380	
Mega S	177, 245, 322	
Mehirume F	273, 380	
Meiji H (E); Y	408; 179, 191, 410-411	
Mei'ou Y	179, 311, 410-411	
Meireki Y	179, 310, 410-411	
Meishou H (E)	H (E) 408	
Meitoku Y	179, 304, 410-411	
Meiwa Y	179, 210, 410-411	
Mekusuwau F	380	
Meme F	199, 380	
Mememe F	177, 273, 380	
Mezurame F	177, 380	
Mibube O	400	
Michi U	394	
Michi'aki N	129, 179, 202, 341	
Michi'ari N	129, 268, 341	
Michi'atsu N	129, 298, 341	
Michichika N	129, 204, 341	
Michifuyu N	128-129, 341	
Michiga'ne N	131, 206, 341	
Michiharu N	127, 129-130, 191, 342-343	
Michihide N	130, 288, 342	
Michihira N	110, 131, 342	
Michihiro N	130, 266, 342	
Michihisa N	119, 130, 342	
Michi'ie N	131, 136, 342	
Michikata N	114, 130, 342	
Michikiyo N	130, 284, 342	
Michimasa N	131, 190, 230, 342	
Michimasu N	130, 222, 342	
Michime F	131, 380	
Michimitsu N	130, 180, 342	
Michimori N	130, 193, 222, 342	
Michi'naga N	111, 131, 289, 342	
Michi'nao N	130, 241, 342	
Michi'nari N	130, 267, 342	
Michi'nobu N	130-131, 233, 342	
Michi'nori N	131-130, 234, 286, 342	
Michi'o N	130, 303, 342	
Michisada N	130, 292, 342	
Michishige N	130, 301, 342	
Michisuke N	130, 186, 305, 342	
Michitada N	130, 300, 342	
Michitaka N	108, 130-131, 225, 342	
Michita'ne N	130, 170, 342	
Michitoki N	122, 130-131, 156, 260, 342	
Michitomo N	125, 130, 280, 342	
Michitoshi N	130, 252, 342	
Michitou N	130, 242, 342	
Michitsugu N	130-131, 187, 207, 342	
Michitsu'na N	131, 276, 342	
Michitsu'ne N	130-131, 261, 342	
Michi'uji N	130, 188, 342	
Michiyasu N (E)	407	
Michiyori N	130, 245, 342	
Michiyoshi N	130, 265, 342	
Michiyuki N	130, 237-238, 342	
Michiza'ne N	131, 290, 342	
Midori F	380	
Mifu S	220, 268, 322	
Mihime F	201, 380	
Mihito N (E)	408	
Mikeshi F	201	
Mikeshime F	380	
Miki S	159, 213, 322	
Mikime F	380	
Miku'ni U	394	
Mime F	176, 380, 254	
Mimi F	380	
Mimime F	201, 380	
Mi'nabe O	400	
Mi'nakawa S	150, 185, 322	
Mi'namime F	105, 380	
Mi'namoto S; U	97, 322, 403; 394	
Mi'nazuki F	214, 380	
Mi'no U	394	
Mi'no no Yatsume U	394	
Mi'nome F	380	
Misumi S	114, 213, 322	
Mitaka P	174, 213	
Mito S	133, 213, 322	
Mitomime F	201, 380	
Mitoshime F	124, 214, 380	
Mitsu F	225, 380	
Mitsu'aki N	223, 262, 342	
Mitsuchika N	180, 204, 223, 342	
Mitsufuji N	163, 223, 342	
Mitsuhide N	180, 223, 288, 342, 404	
Mitsuhiko N	180, 294, 219,v342	
Mitsuhito N (E)	408	
Mitsu'ie N	136, 180, 223, 343	
Mitsuka'ne N	206, 223, 343	
Mitsukazu N	180, 203, 343	
Mitsuko F	180, 380	
Mitsuku'ni N	98, 180, 343	
Mitsumasa N	180, 190, 223, 230, 292, 306, 343	
Mitsumori N	180, 222, 343	
Mitsumoto N	217, 223, 343	
Mitsumu'ne N	180, 262, 343	
Mitsumura N	141, 180, 343	
Mitsu'naga N	111, 181, 343	
Mitsu'naka N	217, 224, 343	
Mitsu'nao N	224, 241, 343

B	Infants & Children	F	Female Names	M	Male Yobina	S	Surname	U	Uji
E	Emperors	H	Chinese Style Names	N	Male Nanori	Y	Era Names	O	Be

Mitsu'nari N	181, 213, 224, 267, 343, 404	
Mitsu'nobu N	181, 233, 343	
Mitsu'nori N	181, 224, 234, 254, 286-7, 343	
Mitsu'nyo F	199, 380	
Mitsusada N	181, 224, 247, 292, 343	
Mitsusato N	140, 181, 343	
Mitsushige N	167, 181, 224, 301, 343	
Mitsusue N	126, 181, 224, 343	
Mitsusuke N	224, 229, 343	
Mitsutada N	224, 241, 343	
Mitsutaka N	107-108, 224, 343	
Mitsuta'ne N	181, 206-207, 224, 343	
Mitsutoki N	122, 181, 343	
Mitsutomo N	125, 224, 343	
Mitsutsugu N	181, 187, 343	
Mitsutsu'na N	224, 276, 343	
Mitsutsu'ne N	181, 224, 261, 343	
Mitsu'uji N	188, 224, 343	
Mitsuwaka B	120	
Mitsuyasu N	181, 209, 343	
Mitsuyori N	224, 245, 343	
Mitsuyoshi N	181, 232, 265, 285, 343	
Mitsuyuki N	181, 224, 237, 253, 343	
Mitsuzumi N	224, 285, 343	
Mi'ura S	149, 213, 322	
Miwabe O	400	
Miwahitobe O	400	
Miwame F	228, 380	
Miyabe O; S	400; 138, 185, 322	
Miyaji U	394	
Miyake U	394	
Miyame F	138, 380	
Miyamoto S	97, 138, 322, 404, 404	
Miyazaki S	138, 146, 322	
Miyome F	380	
Miyoshi S; U	213, 247, 255, 322; 394	
Miyuki F	227, 230	
Miyukime F	158, 201, 213, 244, 380	
Mizoguchi S	100, 144, 322, 404	
Mizu'no S	148, 152, 322	
Mizuta'ni S	147-148, 322	
Mochifusa N	134, 269, 344	
Mochiharu N	127, 269, 344	
Mochi'ie N	136, 269, 344	
Mochikata N	264, 269, 344	
Mochikiyo N	269, 284, 344	
Mochiku'ni N	98, 269, 344	
Mochimasa N	190, 202, 344	
Mochimasu N	221, 270, 344	
Mochime F	177, 242, 380	
Mochimichi N	130, 270, 344	
Mochimitsu N	181, 202, 270	
Mochimitsu N	344	
Mochimori N	202, 222, 344	
Mochimoto N	139, 270, 344	
Mochimu'ne N	262, 270, 344	
Mochi'naga N	111, 270, 344	
Mochi'naka N	218, 270, 344
Mochi'nobu N	233, 270, 344
Mochi'nori N	270, 286, 344
Mochisada N	270, 292, 344
Mochitame N	270, 290, 344
Mochitomo N	125, 270, 344
Mochitoyo N	231, 270, 344
Mochi'uji N	188, 270, 344
Mochiyo N	124, 270, 344
Mochiyori N	245, 270, 344
Mochiyuki N	238, 270, 344
Mochiza'ne N	166, 168, 344
Mogami S	102, 116, 322
Mohitori U	394
Momo F	380
Momoe F	215, 380
Momokawa N	150, 215, 344
Momoko F	160, 215, 381
Momome F	215, 381
Momo'no'i S	131, 160, 322
Momote F	215
Momoteme F	215, 381
Momozo'no H (E)	408
Monmu H (E)	406
Mo'no'nobe O; U	400; 36, 271, 394
Montoku H (E)	407
Mori S	148, 322
Mori'akira N	179, 222, 262, 344
Morichika N	193, 204, 344
Moriga'ne N	206, 222
Moriga'ne N	344
Morihide N	222, 288, 344
Morihira N (E)	407
Morihiro N	106, 222, 344
Morihisa N	119, 222, 344
Morihito N (E)	407
Mori'ie N	136, 222, 344
Morikage N	182, 222, 344
Morika'ne N	206, 222, 344
Morikazu N	203, 222, 344
Moriko F	148, 381
Moriku'ni N	98, 222, 344
Morimasa N	190, 193, 222, 292, 344
Morime F	177, 381
Morimi N	129, 222, 344
Morimitsu N	181, 222, 344
Morimori N	193, 222, 344
Mori'naga N	111, 223, 344
Mori'naka N	218, 223, 344
Mori'nao N	223, 241, 344
Mori'nobu N	105, 193, 223, 233, 344
Morita S	143, 148, 322
Moritaka N	107-108, 223, 344
Moritoki N	122, 193, 223, 344-345
Moritomo N	193, 201, 265, 345
Moritoo N	113, 223, 345
Moritoshi N	223, 252, 345
Moritsugi N	223
Moritsugu N	187, 207, 223, 345
Moritsu'na N	223, 276, 345
Moritsura N	223, 239, 345
Mori'uji N	188, 223, 345
Moriyama S; U	145, 193, 322; 394
Moriyoshi N	223, 295, 345
Moro S	177, 322
Moroai U	394
Moro'aki N	127, 196, 202, 345
Moro'akira N	196, 262, 345
Morochika N	196, 204, 345
Morofusa N	134, 196, 345
Morofuyu N	128, 196, 345
Morohide N	196, 288, 297, 345
Morohira N	110, 196, 345
Morohisa N	119, 196, 231, 345
Moro'ie N	136, 196, 345
Morokage N	182, 196, 345
Moroka'ne N	196, 206, 345
Morokata N	196, 264, 345
Morokawa N	196, 264, 345
Morokazu N	196, 203, 345
Morome F	196, 381
Moromichi N	130, 196, 345
Moromitsu N	181, 196, 345
Moromochi N	167, 196, 345
Moromori N	193, 196, 223, 345
Moromoto N	139, 196, 345
Moro'naga N	111, 196, 345
Moro'naka N	196, 218, 345
Moro'nao N	196, 241, 345
Moro'natsu N	127, 196, 345
Moro'nobu N	196, 233, 345
Moro'nori N	197, 234, 345
Moro'o N	197, 275, 345
Morosada N (E)	407
Moroshige N	167, 197, 301, 345
Morosuke N	194-195, 197, 345
Morotada N	197, 300, 345
Morotoki N	122, 197, 345, 404
Morotsugu N	197, 207, 345
Morotsu'na N	197, 276, 345
Morotsu'ne N	118, 197, 261, 345
Morotsura N	197, 239, 345
Moro'uji N	188, 197, 345
Moroyasu N	197, 209, 345
Moroyori N	197, 245, 345
Moroyoshi N	197, 289, 295, 345
Moroyuki N	197, 237, 346
Moroza'ne N	168, 197, 346
Motegi S	159, 167, 322
Mot'naga N	139
Motochika N	139, 204, 217, 346
Motofusa N	134, 139, 346
Motoharu N	127, 191, 217, 346, 404
Motohide N	139, 288, 346
Motohira N	110, 139, 282, 346
Motohisa N	119, 217, 346
Motohito N (E)	408
Moto'ie N	136, 139, 346

B	Infants & Children	**F**	Female Names	**M**	Male Yobina
E	Emperors	**H**	Chinese Style Names	**N**	Male Nanori

S	Surname	**U**	Uji
Y	Era Names	**O**	Be

Motoka'ne N	139, 206, 346	
Motokiyo N	139, 217, 284, 346	
Motoko F	139, 217, 381	
Motoku'ni N	98, 139, 217, 346	
Motomasa N	139, 190, 217, 230, 346	
Motomichi N	130, 139, 346	
Motomitsu N	181, 217, 346	
Motomori N	139, 223, 346	
Motomu'ne N	139, 262, 346	
Moto'naga N	111, 217, 346	
Moto'nari N	139, 267, 217, 242, 346, 404	
Moto'nobu N	139, 217, 233, 250, 346	
Moto'nori N	139, 234, 286, 346	
Motoshige N	140, 167, 217, 301, 346	
Motosuke N	140, 194-195, 217, 305, 346	
Mototada N	140, 300, 346, 404	
Mototaka N	108, 140, 346	
Motota'ne N	207, 217, 346	
Mototoki N	122, 140, 346, 404	
Mototsugu N	140, 207, 346	
Mototsu'na N	140, 217, 276, 346	
Mototsu'ne N	118, 140, 261, 346	
Mototsura N	217, 239, 346	
Moto'u'emon M	105, 196, 372	
Moto'uji N	97, 140, 188, 217, 346	
Motoyasu N	140, 303, 346	
Motoyori N	140, 245, 346	
Motoyoshi N	140, 217, 254, 265, 289, 295, 346	
Motoyuki N	140, 237, 347	
Motoza'ne N	140, 168, 347	
Motsuza'ne N	168, 202, 347	
Mouri S	177, 293, 322, 404	
Mumatsume F	172, 381	
Mume F	161, 381	
Mu'nakata U	394	
Mu'nawoka S	146, 263, 323	
Mu'ne N	347	
Mu'ne'aki N	127, 189, 347	
Mu'ne'atsu N	262, 299, 347	
Mu'nechika N	204, 262, 347	
Mu'nefuji N	163, 262	
Mu'nehide N	262, 288, 347	
Mu'nehira N	110, 262, 282	
Mu'nehira N	347	
Mu'nehiro N	100, 106, 262-263, 347	
Mu'nehisa N	119, 263, 347	
Mu'nehito N (E)	407	
Mu'nehito N (E)	407	
Mu'ne'ie N	136, 263, 347	
Mu'nekage N	182, 263, 347	
Mu'nekata N	114, 263-264, 347	
Mu'nekiyo N	263, 284, 347	
Mu'neko F	132, 262, 381	
Mu'nemasa N	190, 263, 347	
Mu'nemitsu N	181, 263, 347	
Mu'nemori N	223, 263, 347	
Mu'nemoto N	217, 263, 347	
Mu'ne'naga N	111, 263, 347	
Mu'ne'nari N	263, 298, 347	
Mu'ne'nobu N	233, 250, 263, 347, 404	
Mu'ne'nori N	105, 263, 234, 263, 347	
Mu'nesa'emon M	196, 262, 372	
Mu'neshige N	167, 263, 301, 347, 404	
Mu'nesuke N	194, 229, 263, 347	
Mu'neta N	106, 263, 347	
Mu'netada N	263, 300, 347	
Mu'netaka N	108, 263, 347, 403	
Mu'neta'ne N	207, 263, 347	
Mu'netoki N	122, 263, 347	
Mu'netoo N	113, 263, 347	
Mu'netsu'na N	263, 276, 347	
Mu'netsu'ne N	261, 263, 347	
Mu'ne'uji N	188, 263, 347	
Mu'neyasu N	209, 263, 347	
Mu'neyori N	245, 263, 347	
Mu'neyoshi N	263, 265, 289, 347	
Mu'neyuki N	237, 244, 263, 347	
Mu'neza'ne N	168, 263, 347	
Mura'i S	131, 141, 323	
Murakami H (E); S	407; 102, 141, 323	
Murasaki F	381	
Murasaki'emon F	184, 196	
Murashige N	141, 301, 347	
Murata S	141, 143, 323	
Murayama S	141, 145, 323	
Musashi N; P	404; 138, 257	
Mushime F	174, 381	
Musu F	157, 381	
Musubime F	307, 381	
Muta S	214	
Mutou S	163, 257, 323	
Mutsu F	381	
Mutsuhito N (E)	408	
Mutsuko F	214	
Mutsumi F	214	
Myou'hou'ji P	138, 191	
Myouhoume F	227, 381

N

Nabe F	274, 381	
Nabeshima S	146, 274, 323, 404	
Naeme F	170, 381	
Nagachika N	111, 204, 348	
Nagafuji N	118, 163, 348	
Nagafusa N	111, 134, 348	
Nagahide N	111, 288, 348, 404	
Nagahira N	110, 118, 348	
Nagahiro N	106, 264, 348	
Nagahisa N	111, 119, 348	
Nagahisagimimaru B	120-121	
Nagahito N (E)	408	
Naga'i S	112, 131, 323	
Nagaka'ne N	111, 206, 348	
Nagakata N	111, 114, 348	
Nagakatsu N	111, 118, 257, 348	
Nagakiyo N	111, 284, 348	
Nagako F	111, 117, 381	
Nagakoshinnou F	385	
Nagamasa N	111, 118, 180, 190, 348, 404	
Nagamichi N	111, 130, 348	
Nagamitsu N	112, 181, 306, 348	
Nagamochi N	112, 167, 348	
Nagamori N	112, 193, 223, 348	
Nagamoto N	112, 140, 167, 348	
Naga'nari N	112, 267, 348	
Naga'nori N	404	
Naga'numa S	112, 150, 323	
Naga'o S	112, 176, 323	
Naga'oka S	112, 147, 323	
Naga'oki N	112, 116, 348	
Nagasa S	101, 112, 323	
Nagasada N	112, 247, 348	
Nagasaki S	112, 146, 323	
Nagase S	113, 151, 323	
Nagashige N	112, 301, 348	
Nagasue N	118, 126, 348	
Nagataka N	108, 112, 348	
Nagateru N	112, 179, 348	
Nagatoki N	112, 122, 348, 404	
Nagatoshi N	112, 124, 348	
Nagatoshime F	111, 381	
Nagatsuka S	113, 307, 323	
Naga'uji N	112, 188, 348, 404	
Nagayo N	112, 124, 348	
Nagayori N	112, 245, 348	
Nagayoshi N	112, 254, 289, 306, 348	
Nagayuki N	112, 118, 237, 253, 348	
Nagazawa S	150, 323	
Nageta'ne N	112, 207, 348	
Nagokome F	210, 381	
Nahoi F	241, 381	
Nahoza'ne N	168, 241, 348	
Naitou S	103, 163, 323	
Naka S	272, 308, 323	
Naka'aki N	127, 218, 348	
Nakabumi N	218, 259, 348	
Nakachika N	204, 218, 348	
Nakachiko F	381	
Naka'e S	103, 151, 323	
Nakafusa N	134, 218, 348	
Nakagawa S	103, 150, 323, 404	
Nakahara S	103, 153	
Nakahara S; U	323; 394	
Nakahira N	110, 218, 348	
Naka'i S	103, 131, 323	
Naka'ie N	136, 218, 348	
Nakajou S	103, 189, 323	
Nakaki N	218, 305, 348	
Nakako F	203, 264, 381	
Nakaku'ni N	98, 218, 348	

B	Infants & Children	F	Female Names	M	Male Yobina	S	Surname	U	Uji
E	Emperors	H	Chinese Style Names	N	Male Nanori	Y	Era Names	O	Be

Nakamaro N	165, 187, 218, 348	Narisuke N	194, 267, 349	Nobu'ari N	233, 268, 350
Nakamikado H (E)	408	Narita S	143, 267, 323	Nobuchika N	204, 233, 350
Nakamitsu N	181, 218, 349	Naritada N	298, 300, 349	Nobufusa N	134, 233, 251, 350
Nakamoto N	140, 218, 349	Narita'ne N	207, 267, 349	Nobuharu N	127, 233, 350
Nakamu'ne N	218, 263, 349	Naritoki N	123, 298, 349	Nobuhide N	222, 251, 288, 350
Nakamura S	103, 141, 323, 404	Naritsu'na N	267, 276, 349	Nobuhiro N	101, 233, 350
Naka'nari N	218, 267, 298, 349	Naritsu'ne N	261, 267, 349	Nobuhisa N	119, 233, 350
Naka'no S	103, 152, 323	Naritsura N	239, 298, 349	Nobuhito N (E)	407
Naka'noko F	217, 381	Nari'uji N	188, 267, 349	Nobukado N	233, 290, 350
Nakasada N	218, 292, 349	Nariyoshi N	267, 295, 349	Nobuka'ne N	206, 233, 350
Nakatoki N	122, 218, 349	Nasu S	306, 308, 323	Nobukata N	114, 233, 264, 350
Nakatomi U	36, 391, 394	Natoko F	203, 382	Nobukimi N	193, 233, 350
Nakatomi no Sakahito U	394	Natsu F	127, 306, 382	Nobukiyo N	233, 284, 350
Nakatsu'na N	218, 276, 349	Nawa S	203, 209, 323	Nobuko F	202, 233, 238, 250, 260,
Nakayori N	218, 246, 349	Nebame F	152, 199, 382		382
Nakazawa S	103	Nei F	299, 382	Nobumasa N	180, 190, 233, 350
Namime F	306, 381	Neko F	230, 382	Nobumasu N	222, 233, 350
Na'na F	203, 306, 381	Neme F	167, 382	Nobumitsu N	181, 224, 233, 350
Na'naheme F	381	Nemushime F	167, 382	Nobumoto N	217, 233, 350
Na'name F	381	Ne'ne F	230, 382	Nobu'naga N	233, 350, 404
Nanbu S	105, 185, 323, 404	Ne'neme F	156, 230, 382	Nobu'nari N	233, 267, 233, 298, 350
Na'nimo F	280	Neshime F	152, 227, 382	Nobu'nori N	105, 228, 233, 240, 286,
Na'nimome F	177, 280, 306, 381	Nichiren H	155, 163, 404		350
Na'niwa U	394	Nifuko F	220, 382	Nobusada N	233, 247, 292, 350
Nao'aki N	202, 241, 262, 349	Nigita S	143, 210, 323	Nobusaka N	222, 233, 350
Naoaki N	349	Nihiko F	382	Nobusato N	233, 239, 350
Nao'e S	151, 241, 323	Nihime F	280, 382	Nobushige N	166-167, 234, 301, 350
Nao'ie N	136, 241, 349	Nihofume F	256, 278, 308, 382	Nobusuke N	234, 305, 350
Naomitsu N	181, 241, 349	Niitabe U	395	Nobutada N	234, 300, 350, 404
Naomochi N	241, 270, 349	Nijou H (E)	407	Nobutaka N	108, 234, 350
Nao'nobu N	233, 241, 49	Nikaidou S	134-135, 213, 323	Nobutake N	234, 257, 350
Naosada N	241, 292, 349	Niki S	159, 232, 323	Nobuta'ne N	207, 234, 350
Naoshige N	241, 301, 349	Nikiko F	232, 382	Nobutatsu N	175, 234, 350
Naosuke N	404	Nikkou P	155, 180	Nobuteru N	404
Naotoki N	123, 241, 349	Nikkouhime F	155, 382	Nobutoki N	123, 234, 251, 350
Naotomo N	125, 241, 349	Nikoyame F	280, 382	Nobutomo N	201, 234, 350
Naotsu'ne N	118, 241, 261, 349	Nin'an Y	208, 232, 410	Nobutoo N	113, 234, 350
Nao'uji N	188, 241, 349	Ninga H	232	Nobutora N	171, 234
Naoyori N	241, 246, 349	Ninji Y	191, 232, 410-411	Nobutoshi N	234, 251-252, 350
Naoza'ne N	168, 241, 349	Ninken H (E)	406	Nobutsugi N	218, 234, 350
Naozumi N	231, 285, 349	Ninkou H (E)	408	Nobutsugu N	207, 234, 350
Nara P	289, 306	Ninmyou H (E)	407	Nobutsu'na N	234, 276, 350, 404
Narabigaoka P	147, 213	Ninpei Y	110, 232, 410	Nobutsura N	234, 239, 350
Narame F	308, 381	Nintoku H (E)	405	Nobuyasu N	234, 303, 350
Nariakira N (E)	407	Nishi F	104, 382	Nobuyori N	234, 246, 351
Narichika N	204, 267, 349	Nishigori S	244, 278, 323	Nobuyoshi N	234, 265, 295, 351
Narifusa N	134, 298, 349	Nishigoribe O	37, 401	Nobuyuki N	234, 238, 351
Nariharu N	157, 243, 349	Nishikintoki N	104, 192, 349	Nobuza'ne N	168, 234, 351
Narihito N (E)	407	Nishikin'yasu N	104, 192, 349	Nogami S	102, 152, 324
Nari'ie N	136, 267, 349	Nishikori U	395	Noma S	133, 152, 324
Narika'ne N	206, 298, 349	Nishimura S	104, 141, 323	Nori F	235
Nariko F	240, 298, 307, 381	Nishi'na S	232, 307, 323	Nori'aki N	127, 202, 286, 351
Narimasa N	230, 267, 349	Nishi'o S	104, 176, 323	Norifuji N	163, 234, 286, 351
Narime F	250, 267-268, 381-382	Nishisa'netaka N	104, 169, 349	Norifusa N	134, 235, 286, 351
Narimori N	223, 298, 349	Nishiyama S	104, 145, 323	Norifuyu N	128, 235, 351
Nari'nori N	267, 286, 349	Nitta S	121, 143, 323, 404	Noriharu N	127, 286, 351
Narisada N	247, 267, 349	Nob'naga N	112	Norihira N (E)	407
Narishige N	267, 301, 349	Nobu'aki N	179, 233, 251, 260, 262,	Norihiro N	101, 106, 235, 286, 351
Narisue N	126, 267, 349		350	Norihito N (E)	407

B	Infants & Children	F	Female Names	M	Male Yobina	S	Surname	U	Uji
E	Emperors	H	Chinese Style Names	N	Male Nanori	Y	Era Names	O	Be

Nori'ie N	136, 286, 351	
Norikage N	182, 235, 351	
Norika'ne N	206, 286, 351	
Norikata N	114, 286, 351	
Norikiyo N	235, 284, 287, 351	
Noriko F	228, 260, 382	
Noriku'ni N	98, 286, 351	
Norimasa N	190, 194, 235, 286-287, 351	
Norime F	191, 382	
Norimichi N	130, 235, 351	
Norimitsu N	181, 286, 351	
Norimori N	223, 235, 351	
Norimoto N	140, 167, 235, 287, 351	
Norimu'ne N	263, 286-287, 351	
Norimura N	141, 287, 351	
Nori'naga N; N (E)	112, 286, 351; 408	
Nori'nao N	231, 287; 351	
Nori'oki N	116, 235, 351	
Norisada N	235, 247-248, 287, 351	
Norisaka N	222, 287, 351	
Norishige N	166-167, 235, 268, 286-287, 351	
Norisue N	126, 286, 351	
Norisuke N	194, 229, 286-287, 305, 351	
Noritada N	286-287, 300, 351	
Noritaka N	107-108, 235, 287, 302, 351	
Norita'ne N	207, 287, 351	
Noritoki N	123, 126, 235, 260, 351	
Noritomo N	125, 235, 280, 286, 351-352	
Noritoo N	113, 235, 352	
Noritoyo N	231, 235, 352	
Noritsugu N	207, 235, 352	
Noritsu'ne N	235, 261, 352	
Nori'uji N	127, 188, 286, 352	
Noriyasu N	235, 303, 352	
Noriyori N	246, 262, 286-287, 352	
Noriyuki N	235, 238, 352	
Noriza'ne N	168, 235, 286-287, 352	
Nose S	235, 265, 324	
Nukatabe N (E); O; U	406; 401; 395	
Numada S	143, 150, 324	
Nume F	152, 382	
Nuribe U	395	

O

Obame F	199, 285, 383, 388
Obata S	102, 273, 324
Obito N (E)	406
Obu S	245, 274, 324
Ochi S; U	265, 294, 324; 395
Oda F	201
Oda S	102, 143, 244, 324, 404
Ogasawara S	102, 153, 273, 324, 404
Ogashima S	102, 146, 173, 324
Ogata S	114, 275, 324
Ogawa S	102, 150, 324
Ogimachi H (E)	408
Ogi'no S	152, 164, 324
Ogura S	102, 137, 324
Oguri S	102, 161, 324
Ohari U	395
Oharida U	395
Ohasebe O	401
Ohatsuse U	395
Ohirame F	102, 383
Ohito N (E)	408
Oho'neme F	101, 383
Ohoshika S	151, 220, 324
Ohotsume F	101, 383
Ohoyame F	101, 383
Okabe S	147, 185, 324
Okamoto S	97, 147, 324
Okazaki S	146-147, 324
Okeguchi S	100, 274, 324
Okihito N (E)	408
Okikaze N	116, 158, 352
Okiko F	201, 383
Oki'naga U	395
Okisada N (E)	407
Okita'ne N	116, 207, 352
Okitsu'ne N	116, 118, 352
Oku'ni S	98, 102, 324
Okuyama S	104, 145, 324
Omi P	244, 278
Omi'nako F	198, 383
Omi'nome F	102, 279, 383
Omiyame F	102, 383
O'nigatsurayama P	171
O'niike P	171
O'nitaroume F	383
O'niya'nagi P	160, 171
O'no S; U	102, 152, 324; 395
O'nodera S	102, 138, 152, 324
Oo U	395
Oo'ama no Ouji N (E)	406
Ooba S	101, 142, 324
Oobatake S	101, 142, 324
Oobayashi S	101, 148, 324
Ooda S	101, 143, 324
Oodachi S	101, 137, 324
Oo'e S; U; O	101, 151, 324; 395; 401
Oogimachi S	101, 141, 324
Oohara S	101, 153, 324
Oohime F	101, 383
Oo'i S; N (E)	101, 131, 324; 406
Oo'i'da S	101, 143
Oo'i'da S	324
Ookasuga U	395
Ookoma U	395
Ookura U	395
Oomiwa U	395
Oomiya S	101, 138, 324
Oomori S	101, 148, 324
Oomura S	101, 141, 324
Oo'naka S	101, 103, 324
Oo'nakatomi S	101, 103, 201, 325
Oo'no S; U	101, 152, 269, 325; 395
Oosaki S	101, 146, 325
Ooshiama U	395
Ooshiamame F	101, 383
Ooshiko'uchi U	395
Ooshima S	101, 146, 325
Oosuga S	101, 245, 306, 325
Oosumi U	395
Oota S	106, 143, 325
Ootaka S	101, 107, 325
Ootakume F	383
Oota'ni S	101, 147, 325
Ootomo no Ouji N (E)	406
Ootomo N (E); S; U	407; 101, 201, 325, 404; 36, 395
Ootomobe O	401
Ootsubo S	101, 142, 325
Ootsuka S	101, 139, 325
Ootsume F	383
Oo'uchi S	101, 103, 325, 404
Ooyake U	395
Ooyakeme F	383
Ooyama S	102, 145, 325
Ooya'no S	102, 152, 281, 325
Ooyue U	395
Oozeki S	100, 102, 325
Oribe O	37
Osada S	113, 143, 325
Osafu'ne S	113, 275, 325
Osahito N (E)	408
Osakabe O; U	401; 395
Oshime F	298, 383
Oshi'numi U	395
Oshi'numibe O	401
Otohiko M	200, 219
Otomuro N	219, 307, 352
Otowakamaru B	120-121
Otsuto M	219
Ou'an Y	208, 311, 409, 411
Ouchou Y	111, 311, 410-411
Ou'ei Y	117, 311, 410-411
Ouhou Y	256, 312, 410
Oujin H (E)	405
Ou'name F	383
Ou'nin Y	232, 312, 410-411
Outoku Y	304, 312, 410
Owime F	102, 172, 383
Oyako F	200, 383
Oyama S	102, 145, 325
Oyamada S	102, 143, 145, 325
Ozuki S	102, 162, 325

B Infants & Children	F Female Names	M Male Yobina	S Surname	U Uji
E Emperors	H Chinese Style Names	N Male Nanori	Y Era Names	O Be

R

Raishi F	290, 383
Raku F	253, 383
Reigen H (E)	408
Reizei H (E)	407
Richuu H (E)	405
Rikyuu H	248, 293
Riri F	264, 383
Rokujou H (E)	407
Rokurou M	214, 372
Roppongi P	214
Ryaku'nin Y	232, 311, 410-411
Ryaku'ou Y	311-312, 410-411
Ryuu'nomae F	383
Ryuu'zou'ji S	138, 174, 325

S

Sabame F	151, 175, 199, 383
Saburou M	212, 372
Sachiko F	231, 253, 383
Sada'aki N	202, 292, 352, 404
Sada'akira N (E)	407
Sadabumi N	259, 292, 352
Sadachika N	204, 248, 292, 352
Sada'e N	256, 292, 352
Sadafuji N	163, 292, 352
Sadafusa N	134, 248, 292, 352
Sadahide N	288, 292, 352
Sadahira N	110, 248, 282, 292, 352
Sadahiro N	101, 292, 352
Sadahisa N	119, 292, 352
Sadahito N (E)	407
Sada'ie N	136, 248, 292, 352
Sadakage N	182, 248, 352
Sadakata N	114, 292, 352
Sadakatsu N	248, 257, 352
Sadakiyo N	248, 284, 292, 352
Sadako F	292, 383
Sadaku'ni N	98, 292, 352
Sadamasa N	114, 190, 194, 230, 248, 292, 352-353
Sadami N (E)	407
Sadamichi N	130, 248, 292, 353
Sadamitsu N	181, 224, 292, 353
Sadamori N	223, 292, 353
Sadamu N	248, 353
Sadamu'ne N	263, 292, 353
Sadamura N	141, 292, 353
Sada'naga N	112, 248, 293, 353
Sada'nao N	241, 293, 353
Sada'nori N	124, 248, 286, 293, 353
Sadashige N	167, 248, 268, 293, 301, 353
Sadasue N	126, 293, 353
Sadasuke N	194, 248, 353
Sadataka N	107, 248, 293, 353
Sadata'ne N	207, 293, 353
Sadatoki N	123, 293, 353, 404
Sadatomo N	125, 293, 353
Sadatoshi N	248, 292-293, 353
Sadatsugu N	187, 207, 248, 293, 353
Sadatsu'na N	248, 276, 293, 353
Sadatsu'ne N	261, 293, 353
Sadatsura N	239, 293, 353
Sada'uji N	188, 293, 353
Sadayasu N	209, 248, 293, 303, 353
Sadayo N	124, 293, 353
Sadayori N	246, 248, 293, 353
Sadayoshi N	248, 254, 265, 293, 295, 353
Sadayuki N	237, 253, 293, 353
Sadaza'ne N	169, 248, 353
Sado P	185, 239
Saga H (E)	407
Sagara S	186, 289, 325
Sahara S	153, 195, 325
Saheki U	395
Sa'i U	395
Sai'dai'ji P	104, 138
Saigusa S; U	168, 213, 325; 395
Saigusabe O	401
Saimei H (E)	406
Saitou S	163, 229, 325
Sakabe O; S	37, 401; 185, 274, 325
Sakagami S	102, 129, 325
Sakahito U	395
Saka'i S	131, 274, 325, 404
Sakaibe O; U	401; 395
Sakakibara S	153, 162, 325
Sakame F	307, 383
Sakami F	186, 286, 383
Sakamoto U	395
Saka'no'ue S; U	103, 129, 325; 396
Saka'nyou F	199, 383
Sakata U	396
Saka'uchi S	103, 129, 325
Sakiko F	104, 383
Sakikusabe O; U	401; 396
Sakiyori N	104, 246, 353
Sakuma F; S	166, 383; 119, 133, 195, 325
Sakurada S	143, 160, 325
Sakurai no Tabe U	396
Sakura'i S; U	131, 160, 325; 396
Sakuramachi H (E)	408
Sakurayama S	145, 160, 325
Samejima S	146, 175, 325
Sami U	396
Samiko F	195, 383
Samime F	195, 383
Samukawa S	151, 158, 325
Sa'nada S	143, 195, 290, 306, 325
Sa'ne'atsu N	169, 298, 353
Sa'nechika N	169, 204, 353
Sa'nefusa N	134, 169, 353
Sa'nefuyu N	128, 169, 353
Sa'nehide N	169, 288, 353
Sa'nehira N	110, 169, 353
Sa'nehiro N	169, 266, 353
Sa'neka'ne N	169, 206, 353
Sa'nekatsu N	257, 290, 354
Sa'nekazu N	169, 203, 299, 354
Sa'neku'ni N	98, 169, 354
Sa'nemasa N	169, 190, 230, 354
Sa'nemitsu N	169, 181, 354
Sa'nemori N	169, 223, 354
Sa'nemoto N	140, 169, 354
Sa'nemu'ne N	169, 263, 354
Sa'ne'naga N	112, 118, 169, 354
Sa'ne'naka N	169, 218, 354
Sa'ne'nao N	169, 241, 354
Sa'ne'natsu N	127, 169, 354
Sa'ne'nori N	169, 235, 354
Sa'ne'o N	169, 303, 354
Sa'nesada N	169, 248, 354
Sa'neshige N	167, 169, 301, 354
Sa'netada N	169, 300, 354
Sa'netaka N	108, 169, 354
Sa'netoki N	123, 169, 354
Sa'netomo N	125, 169, 354, 403
Sa'netoshi N	169, 252, 354
Sa'netsugu N	169, 187, 354
Sa'netsu'na N	169, 276, 354
Sa'netsu'ne N	169, 261, 354
Sa'ne'uji N	169, 188, 354
Sa'neyasu N	169, 209, 303, 354
Sa'neyo N	124, 169, 354
Sa'neyori N	169, 246, 354
Sanjou H (E)	407
Sanko F	195, 383
Sanno'ko F	383
Sa'no S	152, 195, 325
Sa'nuki S	195, 298, 325
Sarara no Umakai U	396
Saru F	171
Saruhashi P	171
Sarumaru M	171
Sarume F	157, 383
Sasa F	166
Sasabe S	174, 185, 325
Sasaki S	159, 195, 325, 404
Sasame F	195, 383
Sashime F	151, 227, 384
Sata S	143, 195, 325
Sarake S	162, 195, 326
Satohito N (E)	408
Satoko F	140, 384
Satomi N; S	129; 140, 326
Satomura S	140-141, 326
Satou S	163, 195, 326
Satsukime F	214, 384
Sawa S	150, 326
Sawamura S	141, 150, 326
Sayo F	102, 384

B Infants & Children	F Female Names	M Male Yobina	S Surname	U Uji
E Emperors	H Chinese Style Names	N Male Nanori	Y Era Names	O Be

Name Index   451

Sayome F	195, 384
Sazakibe O; U	401; 396
Seimu H (E)	405
Sei'nei H (E)	406
Seishi F	283, 384
Seiwa H (E)	407
Seki S	100, 326
Sekigahara P	100
Sen F; S	205, 384; 215, 326
Senchiyo F	215, 384
Sendai P	205, 277
Senka H (E)	406
Se'no'o S	176, 201, 326
Senseki S	153, 205, 326
Senzu P	215, 310
Serada S	124, 143, 289, 326
Seto'i S	131, 133, 151, 326
Shiba S	149, 165, 270, 326
Shibata S	143, 164, 326, 404
Shibi U	396
Shibukawa S	100, 150, 326
Shibutsu H	228, 258
Shibuya S	100, 147, 326
Shichirou M	214
Shidzuko F	384
Shiga S	245, 302, 326
Shigechika N	204, 301, 354
Shigefusa N	134, 301, 354
Shigeharu N	127, 166, 354, 404
Shigehira N	110, 167, 282, 301, 354
Shigehiro N	101, 301, 354
Shigehisa N	231, 301, 354
Shigehito N (E)	408
Shigekatsu N	167, 257, 301, 354
Shigekiyo N	284, 301, 354
Shigeko F	245, 267, 301, 384
Shigeku'ni N	98, 301, 354
Shigemasa N	166, 180, 190, 301, 354
Shigeme F	301, 384
Shigemitsu N	167, 181, 301, 354
Shigemochi N	167, 301, 354
Shigemori N	223, 301, 354
Shigemoto N	217, 268, 301, 310, 354-355
Shige'naga N	112, 167, 301, 355
Shige'nari N	267, 301, 355
Shige'no S; U	152, 166, 326; 396
Shige'nobu N	234, 301, 355, 404
Shige'nori N	286, 301, 355
Shige'nosuke M	372
Shigesada N	248, 301, 355
Shigetada N	300-301, 355
Shigetaka N	107-108, 301-302, 355
Shigetake N	257, 302, 355
Shigeta'ne N	207, 302, 355
Shigetoki N	123, 167, 302, 355
Shigetomo N	125, 268, 302, 355
Shigetsugu N	187, 218, 302, 355
Shigetsu'na N	276, 302, 355
Shigetsu'ne N	261, 302, 355
Shige'uji N	166, 188, 268, 302, 355
Shigeyasu N	208, 302, 355
Shigeyori N	246, 302, 355
Shigeyoshi N	265, 268, 295, 302, 355
Shigeyuki N	238, 302, 355
Shigeza'ne N	167, 169, 355
Shigezumi N	284, 302, 355
Shijou H (E)	408
Shijou S	189, 214, 326
Shiki U	396
Shikitame F	302, 384
Shima S	146, 326
Shimada S	144, 146, 326
Shima'i S	131, 147, 326
Shimame F	146, 384
Shima'nushime F	146, 194, 384
Shimatarume F	146, 240, 384
Shimazu S	147-148, 326, 404
Shimotsuke'no U	396
Shimotsuma S	103, 198, 326
Shimotsumichi U	396
Shi'nabe O	401
Shi'nagawa S	151, 277, 326
Shi'na'no P	226
Shingen H	183, 233, 404
Shin'ichi M	220
Shinran H	404
Shinshi F	203, 384
Shiome F	273, 384
Shiozaki S	146, 273, 326
Shiragabe O	401
Shirakabe N (E); U	407; 396
Shirakami F	177
Shirakamime F	184, 384
Shirakawa H (E)	407
Shirimachime F	117, 384
Shiro F	184, 384
Shirou M	372
Shishido S	133, 308, 326
Shishihito U	396
Shitafume F	278, 302, 384
Shitagau N	216, 355
Shitoku Y	304, 313, 410-411
Shitsuori U	396
Shizukagozen F	198, 208
Shizuko F	208, 248, 384
Shou'an Y	208, 291, 410-411
Shouchou Y	111, 291, 410-411
Shouchuu Y	103, 291, 410-411
Shougen Y	217, 291, 410-411
Shouhei Y	110, 291, 410-411
Shouhou Y	256, 291, 410-411
Shouji H; Y	183, 280; 191, 291, 410
Shouka Y	285, 291, 410-411
Shoukei Y	253, 291, 410-411
Shoukou H (E)	408
Shoumu H (E)	406
Shou'ou H; Y	174, 189; 291, 312, 410-411
Shouryaku Y	291, 311, 410
Shoutoku H (E); Y	407; 291, 304, 410-411
Shouwa H (E); Y	408; 179, 210, 291, 410-411
Soga S; U	117, 187, 326; 36, 396
Sogabe O	401
So'ne S	117, 230, 326
Songorou M	200, 214, 372
Sonjirou M	200, 212, 372
So'nobe O	401
So'nobito O	401
So'noda S	142, 144, 326
Soroku M	215
Sosei H	184, 285
Soteme F	184, 282, 384
Sou S	262, 326, 404
Souhou N	404
Sou'ichirou M	262
Soujirou M	212, 262, 372
Souma S	172, 186, 326
Soutan H	222, 226, 262
Sou'un N	404
Sue F	120, 384
Suefusa N	126, 134, 355
Sueka'ne N	126, 206, 355
Sueko F	116, 218, 384
Suemitsu N	126, 181, 355
Sue'naga N	112, 126, 355
Suetada N	116, 300, 355
Suetoki N	123, 126, 355
Suetsugu N	126, 187, 355
Suetsukuribe O	37, 401
Suetsu'na N	126, 276, 355
Suetsu'ne N	126, 261, 355
Sueyasu N	126, 256, 355
Sueyoshi N	126, 265, 355
Suga P	164
Sugadaira P	164
Sugashima P	164
Suga'ura P	164
Sugawara U	396
Sugaya P	164
Sugihara S	153, 160
Sugi'nome P	160, 177
Sugita'ni S	147, 160
Sugurime F	384
Suiko H (E)	406
Sui'nin H (E)	405
Suizei H (E)	405
Sujin H (E)	405
Suke'aki N	179, 229, 305, 355
Sukechika N	204, 229, 305, 355
Sukefuji N	163, 305, 355
Sukefusa N	134, 305, 355
Sukeharu N	127, 229, 355
Sukehide N	195, 288, 355

B	Infants & Children	F	Female Names
E	Emperors	H	Chinese Style Names
M	Male Yobina	S	Surname
N	Male Nanori	Y	Era Names
U	Uji	O	Be

Sukehira N	110, 282, 305, 355-356	
Sukehiro N	106, 195, 356	
Suke'ie N	136, 195, 305, 356	
Sukekage N	182, 194, 356	
Sukekata N	264, 305, 356	
Sukekazu N	195, 203, 356	
Sukekiyo N	229, 284, 305, 356	
Sukeko F	305, 384	
Sukeku'ni N	356	
Sukeku'ni N	98, 195, 305, 195, 264	
Sukemasa N	356	
Sukemitsu N	181, 195, 356	
Sukemochi N	167, 229, 356	
Sukemori N	223, 305, 356	
Sukemoto N	140, 195, 305, 310, 356	
Sukemura N	141, 305, 356	
Suke'na N	203, 305, 356	
Suke'naga N	112, 118, 195, 305, 356, 356	
Suke'nari N	229, 267, 305, 356	
Suke'nobu N	195, 229, 234, 356	
Suke'nori N	229, 287, 356	
Suke'omi N	193, 229, 356	
Sukesada N	248, 305, 356	
Sukesa'emon M	196, 373	
Sukeshige N	167, 195, 229, 302, 356	
Sukesue N	126, 305, 356	
Suketada N	300, 305, 356	
Suketaka N	108, 305, 356	
Suketa'ne N	194, 207, 356	
Suketoki N	123, 229, 305, 356	
Suketomo N	125, 195, 306, 356	
Suketsu'na N	195, 276, 356	
Suketsu'ne N	229, 261, 306, 356	
Suke'uji N	188, 195, 356	
Sukeyasu N	209, 229, 306, 356	
Sukeyori N	246, 306, 356	
Sukeyoshi N	195, 232, 265, 306, 356	
Sukeza'ne N	169, 306, 356	
Sukita no Kurahito U	396	
Sukoteme F	306, 384	
Sukou H (E)	408	
Suku'name F	137, 384	
Sukutame F	384	
Sumitomo N	201, 285, 356	
Suruga S	122, 151	
Sushun H (E)	406	
Susumu N	116, 356	
Sutoku H (E)	407	
Suwa S	240, 251	
Suzaku H (E)	407	
Suzu F	272, 385	
Suzuki S	159, 272	
Suzushiko F	255, 385	

T

Tabara S	144, 153, 327
Tabe O	37, 402
Tachiba'na S; U	114, 161, 168, 327, 404; 396
Tada S	144, 221, 327
Tada'aki N	202, 300, 357
Tadachika N	204, 300, 357
Tadafumi N	259, 300, 357
Tadafusa N	134, 300, 357
Tadafuyu N	128, 241, 357
Tadahira N	110, 256, 300, 357
Tadahisa N	119, 300, 357
Tada'ie N	136, 300, 357
Tadaka'ne N	206, 300, 357
Tadakatsu N	257, 300, 404
Tadakiyo N	284, 300, 357
Tadako F	143, 299, 385
Tadaku'ni N	98, 300, 357
Tadamasa N	190, 230, 292, 300, 357
Tadamichi N	130-131, 300, 357
Tadamitsu N	181, 300, 357
Tadamori N	223, 300, 357
Tadamoto N	168, 300, 357
Tadamu'ne N	226, 263, 300, 357
Tada'nobu N	234, 300, 357
Tada'nori N	216, 300, 357
Tada'oki N	116, 300, 357
Tadasada N	248, 300, 357
Tadashige N	167, 241, 268, 300, 357, 404
Tadasu F	276, 385
Tadasue N	126, 300, 357
Tadatoki N	123, 300, 357
Tadatoo N	113, 293, 357
Tadatoshi N	241, 252, 357
Tadatsugi N	218, 241, 357
Tadatsugu N	207, 300, 357, 404
Tadatsu'na N	269, 276, 300, 357
Tadatsu'ne N	118, 241, 261, 300, 357
Tada'uji N	188, 300, 357
Tadayasu N	241, 256, 357
Tadayori N	246, 270, 300, 357
Tadayoshi N	232, 241, 265, 289, 295, 300, 357
Tadayuki N	237, 300, 357
Tadaza'ne N	169, 300, 357
Tadazumi N	241, 284, 300, 357-358
Taga S	221, 245, 327
Tagima U	396
Taguchi S	100, 144, 327
Tahe F	227, 385
Taheme F	227, 385
Ta'i U	396
Tai'ei Y	101, 117, 410-411
Taifu F	101, 385
Taika Y	409

Taime F	385
Taira S; U	110, 327, 396, 403; 396
Tairakeiko F	385
Taishou H (E); Y	408; 101, 291, 410-411
Tajii U	396
Tajimi N; S	129; 221, 327
Tajiri S	144, 178, 327
Taka'aki N	107-108, 179, 202, 260, 262, 358
Taka'akira M	179
Taka'atsu N	108, 299, 358
Takachika N	107-108, 204, 358
Takafusa N	108, 134, 358
Takaharu F; N (E)	219, 385; 408
Takahashi S; U	108, 144, 327; 396
Takahide N	107, 289, 358
Takahira N; N (E)	107-108, 282, 358; 407
Takahiro N	108, 266, 358
Takahisa N	107, 119, 358
Takahito N (E)	407
Taka'i S	108, 131, 327
Takai F	107, 385
Taka'ie N	107-108, 136, 358
Taka'ishi S	108, 153, 327
Takakage N	107-108, 182-183, 302, 358
Takakai O	402
Takaka'ne N	108, 206, 358
Takakazu N	107, 308, 358
Takaki S	108, 159, 327
Takakiyo N	107-108, 284, 358
Takako F	107, 173, 230, 273, 297, 385
Takaku'ni N	98, 108, 358
Takakura H (E)	407
Takama S	108, 133, 327
Takamasa N	107-108, 190, 358
Takamatsu S	108, 160, 327
Takame F	385
Takamichi N	108, 130, 358
Takamitsu N	107, 181, 358
Takamochi N	107, 254, 358
Takamori N	108, 223, 358
Takamoto N	107-108, 168, 217, 310, 358
Takamuku U	396
Takamu'ne N	107, 263, 302, 358
Taka'naga N	107, 112, 358
Taka'naka N	109, 218, 358
Taka'nao N	107, 241, 358
Taka'nashi S	108, 161, 327
Taka'no P	174
Taka'nobu N	107, 109, 234, 358
Taka'nori N	107, 262, 304, 358
Takara no Himatsuri U	396
Takasada N	107, 293, 358
Takashige N	107, 109, 302, 358

B	Infants & Children	**F**	Female Names	**M** Male Yobina	**S** Surname	**U** Uji
E	Emperors	**H**	Chinese Style Names	**N** Male Nanori	**Y** Era Names	**O** Be

Name Index 453

Takashi'na S; U 108, 134, 327; 397	Tamefuyu N 128, 290, 359	Taruhito N (E) 407
Takasue N 108-109, 126, 302, 358	Tamehide N 289-290, 359	Tarumime F 221, 385
Takasuke N 105, 107, 109, 229, 306, 358	Tamehiro N 101, 290, 359	Tashiro S 124, 144, 327
	Tamehisa N 119, 290, 359	Tasuki U 397
Takata S 108, 144, 327	Tamehito N (E) 407	Tasukime F 143, 385
Takatada N 109, 301, 358	Tame'ie N 136, 290, 359	Tata F 221, 385
Takatoki N 107, 123, 358, 404	Tameka'ne N 206, 290, 359	Tatara S 221, 289, 327
Takatomo N 107, 125, 265, 302, 358	Tamekazu N 290, 308, 359	Tatara U 397
Takatora N 107, 171, 359, 404	Tamemitsu N 181, 290, 359	Tate'nuibe O 37
Takatori S 174, 239, 327	Tamemori N 193, 290, 359	Tatsu'aki N 128, 174, 360
Takatoshi N 109, 159, 252, 359	Tamemoto N 140, 290, 359	Tatsuhisa N 114, 119, 360
Takatsu S 108, 148, 327	Tame'naga N 112, 290, 359	Tatsukawa S 150, 175, 327
Takatsu'na N 107, 276, 359	Tame'nobu N 234, 290, 359, 404	Tatsuko F 156, 385
Takatsu'ne N 107, 109, 261, 359	Tame'nori N 235, 290, 287, 290, 359	Tatsume F 114, 175, 385
Takatsura N 107, 239, 359	Tamesada N 248, 290, 293, 359	Tatsutoshime F 175, 385
Taka'uji N 107, 188, 202, 359, 403	Tameshige N 290, 302, 359	Tawo F 285
Takaya S 108, 147, 245, 327	Tamesuke N 186, 290, 359	Tawome F 221, 285, 385
Takayoshi N 109, 265, 295, 359	Tameta'ne N 170, 290, 359	Tei F 219, 386
Take F 162, 385	Tametoki N 123, 290, 359	Teishi N 197, 248, 360
Takebe O; S 402; 185, 312, 327	Tametomo N 125, 290, 359	Teizou M 219
Takechi U 397	Tame'uji N 188, 290, 359	Temmu H (E) 406
Takeda S 144, 257, 327, 404	Tameyo N 124, 290, 359	Tenbun Y 155, 259, 410-411
Takefusa N 134, 257, 359	Tameyori N 246, 290, 359	Ten'ei Y 117, 155, 410
Takehisamaru B 120-121	Tameyoshi N 290, 295, 359	Tengi Y 155, 254, 410
Takemasa N 190, 257, 359	Tameyuki N 237-238, 290, 359	Tenji H (E); Y 406; 155, 191, 410
Takeme F 162, 385	Tameza'ne N 169, 290, 359	Tenjiku P 155, 163
Takemitsu N 181, 257, 359	Tamiko F 221, 385	Tenju Y 155, 313, 410-411
Takemo'no'me F 385	Tamochime F 176, 385	Tenmei Y 155, 179, 410-411
Take'naka S 103, 162, 327, 404	Tamotsu N 256, 359	Tenna Y 155, 210, 410-411
Take'no S 152, 257, 327	Tamura S 141, 144, 327	Tennin Y 155, 232, 410
Take'o N 257-258, 359	Ta'naka S; U 103, 144, 327; 397	Tenpou Y 155, 256, 272, 410-411
Takeshige N 257, 302, 359	Tanba S 177, 184, 327, 404	Tenpuku Y 155, 253, 410-411
Taketoki N 123, 257, 359	Ta'nefusa N 134, 207, 359	Tenshou Y 155, 291, 311, 410-411
Taketomo N 125, 257, 359	Ta'nehito N (E) 408	Ten'you Y 155, 313, 410
Taketoshi N 126, 242, 257, 359	Ta'ne'ie N 136, 207, 359	Terada S 138, 144, 327
Takewaka B 120	Ta'nemasa N 207, 292, 359	Terame F 138, 386
Takeyoshi N 232, 257, 359	Ta'nemichi N 130-131, 170, 207, 360	Tera'nishi S 104, 138, 327
Takezaki S 146, 162, 327	Ta'nemori N 207, 223, 360	Terasu N 183, 360
Takeza'ne N 169, 257, 359	Ta'nemu'ne N 207, 263, 360	Terazawa S 138, 150, 327
Takezou N 138, 257, 359	Ta'nemura N 141, 170, 360	Teru'aki N 179, 202, 360
Takezumi N 257, 284, 359	Ta'ne'naga N 112, 207, 360, 170	Teruhito N (E) 408
Taki F 221, 385	Ta'ne'nao N 207, 241, 360	Terumoto N 179, 217, 360
Takikawa S 150-151, 327	Ta'ne'nobu N 207, 234, 360	Teshigawara S 151, 153, 242, 251, 327
Takime F 385	Ta'neshige N 170, 302, 360	Teyorime F 176, 240, 386
Taku'an S 404	Ta'nesuke N 170, 195, 360	Toba H (E) 407
Takume F 385	Ta'netomo N 125, 207, 360	Toda S 133, 144, 328
Tama F 272, 385	Ta'netsugu N 170, 187, 360	Togashi S 160, 245, 328
Tama'i S 131, 272, 327	Ta'netsu'na N 207, 276, 360	To'ime F 206, 386
Tamame F 272, 385	Ta'neyasu N 170, 256, 360	Tojime F 281, 309, 386
Tamamushime F 272, 385	Ta'neyori N 207, 246, 360	Tokawa S 133, 150, 328
Tama'noya U 397	Ta'neyoshi N 207, 295, 360	Toki S 115, 153, 328
Tamaru S 106, 144, 327	Ta'neyuki N 207, 237, 360	Toki'aki N 123, 202, 360
Tamatarime F 272, 385	Ta'ni S 147, 327	Toki'akira N 123, 260, 360
Tamate U 397	Tanji U 397	Tokifusa N 123, 134, 360
Tamateme F 272, 385	Tannawa S 226, 282, 327	Tokiharu N 123, 191, 360
Tamatsukuribe O 402	Ta'nushime F 143, 194, 385	Tokihide N 123, 289, 360
Tamatsume F 272, 385	Tarime F 106, 176, 385	Tokihira N 110, 123, 360
Tame U 397	Tarou M 211, 373	Tokihiro N 101, 123, 360
Tame'aki N 179, 290, 359	Tarousa'emon M 196, 211, 373	Tokihito N (E) 407

B	Infants & Children	F	Female Names	M	Male Yobina	S	Surname	U	Uji
E	Emperors	H	Chinese Style Names	N	Male Nanori	Y	Era Names	O	Be

Toki'ie N	123, 136, 360	Tomohisa N	119, 125, 231, 265, 269, 361	Toshihide N	252, 289, 362
Tokika'ne N	123, 206, 360	Tomohito N (E)	408	Toshihira N	110, 252, 282, 362
Tokikiyo N	123, 284, 360	Tomo'ie N	136, 265, 361	Toshihito N	232, 293, 362
Tokiko F	122, 386	Tomokage N	125, 182-183, 201, 361	Toshi'ie N	136, 294, 362, 404
Tokiku'ni N	98, 260, 360	Tomokata N	114, 125, 201, 361	Toshikage N	183, 242, 362
Tokimasa N	123, 190, 360, 404	Tomokatsu N	125, 165, 361	Toshika'ne N	206, 252, 362
Tokimasu N	123, 221, 360	Tomoko F	201, 216, 280, 386	Toshiki N	227, 252, 362
Tokime F	122, 386	Tomomasa N	125, 190, 230, 361	Toshikiyo N	252, 284, 362
Tokimichi N	123, 130, 360	Tomomichi N	130, 280, 361	Toshiko N (E)	408
Tokimochi N	123, 167, 360	Tomomitsu N	125, 181, 361	Toshima S	147, 231, 328
Tokimori N	123, 223, 360	Tomomori N	125, 193, 223, 265, 280, 361	Toshimame F	231, 386
Tokimoto N	123, 140, 360			Toshimasa N	190, 252, 362
Tokimu'ne N	123, 226, 263, 360, 404	Tomomu'ne N	125, 132, 263, 265, 361	Toshimichi N	130, 252, 362
Tokimura N	123, 141, 360			Toshimitsu N	181, 252, 362
Toki'naga N	112, 123, 360			Toshimoto N	140, 252, 362
Toki'nao N	123, 241, 360	Tomomura N	125, 141, 361	Toshi'naga N	112, 252, 294, 362
Toki'nari N	123, 267, 299, 360	Tomo'naga N	112, 236, 361	Toshi'nari N	252, 267, 362
Toki'nobu N	123, 234, 360	Tomo'nao N	125, 241, 361	Toshi'nari'nomusume F	252, 386
Tokisada N	123, 248, 293, 360	Tomo'nari N	125, 299, 361	Toshi'o M	200, 215
Tokishige N	123, 167, 302, 361	Tomo'nori N	125, 216, 235, 265, 280, 286, 201, 287, 361	Toshisuke N	194, 252, 362
Tokisuke N	123, 194, 361			Toshitsu'na N	252, 276, 294, 362
Tokitada N	123, 301, 361	Tomo'oki N	116, 125, 361	Toshitsu'ne N	252, 261, 362
Tokitaka N	107, 109, 123, 361	Tomosada N	125, 248, 265, 293, 361	Toshiyasu N	209, 252, 294, 304, 362
Tokitsugu N	123, 187, 361	Tomoshige N	166, 236, 280, 302, 361	Toshiyori N	246, 252, 362
Tokitsu'na N	123, 276, 361	Tomotada N	125, 301, 361	Toshiyuki N	237, 242, 362
Tokitsura N	123, 239, 361	Tomotarime F	280, 386	Toshiza'ne N	169, 252, 362
Toki'uji N	123, 188, 361	Tomotoki N	124-125, 361	Toto F	133, 386
Tokiwagozen F	118, 198, 386	Tomotoshi N	126, 252, 361	Totome F	238, 240, 386
Tokiyasu N (E)	407	Tomotsume F	265, 386	Totori U	397
Tokiyori N	123, 246, 361, 404	Tomotsu'na N	126, 206, 276, 361	Totoribe O	37, 402
Tokiyoshi N	123, 265, 361	Tomotsu'ne N	118, 126, 236, 261, 362	Toushi F	240, 386
Tokiyuki N	123, 237, 253, 361			Toyama S	145, 245, 328
Tokiza'ne N	123, 169, 361	Tomo'uji N	188, 265, 362	Toyochiyomaru B	121, 124
Tokome F	304, 386	Tomoyasu N	265, 269, 303, 362	Toyoda S	144, 231, 328
Tokoyome F	133, 386	Tomoyuki N	237, 265, 280, 362	Toyofusa N	134, 231, 362
Toku F	304, 386	To'noko F	206, 386	Toyohito N (E)	408
Tokuda S	144, 304, 328	Toochika N	113, 205, 362	Toyome F	173, 231, 386
Tokugawa S	150, 304, 328, 403	Toohira N	110, 113, 362	Toyomichi N	130, 231, 362
Tokuji Y	191, 304, 410-411	Toohito N (E)	408	Toyomitsu N	181, 231, 362
Toku'naga S	118, 304, 328	Tookage N	113, 183, 362	Toyotomi S	231, 245, 328, 403
Toku'nyou F	386	Toomitsu N	113, 181, 362	Tozawa S	133, 150, 328
Tokushima P	146, 304	Toomochi N	113, 167, 362	Tsuchi F	153, 387
Tokutoshime F	304, 386	Toomoto N	113, 217, 362	Tsuchime F	153, 387
Tomareyoshi N	254, 295, 361	Tooru N	306, 362	Tsuchimikado H (E)	407
Tome F	281, 386	Tooyama S	404	Tsuchiya S	137, 153, 328
Tomi no Koujo N (E)	406	Tora F	156, 171, 289, 386	Tsuda S	144, 148, 328
Tomihito N (E)	408	Tora'i'nume F	386	Tsugaru S	148, 226, 328, 404
Tomiji M	213	Torako F	386	Tsuge P	162
Tomiko F	245, 386	Toramasa N	171, 180, 362	Tsugi'naga N	193
Tomime F	245, 281, 386	Toramatsume F	171, 386	Tsugi'nagashinnou N	203
Tomi'no S	152, 245, 328	Torame F	156, 281, 386	Tsugi'o M	213
Tom'naga N	125	Toramori N	171, 223, 362	Tsugiyoshi N	193
Tomo'aki N	260, 265, 361	Torata'ne N	171, 207, 362	Tsugiyoshishinnou N	203
Tomobe O	402	Torayasu N	171, 209, 362	Tsugufusa N	134, 207, 363
Tomoe F	386	Tori'i S	404	Tsuguhito N; N (E)	193; 408
Tomoegozen F	198, 228, 404	Torika(h)ibe O	37, 402	Tsuguhitoshinnou N	203
Tomofusa N	125, 134, 361	Torikime F	386	Tsugume F	218, 387
Tomohiro N	101, 125, 361	Torime F	157, 173, 386	Tsugu'nobu N	187, 234, 363
		Toriyama S	145, 173, 328	Tsugu'nori N	207, 235, 363

B	Infants & Children	F	Female Names	M	Male Yobina	S	Surname	U	Uji
E	Emperors	H	Chinese Style Names	N	Male Nanori	Y	Era Names	O	Be

Name Index 455

Tsukime F	155, 387	Tsutsu'i S	132, 275, 328	u'nebe O	402
Tsuki'nomoto U	397	Tsutsumi S	144, 328	u'neme U	397
Tsukiyo'ne U	397			Unno S	148, 152, 328
Tsukushi U	397	**U**		U'no no Sarara N (E)	406
Tsuma F	198, 387			U'no no Umakai U	397
Tsume F	142, 387	Uchitsu'ne N	103, 262, 364	Urabe O; S	402; 185, 247, 328
Tsumori U	397	Uchiza'ne N	103, 169, 364	Uragami S	102, 149, 328
Tsu'namitsu N	181, 276, 363	Uda H (E); S	407; 132, 221, 328	Urakami S	103, 149, 328
Tsu'nayoshi N	403	Ueki P	167	Urako F	232, 387
Tsu'ne'aki N	202, 261, 363	Ue'no S	103, 152, 328	Urime F	132, 387
Tsu'nechika N	205, 261, 363	Uesugi S	103, 160, 328, 404	Uryuu S	166, 268, 328
Tsu'nefusa N	134, 261, 363	Ueta S	103, 144, 328	Usa S	132, 195, 328
Tsu'nega'ne N	261	Uji U	397	Ushi F	172, 387
Tsu'neharu N	118, 191, 363	Uji'aki N	125, 179, 188, 262, 364	Ushime F	172, 387
Tsu'nehide N	118, 289, 363	Ujibe O	402	Usu'i S	132, 226, 281, 328
Tsu'nehira N	110, 261, 363	Ujifuyu N	128, 188, 364	Usuki S	281, 328
Tsu'nehisa N	119, 261, 363	Ujiharu N	127, 188, 191, 364	Uta F	259, 387
Tsu'nehito N (E)	408	Ujihide N	188, 289, 364	Uteme F	132, 239, 387
Tsu'ne'ie N	136, 261, 363	Ujihiro N	106, 188, 364	Utsu'nomiya S	132, 138, 142, 328
Tsu'nekage N	183, 261, 363	Ujihisa N	119, 188, 364		
Tsu'neka'ne N	206, 261, 363	Uji'ie N; S	136, 188, 364; 136	**W**	
Tsu'neku'ni N	98, 261, 363	Ujikiyo N	188, 284, 364		
Tsu'nemasa N	190, 261, 292, 363	Ujiko F	187, 387	Wada S	144, 209, 329
Tsu'nemi N	129, 261, 363	Ujiku'ni N	98, 188, 364	Wagimome F	187, 201, 387
Tsu'nemichi N	130, 261, 363	Ujimitsu N	181, 188, 224, 364	Wakagozen F	387
Tsu'nemitsu N	181, 261, 363	Ujimori N	188, 223, 364	Wakahito N (E)	407
Tsu'nemori N	118, 223, 261, 363	Ujimu'ne N	188, 263, 364	Waka'i'nukai U	397
Tsu'nemoto N	118, 140, 363	Uji'nao N	188, 241, 364	Waka'i'numaru B	121
Tsu'nemu'ne N	261, 263, 363	Uji'nari N	188, 267, 364	Wakako F	209, 387
Tsu'ne'naga N	112, 118, 261, 363	Uji'nobu N	188, 234, 364	Wakame F	120, 387
Tsu'ne'naka N	218, 261, 363	Uji'no'ko F	387	Wakasa S	101, 120, 329
Tsu'ne'nari N	261, 267, 363	Uji'no'nyou F	387	Wakasakurabe U	397
Tsu'ne'nobu N	234, 251, 261, 363	Uji'nori N	188, 286, 287, 364	Wakayue U	397
Tsu'ne'nori N	235, 261, 363	Ujisato N	140, 188, 364, 404	Wake U	397
Tsu'neshige N	118, 167, 261, 302, 363	Ujishige N	188, 243, 364	Wakeme F	264, 387
		Ujita'ne N	189, 207, 364	Waki S	209, 229, 329
Tsu'nesue N	126, 261, 363	Ujitoki N	124, 189, 364	Wakigeme F	177, 209, 387
Tsu'nesuke N	261, 306, 363	Ujitomo N	126, 189, 364	Wakisaka S	129, 178, 329
Tsu'netada N	261, 301, 363	Ujitoshi N	189, 252, 294, 364	Wakiya S	137, 178, 329
Tsu'netaka N	107, 109, 261, 363	Ujitsu'na N	189, 276, 364	Wakugo F	120, 387
Tsu'neta'ne N	118, 207, 363	Ujitsu'ne N	189, 262, 364	Wakugome F	120, 387
Tsu'netoki N	124, 261, 363, 404	Ujitzugu N	187, 189, 364	Wakume F	209, 387
Tsu'netomo N	118, 185, 363	Ujiyasu N	189, 209, 364	Warahagozen F	387
Tsu'netoshi N	252, 261, 363	Ujiyori N	189, 246, 364	Warahako F	200, 387
Tsu'netsugu N	207, 261, 363	Ujiyoshi N	189, 265, 364	Watasaburou M	373
Tsu'ne'uji N	188, 261, 363	Ujiyuki N	189, 238, 253, 364	Wobame F	199, 285, 383, 388
Tsu'neyasu N	118, 208-209, 261-262, 304, 363	Ukaibe O	225, 402	Wobitome F	266, 388
		Ukita S	132, 221, 254, 328	Wogusome F	102, 178, 388
Tsu'neyori N	114, 118, 246, 262, 363	Ukon F	105, 387	Wohirame F	102, 388
Tsu'neyoshi N	118, 180, 363	Uma F	172, 387	Womame F	285, 388
Tsu'nezumi N	118, 284, 363	Umagome F	132, 387	Womi'nako F	388
Tsu'no U	397	Umakai N	114, 132, 364	Womi'nome F	102, 279, 388
Tsu'nume F	114, 387	Umakaibe O	402	Wonnako F	388
Tsurako F	130, 387	Umame F	172, 387	Wosada S	144, 308, 329
Tsura'uji N	188, 298, 363	Umaraki U	397	Wosame F	111, 388
Tsuru F	174, 387	Umatsume F	172, 387	Woshime F	227, 285, 388
Tsurukome F	174, 387	Umeme F	161, 387	Woto F	388
Tsurume F	174, 387	Umewaka S	120, 161, 328	Wotojime F	281, 285, 309, 388
Tsutomeme F	142, 387	Umishime F	177, 387	Wotome F	102, 221, 388

B	Infants & Children	F	Female Names	M	Male Yobina	S	Surname	U	Uji
E	Emperors	H	Chinese Style Names	N	Male Nanori	Y	Era Names	O	Be

Wou'name F	199, 388	Yasumoto N	140, 304, 365	Yorikazu N	203, 246, 366
Woyame F	285, 388	Yasumu'ne N	263, 304, 365	Yorikiyo N	246, 284, 366
		Yasumura N	141, 209, 365	Yorimasa N	190, 246, 366
Y		Yasu'naga N	112, 304, 365	Yorimasu N	221, 246, 366
		Yasu'nari N	256, 299, 365	Yorime F	240, 388
Yabu'no'uchi S	103, 164, 329	Yasu'nobu N	234, 304, 365	Yorimichi N	130, 246, 366
Yabushime F	126, 200, 388	Yasu'nori N	209, 286, 365	Yorimitsu N	181, 246, 366
Yagi P; S	215; 159, 281, 329	Yasusada N	208-209, 248, 293, 365	Yorimori N	223, 246, 366
Yaguchi P	281	Yasushige N	167, 209, 256, 302, 365	Yorimoto N	140, 217, 246, 366
Yagyuu S	160, 268, 329	Yasutaka N	107, 209, 365	Yorimu'ne N	246, 263, 366
Yahagibe O	37	Yasuta'ne N	207, 209, 365	Yori'naga N	112, 246, 366
Yakako F	136, 388	Yasutoki N	124, 209, 365, 404	Yori'nao N	241, 246, 366
Yakame F	135-136, 388	Yasutomi N; S	245, 304, 365; 208, 245, 329	Yori'nari N	246, 267, 299, 366
Yaka'narime F	136, 388			Yori'nobu N	234, 246, 366
Yakushime F	273, 388	Yasutomo N	126, 209, 365	Yorisada N	246, 293, 366
Yamabe N (E); O; U	407; 402; 398	Yasutoo N	113, 256, 365	Yorishige N	167, 246-247, 302, 366
Yamabukime F	388	Yasutoshi N	208, 252, 304, 365	Yorisuke N	194-195, 247, 366
Yamada S	144-145, 329	Yasutsugi N	208, 218, 365	Yoritada N	247, 301, 366
Yamagata S	99, 145, 226, 329	Yasutsu'na N	209, 276, 365	Yoritaka N	109, 247, 366
Yamagi S	145, 159, 329	Yasutsu'ne N	209, 262, 365	Yorita'ne N	207, 247, 366
Yamaguchi S	100, 145, 329	Yasutsura N	239, 304, 365	Yoritoki N	124, 247, 366
Yamaji U	398	Yasu'uji N	189, 209, 365	Yoritomo N	126, 247, 366, 403
Yamakawa S	145, 150, 329	Yasuurame F	388	Yoritoo N	113, 247, 366
Yamamoribe O	37, 402	Yasuyori N	246, 304, 365	Yoritoshi N	247, 252, 366
Yamamoto S	97, 145, 329	Yasuyuki N	237-238, 246, 304, 365	Yoritsugu N	207, 218, 247, 366, 403
Yama'na S	145, 203	Yasyu'ie N	136	Yoritsu'na N	247, 276, 366
Yama'na S	329	Yatabe O; U	402; 398	Yoritsu'ne N	247, 262, 366, 403
Yama'no U	398	Yatarou M	211, 254; 373	Yori'uji N	189, 247, 366
Yama'nobe S	113, 146, 329	Yatsume U	398	Yoriyasu N	209, 247, 304, 366
Yama'no'uchi S	103, 146, 329	Yawako F	388	Yoriyoshi N	247, 295, 366
Yama'no'ue S	103, 146, 329	Yawe F	229	Yoriyuki N	237-238, 247, 366
Yama'oka S	146-147, 329	Yaweme F	126, 388	Yoriza'ne N	169, 247, 366
Yamashiro S; U	137, 146, 329; 398	Yaya F	120, 254, 388	Yosamime F	177, 240, 388
Yamato S	102, 210, 329	Yayorime F	137, 388	Yoshi N	295, 366
Yamato no Aya U	398	Yochiko F	214, 388	Yoshi'ai N	186, 289, 366
Yamato no Umakai U	398	Yogotarou M	186, 211, 214, 373	Yoshi'aki N	125, 179, 202, 295, 366, 403
Yamato U	398	Yohito N (E)	408		
Yama'uchi S	103, 146, 329, 404	Yo'ichirou M	186	Yoshi'akira N	262, 295, 366, 403
Yamazaki S	146, 329	Yoichirou M	373	Yoshi'ari N	269, 295, 366
Yasu F; S	254, 388; 126, 306, 329	Yo'ichitarou M	211-212, 373	Yoshi'atsu N	295, 298, 366
Yasu'ari N	268, 304, 364	Yokose S	109, 151, 329	Yoshichi N	264, 295, 366
Yasuchika N	205, 209, 304, 364	Yokota S	109, 144, 329	Yoshichika N	205, 295, 366
Yasuda S	144, 208	Yokoyama S	109, 146, 329	Yoshifusa N	134, 289, 295, 366
Yasuda S	329	Yokurou M	186, 215, 373	Yoshifuyu N	128, 295, 366
Yasugimimaru B	121	Yo'neme F	273, 388	Yoshigimimaru B	121
Yasuharu N	209, 364	Yo'ne'nyou F	388	Yoshiharu N	157, 191, 295, 306, 366-367
Yasuhide N	209, 289, 304, 364	Yori'aki N	125, 179, 246, 260, 365		
Yasuhira N	209, 282, 364	Yori'ari N	246, 268, 365	Yoshihide N	254, 265, 289, 295, 367, 403
Yasuhito N (E)	407-408	Yorichika N	205, 246, 365		
Yasu'ie N	136, 209, 256, 364-365	Yorifuji N	163, 246, 365	Yoshihime F	284, 389
Yasukatsu N	257, 304, 365	Yorifusa N	134, 246, 365	Yoshihira N	110, 289, 295, 367
Yasukiyo N	209, 284, 365	Yoriharu N	127, 191, 246, 365	Yoshihiro N	101, 106, 285, 296, 367, 404
Yasuko F	208, 253, 256, 290, 388	Yorihide N	246, 289, 365		
Yasukome F	208, 388	Yorihira N	110, 246, 365	Yoshihisa N	119, 231, 265, 296, 367, 403
Yasumasa N	180, 190, 256, 304, 365	Yorihisa N	119, 231, 246, 365		
Yasume F	388	Yori'ie N	136, 246, 366, 403	Yoshihito N; N (E)	171, 232, 296, 367; 408
Yasumichi N	130, 209, 304, 365	Yorika'ne N	206, 246, 366		
Yasumochi N	270, 304, 365	Yorikata N	114, 246, 366	Yoshi'ie N	136, 296, 367
Yasumori N	209, 223, 256, 304, 365	Yorikawa N	246, 264, 366	Yoshikado N	132, 289-290, 296, 367

B	Infants & Children	**F**	Female Names	**M** Male Yobina	**S** Surname	**U** Uji
E	Emperors	**H**	Chinese Style Names	**N** Male Nanori	**Y** Era Names	**O** Be

Yoshikage N	183, 296, 367, 404	
Yoshika'ne N	206, 272, 296, 367	
Yoshikata N	114, 255, 367	
Yoshikatsu N	257, 296, 367, 403	
Yoshikawa S	150, 232, 329	
Yoshikazu N	203, 266, 296, 299, 367, 403	
Yoshikiyo N	284, 296, 367, 403	
Yoshiko F	121, 158, 284, 389	
Yoshikome F	232, 389	
Yoshiku'ni N	98, 296, 367	
Yoshima S	147, 255, 329	
Yoshimasa N	180, 190, 194, 232, 289, 292, 296, 367, 403	
Yoshime F	225, 232, 389	
Yoshimi N; S	129, 296, 308, 367; 232, 329	
Yoshimichi N	130, 289, 367	
Yoshimi'ne U	398	
Yoshimitsu N	181, 224, 232, 296, 367, 403	
Yoshimizu S	148, 232, 329	
Yoshimochi N	167, 254, 270, 289, 296, 367, 403	
Yoshimori N	223, 266, 296, 367	
Yoshimoto N	140, 168, 217, 289, 296, 367	
Yoshimu'ne N	189, 263, 296, 367, 403	
Yoshimura N	141, 296, 367	
Yoshi'naga N	112, 225, 253, 296, 367	
Yoshi'naka N	218, 266, 296, 367	
Yoshi'nao N	241, 266, 296, 367	
Yoshi'nari N	242, 247, 266-267, 289, 296, 299, 367-368	
Yoshi'natsu N	127, 296, 368	
Yoshi'no U	398	
Yoshi'nobu N	234, 251, 266, 289, 296, 368, 403	
Yoshi'nori N	235, 266, 286-287, 289, 296, 368, 403	
Yoshi'oki N	116, 296, 368	
Yoshirou M	373	
Yoshisada N	248, 289, 293, 296, 368, 404	
Yoshisata N	296	
Yoshisato N	140, 266, 368	
Yoshishige N	166, 243, 296, 302, 368, 404	
Yoshisue N	126, 29, 368	
Yoshisuke N	186, 194-195, 289, 296, 306, 368	
Yoshitada N	241, 255, 264, 296, 301, 368	
Yoshitaka N	107, 109, 232, 266, 296, 302, 368, 404	
Yoshitake N	243, 296, 368	
Yoshita'ne N	167, 170, 207, 296-297, 368, 403	
Yoshitatsu N	175, 297, 368	
Yoshiteru N	181, 297, 368, 403	
Yoshitoki N	124, 297, 368, 404	
Yoshitomo N	126, 297, 368, 404	
Yoshitoo N	109, 297, 368	
Yoshitoshi N	242, 252, 297, 368	
Yoshitoyo N	231, 297, 368	
Yoshitsugu N	187, 207, 289, 297, 368	
Yoshitsuke N	297, 368	
Yoshitsu'na N	276, 297, 368	
Yoshitsu'ne N	118, 262, 289, 297, 368	
Yoshitsura N	239, 297-298 368	
Yoshi'uji N	189, 266, 297, 369	
Yoshiwakamaru B	120-121	
Yoshiyasu N	256, 266, 290, 297, 304, 369	
Yoshiyori N	247, 297, 369	
Yoshiyuki N	237, 253, 297, 369	
Yoshiza'ne N	169, 289, 297, 369	
Yoshizumi N	284-285, 297, 369, 403	
Yotarou M	186, 211, 373	
Youmei H (E)	406	
Youwa Y	210, 313, 410	
Youzei H (E)	407	
Yu'asa S	109, 148, 330	
Yuebe O	402	
Yuge U	398	
Yugebe O	37, 402	
Yu'i S	98, 132, 330	
Yuki'aki N	237, 260, 369	
Yuki'ari N	237, 269, 369	
Yukifuji N	163, 237, 369	
Yukifusa N	134, 237, 369	
Yukihide N	237, 289, 369	
Yukihira N	110, 237, 369	
Yukihiro N	101, 237, 369	
Yukihisa N	119, 237, 369	
Yuki'ie N	136, 237, 369	
Yukikata N	114, 237, 369	
Yukikiyo N	237, 284, 369	
Yukiko F	158, 253, 389	
Yukimasa N	190, 237, 369	
Yukime F	98, 225, 265, 389	
Yukimichi N	130, 237, 369	
Yukimitsu N	181, 237, 369	
Yukimori N	223, 237, 369	
Yukimu'ne N	238, 263, 369	
Yukimura N	141, 238, 253, 369	
Yuki'naga N	112, 238, 369	
Yuki'nao N	238, 241, 369	
Yuki'nari N	238, 267, 369	
Yuki no Tajihi U	398	
Yuki'o N; M	238, 303, 369; 219	
Yukisada N	238, 293, 369	
Yukisuke N	195, 238, 369	
Yukitada N	238, 301, 369	
Yukitaka N	107, 109, 238, 253, 369	
Yukitoki N	124, 238, 369	
Yukitomo N	126, 238, 369	
Yukitsu'na N	238, 276, 369	
Yuki'uji N	189, 238, 253, 369	
Yukiyasu N	209, 238, 304, 369	
Yukiyori N	238, 247, 369	
Yukiyoshi N	238, 297, 369	
Yukiza'ne N	169, 238, 369	
Yura S	98, 289, 330	
Yuri S	98, 293, 330	
Yusa S	195, 240, 330	
Yuta'akira N (E)	407	
Yutahito N (E)	408	
Yutaka M	231	
Yuuki S	137, 244, 330	
Yuuko F	303, 389	
Yuume F	389	
Yuuryaku H (E)	406	
Yuusai N	404	

Z

Zengorou M	214, 247, 373
Zenjirou M	212, 247, 373
Zenni F	229, 389
Zennyo F	199, 389
Zezeme F	269, 389

B	Infants & Children	F	Female Names	M	Male Yobina	S	Surname	U	Uji
E	Emperors	H	Chinese Style Names	N	Male Nanori	Y	Era Names	O	Be

General Index

A

advisors n. 60
agata 39, n. 99, 413
agata no miyatsuko 39, 413
agatanushi 413
agricultural collectives 3, 39
Ainu 1, 14, 63
-ako 49, 413
-akome 49, 413
alchemical elements 56
alliteration/repetition 7, 50
ama- 47, 413
Amaterasu Oomikami 15, 24
amatsu- 47, 413
-ami 50
Amida Buddha 50, 52, 250
Ancient Clans 27-29, 36, 39, 61, 390-398
artisans 8, 14-15, 25-27, 36-39, 42, 53, 68, n. 399-402
artists 5, 26, 29, 42, 53-54
ashigaru 21, 413
Ashikaga 21, 70, 413
Ashikaga Bakufu 18, 21, 27, 413
Ashikaga Tadayoshi 20
Ashikaga Taka'uji 20
Ashikaga Yoshimasa 21
Ashikaga Yoshimi 21
asomi 17, 27-28, 413
ason 27-28, 413
astrology 156
Asuka Period 16
azana 6, 26, 30, 44, 46, 53, 413
Azuchi-Momoyama Period 21

B

bakufu 18-22, 39, 61, 63, 413, 417-418, 420-424
bakufu council see *hyoujoushuu*
bakuhan system 39
battlefield 20, 27, 30, 70
-be 15, 33, 37-39, 51
be 15, 35, 37-39, 51, 413
be-no-miyatsuko 39, 413
beasts and monsters 12, 14, 46-47, 49, 53, 56, 171-175
bhodisatva 250
Bryant, Anthony 41, 68
Buck, Pearl S. 121
Buddha 50, 52, 183, 250
Buddhism 11, 14-17, 25, 42, 45, 50, 52-57, 72, 138, 145, 191, 273, 282, n. 405-406
Buddhist monks 5, 8, 25, 29-30, 44, 52-53
Buddhist names 27, 29, 46, 52
Buddhist temples 12, 16-18, 25, 36, 52-53, 58, 68, 138, 145
buke 3, 17, 20-21, 26-27, 29, 37-39, 41-42, 44-45, 47, 49-50, 61, 67-70, 192, 211, 293, 413

C

calendric system 20, 56, 56-57, 219
capital guards 61
capital police 62-63
cap ranks 17, 28
castle 137
census 3, 7, 16-17, 26-27, 38, 47, 58, 64, 68, 70
Chamberlain, Basil Hall 1
chamei (tea name) 30, 53, 413
chidaijoukanji n. 60
chikakimamori'notsukasa n. 64
childhood 8, 41, 45
children 26, 41-42, 44-45, 70
China 2, 13-14, 17, 27, 31, 35, 45, 53, 57, 68, 71, 98-99, 121, 126, 138, 145, 151, 155-156, 163, 211
Chinese 2-4, 6, 11, 24-25
Chinese dynasties 126
   T'ang 17
   Han 13
   Wei 13-14
Chinese names 11, 24-25
chinjufu 63
-chiyo 45
chokushiden 414
Christian *daimyou* 58-59
Christian names 58-59
Christianity 22, 52, 58
chuu'nagon 60
chuushou 62
clan 4, 6, 14-18, 20, 25-27, 29, 31-32, 35-39, 41-42, 44-46, 49-50, 52, 56, 64, 66, 68, 70
clan names and *tsuushou* 37, 44
clan names and women 19, 61, 139
codes and laws
   Yung-hwui, Code of the 17
   Taihou Code 17, 55, 62
   Yorou Codes 61
   Law of Decorum 66
collectives 15, 31, 39
coming of age 26, 45, 200, 415
Confucian scholars 53
consonants 10
Constitution of Seventeen Articles 406
council of state 60
counsellors 60
counting objects 97
court nobility 7, 17, 25-27, 29, 36, 39, 49, 62

D

daifu 63
daijou see Mahâyâna
daijou daijin 18, n. 60, 403, 414
daijouhou'ou 414

daijoukan 60, 414
daimyou 3, 21-22, 27, 34, 36, 38-39, 414
dai'nagon 60
daizen no daibu 28, 30, 54, 414
Dan no Ura n. 407
Davis, David L. n. 39
Dazaifu 63, 414
densou 414
district 16
Divided Court Period 20, 49, 201
-do'no 49, 65, 68
do'no 63, 68, 414
dougou 8, 53-54, 414
Dragon King 174-175
dynastic naming practices 44

E

eboshi (cap) 26, 414-415
eboshi'na (cap name) 414
eboshi'oya (godfather) 415
Edo Bakufu 26, 415
Edo Period 22, 39, 68
efu 37, 62-63, 415
eji 62
-emon 62-63
emonfu 63
emperor 14-22, 24-27, 29
Emperor and his Family 24
emperors 405-408
   Chijou Tennou 56
   Daigo Tennou 394
   Genmei Tennou 17
   Genshou Tennou 17
   Go-daigo Tennou 16, 19-20, 25, 55, 394
   Go-fukakusa Tennou 19
   Go-ichijou Tennou 56
   Go-kameyama Tennou 21
   Go-murakami Tennou 55
   Go-saga Tennou 19
   Go-toba Tennou 19, 56
   Go-uda Tennou 19
   Ha'nazono Tennou 19
   Ichijou Tennou 56
   Jinmu Tennou 24-25, 56
   Kameyama Tennou 19
   Kanmu Tennou 35, 396
   Kazan Tennou 55
   Kougon Tennou 19
   Koukou Tennou 18
   Koutoku Tennou 57, 409
   Monmu Tennou 17, 55
   Montoku Tennouu 42
   Murakami Tennou 55, 394
   Saga Tennou 394
   Saimei Tennou 16
   Seiwa Tennou 29, 55, 394
   Suiko Tennou 16
   Tenji Tennou 16, 29
   Tenmu Tennou 17, 29
   Uda Tennou 394
   Youmei Tennou 16
   Youzei Tennou 18
empresses 405-408
   Jinguu Kougou 405
   Suiko Tennou 406
   Kougyoku Tennou 406
   Saimei Tennou 406
   Jitou Tennou 406
   Meishou Tennou 408
   Go-Sakuraimachi Tennou 408
employment 28

F

family 3, 5, 7, 15, 17-18, 21, 27, 29-32, 41, 44, 48, 52, 66, 141
family name 4-6, 8, 11, 24-27, 29-32, 34-36, 41, 44, 49-54, 57, 66-68, 70
Farris, William Wayne n. 61
Female Christians 59
feminine names 7-8, 42, 46-47, 50-51
feminine suffixes
   -ako 49, 413
   -akome 49, 413
   -do'no 49, 414
   -gozen 49-50, 415
   -hime 46, 48-49, 416
   -irashime 46, 417
   -kimi 46, 419
   -ko 4, 7, 46, 49, 51, 419
   -kome 49, 419
   -kusu 49
   -machime 49, 420
   -marome 47
   -me 49-50, 420-421
   -mi 50
   -mushime 48-49, 420
   -no'uji 49
   -nomae 49, 421
   -nushime 48
   -nyo 49, 421
   -nyou 49, 421
   -ou 49, 422
   -rame 48
   -shimame 48
   -teme 49, 425
   -tobe 46, 425
   -tojime 49
   -toujime 48
   -tsume 48
   -uji'nome 49
   -ujiko 49
   -ujime 50
   -wakame 48
   -yasame 49, 426
feudal domains 38
foreign *uji* (clans) 36
Fudoki 17, 415
Fujiwara 7, 16-18, 29, 31-32, 36-37, 51, 70, 163, n. 391, 415
Fujiwara Hidesato 37
Fujiwara Mototsune 18
Fujiwara no Fuhito 17
Fujiwara no me 51
Fujiwara no uji 51
Fujiwara Noriyori 67
fumie 58, 415
Funa Watashi Muko 44
furigana 2, 11-12, 415
Furuta Oribe Shige'nari 38
Futodama no Mikoto 36

G

-ga- 34, 40, 415
ge (petition) 415
gechi (*bakufu* edict) 415
gagou 26-27, 30, 53, 415
genfuku 26, 45, 200, 415
Genji 18, 29, 407, 415
Genji Monogatari 72, 156, 273, 282
Genpei War 1, 7, 18, 29, 45, 49, 51-52, 66, n. 407
go- 415
gods and goddesses 24
goke'nin (direct vassal) 415
gouka (noble house) 35, 415
-gozen 49-50, 415
gun (rural district) 40, 415

H

habitats 54
Hakuhou Period 16
Hall, John Whitney n. 39, n. 63
han 22, 39, 415
hanzei (land rights) 416
haru no miya 416
Hearn, Lafcadio 4
Hei'an Period 5, 10, 15, 17-18, 25-27, 35-36, 42, 49-50, 72, 416
Hei'ankyou 17, 42, 416
Heijoukyou 17, 42, 416
heika 29, 416
Heike 18, 29, 36, 407, 416
Heike Monogatari 27-28, 32, 66-67, 416
Heishi 18, 407, 416
Hepburn system 2
high status *kanji*
   -**hito** 26, 44, 232, 416
   kimi- 192, 419
   -**kimi** 193
   kin- 26, 192, 419
   -**tomo** 192, 425
-**hiko** 42
-**hime** 46-48, 416
Hînayâna 52
hiragana 2, 11-12, 54, 58, 69, 416
hisangi n. 60
-**hito** 26, 44, 47, 232, 416
hokuchou 20
honke 416
honmyou 26, 416
honourific *jou'ingou* 55
honourific prefixes 24, 48, 66, 201
Hosokawa Katsumoto 21
hou'ou 407
Hou'ryuu'ji 16
Houjou 7, 18-20, 34, 52, 70
Houjou Tokimasa 18
houmyou 6, 8, 20, 26-27, 29-30, 41, 45-46, 52-55, 71, 193, 416
houses 132
houshinnou 235
hyou'e 62
hyougi 416
hyoujoushuu 416

I

ie 3, 417
iemoto 22, 53, 417
ikki 39, 417
imiki 417
imi'na 30, 52-53, 55, 417
Imibe 15
imiki 17, 417
imperial advisors 60
imperial council see *dajoukan*
imperial family 7, 14-21, 23-26, 35, 37, 39, 42, 44, 48, 55-56, 70, 193
   junior (Southern) line 408
   senior (Northern) line 408
   leaving n. 394, n. 396
imperial palace 189
imperial princes 16, 193, 309
   Ku'ni'naga Shinnou 19
   Mori'naga Shinnou 19-20
   Mu'netaka Shinnou 19
   Nari'naga Shinnou 20
   Tsugi'naga Shinnou 25
imperial princesses
   Kishi Naishinnou 25
   Kyuushi Naishinnou 25
imperial rank 60, 417
imperial titles
   hou'ou 407
   jo'ou 25, 35, 61, 417
   joukou 407, 417
   kougou 405
   koutaishi 63, 419
   koutei 63, 419
   mikado 63, 420
   naishinnou 35, 61, 421
   ou 35, 422
   ouji 16, 63, 422
   shinnou 35, 61, 423
   taishi 63, 425
   tennou 63, 425
   touguu 63, 425
-**in** 55, 417
Inada Hogitaro 32, 53, 68
inaki 15, 17, 417
Inbe 36, 417
India 16, 47, 53, 71, 139, 155
infants 26, 45
ingou 26-27, 55, 417
inkan 417
insei 18-19, 61, 139, n. 407-408, 417

intonation 12
investiture ceremony 21
-**irashime** 46, 417
-**iratsume** 46, 417
isochronicity 12
Iza'nagi no Mikoto 7, 14-15, n. 15
Iza'nami no Mikoto 7, 14-15, n. 15
Izumi Shikibu 48

J

Japanese Society 3, 7-8, 13-14, 17, 20, 30-32, 49, 53, 61, 68
jitou 19, 63, 417
jitsumei 26-27, 68, 417
jo'ou 25, 35, 48, 61, 417
jou'ingou 55, 417
Joudou Shinshuu 52
joukoku 21
joukou n. 407, 417
Joukyuu Disturbance 15, 19, 418
Joumon Period 13
juvenile names 121

K

kabane 17, 27-29, 36, 38-39, 42, 44-45, 48, 61, 417-418
kabane
   asomi 17, 27-28, 413
   ason 27-28, 413
   imiki 17, 417
   inaki 15, 17, 417
   mahito 17, 29, 420
   michi no shi 17, 420
   muraji 15, 17, 36, 420
   omi 15, 17, 36, 420
   suku'ne 17, 424, 424
kaimyou 26-27, 418
Kamakura 19
Kamakura Bakufu 17-18, 20, 418
Kamakura Period 4, 6-7, 15, 18, 27-28, 41-42, 45-46, 49-50, 53, 61, 418
kamei 28, 32, 38, 44, 67-68, 418
-**kami** 66, 418
kamon (herldic device) 31-32, 58, 418
kana 2, 10-12, 69, 418

Kane'mi no Ookimi 62
kanji 11, 33, 43, 56-58, 418
Kannon Bosatsu 250
kanpaku 18, 20-21, 418
ka'ou 418
Kashiwade no Omi 15, 27
Kashiwadebe 15, 38
katakana 2, 11, 54, 58, 418
kazoku 3, 418
Kazuhito Taishi 19
Kazurahara 25
Kazuraki 36
Kazuraki Ouji 29
kebi'ishi 62-63
kemyou 26, 418
Ken'mu Shinsei 20, 419
Kenmu Restoration 16, 19-20, 408
kenza (audience) 28, 419
-**kime** 419
-**kimi** 46, 193, 419
kimi- 192
Kin'kaku'ji 12
kin- 26, 192, 419
Kiyo'u'emon 37
ko'noe 64
ko- 6, 33-34, 42, 46-47, 64
-**ko** 4, 7, 42, 46, 48-49, 51, 419
Kofun Period 14, 419
Kojiki 17, 405
kokka 39
kokujin 39
Kokuki 16
kokushi 62-63, 419
-**kome** 49, 419
ko'noefu n. 64
Koop, Albert James 32, 53, 68
Korea 13-14, 16, 21, 31, 68, 155, 163, 405
koseki 47, 419
kougou 405
Koumyou'in 20
koushi 56
koutaishi 61, 63, 419
koutei 61, 63, 419
kuge 17-18, 26-27, 37-39, 42, 44, 46-49, 60-62, 67-68, 390, 394, 396, 419
kugyou 419
ku'ni 40, 419
ku'ni no miyatsuko 15, 42, 419
ku'ni'nokami n. 60

kunyomi 2, 11-12, 25, 63, 71, 417
-**kusu** 49
Kuzuraki no Ouji 16
Kyuujiki 16, 419

L

labour collective 3, 15, 31, 39
Law of Decorum 66
language 2
long vowels 2

M

-**machime** 49, 420
magatama 13, 420
Mahâyâna 52
mahito 17, 29, 420
male Christians 58
mandokoro 420
-**maro** 41-42, 45-47, 121, 187, 121, 187, 420
-**maru** 41-42, 45, 121, 420
masculine names 6-7, 42, 45, 47, 50-51, 63
masculine suffixes
    -**maro** 41-42, 45-47, 121, 187, 121, 187, 420
    -**hiko** 42
    -**ko** 42, 46, 419
    -**maru** 41, 45
    -**o** 42
    -**OU** 41, 45-46, 49, 422
    -**ROU** 6, 37, 45, 49-51, 67, 70
    -**sa'emon** 37, 45, 62-63, 67, 422
    -**SHI** 7
    -**ue'mon** 37, 62-63, 67, 426
    -**waka** 45-46, 426
    -**yo** 45
masculine *yobina* 4
Mass, Jeffrey 42, 44
-**me** 7-8, 11, 21, 46-47, 49-50, 420
Meiji Restoration 22
men 42
men and clan names 44
men's names 5-6, 42-46
-**mi** 50
Mima'na 16, 420
michi no shi 17, 420
mikado 61, 63, 66, 420

-**mikoto** 61, 420
Mi'namoto 18, 20-21, 28-29, 35-37, 39, 45, 49, 51, 63, 68, 70, 322, 394, 403, 420
Mi'namoto Yoritomo 21, 35, 49, 403
minashiro 37
Mi'natogawa 20
ministers 60-61
ministries 61
mirrors 275
misasagi (tombs) 405
-**miya** 420
miyake (imperial estates) 39, 420
Miyamoto Musashi 27, 138
miyatsuko 38, 420
Mo'no'nobe 36, 401
Momoyama Period 21
-**mon'in** 55
mon'in senge 55
Mongol invasion 18
Mongols 20
monks 8, 17, 19, 26, 29-30, 41, 53-54
monopoly corporation 3, 15-16, 31, 35-39, 48, 70, 185, 309, 399-402
mora 2, 11-12, 48
Morinaga Shinnou 20
Mt. Hiei 17
muko kyougen 44
Munetaka Shinnou 19
muraji 15, 17, 36, 420
Murasaki Shikibu 48
Muromachi Period 7, 20-21, 26-27, 37, 42, 46, 50, 54, 62
-**mushime** 48-49, 420
myoubu 28, 421
myouden 421
myouji 26, 41, 44, 59, 421
myoujigomen 23, 26, 31, 68, 211, 421

N

nagaya 3, 421
naginata 10, 421
Nagoya n. 10
naidaijin 60
naishinnou 25, 35, 48, 61, 421
naishinnou senge 25, 60, 421
Naka no Ooe Koutaish 16

Naka no Ooe Ouji 16
Nakatomi 36
Nakatomi no Kamatari 16
Nakatomi *uji* 15, 394
names 4
    Buddhist 6, 8, 20, 25-26, 27, 29-30, 41, 45-46, 53-57, 71
    chamei 30, 54, 413
    childhood 8, 26, 41
    Chinese 11, 24-25
    Christian 60
    clan 40, 44, 51
    family 4-6, 8, 11, 24-27, 29-32, 34-36, 41, 44, 49-51, 53-55, 58, 66-68, 70
    formal 30
    gagou 26-27, 30, 54, 415
    imi'na 30, 53-56, 417
    juvenile 121
    men 5-7, 42-47, 50-51, 61
    nanori 4, 42-44, 416
    other 8
    osanana 26, 45-46, 422
    okuri'na 56
    patronymics 51
    personal 27
    posthumous 26-27, 29-30, 56, 405
    pseudonym 26
    relational 51
    shimei 26, 41
    songou 26-27, 424
    surnames 4-5, 24-24, 26, 28-29, 31-35, 37-38, 67, 70, 72
    tsuushou 4, 6, 26-28, 35, 40-41, 44-46, 67, 425
    uji 40, 44, 51, 426
    warawana 26, 45-46, 426
    women 7-8, 42, 46-48, 50-51
    yobina 4, 26, 426
Nanboku Period 8, 20, 46, 421
nanori 4-8, 11, 25-30, 32, 35, 37-38, 41-47, 52-54, 57-58, 66-70, 331-369, n. 405, 421
Nara 17, 110, 421
Nara Period 17, 421
nengou 20, 53, 56-57, 409-412, 421
nengu (annual land tax) 421

new clans 36
Nichiren 53
Nihongi 14, n. 405, 421
-no- 34
-no daibu 6
-no jou 6, 62
-no kami 6, 27, 62, 67, n. 19
-no mae 49, 421
-no mikoto n. 15, 421
-no miyatsuko 42
-no sakan 6, 62
-no suke 6, 62-63
-no taifu 62
-no'uji 49
-noe 56
-noto 56
noefu 64
Northern Court 21
Northern Fujiwara n. 64
nushi 28, 66
-nushime 48
-nyo 421
-nyou 49, 421
nyuudou 28 *30*, 54, 421

O

-o 42, 61, 63
o- 7-8, 49-51, 421-422
obito 422
occupational groups 37
Oda Nobunaga 21
Offices 27, 60
okami 61, 422
okami-san 61
Okinawa 1
okuri'na 55
omi 15, 17, 36, 422
onchi (land grants) 422
onomatopoeia 50
onshou 20
onyomi 2, 11, 44-45, 51-52, 55, 67, 71, 422
Oo'ama Ouji 29
oo'omi 36
oomuraji 36
Ootomo 36
Ootomo *uji* n. 16, 395
orthography 2, 11
osanana 26, 45-46
-ou 25, 35, 41, 45-46, 49, 61, 193
Ou'nin Ran 21

ouji 61, 63
Oumi 16
Oumi Mifune 55

P

pagoda 139
Palace Guards 64
patronymics 51
peace 110, 208
personal names 27
phonetic orthography 11
Polynesian 121
posthumous name 11, 24, 26-27, 29-30, 55, 405
pronunciation guide 9-12
provinces 14, 16, 19-21, 27, 40-41
provincial governors n. 60
Pure Land Buddhism 250

R

-rame 48
rank and office 60, 60, 417
regent 16, 18-19, 21
reimei 58, 422
relational names 51
repetition 12
retired emperors 18-19, 139, 414
retirement 18, 45, 54
rhythm 12
ritsuryou system 60-61
Rokuhara 19
-ROU 6, 37, 45, 49-51, 67, 70
rural districts 15
ryouji (princely edicts) 20

S

-sa'emon 63, 67, 422
sa'emondaibu 67, 422
saburau 18
sadaijin 60
samurai 18-19, 22, 26, 50
samuraidokoro 63, 423
sangi n. 60, 423
Sansom, George n. 407
SCA 1, 5-6, 8, 27, 29, 38-39, 41, 45, 55, 61, 67-68, 70
sei'itaishougun 18, 20-22, 27, 60-61, 63-64, 66, 423
Seikamon'in 25

seikamon'in 25
Seiwa Genji 29, n. 394
Sekigahara 1, 7, 21-22, 34, 40, 138
sekimori 61
Sen no Rikyuu 19, 215, 293
Sengoku Period 21, 39
sensei 66, 423
sesshou 16
-SHI 7
shigou 26, 55, 423
-**shikibu** 48, 423
shikken 18-20, 64, 423
-**shimame** 48
shimei 26, 41
-**shinji** 55, 423
shinnou 19-20, 25, 35, 45, 61, 61-63, 193, 203, 235, 423
shinnou senge 25, 45, 60-61
Shinran 52-53
-**shinnyou** 55, 423
Shintoh 24, 38, 283
shisei system 390
shogun see *sei'itaishougun*
shomin 26, 423
shou'en 19, 39, 61, 63, 423-424
shou'nagon 60
shougen 62
shougun 18-19, 21-22, 27, 61, 63-64, 424
shoujou 52, 424
shoushou 62
shousou 62
Shoutoku Taishi 16, 26, n. 406
shugo 19, 21, 27-28, 39, 63-64, 424
shugo daimyou 21, 63
shujin 28, 66, 424
shukke 5
sochi 63
Soga 16, 18, 36, 396
Soga Umako 16
songou 26-27, 424
Southern Court 21
soutsuibushi 19, 424
stupah 139
suku'ne 17, 424
Sumera Mikoto 25
sumou 178
surnames 4-5, 14, 18, 20, 23, 26, 28-29, 41, 67-68, 70, 315-330
syllables 12

T

Tahara no Fujitaka 37
Taihou Code 17, 55, 62
Taika Era 57, 424
Taika Reform 14, 26-27, 36, 38-40, 42, 51, 99, 141, 390, 409, 424
taikou 425
Taira 18, 29, 36, 45, 66, 70, 425
Taira Kiyomori 403
taishi 35, 61, 425
taishou 62, 64
Takeda Shingen 23, 30, 45
tandai 19, 425
Taoist sage 205
-**teme** 49, 425
temple census 58
tennou 25, 61, 63, 425
Tendai 30, 53, 425
tengu 205
Tenjiku 155
Thematic Dictionary 3-8, 23, 25, 56, 67, 70-72
titles 27, 60-64
to'neri 62, 425
-**tobe** 46, 425
-**tojime** 49
Tokugawa 70, 425
Tokugawa Ieyasu 22
tomo 15, 35, 39
-**tomo** 192, 425
tomo no miyatsuko 15, 39, 425
touge 2
touguu 61, 425
-**toujime** 48
Toyotomi Hideyosh 16, 215
trees, felicitous 159
-**tsubone** 425
-**tsume** 48
tsuuji 26, 37, 40, 44, 46, 51, 425
tsuushou 4, 6, 26-28, 35, 37, 41, 44-46, 61, 63, 67, 425
Tumulus Period 14

U

u'emondaibu 67, 70
ubasuteyama n. 50
udaijin 60
-**u'emon** 37, 62-63, 67, 426

uji 14, 18, 20, 26, 35-37, 39, 44-45, 51, 61, 67, 390-398, 426
uji no chouja 14, 426
uji no kami 14, 29, 36, 426
-**uji'nome** 49
-**ujiko** 49
-**ujime** 50
ujizoku 51, 390, 406, 426
Umaya no Ouji 16
Urasenke 53, 426
Utari 1

V

village 15, 26, 39, 141

W

-**waka** 45, 426
-**wakame** 48
warawana 26, 45-46, 426
Warring States Period 21, 28, 47, 54
warrior class 3, 14, 38, 41, 45, 68
warrior families 21, 29, 49
women 3-4, 7-8, 13, 15, 29, 41, 46-51, 54-55, 67-68
women and clan names 51
women's names 7-8, 42, 46-51

Y

-**ya** 31
Yamato Period 24, 47, 49, 426
Yangtze River 99
Yayoi Period 13, 24, 47, 49
Yellow River 151
Yin-Yang 57
yobina 4, 6, 26-27, 29-30, 35, 37-38, 42, 44, 53, 66, 68, 426
yugei (archery companies) 62
Yung-hwui, code of the 17

Z

Zen Buddhism 8, 11, 30, 52-53, 226
zokumyou 41, 44-45, 66-68, 70, 426

About the Author

Barbara Nostrand received a B.A. in philosophy from Central Washington State College where she also studied descriptive linguistics. After completing a B.A. in philosophy, she completed a second major in mathematics also at Central Washington State College. Later, she received M.S. and Ph.D. degrees in mathematics from Northeastern University. After receiving the master's degree, she studied Japanese at Harvard University, George Washington University, John's Hopkins University School of Advanced International Studies, International Christian University, and Omotesandô Nihongo Gakkô, the last two located in Tokyo, Japan.

Barbara Nostrand lived in Japan for six years where she is known as Kitahama Miyuki 北浜美雪. While in Japan, she worked as an engineer for Shinkoh, Ltd. which is a medium size Japanese company. Concurrently, she acted as a consultant for the NEC Printing Corporation. While in Japan, she studied *haiku* composition, calligraphy, tea ceremony, incense ceremony, *kaiseki* cooking, pottery, and kimono wearing. She returned to Northeastern University in 1989 to complete her Ph.D. in mathematics. Dr. Nostrand wrote her dissertation, *Chiral Honeycombs*, under Prof. Dr. Egon Schulte and successfully defended it during the Summer of 1993. She has been a sponsored participant at an NSF institute and a NATO advanced study institute. In 1994, she attended a conference on discrete geometry at Oberwolfach. Barbara Nostrand completed the first edition of *Name Construction in Mediæval Japan* while a visiting assistant professor and research fellow at York University in Toronto during the 1993-94 academic year.

Barbara Nostrand has lectured extensively within the Society for Creative Anachronism where she is known as Solveig Throndardottir. She regularly presents lectures and conducts workshops on Japanese mediæval studies at the annual Pennsic gathering near Slippery Rock, Pennsylvania as well as the Middle Kingdom Heraldic Symposium, the East Kingdom Royal Heraldic & Scribal Symposium at Carolingia, the Known World Heraldic Symposium, the Known World Arts and Sciences Symposium, and East Kingdom University. She has previously published articles on Japanese subjects in *The Northern Regional Arts & Sciences Handbook*, *Pikestaff*, and *The Proceedings of the Known World Heraldic Symposium*. She was written short monographs on diverse Japanese subjects including Japanese theatre arts which will soon be collected in a single volume.

Barbara Nostrand is currently working towards a Master of Arts degree in classical Japanese language and literature at the University of Toronto where she is studying images of women in medieval Japanese theatre. Other current projects include a monograph on late Muromachi period food and food culture including a translation of *Ryôri Monogatari*. She is currently employed as an Assistant Professor of Computer Science and Engineering at SUNY College at Potsdam.

EMAIL: nostrand@deMoivre.org

Dr. Barbara Nostrand
Department of Computer Science
SUNY College at Potsdam
Potsdam, New York 13676

COLOPHON

This monograph was typeset using NISUS® Writer 6.5 on an Apple® Macintosh® iBook® SE with 320 MBytes of memory operating under Mac OS 9.2.2. Electronic prespres was achieved using Adobe® Acrobat® 5.0.5. The main text is printed in Adobe® Garamond and Heiseimincho while display text is in Adobe® Palatino and Heiseimincho. The column header bars are in Adobe® Helvetica. The cover was designed using Adobe® Illustrator® 9.0. The cover is set in Monotype® Truesdell, DynaLab® DFPGyosho, and Adobe® Times. Additional glyphs and included graphics were produced using Macromedia® Fontographer® 4.1.3. Corrections for this printing were achieved using Fontographer 5.2.3, Nisus Writer Pro 2.1.7, Affinity Designer 1.5.5, Adobe® Acrobat® X 10.1.16, Preview Version 9.0 (909.18), and Adobe® Distiller® X Pro 10.1.16 on an Apple® MacBook® Pro with 8 GBytes of memory operating under macOS Sierra 10.12.5.

www.ingramcontent.com/pod-product-compliance
Lightning Source LLC
Chambersburg PA
CBHW081342080526
44588CB00016B/2352